# Building Family Practice Skills

## Methods, Strategies, and Tools

*D. Mark Ragg*
*Eastern Michigan University*

THOMSON
™
BROOKS/COLE

Australia • Brazil • Canada • Mexico • Singapore • Spain
United Kingdom • United States

## THOMSON
™
## BROOKS/COLE

*Building Family Practice Skills: Methods, Strategies, and Tools*
D. Mark Ragg

Executive Editor: *Lisa Gebo*
Assistant Editor: *Monica Arvin*
Editorial Assistant: *Sheila Walsh*
Executive Marketing Manager: *Caroline Concilla*
Marketing Assistant: *Rebecca Weisman*
Senior Marketing Communications Manager:
  *Tami Strang*
Project Manager, Editorial Production: *Christine Sosa*
Creative Director: *Rob Hugel*
Art Director: *Vernon Boes*

Print Buyer: *Barbara Britton*
Permissions Editor: *Sarah Harkrader*
Production Service: *Scratchgravel Publishing Services*
Copy Editor: *Chris Thillen*
Illustrator: *Richard Sheppard*
Cover Designer: *Lisa Devenish*
Cover Image: *Creatas Collection/Picturequest*
Cover Printer: *Thomson West*
Compositor: *Cadmus Professional Communications*
Printer: *Thomson West*

Printed in the United States of America
1  2  3  4  5  6  7  09  08  07  06  05

Library of Congress Control Number: 2005925901

ISBN 0-534-55686-8

Thomson Higher Education
10 Davis Drive
Belmont, CA 94002-3098
USA

For more information about our products, contact us at:
**Thomson Learning Academic Resource Center**
**1-800-423-0563**

For permission to use material from this text or product, submit a request online at
**http://www.thomsonrights.com.**
Any additional questions about permissions can be submitted by e-mail to
**thomsonrights@thomson.com.**

*To the many families who helped me learn my trade,*
*and to my family, Brenda, Jamie, and Devan,*
*for teaching me what families can be*

# Contents

Preface     xv

Introduction: Toward Skills-Focused Learning     xvii

## SECTION I     Thinking Family     1

## CHAPTER 1     Thinking Family: Theories and Frameworks     3

Theoretical Grounding     3
Toward Thinking at the Family Level     4
Using Family Theory     6
Understanding Families From the Developmental Perspective     7
  *Developmental Premises*     7
  *Developmental Problems and Resolutions*     9
Developmental Applications to Family     10
  *Formation of the Adult Relationship*     10
  *Family System Development*     17
Using Systemic Premises to Understand Families     20
  *Systemic Concepts*     21
  *Energy and Energy Management*     21
  *Boundaries and Boundary Management*     23
  *Intermember Exchanges and Control*     26

*Family Interaction Patterns*    29
*System-Subsystem Functions*    30
♦ Exercise 1.1: Identifying Theoretical Assumptions    33
Organizing Theoretical Understandings Into Practice Frameworks    34
Summary    36
Critical Content    36
Suggested Readings    36

# CHAPTER 2    *The Four Parenting Functions*    37

Theoretical Grounding    37
Parental Outcomes    39
*Outcome 1: Promoting Positive Mental Health (Loveable)*    39
*Outcome 2: Instilling Child Limits (Limitable)*    40
The Four Parental Functions    41
The Discipline Function    42
*The Foundation for Limits*    42
*The Strategies of Discipline*    43
The Guidance Function    51
*Expanding Perspectives*    51
*Dealing With Differences, Tension, and Problem Solving*    53
*Developing Boundaries*    55
*Developing Social Roles*    56
*Internalizing Limits*    57
The Nurturing Function    58
*Physical Contact*    59
*Caregiving Acts*    60
*Verbalizations*    61
The Access Function    62
*Providing Support*    63
*Managing Boundaries*    64
♦ Exercise 2.1: Evaluating Parental Functioning    65
Summary    67
Critical Content    68
Suggested Readings    68

# CHAPTER 3    *Cultural Influences on Family Functions*    69

Theoretical Grounding    69
Parenting Functions: The Foundation for Cultural Transmission    71
The Culture Ring: Dimensions of Culture and Impact on Parenting    72
Cultural Influences on Discipline Functions    73
*Abstract Mindedness*    73
*Systems of Sanctioning*    74

Cultural Influences on Guidance Functions     74
    *Experience of Difference*     75
    *Values and Religion*     76
Cultural Influences on Nurturing Functions     77
    *Collectivism Versus Individualism*     77
    *Roles and Expectations*     79
Cultural Influences on Accessibility Functions     79
    *Systems of Support*     80
    *Social and Economic Resources*     81
    *Working With Invisible Cultures*     81
Managing Culture With Issues of Family Violence     83
◆ Exercise 3.1: Cultural Influences     85
Summary     87
Critical Content     87
Suggested Readings     87

## SECTION II  Assessing Families: An Introduction     89

## CHAPTER 4  Exploration and Data Collection With Families     91

Theoretical Grounding     92
Exploring Situations With the Family     93
    *Targeting the Question*     94
    *Setting Up the Question*     96
    *Posing the Question*     97
    *Follow-Up*     102
◆ Exercise 4.1: Transitional Tracking     103
Data Gathering Through Observation     106
    *Observing Family Processing*     107
    *Observing Family Actions and Interactions*     112
◆ Exercise 4.2: Observing Family Processing     118
Using Projective Techniques to Gather Data     121
    *Draw a Family*     122
    *Family Sculpting*     122
    *Family Dances*     123
    *Family Metaphors*     123
Using Standardized or Structured Questionnaires     123
    *Reliability*     124
    *Validity*     124
    *Test Types*     125
Using Data Collection and Exploration Skills     126
Summary     127
Critical Content     128
Suggested Readings     128

# CHAPTER 5    Structuring the Family Exploration        129

Theoretical Grounding      129
Assessment Frameworks        130
The Family Genogram        130
  ◆ Exercise 5.1: Developing a Genogram        134
The Four-Cell Assessment of Inherited Family Models        137
    *Cell 1: Genetic and Biological Influences*        138
    *Cell 2: Environmental Influences*        138
    *Cell 3: Beliefs and Cognitive Influences*        140
    *Cell 4: Behavior and Interactions*        142
    *Using the Four-Cell Model: Finding "Rubs" and "Gaps"*        142
  ◆ Exercise 5.2: Assessing a Romantic Relationship        145
The Parenting Functions Framework        147
    *Assessing the Discipline Function*        147
    *Assessing the Guidance Function*        150
    *Assessing the Nurturing Function*        152
    *Assessing the Access Function*        155
    *Making the Assessment*        158
The Risk Assessment Framework        159
    *Actuarial Approaches to Risk Assessment*        160
    *Psychometric Methods of Risk Assessment*        161
    *Clinical Approaches to Risk Assessment*        162
    *Indicators of High Immediacy*        164
    *Indicators of Potential Dangerousness*        166
    *Assessing the Emergence of Risk*        168
  ◆ Exercise 5.3: Risk Assessment        169
Summary        171
Critical Content        172
Suggested Readings        172


# CHAPTER 6    Moving From Assessment
#                      to Treatment        173

Theoretical Grounding        173
Toward Formalizing the Assessment        174
Identifying Critical Data Themes        174
Attributing Meaning to the Array of Themes        176
    *Organizing the Information*        176
    *Generalizing the Meaning*        177
Inferring Potential Solutions        178
Elements of the Assessment Report        179
    *Sample Family Assessment*        181
  ◆ Exercise 6.1: Formal Assessment Elements        191
Developing Treatment Goals        192
    *Formulating Goal Statements*        193
    *Establishing Objectives*        194

*Additional Contracted Elements*     195
*Sample Plan of Care*     196
 • Exercise 6.2: Goal Setting     199
Summary     201
Critical Content     201
Suggested Readings     201

# SECTION III     Building the Working Alliance     203

# CHAPTER 7     Preliminary Engagement With Family Members     205

Theoretical Grounding     206
The Challenges of Engagement     206
Level 1: Tentative Engagement     208
*Getting People to the Session*     208
*Facilitating Initial Interest*     210
 • Exercise 7.1: Tuning in and Pitching Treatment     212
Level 2: Building Investment in the Working Alliance     214
*Affirming Individuals to Build Family Focus*     214
*Establishing an Atmosphere for Work*     215
 • Exercise 7.2: Toward the Working Relationship: Identifying Areas for Exploration     221
Developing a Sense of Purpose     223
*Building on Perspective Overlaps*     223
*Framing the Situation to Promote Collaboration*     226
 • Exercise 7.3: Toward Building a Sense of Purpose     229
Summary     231
Critical Content     232
Suggested Readings     232

# CHAPTER 8     Interactive Engagement With Family Members     233

Working With Family Energy During Interactive Engagement     233
Blocking Automatic Patterns of Reacting     235
*Interrupting Automatic Responses*     236
*Internalizing the Focus*     237
*Shifting From Action to Processing Systems*     237
*Validating Experiences and Perspectives*     238
Neutralizing Negative Energy     241
*Positive Illumination*     241
*Continued Validation*     241
*Identifying Overlapping Themes*     242
*Cycling Back to Neutral Territory*     242

♦ Exercise 8.1: Blocking Automatic Reactions and Neutralizing Energy    244
Building Common Ground    246
   *Closing Gaps Between Family Members*    246
Developing a Foundation for Change    249
   *Highlighting Shared Needs and Desires*    249
   *Developing a Shared Problem Definition*    249
   *Identifying Direction for Change*    250
♦ Exercise 8.2: Building Common Ground    253
Summary    255
Critical Content    256
Suggested Readings    257

# CHAPTER 9    Positioning Families for Change    259

Theoretical Grounding    259
Toward Positioning for Change    260
Understanding Homeostasis    261
Working With Motivating Affect    261
   *Feelings That Motivate Change*    262
   *Recognizing Feelings and Emotions*    263
♦ Exercise 9.1: Positioning Family Members for Change    263
Developing Two Visions: Change Versus Nonchange    265
   *Identifying the Visions*    265
   *Assessing the Balance*    266
♦ Exercise 9.2: Change and Counterchange Forces    268
Positioning Family Members for Change    270
   *Allying With Motivating Feelings*    270
   *Communicating the Dual Visions*    272
   *Juxtaposing Visions*    273
Strategies of Positioning    274
   *Punctuated Positioning*    274
♦ Exercise 9.3: Using the Two Visions    285
   *Interactive Positioning*    287
♦ Exercise 9.4: Interactive Positioning    291
Summary    293
Critical Content    294
Suggested Readings    294

# SECTION IV    Change-Focused Intervention    295

# CHAPTER 10  Direct Change Strategies for Influencing Family Action Systems    297

Theoretical Grounding    297
Changing Action Systems    299
Actor-Model Strategies    299
   *Modeling Interventions*    300

    *Role-Playing Interventions*    301
  ◆  Exercise 10.1: Actor-Model Strategies    301
  Educator-Coach Strategies    302
    *Maintaining Family Empowerment Through "CARE"*    302
    *Using Educator-Coach Strategies*    303
  ◆  Exercise 10.2: Educator-Coach Strategies    311
  Behavior Interruption Strategies    313
    *Time-Out Strategies*    313
    *Cuing Strategies*    314
    *Scheduling Strategies*    315
    *Pattern Interruption Strategies*    316
  Weight-Shifting Strategies    317
    *Contingency Contracting*    317
    *Establishing Ordeals*    319
    *Pairing Stimuli*    320
    *Behavioral Contracting*    320
    *Reinforcing Behavior*    321
  ◆  Exercise 10.3: Using Behavior Interruption and Weight-Shifting Strategies    321
  Summary    324
  Critical Content    324
  Suggested Readings    325

## CHAPTER 11  *Direct Change Strategies for Influencing Family Processing Systems*  327

  Theoretical Grounding    327
  Identifying Processing Themes and Patterns    329
    *Shifts in Focus*    330
    *Repeated Themes*    330
    *Reaction Intensity*    331
    *Cognitive Distortion*    331
  ◆  Exercise 11.1: Identifying Underlying Processing Elements    332
  Highlighting Processing Themes and Patterns    335
    *Critical Skills for Highlighting*    336
    *Critical Description Skills*    336
    *Critical Reflecting Skills*    340
  ◆  Exercise 11.2: Highlighting Family Processing    341
  Challenging Current Systems of Processing    342
    *Reconstructing Beliefs*    343
    *Overgeneralizing Beliefs*    344
    *Amplifying Beliefs*    345
    *Cognitive Restructuring*    346
    *Direct Challenges*    347
  Altering the Experience of Events    348
    *Influencing Internal and External Dimensions*    350
    *Influencing Positive and Negative Dimensions*    356
  ◆  Exercise 11.3: Challenging Beliefs    360

Summary    362
Critical Content    363
Suggested Readings    363

# CHAPTER 12  Influencing Family Members Through Indirect Strategies of Change    365

Theoretical Grounding    365
Using Indirect Methods of Influence    366
Indirect Resource Activation    366
   *Meaning Attribution Exercises*    367
   *Visualization and Guided Imagery*    368
   *Analogies and Metaphors*    370
   *Storytelling Techniques*    373
   *Symbolic Expressive Interventions*    375
♦ Exercise 12.1: Internal Resource Activation    378
Working Through Others in the Family Environment    379
   *Changing Responding Systems*    380
   *Engaging Supports*    382
   *Negotiating Room for Change*    384
♦ Exercise 12.2: Indirect Intervention Through the Environment    385
Summary    389
Critical Content    390
Suggested Readings    390

# SECTION V  Working With Multiproblem and High-Risk Families    391

# CHAPTER 13  Challenges and Promise    393

Theoretical Grounding    393
Toward Helping Multiproblem and High-Risk Families    395
Challenges to Family Resources    395
   *Educational Achievement and Marketable Skills*    395
   *Financial Resources*    396
   *Available Supports*    397
Challenges of Adaptation    397
   *Intergenerational Family Violence*    398
   *Domestic Violence*    399
   *Ineffective Parenting and Socialization*    402
   *Mental Illness and/or Disability*    403
   *Parental Substance Abuse*    404
♦ Exercise 13.1: Understanding Multiple Stressors    407
Challenges to Traditional Treatment Approaches    409
Promising Approaches to Treatment    411
   *Group Treatment*    411
   *In-Home Support*    412

*Multisystemic Treatment*     412
Summary     413
Critical Content     413
Suggested Readings     414

# CHAPTER 14 Multiagency Work     415

Theoretical Grounding     415
Understanding Systemic Family Stresses     416
Formal Support Services     419
    *The Level of Autonomy*     420
    *The Level of Fit*     420
Collaborative Support Functions With Multiple Helping Systems     423
    *Collaborative Support With Other Professionals*     423
    *Collaborative Support With Family Members*     425
    ◆ Exercise 14.1: Support Functions     432
Case Advocacy     434
    ◆ Exercise 14.2: Case Advocacy     437
Class Advocacy     438
    ◆ Exercise 14.3: Class Advocacy     443
Summary     445
Critical Content     445
Suggested Readings     446

# CHAPTER 15 Support-Focused Intervention     447

Theoretical Grounding     447
Support-Based Interventions     448
Principles for Intervention     448
    *Maintaining a Family Focus*     449
    *Maximizing Support and Mutual Aid*     449
    *Avoiding Traditional Responses*     450
Using Group Work Methods     450
    *Developing the Group Structure*     452
    *Establishing Interpersonal Processes*     455
    ◆ Exercise 15.1: Group Intervention     457
In-Home Work With Families     459
Community-Based Family Interventions     462
    *Working Through Host Settings*     463
    *Working Through Community-Based Partners*     464
Summary     465
Critical Content     465
Suggested Readings     466

References     467

Index     496

# Preface

This text is an integration of research and clinical practice literature. Every chapter incorporates research findings on family dynamics and treatment, providing an empirical foundation for critical treatment concepts. The empirical foundation is integrated with current clinical thinking and approaches to offer a blend of practice wisdom and empirically grounded practice. The empirical and practice concepts are then explored and illustrated at a detailed level so readers can understand the steps and elements inherent in each practice skill. The skills are organized into five separate sections. The text begins with Section I, "Thinking Family." Family practice requires workers to think at the family level in order to understand complex family dynamics. In doing so, they must break with long traditions of individualized thinking. Family-specific theoretical approaches and frameworks are provided to allow readers to develop these abilities to understand families without resorting to individual-based theories and conceptualizations.

Section II, "Assessing Families," is an exploration of assessment issues. This section begins by examining exploratory skills that can be used when working with families. Chapters explore assessment methods, frameworks, and other methods for gathering data from family members. The exploratory skills lead to discussions on how to formulate formal family assessments and negotiate family goals for treatment.

Section III, "Building the Working Alliance," dovetails with Section II to provide a foundation for engaging family members. The three chapters of this section each explore different elements of engagement. The section begins by examining the skills needed to solicit family involvement in treatment. The following chapter presents ways of helping family members to be comfortable and active and how to establish a solid working relationship with the family. The last chapter in this section explores methods of preparing and motivating family members to change.

Section IV, "Change-Focused Intervention," builds on the engagement skills, providing strategies for helping families to change. The three chapters in this section present direct and indirect intervention change strategies. The first chapter explores direct methods of changing behavior and interaction. The next focuses on direct methods for changing family affect and thinking. The third chapter of this section explores indirect methods of achieving family change.

Section V, "Working With Multiproblem and High-Risk Families," focuses on hard-to-serve families. This section builds on the previous skills, exploring where traditional approaches may require additional intervention methods to ensure effective help. Multiproblem and high-risk families require additional skills and strategies for change. Family practitioners must be prepared to work with multiple systems to support and enable change in these families. Support and supplementary interventions are explored.

## Acknowledgments

I would like to thank my many students who helped me with different versions of the material in this book. Without such ongoing input and help, this book would not have been possible.

I would also like to think the following reviewers, who took valuable time to read early draft copies of this book and provide important suggestions and feedback: Arturo Acosta, El Paso Community College; Laura Bronstein, Binghamton University; Betty Garcia, California State University, Fresno; Sheri Golk-Kurn, Baker College Muskegon; Leslie Hollingsworth, University of Michigan; Debra Ingle, Kellogg Community College; and Joanne Whelley, Barry University.

# Introduction: Toward Skills-Focused Learning

There are many approaches to teaching family practice. Some educators prefer a theoretical approach whereby they help students learn theoretical models associated with practice. The assumption of this approach to learning is that students must first understand the thinking associated with family treatment so their interventions can be logically integrated and internally consistent (Fagan, 2002). This approach builds very strong thinking skills to guide practitioner decisions as they enter practice. Students are helped to think beyond individual dynamics by developing an appreciation of larger interacting social units (Liddle & Saba, 1982).

When a student begins by learning theory, there is an inherent challenge of translating the theoretical constructs into practice activities (May, 2004; Maynard, 1996). Often students complain about an overemphasis on the theories of treatment and an underemphasis on the skills and strategies of helping families change (Fagan, 2002). Concurrently, theories are forever transforming (May, 2001). Some theories are tainted by social values that constrain families and must be changed or abandoned (McGoldrick, 1998). Other theories change because new thinking in the field is forever causing integration and alterations to theoretical constructs (Bitter, 2004; Bredehoft, 2001; Watts, 2003).

Increasingly, family practitioners are arguing that core competencies must become part of the family practice continuum (Fagan, 2002). All of the theoretical approaches have common goals of helping families master their life situations, and overlapping skills are needed to help families achieve these goals (Fagan, 2002). In particular, practitioners must be able to respectfully listen to families, understand the situation from the family's perspective, engage families in a change process, and help the family members identify and use their internal resources to master the situation (Carich & Spilman, 2004; Fagan, 2002). A critical element of learning must be how the family practitioner uses herself to help the family change (May, 2001).

This text focuses on the skills and common factors underlying multiple family theories. Consequently, to fully understand how to apply the skills in different situations, readers will want to supplement this learning with additional theoretical knowledge. This approach was selected to take advantage of the many excellent family theory texts on the market. Fewer texts focus on the details of common family practice skills. In adopting this approach, readers must be cautioned to avoid becoming technicians and losing touch with the common tenets of family thinking. Immersing oneself in ungrounded and uncommon techniques may result in isolation and lack of support in practice (Stevens, 2000). It is important for the family practitioner to be able to describe his practice and engage with others in supervisory and consultative relationships. If he becomes too immersed in ungrounded technique, this can become a risk.

It is critical to adopt a balanced approach to family practice. Theories help the practitioner to think about families, and individuals within families, from a systemic rather than individualistic perspective. Consequently, this text opens with a section outlining commonly held theoretical assumptions. Although this section is not exhaustive of the available family theories, it can deepen appreciation of the need for theoretical grounding. Ideally, because the primary focus here is on practice skills, readers will have taken a course in family theory before reading this text. Readers who have not studied family theories may want to supplement the readings of this text with additional reading material to stimulate theoretical thinking in concert with the practice material.

To help identify important theoretical materials associated with the various chapters, Table I.1 is provided to allow readers to identify theoretical approaches relating to each chapter as well as note the significant authors associated with each approach. For authors cited in the table, note that complete references are contained in the bibliography of this text. Note also that most of the references in the table refer to books. Books have been selected because they offer the most in-depth analysis of the theoretical approaches. Each text chapter provides additional references, identifying chapters and journal articles that summarize different approaches to family practice. Readers are advised to consult the suggested reading materials to supplement their thinking about practice. For more in-depth material, select from Table I.1.

---

**TABLE I.1**
**Chapter Content and Theoretically Focused Materials**

| Chapter Focus | Related Theoretical Approaches | Important Authors |
| --- | --- | --- |
| 1. Theories and frameworks | Family systems therapy<br>Intergenerational family therapy | Bowen, 1978; Framo, 1992; Carter & McGoldrick, 2005 |
| 2. Parenting | Intergenerational family therapy<br>Family systems therapy | Bross, 1982; Carter & McGoldrick, 2005; Minuchin, 1974 |

| Chapter Focus | Related Theoretical Approaches | Important Authors |
|---|---|---|
| 3. Cultural influences | Multicultural family therapy | Laird & Green, 1996; McGoldrick, Giordano, & Pearce, 1996; McGoldrick, 1998; Walsh, 1996 |
| 4. Exploring family processes | Narrative family therapy<br>Strategic family therapy<br>Symbolic experiential family therapy | Napier & Whitaker, 1978; Penn, 1982, 1985 |
| 5. Structuring exploration | Family systems therapy—Bowen (genograms)<br>Symbolic experiential family therapy<br>Cognitive-behavioral family therapy<br>Communications approach | Haley, 1987; Madanes, 1984; McGoldrick & Gerson, 1985; Satir & Baldwin, 1983; Bowen, 1978 |
| 6. Formal assessment and contracting | Structural family therapy<br>Family systems therapy | Minuchin, 1974; Satir & Baldwin, 1983 |
| 7. Preliminary engagement | Structural family therapy<br>Narrative family therapy | Minuchin & Fishman, 1981; Nichols, 1987 |
| 8. Interactive engagement | Narrative family therapy<br>Constructivist (postmodern) family therapy<br>Communication approach (Satir) | Friedman, 1993; Teyber, 1989; White & Epston, 1990 |
| 9. Positioning | Solution-focused family therapy<br>Strategic family therapy<br>Narrative family therapy | de Shazer, 1985; Watzlawick, Weakland, & Fisch, 1974; White & Epston, 1990 |
| 10. Changing action systems | Behavioral family therapy<br>Strategic family therapy | Falloon, 1988; Madanes, 1981; Selvini-Palazzoli, Boscolo, Cecchin, & Prata, 1978; Watzlawick, Beavin, & Jackson, 1967 |
| 11. Changing processing systems | Narrative family therapy<br>Cognitive-behavioral family therapy<br>Cognitive family therapy<br>Solution-focused family therapy | de Shazer, 1985; Donovan, 2004; Epstein, Schlesinger, & Dryden, 1988; Greenberg & Johnson, 1988; Hudson & O'Hanlon, 1992; White & Epston, 1990 |
| 12. Indirect change strategies | Narrative family therapy<br>Strategic family therapy | Haley, 1973; Lankton, Lankton, & Matthews, 1991 |
| 13. Working with multiproblem families | Multisystemic therapy<br>Family ecosystems approach<br>Family preservation | Aponte, 1994; Minuchin, Colapinto, & Minuchin, 1998 |
| 14. Multiagency work | Empowerment theory<br>Multisystemic therapy<br>Family preservation | Aponte, 1994; Henggeler & Borduin, 1990 |
| 15. Support-based interventions | Multiple-family group treatment<br>Family empowerment approach<br>Family preservation | Henggeler & Borduin, 1990 |

## SECTION I

# THINKING FAMILY

This first section is an exploration of family-based concepts as a foundation for thinking at the family level. Most practitioners are well grounded in individual theory and practice knowledge. This individualistic mode of thinking is reinforced through education, social influences, and past experience. The pervasiveness of individualistic thinking provides a default setting that practitioners often use as a first approach to understanding clinical situations. Such thinking can lead practitioners astray when working with families. This section seeks to provide an alternative set of concepts that can allow for a new approach to understanding clinical situations.

Chapter 1 presents family-based theoretical concepts. The concepts are general to many family theories and do not delve into the specifics of any one theory. To broaden your understanding, you may want to find articles or books that describe specific theories. Because this text is not a theoretical work, it provides only the basic theoretical constructs. Chapter 2 focuses directly on parental functioning. Many family practice situations are parent-child based. In this chapter we explore the nuances of parental functioning through providing a framework for understanding and assessment. In Chapter 3 we explore the influence of culture on family functioning. With families being the main source of cultural transmission, it is important to adjust theoretical understandings to accommodate culture. The chapter focuses primarily on how culture influences parent-child relationships.

Together, these three chapters serve as a foundation for conducting family assessments. The concepts introduced in Section I are central to understanding the rest of the text. As a human services worker and family practitioner, you will want to achieve a comfort level with the concepts and thinking that are central to family work. Without an ability to think at the family level, you may develop practice approaches and strategies that are unlikely to succeed. Spend time with each chapter to become comfortable with each concept.

Chapter 1

# Thinking Family: Theories and Frameworks

In this chapter we explore several common family constructs that must be understood in order to conceptualize problems using a family-based framework. Both systemic and developmental premises are explored to help the reader understand two types of theories often associated with family practice.

## Theoretical Grounding

Throughout this chapter, constructs from different family theories are used to provide a foundation for thinking. Because the chapter is only an overview of the theoretical constructs, many readers will want to deepen their understanding of these constructs. The preface contains recommendations for in-depth sources of information for each chapter, and Table 1.1 outlines specific concepts and indicates the theoretical bases that can expand the discussion and your understanding. A review of the chapters indicated in the recommended reading will provide additional information that can enhance the thinking discussed in this chapter.

Table 1.1 presents theoretical models and supplementary reading options because this text contains little discussion of theory. Although theory is important, the focus of this text is on the skills and strategies needed for professional practice. Because many skills and strategies are used across theoretical models, in this text we will not examine the models' specific nuances and rationale. If the concepts appear incomplete or confusing, you can easily access one of the recommended texts and

**TABLE 1.1**
**Chapter Constructs, Theories, and Sources**

| Chapter Constructs | Theoretical Base | Recommended Reading |
|---|---|---|
| Stages of development | Family development model | Goldenberg & Goldenberg, Chapters 2, 8<br>Horne, Chapters 10, 11<br>Nichols & Schwartz, Chapters 5, 6, 9 |
| Intergenerational effects | Intergenerational model | Goldenberg & Goldenberg, Chapter 6<br>Nichols & Schwartz, Chapters 5, 9 |
| Family interaction | Communication model | Goldenberg & Goldenberg, Chapters 1, 7, 8, 10<br>Nichols & Schwartz, Chapters 4, 5, 7 |
| Energy and energy management | Family systems model | Goldenberg & Goldenberg, Chapters 4, 8, 10<br>Nichols & Schwartz, Chapters 4, 5, 7, 8 |
| Boundaries and boundary management | Family systems model<br>Structural model | Goldenberg & Goldenberg, Chapter 9<br>Nichols & Schwartz, Chapters 4, 5, 7 |
| Intermember exchanges and control | Structural model | Goldenberg & Goldenberg, Chapters 1, 4, 9<br>Nichols & Schwartz, Chapters 4, 5, 7, 8 |
| System-subsystem functions | Family systems model<br>Structural model | Goldenberg & Goldenberg, Chapters 1, 4, 9<br>Nichols & Schwartz, Chapters 4, 5, 7 |

review the chapters indicated. Table 1.1 specifies the following three textbooks merely to optimize your chances of obtaining at least one of them at a local library:

◆ *The Essentials of Family Therapy* (2nd ed.), by M. P. Nichols & R. C. Schwartz, 2005, Boston: Allyn & Bacon.
◆ *Family Counseling and Therapy* (3rd ed.), by A. M. Horne, 2000, Pacific Grove, CA: Brooks/Cole.
◆ *Family Therapy: An Overview* (6th ed.), by I. Goldenberg & H. Goldenberg, 2004, Pacific Grove, CA: Brooks/Cole.

# Toward Thinking at the Family Level

As helping professionals approach the field of family practice, they often struggle to shift their paradigms of understanding from an individual to a family framework. This struggle stems from the predominance of individualistic frameworks for understanding interpersonal situations. Practitioners are typically well versed in models of individual development and adjustment. Such models frequently use the family as a context for individual functioning and do not highlight family processes. A paradigm struggle occurs as practitioners work to focus primarily on family processes.

Contributing to this cognitive struggle, North American culture promotes a focus on the individual. The competitive dog-eat-dog atmosphere, where one person must rise above the others, not only promotes individualism but also makes collectivist thinking suspect. Relational thinking is frequently regarded as a feminist concern;

similarly, collectivist thinking is considered socialist. Such dismissal of nonindividualistic frameworks inhibits exploration of the larger system processes. Consequently, family problems yield attributions of individual responsibility.

Even larger system paradigms are subject to individualistic thinking. You are probably familiar with the notion that a team is only as strong as its weakest member. Notice that in this framework for understanding a team, individualistic thinking controls the interpretation of team problems. There is no consideration of how team members must balance and complement the strengths and liabilities of the other members. This same tendency is common when approaching family situations, where practitioners seek to identify one member of the family who is "dysfunctional" and place the responsibility for family problems on the shoulders of this individual.

---

## CASE EXAMPLE

A mental health worker has been working with a depressed woman for several months with no progress. He has noticed that the woman complains about her husband frequently, so he refers her to a marital worker. In describing the problem to the new worker, the mental health worker says, "She just can't make any progress because her husband is such a jerk. He comes home from work and falls asleep every day. Can you meet with them and smarten this guy up so she can get over her depression?"

---

Notice in the example that even when viewing the problem as a marital issue, the mental health worker uses individual frameworks of understanding to present the problem. It is almost as if individual-based understandings are our default settings for thinking about interpersonal situations. The term *default setting* suggests that in the absence of an alternate framework for understanding, people will naturally revert to individualistic thinking. Consequently, family practitioners must develop methods for "resetting" their interpretive frameworks. Such resetting must be purposeful, to avoid inadvertently operating from the default settings through a lack of conscious attention.

The challenge to family thinking is most pronounced when you, as a family practitioner, are not working with a full family unit. In such situations, you may be working with an individual but need to interpret the situation from a larger family perspective. Some job classifications make this difficult, especially if the mandate has an individual focus. For example, in child welfare, you must work with individual children given that they are the main clients. However, you must also work with the families and think at the family level. If you cannot balance both perspectives, there is a risk that you will rely on default understandings and make decisions that might compromise the family members.

**CASE EXAMPLE**

A child welfare worker is working with a family in which there has been frequent spousal assault against the woman. The child welfare worker is very concerned about the children's aggression and destructiveness in the community. She has identified that the violence in the home is traumatizing the children and has threatened to remove the children unless the woman leaves the man. The woman consequently leaves the batterer, but the children's behaviors have not decreased. Rather, there is a drastic increase because the woman is not able to get the children to follow any rules. The children are running the streets all night and becoming very active in gang activity. Eventually, the children enter the juvenile justice system and are removed from the mother.

In this example you can see that the worker's individual-level thinking, though accurate, demonstrates an incomplete understanding of the situation. Yes, the children were traumatized by the violence, but the worker failed to see that the coercive discipline system developed by the batterer was the only mechanism of control in the family. The worker also failed to understand that undermining the woman's authority in the family (common in domestically violent homes) left the woman unable to control the children without redressing the systemic impact of the violence.

It is important for family practitioners to think both at the individual and family levels to understand how individual family members and the rest of the system develop mechanisms for coexistence. The system accommodates the individuals in the family while they, in turn, adapt to larger family dynamics (Bowen, 1978). There is a constant flow of influence between the family as a system and the individuals within the system as each element adapts and influences the other. This is the crux of family practice. Figure 1.1 illustrates how, even when working with an individual, the family practitioner must maintain the system as a second client. Likewise, when working with the family system, the worker can never lose sight of the individuals. Family practitioners develop skills for working and thinking on both the individual and family level.

# Using Family Theory

Just as individual theory helps practitioners interpret and respond to clients, family theories provide tools for expanding your default thinking to include a family-based framework. Many family theories are available to explore, and you can often find entire texts dedicated to explaining the different theoretical approaches. As mentioned earlier, this text seeks to focus on family practice skills and will not explicate every theoretical approach. Rather, this text builds on common understandings, skills, and

**Figure 1.1** Working With the Family as a Second Client

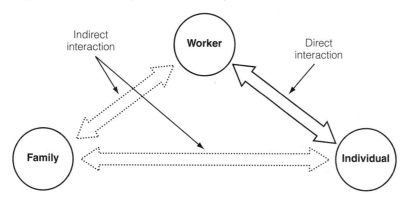

strategies that promote family practice. It is recommended that students read many sources on family practice to glean an understanding of the different theories.

In reading different theoretical approaches, you will discover overlaps and commonalities among the theories. This chapter identifies some commonalities among family theories. Two broad types of theory apply to family practice: developmental and systemic theories. By reading the following discussions of each broad theory type, you can gain some appreciation of the core assumptions of that theory. While reviewing the different approaches, you can identify whether developmental or systemic assumptions are inherent in each approach. Later chapters will build on other commonalties and overlaps among the theoretical approaches to provide a foundation of skills inherent in family practice.

# Understanding Families From the Developmental Perspective

There are many developmental models for understanding how family units change over time. Typically, these models begin with an exploration of unattached adults and progress to aging adults who have launched their adult children (McGoldrick, 2003). Although most family development models have significant cultural and heterosexual biases, it is generally understood that families develop and change from a couple relationship to a family system that involves children. As the children age, the family configurations adjust, and eventually the children launch from the family to form their own family units.

## Developmental Premises

When considering any theory, it is useful to understand the underlying assumptions. Developmental theories tend to share core assumptions. In this section we explore some of the common developmental assumptions inherent in family development theories. Three core assumptions of developmental theories are

1. Optimal direction
2. Stages/tasks
3. The epigenetic principle

***The Assumption of Optimal Direction*** All developmental theories are based on the assumption that development should follow a specific direction for optimal outcomes. They further assume that the natural order of things should correct misdirection and bring development back to the proper developmental path. The metaphor often used in explaining this assumption is the seed. Even when seeds are planted upside down, they will still grow up through the ground toward the light source.

The directional assumption is inherent in many theories that explain growth or adaptation. As a human services student, you are well acquainted with theories of psychosocial development, grieving, and moral development. In each of these theories you can observe that people progress in a prescribed direction if they are to achieve the end result of healthy adjustment. Alternate paths to healthy adjustment are not considered; there is but one single direction.

Relationship and family development theories make this same assumption. In relationship theories, the individual is expected to make the transition from a sense of singleness by entering a mature and committed relationship. This relationship is often viewed as the foundation for the family system. This central relationship transforms when the couple is raising children. Eventually, the children are launched as young adults. Variants such as multiple committed partners, homosexual or lesbian families, childless couples, or single-parent families are seldom included in the assumptions of a proper direction. Such family formations are often viewed as less optimal or less healthy than is the committed heterosexual couple with children (Mayadas & Duehn, 1976; Robin, 1979; Schumm, 2004).

The prerequisites for health in most family development theories assume that an individual follows the developmental path as outlined in the theoretical model. Variations tend to be described as deviations or incomplete (arrested) development, conveying that proper development has failed. The end product is consequently considered flawed or incomplete (Gottlieb, 1991). If you hear a worker describing a family in such terms, you can assume that developmental premises are being used to assess the family's health.

***The Assumption of Stages and Tasks*** The second core assumption of a developmental theory is that development occurs through a series of stages. Each stage requires the mastery of specific developmental tasks. People and systems evolve through several stages, moving from an initial simple state to a more evolved or complete stage of development. The stages are typically identifiable through features and accomplishments. These accomplishments are indicators that some development has occurred. Based on these indicators, family practitioners can identify both the current level of development and the stages that are currently incomplete.

At each stage of development, it is assumed that the individual or system will achieve specific tasks and skills. These are often referred to as *developmental tasks*. Typically, each stage has a specific developmental task that once mastered will lead to the ability to move to the next stage of development. Mastery of the task thus provides indicators that mark a developmental milestone. Theories frequently outline the consequences of failing to achieve developmental tasks. Frequently, success and failure are presented in a polarized manner; the individual or system either continues along the optimal developmental path or deviates into problems. When specific tasks or accomplishments are not achieved, future development is compromised.

Resolving a stage-specific task is frequently presented as a developmental crisis. The crisis implies the importance of resolving the polarized pulls to achieve mastery (or failure). Also implied is a need to reorganize slightly to prepare for the demands of the next stage. Health is implied when the individual or system resolves the crisis in a manner consistent with the theoretical direction. Pathology is typically implied when the person or system deviates from the direction.

*The Assumption of an Epigenetic Principle*   All developmental theories tend to expect one stage of development to provide a foundation for future stages of development. Each stage thus provides changes (skills, competencies, etc.) that allow the next stage to occur. Consequently, it is assumed that the individual or system cannot successfully develop at the more advanced stages without mastering the earlier stages. This is referred to as the *epigenetic principle*.

Workers using developmental premises can usually identify the stage that was failed by observing the lack of specific skills or areas of mastery. The epigenetic principle often promotes such retrospective inquiry, given that the crux of the problem is assumed to be at an earlier stage of development. All development beyond the point where development was disrupted is considered compromised because it is built upon a faulty foundation. Even functional behavior at the higher levels is considered illusionary unless the earlier stages of development are successfully mastered.

## Developmental Problems and Resolutions

Professionals using developmental theories typically frame problems as stemming from failed developmental tasks. When the task is not accomplished, the foundation for future growth and development is compromised. Such compromises influence all future development. Inherently, the failed task sets the stage for future problems and developmental failures (Proudfit, 1984). It is assumed that the individual must rectify the developmental lack by reworking earlier stages of development and mastering the tasks and skills needed for healthier development.

Resolution of developmental problems often requires that the clinical practitioner take the family or family member back to an earlier stage of development so the failed tasks can be successfully completed. You do this by focusing on the developmental tasks that have failed and helping the client to acquire the necessary skills and competencies. After the initial task has been accomplished, you can then redress the ensuing problems so that each stage's critical tasks can be successfully accomplished.

As you can see, intervention is very focused and comprehensive when using developmental theories. Treatment is often long term because the individual or family must first work through the initial problem and then rework the other developmental tasks to assure proper functioning in the present. For example, in working with a volatile and chaotic family, you might start with trying to develop a stable adult relationship—assuming that the couple has not been able to function at a mature level. You can then build on the relationship to help the couple learn to nurture and discipline their children.

# Developmental Applications to Family

When applying developmental premises to families, theorists attempt to explain two areas of family functioning. First, they often concentrate on the adult relationship. This focus promotes theories used by marriage therapists to understand and treat couple problems. The second theoretical thrust emphasizes family system development. Although this focus overlaps with the couple relationship focus (as a first stage), the stages tend to build on the couple relationship as a relational foundation and then focus attention on larger family developments. In this section we explore both types of family development theory to examine some common developmental themes in the marriage and family therapy field.

## Formation of the Adult Relationship

When focusing on family development, the family practitioner cannot ignore the issue of relationship development. Families evolve from a relationship between two adults. As the relationship develops, permanence occurs, and the relationship becomes the foundation for the developing family. This core relationship is often referred to as the *spousal relationship* (based on the traditional family patterns of heterosexual spouses). Regardless of sexual orientation, most families have an adult relationship that anchors the family. Like families, this relationship evolves through several stages of development. Figure 1.2 illustrates a basic developmental sequence including the thresholds (developmental tasks) needed for optimal development.

*Stage 1: Attraction Formation*   The first stage of the adult relationship involves the development of an initial connection between the two adults. This frequently begins with some form of incidental contact. In this initial contact, two sets of considerations occur as each person decides whether to engage in a process of exploration with the other. First, each must decide whether there is sufficient attraction to warrant a meaningful exploration of the other (see Figure 1.2). If the person is sufficiently attractive (at one or more levels), exploration begins by one person engaging the other in conversation. The second person, if sufficiently attracted, will engage in the conversation.

**Figure 1.2** Relationship Formation

---

**Attraction formation**

1. Can attraction to person be maintained in comparison to options?
   - Physical attractiveness (e.g., nice eyes, fit body, etc.)
   - Status attractiveness (e.g., money, car, community)
   - Transference reactions (e.g., like someone else)
   - Utility attractiveness (e.g., make others jealous, protector)
   - Externalized need (e.g., attentive, good listener)
2. Can the attraction to the relationship be maintained in comparison to options?
   - Sexual relations (e.g., sensitivity, level of adventure)
   - Commonalities (e.g., interests, experiences)
   - Validations (e.g., appreciations, accommodations)
   - Infatuation and passion (e.g., prolonged romanticism, hot/cold reactions)
   - Self-completion (e.g., does the person balance out personal deficits)

---

Judgment of desirability

---

**Relationship boundary formation**

1. Can the couple form reasonable boundaries for self and other?
   - Freedom (patterns of accessing and exiting mutual time)
   - Dependence vs. independence balance (meeting needs through other)
   - Negotiate spheres of control (control, influence, no control)
   - Development of ontic quality in the relationship (special identity)
2. Can the the couple achieve a mutual and respectful balance?
   - Negotiated and mutually agreed-on balance (needs, desires, expectations)
   - Aquiescent balance (one gives in to the other)
   - Manipulated balance (setups, guilting, etc. to gain concessions)
   - False self-balance (pretend to be someone you can't maintain)

---

Judgment of acceptability

---

**Formalization of the relationship**

1. Can the couple's models of relationship and family coincide?
   - Default models (compatible or in conflict)
   - Gaps (models must be functional when joined)
2. How are the models brought together to form a new model for the couple and family?
   - Equality (dominance vs. subservience as models combine)
   - Competition (versus developing a mutual model)
   - Negotiation (developing a mutual model)

---

In the discussions and exchanges that follow the initial attraction decision, the two people begin to explore aspects of each other to determine whether there is sufficient compatibility or common ground to form a relationship (Duck, 1985; Neimeyer & Hudson, 1985). In this deepening exploration, both people track and assess the following areas:

◆ **Commonalities** (Caspi & Herbener, 1990; Feeney & Noller, 1990). There is a tendency for people to seek out traits, interests, values, and experiences that are similar or at least familiar (Waring, 1990). This may not always be a conscious choice, but rather a predisposition toward similar patterns of understanding and behavior. Alternatively, some people will seek people who are divergent from elements of their current or past situations. Both outcomes require the individuals to explore and make judgments about the desirability of commonalities.

◆ **Cultural and subcultural influences.** Depending on their cultural background, people are differentially attracted to others. For example, men in the dominant culture prioritize physical attributes of the love object in their attraction, whereas women have been found to prioritize the socioeconomic potential of the male (Buss & Barnes, 1986). Concurrently, people stress aspects that are consistent with their cultural beliefs to determine how the other will respond as they decide on relationship continuation (O'Heron & Orlofsky, 1990).

◆ **Social fit.** People tend to assess potential partners for fit with their friends and family (Duck, 1985; Sprecher, 1988). Early in the relationship, each person is primary affiliated with his or her social network. Consequently, negative feedback about the relationship can cause its dissolution. The ease of such influence suggests that relationship boundaries are not established at this early point.

In the ongoing exploration, each person requires feedback from the other to establish relationship values. This occurs as each person identifies traits he or she values; and through their interaction and behavior, the couple validates these critical traits within the relationship. As each person identifies and validates traits in the other, they create personal meaning in the relationship through moments of acceptance and celebration (Neimeyer & Hudson, 1985). Establishing personalized meaning in each other increases the likelihood of continued relationship development for the two people (Neimeyer & Neimeyer, 1985).

Initially, the validation process is a romantic venture as each person discloses aspects of himself or herself, prompting experiences of being valued and validated. Such romance and newness often result in a desire to please each other (Berg & McQuinn, 1986; Carter & McGoldrick, 2005). Over time, patterns of interaction and behavior develop in the relationship (Watanabe-Hammond, 1990). If the evolving behavior patterns are complementary, a feeling of affiliation develops (Bluhm, Widger, & Miele, 1990). The sense of affiliation frequently results in each person adjusting his or her individual behaviors to suit the other person (Berg & McQuinn, 1986).

Based on the shared information, experience of validation, and developing affiliation, each person reflects on the relationship and decides whether the other person is sufficiently desirable to forsake potential relationships with other people. Such decisions involve affective experience, values, ambitions, and other considerations as each person envisions how the relationship can meet their long-term aspirations. This decision results in each person deciding to continue meeting with and exploring the other.

In this earliest stage of the relationship, problems can occur depending on each person's conduct when with the other. Four common problems occur at this stage of relationship development.

1. **Idealization.** When one member of the relationship idealizes the other rather than objectively assessing the potential partner (Carter & McGoldrick, 2005), the attraction decisions are made based on idealized illusions. In such situations, one person acts as if the other fits the ideal, even though this is not objectively confirmed.

2. **Acquiescence.** A second problematic behavior involves one partner pressuring the other into assuming traits or behaviors that are not inherent in the individual (Firestone, 1987; Green & Brown-Standridge, 1989). When that person acquiesces to the pressure, he (or she) cannot be himself (or herself) in the relationship. Again, the decisions are based on illusions rather than reality. This dynamic will interfere with continued satisfaction in the relationship (Neimeyer & Neimeyer, 1985).

3. **Image management.** Sometimes one person may promote and seek validation for a desired self-image (Firestone, 1987). This often involves extreme self-presentations (e.g., always being nice or gracious). However, such promotion may break down and lead to volatility when issues of separateness and rejection emerge in the relationship (Schlenker & Trudeau, 1990). If personal identity issues predominate for one of the members, energy is channeled into individual needs rather than into the creation of a relationship system.

4. **Lack of scrutiny.** Sometimes couples fail to scrutinize the relationship for a realistic appraisal of fit. This is common when other factors motivate the couple to continue or speed up relationship development. In such situations, the relationship may be seen as an answer to problems. Possible contributing factors include

   ◆ Escaping from an unhappy family of origin
   ◆ Escaping from personal pain or experiences of rejection
   ◆ Manipulating acceptance from the family of origin
   ◆ Competition with friends or family
   ◆ Overvaluing the visual or symbolic meaning of the other
   ◆ Pregnancy or catastrophic occurrences that push development prematurely
   ◆ Lack of emotional autonomy and maturity

*Stage 2: Relationship Boundary Formation*   As the relationship continues to develop, boundaries are negotiated. In this negotiation there is a relaxation of personal or individual boundaries concurrent with restricting the flow of emotional energy outside of the relationship. Individually, boundaries build on affiliation as each person yields elements of his or her individual boundaries to form a sense of unity and an identifiable relationship. In this negotiation, patterns of closeness, vulnerability, and separateness evolve (Houle & Kiely, 1984; O'Connell, 1972). The emerging couple begins to establish the basic relationship expectations and codes for being together.

Concurrent with the individual boundary adjustments, boundaries between the couple and the environment must be established to achieve a relationship identity

(Carter & McGoldrick, 2005). Decisions must be made about which friends and family members will influence the system. Parameters for the nature of influence and protocols for accessing people across the boundary develop. This can be a difficult time for the couple as each person adjusts old relationships to permit emotional energy for the new relationship. During this period of adjustment, conflicts of loyalty may emerge when people on either side of the relationship exert pressures to minimize the changes or sacrifices being made to develop relationship boundaries. Most readers have experienced or witnessed relationships in which partners or friends create competition and conflicts as they vie for more exclusive time with a person in a new relationship.

Successful negotiation of relationship boundaries requires maturity in all of the people involved with the couple. If competition emerges, triangulation occurs, wherein people slander each other and set up members of the relationship so they must make difficult choices and selections. Decisions can become even more difficult when unfavorable selections are interpreted as rejection. The ongoing vying for influence and refusal to renegotiate past relationships are usually inherent in boundary problems.

Four frequent problems are associated with this stage of development. These problems tend to prompt referrals for service at later stages of family development. At the point of referral there is usually a long history of arguing about family or friends and deep feelings of resentment between the members of the relationship. The four common problems are as follows:

1. **Failure to discuss** situations in a manner that allows both individuals to be honest (Zusman & Knox, 1998). When individual reactions to differences (e.g., volatility, withdrawal, acquiescence, learned helplessness) cause one member to edit his or her input, boundaries are not based on equal and honest feedback. The resulting boundaries tend to be influenced by hidden elements.

2. **Feelings of obligation** or loyalty that elevate the priority of prior relationships and inhibit boundary development (Nix, 1999). Friends and family often create guilt or other emotional reactions that elevate their power and influence over one of the relationship partners. This in turn yields great influence over the relationship and ensuing development.

3. **Failure to relinquish individual autonomy** in service to the relationship (Zimmer-Gembeck, 2002). Sometimes relationship partners attempt to retain their same level of individual functioning and autonomy after they have entered a relationship. If one person refuses to sacrifice on behalf of the relationship, the other member often compensates by increasing their level of sacrifice. If both members attempt to retain single functioning, a relationship of low commitment can be maintained; but this relationship establishes a poor foundation for family development.

4. **False representation** of one member during formative stages (Neimeyer & Hall, 1988; Rowatt, Cunningham, & Druen, 1999). If one member presents a false self or has not fully formed an autonomous identity, boundaries may be established that subsequently do not fit the couple. This is because the negotiation of the boundary is based on spurious input.

At the conclusion of this stage of development, the couple has established a relationship identity and system of interacting with the environment. This allows both relationship partners to make a judgment about the relationship and decide whether the situation is acceptable. If each person accepts the relationship system (either explicitly or implicitly), then development continues. If elements are identified as unacceptable, the couple either terminates the relationship or renegotiates the elements that are identified as unacceptable.

*Stage 3: Formalization of the Relationship*  The final stage of relationship development is relationship formalization. It is during this stage that the patterns of ongoing operation are established for the couple system. Expectations and norms are developed, so that each person increasingly knows what to expect from the other. The formalization affects all of the response systems (action, interaction, beliefs and thinking, and affect). Table 1.2 captures some of the areas of formalization within each response system. Note in reviewing Table 1.2 that many of the patterns that will characterize the relationship emerge during this stage. In reviewing the table, you can see that the actions and sharing between the relationship members set the stage for ongoing expectations.

The formal structures that begin to emerge in the relationship are often predicated on earlier events or precedents. Consequently, healthy development requires each member of the relationship to share his or her reactions in an open and honest manner. There is an implicit assumption of equal partnership wherein each person is free and willing to share his or her thoughts and responses to ensure that the structures are fair to each other. When one member of the relationship censors what he or she says or elects to have no response to events, formal structures can form in a manner that disadvantages one person in favor of the other. Over time, this disadvantage becomes part of the negotiated relationship system and may lead to eventual problems.

The shift from one's family of origin model to a new model occurs as both members of the couple identify elements in each family that they want to keep or reject. Ideally, the models of both individuals should be complete and reasonably healthy. Problems can occur when each person's model of family lacks important elements needed to contribute to a healthy relationship. For example, suppose in one couple that the man comes from a violent family whose members respond to differences with volatile reactions. He will have learned that differences are bad and that tension associated with differences must be avoided. If the woman in that couple is from a family with no functional system for resolving differences (e.g., the parents never argued in front of the children), neither person will have a system for solving problems. This can create difficulties because neither model of family has the important element of problem solving.

A second issue associated with the family models inherited from a person's family of origin is incompatibilities in the original models. For example, one partner grew up in a family where differences were welcomed and the family enjoyed long debates and friendly arguments. The other partner, however, grew up in a verbally abusive family where expressions of difference yielded attacks. In such situations, one member will believe that arguing is healthy and the other may experience anxiety and feel

**TABLE 1.2**
**Response System Adaptations During Formalization**

| Response Systems | Formalization Function |
|---|---|
| Interaction | ◆ **Patterns of decision making.** The couple develops repeated patterns for making decisions.<br>◆ **Managing conflict and difference.** The couple experiences and resolves differences, setting precedents for how conflict will be handled in the future.<br>◆ **Support provision.** The couple develops mechanisms for triggering support provision and nurturing responses. |
| Behavior | ◆ **Role structures.** Individuals develop roles for attending to the relationship needs and managing the boundaries.<br>◆ **Behavioral tolerances.** Through precedence, the couple develops tolerances for each other's behaviors. Standards of what is or is not acceptable develop.<br>◆ **Rituals.** The couple develops rituals for marking special events and occasions. These become part of the relationship system for celebration, grieving, and so forth. |
| Affect | ◆ **Expressive systems.** Each member of the relationship develops his or her own method of expressing affect. The other person's response to these expressions sets the stage for ongoing patterns.<br>◆ **Proximity management.** The couple develops methods of tracking each other, including setting tolerances for how long and how far each can stray from the other.<br>◆ **Tension management.** The couple develops a system for monitoring and responding to tension in the relationship.<br>◆ **Replenishment systems.** The couple develops methods of soothing and replenishing emotionally within the relationship. The role of each person becomes prescribed by his or her responses. |
| Beliefs | ◆ **Establishing shared values.** The couple highlights important values that guide them in their behavior and interactions. Shared goals emerge based on these values.<br>◆ **Establishing shared beliefs.** The couple develops beliefs used for interpreting their environment and understanding situations.<br>◆ **Establishing resource priorities** (time, money, etc.). Based on values and beliefs, the couple sets up priorities on how resources, such as time and money, are to be invested. |

that arguing is bad. To develop a new system that works for both people in the forming family, these significant differences must be discussed.

The requirement for honest input into how the relationship structures emerge gives rise to three common types of problems associated with this stage (Firestone, 1987). These include withholding, undermining, or sanctioning input.

1. **Withholding input.** Sometimes one member will not provide feedback or input to the other while the relationship norms are forming. For example, one member might have a long history of being abused, so learned helplessness causes him to believe that his reactions do not matter.

2. **Undermining input.** Sometimes one member will discredit, manipulate, or otherwise criticize the input of the other member. In such situations,

devaluing one position allows the other position to have unfair weight in forming the relationship norms.

3. **Sanctioning input.** Sometimes one member will punish or attack the other when she responds to relationship events. This type of reaction causes the member who is attacked to withhold honest feedback that could shape the relationship norms.

With relationship formalization, the couple moves into a committed relationship with some expectation that they will remain together into the future. The couple begins to develop a vision for what their relationship will be like in the future and how each person will be able to meet his or her needs within the relationship. There is often contemplation of cohabitation and engaging in rituals such as marriage. Note in the sequence of events just described that this developmental sequence is heavily influenced by the dominant North American culture. With other cultural groups, different sequences will occur, especially if cultural expectations involve parental selection of spouses or there are cultural group pressures toward homogeneity. It is possible to generate different models for multiple groups, each beginning with an initial connection and ending with formalization.

Most interesting in models of relationship development are the patterns of connection and progress in the relationship. Regardless of culture, sexual orientation, race, or other demographic groupings, every committed adult relationship progresses through a series of stages as relationship members evolve from two individuals to a couple. It is intriguing that the decisions and patterns developed in the early stages of a relationship often directly influence the couple-based problems that emerge later in the relationship. Many family-system problems are also indirectly associated with early couple development.

## Family System Development

As a committed couple moves into the future together, they often begin to form a family system. As in the couple development sequence just described, developmental concepts can be applied to the family as a system. Typical models of family system development begin with a childless couple and conclude with older adults with adult children (White, 1991). There are multiple models of family development, ranging from four to ten stages of development depending on the complexity used by the author when describing the developmental stages (Bross, 1982). In most models of family development, thematic patterns are evident. Within each thematic cluster of activities, certain changes occur as family members age and as the environmental expectations change, eventually leading to young family members differentiating from the family system (Bowen, 1974). Following are some of the thematic clusters:

◆ The adult(s) must develop sufficient supports to cope simultaneously with environmental demands and internal family demands (Goldman, Gier, & Smith, 1981; Olson, 1988; Bross, 1982).

◆ The adult(s) must develop systems for meeting the basic needs of family members who are dependent (Fishbein, 1982).

◆ The adult(s) must develop systems for enhancing the autonomy and competence of family members over time (Shapiro, 1988).

◆ The adult(s) and youth must promote individuation of family members so that the developmental cycle can be repeated in the next generation (Bowen, 1978).

Family development adapts and fluctuates with the individual development of family members (Hareven, 1986; Hooper & Hooper, 1985; Bross, 1982). Developmental processes initially change as a system with adult members adds highly dependent young members. The dependence of children requires the adults to adapt and change. More adaptation is required as the highly dependent members increase their ability for autonomous thinking and action. This change in the children requires retooling of the adult systems that responded to dependency. As the children expand their sphere of operations and assume increased control of their lives, again adult systems must adapt. Eventually, the family must adapt to membership changes as children form their own adult relationships and assume independent functioning. Similarly, the family system must adapt to job, health, and goal changes in the adults. When many families adapt the same way in similar situations, it is considered to be part of normal family development. The following seven stages are typical of many family development models.

1. Family systems comprised of the adult couple
2. Family systems with infants and very young children
3. Family systems with school-age children
4. Family systems with adolescents
5. Family systems with young adult children
6. Families where children have left the nuclear system
7. Family systems with aging parents

Without subscribing to a specific developmental model, it is important to understand some of the common changes that occur in family systems as members develop and grow. These changes are described next, based on functions and common family processes rather than presented as discrete developmental stages. This approach is appropriate because no single model of development is sufficient to understand the vicissitudes of family development. Rather, it is important to be able to understand how and why families are adapting (or not adapting) based on the needs and demands of the individual family members and the environment in which the family develops (McCubbin & Lavee, 1986). Here are some of the common adaptive changes:

1. **Interactive system changes** (Wynne, 1984; Zuk, 1971). Interaction must adapt and change over the family life cycle. Initially there is only adult interaction, which is frequently dyadic in nature. This one-to-one system of communication is simple in many respects. People must deal with each other somewhat directly given that there are limited alternatives. If the relationship is to continue, the partners must interact. When a family system adds

more members (possibly through birth or adoption, or when relatives move in, thus joining two systems with more than one person), interaction becomes more complex because triangles become common. Family members must be able to adapt their interaction systems to accommodate potential triangles without disrupting the health of the system. In families where this accommodation does not occur, it is common to find indirect communication, collusion among the family members, and triangulation of conflicts.

2. **Hierarchal system changes** (Skynner, 1976; Wynne, 1984). When individuals join to form a family, there is movement from autonomous functioning to some form of partnership. Power and authority must be adapted so that each person can move from the individual stage to the point where he or she can accommodate another person. Many people struggle with the move from being the "king" or "queen" of their own life to a partnership situation where they must accommodate another person. Adaptation must again occur with the addition of children, because adult members must assume leadership and authority over the children. Family members need to determine the system of power and authority that will be used. As children decrease in their dependence, hierarchal systems must adapt to support individuation and the development of autonomy.

3. **Support function changes** (Bertram, 2000; Kagan & Weissbourd, 1994). As people in a family system age, the nature and types of support needed to survive and grow change. With very young children, support is total and involves emotional, instrumental, informational, and appraisal forms of support. As the children develop, they begin to garner emotional and appraisal support from peers rather than from parents, but instrumental support often remains a parenting function.

4. **Boundary maintenance changes** (Skynner, 1976). As families develop, boundaries tend to change. When the family is a couple, the boundaries are very open to friends of all sorts. With the addition of children, some of the friends may be screened out, and extended family members may be allowed greater access. When children reach school age, teachers and other systems increase their influence. It is easy to see how different levels of development require boundary adjustments.

5. **Ontic relationship changes** (Bross, 1982). The sense that the relationship is special changes throughout the family's life. With a couple, the sense of specialness (ontic quality) comes from the romance, closeness, and sharing in the relationship. When children are part of the family, some of the feelings that the family is a special place are derived from the children's accomplishments.

6. **Role function changes** (Lu & Lin, 1998; Mederer & Hill, 1983). As the family changes over time, new roles are assumed and old roles are often discarded. With the addition of children, parents acquire many new roles, often leading to role conflicts. At this time, each parent may attempt to impose his or her inherited family roles, requiring significant negotiation of the role systems.

7. **Processing of difference changes** (Bowen, 1974, 1978). At different points of family development, the systems of processing and accepting difference must change. Early in the relationship, couples tend to focus on similarities because differences might threaten the relationship. Over time, the parents must adapt to differences without experiencing threat in order for the children to become autonomous.

These changes occur at each stage of development. Critical times that necessitate these changes include the addition of children (births, adoption), adding other adult members (e.g., remarriage, caring for elderly parents), expanding child autonomy (e.g., going to school, becoming teens, getting married), and expanding systemic linkages (e.g., when children go to school, families must deal with school systems, teams, and so forth). As each developmental situation occurs, the developmental structures must adapt to ensure that the system remains functional.

Although developmental premises suggest that adaptation follows a predictable sequence, not all adaptations occur according to developmental models. Divorce, illness or disability, death of a family member, and changes in the family environment all will require systemic adaptation. Increasingly, changes to developmental models are proposed to include elder care, chronic diseases, marital changes, and single parenting (Mills, 1984; Nichols & Pace-Nichols, 1993). Such alterations to the basic developmental model suggest that family development is inherently complex and must be approached with respect to family subtleties rather than with the assumption that family development follows a simple path.

In the next section we explore some of the systemic concepts that will help you gain an understanding of such adaptation. Between the developmental concepts of this section and the systemic concepts of the next, most family-based theories are subsumed. Remember that the discussions in this chapter cannot provide a full theoretical exploration. You are encouraged to explore many theories to broaden your thinking and knowledge.

# Using Systemic Premises to Understand Families

The second type of family theory is based on the systemic paradigm. This type of theory focuses on how the family as a unit operates at any given time and how systems adapt to their environment. Systemic theories describe interactions, processing, and dynamics, but they do not have a clear sense of right and wrong or cause and effect. Although it is important to understand the system-based theories that influence family practice, this chapter provides only a brief discussion to highlight common systemic concepts that will bear influence on practice. Because this is a practice text, it is assumed that students will have taken theory courses either concurrent with or prior to the current course.

It is useful to note that many theories focus on subsystems or smaller systemic concepts and present themselves as unique family theories. Recent advances in our understanding of how family members attribute meaning to their experiences are often discussed as radically new theories, yet they still build on the basic systemic constructs and premises. By understanding these core constructs, you can read and understand new theoretical developments within a larger context.

## Systemic Concepts

In any system-based theory, some consistent assumptions underlie the theoretical understanding. In practice, it is important to be clear about such assumptions because they provide a foundation for the interventions selected. In this section we examine some of the critical systemic concepts in order to provide a blueprint for understanding systemic functioning in the here and now. The concepts do not explain how the system came to function in a given manner, but they do document the current systemic functioning.

Systemic theories are based on five critical concepts. Different theories will focus on or prioritize different elements, but the following five concepts are quite consistent across the many systemic theories:

1. Energy and energy management (Jackson, 1957)
2. Boundaries and boundary management (von Bertalanffy, 1950; Minuchin, 1974)
3. Intermember exchanges and control (Jackson, 1959)
4. Interaction patterns (Minuchin, 1974)
5. System-subsystem functions (Minuchin, 1974)

## Energy and Energy Management

Most systemic theories have some concept of energy or balance. It is assumed that systems require energy to survive. It is also assumed that energy is balanced, so that things do not become too chaotic or too stagnant. If there is too much energy, system members cannot function properly because there is too much to attend to. Likewise, too little energy will lead to lethargy and atrophy. In family systems, energy is exchanged across boundaries.

The family system contains mechanisms that serve to manage the ways that energy is expressed and managed among the family members. Family practitioners pay attention to how energy is managed in the family system. Here are some of the family indicators or energy processes:

1. **Affiliation systems.** To understand the energy exchanges in family relationships, family practitioners often focus on patterns of affiliation (how family members feel toward each other). When members are closely aligned they interact more, support each other, and express positive affect toward each other (Allcorn & Diamond, 1997; Biringen, 1990; Boverie, 1991; Ray, Upson, & Henderson, 1977; Wheelan et al., 1994). Concurrently, there are patterns

of negative affiliation wherein some members dislike other members. Such energy exchanges provide important information about family systems.

2. **Atmosphere and morale.** In families, there is often shared emotion or affect (Allcorn, 1995; Robbins, 1993; Forgatch, 1989). Such emotional energy is often displayed through nonverbal messages. Positive energy is often displayed through playfulness and laughter; negative energy is often shown through silence and negativity. Family practitioners pay close attention to the nature of family energy expressed by people in the family system.

3. **Belief and meaning systems.** Family systems transmit values and beliefs from the adult generation to the children (Bagarozzi & Anderson, 1989). Such transmission occurs through repetitive messages and themes produced by the adult members of the families. The themes may provide positive examples for the members, or they may illustrate how members should not respond. Such themes are often embedded in family stories that are repeated among the membership. Inherent in these repeated stories are the scapegoats, heroes, and themes that instruct system members on how to interpret and respond to situations (Byng-Hall, 1988). These instructions outline the desirable and prohibited energy exchanges by attaching interpretation guides. Concurrent with family-influenced belief generation, individuals in the family also attribute meaning to their experiences. Increasingly, family practitioners explore the individual-level attributions and meanings based on the individual-level stories (Firestone, Firestone, & Catlett, 2003).

4. **Tension management.** Families constantly adjust the tension and energy in the system to maintain equilibrium. When tension becomes too high for the system, family members will trigger mechanisms to assure that tension is brought back within an acceptable range. If there is not enough tension to keep the family active, a family member will also stimulate the family. Practitioners seek to understand how tension is managed in the family and who in the family triggers the tension release and activation functions. In many families the tension management systems and role structures can blend, resulting in scapegoats and heroes in the family. The key to understanding these tension management systems is to tune into the whole-system impact of the tension.

5. **Family rituals** (Albert, Amgott, Krakow, & Marcus, 1979; Richlin-Klonsky & Bengston, 1996). Rituals are patterned behavior occurring on a repeated basis. The rituals may be positive or negative in meaning but will tend to contain some power in how the family channels energy associated with specific events. Family practitioners pay close attention to ritual activities to determine the function of the activity at the family level. Here are two common rituals:

    ◆ **Special occasion rituals.** These rituals are used to channel energy when expectable events arise (e.g., Christmas dinner, meeting the parents). Such rituals provide a mechanism for controlling energy exchanges.

◆ **Routine rituals.** These rituals often are used to control the energy levels during specific times of the day, when energy might become misdirected or otherwise problematic (e.g., bedtime routines). Routine rituals may also be used to create a desired type of energy through routinely engaging all family members in a specific act (e.g., Sunday dinners).

## Boundaries and Boundary Management

Systems theories will contain some sense of boundary between different systems, subsystems, or levels within a system. Elements are viewed as part of a much larger network of systems, all of which operate in some sort of balance. The view can expand to the universal level or be microscopic and focus on how cells operate. In families, boundaries refer to the structures and methods that family members use to separate the family unit from its environment and one subsystem from the other (Bowen, 1978; Minuchin, 1974). When exploring boundaries, the family practitioner assesses the boundary placement and boundary maintenance within the family system. Boundary placement focuses on who is included within the boundary. Some families may include friends as part of the parenting system or will operate on an extended kinship model of family. Consequently, workers want to understand who is included within each system or subsystem.

Concurrent with understanding boundary placement, the family practitioner also needs to understand the permeability of the boundary. *Permeability* refers to the ease with which people external to the boundary can enter and influence the system. If people outside the system (or subsystem) can too easily exert influence across boundaries, it is often a sign of problems. For example, when children begin assuming parental functions it is sometimes a sign of inadequate parental functioning. Similarly, if friends or extended family members have great influence on family decisions, it is a sign that the boundary around the family is highly permeable. In any given situation, the impact of boundary permeability may be either helpful or harmful. Workers must assess the permeability and the outcomes to understand how the boundaries are functioning for the family.

Some families are very rigid and do not allow outsiders to know what is occurring inside the family. Such boundaries are referred to as *rigid*. Other families appear chaotic with outside people cycling through important roles with little apparent thought. Such boundaries are often referred to as *loose* or *highly permeable*. When interpreting how family boundaries are functioning, family practitioners must consider issues of culture and vulnerability before assuming that the boundaries are problematic. Some cultures are highly collectivist, resulting in many people having influence within the family boundary. Similarly, families living below the poverty line often must loosen their boundaries to function because there are not enough monetary resources entering the family to allow it to function effectively. In such situations, children watching children may occur because there is not enough money to hire a caregiver.

In any family, there are multiple boundaries. To organize the thinking about boundaries, family theorists have identified critical boundaries for understanding family functioning. In family systems, theorists most often look at these boundaries:

◆ **Family-environment boundary.** How easily others can enter and influence the family functioning.
◆ **Generational boundaries.** How access and influence occur between the adults and children within any generational system. This includes the access and influence between adult children and their parents.
◆ **Subsystem boundaries.** How the different subsystems within a family (spousal systems, parental systems, sibling systems) influence and respond to each other.

*The Family-Environment Boundary*   The family-environment boundary distinguishes who is considered a family member; this includes both kin and fictive kin (Bowen, 1978; Minuchin, 1974). Practitioners must be careful in making assumptions about this boundary, because each family system controls who will be included in important family decisions. It is very common for people with no blood relationship to family members to occupy a role in the family system. These people are often referred to as *fictive kin*. Such people act like extended kin within the family system and will have access comparable to that of blood-related family members.

When people such as fictive kin are included in the family, practitioners are often interested in how such people were selected and how many people are able to occupy such central roles in the family system. In families where fictive kin cycle through the family one often becomes concerned about how well people are screened as they enter the family system. When there are multiple people occupying fictive kin roles, practitioners often are interested in how the family members manage these multiple influences.

In all of these assessments, the critical consideration is how well the family is functioning as a unit. If things are chaotic and rules change based on who is in the room at the time, the family's boundaries might be considered too permeable. Conversely, if nobody is allowed into the home and family members are not permitted to share family information with people outside of the family, the concern may be that the family is too insulated from external influences and at risk of being shut off. Each situation must be explored within the cultural, subcultural, and economic realities of the family to determine whether the boundaries are creating problems.

*Generational Boundaries*   Generational boundaries are drawn between the child and adult levels of the family. There are generational boundaries between the young children and their parents as well as the adults in the family and their parents (Minuchin, 1974). Related to the generational boundary is the system's mechanism for making decisions and accomplishing tasks (Godwin & Scanzoni, 1989; Rusbult, Johnson, & Morrow, 1986). It is important to identify family decision-making processes and power structures and how they relate to the generational boundaries. Often, the family decision making involves a hierarchy with the parents, grandparents, or other adult members assuming critical leadership functions. If children are assuming the critical decision-making functions, the practitioner will want to explore the placement and permeability of the generational boundary.

The generational hierarchy reflects the roles that people assume within the family system. For example, in some families parents may make all decisions. In some families this role is split according to gender, with male parents making some types of decision and female parents making others. The decision-making power may even reside in the extended kin system. When engaging such families, workers must make sure that the critical decision makers have had input and agree to the direction of service. If they are not engaged, their influence over the rest of the system may result in failed engagement.

When a hierarchy is lacking, decision-making power changes from situation to situation. Typically, several family members may have input into decisions. When critical situations arise, the family may lack the leadership needed for an effective response. Such family systems are difficult to engage because decisions may shift with priorities. With no clear leadership, it is hard to ensure continued work toward goals.

*Subsystem Boundaries*   In a stereotypical family system, there are three common subsystems. Although these subsystems are discussed in terms of common patterns, the subsystems may look different based on the roles of fictive kin and family living arrangements. The common subsystems include parental, spousal, and sibling subsystems. Each subsystem has its own functions, which we will explore later in the chapter. In this discussion, it is important to understand that there are boundaries between the subsystems isolating subsystem functions and separating the role expectations of family members.

Subsystem boundaries are associated with role structures that dictate expectations and privileges available to the family members (Minuchin, 1974). Some roles and privileges are limited to specific subsystems. For example, child-rearing roles such as disciplinarian and nurturer are most often reserved for people within the parental subsystem. Likewise, the roles of lover and/or sexual partner are commonly reserved for the spousal subsystem. At the child level, frequent roles include distracter, clown, and dependent roles. Given the nature of these roles and functions, it is easy to understand the importance of maintaining subsystem boundaries. When family members cross these boundaries, problems can occur. This is especially true when the family system begins to rely on boundary breaches to maintain long-term functioning.

When observing subsystem boundaries, it is often important to understand the mechanisms that people use for accessing people and functions across the boundaries. Children must be able to reach across the boundaries to activate needed parental responses. If the boundary is too rigid, activating parental responses will be difficult. Children may then have to resort to destructive means of gaining parental input. If the boundary is too permeable, parents intrude on the children's autonomy and interfere with their ability to function. Families must achieve a delicate balance that preserves boundaries while allowing family members to meet each other's needs.

To understand the multiple areas of balance, view the circles in Figure 1.3. Also envision the circles moving to different positions. For example, if the mother's circle

**Figure 1.3**   Boundary Maintenance Systems

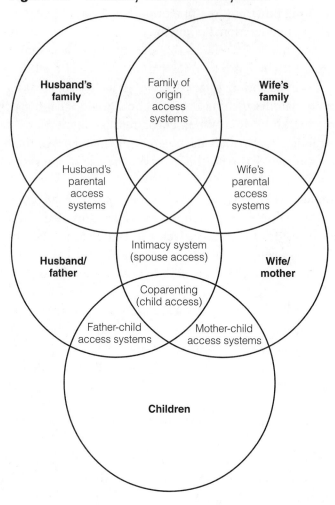

moves up into her family of origin, the overlap between the families of origin increases, while the overlap with the spouse decreases. The wife in such situations can be expected to be more influenced by her family of origin than by her family of procreation. Moving circles in such a manner helps to identify potential problems associated with boundaries.

## Intermember Exchanges and Control

A third concept of systemic theories is *exchanges* across boundaries. This concept builds on the concepts of boundaries and energy. The concept of exchange is inherent in the development of boundaries. Every system must bring in resources from its environment or external systems in order to survive (Jackson, 1959). The concept of exchange explores how important resources are acquired and distributed within the family system. Common exchanges include money, sustenance needs, information, support, and recreational opportunities. These elements allow for an exchange whereby family members expend energy in order to acquire something that meets their needs. Inherent in the concept of exchange is the understanding that as something enters the system, something is given up by the system to accommodate and acquire the resource. For example, in order to get money, one of the family members must agree to give up something (e.g., time, dignity) so that the other system will release the money to the system.

Exchanges are often governed by family norms. Family norms are patterns of exchange that have become second nature in families. Consequently, each member knows what is expected of him or her based on the actions of the other members. When family members deviate from the norms, tension is introduced and family members act to bring the family member back into "normal" behavior (Jackson, 1959). Corrective acts often involve informal pressures such as ostracizing the member or increasing tension to reestablish expectable behavior. Family norms differ greatly across families. For example, some families argue loudly and don't consider a person serious unless he or she is vehement about their position. Other families may view volume as indicating anger. Regardless of the behavior, no inferences can be drawn without knowing what is normal within the family. Here are some specific areas in which practitioners may want to explore normative behavior:

◆ Expressions of emotion (e.g., intimacy and closeness, anger, tension)
◆ Granting of privileges and freedoms (e.g., special treatment, who gets to do what)
◆ Reinforcing standards (e.g., what is good enough, what is good and bad)
◆ Providing support (e.g., who is worthy of support, how a member gets support)

When norms are seriously violated, family control mechanisms are enacted. *Control mechanisms* refer to the methods that the family system uses to control the acts of members. Control mechanisms are central to the action system because they reinforce desirable behavior and/or dissuade problem behaviors in the system. It is important that the mechanisms be consistently applied with a rationale endorsed by most people within the system (Lansberg, 1988; Smith, Kamistein, & Makadok, 1995). Some family systems have no control mechanisms, allowing behavior from family members to be expressed with no attempt to influence or limit the behavior. Such systems often become the focus of external scrutiny, and society is usually expected to control or change the family to ensure that the lack of limits does not impinge on other systems.

Multiple forms of power and control occur in the family system. The following list is a brief exploration of the different power systems that can occur within the family. Note that each type of power has limitations and conditions.

◆ **Coercive power** (French & Raven, 1959). This strategy of gaining power usurps power from others by creating fear. One member exerts power and authority based on his ability to punish or harm others. For example, abusers usurp power from other family members by threatening (or enacting) violent behavior. Coercive power relies on the person being a viable threat to other family members. If the threats are empty, the power will dissipate.

◆ **Positional power** (Blanton & Vandergriff-Avery, 2001). *Positional power* refers to the power inherent in the person's position in the family. For example, parents have some power because they are the signatories in the family. They sign permission slips and are externally viewed as the administrators of the family. In some families, the power of the parental position is unchallenged; parents can take the position, "I am the parent, and I say . . ." In other families, positional power is very weak. Positional power relies on other people honoring and respecting the position.

◆ **Expert power** (French & Raven, 1959). When family members see one person as having exceptional skills or knowledge, that person is given *expert power;* other people will follow her advice. Sometimes parents have expert power because they have more experience. Older siblings can also garner this type of power. Expert power relies on other family members recognizing the expertise. If the expertise is weak or unrecognized, power will dissipate.

◆ **Reward power** (French & Raven, 1959). This strategy of gaining power creates an exchange whereby members will grant power and authority to a member based on the rewards that will be gained by giving up authority or autonomy. For example, many parents use privileges such as outings, snacks, and use of the car to reward compliance of other family members. This type of power relies on the person having sole access to desired resources or the ability to restrict privileges of the other family members.

◆ **Referent or charismatic power** (French & Raven, 1959). This strategy relies on the personality and persuasive nature of the individual. In such power strategies, the individual gains compliance of others based on the power of his personality and other people's desire to please or emulate him. For example, some children want to be like their parents and will copy their behaviors and mannerisms in an attempt to emulate the parent. This type of power relies on the other family members wanting to please or to be like the person.

◆ **Disruptive power** (Goldberg, 1990). Similar to coercive power, this strategy usurps power from other family members by creating tension. One member exerts power and authority based on her ability to disrupt accomplishments of others and create hassles. For example, many children learn that they can get parents to give in by arguing, pestering, or repeated questioning. This type of power relies on the ongoing success of the strategy. If the disruptions are not rewarded with positive outcomes, the power dissipates.

◆ **Relational power** (Blanton & Vandergriff-Avery, 2001). People control themselves within the system because they do not want to disappoint other people in the system. People in such systems tend to be open about their thoughts and plans and seek input before taking action. The power that motivates the self-control is inherent in the respect that people hold for each other within the system. This type of power is reliant on positive exchanges and affiliation among the family members.

# Family Interaction Patterns

Families are subject to constant interaction. Workers pay attention to the sources and patterns of interaction within systems and between system members and others in the environment. Workers will monitor for the affect, frequency, content, and modes of interaction as they occur in the family. Inherent in the interactions, information can be gleaned about the boundary systems and the relationships among system members and across system boundaries.

In family systems, interaction operates like energy. Some form (verbal or nonverbal) of interaction is always occurring. Interactions can occur between people, people and systems, systems and systems, or people and things. For example, when parents of a learning-disabled child must deal with the education system, interactions are occurring on the individual-to-system and system-to-system levels. Practitioners focus on both types of interaction when trying to understand the nature of the interaction. Much can be inferred about relationships from the interactions that occur within systems.

People's patterns of interaction within the system are important in understanding the relationships among family members. Family practitioners focus on the interaction patterns to glean an understanding of the family dynamics, which include

- ◆ **Patterns of interaction** (Watzlawick, Beavin, & Jackson, 1967). Who talks to whom, and who tends to be left out of the interactions.
- ◆ **Frequency of interaction** (Green & Brown-Standridge, 1989). How frequently different members speak to each other in the system often indicates affiliation.
- ◆ **Content of interaction** (Watzlawick et al., 1967). Concurrent with frequency, the practitioner needs to consider the content of member disclosures because it indicates important information about the relationship.
- ◆ **Nonverbal content in interaction** (Watzlawick et al., 1967). The content of interaction is often qualified, disqualified, or otherwise altered by the nonverbal communication that occurs simultaneously with the verbal message.
- ◆ **Polarity of interaction** (Forgatch, 1989). What is the positive, neutral, or negative affect expressed in the interaction?

One of the most problematic interaction patterns in families is triangulation (Bowen, 1978). Triangulation occurs when interaction between two people becomes routed through a third. Perhaps the most common triangle is the victim-persecutor-rescuer triangle. In this triangle, a problem between two people (victim and persecutor) involves a third person who takes the side of the victim. The result is the victim and rescuer allying themselves against the perceived persecutor.

For example, a six-year-old child is angry that she did not win a Monopoly game. She begins yelling, throws down the pieces, and stomps out of the room. Her mother starts yelling at her and tells her to go to bed. The father steps in and begins yelling at the mother for chastising the child. Notice that as soon as the father intervenes, a triangle is formed, pitting the daughter and father against the mother. In this triangle, the daughter's behavior becomes lost to the mother's chastisement of the daughter.

**Figure 1.4**  Triangulation

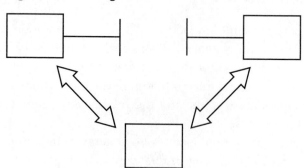

Although the victim-persecutor-rescuer triangle is most common, many other triangles occur in family relationships. Frequently love triangles (competing for attention), diverted anger triangles, and other emotionally laden situations occur in which the emotional energy between two individuals becomes diverted through a third (see Figure 1.4). Often this pattern of interaction allows two people with intense feelings (e.g., anger) to indirectly express their affect. However, the third person in the triangle is both compromised and empowered. He is compromised because he has no legitimate stake in the emotional situation. He is empowered because he can use his position to manipulate the others.

## System-Subsystem Functions

Within systems and subsystems there are functions that must be met for the system to be successful and to maintain balance with the larger environment. Critical subsystems that the practitioner considers when approaching families are the spousal-relational, parental, and sibling subsystems.

*Spousal Subsystem*   As the family forms, the initial subsystem is the spousal subsystem. Most families evolve through two adults meeting and forming a relationship. This relationship over time develops boundaries and a sense of specialness for members of the relationship. As the relationship persists, the adults ideally begin to meet certain needs in the relationship. In single-parent families such need-fulfilling functions remain important and are often relegated to friends or kin. Critical spousal subsystem functions include the following:

1. **Cooperation and support**. Adult family members must receive cooperation and support to sustain themselves. Support includes emotional, informational, instrumental, and appraisal support. Such support allows the adult members to manage

   ◆ Demands of life
   ◆ Achievement of life goals
   ◆ Maintenance of personal and relational stability
   ◆ Maintenance of personal history within the context of the family

2. **Transformation.** The adult individuals must yield part of self to form the new system. Spousal partners need to blend parts of themselves and their family models to achieve a new union and develop a new system. The new system contains attributes of both spouse's family and relationship models. If one member of the spousal subsystem fails to yield part of him- or herself, resentment and tension are likely outcomes. Such outcomes interfere with the other subsystem functions.

3. **Achieving a balance of intimacy and autonomy.** Spousal partners need to be able to feel close and validated by the other person without emotional dependence or loss of autonomous functioning. Deep sharing and knowledge between the spousal subsystem members provides a base where each knows the other and is available to support the other and to meet his or her deepest needs. Spouses who achieve a healthy balance between intimacy and autonomy often refer to each other as their "best friends." If a healthy balance is not achieved, partners must go outside of the subsystem to meet their needs. This movement outside of the spousal system often results in conflicted loyalties, affairs, and inappropriate parent-child relationships. Although sexual intimacy is an element of this function, it is only one element. If sexual intimacy is given high priority (e.g., equated with love), it can result in politics and pressures within the relationship.

4. **Establishing generational boundaries.** The spousal subsystem develops the family and relationship as something operationally separate from the families of origin as well as concurrently separate from the children within the family. Some information and activity is reserved just for the subsystem and not shared with other generations. This provides spousal autonomy and a forum for providing support among the spousal subsystem members.

5. **Achieving systemic maintenance tasks.** Spousal partners must assure that sufficient resources enter the system to maintain the system (e.g., food, money, support, etc.). Such resources meet the entire family system's basic needs for shelter, safety, food, and clothing. This function is inherent in the spousal system because the family is built on this relationship foundation. If the adult couple cannot sustain itself, the family is in jeopardy.

*Parental Subsystem*    The second adult subsystem, the parental subsystem, involves adults fulfilling the parenting functions. To help understand the parental subsystem tasks, it is first useful to understand the outcomes of parenting. Within every culture, parenting is an outcome-driven enterprise. The first outcome of successful parenting involves having children grow up emotionally well adjusted. This requires the child to internalize self-worth, self-respect, self-care, self-esteem, and self-reliance. The second outcome involves the children internalizing a sense that they must follow rules and tailor their behavior for living in a civilized society (adhering to the general laws of society and making moral decisions). These two outcomes are referred to as growing up *loveable* and *limitable* for the purposes of the ensuing discussion. The concepts form a simple framework of "loveable and limitable" that, if achieved, will indicate successful parenting outcomes.

The outcomes of becoming loveable and limitable are achieved through four parental functions (Bross, 1982):

1. Discipline
2. Guidance
3. Accessibility
4. Nurturance

The first two functions help the child internalize limits (limitable). The second two help the child develop a positive sense of self (loveable). With any of the tasks, parents can err through over- or underperformance depending on how well they are functioning. A description of each parental function follows.

◆ **Discipline.** The function that brings most parents into treatment is the discipline function. Discipline describes the parental behaviors that help the child conform to externally set limits. Such conformity is necessary for social adaptation. Children who cannot adhere to limits develop omnipotent beliefs that rules do not apply to them and they can do whatever is necessary to meet their needs. If such beliefs become the code through which the child's behavior is set, society most often will move in to take control and place the child in a setting where the omnipotence does not harm others.

◆ **Guidance.** The task of parental guidance requires parents to help children understand rules, limits, and expectations. This task includes activities such as helping with homework, processing social problems, and verbally discussing limits and expectations with their children. The nature of the guidance function is proactive and noncoercive. This approach to helping children learn is instrumental in helping children internalize rules and expectations (Boyum & Parke, 1995; Kochanska, 1995; Nachmias, Gunnar, Mangelsdorf, Parritz, & Buss, 1996; Spoth & Redmond, 1996). Disempowered parents often miss this function because they are often too absorbed with their own life situations. With embattled parents, guidance functions often involve blaming or negatively focused overcorrecting, promoting negative parent-child interactions (Mash & Johnson, 1990; Whipple & Webster-Stratton, 1991). Highly negative parent-child interaction promotes negative and externalized systems of childhood coping (Kolko, Kazdin, Thomas, & Day, 1993; Wolfe, 1987).

◆ **Access.** In access functions, the embattled parent tends to be constantly present and engaged in correcting, reminding, and prompting the child. The parental consistency in this pattern often results in intrusive interactions in public situations where the child becomes easily embarrassed. The intrusive nature of the parental interaction interferes with the internalization of expectations and is associated with anxiously attached children (Nachmias et al., 1996). Maternal intrusiveness has also been associated with the development of aggression in the child (Lyons-Ruth, 1996). The disempowered parent, on the other hand, often does not tune into the child's expressed cues designed to engage the parent. Consequently, children often become demanding or act out to gain parental input, leading to negative parent-child interaction (Camras et al., 1990; Dadds, 1987; Donovan & Leavitt, 1989; Kolko et al., 1993; Olson, Bates, & Bayles, 1990). This pattern is common where the parent has been abused in his or her own childhood (Burkett, 1991).

◆ **Nurturance.** Nurturance tasks are important in helping children develop a sense of self-worth. Nurturance requires the parent to express positive emotion toward the child. The expression of affect must be consistent across the child's senses. The child must see, hear, and feel that he is loved. One cannot just say "I love you" and never hug, kiss, or admire the child. Nurturance is particularly important between children and their same-sex parent (Boyum & Parke, 1995).

*Sibling Subsystem*    The third family subsystem, the sibling subsystem, includes the children. Like the other subsystems, the sibling subsystem helps children adapt and grow. Three critical considerations help the children interact successfully with others (Bross, 1982):

1. **Competition.** Sibling relationships help children learn to compete and still maintain relationships with the objects of competition. This ability sets the stage for success in many school, work, and recreational ventures.
2. **Cooperation.** Sibling relationships help children learn how to work together toward mutual goals. The basic skills of teamwork, collaboration, and achieving harmony are all subsumed in the ability to cooperate.
3. **Negotiation.** Sibling relationships help children learn how to meet their needs with equal-power peers without the need for coercion or manipulation. The ability to negotiate and compromise with other people is a critical social skill for future success.

## ◆ EXERCISE 1.1    IDENTIFYING THEORETICAL ASSUMPTIONS

You are meeting with a child protective service worker who reports to you that she has concerns about a family on your caseload. As you discuss the situation, she says, "I think the family is really messing up this child. There are people in and out of the house all the time, and I'm afraid that the child will bond to too many adults rather than to her parents. I think that this will mess her up when she gets older and make it difficult for her to have stable relationships."

1. Identify whether this worker is using developmental or systemic premises.

2. List the worker's assertions that correspond to the core assumptions of the theoretical approach.

You are meeting with the same worker at a later date and she continues to discuss the same family. This time she says, "The family is so chaotic. With people coming and going all the time, people don't talk to each other and things just don't get done. Nobody knows who is supposed to do what. It is just always crazy and disorganized. It is a wonder that the kids even get fed."

1. What theoretical approach is being used by this worker?

2. List the worker's assertions that correspond to the core assumptions of the theoretical approach.

# Organizing Theoretical Understandings Into Practice Frameworks

Applying theory in practice situations can be overwhelming, because each theory has concepts and information that are highly abstract and difficult to apply when working with family members. It is consequently helpful to use application frameworks to organize and apply theoretical information through practice skills. This book is organized into a practice framework known as the response system framework. This framework is transtheoretical, meaning that it can be applied using many theoretical approaches.

**Figure 1.5**  The Response System Framework

| Processing systems | Action systems |
|---|---|
| **Thinking**<br>• How members interpret situations outside of family<br>• How members interpret each other's actions<br>• Shared family values<br>• Codes for living together<br>• Belief systems<br>• Myths about family and nonfamily<br>• Attributions<br>• Inherited family model<br>• Family rules | **Behavior**<br>• Observable behaviors<br>• Methods for meeting family needs<br>• Behavioral tolerances<br>• Boundary maintenance<br>• Family task accomplishment<br>• Family routines<br>• Family rituals |
| **Feeling**<br>• Visceral reactions to situations<br>• Feeling states<br>• Family atmosphere and morale<br>• Family pride/shame<br>• Tension management systems<br>• Intimacy management systems | **Interactions and relationships**<br>• How people relate to others (close, warm, etc.)<br>• Patterns of interaction and responding<br>• Allowable topics<br>• How members say things<br>• Systems of support activation<br>• Emotional expressiveness<br>• Patterns of affiliation |

*Note:* Based on the response system framework in *Building Effective Helping Skills: The Foundation of Generalist Practice,* by D. M. Ragg, 2001, Newbury Park, MA: Allyn & Bacon.

The response system framework assumes that responses to situations give rise to family problems. As the practitioner, you can focus on the situation (e.g., the family is at risk of breaking up, father is losing his job, they are at risk of losing their home) and try to rectify it. Alternatively, you can focus on how the family is responding within the situation and work on family responses. Frequently, the method of family response is the impetus for entering into service.

The response system framework helps workers focus on the family's systems of responding. There are two categories of response systems: action systems and processing systems. Action systems focus on two response systems: behavioral responses, or what family members do; and interactions, or what family members say and how they relate (Sundel & Sundel, 1999; Thyer & Myers, 1999). Processing systems focus on two subsystems: feelings and thinking. These processing systems often underlie the family action responses (Berlin, 1996; Carpenter, 1996; Greenberg, Rice, & Elliott, 1996). Observe in Figure 1.5 how different dynamics are subsumed and organized under the response system framework. This framework serves to organize the theoretical elements discussed in the chapter into domains. These domains can be used to focus practitioner thinking and understanding in practice situations.

Throughout this book, the response system framework will be used to organize thinking and interventions. Inherent in the use of the response systems, the developmental and systemic processes outlined in this chapter will be applied with a focus on using your knowledge to understand and intervene with families.

# Summary

Although sidestepping a fuller discussion of theoretical principles, the material of this chapter provides a partial foundation for exploring family practice. All of the chapters in this text assume knowledge of developmental and systemic processes and an ability to "think family." A focus on the systemic level, through either systemic theory or developmental theory, is required to understand family dynamics. Without such an understanding, it is likely that individualistic thinking will interfere with intervention.

The assessment and intervention methods described in the following chapters build directly on this chapter to provide a model of how to use these theories to build an understanding of family problems. Response systems will be used to focus theoretical applications. You will need to know the premises of developmental and systemic theories to comfortably conduct assessments. You will then need to use the response system framework for organizing the assessment understanding.

# Critical Content

1. There are two types of family theory: developmental and systems theory.
2. The constructs in these theories provide a foundation for thinking at the family level.
3. Family practitioners are well versed in these theories and can apply them in practice.
4. Frameworks are often used to organize theoretical information for use in practice.
5. The parental functions and response systems are frameworks that will be applied through this text.
6. You will need to work continuously on breaking individualistic thinking and applying family principles in case conceptualizations.

# Suggested Readings

Braithwaite, D. O., Olson, L. N., Golish, T. D., Soukup, C., & Turman, P. (2001). "Becoming a family": Developmental processes represented in blended family discourse. *Journal of Applied Communication Research, 29,* 221–247.

Moore, S. I. (1990). Family systems theory and family care: An examination of the implications of Bowen theory. *Community Alternatives: International Journal of Family Care, 2,* 75–86.

Wark, L., Thomas, M., & Peterson, S. (2001). Internal family systems therapy for children in family therapy. *Journal of Marital and Family Therapy, 27,* 189–200.

Zilbach, J. (2003). The family life cycle: A framework for understanding family development. In G. P. Sholevar (Ed.), *Textbook of family and couple therapy: Clinical applications* (pp. 303–316). Washington, DC: American Psychiatric Publishing.

## Chapter 2

# The Four Parenting Functions

The models we explored in Chapter 1 provided different approaches to understanding families. Although the two major theoretical approaches each offer a unique view of the family, practitioners often use the two types of theory in concert with each other through frameworks of understanding that allow the theories to be applied. The response system framework described at the end of Chapter 1 is one such approach. In this chapter we explore a new framework focused on the functions of parenting.

## Theoretical Grounding

Most of the theories associated with parenting are embedded in family systems theories. This chapter draws heavily on various family theories from a functional perspective. The core assumption of the chapter is that parenting is an outcome-driven enterprise wherein the adult members of the family attempt to help children socialize to the broader societal expectations and develop in a manner that maximizes positive mental health. Many of the theories underpinning this chapter are presented in Table 2.1. In reviewing the table you can see there are many theories, all of which stress the importance of parenting. The theories have different nuances, but the parental functions outlined in this chapter are consistent with most theoretical approaches. The texts referenced in Table 2.1 are listed here, to help students identify alternative resources for expanding knowledge.

**TABLE 2.1**
**Chapter Concepts, Theoretical Models, and Sources**

| Chapter Concepts | Theoretical Model(s) | Recommended Reading |
|---|---|---|
| Parenting is an outcome-driven enterprise. | Structural family model<br>Psychodynamic models<br>Family systems model (Bowen)<br>Strategic family model<br>Adlerian model | Goldenberg & Goldenberg, Chapters 8, 9, 10<br>Horne, Chapters 6, 7, 10, 13<br>Nichols & Schwartz, Chapters 5, 6, 7 |
| Discipline is important. | Structural family model<br>Psychodynamic models<br>Family systems model (Bowen)<br>Strategic family model | Goldenberg & Goldenberg, Chapters 6, 8, 9, 10<br>Horne, Chapters 6, 7, 10, 11, 13<br>Nichols & Schwartz, Chapters 5, 6, 7, 9 |
| Guidance is important. | Structural family model<br>Psychodynamic models<br>Family systems model (Bowen)<br>Strategic family model | Goldenberg & Goldenberg, Chapters 6, 8, 9, 10<br>Horne, Chapters 6, 7, 10, 11, 13<br>Nichols & Schwartz, Chapters 5, 6, 7, 9 |
| Parents must be accessible. | Structural family model<br>Psychodynamic models<br>Family systems model (Bowen)<br>Strategic family model | Goldenberg & Goldenberg, Chapters 6, 8, 9<br>Horne, Chapters 6, 7, 10, 11<br>Nichols & Schwartz, Chapters 5, 6, 7, 9 |
| Parents must nurture children. | Structural family model<br>Psychodynamic models<br>Family systems model (Bowen)<br>Strategic family model | Goldenberg & Goldenberg, Chapters 6, 8, 9, 10<br>Horne, Chapters 6, 7, 10, 11<br>Nichols & Schwartz, Chapters 5, 6, 7, 9 |

- *The Essentials of Family Therapy* (2nd ed.), by M. P. Nichols & R. C. Schwartz, 2005, Boston: Allyn & Bacon.
- *Family Counseling and Therapy* (3rd ed.), by A. M. Horne, 2000, Pacific Grove, CA: Brooks/Cole.
- *Family Therapy: An Overview* (6th ed.), by I. Goldenberg & H. Goldenberg, 2004, Pacific Grove, CA: Brooks/Cole.

In family service situations, practitioners frequently face clinical challenges associated with parenting functions. The frequency of parent-related problems in practice is partially due to the primacy of the parenting roles in overall family functioning. Sibling functions tend to be directly associated with how the parent functions are performed. Concurrently, if the spousal system has problems, they will frequently interfere with parenting functions. Family practitioners use their knowledge of parenting functions to identify areas of parental strength and challenge in the family system.

# Parental Outcomes

To understand the issues associated with parental functioning, it is important to explore some influences and outcomes of each parental function. Although these functions are briefly described in Chapter 1, the level of discussion has at this point been cursory. In this chapter we will review and explore each parental function in order to achieve a broader understanding of this most important family subsystem. Our exploration begins with a look at parental outcomes; we then explore how each parental function promotes positive child outcomes.

## Outcome 1: Promoting Positive Mental Health (Loveable)

Almost all parents want their children to be well adjusted. Parents do not purposely pursue poor mental health for their child. Even when parents actively interfere with their children's mental health, they are typically attempting to achieve nobler goals. In this author's clinical practice with parents, no parent has ever said, "I want my child to be depressed, miserable, and potentially suicidal when he grows up." Rather, most parents talk about wanting their child to be happy and well adjusted. This almost universal assertion leads to the first parenting outcome of promoting positive child mental health. For brevity, this outcome is referred to as being *loveable*.

Helping the child feel loveable involves several cognitive-emotional elements that combine to help her to internalize a sense that she is a competent, worthwhile, and valuable human being. Here are some of these elements:

- ◆ **Developing a positive self-concept.** A child needs to become aware of her strengths and positive traits so that when negative events occur, she can draw on areas of strength to maintain a positive identity.
- ◆ **Achieving happiness.** A child needs to be able to celebrate his successes and to find areas of joy in his life. Sources of happiness and celebration need to be located inside the child rather than externally located and controlled by others.
- ◆ **Developing negative mood regulation.** A child needs to develop an ability to manage negative moods using positive thinking, past experiences, and other methods of internalizing emotional control.
- ◆ **Developing a tolerance for anxiety and uncertainty.** A child needs to develop a basic trust that she will be all right in the world. This trust allows the child to manage anxiety and uncertainty.
- ◆ **Developing a tolerance for differences.** A child needs to develop a sense of himself apart from other people and begin to appreciate that differences between himself and others are value free and do not diminish his worth.

Notice in the list that the cognitive-emotional elements all promote a sense of self-worth and efficacy in the child. This focus on internalization is important because it is the messages that the child takes in that are important. If positive messages become housed in other people, the child cannot easily internalize them—for example, a father tells a child she is good when her behavior pleases him, but says she is bad when misbehavior occurs. Notice in this example how the father controls the child's feelings of worth. The child consequently internalizes the sense that she is worthless unless she makes other people happy. The child does not achieve the outcome of being loveable in this configuration, because it undermines her internalized sense of self-worth.

## Outcome 2: Instilling Child Limits (Limitable)

Concurrent with helping the child develop positive mental health, parents are challenged to help the child adjust his behavior to achieve harmonious coexistence with other people. Just as no parents have announced to this author that they want their child to be miserable, no parents have stated that they want their child to be in prison when he grows up. Parents typically want their children to take in certain rules for living, so they can survive in the world without the need for society to restrict their access to other people. Here are some important skills associated with limitable outcomes:

- **Curbing violent tendencies.** A child needs to learn how to interact without being physically or emotionally harmful to other people. Although parents may promote assertion (standing up for yourself), children must curb unfettered violence and active hostility toward others.
- **Balancing self-rights with the rights of others.** A child needs to understand the rights of other people and begin to tailor her interactions to respect other people's rights (e.g., to privacy, respect, etc.).
- **Achieving social appropriateness.** A child needs to be able to read social situations and respond in a manner that does not offend other people or cause him to be ostracized.
- **Developing contractual skills.** A child must learn to negotiate with her environment in a way that promotes mutual compromises, clarity of expectations, and achievement of outcomes according to stated commitments.
- **Developing success promotion skills.** A child must learn how to read the rules and tailor his behavior in a way that will promote success. This set of skills involves understanding the situation, identifying rules and expectations, balancing goals with the situational parameters, and maximizing his potential for success.

Like the loveable outcomes, the quest to help children to become limitable involves helping them to internalize rules for living. In this outcome the internalization involves understanding the perspectives of other people and balancing personal wants and needs with the rights and positions of other people in the situation. The child learns rules for living and develops methods for meeting her needs without compromising the rights of other people.

# The Four Parental Functions

The child outcomes are achieved through four parental functions. These include discipline, guidance, nurturance, and accessibility (Bross, 1982). In Figure 2.1 you can see that the four tasks serve as the interface between the parent functioning and the child outcomes. The functions of discipline and guidance are critical to developing the child's ability to respect and adhere to limits. The discipline function incorporates all of the parental activities that set and maintain limits for the child. Guidance functions support the establishment of limits by interpreting and supplying rationale for parental limits. These functions help the child internalize limits and abide by societal standards.

The parenting functions of nurturing and access help the child develop a sense that he is inherently loveable. Nurturing involves parental actions that help the child feel important and loved because of something inside of himself rather than because someone happens to be pleased with his behavior. Accessibility refers to the parent's physical and emotional availability.

To understand the four parenting functions, it is useful to discuss them independently. In the following sections we consider each parenting function and devote attention to the different balances of parental empowerment. In each section we first explore the requirements of the function, examining how that function contributes to the desired child outcomes of feeling both loveable and limitable. Then we explore the differences in empowerment positions to see how the forms of disempowerment can influence parental functioning.

**Figure 2.1**   Parenting Functions and Outcomes

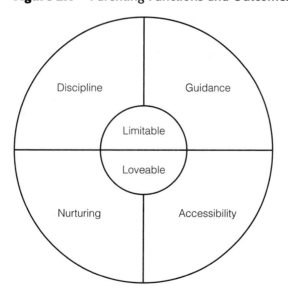

# The Discipline Function

Discipline is one of the most critical functions for parents. Discipline helps children internalize limits to their behavior. Such conformity is necessary for social adaptation (Barnett, Quackenbush, & Sinisi, 1996). Children who fail to adhere to limits often become increasingly unmanageable and feel that rules do not apply to them (Dadds & Salmon, 2003; Nagaraja, 1984; Snyder & Brown, 1983). If such beliefs become the code through which a child's behavior is set, society most often will move in to take control and place him in a setting where the omnipotence does not harm others.

Discipline functions disrupt the development of omnipotent positions through instilling a sense that the child must operate within externally developed parameters. Whenever the child exceeds the parameters, parental discipline is enacted to bring her back into an acceptable range of behavior. As such, the discipline functions are guided by predetermined limits for child behavior. Over time, the child internalizes the limits that are consistently reinforced by the parent.

## The Foundation for Limits

There are two categories of limits. The first type of limit exists to ensure that the child remains alive. These are often called safety rules. Generally some of the rules pertain to the child's individual behavior, such as not smoking or doing drugs. The other rules are more situational, such as prohibitions against playing in high-traffic areas. The second type of limit focuses on helping the child to succeed in life. Issues of politeness, responsibility, punctuality, and morality often enter into the second type of limit.

The priority given to both types of limits tends to be associated with the parent's upbringing. For example, if a parent was raised in a farm family with dangerous machinery and animals nearby, limits associated with safety were likely stressed. As an adult it would be common for that parent to monitor safety limits carefully. Likewise, if the parent was raised in a family where punctuality was important (e.g., having dinner on time, complying with curfew), we can expect that parent to place a high value on time and prioritize success-focused limits. This passing of limit-oriented beliefs from generation to generation occurs on an unconscious level with the parent simply believing that the belief structure is right.

In the same way that limit-related belief structures are passed from generation to generation, the opposite is sometimes true. Some adults reject aspects of some limit-setting beliefs that they found distasteful in their family of origin. For example, a parent raised in a home where yelling and verbal abuse occurred whenever there was disagreement might consciously decide to prevent such interactions in his family by avoiding disagreements. Consequently, that parent develops limits in the family about how well people must cooperate and how much tension is permissible among family members. Although such limits are more conscious in development, often an unconscious element is associated with the anxiety or feelings that caused the limit to be developed.

## The Strategies of Discipline

To enforce and reinforce limits, parents must become actively involved with the child. The nature of the parental involvement in discipline influences how the children attend to different sets of limits. Activities used to enforce and reinforce limits involve both positive and negative action initiated by the parent for the good of the child (Frank, 1983).

Many parents confuse discipline with punishment. Punishment is one action used to discipline a child. Most often, punishment inflicts pain or discomfort on the child based on an assumption that the child's desire to escape pain will motivate her to cease certain behaviors. Unfortunately, punishment does not always result in permanent change. This creates a problem for parents who are punishment oriented because they are constantly challenged to develop new and/or more painful punishments.

It's clear that having a full range of discipline strategies is important for parents (Frank, 1983). With a choice of many strategies, the parent can respond to multiple behaviors without the constraints inherent in a single-strategy approach such as punishment. In this chapter, we look at the full range of discipline strategies. For our purposes, the term *discipline* describes all parental actions designed to increase a child's motivation to comply with a set of limits. When considered this way, discipline is an investment whereby consistent input over time creates a child who remains safe and respectful.

Many disciplinary approaches are available to parents. Here are eight common strategies:

1. Triangulation
2. Inscription
3. Withdrawal of love
4. Reinforcement
5. Power assertion
6. Strategic approaches
7. Social illumination
8. Induction

On the following pages, we explore each disciplinary strategy to gain an understanding of the basic assumptions and associated behaviors.

***Triangulation Strategies*** *Triangulation* is an indirect approach to discipline in which the parent enlists another person's assistance in shaping the child's responses. Disempowered parents often tend to use this strategy indiscriminately because they feel that they cannot influence the situation without having to draw on another person's power. Triangulation can be a useful strategy when the other person has more information or expertise in a given area. However, parents should be careful not to overuse this strategy, because it could decrease their influence over the child. An example of this strategy is having a child's friend talk to him about the swim team with the hope that he might be motivated to join.

Although triangulation can be used in certain situations, the strategy is indirect and has some problems. The greatest problem is that the parent actually loses influence by using the strategy. This loss of influence occurs because the parent gives another person control over the interaction with the child. The parent cannot control what is being said by the third person. Parents may feel betrayed when using this strategy because the third person either may see the child's side or may not carry out the parent's agenda. When this occurs, the parent often becomes angry with the ally; arguing may occur, allowing the child to emerge as a winner.

Family practitioners often serve as the third party in parental triangulation strategies. Frequently, parents approach a practitioner by stating that they have tried everything and asking the professional to speak to the child. Parents often end their request by saying, "Maybe she will listen to you." In such situations, the practitioner must be careful to sidestep the inherent conflicts associated with triangulation and seek to promote effective parent-child interaction and discipline.

***Inscription Strategies*** *Inscription* occurs when all family members (or at least the most influential) are expected to engage in the same behavior at a given time. The cohesion surrounding the activity serves to motivate the child to engage. Family rituals and traits come from inscription strategies. For example, religious families all go to church together, and sports-minded families are all involved in sporting activities. The inclusiveness of the inscription renders the child as somewhat of an outsider if he does not engage. Resistance to engage is often met with an attitude of "we are all going, so you have to come too," which actively promotes some level of engagement. Empowered parents tend to use inscription often. The parents usually decide on which outcomes they want in their children and then plan the family's activities to achieve these outcomes. Common patterns include

- ◆ **Values-based outcomes.** Parents guide the family in activities such as going to church or attending cultural events.
- ◆ **Health-related outcomes.** Parents engage the family in activities such as hiking, sports, or canoeing to ensure an active lifestyle.
- ◆ **Learning-based outcomes.** Parents have the family participate in trips, games, watching programs, or outings that provide learning or enrichment.
- ◆ **Cohesion-building outcomes.** Parents engage the family in activities such as camping trips or family entertainment activities.

In each of these patterns, the parents have a desired outcome identified in loose terms, for example, "Wouldn't it be nice to see what Niagara Falls looks like?" The general outcome becomes the impetus for planning the family activity. You can see the clear leadership and planning involved in this type of discipline.

***Withdrawal-of-Love Strategies (Hoffman, 1963)*** *Withdrawal-of-love strategies* include several common forms of discipline that manipulate parental attention levels to shape child behavior. The most nonintrusive example of this strategy is ignoring. Ignoring operates on the belief that if a parent withdraws attention concerning some of their child's behaviors, the behaviors will not be reinforced and they are less likely to reoccur. Other common procedures included in this strategy are imposing a time-out, removing a possession, and withdrawing privileges. The critical feature in such strategies is to apply less positive parental attention in response to the child's behavior. Here, *attention* means rewards, positive verbal expressions, and parental engagement.

This strategy requires the parent to engage frequently with the child when his behavior is appropriate. If parental attention is inconsistent or infrequent, the child will not notice if the parent is purposefully ignoring him. Consequently, the use of subtle withdrawal strategies such as ignoring the child's behavior or not attending to his needs must diverge from the family norms enough to influence him. Parents also need some empowerment to use this type of strategy effectively. A low power base is problematic when a parent uses withdrawal of privileges and time-out strategies because children are likely to test the parent's resolve. The parent may have to expend energy consistently over a period of time to withstand the child's testing and whining as he tries to break the parental will.

---

## CASE EXAMPLE

A parent reported that she had grounded her daughter for the weekend due to curfew violations the previous weekend. But her daughter wanted to go to the movie with friends, and although she was grounded, she asked her mother if she could go. The mother first said no; yet the daughter was unrelenting. For about 15 minutes, the daughter described how great the movie was, how it was not in town for long, how her friends were going, how sorry she was for being late, and how "it will never happen again." When the mother stood firm in her position, the child phoned her friend and started crying. She told her friend how terrible she felt, and how mean her mother was. The mother stood firm until after the phone call, when the daughter sat silently at the kitchen table while the mother made dinner. When the two of them sat down for dinner, the mother asked, "If I let you go tonight, do you promise you won't break curfew again?" The daughter agreed and gleefully called her friend back with the good news.

---

When using withdrawal-of-love strategies, parents need to avoid emotional reactivity during the disciplinary process. First, parents must be careful to avoid emotionality when they withdraw the attention, so the child does not experience the action as emotional rejection. Rather, the child needs to realize that her behavior is causing a lack of attention. Parents must also remain calm and unemotional in withstanding the child's strategies to change the decision. It is then that the parents need to be most consistent in sticking to their position. If the parent becomes emotionally invested in the situation, control shifts from the parent to the child and may cause escalation or a change in the parent's position.

*Reinforcement Strategies (Horne, 1974)*   Reinforcement strategies are somewhat similar to withdrawal-of-love strategies. In reinforcement, the parents may use withdrawal of some privilege as part of the strategy; but they can also use *positive reinforcement* to reward appropriate behaviors. The critical element to reinforcement is being clear about the behaviors that the parent wishes to promote or dissuade (Horne, 1974; Dix & Grusec, 1983). When promoting behaviors, the parent first observes the behavior and then uses some form of reward to reinforce the continued use of the behavior. Here are some different types of rewards:

- **Token rewards.** Token rewards involve providing some concrete incentive such as allowance, toys, trips, and so forth, contingent on the child's achieving a behavioral outcome. For example, a parent was having difficulty getting her two children to clean up after themselves. She decided to put $14.00 in two envelopes every week. This allotted $7.00 for each child. She informed the children that the money was for cleaning up after themselves. If they picked up their belongings every day and cleared their dishes from the supper table, the money would be theirs. However, if she had to pick up after them, she would remove one dollar for each day she had to wait on them. If she had to pick up after just one child, the money would come only from that child's envelope. If she picked up after both of them, they would both lose money.

- **Token economies.** A token economy uses token rewards in a very structured way to motivate the child to engage in several behaviors or expectations. Point systems are a good example of this strategy. In using point systems, or token economies, the parent lays out a structured list of expectations for the child. The child receives points for expectations that are met, but no points for unmet expectations. The child can then use her points to "buy" privileges or token rewards.

- **Situational rewards.** Situational rewards provide a concrete incentive that is derived from the situation. For example, when coming home from an outing at the beach a parent might say, "You guys have been so well behaved that I want to treat you to an ice cream on the way home." Typically, situational rewards are not negotiated ahead of time; rather, they emerge when the situation allows.

- **Child-identified rewards.** Child-identified rewards involve the parent picking up on a child-identified goal and using the child's motivation to promote positive behavior. For example, an adolescent boy wanted to go on a school trip that would cost a lot of money. The parents informed their son that they would help fund the trip if he would help out with cleaning the house. The boy agreed to vacuum the living room twice per week, and his parents agreed to put $10.00 per week into the trip fund.

- **Praise-focused rewards.** Praise-focused rewards are verbal rewards, such as praising and sharing observations that the child is doing well. For this type of reward, the parent must first notice positive behavior and then make mention of the behavior so the child can self-observe the desired actions. When using praise-focused rewards, it helps to be very descriptive so the child can understand what is being rewarded. For example, a sibling pair was playing a game very calmly and cooperatively. Their father noticed and said, "I am impressed with how well you are taking turns with each other today. You are both very gentle and calm about waiting for the other."

◆ **Verbal shaping rewards.** This type of reward is similar to praise but is smaller and more frequent. In using verbal shaping, the parent catches the child doing something right and then briefly highlights that child's success. For example, a 10-year-old boy came straight home from school and started doing homework without being told. His mother noticed and briefly stated, "You must be getting older. You got started on your homework all by yourself." Notice that unlike the praise reward, which uses a full descriptive statement, the verbal shaping reward involves very brief statements.

A second type of reinforcement strategy is negative reinforcement. This is most often where punishment enters into the disciplinary picture, because this type of parental activity tends to be negative. Rather than rewarding positive behavior, *negative reinforcement* inflicts a cost or consequence on the child for misbehavior (Miller, 1984). Even though this type of response is negative, it is important for the parents to remain calm and in control of their emotions to ensure that the response is a measured response to behavior rather than an opportunity for the parent to achieve emotional release. Parents tend to use three common types of negative reinforcement:

1. **Natural consequences** (Sweeney, 1998). When using natural consequences, the parent allows negative outcomes to occur as a consequence of the child's decisions or behavior. For example, the child dawdles in the morning and misses a school outing. This type of consequence works best when there is an outside event or system that will provide the consequence and it will not inconvenience the parent.

2. **Logical consequences** (Sweeney, 1998). When using logical consequences, the parent considers the child's transgression and provides a consequence that is logically linked to the transgression. For example, the child dawdles in the morning and misses the school bus, requiring the parent to drive the child. After school, the parent has the child wash the car before he can go out to play.

3. **Constructed consequences.** When using constructed consequences, the parent creates a system where specific events occur whenever the child transgresses. For example, a parent trying to decrease a child's failure to complete homework sets aside five dollars for allowance per week. The parent informs the child that every time she forgets her homework, one dollar will be deducted from her allowance.

Parents often use multiple reinforcement strategies. Blending different types of reward is important, for example, delivering verbal rewards along with more concrete rewards. This keeps a steady flow of feedback and reinforcement directed at the children and creates a situation wherein parents do not have to rely on a single type of reward. Over time, the children feel that their positive behaviors are noticed and bring them rewards. The children start to identify with the positive statements and actively try to promote more reinforcement. Effective parents also incorporate consequences into their reinforcement strategies, so the children also understand that limits exist (Horne & Van Dyke, 1983).

---

**CASE EXAMPLE**

As a mother and child enter a department store, they walk by the gumball machines and the child slows down. The mother responds, "If you listen well, you can get something on the way out." Later, as they are leaving the store, the child asks for a quarter. The parent responds, "You have been great while we were shopping, so of course you can have a quarter." The child then buys something from the machines and they continue on their way.

---

Parents must also be comfortable with denying requests when they feel that the child's behavior should not be rewarded. In the testing afterward, the empowered parent does not engage in arguing. Rather, the parent limits discussion either by not responding or by making statements such as "I have already given you my answer" and "What did I just tell you?"

***Power Assertion Strategies (Hoffman, 1963)***   Parental strategies using *power assertion* have a long history. Until recently, society has endorsed the idea of parents spanking their child. Spanking is the most common power assertion strategy, but parents also use actions that include restraining or physically moving a child. Such strategies rely on the parent having more power than the child does, in order to force him into complying with parental desires. The strategy becomes less effective as the child grows and gains strength, because he can begin to overpower the parent.

When a parent relies too much on power assertion strategies, they can be problematic. Logically, no single strategy will work in every situation, so when one strategy stops working, a parent must choose another strategy. Often the selection of the new strategy occurs along a continuum that ranges from very nonintrusive strategies to power assertion. If a parent overuses power assertion, options become limited when the strategy stops working. Parents must then increase the frequency or the intensity of power assertion. Consequently, as effectiveness wanes, the risk of abusing the child increases.

Critics of power assertion strategies point out that along with their limited effectiveness, power assertion strategies teach children that violence can be used in supposedly loving relationships to gain compliance. There is ample research to indicate that power assertion strategies such as spanking can be harmful to child development (Simons, Whitbeck, Conger, & Chyi-In, 1991). As a family practitioner, you will consequently want to help parents decrease their reliance on this type of strategy so that they can make use of a full continuum of disciplinary behaviors.

Empowered parents most often use power assertion strategies as a last resort. Noncoercive strategies are applied first; and if they are unsuccessful, the parents consider using power assertion strategies. A critical factor in the decision making of empowered parents is the type of limit that they are trying to enforce. It is often not appropriate to use power assertion on limits that promote success, such as school grades or social behavior. Typically, empowered parents use power assertion strategies to impose limits associated with safety.

---

**CASE EXAMPLE**

Vang, a parent, is experiencing some difficulty with his daughter while at the mall. Bao, who is about three years old, keeps wandering off while in the stores whenever Vang's attention is diverted. Vang continually tells Bao to stay with him, but she ignores his verbal prompts. Vang responds by having Bao hold his hand for a few minutes until she promises that she will stay near. Vang tells Bao that she will have a time-out in the car if she does not keep her promise. She repeats her promise, so her father lets go of her hand. Shortly afterward, Bao wanders off and hides under a clothing rack. Vang is somewhat panicked when looking for his daughter; upon finding her, he picks her up and carries her, kicking and screaming, to the car in the parking lot for the agreed-upon time-out.

---

*Strategic Approaches (Efron & Rowe, 1987)*  *Strategic discipline* requires parents to respond very purposefully to the child. This type of strategy always keeps the long-term desired outcomes in mind (loveable and limitable). It requires a high level of parental openness and flexibility as the parents approach each situation by looking for opportunities to promote the goals of encouraging their child's feelings of being loveable and of working within limits. This type of strategy works with the situation in a way that shapes the meaning of the behavior into something that can promote the two desired outcomes.

In a strategic approach, the parent first looks at the situation and then tries to approach the child in a way that promotes success. Specific strategies include preempting problems by providing warnings (e.g., "We will be leaving the park in 10 minutes"); prescribing the inescapable (e.g., "I want you to put on your sad face now because it is time to go"); and reframing behavior as positive (e.g., "You know, you have a great argument . . . you could be a lawyer . . . but it is still time to go"). The strategies all focus on the desired outcomes of parenting while still reinforcing the limits needed in the current situation.

Empowered parents often use strategic discipline because the approach respects both the parent and child power base. Using the desired outcomes as a guide, the empowered parent intervenes selectively, allowing the child to control most aspects of his life while influencing other aspects as needed to accomplish the desired outcomes. The child's reactions to the parent are not interpreted as slights or challenges, but rather as natural reactions.

## CASE EXAMPLE

Beate, a mother, is struggling with some emotional reactivity with her daughter Elfie, who pouts whenever she does not get her own way. Beate wants to break the habit before it becomes an instant reaction to the setting of limits. To move toward influencing the reactivity, Beate begins labeling the emotional faces Elfie makes. In a short time, mother and child have made a game of different-feeling faces—including mad, sad, happy, and goofy. When Beate sets a limit that Elfie does not like, resulting in a sad face, Beate praises the sad face. To further distract her daughter, Beate then encourages Elfie to make other faces, like a mad or goofy face. At other times, when Elfie persists with her pout, Beate describes some of the great features that go into creating a mad face or a smile. Either way, the game begins. Eight years later, Beate is still using this strategy with great success.

*Social Illumination*   Social illumination strategies highlight a child's transgressions in a public manner, so that broader social judgment becomes a consequence for his behavior. If social illumination is applied to a specific behavior, it generates feelings of guilt in the child. These feelings become the motivation to cease the behavior. If the social illumination focuses on the child as a whole, the feeling generated tends to be shame (Tangney & Dearing, 2002).

Empowered parents tend to use social illumination in a covert manner, allowing social consequences to occur (e.g., when the child is rude to someone, inviting the person to provide feedback). As the parents become more active in generating the social reaction, feelings of guilt and shame occur. At the malevolent end of the continuum, the parents shame the child through caustic comments, public humiliation, and negative labeling. Although guilt tends to inhibit behaviors, shaming approaches often lead to adjustment problems in the child (Dutton, van Ginkel, & Starzomski, 1995; Ferguson, Stegge, Miller, & Olsen, 1999).

*Induction Strategies (Hoffman, 1963)*   Induction strategies of discipline use the parent-child relationship to help the child understand rules and learn from her misbehavior. This approach to discipline uses reasoning, clear expectations, fitting consequences to the behavior, and attending to the child's full relationship system. For it to be effective, parents must be highly engaged with the child and in constant interaction. *Induction* is defined in the literature as the most effective and desirable approach to discipline, yielding the most pro-social outcomes in the child (M. A. Barnett et al., 1996).

Induction involves some elements of the reinforcement, strategic, and inscription strategies of discipline; however, induction takes the discipline one step beyond simply shaping behavior. When using induction, parents are very clear about limits and the reasons for each expectation. This allows the child to engage with the parent to discuss aspects of the rules and even challenge the parent to provide a strong rationale. Parents must be secure and rational in using this approach, because logical cohesiveness is its most important element. Parents must be able to outline why rules exist and alter the rules when they are inconsistent with the logic.

When using an induction approach to discipline, a parent incorporates both the discipline and guidance function to address behavioral concerns concurrent with the child's moral development. To truly understand induction approaches to discipline, it is necessary to understand elements of all disciplinary approaches and then combine the strengths of the different methods with the guidance functions described in the following section.

# The Guidance Function

Guidance functions operate in concert with discipline to help the child understand the need for limits and codes of conduct. Whereas the discipline function requires energy for investment, the guidance function requires time. Because of the time commitment, guidance functions are often neglected in today's busy families, and parents come to assume that discipline alone can help a child achieve the desirable outcomes. The most successful and well-balanced children all seem to have parents who are willing to invest in the guidance function. In families of antisocial children, guidance functions are often missed in favor of blaming the child and having negative parent-child interactions (Mash & Johnson, 1990; Whipple & Webster-Stratton, 1991). This situation promotes negative and externalized systems of childhood coping (Kolko et al., 1993; Wolfe, 1987).

The guidance function includes activities such as helping with homework, processing social problems, and verbally discussing limits and expectations with the child. The nature of the guidance function is proactive and noncoercive. This approach to helping children learn is instrumental in helping children internalize rules and expectations (Boyum & Parke, 1995; Kochanska, 1995; Nachmias et al., 1996; Spoth & Redmond, 1996). The guidance function also prepares the child for success in social relationships.

There are five areas of guidance to consider in the parental function. Each of these guidance activities equips the child to function effectively in the social environment:

1. Expanding the child's perspective
2. Dealing with differences and tension (problem solving)
3. Developing personal boundaries
4. Developing social roles
5. Internalizing limits

## Expanding Perspectives

To function effectively in social situations, the child must learn to broaden his perspectives to include other people. Children are born with an egocentric view; they are primarily focused on themselves. It becomes the parent's job to help the child move

**TABLE 2.2**
**Perspective-Taking Capacities and Child Development**

| Age Range | Perspective-Taking Capacity |
|---|---|
| Infancy | No capacity because no real sense of self being different from others; tends to be demanding in relationships to meet own needs |
| Preschool-age | Beginning capacity as child becomes aware of self and others; relatedness tends to come through identifying with others |
| School-age | Starting to respect individuality; struggling with resolving differences and conflict with others |
| Preadolescent | Appreciates and is sensitive to the needs of others; still dependent in relationships |
| Adolescent | Increasing appreciation for autonomy and differences; allows for fuller taking of perspective |

beyond this selfish state as he develops. This is a delicate balance, because social capacity changes with the child's age. Parents must therefore have some appreciation of how the child's capacity to relate, and take perspective, changes through his development. Table 2.2 is a rough description of how abilities to take perspective and relate to others changes with the child's age range. Although the table is organized in broad age ranges that lose some of the subtle changes, as a general pattern it can guide parents' expectations.

To help children take perspective, three demands are placed on the parents. First, the parents must be available for talking with the child about her social situations. This is important, because the child's learning will come from problems she experiences with others. The second prerequisite is that parents need to be emotionally open and nondefensive. If parents see social mistakes as a personal reflection on themselves, they will react in a manner that causes the child to stop sharing. Finally, the parents need to help the child view situations from the perspective of others who are involved in the situation.

Empowered parents tend to ask their children about their days, and they routinely take time to listen to their children. It is almost as if that time becomes structured into the day. Such parents also tend to track their children's moods and will ask a child about changes in his moods. Even when the child denies that there is something that should be discussed, empowered parents persist until they feel satisfied that he is all right.

## CASE EXAMPLE

After out-of-town relatives have returned home, Abia, a school-age girl, begins being nasty to her younger sister and continues for most of the evening. This behavior is somewhat puzzling to Abia's father, Dagan, because the relatives had been at the house for the weekend, and people were playing games and generally having fun the entire time. Dagan asks his daughter several times what is wrong, but Abia says there is no problem. When the behavior persists, Dagan suggests that Abia is overtired and needs an early bedtime. Upon tucking Abia into bed, Dagan comments that her behavior has been unusual because she is always exceptionally good. The child begins talking about how hard it was that everyone laughed at her sister when she said things; but when she said the same things, they were considered sassy. Over the next 10 minutes, Dagan encourages Abia to remember when she was small and how people responded to her as being cute. This talk leads to a discussion of some different expectations and privileges associated with being older.

## Dealing With Differences, Tension, and Problem Solving

Differences and tension are two of the most troublesome areas in relationships. Consequently, they are critical areas of guidance in working with a developing child. Parents most often teach children how to deal with tension and differences through their own behavior. If parents are comfortable dealing with differences, they will naturally accept differing positions in others and adapt their approach in light of differences encountered. However, if parents are uncomfortable with differences, tension results. Depending on the parents' level of empowerment, they may give in to the difference in attempting to avoid tension; alternatively, they may perceive the difference as an affront to their position. Through such reactions, children learn that differences are somehow bad or something to be avoided.

To help children deal effectively with differences and tension, parents need to acknowledge differences openly, without attaching value or meaning to the difference. Doing so often requires the parents to be in control of the effects of their own childhood, because these effects create most of the additional meanings attached to difference. In helping children deal with differences, the traditional model of problem solving is useful (see Table 2.3).

Empowered parents try to approach differences by being open about the meaning of the difference. There is no predetermined interpretation of differences as being negative. This does not mean that the parents believe all differences are good; they do, however, judge differences as they arise. Consequently, the child feels free to express differences of opinion and propose options to the parents' position. As the child expresses such differences, the empowered parent uses the desired outcomes (loveable and limitable) as the framework for assessing differences. When a child's divergent desires might jeopardize the child's sense of being loveable or pose a risk to the child's well-being, the parents maintains a firm position, explaining their rationale. Differences of opinion that are consistent with the desired outcomes result in a more flexible parental response.

Empowered parents are also able to withstand tension. They approach tension-producing aspects of parenting as necessary parts of their job and engage in topic areas that other parents may avoid. As the parents engage in difficult topics, they must be

**T A B L E 2.3**
**Problem-Solving Steps and Common Difficulties With Each Step**

| Step | Common Problems |
|---|---|
| 1. Define the problem. | Often two people define the problem differently, each basing the definition on their own perceptions of the situation. If they do not check with each other to find a mutually agreed upon problem, each tries to solve a different problem. The problem will escalate because the solutions for one problem don't fit with the solutions for the other, causing them to compete with each other. |
| 2. List possible solutions. | Most commonly, people do not get a complete list. Rather, the two people each pick one solution and try to get the other to accept it. They need to compile an exhaustive list before even starting to discuss the merits of each possible solution. |
| 3. Assess each solution. | Each solution listed in step 2 must be explored for requirements and consequences of the solution. Some solutions require resources or the involvement of other people. Other solutions can result in outcomes that are not acceptable to one of the people. These need to be listed beside each solution to help decide on directions. |
| 4. Reject the unacceptable. | After each solution has been discussed, clearly unacceptable suggestions are rejected, leaving only solutions that are acceptable to both people. |
| 5. Develop a plan. | From the acceptable solutions, one or a combination of solutions are kept and developed into a plan of what will be tried first to solve the problem. In the plan, the people should discuss how and when it will be implemented and how and when they will know if the solution worked. |

prepared to take the unpopular position while giving the child permission to adopt a different position. In the ensuing debate, an empowered parent allows the child to speak her mind and will be able to reflect an understanding of the child's feelings. Compromises sometimes evolve whereby the parents' concerns for the desired outcomes can be met without blocking the child's engagement in an activity.

---

### CASE EXAMPLE

Maria, a 14-year-old girl, wants to go to a party at her friend's house. However, Maria's mother, Olivia, knows that the parents are out of town and suspects that problems may occur with older youths bringing in alcohol and setting the stage for an out-of-control event. Consequently, Olivia responds, "Well—I don't know if that will be good" and explains her concerns. Maria at first denies that drinking and extreme partying might occur; but Olivia says she will not take that risk. In the conversation, Maria keeps saying that she doesn't want to be the only one to miss the party; and Olivia continues to state her concerns for Maria's safety. Eventually, Olivia says that in order to go to the party, Maria has to negotiate a safety plan to address her mother's concerns. Maria agrees to allow her mother to drive by her friend's house and monitor the situation. Maria then agrees to leave the party immediately if Olivia calls her on the cell phone. If there is no answer, they agree that Olivia will come to the door and Maria will leave, stating that her ride has arrived.

---

In this case example, you can see that the parent and child each have a legitimate, but different, concern about the party. By not allowing the concerns to compete for importance, Olivia and her daughter are able to come up with a plan that accommodates both concerns. Olivia is willing to invest segments of her time to monitor the party at a distance, and Maria is willing to postpone any kind of embarrassment or frustrated reactions if her mother comes to the door to collect her. By discussing the situation with her daughter, Olivia was able to model problem solving; by having Maria negotiate a safety plan, Olivia coached her daughter in dealing with differences.

## Developing Boundaries

Children require constant parental guidance to distinguish their wants and needs from the wants and needs of other people. This is a critical skill in preventing emotional problems, traumatic events, and relationship problems. Unclear personal boundaries have been associated with psychological and emotional problems such as depression, anxiety, and addiction (Lowe & Sibley, 1991; Reinhard, 1990). Similar boundary problems are associated with risk of child sexual abuse, when adults manipulate children to put their needs above the child's own needs (Finkelhor, 1978). Given these associations, guiding child development in this area is of paramount importance.

Personal boundaries take many years to develop. Children are born with no sense of personal boundary, and over time, they begin to distinguish themselves from others. The sophistication of child individuation increases with cognitive abilities as children begin to identify differences in values, rights, and priorities in their relationships with other people (Archer, 1985; Waterman, 1985). Parents are instrumental in guiding this development, which occurs through both verbal and nonverbal channels of interaction.

Verbally, parents instruct children regarding their rights, responsibilities, and relationships with others. Such verbal guidance promotes respect for self and others. Parents are constantly explaining to their children why they should not intrude into other people's conversations or belongings. Parents also reinforce emotional and physical boundaries with the child's peer group. Often peers expect to be able to infringe on a child's boundaries by eating his snacks, taking things from his room, touching him in uncomfortable ways, and expecting him to attend to their emotional needs at the expense of his own. The parental exploration of these boundary intrusions helps the child to understand and negotiate his boundaries.

A parent's nonverbal interaction with the child also guides the development of personal boundaries. Boundary reinforcement includes such actions as

- Knocking on the child's door and waiting rather than entering her room
- Avoiding contact with private parts when bathing young children (use hand on hand) and allowing privacy in the bathroom with older children
- Allowing privacy when children are with their friends
- Balancing discipline monitoring with intrusive information gathering to ensure that safety and other limits are met but the child does not feel that the parent is controlling all aspects of his life
- Letting the child organize her time to accomplish her tasks (e.g., homework, chores, etc.) and working with her on better organization when she fails
- Allowing the child to express his own opinion about what he would like and letting it occur whenever it will not compromise desired outcomes
- Letting the child decorate her own room, choose her own clothes, and dress herself within clear negotiated parameters
- Enrolling the child in activities that reflect his strengths rather than in activities for all of the children or those other parents are considering

In each of the parent actions just listed, there is a clear acknowledgement of the child as a separate person. Such acknowledgement promotes an autonomous identity in the child while still identifying him or her as a family member.

## Developing Social Roles

Parents are perpetually involved in helping their children acquire and succeed in their social roles. The most common parental activity in this area is helping children understand and complete their homework assignments. Other common forms of engaging in this type of guidance include discussing the child's performance after she has played a team game or performed in a play or recital. This type of guidance tends to involve five parental activities:

1. Helping the child understand the responsibilities that accompany the role
2. Helping the child understand the performance expectations that others are placing on her
3. Helping the child develop a plan to meet her responsibilities and expectations
4. Supporting the child by providing resources to help her implement the plan
5. Supporting the child through emotional support, advice, and resources to adjust the plan when it fails to achieve the expectations of the role

The second area of parental guidance in social roles is in the friendship relationships. Friendships are a complex system of roles, expectations, and responsibilities that are often unspoken. Parents often notice mood changes in their children, and upon investigation they find that something is occurring within the child's network of friends. Parents are active in helping the child determine the expectations, agendas, and obligations occurring in her relationships while still allowing the child to make her own decisions.

The parent must be respectful of the child's autonomy when moving into the guidance function, lest the child feel that the parent is trying to tell him what to do. The logical approach with such a child is first to help him sort out the responsibilities and expectations in the social situation and then help him to see how others may not be ready for his autonomy and self-directedness.

---

**CASE EXAMPLE**

A parent, Peter, is most concerned about his son Jacob, who changes friends very often. Whenever Peter tries to explore the problems that might have precipitated the change, Jacob denies any problems and says he is just tired of that friend. One evening Jacob comes home seeming somewhat distraught, and his father is able to get him to talk. In the discussion, Jacob says that the other kids always want to have their own way and won't do what he wants, so he tells them he doesn't want to play with them anymore. Peter explores the autonomy Jacob has gained in the family. Then Peter compares Jacob's autonomy to that of other children, who have to make deals with each other to get along. Within this framework, Jacob is able to think differently about the rules of friendships and deal with the friendships differently.

---

## Internalizing Limits

Internalizing limits is perhaps the easiest but most overlooked aspect of guidance. This area is heavily associated with discipline; often, the discipline function is performed and the issue is considered complete without attending to the guidance function. This function involves verbal engagement, providing the rationale for limit setting. Such verbal exchanges help the child better understand the function of limits. By making sense of limits, children can understand how following the limits will help them in their lives. This makes the limit logical and promotes the internalization of rules and injunctions.

Internalizing limits is simple in form, but it is demanding in practice. To help a child internalize limits, parents need to develop a consistent pattern of interpreting their disciplinary acts with the child every time they apply discipline. Parents need to follow up discipline and punishment with a discussion of why the limits exist, and how they promote the desired outcomes of loveable and limitable. The following examples illustrate how these themes coexist with the internalizing function of guidance.

◆ Knowing that the parent still very much loves the child, even though discipline was required (e.g., "Hey, even when I send you to your room, I love you . . . that never goes away . . . but I still can't let you throw toys at your sister. When you do that, I will keep putting you in your room until you calm down so nobody gets hurt . . . and while you are up there and angry with me, I will keep loving you.")

- Explaining how the child's attitude or behavior compromises the desired outcomes for the child (e.g., "if you keep doing that it will cause others to treat you badly"; "you are a good child and I don't understand why you threw that toy")
- Affirming the child's wants, needs, and thinking in the problematic situation but maintaining limits and desired outcomes (e.g., "I know you want to watch the movie, but you have an important test tomorrow. I will tape the movie so you can watch it later.")

In each of these examples, the desired outcomes serve as the central rationale for the parent's action. Verbally connecting the parent action to the desired outcome provides a framework to help the child internalize the limits. In the first example the parent follows up discipline with assurances that the child is loveable. In the example, the child became angry and needed to be reassured that although limits are needed, she remains loveable. The second example is similar, but a more direct link is made to the desired outcomes. The examples stress that the child is loveable and limitable and that his behavior should be consistent with this reality. The third example simply respects the child's position and works toward a compromise that enforces the limit but still affirms the child's reality.

The functions of discipline and guidance directly influence the limitability outcomes in the child. Discipline highlights desirable and undesirable behaviors. Such illumination helps the child to identify limits. Guidance provides the rationale for limits. This function helps the child understand and internalize the limits. The next two parenting functions focus on the loveable outcomes in the child. Nurturing and accessibility help the child to feel important and secure in the family.

## The Nurturing Function

Parental nurturing functions develop a child's sense of self-worth and emotional well-being. *Nurturance* requires the parent to behave and talk in ways that create positive experiences in the child while imparting a sense that the child is special or deserving of the experiences. It is important for children to take in messages that others value them and are confident in their abilities. Such positive parental messages and responsiveness help the child internalize feelings of self-worth, confidence, and esteem (Beckwith & Cohen, 1989; Rand, 1995). Parental responsiveness is also associated with moral development in the child (Kochanska, 2002).

The parental activities of nurturing change greatly over the life of the child. As an infant, the child's nurturing is often associated with feeding and hygiene activities when the parent feeds, strokes, and talks warmly to the baby. When the child becomes more mobile, her parents add verbal encouragement and celebrations of success to the holding and stroking. From this point on, the blend of holding, stroking, and verbal nurturing shifts gradually in balance as the child assumes more and more autonomous functions. By the child's adolescence, hearing key words and phrases from her parents can create in her the same warm feelings that once took minutes of praising and hugging.

The positive messages internalized by the child provide building blocks for a mental self-image. If this internal mental image is positive, the child uses it to balance failures and negative events in her life (Brown & Dutton, 1995; McWhirter, McWhirter, McWhirter, & McWhirter, 1994). The child also uses the positive internalized image to withstand social pressures. The nature of the parental input is critical in building a positive self-image in the child. Parents cannot simply tell the child that she is good and expect her to develop a positive self-image. The child must see, hear, and feel that she is loved. This is particularly important between parents and children of the same gender (Boyum & Parke, 1995).

Parents commonly use four types of activity in nurturing their children:

1. **Physical contact.** Feelings of worth and security come through the level and nature of physical contact between the parent and child.
2. **Caregiving acts.** Feeding, grooming, health care, and other activities whereby the parent cares for the child's well-being produce messages that his well-being is important.
3. **Verbalizations.** The things that parents say about their children, and the manner of presentation, supply direct messages about the child's worth and value to the parent.
4. **Support.** When parents support their children in achieving tasks and enterprises without trying to take over or control the activity, they transmit a message of faith in their children's ability.

This list of nurturing activities is not exhaustive, but it does represent actions (and inactions) that are common to most parenting situations. To understand the breadth of each activity, we examine them separately in the following sections.

## Physical Contact

It is generally accepted that all children crave physical contact, from the time of birth onward through life. The nature of the physical contact and the child's reactions to the contact lay the foundation for the child's experience of himself in relation to his parents (de Chateau, 1976; Shields & Sparling, 1993). If the holding is too restrictive or rough, the infant experiences the contact as negative or intrusive. He will then resist certain types of contact. Likewise, if the physical contact at this stage is soothing and positive, the child develops a comfort with his body and the interaction with others. In this comfort, the child begins to trust that good feelings will result from contact with others.

As children age, the stroking and cuddling received become internalized as several messages. First, the child begins to experience esteem for and pleasure from her body. This lays the foundation for body appreciation. Second, the child's need for physical closeness is met with enough consistency that she begins to believe that these needs will be met (Rand, 1995). The nonintrusive and comforting physical exchanges give the child a secure feeling that she can get comfort from parents when needed. This security, in time, allows the child to wait to get her needs met because she trusts that her parents will eventually tend to them. Children also engage in self-soothing behavior that is modeled after the parental responses.

---

**CASE EXAMPLE**

Margot, a three-year-old child who is used to being held and stroked, is observed after a cat has scratched her on the arm. Margot whimpers slightly, but notices that both parents are in other areas of the house and are not able to respond immediately. She consequently kisses her forearm and says to herself, "there . . . all better now . . . I love you." She then occupies herself by playing with toys.

---

Children who grow up with intrusive and negative physical contacts often experience confusion about touch and body sensations. If they have been physically or sexually abused, they may also develop negative feelings about their bodies. Self-mutilation and various eating problems have been associated with past abuse of the child (White, Leggett, & Beech, 1999). Such experiences may also erode trust that touch from others will be comforting. Rather, the child may begin to withdraw from others when other children would approach adults for comfort. Finally, such children are less able to discriminate good from bad touches. This places them at some risk because they must rely on the adult's integrity to be sure that touch is nurturing rather than self-gratifying for the adult.

## Caregiving Acts

Basic activities of parenting—such as feeding, grooming, housing, and clothing the child—are opportunities for empowered nurturing. Parents can convey powerful messages to promote self-worth in the child through such simple acts. With infants, feeding and changing the child become times for sharing closeness and warmth. As the child grows, caregiving broadens in focus, as do the opportunities to convey messages of the child's value. Some opportunities occur when parents allow the child to express his individuality by letting him choose his own clothes and decorate his own room. Other activities require special extensions of caregiving, such as picking up the child at school when it is raining or cooking his favorite dinner.

Inherent in caregiving is the principle that parents must be consistent. Consistency requires the parents to fulfill their functions in an expectable manner. If children do not know when the parent will feed them or if the parent will pick them up from school, anxiety and behavior problems may emerge. If the parent is consistent, the child is able to predict the pattern of her day. Such predictability enables the child to relax and focus on her developmental tasks, such as succeeding in school.

Parents can use the caregiving functions to enhance the child's sense of self-worth. Although many of the functions are tedious and may feel like impositions, parents can communicate value. Some activities communicate caring when the parent initiates them, for example:

- Buying favorite foods
- Buying items that the child needs or wants when out shopping
- Bringing homework projects to the school when the child leaves them at home
- Offering to drive the child to see friends when he seems bored
- Suggesting that the child invite a friend for a sleepover

Other activities communicate caring through the parental response to the event. This is most common in the daily activities and chores that the parent must perform. In carrying out such activities, the parent can choose to treat the chore as a welcome event or a burden. If the child perceives that the event is welcomed, she feels important. But if parents performing child-related tasks communicate that they are a burden, the child may feel that she is a problem to the parent.

---

**CASE EXAMPLE**

A family decides to approach tucking their child into bed as a privilege rather than a burden. When the child's bedtime approaches, one parent asks the child if they can be the one to tuck him in bed. The other parent then feigns an argument and says that they want to put the child to bed. Over time, the child begins offering his parents the opportunity to tuck him in as a reward to the parents, or he engages in a rhyme to see which parent will win the opportunity. The child develops a strong sense of self-worth, and there are never any problems with bedtime.

---

## Verbalizations

Children take in what their parents say about them, and they start to form a foundation for what they believe about themselves. Children listen to what adults say about them even when they are not part of the conversation. Consequently, their self-concept is built not just through direct statements intended for the child, but through indirect statements the parents make to others about the child.

Giving *direct feedback* to a child is most powerful when the parent is concrete. For example, if the father is commenting on a picture, he will describe what he likes about it (e.g., nice bright colors, strong lines). This allows the child to internalize very specific information. General evaluative statements such as "nice picture" do not internalize as readily because they are too broad. The child cannot internalize what she did, so the picture becomes "nice"; but she does not internalize feelings of being a skilled artist. The need to be descriptive also pertains to giving praise and appreciation. When parents describe what they appreciate in the child, she is able to validate the parent statement through her own experience. The combination of hearing her parents' description and internal validation make it easer for the child to internalize the feedback into her self-image.

A second area of direct verbal input involves the *positive-negative value* of parental statements. Some parents monitor their child for mistakes and intervene in a corrective manner. In such families good behavior may be ignored, shifting most of the parental attention in a negative direction. Children in families where most of the attention is negative may start to feel deficient or bad (Berg-Nielson, Vikan, & Dahl, 2002). In other families, parents focus on positive behaviors and child strengths. In such families, children internalize beliefs that they are competent and worthwhile.

The child gets *indirect feedback* when his parents talk about him with other people. Often, children listen intently to parental discussions with others to find out how their parents talk about them. Children may even give more credence to this indirect feedback because it is not directed at them. If parents are aware that their children are listening, they can use this fact to their advantage. Parents can look for opportunities to talk well of their children, knowing that as a child overhears the conversation he will take in messages promoting positive self-worth.

## The Access Function

The final parenting function is access. To promote optimal development in their children, parents must be available and responsive to their children (Kochanska, 2002). The two types of access a child needs are geographic access and emotional availability. *Geographic access* means that the parents remain in sufficient proximity to monitor child well-being and respond to child needs. Emotional availability involves the parents' being able to experience and respond to the child as a person with separate needs, rights, and desires.

There are really two levels of geographic access. First, parents must be physically available, so that the parent and child can access each other. Physical availability does not require parents to be immediately present at all times. Rather, it implies that the parents have ensured that they and their children are mutually aware of each other's movements and activities. This availability requires both parents and children to communicate changes of location, so they can access each other when needed. Geographic access also requires parents to attend child-related functions such as sporting events and parent-teacher conferences.

The second aspect of geographic access involves awareness. Sometimes parents are geographically present, but they have no idea what their children are doing. Awareness requires the parents to continually shift their attention back to the child to monitor his activities and needs. Even when engaged with other people, responsible parents monitor their children. Such parents often break off conversations to respond to a child's needs and then shift back to the discussion.

*Emotional availability* refers to the parent's openness to hearing what their child is trying to communicate. Emotional availability requires the parent to listen carefully, understand the child as an individual, and avoid reacting or dismissing the child's concerns. This is sometimes difficult, given that parents are often busy preparing meals at the same time that they reconnect with children after school. Parents must often consciously stop themselves from shutting down the child through dismissive responses.

If parents are not available on these two levels, children will begin to distance themselves from their parents and find other people to fulfill these functions. This diminishes the parents' ability to influence their child. Although the alternate sources may be helpful for the child, the child may be vulnerable depending on the available support people.

Parents engage in two types of tasks while performing the access function: supportive tasks and boundary maintenance tasks. Although the descriptions of these tasks are not exhaustive, you can see the types of parental behaviors that occur while fulfilling the access function. Notice how these behaviors convey a sense of importance and competence in the child.

## Providing Support

Supportive functions involve a blend of geographic and emotional access. Geographically, the parents must be present and engaged in the child's situation. On the emotional level, the parents must understand the details of the child's situation so they can tailor a response that enhances the desired parental outcomes. The following supportive behaviors help the child develop competence while still relying on parental responses.

*Empowerment-Enhancing Support*   Parents help the child develop skills and competencies by remaining available for the child while also allowing the child to take charge of her own life.

---

**CASE EXAMPLE**

A child, Tonja, comes to her mother, Kenyatta, upset that a wheel has fallen off her toy carriage. Kenyatta asks the child where she has gone with the carriage and then suggests that Tonja retrace her steps to look for the wheel. Kanyatta says that if going back does not work, she will then help Tonja search. Tonja finds the wheel within minutes.

---

*Active Support*   Parents must often become active in helping children accomplish tasks and chores. In the example just described, the parent is prepared to become active if her child is not successful. This is an important stance because children must learn all competencies at some point in their lives, and not all of those competencies will be easy. When providing active support, parents must resist the temptation to take over the situation or rescue the child; still, they should participate in helping the child master the situation. Helping with homework is perhaps the most common form of active support.

*Mediation Support*   One important type of support is mediation. Parents must be prepared to help children resolve differences with other people and systems by ensuring that problem-solving discussions occur. Mediation typically involves bringing two parties together to discuss a situation and then build on common ground to resolve potential problems.

---

**CASE EXAMPLE**

A child, Anthony, is upset that he always has to play defense for his soccer team and wants to start playing forward. His father, Leon, suggests that he talk with his coach, but no discussions ensue. After a game, Leon is talking with Anthony and the coach and asks Anthony, "Did you ever talk to Tony (the coach) about wanting to try some new positions?" The coach picks up on the comment and prompts Anthony to discuss his desires. After explaining to Anthony that he is the team's best defensive player, the coach promises to try him in new positions when he isn't needed for defense.

---

*Advocacy Support*   Parents must be prepared to assert themselves on behalf of their children. Because children are often in contact with systems and people much more powerful than they are, they must be able to count on parental support when treated unfairly.

---

**CASE EXAMPLE**

Tadako, a young girl starting grade one, comes home upset that her teacher is yelling at the class. Her father, Kaede, after first exploring the situation with Tadako, realizes that the teacher is really yelling at other children; so he explains the difference to his daughter. Kaede then writes to the teacher, informing her that his daughter has been upset and asking for feedback so he can help Tadako adjust to the teacher's expectations. For the next two days the child returns home upset, saying that the teacher has called the class a bunch of babies. Kaede then phones the principal and asks to have Tadako moved to another classroom. The principal meets with the teacher, child, and parent to discuss the situation. In the meeting, Kaede describes how the yelling is affecting his child and insists that some changes be made. Although the teacher is resistant to changing, Kaede stresses the impact on his child and enlists the principal to help alter the tone in the classroom.

---

## Managing Boundaries

The second type of activity associated with access functions is managing the parent-child boundaries. Parents need to ensure that a flow of information is maintained with the child while still allowing some child autonomy and individuation. The following three activities are common boundary management behaviors.

*Checking In*   Parents and children need to check in with each other once in a while. The act of checking in communicates importance and assures each other that the presence is being maintained. Empowered parents often insist that their children phone home periodically when they are out with friends to update the parents on their location and ensure that the child is all right. Parents may also check in with other people associated with the child (e.g., teachers) to ensure that situations are safe and healthy for the child.

*Updating*   In an activity similar to having their child check in, empowered parents do an update with their children to ensure that each child understands life events and activities. Whereas checking in is a very brief exchange that updates safety and proximity, updates more deeply explore the content of the child's activities. Some parents spend time after school or activities asking their child about the day; others use bedtime routines as an opportunity to review the child's life events and responses. Parents also do updates with other people in the child's life by meeting with teachers or others important to the child's health and well-being.

*Probing*   When children are upset, they may try to avoid discussion. At such times parents probe to ensure that important details are discussed. Probing is often experienced as pressure by the child, but this activity is an important element of ensuring that the child is safe and secure. Parents must use probing carefully, to ensure that the child has some psychological autonomy. Empowered parents tend to apply this function when children seem withdrawn or upset about situations that are not immediately apparent.

◆ **EXERCISE 2.1   EVALUATING PARENTAL FUNCTIONING**

You are working in a child guidance clinic. You are meeting with a mother (Melissa) and father (Jack) who were referred because of their child's misbehavior. The son, Frank, is diagnosed as ADD/HD. He struggles in school and often gets into trouble for wandering around the room during class and talking out of turn. Frank is very impulsive and often engages in dangerous behaviors (e.g., running into traffic) because he doesn't think about things. His father has tried grounding him and sending him to his room to help him think about things but this has not been effective. The school wants Frank put on medication, but Melissa does not want to use drugs to control her son.

Melissa describes her childhood as being fraught with all types of abuse. Her mother reportedly was physically and emotionally abusive to the children. Melissa states that she never wants to be like her mother. She shares that her approach is to provide love, because she feels that she did not get enough love as a child. She expresses concerns about Jack, who tends to be very strict. She confides in you that she often cuts the children slack and lets them off their punishments because she believes that Jack is too harsh. This often leads to conflict between the two of them, because Jack feels undermined when he discovers that Melissa does not support his punishments. She insists that Frank is a good boy and just needs to understand how his behavior affects other people.

Jack describes his parents as being very stern. His father was the main disciplinarian and ruled the family with an iron hand. Jack expresses pride that none of the kids get into trouble with the law and that they all are ideal citizens. In describing the parental approaches in his family, Jack reveals that his father used belittlement and yelling as his prime source of punishment. Jack and his brothers competed for their father's approval. Jack's mother was a stay-at-home mother who was always available. She did not use punishment and would often tell the boys that she was going to tell their father about misbehaviors, but she would forget by the time he came home. Jack states that he agrees with his father's strict approach and expresses dismay that his wife constantly undermines his punishments. He states that he often elevates his strictness to compensate for her letting their son get away with misbehavior. Jack states that Frank simply needs to learn the rules for living. He states that he is trying to help him learn, but he gets no support from Melissa.

Using the following table, list the strengths and challenges inherent in the parenting approaches of this mother and father.

| Parental Function | Mother's Functioning | Father's Functioning |
|---|---|---|
| Discipline | | |
| Guidance | | |
| Nurturing | | |
| Access | | |

1.  Based on the strengths and challenges identified in the table, what influence does the parenting appear to have on Frank's behavior problems?

2.  Given the strengths, challenges, and impact on child behavior, what changes in the parental functions would you recommend?

3.  Identify alternative discipline methods that may be consistent with the mother's approach.

---

## Summary

The parenting functions we have explored throughout this chapter provide a framework with which family practitioners can understand parental functioning. Many family problems that are presented to a family practitioner will require an understanding of the parental functioning. This framework provides an easy-to-follow model that a practitioner can use to explore and understand the multiple dynamics of parenting. The four functions give practitioners a focused understanding that can promote a direction for intervention.

# Critical Content

1. Two desired outcomes are associated with parenting: helping internalize a sense of being loveable and promoting internalized rules.
2. The four parental functions of nurturing, access, discipline, and guidance promote these outcomes.
3. The parental functions of nurturing and access promote a feeling of being loveable in the child.
4. The parental functions of discipline and guidance promote the child's internalization of rules and limits.
5. Multiple strategies, tasks, and behaviors occur within each function to promote the parental outcomes.
6. Some functions and tasks will be over- or underperformed by a parent. The pattern of performance will indicate the nature of the problems and focus of intervention.

# Suggested Readings

Benjet, C., & Kazdin, A. E. (2003). Spanking children: The controversies, findings, and new directions. *Clinical Psychology Review, 23,* 197–224.

Berg-Nielsen, T. S., Vikan, A., & Dahl, A. A. (2002). Parenting related to child and parental psychopathology: A descriptive review of the literature. *Clinical Child Psychology & Psychiatry, 7,* 529–552.

Dadds, M. R., & Salmon, K. (2003). Punishment insensitivity and parenting: Temperament and learning as interacting risks for antisocial behavior. *Clinical Child & Family Psychology Review, 6,* 69–86.

Chapter 3

# Cultural Influences on Family Functions

Family practitioners work with culture on a daily basis. You cannot escape cultural considerations when working with families, because the family is the conduit of culture. As adult family members socialize children into shared beliefs, behaviors, and traditions, they impart cultural patterns and beliefs. Given this ongoing enculturation process, it is not possible to work with families without working simultaneously with culture. This chapter, in which we explore the role of culture in family-based thinking, provides a framework that family practitioners can use to organize cultural information.

## Theoretical Grounding

There is no official theory associated with understanding culture, but there is a concept of cultural competence that leads practitioners to actively consider cultural influences in understanding and responding to family situations. Culture is central to family life; appreciating its role calls for both sensitivity and mastery when interacting with families. Additional reading materials are recommended in Table 3.1 and in Table I.1 of the Introduction to further enhance your cultural competence.

Although culture is a central element of family practice, it is an aspect of family life frequently missed by family practitioners. Cultural omissions often flow from worker assumptions, based on their own culturally steeped family experiences. Such assumptions typically go unnoticed by practitioners because the family experiences

**TABLE 3.1**
**Chapter Concepts, Theoretical Models, and Sources**

| Chapter Concepts | Theoretical Model(s) | Recommended Reading |
|---|---|---|
| Need to consider culture | Cultural competence | Goldenberg & Goldenberg, Chapter 3<br>Nichols & Schwartz, Chapter 11 |
| Need to consider racial issues | Cultural competence | Goldenberg & Goldenberg, Chapter 3<br>Nichols & Schwartz, Chapter 11 |
| Need to consider religion and spirituality | Cultural competence | Goldenberg & Goldenberg, Chapter 3<br>Nichols & Schwartz, Chapter 11 |
| Gender roles and culture | Cultural competence | Goldenberg & Goldenberg, Chapter 3<br>Nichols & Schwartz, Chapter 11 |
| Values and culture | Cultural competence | Goldenberg & Goldenberg, Chapter 3<br>Nichols & Schwartz, Chapter 11 |
| Culturally distributed resources | Cultural competence | Goldenberg & Goldenberg, Chapter 3<br>Nichols & Schwartz, Chapter 11 |
| Impact of culture on parenting | Cultural competence | Goldenberg & Goldenberg, Chapter 3<br>Nichols & Schwartz, Chapter 11 |

and cultural models tend to blend into one. Consequently, expectations of family contain an embedded cultural context. When working with a family from your own cultural background, these assumptions and expectations fit. As the client family's culture diverges from your experience, you must consciously adjust assumptions to avoid superimposing your cultural system onto clients and families.

To avoid assumption-based errors, family practitioners must understand other cultures. This involves learning about different cultural groups, so that as a practitioner you can tune into the beliefs, experiences, actions, and interactions common in the cultural group. You can then adjust your assumptions and responses for each family. To accomplish this task, you will need to glean information about other cultures and apply the information in family intervention.

Gathering and applying cultural knowledge can be a challenge. First, you must acquire knowledge about a culture. Such gathering often results in stereotyping because information sources typically provide commonly shared traits inherent in a culture. Consequently you must not only gather information about cultural trends but also temper that knowledge with an appreciation of diversities within the cultural group. Family practitioners apply their cultural knowledge to adjust theoretical frameworks and understandings of what might be normal. This is a complex task because cultural understandings are often very rich and not necessarily organized for application to families. For this reason, practice applications often require frameworks to guide the cultural application.

In this chapter you will find a framework for understanding the cultural influences on the family system. The framework identifies aspects of culture that influence the parental tasks or functions outlined in Chapter 2. Family practitioners can use the framework to identify important cultural elements and then reflect on how these elements influence the parents' behaviors with their children. By understanding how cultural elements influence parenting functions, you can begin to consider how different cultures are influencing families coming into service. Such a differential understanding can help systematically adjust your assumptions, assessments, and planning according to the family's cultural dimensions.

# Parenting Functions: The Foundation for Cultural Transmission

To understand cultural influences on parenting, it is first useful to recap parenting functions in the family (covered in Chapter 2). This summary is brief, serving as an anchor for the cultural application. If any element of the model remains confusing, you may want to review Chapter 2 before applying the culture ring.

In Chapter 2 we learned that the tasks involved in the parenting functions are driven by desired outcomes in the child. Within every culture, parenting is an outcome-driven enterprise. Two desired outcomes extend across multiple cultures:

1. **Loveable.** The children will grow up emotionally well adjusted (assumes good mental health, self-worth, self-respect, and emotional contentment).
2. **Limitable.** The children will grow up with a respect for rules and the rights of others (operate within the general laws of society, act responsibly, and make sound moral decisions).

The two outcomes form a simple framework of loveable and limitable that, if achieved, will indicate successful parenting outcomes.

Parents achieve these outcomes by means of four parenting functions: discipline, guidance, nurturance, and accessibility (Bross, 1982).

1. **The discipline function.** The discipline function describes parenting behaviors that help the child conform to externally set limits, so that social adaptation can occur.
2. **The guidance function.** The guidance function requires parents to help children understand rules, limits, and expectations. This task includes activities such as helping with homework, processing social situations, and verbally discussing limits and expectations with children.
3. **The nurturance function.** Parenting tasks that develop child self-worth through responsiveness to the child's biological, emotional, and developmental needs are all acts of nurturance. Nurturing activities also require the parent to express positive emotion and intent toward the child.
4. **The accessibility function.** The accessibility function requires parents to be geographically and emotionally available to their children. Doing so includes being home to spend time with children, attending children's functions, allowing children to express themselves, and being responsive to children's requests.

# The Culture Ring: Dimensions of Culture and Impact on Parenting

Parenting functions vary considerably, depending on cultural influences. Most family practitioners observe differences in discipline strategies and nurturing across cultural groups. Practitioners also note values-based differences in how parents are expected to respond to their children. Clearly, the family system is subject to a multidimensional set of influences.

The culture ring highlights eight dimensions that influence the parental functions. Although this list of dimensions is not exhaustive, it does capture some consistent influences on how parenting occurs within a given culture. The eight dimensions are depicted as being associated with specific functions (see Figure 3.1). Notice that there is some overlap between the dimensions and their functional impacts.

In reviewing Figure 3.1, you can see that the culture ring provides a context for the influences on parenting functions and outcomes. Thus we can expect each culture to have a vision for the ideal child's loveable and limitable qualities. Some cultures will value different aspects of mental health while devaluing others. For example, in the dominant North American culture, independence is highly valued; therefore, confidence will be important in the loveable outcomes, and autonomous functioning will

**Figure 3.1** The Culture Ring

be expected in the limitable outcomes. However, in Ojibwa tribes, connections with both nature and community are more highly valued. In this context, connection and spirituality are stressed in the loveable outcomes; sensitivity to community needs is the focus of the limitable outcomes.

When you are working with family systems, it is important to understand the shifting emphasis and mechanisms of socialization within various cultures. If you do not understand cultural influences, you are at risk of making ethnocentric decisions (Laird, 2000). It is beyond the scope of this chapter to explore individual cultures, but the culture-ring framework can be helpful for organizing information when learning about various cultural groups. In this chapter we explore the cultural dimensions within the culture-ring framework and consider how each influences the parental functions. When you begin working with other cultural groups as a family practitioner, you will need to learn about each group and to understand how each of its dimensions affects the parent-child dynamics.

# Cultural Influences on Discipline Functions

Discipline functions are instrumental in helping children learn and internalize the rules of living. Different cultures have different methods of helping the children learn such rules. When you are working with cultural groups, it is helpful to consider two cultural dimensions that influence the disciplinary functioning of parents: abstract mindedness and sanctioning systems.

## Abstract Mindedness

Inherent in every culture, there is a continuum of concreteness. Some cultures are very concrete in how they understand the world. This view may be indicated by a connection to the material world, as seen in agrarian cultures that work closely with the land. A culture's concreteness may also be indicated by how its people understand rules and sanctions. Some cultures have a very strict code of living. For example, theocratic cultures often enforce rigid adherence to a religious dogma. On the other end of the continuum, some cultures are very abstract and make sense out of events and situations by creating mental frameworks or stories.

The frameworks used by a culture for understanding situations provide important information for the family practitioner (Helms, 1995). For example, if you are working with a Native American family, the cultural pattern of making sense out of situations using stories and legends can be very important. The principles for living— harmony with nature, community, and other important cultural precepts—are embedded in the cultural stories. This is a fairly abstract system of sharing an understanding of the world. To understand what the family is communicating, you must listen carefully to the stories that family members share with you. Concurrently, you must be careful not to be too blunt or concrete in your approach.

Not all cultures interpret situations and pass on knowledge through abstract principles. On the other end of the continuum, many cultures are concrete. Such cultures are often rule bound, with strict codes of acceptable versus unacceptable behavior. The rationale for the behavior may not be important in the culture. Rather, rules or customs are accepted as rote. Such cultures allow no discussion of rationale; they simply obey a rule. Some of these cultures do not allow people in certain circumstances to look others in the eye, to speak, or to dress in certain ways. Practitioners working with such cultures must listen for the rules governing the situation and be prepared to offer very specific, concrete solutions.

At the parental level, abstract mindedness influences how parents respond to the child's behavior. Cultures with high levels of abstraction are often permissive, allowing children to experience life and learn from their experiences. Such cultures may also delve into the gray areas of behavior and treat each behavioral infraction case by case, exploring the situation before rendering discipline. Concrete cultures, on the other hand, tend to be more controlling of children's behavior and often insist on compliance to rules. Disciplinary action is apt to be very consistent and concrete in its approach.

## Systems of Sanctioning

Along with the continuum of concreteness, cultures contain permission for different types of punishment and disciplinary behaviors. These cultural systems of sanctioning influence the disciplinary acts taken by parents. Cultures often have accepted prohibitions, limits, or encouragement to use certain behaviors (Waldman, 1999). These sanctioning systems evolve from the cultural values governing behavior within the cultural group.

Some cultures sanction behavior through resources (e.g., dowries, inheritances), some through relationships (e.g., disowning, ostracizing), and some through corporal systems (e.g., cutting off limbs, caning, killing). Depending on the culture, the systems of shaping behavior can vary greatly. Members of more extreme cultures may be repressive and use corporal systems of control. Other cultures may be lenient and flexible in their approach. Regardless of the nature of sanctioning behaviors, culture will influence the behaviors considered acceptable for influencing other people.

In Chapter 2, we explored several disciplinary strategies. Notice that some cultures tend to endorse some strategies and not others. When you are reviewing these discipline strategies, consider each one on a continuum from benign to malevolent. Although most discipline occurs in the middle ranges, it is important to understand that any strategy can range from potentially helpful to potentially harmful. For example, power assertion can easily become abuse when overapplied, and withdrawal of love may become neglect. The culture will identify the acceptable ranges of each behavior.

# Cultural Influences on Guidance Functions

Whereas discipline involves the parental actions used to shape the child's behaviors, guidance focuses on helping the child to understand and internalize the rules for living. Two cultural dimensions commonly influence the guidance functions. The first dimension involves how the parent interprets and explains cultural differences. Most critically, parents must explain to their children the relationship between the family culture and the dominant culture. The second dimension focuses on the values and religious influences of the cultural group.

## Experience of Difference

When a cultural group is visibly, socially, or economically different from the dominant culture, the difference is obvious. In such situations, parents help children interpret and make sense of the differences between themselves and other children. The messages the child receives from his parents about the meaning of difference in society shape the way the child approaches the dominant cultural group and people of other cultural groups.

Society places different values on between-group differences. These values, though constantly changing, reflect the relationship between the cultural and ethnic groups in society. Many people are aware of the historical devaluation of African American citizens in the United States. Through their devaluing statements, people influential in the dominant culture justified slavery, discrimination, and disenfranchisement. As the society became more enlightened, new value statements emerged to re-explain the differences. Some new statements common in the dominant culture declare that "we are all the same underneath," "race doesn't really matter," and "things are much better now."

Notice that the statements identified with the dominant culture tend to be somewhat dismissive about the differences. People in the dominant society have the luxury of making such dismissive statements because members of the dominant culture typically are not negatively affected by the difference. Parents within minority cultures must be more engaged in helping children understand differences. Children who physically look different from members of the dominant group often experience ignorant or hurtful interactions. When children come home after such experiences, their parents must help them understand and process the situation so the children can remain physically and emotionally safe in future interactions.

Visible differences require parental input about the meaning of difference, and so do other differences experienced by children. Differences occur on many dimensions (e.g., visual, social, and economic). Multiple differences accentuate the need for members of a cultural group to work with their young to help understand the differences. For example, if you are from a visible minority culture and also poor, the complexities of helping your children understand the differences increase. When members of your cultural group experience racism and oppression, the task of helping affected children understand the difference becomes more difficult (Fiske, 1995). The all-encompassing judgments inherent in racism cannot be easily explained, nor can the inconsistencies among members of the dominant culture.

Economic oppression can greatly complicate the processing of cultural differences. When members of a nondominant culture notice that their economic resources are not equal to those of the dominant culture, resentment results. It is difficult to explain to children why the dominant group has high-paying positions when another group must perform menial tasks for long hours with little pay. Concurrent with the social impacts of poverty and economic oppression, economically vulnerable groups are also exposed to higher levels of pollution, environmental stress, and health risks (Anderson & Armstead, 1995; Link & Phelan, 1995). It is difficult to find positive frameworks for understanding such differences.

For some cultural groups, the challenges just described are exacerbated by broad public acceptance of an unfair situation. Such acceptance by the dominant culture is often interpreted as purposeful indifference that supports and legitimizes the oppression. This view leads to stigma and anger among members of the nondominant culture, who feel hopeless and powerless about the overwhelming differences. Children will notice these social dynamics and require parental guidance in interpreting the social events.

## Values and Religion

As they engage their children in learning about the world, the parents' cultural values and beliefs influence their guidance themes and priorities. Concurrently, the values-based institutions that most strongly influence child socialization will have a cultural base (Betancourt & Lopez, 1995). Included in culturally significant institutions are the church, education system, government, and economic system. The centrality of these different institutions in the family's life will change across cultural groups. Children observe the parental preference for the institutions and form their opinions.

---

**CASE EXAMPLE**

In the dominant American society, the capitalist economic system is very powerful. In this economic system, efficiency and hard work are valued. Those who work hard and achieve good outcomes are considered worthwhile. This cultural value influences both the education and family systems. In U.S. schools, teachers promote hard work, business-related subjects, and good grades. There is often a competitive atmosphere that pressures children to succeed and be noticed for excellent achievements. Families with school-age children support that cultural value by promoting good grades and completion of homework. The parents believe that such effort will promote the child's later success. In more collectivist cultures, values of cooperation and mutual support yield a different emphasis in school and family life. Values such as excelling for the larger good rather than for individual success are likely to be emphasized (Sue & Sue, 1992).

---

Family members, through their relationships with cultural institutions, shape their children's value systems. Children observe the institutional role, parental priorities, and the cost-benefit exchange between the family and cultural institutions. From a very young age, children decide how important the institution and related values are in their lives. If school is important to the family, children learn how to be good students. Likewise, the church and economic systems will all exert influence on the child's eventual priorities as well as on the issues stressed by the parents.

Family practitioners explore the family's culturally related beliefs when trying to understand different rules and expectations. This exploration is critical because without the cultural context, practitioners may confuse indicators of health with problems. For example, a son may not be able to attend a school trip because the parents insist that he earn the money on his own. The parents value self-sufficiency and believe that the child must learn to make it on his own. Alternatively, a child may not work up to her "potential" because she is not driven to excel. This may conflict with a family practitioner's belief that education is important and children should be exposed to broad stimuli to learn.

# Cultural Influences on Nurturing Functions

Nurturing functions help children to develop a sense of self-worth and emotional well-being. Parents promote these affective outcomes in children by demonstrating behaviors that assure the child is soothed, fed, and knowingly cared about. As the child internalizes the caring messages, she begins to develop a sense of worth that helps her cope with the stresses and tribulations of living. In the dominant culture in North America, nuclear parents fulfill most nurturing functions. This pattern is not true for all cultures. Two cultural dimensions influence the provision of nurturing. First, the collectivist (versus individualistic) nature of the culture influences how many people become involved in fulfilling parental functions. Second, the role expectations associated with the culture dictate how people fulfill their parental functions.

## Collectivism Versus Individualism

Some cultures have high levels of obligation to the collective group, whereas others tend to be very individualistic (Sue & Sue, 1992). On the collectivist continuum, two aspects influence parenting. First is the individual-collectivist value set. Individualistic cultures tend to be competitive and view success through individual achievements and acquisitions. They pay little attention to the impact of individual strivings on the larger social systems. In contrast, collectivist cultures place a higher value on the social group. Collaboration and harmony are more highly valued. The concept of individual success is often not present, because success is measured by the conditions of the larger group.

In working with families from collectivist cultures, you may find that they frequently will acquiesce to the larger group when making decisions. Concurrently, their self-concepts may be heavily influenced by the obligations and attitudes of others within the cultural group (Triandis, 1995). Parents in such cultures will work with the children to help them identify and respond to the needs and obligations of the larger group. Individual needs for nurturance, being less valued than the collective needs, will not take a priority in the family. Consequently, many expressed needs of the child will be unheeded, or even responded to with discipline to shape the expression of needs.

As noted earlier, in individualistic cultures such as the United States, people highly value individual achievement. Parents frequently cater to the expressed needs of children by providing stimulation, toys, and nurturing upon demand. Parents identify their child's unique qualities and abilities and hone them so the child can excel in future endeavors. Getting children into the best schools and the best teams is frequently a concern as parents nurture each child's exceptional talents. Parents tend not to focus on the greater needs of the social group and how the child should adapt to those collective needs.

In an individualistic culture, parents are often competitive in gaining advantage for their children. As their children gain advantage, such parents have little regard for whether other children's abilities will develop. To enhance a child's feelings of competence, parents sometimes use comparisons between their child and children of lesser skill. Competition in grades, athletic ability, and other skills are often used to demonstrate that the child is special. Higher education systems are designed to reward these skills through scholarships and other forms of support. This individualistic value is illustrated in the recent challenges to affirmative action in higher education. Affirmative action is a collectivist solution that does not fit well into the dominant individualistic culture.

The second influence inherent in a collectivist culture is the caregiving system. In collectivist cultures, children are raised by extended systems of support. Children can often run freely within the community, and all people will know the children and be mandated to intervene on their behalf if they need anything (e.g., discipline or shelter). The famous adage, "It takes a village to raise a child" reflects collectivist thinking. Not surprisingly, Hillary Rodham Clinton's assertions of this value have not been widely accepted in the highly individualistic culture of the United States.

Collectivist cultures involve multiple systems in the parental functions. A common practice is to use extended and fictive kin systems to ensure that the child's nurturing needs are met. Frequently, extended kin groups live in the same home or neighborhood and support each other daily. Other caregiving systems common in collectivist cultures include socialized day care, after-school programs, and other group systems of child care.

In contrast, individualistic cultures tend to rely on a very limited number of people. Typically, parents are charged with the sole responsibility for ensuring their children's safety, well-being, and nurturance. Public assistance is provided only in emergencies, and parents tend to be stigmatized if they need help in fulfilling their obligations. When parents must balance external demands such as work, they enlist supports such as siblings, neighbors, and paid caregivers to help fulfill their obligations.

## Roles and Expectations

Family role structures are often the focus of intervention. Culture heavily influences social, family, and gender roles through culturally determined expectations of how such roles should be performed (Devaux, 1995). Every culture has a model of the ideal family (Montague, 1996). Through this model, cultures dictate gender expectations, family structures, and adequate role functioning. When family performance deviates from the culturally prescribed norms, tension emerges in the larger group, causing cultural leaders to either change the role-perceptions or reestablish the norms. Such social pressures are evident in the United States as traditional family values emerge in political debates, and federal funding programs seek to motivate populations to more closely subscribe to the "ideal" vision of the family.

These cultural models determine a society's images of mothers, fathers, and children (McCollum, 1997). In some cultures, there are clear distinctions and divisions of labor for different roles in the family. For example, in some cultures women are expected to defer important decisions to the male head of the household. Such cultural models invest power and privilege in the male role. Women in these cultures may have fewer rights and more obligations than males do. This cultural model is very different from the North American egalitarian model of families. Differences between models can create tension when a minority culture's model comes into conflict with the dominant culture.

By its association with family roles, culture influences the broader gender roles. Images of maleness and femaleness are largely culturally determined. Male-dominated cultures have a prescription for males to be assertive and decisive; concurrently, there is a prescription for females to be submissive. Each of these gender role prescriptions has implications for allowable gender-specific behaviors and interactions within the culture. Notably, prescriptions are accompanied by power, autonomy, and prestige differences across the genders.

All of the culturally bound role expectations influence nurturing functions in the family. In some cultures males do very little nurturing, but they may remain the ultimate authority when discipline is applied. Additionally, males may be largely absent due to expectations that they earn money for the family. In more collectivist cultures, females tend to be more active outside of the home, and tasks within the home are more evenly distributed. Children observe and model these roles in the home, basing their expectations on the family's balance of roles and expectations. If the culture allows diversity, children are able to assess the family models, contrast them with alternatives, and then select their own model.

# Cultural Influences on Accessibility Functions

Adults must be accessible to their children in order to help them process and understand the world. In some cultures this function is largely met by the parents; in others, the access systems are more broadly defined. We must also consider the culture within the society in order to understand how parents are able to maintain accessibility for their children. Parental accessibility has two major influences: systems of support and socioeconomic resources.

## Systems of Support

Cultures provide varied systems of support for individuals and families. Some cultures promote kinship as the first level of support (Scannapieco & Jackson, 1996; Weaver & White, 1997). This emphasis can occur independently of the culture's collectivist versus individualistic features. For example, in the United States, a highly individualistic country, people are stigmatized for using public support systems; there is an insistence that families take care of "their own." Inherent in such cultures are expectations that families provide necessary resources and services. Other systems of support are less valued and viewed as systems of last resort.

In cultures where the family is considered the legitimate avenue of support, there are mechanisms to promote the family supports as being more favorable than alternatives. For example, society may offer enticements for staying in a marriage or impose punishments for separation and divorce. Concurrently, cultural values motivate people to use family members by stigmatizing alternative sources of support.

In collectivist cultures, mechanisms focus less on the nuclear family because provisions are made for broader systems of support. However, it is common for such cultures to have a hierarchy of supports. Some cultures have internal systems of support through which people within the cultural group are expected to help each other. Some cultures have their own agency systems (e.g., Jewish Family Services). These agencies supplement the family by providing services that are consistent with the culture's beliefs and values. These formal support systems are often viewed as more desirable than the supports provided by the dominant society.

Many cultures have injunctions about using formal supports. In such situations, entering service is viewed as a sign of selling out or failure. Families in such cultures try to find all supports either internally or through their culture. Doing so can become problematic if the cultural group is small, because there are fewer support options. Families may rely on inadequate supports rather than face the stigma of using societal support systems. This approach can result in families receiving inadequate resources, including fewer opportunities to obtain child care, money, emotional support, and advice.

In cultural groups where formal supports are the norm, there is much less informal support, and children have fewer accessible adults. For example, in cultures that promote the nuclear family system, families often use day-care services rather than kin for their children's caregivers. Kin often become an avenue of last resort. In these cultures it is also common for families to move away from kinship systems, leaving few adults available for informal support. In times of economic stress, families may find themselves not only without money for formal supports but also without informal supports. In such situations, children frequently are brought to work or left minimally attended.

## Social and Economic Resources

Although cultural systems provide supportive resources, cultural economic issues are also associated with access. Every family has minimum resource requirements for meeting personal and family goals. Culture affects these minimum requirements in two ways. First, some cultures encourage families to exceed the minimum requirements by placing a value on accumulated wealth. In such cultures, a person's success is often measured by the amount of wealth that she is able to accumulate. The second cultural effect stems from differential access to resources. If a cultural group, through disparate access, does not have enough resources, members of the group must work extra hours just to achieve the minimum resource level (e.g., take two jobs).

If a family has sufficient resources, access functions are enhanced; extra time and resources are available for family life. For example, some families have enough resources so that only one person is required to seek outside employment. In these families, surplus time resources (time exceeding what is required for subsistence) allow children increased access with one of the parents. Similarly, if financial resources are above the minimum requirement, there is a surplus that allows family members to attend camps, participate in athletics, or take family vacations.

Families in cultural groups with compromised access to resources often have multiple family members working outside of the home. This situation diminishes the access function because able-bodied adults and older siblings are needed to meet the basic resource requirement. Access is further diminished if family members return from work exhausted, thus limiting emotional access. The kind of work typically available to minority cultural groups is less desirable, physically hard, and yields minimal compensation. Family members must work longer hours to achieve basic needs.

In such families, the level of energy invested in meeting basic needs limits the family options (Fiske, 1995). When multiple families in a specific cultural group are in this position, there is a clear cultural influence. The relationship is not direct, but there is a clear tendency for members of the dominant culture to have much higher levels of resources. Many people in nondominant cultural groups do not have resource levels sufficient to meet their personal and family goals (Falicov, 1998).

## Working With Invisible Cultures

The concept of culture is most often applied to groups of people who are visibly and/or ethnically different from the dominant group in society. There are, however, some cultural groups that look identical to those in the dominant group yet have shared experiences and beliefs that form a group separate from the dominant group. It is possible for family therapists to begin working with such cultural groups without noticing that the family is different from the dominant group.

Two invisible cultures in North American society are gay or lesbian families and families identified from fundamental or conservative religions. Although these two groups have very different beliefs and experiences, they share the traits of invisibility, divergence from the mainstream groups, and a history of being misunderstood. Both cultural groups also raise children and live in family units, fulfilling all of the functions described in the first two chapters of this text.

To identify how these invisible cultures influence family functioning, Table 3.2 presents the elements of the culture ring, along with trends and tendencies for both populations. Remember that although the tendencies are common within a cultural group, families within each group are likely to vary greatly from these central tendencies. When working with families from either group, practitioners must approach the family with a solid knowledge about the group—concurrent with a naïve approach of letting each family be the experts in their own reality.

In Table 3.2, you can observe how both conservative religious families and gay-lesbian families are influenced by cultural elements. The cultural elements have implications for parents within each group. Notice that one group is apt to be more lenient in discipline, while the other may have more rigid expectations based on the shared beliefs

---

**TABLE 3.2**
**Culture-Ring Application to Invisible Cultural Groups**

|  | Conservative Religious Groups | Gay or Lesbian |
|---|---|---|
| Resources | Strong fund-raising and church structures; often very wealthy and willing to contribute to the cause. | Hidden population and economically diverse; few organized resources. |
| Supports | Church structures and congregations provide highly available although sometimes judgmental supports. | Due to phobic reactions, not highly visible; supports are often more informal. |
| Systems of Sanction | Often adhere rigidly to church dogma and rules; "spare the rod and spoil the child" approach. | Many parents are no different from the mainstream; tendency to be somewhat lenient. |
| Abstract Mindedness | Tendency toward concrete interpretations and religious dogma; view things as black and white versus gray. | Frequently educated and abstract thinkers. |
| Roles and Expectations | Belief in traditional family values and roles; expect family members to do their part. | With divergence from traditional family format come flexible roles. |
| Individual Versus Collective | Blended with a focus on individual rights and responsibility concurrent with importance placed on the congregation. | Largely collectivist with a large focus on the gay-lesbian community. |
| Experience of Difference | Tendency to feel closer to God and morally superior; differences are processed in terms of enlightenment. | Safety issues are frequently associated with difference; often persecuted and attacked. |
| Values and Religion | Religion provides guidance and the code for living. People are expected to live according to the accepted interpretation of the Bible and church doctrine. | Often humanistic in values; acceptance, openness, and respect are important. |

within the cultural group. Notice also how each group adopts a different approach to handling differences. Based on these cultural differences, children within each group will inherit different messages about themselves, other people, and family life.

# Managing Culture With Issues of Family Violence

Cultural competence can be a difficult balance when the norms of the dominant society and the norms of a minority cultural group conflict. Such conflicts most often emerge in the way power and privileges are distributed among the family members. In some cultures, power is vested in one individual or role within the family. This autocratic vesting of power often offends the values of the dominant culture. When there are also differences in the way power can be used among the family members, additional problems are sure to arise.

Cultural conflicts frequently occur when issues of violence and/or abuse emerge. Conflicts are inevitable because the judgment about what is abusive is a cultural decision. Consequently, issues of violence can never be divorced from culture, because cultural groups will vary in their definitions of the problem. In situations where there is a law governing the worker response, cultural competence requires practitioners to honor the family's culture while still upholding the culturally bound laws of the dominant group.

Due to the nature of many conflicts, it is useful to understand how cultural values and family policy intersect. Laws of the dominant culture always reflect aspects of the dominant ideology and competing interests in the society. Figure 3.2 depicts the various constituencies that influence the passage of violence-related legislation.

Notice in Figure 3.2 that many groups and political forces intersect when forming the final legislation. These interests have a long-term influence on legislation. Typically, a single group within the dominant culture identifies a problem and initiates action to promote the legislation. Through this group's efforts, acceptance of the issue as a social problem grows. Through this growing awareness, other segments of the population support the advocacy, thus giving it legitimacy within the dominant culture.

As efforts to form legislation progress, other groups vie for influence. The blending of multiple self-interested groups changes the initial spirit of the legislation through compromise and competition for privilege in the outcome. Eventually, a compromised law is passed. With the legislation, political legitimacy is achieved; but changes may not occur. It is often left to the initial groups to monitor the situation to ensure that the law is enacted and effective. Doing so involves many years of working with people within the system to standardize and implement the law.

Given the forces that influence violence-related legislation, the dominant cultural values cannot be separated from the legislation. This situation influences the framework, the problem definition, and ultimately the legal response to the problem. It frequently results in a culturally insensitive legal response because the resulting legislation contains language specific to the intergroup compromises and politics that emerged during the development of the legislation.

**Figure 3.2** Development of Violence-Related Legislation

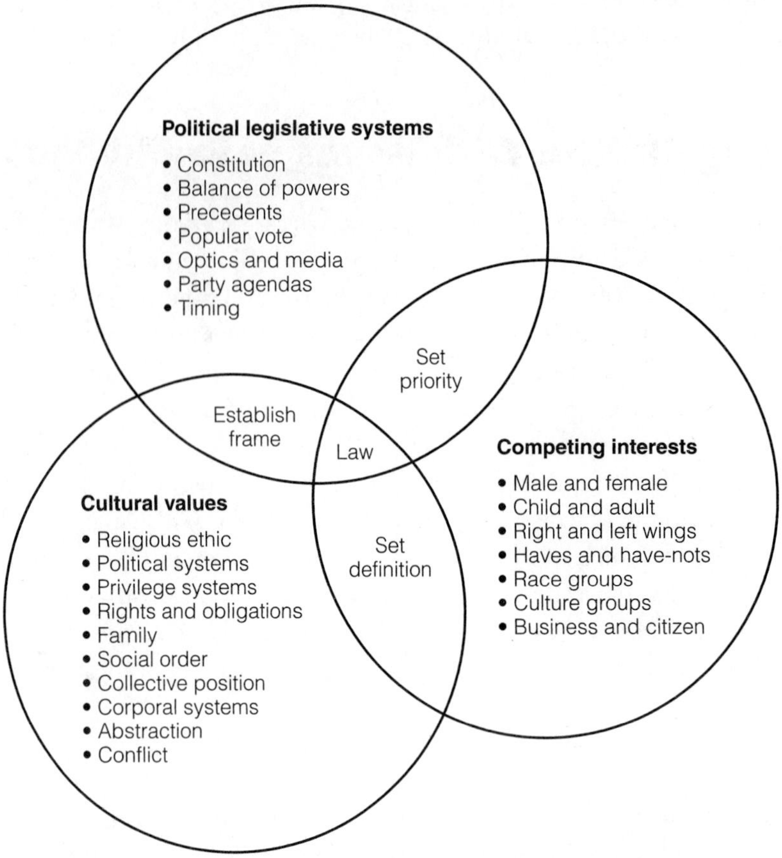

**Political legislative systems**
- Constitution
- Balance of powers
- Precedents
- Popular vote
- Optics and media
- Party agendas
- Timing

Set priority

Establish frame

Law

**Competing interests**
- Male and female
- Child and adult
- Right and left wings
- Haves and have-nots
- Race groups
- Culture groups
- Business and citizen

**Cultural values**
- Religious ethic
- Political systems
- Privilege systems
- Rights and obligations
- Family
- Social order
- Collective position
- Corporal systems
- Abstraction
- Conflict

Set definition

As a practitioner, you have little flexibility here; but you can help people from different cultures find culturally sound alternatives to the prohibited violent act (e.g., hitting children or spouses). You can also reinforce the idea that the law is part of the social structure and outside of most people's control. Helping people access political systems can help them exercise their rights to express concern, but family practitioners cannot ignore the law.

The cultural insensitivity inherent in the legal definitions and responses extends to the service system, because services are grounded in the legislation. All programs are bound in that they cannot alter the legal definitions. Programs, however, can work with different cultural groups to identify frames and operational definitions (e.g., when hitting someone leaves a bruise) that allow clients to understand the subtleties so they can incorporate the legal injunctions into a cultural framework. In such conflicted situations, the culture ring can help practitioners to identify alternatives that will be consistent with cultural norms.

## ◆ EXERCISE 3.1 CULTURAL INFLUENCES

In this exercise, you must first identify a cultural affiliation. Your cultural affiliation will be influenced by your race and ancestry. For example, if you are Caucasian and were born in the United States, your culture is probably the dominant culture. However, if you are African American, you will be identified differently because you have had very different life experiences. Spend some time thinking about your life experiences, ancestry, and cultural background; then identify your cultural group.

After you have identified your cultural affiliation, use the following prompts to think about your culture and how its influences affect parenting within the culture. For each cultural element, first think about the questions and then enter some of your observations in the following cultural chart.

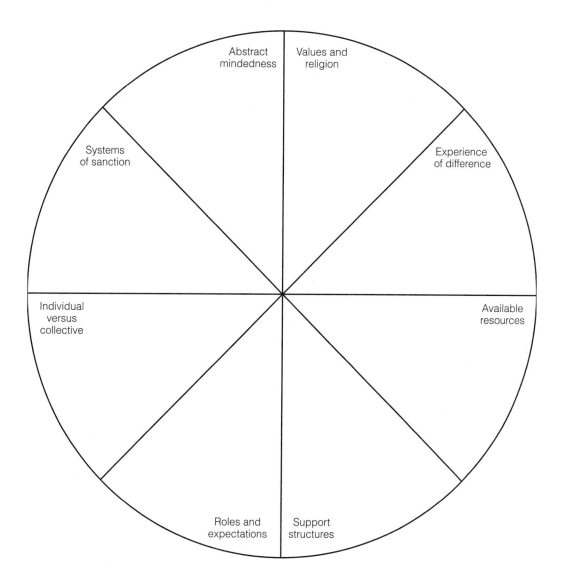

1. **Abstract mindedness.** In your culture, how much do people rely on principles, symbols, and so forth to convey cultural values? Are there clear rules that people must follow? How do you tell if someone is successful—through symbols, position, actions, or some other indication? How do you tend to be influenced by this aspect of your culture? Enter your observations in the chart.

2. **Experience of difference.** How are people in your culture different from others? How have people in your life made sense of the differences? Do people talk about the differences, or do they avoid this topic or brush it aside? How are the resource differences between different cultures explained? How do issues of difference influence your responses to situations? Enter your observations in the chart.

3. **Values and religion.** What are the most important cultural institutions for your people? What are the institutions that people defend in the news? What are the practices that people within the culture engage in to promote the institutions? How have the important values and institutions influenced your responses to situations? Enter your observations in the chart.

4. **Individualistic versus collectivistic.** In your culture, are common rights or individual rights more important? Do people have responsibilities to the larger group? How is this value (individual versus group) expressed? How does it influence people's thinking and behaviors? How has it influenced your responses? Enter your observations in the chart.

5. **Roles and expectations.** What roles are most respected in your culture? How are people expected to treat people within those roles? What family roles are important? Is there an ideal family structure in your culture? What cultural history seems to influence the ideal or actual family structures? How have the roles and expectations influenced your response to situations? Enter your observations in the chart.

6. **Available resources.** In your culture, as compared to others, do people tend to have enough resources to achieve their goals? How important are resources in your culture? How are resources used in your culture? How have these cultural influences influenced your responses to situations? Enter your observations in the chart.

7. **Support structures.** Where do people within your culture get support? Are there any common types of support that might not be valued in other cultures? Are people judged if they use certain sources of support? Are there any stigmas about using different types of support? How does this influence you when you want support? Enter your observations in the chart.

8. **Systems of sanctioning.** In your culture, how do people hold each other accountable when problems occur? Do people deal with each other directly, or do they use a third party? What are the worst sanctions? What are the most common sanctions? How does the culture reward people who are doing well? How does this shape your responses? Enter your observations in the chart.

# Summary

Family practitioners must be sensitive to the general tendencies within the various cultural groups. Such awareness helps professionals prepare for working with the family. In this preparation, family practitioners reflect on the common patterns of parenting, belief and interpretation systems, and external systems of input and support. Although each family will be unique, family practitioners need a basic knowledge from which to diverge. When meeting families, however, the practitioner must approach each one as if it is totally new; they must allow the family to inform them of how they integrate the cultural influences into a unique family structure.

The culture ring presented in this chapter gives family practitioners a framework for organizing and understanding the influence of various cultures. When using the culture ring, remember that the various cultural elements have implications for many parental functions. Application of the culture ring in this chapter presents each element as relating to a single parental function, but in practice you will find multiple linkages and implications. Even if the primary implication focuses on a single parenting function, remember that multiple functions are affected by every cultural element.

# Critical Content

1. Families serve as conduits of culture as they transmit cultural beliefs to the children.
2. All families are unique, but elements of the culture influence how parents fulfill each parenting function.
3. To ensure openness with families, family practitioners must develop a sound knowledge base about multiple diverse cultures.
4. Family practitioners must approach families with cultural knowledge in abeyance, allowing each family to be unique.
5. The culture ring can help family practitioners to organize and track cultural influences.
6. Not all cultures are visible; some, like gay-lesbian and conservative religious groups, are invisible.

# Suggested Readings

Bateson, M. C. (1985). We are the world, we are the parents. *Family Therapy Networker, 9*, 42–45.

Laird, J. (2000). Gender in lesbian relationships: Cultural, feminist, and constructionist reflections. *Journal of Marital & Family Therapy, 26*, 455–467.

Waldman, F. (1999). Violence or discipline? Working with multicultural court-ordered clients. *Journal of Marital & Family Therapy, 25*, 503–515.

# SECTION II

# ASSESSING FAMILIES: AN INTRODUCTION

In Section II of this text, we explore the process of assessing families. After reading an overview of the skills required for exploring family dynamics and stories, you will learn about frameworks and tools for organizing and structuring assessment sessions. Finally, you will examine a model for writing family assessments and beginning the transition from exploration to change-focused work. The content in this section builds on the theories and models provided in Section I. By studying these sections, you will learn how to use theory to guide exploration and formulate an understanding of family problems.

In Chapter 4 of this section, you will consider strategies for exploring family stories and processes. We begin with a description of exploratory questioning, a critical skill that provides a foundation for all future skills. After reading about the questioning strategies, you will learn observational techniques for identifying potential family issues through intermember transactions. These interactive strategies are followed by descriptions of other data collections strategies. We then consider the benefits and limitations of using projective techniques (such as family sculpting) and structured questionnaires.

Chapter 5 in this section presents four tools that can help structure your data collection. First we look at the genogram, a common tool in family practice. You will learn basic techniques for making and using genograms. Next we examine the four-cell couple assessment model, which is useful for assessing intimate partners and parental dyads. Third is a parental assessment tool that builds on the content in Chapter 2. Finally, we consider a model for assessing risk in the family system.

In Chapter 6 of this section, we explore the writing of formal assessments and contracting for change. First you will examine, task by task, a model for formal family assessments. To illustrate each stage of the model, the chapter contains a sample assessment. Next you will explore issues of goal formation and treatment objectives. In this discussion, we consider contracting skills and examine a sample plan of care based on agency practice.

## Chapter 4

# Exploration and Data Collection With Families

When families enter treatment, the family practitioner begins by exploring the family situation in order to identify elements that contribute to the family's problems. While examining various aspects of the family and its situation, the practitioner, in partnership with family members, identifies elements that might explain the problem situation. If formal assessments are required, the practitioner then applies her knowledge and theories in order to understand the family's problems and develop a treatment direction.

Formal assessments are often unnecessary for family practitioners in private practice, especially if the practitioner is using narrative or solution-focused approaches to treatment. Such practitioners partner with the family to co-construct an understanding of the family situation. However, for many practitioners in agency practice or practitioners who must defend their understanding to external authorities (e.g., courts, third-party sources of payment), a rigorous system of gathering and documenting data is needed. In this chapter and in Chapters 5 and 6, we examine methods needed for both informal and formal assessment of family situations.

Family-based exploration can seem confusing. When family members enter treatment, they have a long history with the problem. Consequently, family members have formed rigid patterns of responding to and interpreting the situation (White, 1983, 1984). The practitioner must explore each family member's perspective to determine the unique and shared versions of family events. As such exploration unfolds, important information, dynamics, and belief systems will emerge to reveal the nature of the family's problems.

# Theoretical Grounding

The concepts we consider in this chapter are unevenly endorsed by different family models. Some theoretical models use questioning techniques, but never use structured questionnaires; other models believe in using objective means during the assessment phase. You will find that many models do not even include assessment as a phase of treatment. Because most family practitioners in agency practice must perform some sort of assessment as part of their job requirements, we examine various family exploration and assessment techniques throughout this chapter. As you delve into the specifics of a theoretical model, you will endorse some techniques while discarding others. To aid you in making informed decisions about models and techniques, refer to Table 4.1, which correlates chapter concepts with various theoretical models. Recommended reading in this table focuses on the broadly available texts:

- *The Essentials of Family Therapy* (2nd ed.), by M. P. Nichols & R. C. Schwartz, 2005, Boston: Allyn & Bacon.
- *Family Counseling and Therapy* (3rd ed.), by A. M. Horne, 2000, Pacific Grove, CA: Brooks/Cole.
- *Family Therapy: An Overview* (6th ed.), by I. Goldenberg & H. Goldenberg, 2004, Pacific Grove, CA: Brooks/Cole.

**TABLE 4.1**
**Chapter Concepts, Theoretical Models, and Sources**

| Chapter Concepts | Theoretical Model(s) | Recommended Reading |
|---|---|---|
| Need for exploration | Structural model<br>Family systems model | Goldenberg & Goldenberg, Chapters 4, 8<br>Horne, Chapters 6, 10<br>Nichols & Schwartz, Chapters 5, 6, 7 |
| Family-based questioning | Milan model<br>Strategic model<br>Narrative model | Goldenberg & Goldenberg, Chapters 10, 11, 13, 14<br>Horne, Chapter 8<br>Nichols & Schwartz, Chapters 6, 13 |
| Observing family processes | Communications model<br>Symbolic experiential model and Satir<br>In-home models<br>Behavioral models<br>Integrative models<br>Structural model<br>Family systems model (Bowen) | Goldenberg & Goldenberg, Chapters 4, 7, 8<br>Horne, Chapters 4, 10, 15<br>Nichols & Schwartz, Chapters 7, 8, 11, 14 |
| Measuring family processes: structured questionnaires | Behavioral models<br>Psychometric models | Goldenberg & Goldenberg, Chapters 11, 16<br>Horne, Chapter 15<br>Nichols & Schwartz, Chapter 10 |

In this chapter you will focus on the different skills and strategies that family practitioners use to explore the family situation and collect data that can help explain family problems. Family practitioners beginning the exploration process with a family are guided by the theories and knowledge outlined in Section I of this text. Such thinking is crucial when selecting strategies for exploration and data collection. Multiple data collection methods are available for family practitioners. Following are some common assessment techniques. We explore these strategies in detail throughout this chapter.

◆ **Exploring situations with the family.** Workers frequently meet with families to conduct assessment interviews. In the interview, the purpose is to glean an understanding of the situation. Typically, workers will have a framework of questions to ensure that they obtain all of the critical information. Some organizations structure the interviews to guarantee that the agency-mandated information is collected.

◆ **Observation.** Workers sometimes select the option of observing families while interacting or when performing some task. The tasks or interactions may be timed, or a system of interpreting the meaning of actions and interactions (e.g., types of words used, frequency of themes and behaviors) can be applied. Some workers like to remain in the room; others may observe from a distance or through a one-way mirror.

◆ **Projective techniques.** Workers frequently use projective techniques to gather focused data from families. Perhaps the most famous example of such a strategy is the Rorschach inkblot test. Other techniques are more frequently used, such as sharing three wishes, completing sentences, sharing repetitive dreams, responding to pictures or stories, and completing a story. In using these techniques, the worker presents a vague picture or an open-ended narrative and asks the family to respond. The worker then helps interpret the themes in the family's response. This type of data can be heavily influenced by worker fantasies and/or misinterpretations due to the vagueness of information gathered.

◆ **Structured questionnaires.** Structured questionnaires tend to use a list of questions or statements. Frequently, all of the questions will have an underlying theme (e.g., all about alcohol use, anxiety, etc.). Some questionnaires will have several scales with a common theme (e.g., the Child Behavior Checklist has multiple scales). Families are most often asked to provide their agreement or reaction to each item on the questionnaire and mark their response on some sort of scale. These questionnaires are often referred to as *standardized measures*.

# Exploring Situations With the Family

A family interview is a rich and dynamic source of information. The multiple people, relationships, and perspectives produce dynamics in the session that never occur in individual meetings. For example, when you are interviewing one family member, other members may begin arguing. If you are not prepared for such interactive energy, it can be overwhelming. At times, the practitioner may need to harness and direct family members to ensure a productive interview.

The potential for interaction and multiple relationships requires specialized interview strategies. These strategies build on the skills used in individual treatment through specialized questioning strategies to maximize interactive information and focus the family energy. In a family session, you can direct communication to one family member while talking to another. This is possible because all family members are present and either actively or vicariously involved in all conversations.

Family-based exploration often uses questions that yield information while at the same time giving the family feedback (Palazzoli, Boscolo, Cecchin, & Prata, 1980; Tomm, 1987a, 1987b). For practitioners, the simultaneous development of information and feedback does more than gather information; it also enhances the working alliance by promoting insights (Adams, 1997; Dozier, Hicks, & Cornille, 1998). Family practitioners have pioneered the art of asking questions that can promote change during the exploration process (Brown, 1997).

Family-based questions are frequently complex. Family practitioners must consider many elements as questions are conceived and delivered. Whereas therapist thinking and questioning tend to occur instantaneously, it is important to understand the four elements of family-based questions:

1. **Targeting the question.** What are you trying to accomplish, and how?
2. **Setting up the question.** What do you need to put on the table for optimum effect?
3. **Posing the question.** How do you want to phrase the question?
4. **Follow-up.** Where do you want the follow-up discussion to take the response to the question?

Because most family-based questions involve some sophistication in setup and delivery, we will discuss each of these four elements in detail.

## Targeting the Question

The technique of targeting a question involves two elements. In session with a family, you must first select a person in the family to respond to the question. This will most likely be the family member having the strongest capacity to influence others with his or her answer. Sometimes the desired effect of a question is to elicit specific information. At other times, you may seek to infuse new information or feedback into the family system. When selecting a respondent, you will consider three elements:

1. Choosing a respondent who will not be discounted
2. Choosing people who are likely to have critical information
3. Choosing a family member whose perspective will introduce information in a disarming or influential manner

## CASE EXAMPLE

A practitioner is working with a family under significant financial stress. She knows the parents are arguing about money and is concerned about the impact on the children. The parents seem unaware that their five-year-old is becoming anxious, and the practitioner wants to elicit information in a way that will help the parents to see the girl's plight. She consequently asks the child, "Your mom and dad seem concerned about the money. When they argue about money, what do you do?" The child begins talking about feeling scared and hiding in her room.

In this case example, the practitioner selects a specific target—the child, who can get critical information on the table while also highlighting the emotional impact that the problem is having on the children. If she had wanted information about the details of financial stress in the family, the therapist would not have selected a child as the target, because he or she would not have the information and might be discounted. Given the goal, targeting the child is effective because she has knowledge, will not likely be discounted, and has a new perspective to add to the issue.

The second element of targeting involves determining the desired effect of the information. Typically, when you ask a family-based question, you are attempting to influence the family while gathering information. Thus you must focus the question so that the person who responds will offer relevant and influential information. Most often, the desired effect emerges from the therapist's hunches. For example, if a family member repeatedly states that people in the family get along well, you may suspect there is some rule about getting along. Acting on this hunch, you can target a question about how the rule operates in the system.

When targeting a question, the family practitioner can use the family response systems to help direct the desired effect. The response system framework provides a crosshair system that allows you to identify specific areas for exploration. Notice how each response system yields different types of information.

- ◆ **Cognitive systems** yield information about the beliefs associated with a rule. Example: "How important is it for people in the family to get along?"
- ◆ **Affective systems** yield information about the feelings underlying the rule or the rule enforcement. Example: "When people don't get along, who becomes most upset?"
- ◆ **Behavior systems** yield information about how the rule is enforced. Example: "What happens when the children in this family are unable to get along with each other?"
- ◆ **Interaction systems** yield information about how the rule is communicated and the relational structures underlying the rule. Example: "How do your parents remind you children about getting along with others?"

During family-based exploration, therapists often focus initially on a response system that will be easiest to access and provide information for further discussion. Later, the therapist attempts to elicit the most strategic information. Frequently, it is useful to focus on the processing systems (feeling and thinking) early in the exploration because they underlie behaviors and provide critical information about the belief systems that support the problem (de Shazer, 1997).

## Setting Up the Question

As a practitioner, it is important that you set up the question to focus the family energy. A setup line can maximize the desired effect by providing a context, adjusting emotions, activating thinking, and disarming resistance. If questions are not set up properly, family members may resist answering or give you information that is superfluous to the desired effect. Setting up a question involves two steps:

1. **Linking.** Often, practitioners use part of the family member's last statement to build the setup. This makes the question a continuation of the last client statement rather than a new direction. Doing so can also affirm the family member. In the preceding case example, the setup involves a simple reflection to the child that her parents are concerned about their finances.
2. **Modulating.** After linking to the family member's last statement, the therapist introduces new elements to modulate the focus or meaning. This step involves stressing specific response systems (thought, feeling, interaction and relationship, action theme) to build a transition toward the new information the therapist wants to develop. In the case example, the practitioner focuses on the affect system and selects the word *concern* to tune the parents into their feelings.

The setup is presented as a brief statement immediately preceding the delivery of the question. Typically, practitioners avoid using long setup statements, which may confuse the family by providing too much information and thus detract from the desired effect. The following setups are commonly used in family practice. When reading the examples that accompany the discussions, note the italicized wording, which indicates the setup lines.

- ◆ **The presupposition setup** (Patton, 1980). A presupposition setup is useful when you are asking about difficult or sensitive behaviors. Presupposition precludes denial by embedding an assumption that something is occurring. The question then focuses on the degree or intensity of the behavior. Example setup: "Dad, *when you and your partner fight,* how often does it escalate to the point of screaming?"
- ◆ **The balanced setup** (Patton, 1980). Balanced setups allow for both positive and negative extremes. The range of permissible behavior encourages a response because potential concerns about negative judgments are neutralized. Example: "John, *arguing can be growth enhancing and at times disruptive in families.* How does arguing affect people in your family?"

◆ **The illustrative examples setup** (Patton, 1980). At times you will want to give an example of the possible options when setting up a question. Example: "I know that *all couples disagree with each other and have conflict. In some families the conflict even leads to behaviors such as swearing, grabbing, and shoving.* In your relationship, how do you deal with conflict?"

◆ **The validation setup.** Frequently, you will want to validate the respondent, making her feel comfortable when responding to the question. In validating the respondent, you will often seek to highlight her strengths and increase the credibility of her answer. Example: "Mom, *I know that you have made many sacrifices for the children over the years.* How have they shown you their appreciation?" Notice that the validation setup establishes a tone for the question.

◆ **The summary setup.** When setting up many questions, you will want to affirm an issue or topic that a family member has put on the table. In this type of setup, the practitioner repeats or summarizes information provided by the family to focus the question. Example: "Mom, *you stated that the kids don't seem to respect you.* What do they do that shows disrespect?"

◆ **The contextual change setup** (Tomm, 1987a, 1987b). To explore the impact of context on a situation, the therapist can alter the context of the setup to see if the family response changes. Example: "*If it was your son coming home an hour after curfew,* would you be as worried?"

## Posing the Question

After setting up the question, you must pose the question to the family. The way that you pose the question will cause the family to focus, think, and respond in different ways (McGee, 2000). All individual-focused questions can still be used, but be aware that asking unique, family-based questions can yield very different results. Several questioning options are available for family-based exploratory questioning.

In the field of family therapy, the questioning typologies can be confusing. The following five questioning types are often referenced:

1. **Direct.** Direct questions are typically used for investigating family situations. The question is posed directly to a family member, soliciting his opinion or knowledge on a subject. Example: "John, how do you influence the rules that your family makes?" Notice that this question yields information on the person's perceptions of his own position in the family decision making. Direct questioning is useful when the therapist believes the person will share important information about the family without attempting to disguise or elude critical issues.

2. **Triadic.** Triadic questions ask one family member to report on the relationship or behaviors of other family members (Penn, 1982). With a triadic question, the respondent is not the focus of the desired impact. Consequently, the respondent is in a position to report on relationships or exchanges

between other members of the family. Example: "John, when mom wants to do something and dad wants to do something else, who tends to get their own way?" Notice that this question yields information about the problem solving in the parental relationship. This style of questioning is useful when direct questioning may yield elusive responses.

3. **Circular.** Circular questioning is useful for exploring family dynamics (Tomm, 1987a). The therapist targets multiple respondents, inviting each person to contribute information from his or her own perspective (Penn, 1982). This type of questioning often yields information about relationships, differences, and coalitions in the family. Example: "John, when your mother wants to do something and your father doesn't, who tends to get their own way? . . . Mary, from where you sit in this family, who tends to get their own way when mom wants to do something and dad does not?" Notice how the worker gathers information from one person and then shifts to another person to solicit her perspective. All perspectives are considered valid.

4. **Reflexive.** Reflexive questions solicit information in a manner that facilitates a deeper understanding of the situation among the family members (Tomm, 1987b). Reflexive questions tend to expand the family's understanding by eliciting information about connections; or, they may constrain the family's understanding by eliciting distinctions (Brown, 1997). As the family member answers the question, new information is presented. As the family members integrate the new information into the past conceptualization, a foundation for change is created.

5. **Lineal.** Lineal questions seek information about interaction and interpretation sequences (Tomm, 1987b). Such questions track the step-by-step interactions or interpretations that occur during family exchanges (Ragg, 2001). The purpose of sequential questions is to slow the family down so its members can better understand their interaction sequences. It is assumed that actions taken at one step of the process cause the subsequent actions. By tracking each action and/or the thinking that underlies each action, the practitioner can identify the patterns of family interaction.

These five different methods of posing a question can be used with multiple questioning strategies. A questioning strategy controls the focus of the question. Some questioning strategies are useful for exploring processing systems, whereas others tend to focus on action systems. Each strategy can make use of the five questioning methods, allowing for great diversity in how questions are posed. In the following sections, we explore different questioning strategies that you will find useful with families. The strategies are organized according to response systems.

*Interaction System Questioning Strategies*   In your work with family members, it is important to glean an understanding of the interactions and relationships existing among the family members. The relationship system not only can be very complex but also can be viewed differently from the various positions in the family.

The following questioning strategies have proven useful in gleaning relational information:

- ◆ **Interaction sequencing questions** (Ragg, 2001). Family practitioners often want to delineate repeated patterns of interaction. Interaction sequence questioning begins with the context of an exchange and then asks a series of questions step-by-step to identify discrete phases of the interaction. This strategy is commonly used when you want to know how each family member responds in a specific situation. Sequencing and timing are explored to create a clear picture of the problem. Example: "When Marty and your mom begin to fight, where are you? . . . What is said first? . . . By whom?" . . . "Dad, where are you when this is happening? . . . Dad, what do you say when you see the argument begin?" . . . "Mom, when your husband says these things, what do you most often do?" You will track these questions until the full pattern unfolds and you can account for the actions of all family members.

- ◆ **Process identification questions** (Yalom, 2002; Ragg, 2001). In a strategy similar to that of the sequence questions, family practitioners often want to identify interpersonal processes without tracking the details. In such situations, process identification questions invite family members to comment on the interpersonal processes that they observe in the family. Example: "Mary, do you notice that whenever you say 'I don't know,' your mother rolls her eyes back in her head? . . . Does she also do this at other times?" A triadic formulation of the same question would be, "Dad, what did you notice your wife doing when Mary said 'I don't know'?"

- ◆ **Coalition and alignment questions** (Tomm, 1987a, 1987b; Penn, 1982). Coalition and alignment questions often use the triadic formulation to engage one family member in commenting on coalitions among other members. Families often form coalitions and alignments in which two or more family members take sides against another family member. Workers are often challenged to determine which members are siding against other members. Coalition and alignment questions ask family members to reflect on the family's side-taking structures. For example, in a family where the children are becoming involved in parental problems, a worker may address the children with the following question: "Mary, when your mom and dad argue, who in the family takes mom's side? . . . And who in the family will take your father's side?"

*Behavioral Questioning Strategies*   When working with families, you will often want to explore the action systems of the family to determine what kinds of behavior are common in the family system. Most practitioners have a repertoire of behavior-based questions (e.g., descriptive: "What would I see when I come over to your house?") that can be used with individuals either separately or during a family interview. Family practitioners most commonly use the following four types of behavior-based questions to elicit information about family dynamics or behavior within the family:

1. **Normative questions** (Penn, 1982; Tomm, 1987a, 1987b). Normative comparisons ask family members to reflect on normal processes within the

family. To gather such information, therapists often ask family members to reflect on who in the family performs different functions. Example: "Mary, out of all the people in the family, who is the person who tries to make you feel better when you are sad?" Notice that this question compares the normative behavior of one person to that of others in the family.

2.  **Observational perspective questions** (Tomm, 1987a, 1987b). A frequent type of question involves asking the respondent to share what he observes with his own senses. You can ask the respondent to report his own observations directly ("When mom and dad fight, what do you see mom doing?") or to shift his perspective to an external observer ("If I were a fly on the wall when mom and dad fight, what would I see them doing?")

3.  **Comparative questions** (Penn, 1982; Tomm, 1987a, 1987b, 1988). A third type of behavior-focused question explores the behavioral differences among family members. You can either combine this with normative questions to compare common patterns or limit the questions to a specific situation. Example: "Mom, you said that Tommy is a very hard worker. How is that different from the other children in the family?"

4.  **Future orientation questions** (Tomm, 1987a, 1987b). You will often want to ask family members to reflect on the future implications of their behavior. Ask them to think about the future and imagine how their current behavior might influence their future. Example: "If you keep fighting the way you have been for the last six months, what will your relationship be like five years from now?"

*Thinking and Belief System Questions*  Families have belief systems, values, and patterns of interpretation that are idiosyncratic to the family system. Family practitioners want to understand how the beliefs influence family members through formal and informal rules. Here are some common questions that can begin to highlight such belief systems:

◆ **Injunction questions** (Tomm, 1987a, 1987b). Families often have injunctions or rules that limit family members' response repertoires. Such injunctions can be overt or covert. Often family rules and injunctions occur in response to the needs and actions of a specific family member. Family practitioners seek to understand the nature of the family injunctions by understanding the rule and the individual or subsystem promoting the rule. Example: "If mom becomes upset, what do people in this family do to let you know that is not okay?"

◆ **Cognitive sequencing questions** (Ragg, 2001). Cognitive sequencing questions are a lineal type of question whereby the practitioner attempts to highlight the interpretations and beliefs underlying family interactions. This type of question often works in concert with the interaction pattern questions. After tracking an interaction sequence, you can retrace the sequence, asking family members what their thinking was at each step of the interaction. This approach is useful in helping family members understand the interpretations underlying problematic exchanges. Example: "Mom, when you are going into the room to ask Mary to go to bed, what thoughts go through your head before you speak?" . . . "Mary, when you hear your mom ask you to go to bed, what thoughts go through your head?"

◆ **Perspective-taking questions** (Penn, 1982; Tomm, 1987a, 1987b, 1988). With multiple relationships, you will often want to assess the misunderstandings between the members and gather information on the types of misunderstandings in the family. You can do so by having family members answer from another person's perspective. Perspective-taking questions are a triadic type of question that asks a family member to adopt the interpretation system of another person in the family and answer from their perspective. Example: "Larry, when Pam says that you are not doing your chores, what chores do you think she is referring to?"

*Affect System Questions*   In addition to seeking information on thinking and beliefs, you will want to explore how affect is managed in the family system. When one person is always experiencing a certain emotion, or others are not allowed to express emotions, family problems can occur. In conducting the assessment, workers often want to determine the patterns of experiencing and processing affect in the family.

◆ **Normative questions** (Penn, 1982; Tomm, 1988). Normative questions were discussed in the discussion of behavioral questioning strategies. Just as family practitioners seek to identify normative behavior in the family, it is important to understand the emotional norms. Example: "Who seems to be the happiest person in this family?"

◆ **Comparative questions** (Penn, 1982; Tomm, 1988). In using comparative questions, as with behavior-based questions, the practitioner often wants to compare and contrast emotional responses across the different family members. Example: "If Anthony is the happiest person in the family, who is the least happy?"

◆ **Affective processing questions.** The family practitioner frequently wants to identify the affective processes occurring among family members. Affective processing questions seek to understand how different family members deal with affective material. The worker explores both the affective experience and how the family member reacts to the affect. Example: "Norm, I saw you become quiet when Mary said she didn't like the gift you gave her. What feeling did you experience when you heard her words?"

◆ **Primary feeling questions.** Often in families, past interactions lead people to cover up more vulnerable feelings and hide them using feelings such as anger. When such secondary emotions are expressed (e.g., anger), the worker often wants to identify the underlying primary feeling. Typically, this involves asking the family member to identify the feeling that accompanies the secondary emotion. Example: "Tom, I hear in your voice that you are getting frustrated. What is the feeling that you find underneath your frustration?"

◆ **Scaling questions** (de Shazer, 1982). Family practitioners often seek to understand the magnitude or impact of a feeling or event. In such situations, scaling questions are very useful for having family members assess the feeling or impact. This type of question can be direct; for example: "On a scale of one to ten, with one being not upset at all and ten being extremely upset, how upset do you get when Tanya lies to you?" Practitioners can also use triadic approaches to gather impressions of how upset others are in a given situation. Example: "How upset does your mother become when Tanya lies to her?"

## Follow-Up

After asking a question, the practitioner follows up the question with further exploration. The direction of the follow-up will change depending on the treatment goals and impact of the question. The worker must be able to take the family member's response to the question, validate his or her position, and then build on the response to explore the situation more fully.

---

**CASE EXAMPLE**

The following exchange is from a family assessment meeting that includes a father, mother, and son. The family was referred for treatment to help with the high level of conflict in the home. This sequence involves an exploration of a repeated fight theme that occurs when the son ignores his mother's requests to help clean up the house.

*WORKER:* Mr. Alvarez, you said that Juan does not listen to Marie (mother); what do you do when you notice Juan ignoring her?

*FATHER:* At first I watch to see what she will do.

*WORKER:* What do you see her doing?

*FATHER:* Nothing . . . she just natters at him and he goes on doing whatever he wants.

*WORKER:* When this occurs, what are the thoughts that go through your head?

*FATHER:* I think . . . here we go again. Why can't she just take control of him? I never have these problems with him.

*WORKER:* So you are able to make him listen?

*FATHER:* Yeah.

*WORKER:* What do you tell Marie to help her make him listen?

*FATHER:* I say why do you put up with him like that? You need to take charge.

*WORKER:* . . . and her response to you is?

*FATHER:* She starts to cry and says, "He won't listen to me. I can't take charge. I am not like you."

*WORKER:* Juan, when mom and dad start arguing about how to make you listen, what do you do?

*JUAN:* Nothing.

*WORKER:* Nothing because you are frozen with fear, or, nothing because this is a pretty familiar pattern?

*JUAN:* It is a familiar pattern. They are always fighting about me.

*WORKER:* Who usually wins the fight?

*JUAN:* Nobody; mom goes crying to her room and dad gets mad and watches TV.

*WORKER:* . . . and where do you go?

*JUAN:* I go out with my friends.

*WORKER:* When you come home, what is said about the fight?

*JUAN:* Nothing.

*WORKER:* Nothing?

*JUAN:* Yeah, nothing.

*WORKER:* Marie, do you and Tony talk about the fight when Juan is out?

*MOTHER:* No. I stay in my room and Tony watches TV.

*WORKER:* How do you two get back together in the same room?

*MOTHER:* After I go to bed, Tony comes in and goes to sleep.

*WORKER:* Where does all of the tension go when you wake up the next day?

*MOTHER:* We talk about other things and then it goes away.

---

Notice in this case how the worker is using direct questioning strategies to determine the pattern of arguing. Notice also how each question uses part of the client's response to launch the next question. This linking of the question to the family member's response is known as *transitional tracking* (Ragg, 2001). When you are exploring a situation, this method of linking questions is useful to ensure that exploration occurs in small increments that are paced to the family members. In the assessment stage, practitioners use transitional tracking to determine the problematic patterns that are contributing to the family problems.

## ◆ EXERCISE 4.1  TRANSITIONAL TRACKING

You are working in a family service agency with a contract for helping families stay together. Your agency is new and funded through the new religious-based partnership incentives provided by the federal government. You are working with a family that has high levels of conflict. Although there is no physical violence, the adults are highly reactive to each other and tend to personalize comments. The children are beginning to act out in school and have been identified as needing intervention. The family is comprised of a 40-year-old father, who works in an auto parts manufacturing plant; a 35-year-old mother working in the same plant; an 11-year-old male child in grade five; and his 9-year-old sister, who is in grade three. You are meeting with the entire family and want to explore the dynamics of the arguments. Specifically, you want to understand how the problems start, the pattern of the arguing, how the arguments are terminated, and then how people resolve the tension.

1. Start with a direct questioning strategy focused on the behaviors associated with the fighting. Use this question to understand how volatile the arguing becomes.

2. Now use a triadic question to begin assessing either the family alliances or the reactivity in the adult members of the family. Focus the question on one of the children, but select a triadic format to solicit information about the parents.

3. Based on a possible response to the triadic question, use circular questioning to explore how each person responds to the start of the argument. Write a question that you would address to each of the family members to get at their unique experiences of the fighting.

You are working with a young couple who are having difficulty adjusting to marriage. They have been married for about six months, and they are still struggling with forming their relationship. You suspect that they need to negotiate their own model of being together, but they are still being heavily influenced by their families. You want to explore how each family exerts influence on the couple and how they respond to the influence attempts. You also want to understand how they are negotiating the differences between their family models.

1. Using a direct question, ask one of the people to share his or her beliefs about the differences between the two families.

2. Using a triadic question, have one of the people assess who in a family of origin is most invested in shaping this new family, or who would be most affected if the couple became autonomous. Focus this question across families, so the person reports on his or her partner's family.

3. Use a circular questioning strategy to engage the other person in the exploration.

# Data Gathering Through Observation

Family data collection often involves observing family processes. Observation of family interactions and transactions can give you critical information about family functioning. Some family practitioners assign a family a task so they can observe family processes. For example, a family therapist instructed the family to determine the meaning of the statement, "A rolling stone gathers no moss." The therapist then left the room to observe the family through a one-way mirror. Other practitioners make home visits to see how the family acts in its natural environment. You also will have ample opportunity to observe family processes during interviews.

Regardless of how you set up opportunities to observe family members, you will want to include such data in the assessment. The following elements can be observed in family systems. Although you can ask questions about these areas of family functioning, you will often observe an exchange or pattern in the family first and use that observation to set up questioning. As with questioning strategies, to focus their observations workers can concentrate on the different response systems.

When observing families, practitioners focus on both the action systems and processing systems in the family. The *action systems* include interactions and behaviors. *Processing systems* include (a) thinking and beliefs and (b) affect. These two types of response system control how the family members respond to situations and events.

## Observing Family Processing

Workers gather data on belief systems through questioning; and they use observational skills to gather data identifying patterns of affect and interpretation that indicate important dynamics in the family. During interaction, family members will experience and express different emotions. Family practitioners track patterns of emotional processing to understand how the family manages different types of emotion. The following specific areas of emotional processing are often of interest:

- Intimacy and sharing
- Belief and value systems
- Tension management
- Affective expression

*Intimacy and Sharing*   Intimacy refers to how close or distant family members are with each other. Intimacy can occur physically through touch or emotionally through sharing. Family practitioners are interested in the level and patterns of expression among the family members for both physical and emotional intimacy. Family practitioners commonly use the following indicators for observing the patterns of intimacy and sharing in a family:

- **Aloofness.** Some family members tend to be aloof and emotionally distant with other people in the family (Dillard & Protinsky, 1985). Such aloofness often indicates lower levels of intimacy with that individual. Practitioners monitor for patterns of aloofness to determine which member is close to whom, and which member tends to be isolated in the family.
- **Personal knowledge.** The level of information that family members have about each other's personal lives is a strong indicator of the level of sharing and intimacy among the family members. When people know the details of each other's lives, you can assume they have higher levels of closeness.
- **Physical closeness.** How family members position themselves with each other can indicate patterns of closeness (Sigelman & Adams, 1990). People who are comfortable with another sitting close enough to touch are often fond of that person. Workers frequently observe who sits near whom to determine close versus distant relationships.
- **Postures.** The way that family members hold their bodies and respond to touch can provide a lot of information about intimacy in the family. People who sit stiffly with their arms closed are often distant from others. If people stiffen when touched, this can also indicate some emotional distance.

Likewise, if people relax when touched you can anticipate that they have some comfort with closeness.

◆ **Rituals.** Families have rituals that are important to maintaining the sense of family cohesion, for example, Sunday dinners, game night, birthday celebrations, and vacations (Dickstein, 2002; Eaker & Walters, 2002). Although you cannot often directly observe rituals, you can track content themes and stories to understand what rituals occur in the family. The pattern and frequency of rituals can provide rich information about the affective exchanges among family members.

*Belief and Value Systems*   Families have belief systems that provide a rationale for family actions and interactions (Teichman, 1984; Whitbeck & Gecas, 1988). Family practitioners monitor belief systems to understand how attributions, interpretations, and values influence family members. Belief systems are not always easy to identify, because beliefs are often embedded in stories and patterns of responding. The following indicators frequently provide information about family belief systems:

1. **Responsibility attributions.** Families often have consistent patterns of attributing responsibility for positive and negative events (Bradbury & Fincham, 1992). For example, a family may blame negative events on other people but believe that they are responsible for positive situations. Family practitioners monitor themes to determine the family patterns of belief. Here are four critical themes:
    ◆ *Internal versus external* (Wicki, 2000). Families identify forces either internal to the family or external to the family as being responsible for events.
    ◆ *General versus specific* (Wicki, 2000). Families identify the impact of an event as either having implications beyond the immediate situation or being limited to the specific event.
    ◆ *Intentional versus unintentional.* Families believe that events either occur with intent or are serendipitous and random.
    ◆ *Positive versus negative.* Families will label some thoughts, behaviors, and events as positive and others as negative depending on the family values and beliefs.
2. **Family stories.** Families share stories among themselves and with others who are important to the family (Connell, Mitten, & Whitaker, 1993). Stories are often designed to reinforce beliefs that the family members hold as important. Practitioners listen to family stories and monitor (a) the attribution and value themes in the story; (b) the individuals included in the story; and (c) the implicit moral of the story. These elements of the stories provide information about the family processing of situations and events. Three story types frequently occur in the family (Byng-Hall, 1988; Papp & Imber-Black, 1996):
    ◆ *Stories shared by all family members.* These stories tend to indicate themes and beliefs that are important to the entire family system.

Implications are often general to all members or to the family system as a whole.

- ◆ *Stories shared by one person.* These stories tend to have meaning only for the person telling the story. You can often glean information about what issues are important to the individual family member and to her relationships with other family members.
- ◆ *Family legends.* Families have legends, featuring heroes and villains, that are shared among the family members to identify people and behaviors that are valued by the family system (e.g., Tom is a doctor; Mary is an addict). The family frequently shares the legendary stories about these people in order to reinforce desirable and undesirable models.

3. **Family mantras and slogans.** Families often have repeated slogans or sayings that become generally accepted by all family members (e.g., keep the babies safe; education is important). Such repeated statements reinforce important beliefs and values in the family. Practitioners listen for repeated sayings to identify underlying beliefs and values.

4. **Investments.** Families invest time and energy in specific pursuits. Inherent in the investment of family energy is a family value. To identify what outcomes the family values most highly, practitioners observe how families invest their time, money, and emotional energy (Napier & Whitaker, 1978).

5. **Privilege hierarchies.** Families often make allowances for some members but not for others. These allowances create double standards and privilege hierarchies that indicate values within the family system (Bograd, 1986). For example, some families allow boys to stay out later than girls. Inherent in this double standard is the message that one gender is more valued than the other is. Once they have noted such hierarchies, practitioners can explore them to determine the inherent meaning in the double standard.

6. **Standards and rules.** Through the themes and issues presented, you can often identify specific standards that guide the family. Family members use standards to identify behaviors or interactions that are considered problematic and nonproblematic (Jackson, 1965). It is important for workers to understand the standards that are important to the family. Standards may be established for areas such as behavior, loyalty, public sharing, individuation, punctuality, and attitude.

7. **Avoidance patterns.** Families will often tend to avoid events, situations, or emotional states (e.g., tension). Active avoidance of situations tends to indicate that there is a rule about the situation (Jackson, 1965). Rules indicate some value or injunction about the situation. Practitioners monitor for patterns of avoidance to identify the values underlying the rules (e.g., "tension is bad").

8. **Punishment patterns.** Like avoidance patterns, punishment patterns indicate informal (or formal) rules that govern the family. When one type of rule is more vehemently sanctioned than are other types of rules, hierarchies are

developed (Jackson, 1965). The pattern of the hierarchy indicates an underlying value. Here are some types of rules:

◆ *Safety rules.* These rules ensure that family members are safe (e.g., don't play in the street; let me know where you are).

◆ *Presentation rules.* These rules dictate how family members are to present themselves to other people (e.g., be on time; wear clean clothes; say please and thank-you).

◆ *Respect rules.* These rules instruct family members on how to treat other people (e.g., don't talk back).

◆ *Boundary rules.* These rules dictate the nature of the information and access flow across system and subsystem boundaries (e.g., don't talk about the family to others).

*Tension Management*   Tension occurs in every family. However, some families have difficulty managing the tension. Family practitioners pay close attention to issues of tension because they can create many problematic dynamics in the family (Grinker, 1971). Tension-related reactions are often observed in the family rather than shared openly through verbal disclosures. Here are some tension management mechanisms that can be observed in the family system:

◆ **Agitation.** When tension occurs in a family, some family members may become agitated. Indicators of agitation include changing the subject, nervous behavior, and/or reactive statements designed to decrease the tension (e.g., "You don't have to tell me twice"). Such dynamics indicate that the family does not have strong mechanisms for decreasing or managing tension (Napier & Whitaker, 1978).

◆ **Acquiescence and dominance hierarchies.** In some families, people deal with tension by giving in or catering to the family members who generate tension. In such situations, some family members gain power through the tension and others give up their power (Whitaker, 1975). Practitioners observe families for patterns of acquiescence and catering to identify potential situations where tension management has created power hierarchies in the family.

◆ **Problem solving.** In well-functioning families, one or more family members are able to identify issues that are creating tension and "put them on the table" for discussion (Napier & Whitaker, 1978). This is a problem-solving approach wherein situations are openly discussed and options explored. Practitioners watch for family members who identify and speak openly about issues that are generating family tension.

◆ **Playfulness.** Family play and joking are strong antidotes to tension buildup. Families whose members are able to play with each other do not tend to take things personally or perceive slights easily. This keeps tension levels low and provides mechanisms to draw off tension (Winnicott, 1971). Practitioners tend to watch for family joking and levity.

◆ **Ignore and explode cycles.** Some families have patterns in which they ignore tension until it is unbearable, at which point explosive exchanges occur. This is common in families where some of the members have a history with family violence or abusiveness (Whitaker, 1975). Practitioners monitor for patterns of dismissing or avoiding small problems followed by volatile moments.

◆ **Distraction.** When tension rises in the family, some family members often attempt to distract the attention of others to draw off the tension. Sometimes children who act out or get into trouble are fulfilling this function for their families (Napier & Whitaker, 1978). Practitioners watch for patterns of tension rising and being siphoned off through behaviors that cause tension to be put onto an individual family member.

*Affective Expression* A final element that family practitioners focus on when observing family processing systems is affective expression. All families have systems for expressing emotion (Bowen, 1978). Some families are not comfortable with emotion and channel expression indirectly; other families openly express emotion. With some families, methods for expressing positive emotion differ from those used to express negative emotion. Many rules and patterns associated with affective expression can be observed (Papero, 1990):

◆ **Affective channeling.** Workers often look for how people respond to others affectively, and how the affect is expressed. Some members express feelings verbally; others channel their emotions physically (Bowen, 1978). Practitioners observe for methods of expression. People who express emotion physically often have physical reactions (such as stiffening, gesturing, looking down), whereas others will talk openly. Patterns of reactivity provide important information about the affective processes in the family.

◆ **Acting out.** In some families, one or more member will act out the family emotion (Papero, 1990). In such situations a family member will engage in emotionally expressive behavior that allows everyone in the family to vicariously experience the emotional expression. You can observe this dynamic when a family member engages in an emotionally expressive behavior (e.g., swearing at their teacher), but nobody in the family takes effective action to dissuade the family member from, or outline consequences for, the behavior.

◆ **Somatizing.** When a family member is highly uncomfortable with emotion, she may internalize the affect and express it through physical symptoms (Bowen, 1978; Minuchin, 1974). Such symptoms may include illness, fainting, and aches or pains. This pattern most often occurs when negative emotions are involved, allowing that family member to influence the family dynamics without experiencing the vulnerability of directly expressing the emotion.

◆ **Dramatizing.** Some family members may become overly dramatic when emotional issues arise. Such people tend to polarize situations and passionately defend one polar position in opposition to the other (Greenberg & Johnson, 1988). When emotionally laden situations promote a black-and-white presentation of issues, you may be dealing with family systems in which some people dramatize the issues.

◆ **Amplifying.** Sometimes family members amplify emotional situations and get caught up in the emotional "high." Such people often yell, shriek, dance, or otherwise create a loud, expressive scene when emotional situations arise (Bowen, 1978). This high level of expressiveness can be easily observed when working with families.

◆ **Shifting to secondary emotion.** Primary feelings such as helplessness, powerlessness, joy, and intimacy sometimes feel overwhelming for family members. In such situations, some family members will transform the primary feeling into a secondary emotion such as anger or horniness (Greenberg & Johnson, 1988). Secondary emotions have the illusion of controllability because they shift focus onto another person, who is credited with causing the emotion. You can observe this type of process through externalized themes, whereby someone else always causes the emotional state of a family member.

◆ **Direct expression.** Some families engage in direct emotional expression in which they identify the internal affect, label it, and share it openly with other family members. Such processes are easy to identify, because family members are open and honest about their emotional experience and their impact on the emotional experience of others (Greenberg & Johnson, 1988).

◆ **Symbolic expression.** Some families engage in token expressions to share emotion. Actions such as giving flowers and doing favors are often a symbolic expression of caring. Similarly, negative emotions may result in undermining another person, breaking another person's belongings, or acting in a way that might hurt the other person's feelings (Napier & Whitaker, 1978). This type of emotional expression may result in triangulation, wherein emotions are channeled through a third person (Bowen, 1978).

## Observing Family Actions and Interactions

Action systems include the interaction and behavioral responses in the family. Interactive processes are most easily observed because family members are frequently interacting with each other during family treatment. As a worker, consequently, you have ample opportunity to observe interaction during the family session. Behaviors are easy to observe, but you may be challenged to set up situations to observe important behaviors. Sometimes you can elicit behaviors in a family interview; but you must often go into the home or engage families in an exercise in order to observe some of the behaviors. Action system dynamics include such elements as the following:

◆ Accomplishing tasks
◆ Using control mechanisms
◆ Communicating

◆ Providing support
◆ Managing differences

*Accomplishing Tasks*    Families must be able to achieve certain tasks in order to assure survival. These tasks include securing an income, keeping order in the home, meeting survival needs, and so forth. How these tasks are met provides valuable information about how the family is functioning (Schwebel & Fine, 1994). Many elements can interfere with a family's ability to accomplish tasks. Such elements include poverty, substance abuse, illness, external constraints (e.g., structural racism, intergenerational problems, stress), and economic shortfalls (Kilpatrick & Holland, 1999). Frequently, you must go into the family's home to observe how well task accomplishment is occurring. The following elements can influence how survival tasks are accomplished by family members (Beavers & Hampson, 1990; Kilpatrick & Holland, 1999):

◆ **Physical environment.** The home environment often provides clues about the task accomplishment of the family. If there are sufficient resources and nothing is interfering with the task accomplishment, the physical environment is typically free from hazards (Kilpatrick & Holland, 1999).

◆ **Physical development.** The development of the family members (e.g., children who thrive) yields information about task accomplishment. Practitioners often observe how individual family members look compared to population norms to determine functioning in this area.

◆ **Physical health.** Practitioners often look for patterns of health concerns, bruises, and other physical manifestations of health or illness to identify concerns related to task accomplishment (Krysan, Moore, & Zill, 1990).

◆ **Decision making.** The ability to make decisions is a prerequisite for families to respond to environmental situations and opportunities. Consequently, decision-making ability is an indicator of how well families are functioning in the area of task accomplishment (Beavers & Hampson, 1990; Krysan et al., 1990). Practitioners observe family decision making and planning to understand how adaptable the family might be.

◆ **Crisis responses.** Family life yields many crises that can interfere with task accomplishment. Family practitioners are concerned with family members' abilities to respond to critical events (Krysan et al., 1990; Kilpatrick & Holland, 1999). If families stop functioning at times of crisis or become volatile, task accomplishment may be compromised. However, if families can deal with crises without volatility or depressive reactions, task accomplishment may remain intact.

◆ **Resource acquisition.** When families have enough resources to survive, task accomplishment is enhanced. When there are too few resources to meet the family's survival needs, task accomplishment is compromised because family members must either make do with insufficient resources or forsake some elements of the task in order to supplement resource acquisition functions (Kilpatrick & Holland, 1999).

- ◆ **Role functioning.** Family roles have many role expectations (see "System-Subsystem Functions" in Chapter 1). Family practitioners monitor the extent to which family role expectations are met. If the family functioning suggests that some role functions are not met (e.g., no discipline), task accomplishment will be compromised (Krysan et al., 1990).
- ◆ **Boundary maintenance.** Families have patterns of access across boundaries. You can observe how (and how easily) people can enter and influence the family system and how firm subsystem boundaries are in the family. When practitioners note that multiple people have easy access to people in the system and influence how the family functions, worries about task accomplishment emerge (Minuchin, 1974).

*Using Control Mechanisms*   All families have systems for controlling the behavior and interaction of other people in the family unit. When a family member diverges from what is considered acceptable, other family members act in ways that will bring the family member back into line with what is expected. Practitioners observe families to understand which family members enact the control functions and what mechanisms they use to control others.

Inherent in the control mechanisms are the formal and informal rule structures governing the family. In observing a family for rules, practitioners watch for repeated themes associated with problematic behaviors or stories shared about problems. Practitioners also observe for areas of sensitivity in which family members avoid actions or issues. The following control mechanisms are commonly observed in families:

- ◆ **Monopolizing.** One family member takes over the conversation, focusing all of the attention on their version of what should occur (Patterson, 1982). Other family members allow this focus shift and follow the family member. Monopolizing can be observed as one member begins to talk for others, and the others move into a silent mode.
- ◆ **Pressuring.** One or more family members will harass or pester another family member to go along with their desires. Pressuring can be observed when family members make frequent comments or expressions to another, attempting to engage them in desired actions or interactions (Patterson, 1982).
- ◆ **Reinforcing.** When a member engages in a desired behavior, other family members provide benefits or privileges that reward the performance (Horne, 1974).
- ◆ **Retaliating.** When a member transgresses against other family members, there may be efforts to punish the transgressing member with retaliatory acts such as withholding privileges or punishing (Horne, 1974).
- ◆ **Coercing.** Sometimes family members will use threats or violent behavior to control other members to give into their desires (Horne, 1974; Patterson, 1982). Although practitioners seldom observe the actual violence in families, coercive processes can be detected when one member gestures, glares, or makes comments to others who immediately fall silent and acquiesce.

- ◆ **Discounting.** Sometimes family members discount the contributions of another family member to try to change their position (Patterson, 1982). Discounting can be observed when people ridicule, dismiss, or otherwise put down what another person wants.

- ◆ **Withdrawing.** Some family members will attempt to control others by withdrawing from the relationship (Patterson, 1982). Withdrawing can be observed through sudden changes in activity level with the member. When somebody stops participating and a shift in family interaction occurs, an attempt to control others is likely occurring. In such situations, practitioners try to recall the content immediately before the shift in order to understand the potential meaning of the shift.

- ◆ **Disengaging.** Beyond withdrawal, sometimes family members disengage from the family and seek to meet their needs outside the family unit. Disengaging can be observed when family members spend large amounts of time with other people or engage largely in nonfamily-related pursuits. This is normal for adolescents because they must individuate, but it is less normal for adult partners. Family practitioners explore the patterns of disengagement to determine whether a member's absence from the family is a possible control dynamic.

- ◆ **Elevating tension.** Family members can use gesturing (e.g., throwing up their hands) and other forms of nonverbal communication (e.g., sighing, crossing arms across chest) to elevate the tension during family interaction (Patterson, 1982). When family practitioners find a shift in tension levels, it is useful to look for such nonverbal expressions to determine the control dynamics occurring in the family.

- ◆ **Developing dependence.** Some family members develop dependent relationships as a method of controlling the behavior of others (e.g., maximizing illness, failing to master autonomous tasks, drawing others into their problems). Dependence can be observed when one or more family members appear locked into roles that appear to benefit an individual family member at the expense of their own autonomy.

*Communicating*    Communication is an area of family functioning that family practitioners are consistently observing while in session to identify targets for intervention. Communicating and interacting are often central to family problems because most problems eventually affect the interactions among family members. When observing communication and interaction, family practitioners are often focusing on patterned communications that repeat. When such patterns appear to be associated with family problems, family practitioners pick up on the communication and explore the underlying dynamics to better understand the family problems. These elements of communication are often observed in family interactions (Watzlawick et al., 1967):

- ◆ **Content patterns.** Specific content is repeated during family discussions. Family practitioners listen for repeated words, phrases, and content themes to identify hot or unresolved issues for family members.

- **Alliance patterns.** Some family members side with each other in opposition to other members of the family. Family practitioners monitor who sides with whom in the family; they also note the frequency of alliances. When two or more members of the family ally with each other on specific issues, practitioners tend to consider this a pattern of alliance. However, when the alliances persist regardless of the issues being discussed, practitioners become concerned that there may be coalitions among the family members.
- **Divergence patterns.** Divergence patterns occur when communication has been progressing in one direction and then a family member changes the subject. When all family members follow the new direction, there may be some family-level reason that the divergence has occurred. Practitioners note the pattern and then monitor for content patterns that may be associated with the divergence.
- **Escalation patterns.** When families have difficulty with problem solving, patterns of escalation may exist. Family practitioners monitor for power struggles in which two or more members of the family engage in a tit-for-tat pattern of one-upping each other. Family practitioners are interested in the pattern of escalation as well as in how the escalation terminates (e.g., in violence, people leaving, people giving in).
- **Distortion patterns.** In family communication, it is common for one member to experience some sort of slight in the messages communicated by other family members. The communication patterns change immediately after the person perceives the slight. Such changes can include defensive or angry themes. Family practitioners monitor for such shifts in communication to identify interpretations and issues that seem to underlie the family problems.
- **Congruence patterns.** Communication occurs on both the verbal and nonverbal levels. Family practitioners observe family members on both levels of communication to determine whether the family members are communicating the same message. When communication on one level is inconsistent with communication on the other, the lack of congruence is often considered an area for further exploration.

*Providing Support*   Supporting each other is a central function of families. Given the importance of this function, family practitioners try to observe how support functions are being fulfilled in the family. When observing support functions, you will find there are two areas of concern. First, you must seek to understand how family members activate support provision from others in the family. Second, you must seek to understand the conditions and parameters that the family sets for providing support (Bross, 1982).

- **Provision injunctions and conditions.** Family members commonly have rules about how, and to whom, support can be provided. Family practitioners are interested in observing not only who gets support, but the family's rationale for the patterns of provision. Some families exclude members based on age, sex, performance, or other reasons.

- ◆ **Types of support provided.** There are four types of support: emotional, instrumental, informational, and appraisal. Family practitioners seek to understand the types of support provided among the family members. If one type of support appears to be less available, this is an area for further exploration to understand the family's beliefs about support provision.
- ◆ **Provision patterns.** In some families there is a division of labor as to who provides what types of support. For example, in some families the females give emotional support while the males give feedback and appraisal support. These patterns of support provision can reveal important information about both action and processing systems in the family.
- ◆ **Solicitation patterns.** Just as support provision has patterns, solicitation of support also has patterns. Family members are likely to differ in their directness and focus when seeking support. Some family members may brag about their accomplishments; others might sulk. Both are solicitation methods, but one is direct and the other indirect. The solicitation methods and types of support solicited may also affect whom each member approaches for support. Family practitioners look for such patterns in the family interactions and family stories.

*Managing Differences* The final area of observation in the family is to see how its members manage differences. All families must find methods for dealing with differences of opinion regarding member behaviors, desires, and interactions. Families that are very comfortable with difference will engage members in discussions; other families attempt to quell any expression of difference (Bowen, 1978). All families develop mechanisms for dealing with differences. Family practitioners observe these mechanisms when monitoring for areas of problem functioning. Unfortunately, this is an area where many families do run into problems. The following family dynamics may indicate problems with member differentiation (Bowen, 1978)

- ◆ **Minimizing differences.** In some families, family members attempt to deny that differences exist and will convince themselves that the difference is illusionary or will ignore any expressions of difference. Such mechanisms are usually obvious in the family interaction, because some members will express opinions and receive no validation that they have even spoken.
- ◆ **Squelching differences.** Some families take very active approaches to expressions of difference by immediately attempting to correct the person who expresses the difference. Depending on how strongly people hold to the divergent position and the level of perceived threat by the family, attempts to correct may include arguing, ridiculing, ostracizing, or even coercion.
- ◆ **Engaging differences.** Some families seem to enjoy differences and actively engage expressions of difference in friendly debates. In such families, ideas and opinions are viewed as separate from the individuals so there is no perceived threat in the expression of difference. In those families, you will observe the invitation for varying positions and attempts to incorporate

multiple perspectives into decision making. Compromises and changes of plans are frequent in such families.

♦ **Solving problems.** Families often have clear patterns of decision making and problem solving that you can observe. To solve problems, however, families must first acknowledge and engage themselves with the differences. When families are solving problems, family practitioners observe for how well family members (a) agree on problem definitions, (b) generate options, (c) agree on options, and (d) implement a plan.

## ♦ EXERCISE 4.2 OBSERVING FAMILY PROCESSING

You are working in a children's mental health clinic at the community center of a small town. You are working with two parents, Sam and Janet, and their 13-year-old daughter Flo. You are starting immediately with the family because the daughter was recently playing with a friend on the ice of a river when they both fell in. Flo's friend drowned; and Janet, her mother, is concerned about the impact her friend's death might have on Flo. This family, which the agency has known since Flo was eight years old, had been out of service for only about a month before the present crisis occurred.

When the family enters the session, the mother, Janet, begins by describing the drowning and how her daughter Flo had tried to save her friend; but she had to let go of the girl's coat collar in order to save herself. Janet describes how upset Flo has been, and shares that Flo has been having visions of where the body is under the ice. Janet goes into great detail about the location of the body and how it is consistent with Flo's dreams. During this time, Flo and her father, Sam, sit silently in the room, allowing Janet to do all of the talking. When you ask Sam his opinion, he sighs and the following discussion ensues.

> *SAM:* I drive them to these appointments, but nobody has asked me for an opinion before.
>
> *THERAPIST:* Well, now is your chance. What do you see as being needed to help your family?
>
> *SAM:* I think we need to get along.
>
> *THERAPIST:* Who needs to get along?
>
> *JANET:* Flo is very high strung and needs a lot of help. She doesn't always like the things we need to do. She is very upset about the death of her friend.

You then attempt to engage Flo in the discussion by asking her how she is doing with the death of her friend. Janet immediately answers, outlining how the girls had been best friends for a long time and Flo feels guilty for not being able to save her. You ask Flo for validation and she answers (flatly), "Yeah." Janet then outlines how the anxiety has made Flo's asthma so bad that they had to take her to the emergency room on the weekend. Janet shares how they have a new doctor, so she had to give him Flo's medical and counseling history. Janet starts to share the details with you, including Flo's sexual abuse at the age of eight, behavior problems at school, learning disabilities, and several health concerns.

You listen politely for a period of time and then inform Janet that you want to hear from Flo. You turn to Flo and start the following exchange.

THERAPIST: You have had so much going on in your life and so many people meddling with you. Is it uncomfortable having your life be an open book?

FLO: Yeah.

THERAPIST: If you could limit what I learn about you, what would you limit it to?

FLO: I would limit it to everything.

THERAPIST: So you wouldn't want me learning about you.

FLO: Right.

THERAPIST: You need a little more privacy.

FLO: Yeah. I am tired of everyone knowing my business.

JANET: People need to know about you. How else can they help?

FLO: (louder voice) I don't need help. I am just fine.

JANET: You are not just fine. You have problems, and you need to deal with them.

FLO: (louder still) I don't have any problems!

SAM: (to Flo) Don't you yell at your mother.

THERAPIST: Flo. You say you don't have problems, but your mom and dad seem concerned about you. What do you think they are concerned about?

FLO: They are always concerned about something, but I just want to be left alone.

JANET: Flo . . . we care about you and are doing this for your own good.

THERAPIST: Janet. How do you think Flo experiences this caring?

JANET: Deep down she knows this is the best thing for her, but she just won't admit it to herself.

FLO: Yeah . . . right.

JANET: Come on. Tell the therapist about what is really going on so you can get help.

FLO: (loudly) I don't need any help!

SAM: (to Flo) Hey. None of that.

1. This family appears to have some rules about expressed emotion. What did you observe about these possible rules?

2. One of these family members may have difficulty with differences. Who would this be, and what did you observe when identifying this person?

3. Think about patterns of support seeking. How does this mother tend to seek support?

4. What communication patterns do you notice among all of the family members?

5. What appear to be the control mechanisms in the family, and what did you observe to reach that conclusion?

---

# Using Projective Techniques to Gather Data

Practitioners frequently gather family data by using *projective techniques*, in which family members create some product onto which family issues are unconsciously projected or expressed. The worker uses the product to identify elements of the family functioning for further exploration.

As a practitioner, you must be cautious when using projective techniques. If you are doing the interpretation rather than engaging family members in interpreting their own material, it is too easy to read your own issues into the product, resulting in a blending of your projections with those of the family. You are well advised to try engaging family members in describing their product and in helping them to understand the meanings of different features. The projective technique is simply a tool for getting issues on the table for further exploration.

Four common projective strategies are used with families. You must be comfortable with engaging families in the specific activity as well as with giving clear instructions on how the activity is to proceed. These strategies come from expressive therapy techniques and often require you to engage the family in some activity:

1. Draw a family
2. Family sculpting

3. Family dances
4. Family metaphors

In the following sections, we explore each of these projective strategies separately.

## Draw a Family

The draw-a-family strategy involves the worker engaging each family member in drawing a picture of the family (Deren, 1975; Geddes & Medway, 1977; Spigelman, Spigelman, & Engelsson, 1992). The worker then has each family member share his or her picture with the rest of the family. When each person shares their picture, the worker shares his observations of the following details and uses the shared observations to engage the family in further discussion.

◆ Position of family members in relation to each other
◆ Features of each family member
◆ Expression of each family member
◆ Color choices and detail used with each family member
◆ Inclusions or exclusions of people

After each person shares his or her picture, the worker often engages the family in a discussion of the similarities and differences among the pictures and the themes that appeared important during the individual presentations. Issues that appear important are highlighted and explored with the family to determine the need for work in those areas. A variation of this technique is to have the family conjointly draw a picture (Bing, 1970).

## Family Sculpting

Family sculpting is similar to the draw-a-family technique; but with sculpting, the family members use each other to form a visual representation of the family (Duhl, Kantor, & Duhl, 1973; Hearn & Lawrence, 1985; Hernandez, 1998). In using this technique, the worker has each family member take a turn positioning people in the family to form a sculpture that they feel represents the family. She may want to direct the situation slightly and ask that the sculpture represent a certain aspect of family life (e.g., having fun, fighting, or discussing report cards). With each sculpture, the worker observes the following elements:

◆ Placement of each family member in relation to the others
◆ Body positioning (arms, legs, facing front or back, etc.) of each family member
◆ Expressions and visual impact of the different family members in the sculpture

As with the draw-a-family strategy, the worker can comment on the different features of each sculpture and engage the family in discussing the differences and similarities of the sculptures.

## Family Dances

Family dances are very similar to sculpting, except movement is incorporated into the sculpture (Watanabe-Hammond, 1990). With family dances, the worker sets up the exercise just like the family sculpture exercise (engaging members in positioning bodies, setting the situation) but adds that the family must have a motion that represents that person in the situation. Motions may include the following:

◆ Fist waving
◆ Finger wagging
◆ Pulling at other family members
◆ Trying to leave
◆ Reading the paper
◆ Acting goofy
◆ Covering ears, eyes, and so forth

The addition of action in the family dance allows interactive sequences to be included in the exercise. When debriefing the exercise with family members, the worker will explore people's reactions to their action sequences (and those of others) while exploring how well each dance captured the family issues.

## Family Metaphors

Two types of metaphor tend to be used in assessing families. First, you can use variations on any of the preceding exercises to create metaphoric families. For example, you may have a basket of animals or puppets and ask the family members to use the animals to create a family situation or story (Irwin & Malloy, 1975). The choice of animals along with all of the sculpting and dance considerations can be used to pull out family issues.

The second type of metaphor is that of family-generated metaphors (Cade & O'Hanlon, 1993). Many families will spontaneously share metaphors for their functioning (e.g., "It's like living in a hurricane"). When families create a metaphor, you can then use it to explore how the family fits the chosen image. Some workers ask families to generate a metaphor by having them complete a sentence such as, "Living in our home is just like living in a _____." It is sometimes helpful to have family members share their metaphor for the family. After each member has presented his or her metaphor, you can explore the themes and differences inherent in the metaphors to highlight issues for treatment.

# Using Standardized or Structured Questionnaires

Standardized questionnaires are commonly used to conduct family assessments. When using standardized systems of gathering data (such as scales or psychometric instruments), you have several issues to consider. First, you must consider the reliability of the data collection instrument (Cox & Anderson, 2003). Many agencies use questionnaires and measures that have not been tested for reliability. You can never be confident that the scales are providing accurate information. The second critical issue is the validity of the measure. Without established validity, you really cannot be sure what you are measuring.

## Reliability

*Reliability* refers to how consistently the scale measures the same thing across families. Reliability is scored on a scale from 0 to 1.0; scores close to 0 indicate a very inconsistent scale, and scores near 1.0 indicate a highly reliable measure. In making clinical judgments about a family, you will want to ensure that the reliability of the scale is .80 or higher.

Four types of reliability are commonly cited. The following brief descriptions of the four reliability types will give you a sense of the different forms of reliability. However, reliability is very complex, and these descriptions are rudimentary. For further information about reliability, you may want to explore the complexities in a research or quantitative measurement text.

1. **Test-retest.** This reliability type occurs when the measure has been administered to the same people at two different times (when things should not have changed) and the amount of change between the two times is assessed. If there is very little change, the measure is considered reliable.
2. **Inter-rater.** This reliability type describes the situation when more than one person has used the measure on the same subject, and the level of agreement across assessors has been evaluated. Higher levels of agreement indicate higher inter-rater reliability.
3. **Split half.** This type of reliability occurs when the items on the scale have been spit into two separate scales and the relationship between the two halves has been assessed.
4. **Cronbach's alpha.** In this reliability type, the split-half procedure is repeated so that all possible combinations have been assessed; the average score is used.

## Validity

A second consideration when using standardized measures is the validity of the measure. *Validity* refers to whether the scale is measuring what it is supposed to measure. Even if a measure consistently measures the same way (reliability), you need to be concerned that it is measuring what it is supposed to assess. Scale developers are supposed to assess the validity of a scale before allowing it to be used for clinical purposes. You would not want to be assessing a child's behavior and find out later that the parent's level of depression was the real problem.

Like reliability, validity has many forms. The most important type of validity will change according to what you are attempting to assess. If you are trying to assess levels of some attribute (e.g., depression, anxiety, violent behavior), construct validity will be important. However, if you want to assess risk (e.g., of abuse, relapse, or suicide), predictive validity will be most important. Here are some of the most common forms of validity:

- **Construct validity** assures that the test measures what it claims by testing it against other scales that measure similar constructs and others that should not be related at all. These results are often called *divergent* and *convergent* validity.
- **Content or criterion validity** uses groups of experts to assess whether the item content and construction seem logical or complete.
- **Known groups validity** makes sure the measure can discriminate across groups of families that differ in the attribute measured.
- **Predictive (or discriminant) validity** tests to make sure the measure can distinguish groups in which there are problems from groups that have no problems.

## Test Types

A final consideration when selecting a standardized instrument for assessing families is the type of test.

*Normed Test*    Some tests allow you to compare a family to a population of people. This is called a *normed* test. Typically the results on a family can be graphed, so you can see whether and how the family differs from people who are considered normal. If the family scores higher than the normal group, you might infer that a problem exists. Likewise, if the family is in the normal or below the normal range, you can infer that the family has some strengths. When using this type of scale, you need to be clear about the normal group to determine whether the comparison is appropriate. For example, if the scale is normed on White university sophomores, and you are assessing an uneducated 16-year-old African American youth from the center city, the comparison may make the youth look less adaptive based on population differences rather than problem differences.

*Cutting Score Scale*    A second type of measure is known as a *cutting score* scale. This type of measure has critical scores that indicate whether the family is in a problem range. Typically, cutting scores are developed by comparing groups that have a trait with groups that are free from the trait. Where one group's scores drop off and the other group begins, the cutting score is developed. These types of scales are the easiest to interpret. When considering this type of scale, you will want to explore how the cutting scores are determined (what were the groups) to ensure they make sense for the family to be assessed. You will also want to carefully consider the family score, because false positives or negatives will occur frequently as a score nears the cutting scores.

*Descriptive Measures*    A final type of measure is referred to as *descriptive measures*. These scales are not sufficiently developed to provide norms or cutting scores; they simply indicate the level of the attribute that the scale measures. These are best used for assessing the family before service, and then again after service, to determine the level of change. This allows a family member to compare the family to himself or herself before and after treatment. Although the other scales can also be used for pretesting and posttesting, they also have some features that make them independently useful for the assessment phase. Descriptive tests are less useful given the lack of comparisons built into the test.

When using any type of standardized tests, family practitioners must be mindful of the scale directions. On some scales, higher numbers indicate problems, whereas on other scales high scores will indicate health. Concurrently, some items are referred to as *reverse-scored* items, for which workers will have to change the scores so that all items are scaled in the same direction. Reverse-scored items are scaled in a different direction to assure that families read each item and don't just check one number on all items. Workers must also watch for missing items and as well as for situations that might make the scales hard to interpret (e.g., vague items, one scale with many more items, and culturally insensitive items or scales).

## Using Data Collection and Exploration Skills

The skills for gathering information are critical in conducting an assessment. However, these skills go far beyond initial assessment methodology. Exploration is an ongoing process with families. Consequently, family practitioners will continue to use questioning, observation, and other skills at every stage of the helping process. What makes the initial assessment process unique is that this is the first exploration with the family. At this first moment you, the practitioner, are still foreign to the family. As such, you must be very skilled in gathering accurate information in a nonthreatening approach. The following suggestions can be helpful in shaping your exploratory style:

◆ **Include all family members who are in the room.** It is important for all family members to have some input into providing information and shaping the understanding. Even if the family member simply nods, each person needs to feel she is part of creating a unified understanding.

◆ **Validate every contribution.** When a family member provides input, he must be validated for his contribution even if it does not appear important. Look for areas of strength, and highlight them immediately in your response.

◆ **Acknowledge each different perspective.** There will be multiple perspectives on what is occurring in the family. Acknowledge each person's perspective without putting it in competition with other family members' perspectives.

◆ **Avoid taking sides.** Early in the exploration, family members will want you to take their side. Be careful when validating each member that you validate her as a person rather than by her position on the family problems. Let people know that the early exploration is designed to arrive at some shared understanding of the problems.

- ◆ **Let the family interact.** To observe their interactions, you must allow family members to interact. However, interaction will create some tension as family members lapse into their regular patterns. When this occurs, interrupt the interaction and tie it to the family challenges. Let the family members identify whether the pattern is part of the family problems. If so, explore the patterns using the family members as observers.
- ◆ **Slow down the fix.** Families will put some pressure on practitioners to provide immediate answers for the problems. Avoid this trap by slowing the situation down and maintaining the position that the family needs to arrive at a shared vision of what is needed. Do not offer them easy solutions, because they have probably tried them already. If you try to give them a solution, you are likely to be challenged later, when they inform you that it did not work.
- ◆ **Reference the family strengths and capacities.** Make frequent comments about areas of family strength and obvious capacities. All families have been working on their problems long before coming into service. When you identify these areas of strength in the exploration, family members will experience a better balance. You can then use these strengths as references for why you need the family to arrive at a shared vision.

As the exploration continues over time, a relationship between the worker and family will develop. This relationship and the eventual focus for service will provide a later context for using exploratory and data collection skills. Although the formal assessment phase is likely to be over, data collection and exploration will be ongoing as information emerges and is explored at every phase of service. In the later stages, the exploration will be an element that helps family members to expand insights and develop new understandings.

Several methods of data collection and exploration are outlined here; but in practice, you may not be required to use all methods. Depending on agency protocols and your eventual theoretical model, some methods will be emphasized and others deemphasized. Many family theoretical models use observation and questioning but do not use more formal or structured methods. However, some agencies insist on using formal methods. As your professional career progresses, patterns will emerge in how exploration and data collection occur.

# Summary

Multiple methods are used in assessing family systems. Some methods are similar to those used for individual assessments; but with families, you will use specific techniques and strategies during the assessment. Family practitioners use many of the methods described in this chapter to gather information on the family processes and experiences of individual family members. Data collection is directed by the goals and problems identified when family members enter service. All data collected should have the purpose of illuminating the problems identified by the family.

# Critical Content

1. Many methods are used when collecting information and exploring family processes. These include direct interviews, observation, projective techniques, and psychometric testing.

2. When you are interviewing a family, you will use specialized questioning formats to capitalize on the relationships and on the multiple people in the room. Family practitioners must be skilled in targeting, setting up, delivering, and following up these types of questions.

3. To gather information on interaction, you often must observe the family. There are many interactive and content-related methods of observing family processes.

4. Projective methods can employ almost gamelike methods to have family members create metaphors or other symbols of the family. These methods can be used to identify potential issues and strengths in the family.

5. Many psychometric tests are available for assessing family processes. When you are using tests, make sure they are valid and reliable. Also ensure that the focus of the test provides what is needed for the assessment.

# Suggested Readings

Brown, J. (1997). Circular questioning: An introductory guide. *Australian & New Zealand Journal of Family Therapy, 18,* 109–114.

Cox, R. P., & Anderson, H. (2003). Family assessment tools. In R. P. Cox (Ed.), *Health related counseling with families of diverse cultures: Family, health, and cultural competencies* (pp. 145–167). Westport, CT: Greenwood Press.

Deacon, S. A., & Piercy, F. P. (2001). Qualitative methods in family evaluation: Creative assessment techniques. *American Journal of Family Therapy, 29,* 39–73.

Locke, L. M., & Prinz, R. (2002). Measurement of parental discipline and nurturance. *Clinical Psychology Review, 22,* 895–930.

## Chapter 5

# Structuring the Family Exploration

In Chapter 4 we looked at the first step of the assessment process, exploration and data collection. You learned strategies for collecting family information, including family-based questioning, measurement, and observation strategies. In this chapter we build on those earlier discussions by considering frameworks for organizing exploration activities. When data are collected, it is important to organize the data to promote a family-specific understanding. The frameworks provided in this chapter structure the data collection efforts and organize theoretical concepts into usable systems.

## Theoretical Grounding

Most of the concepts included in this chapter are applications rather than theoretically driven knowledge. Consequently, you will need to understand the theoretically based thinking and then identify how the thinking is used within the assessment protocols we examine in the chapter. The theories underlying the assessment techniques are provided in Table 5.1. To become comfortable with the thinking associated with the assessment techniques contained in this chapter, you may want to read more on the underlying theoretical models.

**TABLE 5.1**
**Chapter Concepts, Theoretical Models, and Sources**

| Chapter Concepts | Theoretical Model | Recommended Reading |
|---|---|---|
| Using a genogram to structure assessment | Family systems model | Goldenberg & Goldenberg, Chapter 8<br>Horne, Chapters 3, 10<br>Nichols & Schwartz, Chapter 5 |
| Using the four-cell model | Cognitive-behavioral model<br>Intergenerational model<br>Narrative model | Goldenberg & Goldenberg, Chapter 8, 12, 14<br>Horne, Chapter 8, 9, 10<br>Nichols & Schwartz, Chapters 5, 10, 11 |
| Parental functions assessment | Structural model | Goldenberg & Goldenberg, Chapter 9<br>Horne, Chapters 6, 7<br>Nichols & Schwartz, Chapter 7 |
| Risk assessment | Cognitive-behavioral model | Goldenberg & Goldenberg, Chapter 12<br>Nichols & Schwartz, Chapters 3, 10 |

# Assessment Frameworks

Four frameworks are provided in this chapter to help you in organizing, focusing, and interpreting family information. Each framework allows the family practitioner to organize large amounts of family information for easy understanding. Notice that each framework offers a slightly different view of the family system, ranging from a whole-system view to specific subsystems or dynamics within the family. Depending on the family's presenting concerns, you can select the framework that best explores and organizes information pertinent to the presenting problems. Here are the four frameworks:

1. **The family genogram** captures full family information.
2. **The four-cell model** captures couple-related information.
3. **The parental functions grid** captures parental subsystem information.
4. **The risk assessment framework** captures indicators of violence risk.

Each of these frameworks can be used to guide exploration during the assessment phase of family treatment. The first two frameworks use developmental premises to assess family system development, and the next two focus on specific elements of systemic functioning.

# The Family Genogram

Murray Bowen (1978) developed the *family genogram* framework, which has been broadly used in family-based practice. Although the genogram was initially associated with the family-system approach to treatment, practitioners frequently use it with divergent approaches because it concisely captures a wealth of family information. Because many books are available that outline the use of genograms in practice (see McGoldrick, Gerson, & Shellenberger, 1999), this discussion is cursory. It introduces you to the basic concepts, symbols, and use of genograms in practice.

Practitioners use genograms to collect information on all members of the family system, including information on extended family systems. In a genogram, circles and squares are the symbols for family members. Circles represent female family members, and squares represent males. To clearly identify the family member represented by each circle and square, you will often place a name under each symbol and record that person's age inside the circle or square. When using the genogram, you will also distinguish membership in specific generations (e.g., children, parents, grandparents) by placing the eldest generation at the top of the page and the youngest generation at the bottom.

At each generational level, there are procedures for organizing the circles and squares. The procedure for adult couples is to place the males consistently on one side and the females on the other. Many recommend placing the males on the left, but consistency is most important because it lets you more easily view patterns across generations and within the male and female family systems. Books with rules and conventions for writing the genogram can provide very specific recommendations (see McGoldrick et al., 1999). For the purposes of this introduction, you are advised to ensure that you understand the basic premises of the genogram and are consistent in using the symbols.

In genograms, an adult couple is most often indicated by drawing two lines, one dropping down from each symbol, and then making right angles to connect the two lines. If the adult couple is married, the line is solid. Affairs and common-law relationships are often indicated by dotted lines joining the couple. It is useful to note the starting and ending dates of the relationships, to establish a time reference for relationship milestones. If the couple is heterosexual, a circle and square are joined. Lesbian couples are shown as two circles and gay male couples are shown as two squares, each with an upside-down triangle in the circle or square. Figure 5.1 illustrates a heterosexual couple.

If a couple is divorced, you will draw a double slash through the line connecting them. This indicates that the relationship has been severed. Separations without divorce can be depicted by a single slash. If there has been separation or divorce and then reconciliation, you simply cross out the slash with a single slash in the opposite direction (e.g., ⚓). Most practitioners enter the date of the separation or divorce near

**Figure 5.1**   Drawing the Couple

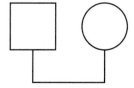

**Figure 5.2**  Depicting Multiple Adult Partnerships

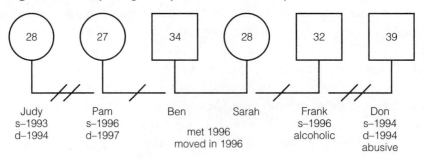

the slash line, to identify when the relationship ended. You can also enter additional information that might be useful. For example, you may want to note the date of the separation and the date of divorce if the time between the two events is important. You may also want to record the reasons for separation. Such details can be jotted down as notes near the slash line to help remember details. For couples that have had multiple partnerships, you can extend the connecting "couple lines" to include additional partners (see Figure 5.2).

In Figure 5.2, you can see how multiple relationships can be documented along with basic information about the relationship timelines. Notice, for the intact relationship between Ben and Sarah, that some information was included about the beginning of their relationship; also notice that terminated relationships contain information about separations (denoted as *s*) and divorces (*d*). When creating a genogram, you can add such notes at any time.

Drawing children is slightly different from drawing the adult couple. You will indicate the eldest offspring by dropping a line from the couple line, near the left end of the line. A short line up from the child's circle or square connects the child to the adult union, indicating parenthood. For twins, drop two lines at angles so the children can be depicted as intersecting the adult relationship line at the same point in time. Note in Figure 5.3 that you can identify children resulting from any of the adult unions.

When drawing complex genograms, you will usually want to indicate who is living together or forming the family unit. This can be accomplished by drawing a dotted

**Figure 5.3**  Depicting Parental Relationships

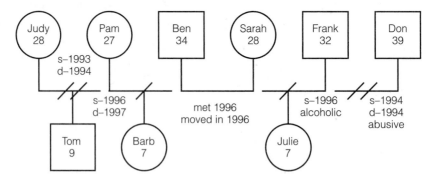

line around the cohabiting group. You can also use lines to identify relationship qualities. While reviewing the genogram in Figure 5.4, note the following features:

- The cohabiting group (at the bottom, bounded by the dotted line) was formed from people who had not been in previous family units that have ended through separation or divorce.
- One mother died (shown by an X).
- The parents on the other side of the family are divorced (shown by the slash breaking the couple line).
- There is mutual hostility between the husband's divorced parents and between one daughter and a paternal aunt (crooked lines).
- The eldest son is very close with the same paternal aunt (double line).
- The father in the cohabiting group is cut off from his mother (line with slashes indicating a break).
- The mother in the cohabiting group is distant with her father (dotted line), but is close with her husband's father (double line).

Notice in Figure 5.4 that a three-generational genogram was used. Family practitioners frequently want to assess families using three generations to understand the

**Figure 5.4**  A Three-Generation Genogram

| | |
|---|---|
| ═══════════ | Very close |
| ───┤├─── | Cut off |
| - - - - - - - - | Distant or tenuous |
| ∿∿∿∿∿ | Hostile |

**Figure 5.5** Common Relationship Lines Used in Genograms

| Type of relationship | Figure |
|---|---|
| Positive | ————————— |
| Distant | - - - - - - - - - - - - - - - |
| Close | ═══════════ |
| Hostile | ∧∧∧∧∧∧∧∧ |
| Fused | ═══════════ |
| Cut-off | ——⊣ ⊢—— |
| Abuse (dark arrowhead) | ∧∧∧∧∧∧→ |

Note: Adapted from *Genograms: Assessment and Intervention* (2nd ed.), by
M. McGoldrick, R. Gerson, & S. Shellenberger, 1999, New York: Norton.

patterns, boundaries, and relationships across generations. The three-generational genogram places the eldest family members at the top and the youngest at the bottom.

Relationships among family members are depicted on the genogram using different lines. Typical relationships include conflicted relationships, close relationships, distant or tenuous relationships, and cut-off relationships (no longer talking to each other). Many more types of relationships can be included in a genogram, but these four are enough for our purposes. If you want to include other relationship types, simply add more types of lines to the legend and then use them in the genogram. Figure 5.5 illustrates some of the most common relationship lines.

In genograms, the direction of emotional energy can be indicated with arrowheads. If the feelings are mutual, draw arrowheads at both ends of the line. If the feeling flows in one direction, draw the arrowhead so it points to the family member who receives the emotion. For example, if a woman is always angry with her son, but the feeling is not reciprocal, the arrowhead will point from the mother to the son.

It is often useful to construct a genogram when you are first meeting with a family, in order to document the relationships and family members involved. You can also identify extended kin who remain involved with the family. Many clinical settings use genograms when conducting supervision or case conferences because the drawings can convey a wealth of information very quickly.

## ◆ EXERCISE 5.1    DEVELOPING A GENOGRAM

This exercise gives you an opportunity to apply some basic genogram principles. Although there is much to learn about genograms, this exercise will help to refine your skills.

## Making Your Genogram

1. In the space provided, draw your parents by making a square for your father and a circle for your mother. Keep the circle and square far enough apart to leave room for the children in your family. Try to put your father near the left side and your mother near the right side of the page. If your family has more than one father or mother figure, include them by extending the lines out from the mother and father, as indicated in Figure 5.2.

2. After drawing the circle and square, draw a short line down from the middle of the circle and then from the square, and draw a horizontal connecting line that joins the bottoms of those two lines.

3. For each child in your family, draw a line down from the connecting line and make a circle or a square to indicate whether the child is male or female. Start with the eldest child on the left and proceed in order to the youngest on the right. Make sure you leave enough space between siblings to provide information about them.

4. After you have represented all of the family members, look at your picture. Start to make notes and changes that indicate the unique nature of your family. Put people's ages in each circle and square. If anyone has died, draw an X through the circle or square and then make a note to the side indicating the cause of death. Make other notes that you consider important (e.g., family roles, behaviors that are concerning, etc.).

5. For each family member write down information about the roles he or she plays in the family (e.g., hero, clown) and any other information that describes how the person functions in the family.

6. For yourself and your siblings include spouses and children (if any). To indicate significant relationships, create smaller genograms attached to each sibling.

7. Add information on roles and other notations for these relationships.

8. Look at the array of people in the family, and draw a jagged line between members who are often in conflict. Next, draw a double line between members who are closely aligned with each other. Finally, draw a dotted line between members who are distant and tenuous with each other.

9. Finally, look at your genogram and think about the pattern of relationships among your family members. Make notes on your conclusions at the bottom of the page.

# The Four-Cell Assessment of Inherited Family Models

The four-cell framework for organizing data collection focuses on the inherited models of understanding and behaving for the two adult members of the family (Ragg, 2001). This framework is useful not only when working with couples but also if the family problems appear to be associated with differences in the approaches of two adult members. The framework uses four dimensions of development to explore the model of "family" for each person (Figure 5.6). To help with this exploration, we next discuss each of the four cells in more detail.

**Figure 5.6**  The Four Cells of an Inherited Family Model

| Genetics and biology | Environment |
|---|---|
| • Ability or disability<br>• Race<br>• Intelligence<br>• Attractiveness<br>• Temperament<br>• Neurological processing<br>• Parental identification<br>• Metabolism<br>• Aptitudes<br>• Looks and features | *Family*<br>• Problem solving<br>• Alcohol or drug abuse<br>• Processing tension<br>• Self-other orientation<br>• Positivity or negativity<br>• Closeness or distance<br>• Violence or abuse<br>• Gender roles<br>• Autonomy or dependency<br>• Expressive or repressive<br>• Good or bad standards<br>• Culture and assimilation<br>• Handling of difference<br>• Gender dominance patterns<br>• Adequacy beliefs<br><br>*Social*<br>• Oppression or privilege<br>• Discrimination or acceptance<br>• Ostracization or inclusion<br>• Economic options<br>• Culture<br>• Neighborhood |
| **Beliefs** | **Behavior** |
| • Tension tolerance<br>• Beliefs about differences<br>• Gender roles<br>• Self-concept<br>• Beliefs about competence<br>• Locus of control<br>• Standards of cleanliness<br>• Standards of behavior<br>• Standards of punctuality<br>• Beliefs about others<br>• Sex attributions<br>• Beliefs about communication<br>• Emotional expressiveness<br>• Cultural values<br>• Trustworthiness of others | • Problem solving<br>• Handling tension<br>• Reactivity<br>• Affiliative responses<br>• Distaste of others<br>• Avoidance behavior<br>• Side taking<br>• Dismissing concerns<br>• Handling anger<br>• Use of humor<br>• Reactivity<br>• Validation seeking<br>• Discimination (sex, age, ethnic, cultural, sexual orientation, gender ascription, economic, educational, attractiveness, able-bodied, values based)<br>• Acceptance and rejection patterns<br>• Flirting<br>• Performing expectations<br>• Punctuality and time beliefs |

## Cell 1: Genetic and Biological Influences

The first cell is an exploration of the biological traits and genetic traits that we inherit from our parents. Most people look, act, or have identifiable traits that are similar to those of their parents. This cell is a good starting point for exploration because it gets at biologically based strengths and weaknesses that are easy to share. These traits are likely to be difficult to change, so it is worth noting them first. When exploring this cell, you will ask questions about the following areas:

- Physical similarities to each parent and the family member's experience of these similarities (e.g., were they sources of pride? how does the person identify with the parent?)
- Biologically based strengths and weaknesses (e.g., learning abilities, physical abilities) and the family member's experience of these traits when growing up
- Coping and attitude (e.g., dealing with pressure)

This exploration sets the stage for the second cell, which examines environmental influences and their effect on the family members when growing up.

## Cell 2: Environmental Influences

After exploring their inherited traits, clients tend to merge immediately into discussions of their family environment. This transition occurs seamlessly, because clients do not distinguish between biological and environmental influences. As the person begins discussing her parents, the family practitioner begins exploring multiple family influences. Consequently, the second cell considers the environment. When focused on the environment, family practitioners explore the childhood family environments of each adult. Such exploration focuses on family atmosphere and dynamics as well as on broader social variables like community. In family practice, you might explore these specific influences with your clients:

- **Family rules.** Ask clients to reflect on how rules were set in their family. In this exploration, try to discriminate formal rules from informal rules (e.g., don't make mom upset). It is useful to explore what infractions tend to yield the most severe punishments, to get some indication of a rule hierarchy. Similarly, most families have some rules that exist but are never enforced. Issues of consistency (across rules and people) are often important, because you can also elicit information about other relationships and how tension was managed in the other person's family. If some people were immune to rules (by either negotiating, using witnesses, or applying double standards), that information is important.
- **Family standards.** When discussing rules with your clients, you can also explore issues of family standards. Take time to understand the standards about cleanliness, grooming, keeping commitments, talking to others, telling the truth, and punctuality. By exploring how standards were enforced, you can often get some sense of family values.
- **Family problem solving.** Family problem solving is a critical area of exploration. It focuses on how the family experienced differences as well as on its

methods for solving difficulties. For example, did the parents fight, or did they hide their problems from the children? What about problems between parents and children; how were they resolved? In this exploration, you are trying to determine how problems were raised and then resolved in the family. Some families try to ignore problems, while others are able to put issues on the table. By exploring how problems are raised, you can access information on how tension was managed in the family. Try to determine the patterns and feelings that were evoked during problem solving. This exploration includes understanding the level of directness.

- **Emotional expression.** Take time to find out how emotions were expressed in the family. In this exploration, try to determine patterns of who was allowed to express which types of emotion, and how openly different people were willing or able to express their feelings. In many families, some feelings are hidden. Exploring the taboo feelings and acceptable feelings allows you to understand some of the family beliefs and values. Some critical feelings to explore include inadequacy, powerlessness, hopelessness, and helplessness, because these are primary feelings that are often covered up with anger. Typically, during this exploration you can also find out how emotional support was provided in the family.

- **Family roles.** Given that people tend to reassert their family models in their new relationships, it is important to understand the family roles in their model. In exploring the family roles, consider the array of roles that different family members played; try to determine the flexibility of roles, how they were assigned, who assumed burdensome roles, and whether privileges were associated with any roles. Also be sure to explore the possible deviant roles and how they served the family equilibrium.

- **Support seeking.** Take time to understand how people activated support in their family. Many families have beliefs about support giving and seeking. In some families, members get support only when they are sick, because support seeking is viewed as a weakness; other families unconditionally allow support seeking. By knowing how support was solicited and granted in the family, you can begin to understand beliefs and patterns that might be important in the current situation.

- **Relating to others.** Have family members talk about how people in the family related to each other. In the exploration, tease out hierarchies (e.g., one family member is demanding) and expectations of how people should relate to each other. During this type of exploration, you can identify expectations of loyalty and expressions of difference. You can also explore sanctions that would be used if a family member failed to relate as expected. In this exploration, be sure to determine how family members influenced each other (threats, tension, open communication, guilt, shame, pouting, etc.) and how others responded. When exploring these relationships, also explore relationships with friends and others who influenced the family. Try to understand how people from outside the family were able to access and influence the family.

Concurrent with the family dynamics just listed, you will use data on the community and neighborhood in order to understand the family context. Family dynamics may have different meaning if the family was poor rather than wealthy. Some patterns will also take on different meanings depending on the level of safety in the community. Important community elements include:

◆ **Neighborhood.** Practitioners often explore neighbor relationships to determine the web of nonfamily relationships that influenced family development. In this exploration, you will seek to determine the sources of emotional, instrumental, informational, and appraisal supports provided to the family. You will also seek to understand issues of safety and stress that were inherent in the community by tracking themes of conflict, danger, respect, and stigma.

◆ **Culture.** In Chapter 3, we considered cultural influences. Culture provides a context for child and family development. During the assessment, you will explore the family's cultural linkages and background. Pay close attention to the kinds of messages that the family experienced based on its culture. Even if they have not been identified, cultural expectations and values can be very influential.

◆ **Social institutions.** Past family experiences with social institutions can influence child and family development. Listen for references to societal institutions that influenced the family (e.g., school, church, police, neighborhood organizations, clubs, social welfare institutions, economic institutions). Try to determine the relationship between the family and the institutions to determine levels of intrusion, negativity, and supportiveness.

As each adult tells his or her family story, the family practitioner tracks messages and themes. Initially, the important themes involve incidents and dynamics that shape the belief systems and codes for living. As the story is told, you will find it helpful to jot down critical words, experiences, and patterns. These critical themes provide the foundation for further exploration using other cells.

## Cell 3: Beliefs and Cognitive Influences

As one by one the adults tell their family story, the family practitioner leads them through an exploration of the family dynamics. Throughout the story, you will glean an understanding of the important elements that each client inherits from the family. These important elements control how the client interprets situations, attributes meaning, and sets standards for living. You will be tracking the patterns of thoughts that emerge during the client discussion of the first two cells. This is a very inductive process whereby the themes of the client's story can be shared and validated. As the discussion evolves, you will identify critical codes and thinking that govern the client's behavior. Here are some critical areas for exploration that can help you in drawing linkages between the past and present:

◆ **Rules and standards.** You are seeking to identify the rules that the clients developed to guide their actions when growing up in their family. Because these inherited rules will affect their standards of punctuality, cleanliness, appearance, maintaining commitments, and so forth, be sure to explore all of the areas. Try to determine how rigid the rules are at this time in their life and how strongly they subscribe to each rule. In this exploration, try to identify how strongly a client feels about rule violations.

◆ **Self-concept.** Inherent in the clients' story will be implications for their self-conception. You will try to clarify messages that the clients received about themselves. In this exploration, try to determine (a) how positive or negative the pervasive messages were, (b) how much power others had over each client's feelings of self-worth, and (c) how quickly others can disturb the client's feelings of self-worth. From this exploration, it is helpful to monitor powerful themes that threaten the self-concept (e.g., inadequacy, powerlessness, hopelessness).

◆ **Relating to others.** As with self-related beliefs, the beliefs that clients inherit about other people are important to understand. Beliefs about the safety and trustworthiness of others are often inherited. Concurrent with issues of safety and trust, you will want to explore beliefs about entitlement, loyalty, and worthiness (look for changes based on gender, age, race, or sexual orientation).

◆ **Roles.** Many clients inherit models of ideal (and problematic) family roles. Even if a client does not agree with the models from the family, the role structures will influence her beliefs by serving as a rejected model. Typically, models of maleness and femaleness are included in a client's inherited role expectations. Given that many families have one parent who is dominant in decision making, it will be important to tease out how each gender functioned in the family of origin. Explore expectations, oppression, privilege, and burdens borne by different people in the family. Concurrent with the role structures, pay attention to the use of scapegoating and triangulation in the family to determine the family maintenance roles.

◆ **Problem solving.** Inherent in each person's story are beliefs about differences and problem solving. Some families embrace differences and solve problems openly; others avoid expressions of difference and seldom model problem solving. When exploring this area, you will find it useful to pay attention to tension-related beliefs. Problems cannot be solved without increasing tension. If the client's family believed that tension was bad, its approach to problem solving will be affected. Monitor for patterns of collaboration versus isolation, blaming versus responsibility taking, and avoidance versus engagement. With each area of belief, explore how strongly the belief is associated with the client's inherited model of family.

◆ **Emotional expression.** The client's story will convey implications for emotional expression. Inherited beliefs about emotionality often cause clients to have feelings about certain emotional states and modes of expression. Try to tease out the beliefs about certain feelings (e.g., sadness, insecurity). Also explore how feelings should be expressed according to the inherited model. Some families encourage direct expression of feelings whereas others insist on keeping feelings inside and using indirect methods of expression. Help the clients articulate how their family showed both positive and negative feelings.

## Cell 4: Behavior and Interactions

After exploring the beliefs that each person has inherited from his or her family of origin, the practitioner shifts focus to understand how each critical belief translates into behavior. Most behavior patterns have underlying beliefs. When you are working with clients to change difficult behaviors or interactions, it is useful to pair the behaviors with corresponding beliefs (McGoldrick & Carter, 2001). When translating beliefs into behavior with clients, it is helpful to focus first on the most pronounced beliefs and explore their associated actions and/or interactions. After developing a list of the clients' critical beliefs, you can explore them one by one to identify the behavioral and interactive aspects of each belief.

An exploration of action systems occurs at the end of the four-cell framework, because it is important to move from the client story through the associated beliefs before focusing on behavior. Such sequencing is important because behaviors are often the focus of family arguments and fights. By first providing a historical context and belief system foundation, you can shift discussions back and forth from behaviors to beliefs and context to manage tension in the room. This approach can prevent escalation during the assessment process.

A second benefit of this type of assessment is the ability to reframe behaviors as part of an inherited model rather than as something inherently defective in the individual. Many couples and families enter treatment with a history of fighting about each other's behavior. Most often this fighting includes the tendency to identify the core problem as inherent in other people's personalities. The inherited model framework shifts the focus from current behavior and personalities to inherited models. You can then explore with the clients how, by thinking through the model they want their family to have, they can take control of the model their children will inherit.

After outlining a model and discussing all four cells, you will find it useful to summarize each cell for your clients. Highlight the critical events, beliefs, and behaviors. In this summary, it is important to check your understandings with the clients to ensure that the model reflects their lived experience. By summarizing cells and checking understanding, you can frame the clients' problematic beliefs and behaviors as elements of the inherited model. This shift in meaning can lay the groundwork for a new definition of the problem.

## Using the Four-Cell Model: Finding "Rubs" and "Gaps"

When you are using this assessment framework in couple therapy, it is useful to have one person explore her model first, while the other listens, and then reverse positions. As each person describes his or her story and the model unfolds, you may find it necessary to restrain input and argument from the partner. Restraint is important because each person must be the expert on his or her experience. If strong reactions occur, you can ask the person whose model is being explored to comment on the differences of opinion; but try to avoid debates and competitions about who is the expert on each person's model.

When both models are developed, you can see where problems of fit exist between them. In this discussion, we refer to problems of fit as *rubs* and *gaps*. Rubs exist where significant differences occur between the models. Gaps occur when similarities in the two models cause important abilities to be missing for both adults. The rubs and gaps are identified quickly in the belief and behavior cells (see Figure 5.7). There is little use in comparing the other two cells, because they are background to each person's model. When identifying the rubs and gaps, you may find it useful to list them side by side so the adult partners can see how each rub and gap contributes to the family problems. As you review each person's beliefs and corresponding behaviors, the similarities often give clues about skill or capacity gaps where each person's model leaves some important ability undeveloped. Likewise with the differences, many rubs are found where important beliefs lead to divergent ways of acting.

Assessment of rubs and gaps begins with identifying the differences that emerge in the area of beliefs. Frequently, critical beliefs in one person's model "rub violently"

**Figure 5.7**   Four-Cell Family Model: Assessing Rubs and Gaps

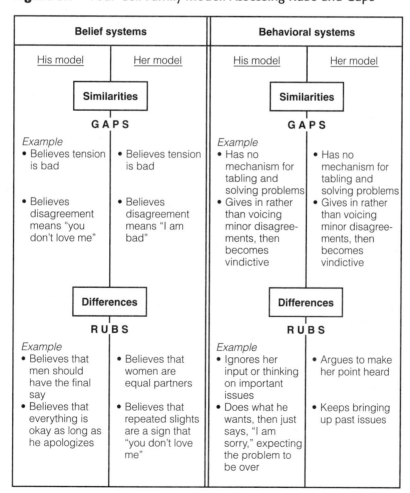

against important beliefs in the partner's model. These rubs are the areas where the adults will focus repeated fights. When the rubs become apparent, during a session you will find it useful to reframe the issues as spots where the two models do not fit comfortably together. This reframing allows for a new definition of recurrent fights. After exploring differences in the couple's belief systems, you can assess potential gaps in these belief systems. Gaps emerge when both models have beliefs that inhibit important couple or family functions.

After exploring with the couple the similarities and differences in their belief systems, you can then highlight the corresponding behaviors. By discussing behaviors as outgrowths of the couple's models, and exploring the rubs and gaps in behavioral terms, you can describe most of the difficulties between the partners. This discussion finalizes the shift from the couple's old definition of the problem to a new definition that describes the recurring behaviors as outgrowths of inherited beliefs. The problems are no longer located in the individual partners, but rather are defined as being inherent in the family model each person brings into the relationship.

## CASE EXAMPLE

A lesbian couple enters treatment because one partner, Joyce, is thinking of leaving, stating that her partner, Barb, is unresponsive. The two have been drifting apart for about three years. In the assessment, Joyce shares her story of growing up in an abusive home. Her model includes beliefs that problems are dangerous, and tension should be avoided. Inherently, her model lacks an ability to solve problems because tension is avoided by ignoring problems. Her partner Barb comes from a home where the parents never argued. She cannot recall a time when her parents had significant differences. Everybody in her family cooperated and gave in to each other rather than asserting differences. Although the models are very different, they share the belief that tension is not good. One belief emerged through too much tension, the other through an absence of tension. Regardless of the model specifics, the beliefs have created a gap in the current relationship that inhibits effective problem solving. Neither member is comfortable with stating an opinion; and whenever differences arise, both partners retreat from the conversation. Each woman views the other as being unresponsive and disinterested, and both women feel unfulfilled in the relationship.

In this case example, we can see that a gap exists where problem solving should be. The couple cannot express differences and certainly cannot resolve differences. When gaps occur, it is important to highlight the lack of an important function in the family models and frame the situation accordingly. This reframe is useful because the problem becomes understood as a lack in the inherited models rather than something inherent in the individuals.

## ◆ EXERCISE 5.2   ASSESSING A ROMANTIC RELATIONSHIP

1. In the following four-cell forms, label one form for yourself and the other for a past dating or romantic relationship that did not work out so well.
2. In your form, start with the biology cell and jot down any features that you have that are similar to those of your biological parents. If you were adopted or do not know your biological parents, leave this cell blank.
3. After completing the biology cell, proceed to the environment cell. In this space, think about your family environment when you were growing up, reread the environmental influences listed earlier, and jot down brief notes on your family environment. Be sure to reflect on the rules, role models, opportunities, and values that were stressed in your family.

Name: _____

| Biology | Environment |
|---|---|
| | |
| Beliefs | Behaviors |
| | |

4. After completing your environment cell, review the cell 3 (beliefs and cognitions) information presented earlier. After reviewing this information, reflect on how your environment promoted specific codes for living, values, and important beliefs. Jot down about five of the most critical beliefs that you use to organize your life.
5. After identifying about five critical beliefs, reflect on how these beliefs translate into patterns of behavior and relating with others. Identify a critical behavior pattern that relates to each belief.
6. Repeat steps 2, 3, 4, and 5 for the romantic partner.
7. After completing your romantic partner's model, reflect on the differences between your model and your partner's. Try to identify in the models some reasons that the relationship may have failed.

Name: _____

| Biology | Environment |
|---|---|
| | |
| **Beliefs** | **Behaviors** |
| | |

# The Parenting Functions Framework

We have explored the parenting functions framework in other chapters as a structure for focusing practice. In this section, we use the framework as an assessment tool. When assessing the parental functioning, the practitioner most often wants to understand how each parent is fulfilling the parenting functions. It is not unusual for each parent to have his or her own parenting approach. Thus, as the family practitioner, you will explore each parent's approach to the parenting functions in order to compare and contrast them.

## Assessing the Discipline Function

When assessing the discipline function, the family practitioner seeks to understand how each parent responds to the child's needs for limits. Different issues associated with thinking, feeling, interacting, and behaving are important in understanding each parent's approach to discipline.

*Thinking Elements*  Each parent's interpretations of child behavior and beliefs about discipline influence how they fulfill the disciplinary function. To better understand a parent's selection of disciplinary strategies, you will frequently want to understand that parent's interpretation systems. Although there are multiple cognitive influences on discipline, family practitioners commonly focus on the following five thinking elements when assessing the discipline function:

- ◆ **Family loyalties.** Parents often refer to how they were disciplined and assume that it was the right method because it was inherited from their parents. Issues of loyalty tend to emerge when one parent seeks to change the other's disciplinary behaviors.
- ◆ **Utility of punishment.** Some parents believe that punishment is important and will focus on punishing responses rather than using a wider range of disciplinary strategies. Other parents do not believe that punishment is appropriate and may elect to avoid disciplinary activities.
- ◆ **Rule hierarchies.** Parents may have hierarchies of rules that often depend on the severity of the discipline attached to different child infractions. Knowing the hierarchy of rules is important to understanding how discipline is being applied.
- ◆ **Responsibility.** Parents frequently have different beliefs about responsibility. This includes beliefs about their responsibilities to discipline as well as their child's responsibility for his own actions. It is useful to notice how responsibility themes emerge with the parent. As the themes emerge, you can monitor for externalization and blaming versus internalization and assuming responsibility for solutions.
- ◆ **Normalcy.** Parents sometimes differ on what is considered normal behavior for children. If a parent believes that something is normal, she is not likely to discipline the child in that situation.

*Affective Elements*   Parental emotions frequently influence how, and when, they apply discipline. Family practitioners seek to understand the role of parental affect when applying discipline. The following aspects of parental emotion frequently influence disciplinary functioning:

♦ **Emotional investment.** Parents must have some level of emotional investment in their children in order to even care about how the child is behaving. Some parents are overinvested and feel responsible for their children. Other parents are minimally invested and intervene only when the child's behavior negatively affects their goals.

♦ **Negative-positive predisposition.** Some parents take a very positive approach to discipline and use methods such as rewarding children. Such parents do use punishment and other strategies, but they frequently combine the discipline with expressions of love and caring. Other parents tend to be more negative and punitive in their approach.

♦ **Conflicted emotions.** Sometimes parents have mixed emotions about discipline. This creates parental guilt and confusion when discipline is necessary. Such emotions can interfere with disciplinary effectiveness. For example, the parent who feels that punishment is bad may overlook behaviors until they become critical.

♦ **Stress.** When parents are under a lot of stress, discipline often becomes more severe and negative because the tension associated with stress becomes channeled into the disciplinary functions. For example, a parent who is concentrating on trying to balance an inadequate budget may overreact to the children making noise.

♦ **Overcompensation.** Sometimes parents feel bad for their children because of other people's actions. This emotion can influence discipline, because the parent may elect not to act or may apply inconsistent discipline as a compensatory measure for other events. For example, a mother may let the children break curfew to make up for their father's extreme discipline the day before.

*Interactive Elements*   Because discipline is an interactive activity, family practitioners are interested in the interactions surrounding discipline. Attention is focused on interparental and parent-child interactions. The following interactive elements commonly influence how discipline is provided in the family:

♦ **Collaboration.** It is important for parents to collaborate in applying discipline. This element includes the level of agreement about rules and disciplinary strategies. When parents do not collaborate, competition between the parent figures often exists. Such dynamics undermine parenting effectiveness.

♦ **Triangulation.** Frequently, parents and children become triangulated, resulting in adult issues being expressed through disciplinary activities. For example, one parent may become angry with the other, but express her anger by harshly disciplining the child. In such situations, emotions occurring between the adults become a compelling element in the disciplinary interactions.

- ◆ **Engagement.** A critical child-parent interaction is engagement. To be effective in disciplining, parents ideally need to be focused on the child and in full understanding of the situation. Parents who sit on the couch watching television and barking orders at the child are examples of disengaged parents. Such approaches are ineffective.

- ◆ **Undermining.** Sometimes a parent figure undermines other adults by giving the child messages that they do not need to listen to the other parent. Such messages tend to be self-serving and do not focus on achieving positive child outcomes.

- ◆ **Intrusiveness.** A final interactive dynamic is intrusive parenting. Such parenting involves constantly correcting and intruding into the child's life. Parents who too closely supervise and constantly correct their child often promote resentment and anger in the child.

*Behavioral Elements*   Family practitioners pay close attention to each parent's disciplinary behaviors. When there are parental behavioral problems, some behaviors, such as abuse, require you to take immediate action; other behaviors may become the goals of intervention. During the assessment, the family practitioner monitors the following disciplinary behaviors:

- ◆ **Styles of discipline.** A central concern for practitioners involves the styles or strategies of discipline used by the parents. We examined a list of disciplinary styles in Chapter 2. Some approaches undermine parenting effectiveness when overused. It is important for practitioners to be aware of the different disciplinary strategies.

- ◆ **Continuum of discipline.** Parents sometimes need to have many strategies of discipline. These strategies exist on a continuum from doing nothing to frequent hitting. You will want to ensure that parents do not stick to a single strategy (especially corporal types of punishment), because strategies may be hard to adjust when they do not work.

- ◆ **Consistency.** Discipline is most effective when it is consistently applied. If discipline is inconsistent, it is easy for children to become confused; sometimes their behavior is acceptable to the parent, but at other times it yields a disciplinary response. When parents are inconsistent, children learn less about limits and more about how to manipulate the parent.

- ◆ **Efficiency.** To be effective, discipline needs to have outcomes. You will find it useful to monitor the amount of energy that the parents are investing when applying the discipline and compare that input to the outcomes. If the outcomes do not match the energy investment, some changes may be needed.

- ◆ **Activation issues.** Sometimes certain behaviors or tones in the child's interaction yield an immediate response. It is useful to explore the events that activate parental discipline in order to understand hierarchies and disciplinary priorities. Activation patterns may also provide information about hidden beliefs or relational issues.

## Assessing the Guidance Function

When assessing the guidance functions, family practitioners usually explore the inter-actions and parenting processes surrounding the parents' attempts to teach children right from wrong. Guidance thus has an association to discipline, but it tends to focus on attempts to help the child understand the rules rather than on attempts to enforce the rules. In the following sections, we examine the response system elements associ-ated with guidance.

*Thinking Elements*   Because it involves the parents in constructing and sharing their rationale for rules and standards for living, guidance hinges heavily on parental think-ing and beliefs. Parents first need to be able to identify themselves in a guiding role and then be able to think through complex issues in order to adequately guide the child. Family practitioners focus on how effectively parents approach and process child situations that require guidance.

- ◆ **Role expectations.** Parental involvement in guidance is heavily influenced by the parents' beliefs about their own roles and the roles of others. Some parents do not feel that it is their job to help the child in specific areas. For example, some parents do not help children with homework because they believe it is the school's job to teach the child.
- ◆ **Problem solving.** To effectively help children to handle life events, parents must be able to help them understand problem situations and then generate options. This task requires the parent to be able to identify options and then to help the child select and thoughtfully implement her options. For exam-ple, if a child has been ridiculed at school, a parent may help her to under-stand the possible reasons or meaning of the ridicule and then identify potential responses. This is in contrast to a parent who always responds with advice such as, "Just don't hang around with those children."
- ◆ **Strength focused.** Ideally, guidance functions will involve working with chil-dren's areas of strength and competence so they can develop self-efficacy and successfully deal with life situations. This task requires parents to be able to identify and use their child's strengths. Parents who cannot see the strengths in their child will struggle with identifying viable options for him.
- ◆ **Proactive positioning.** When helping children cope with and manage life's demands, parents must be able to foresee issues and help the child plan for them in advance. Achieving this proactive position requires parents to think clearly through the range of potential situations. Some parents struggle with this task and come across as paranoid or anxious; others tend to be blind-sided by events that they might have predicted.

*Affective Elements*   The cognitive nature of the guidance function requires parents to be levelheaded. This requirement has implications for the parents' emotional functioning because emotionality can interfere with the logical processes needed to guide chil-dren. Family practitioners monitor the parents' emotional expressions and reactivity in order to understand the parental experiences that may interfere with guidance functions. Here are some affective issues that can influence guidance functions:

◆ **Emotional self-control.** When fulfilling guidance functions, parents must remain somewhat calm and rational to be effective. Too much emotionality will interfere with their logical processes and will concurrently cause the child to start shutting them out and discounting their concerns.

◆ **Affective investment.** Although emotional control is important, parents also must have some emotional investment or caring to be effective in the guidance function. If parents do not care, they will not invest the energy in identifying options or helping the child solve problems.

◆ **Positive-negative balance.** Guidance works best when it is balanced. If parents approach the child only with negative messages, problems are likely to result. Similarly, if the parent provides only positive messages, corrective feedback is lacking. Parents must consequently manage their tendencies to overextend in either direction.

◆ **Impartiality.** While maintaining the caring and investment, parents must be able to let their child make mistakes and help her to learn from her mistakes. The goal of guidance—helping children learn, not controlling the outcomes—is sometimes difficult for parents to achieve.

*Interactive Elements*   For guidance to succeed, interaction must occur. Family practitioners pay close attention to the level and type of parent-child interaction when assessing this function. Some parents tend to be underinvolved and respond to the child in ways that end discussion or dismiss the child's concerns. Other parents become intrusive as the child tries to generate his own responses to situations. An optimal balance allows the child to make his own decisions with support when needed. Family practitioners monitor the following interactions when assessing the guidance function:

◆ **Engagement.** Parents must engage with the child to help him understand and think through his responses to life situations. Parents who simply give the child advice or dismiss his concerns tend to be disengaged. Parents who take things personally or overreact to situations may be overengaged. A balanced engagement is optimal.

◆ **Teaching.** When children do not know something important, it falls to the parent to teach them. This interaction includes such activities as helping the child with homework, explaining use of utensils in a restaurant, and using the public transportation system. Again, a balance is needed so the child can engage in self-learning but still have parental support.

◆ **Coaching.** Teaching largely involves explaining or showing the child what to do. At times the parent must accompany the child, watching how she performs tasks and intervening only when she needs further input. This more active shaping is referred to as coaching. Typically, coaching is focused on skill development more than knowledge building.

◆ **Follow-up.** When children have had a concern, parents often need to follow up to see how the situation has evolved. Parents also need to seek out a child when something seems to be bothering him. By following up on the child's concerns and issues, the parents communicate his importance to them and ensure support throughout the situation.

*Behavioral Elements* Guidance functions require parents to actively involve themselves in their child's life. Parents cannot fulfill this function by sitting on a couch watching television and listening to the child only during commercials. Parents frequently must leave the couch, and sometimes even the home, to ensure that the guidance functions are adequately met. Many of the behaviors associated with guidance functions lead to opportunities to interact. Here are some critical behaviors:

◆ **Seeking out.** When children are away from the home or seem isolated, parents need to seek out the child and check in with him. The spirit of checking in is to ensure that the child is okay and that he knows support is available. Some parents check up on the child rather than checking in, which undermines his autonomy. Family practitioners focus on the frequency and nature of seeking-out interactions.

◆ **Outreach.** Similar to checking in with the child, parents must reach out to other people involved with the child. To support their child's activities, parents talk with coaches, teachers, club leaders, and so forth.

◆ **Attending.** Parents need to attend child events such as concerts, parent-teacher conferences, required meetings, and sporting events. When assessing the attending behaviors, family practitioners focus on the frequency of attending, the reasons used to justify nonattendance, and the relationships developed with child supports outside of the family.

◆ **Demonstrating.** When children are unclear about a behavior or skill, parents often demonstrate the behavior and then discuss the skill to help the child learn. Demonstration and participation in skill-related practice is instrumental in helping children to learn concrete skills. When assessing this behavior, family practitioners tend to focus on the frequency of engagement.

## Assessing the Nurturing Function

Family practitioners try to understand how parents fulfill the nurturing functions. The patterns of caregiving and responding to the child are important to understand when assessing the parents. Some parents are very warm and caring with their children. Others tend to be hostile and rejecting. You will want to understand where the parents are on this continuum. The following elements are important when conducting the assessment.

*Thinking Elements* The beliefs parents hold about their children influence how nurturing functions are performed. In assessing parental functioning, family practitioners frequently tune into the parents' patterns of thinking and interpreting their children's situations. Family practitioners are also interested in the parents' interpretations of their own roles in raising the children. The following areas of belief are often important in making an assessment:

- **Autonomy beliefs.** The parents' belief about how much support children should receive and how much they should be able to do on their own influences parental patterns of responding. Some parents believe that children should be able to take care of themselves at a very young age. Such parents often hold back on nurturing activities. Other parents tend to be very nurturing and take over situations that the child can manage alone. The beliefs underlying such patterns are of great interest to family practitioners.

- **Role beliefs.** The beliefs parents hold about what they should (and should not) be doing as a parent influence how they respond to their child. For example, some men say they are babysitting when they stay home with their children. Such statements indicate a belief that these men do not see child care as part of their parental role. Such parental beliefs form a job description in their minds, and parental activities frequently follow the job requirements quite closely. When you are trying to assess parental functioning, it is important to know each parent's role expectations.

- **Distortions.** Sometimes their belief systems may cause parents to overreact to child situations. This distortion often results from holding extreme beliefs or cognitive injunctions. Family practitioners look for patterns of personalizing, catastrophizing, and overgeneralizing that may affect parental responses.

- **Tuning in.** An important parenting ability is to tune into the child's experience. If parents are able to understand the child's internal experience, they can frequently affirm and respond to her emotional needs. However, if parents cannot understand situations from the child's perspective, they are often at risk of missing elements that are important to her. Such responses are often invalidating to the child.

*Affective Elements* Parental emotionality can have consequences for the nurturing functions. Extreme negative emotions will inhibit the expression of positive affect toward the child and may even generate hostile or negative messages to the child. Conversely, positive affective expressions often convey messages of caring and celebration to the child. Family practitioners pay close attention to how the parental emotions are expressed with the children. The following areas of parental emotionality are often taken into consideration when making an assessment.

- **Vulnerability tolerance.** Parents must be able to withstand the strains of child individuation. As children grow, they challenge parental positions and often express negative affect about parental behaviors or positions. Such events are part of normal child development. Some parents react to these developmental events as personal attacks, while others manage to remain emotionally calm. How parents manage their feelings of vulnerability in relation to their children is important when you are seeking to understand how the parenting functions are being fulfilled.

◆ **Positive-negative balance.** The nature of parental emotion is critical in understanding the nurturing functions in the family. If parents are very negative, the messages they give may undermine feelings of competence and self-worth in the child. Some parents are too positive and fail to see a balanced picture of their child. Such parents may promote messages that the child is beyond reproach and create an inflated sense of worth or entitlement in the child.

◆ **Playfulness.** Parents who play with their children provide important messages and experiences that the children internalize. Children learn how to shift from serious to playful and can experience authority figures in a balanced or well-rounded manner. In families where the parents cannot joke around or be playful, messages tend to become somber and may seem negative because people take situations too seriously. In families where people never take situations seriously, there may be cause for worry about the child failing to understand the experiences of others.

◆ **Investment.** Parents must have some emotional investment in their child's well-being. Without such investment, parents would not care about child activities or situations. Similarly, too much investment may cause the parent to overidentify in situations and fail to separate their own feelings from those of the child.

*Interactive Elements*    The interactive elements of nurturing focus on how the parent relates to the child. Family practitioners are concerned about levels of support, succor, and the nature of messages generated about the child. In the parental interactions, practitioners want to ensure that the parent communicates messages that the child is valued. Practitioners also want to ensure that the parents are able to understand the child's needs separate from their own desires and wants. Here are some areas used to assess the interactive elements of nurturing:

◆ **Boundary maintenance.** For children to develop a positive and autonomous self-concept, it is important that the parent allow the child to individuate. Some parents struggle with this and expect their child to hold the same values, beliefs, and priorities that his parents have. Other parents encourage individuality and expressions of difference in their child from a very young age.

◆ **Reflections of value.** Nurturing parents often make statements or comments on how important the child is to the family by expressing appreciation, love, and celebration, or by highlighting successes. When hearing such statements, the child internalizes a sense of emotional well-being and value.

◆ **Celebration of accomplishments.** When a child achieves milestones or accomplishments, it is important for parents to acknowledge and celebrate his achievements. Even small achievements, such as putting his books away, can be powerful influences if parents express appreciation.

- ◆ **Support.** One of the most critical interactive elements in the parent-child relationship is support. Parents must provide emotional, informational, instrumental, and appraisal support for the child. In making the assessment, the practitioner seeks to understand how each type of support is provided and how the child activates the supportive response.

*Behavioral Elements*   Parental nurturing behaviors are a critical feature in assessing nurturing because nonverbal communication is often a central feature of the messages internalized by the child. If a parent looks away from the child when saying "I love you," the nonverbal communication undermines the verbal communication. Consequently, family practitioners pay attention to the parental actions that accompany nurturing. The following behavioral elements are often considered when assessing the parental nurturing behaviors:

- ◆ **Touch.** When a parent hugs his child, touches her shoulder, tussles her hair or smiles when with the child, he communicates an attitude of caring. Similarly, if a parent never touches his child except when angry, a totally different message is communicated to the child. Practitioners also pay attention to whose needs are being met when touching occurs.
- ◆ **Play.** Parents who are able to play with their children communicate acceptance. Given that play is the child's major mode of experiencing life, when parents play with the child, they actually enter the child's life and communicate on a level that is easily internalized by the child.
- ◆ **Attending to needs.** Practitioners pay attention to how parents identify and respond to child needs. When children express needs, they often do so indirectly. Some children become cranky when hungry, or clingy when scared. Parent responses to such expressions convey important information. Likewise, parents must often be active in the child's daily routines. Hygiene, homework, getting to places, and going to bed often involve parental actions. Practitioners pay attention to how parents become involved and the messages that are communicated surrounding such involvement.
- ◆ **Protection.** Parents must sometimes act to protect their child. This behavior occurs as part of daily routines, such as ensuring that a young child is attended when bathing. Protective moments also occur when others impinge on the child's development. Often parents must mediate the influence of teachers, other parents, children, animals, and environmental hazards. Practitioners consider how the parent monitors and actively mitigates the environmental influences that could prove harmful to the child.

## Assessing the Access Function

For children to achieve optimal development, parents must be geographically, psychologically, and emotionally available for the child. When assessing this function, you will seek to determine the level of such availability for each parent figure. The following areas are considered when making this assessment.

*Cognitive Elements*    Parental interpretations of the child's needs and their own roles in relation to the child influence how they make themselves available. If parents harbor beliefs that result in separate child and adult spheres of operation, access functions are likely to be neglected. Such beliefs may come from inherited models or may be necessitated by life's demands, such as work schedules. Here are some cognitive elements to consider when assessing the parents' access behaviors:

◆ **Attentiveness.** Some parents are oblivious to their child's whereabouts, while others have finely tuned radar that helps them know roughly where their child is and should be at all times. This attentiveness is critical for understanding accessibility. If parents are constantly distracted by other demands, wants, or activities, they cannot adequately fulfill this function. In such situations, practitioners look for other adults who have been available for the child to access.

◆ **Beliefs about child engagement.** In homes where parents believe that children should been seen but not heard, or that children normally need to be outside exploring the world, access functions are likely to be a low priority. In such situations, you may want to explore the belief systems to determine their origin and level of influence. In some families, beliefs about parent-child engagement result in the parents being too available or intrusive in the child's life.

◆ **Values rigidity.** The values held by parents can interfere with psychological access if the parent's belief systems are too rigid to allow them to hear the child's concerns or assertions. Some parents' beliefs systems screen out child positions that are counter to their worldview, effectively rejecting child-generated thinking.

◆ **Causal attributions.** Some parents believe that their children interrupt them or seek access just to drive the parent crazy. Such attributions convey rejections and anger whenever the child attempts to initiate the access function. Other parents interpret child access behaviors as expressions of need and see it as their obligation to respond.

*Affective Elements*    Parental affect can inhibit or expand the parental access behaviors. When parents are self-absorbed in their emotions, they are likely to be either unresponsive due to ignoring the child, or intrusive because of overresponding to resolve the child's emotional state. Either extreme can interfere with access functioning. Here are some specific areas for assessment:

◆ **Negative-positive tenor.** Positive parental emotion promotes child access, because the child is more likely to be validated and receive positive attention. Negative emotion is more likely to result in rejection and criticism of the child.

◆ **Emotional reserves.** When parents are emotionally depleted, they have little emotional energy to invest in parenting. Consequently, they disengage from the child and do not respond to access attempts or opportunities. If this is prolonged, children will seek other adults for attention or adopt alternate systems of meeting their needs.

- **Stress levels.** Stress can greatly interfere with a parent's ability to respond to his or her children. Stress causes emotional energy to be drawn into the source of stress (e.g., relationship problems, financial crises, job-related issues). This limits the emotional energy available for investing in the children. Long-term stress will dissuade children from attempting to engage the adult or will promote more extreme attention-seeking that may result in escalation and problems.
- **Anxiety.** Although most of the emotional issues just described result in decreased attentiveness, anxiety can create increased access behavior in the parent. If the parent is fearful or anxious, she may make frequent phone calls to access the child or check up on him more frequently than is necessary. These intrusive acts can inhibit the development of child autonomy and may undermine positive self-conceptions in the child.

*Interactive Elements*   Access functions require interaction or exchanges between the parent and child. Some can occur on the nonverbal level (e.g., the parent sees the child, waves, and smiles), but many exchanges involve the child coming to the parent wanting some sort of attention. Family practitioners are often interested in the nature of the ongoing but minor (e.g., not guidance related) exchanges between the parent and child. Here are some areas you will want to assess:

- **Checking-in routines.** Parents and children often devise some system of checking in. Common patterns of checking in include after-school contact, end-of-day routines, and schooltime send-offs. Note that at each juncture, the parent has the opportunity to ensure that the child has what she needs (materials, advice, comfort) to be successful. Some families have no checking-in routines; they leave the child to manage transitions on his own. In other families the parent ensures that some form of checking in occurs when the child goes through regular transitions such as coming home, leaving home, and going to bed.
- **Engagement.** When children approach a parent, they expect to achieve some level of engagement. The child wants to be acknowledged and have her presence welcomed. In families that encourage child contact with the parent, children become secure in their relationship. Rejecting messages and negative or hostile reactions can have the opposite effect (Allen, Gabbard, Newsom, & Coyne, 1990; Bischoff & Tracey, 1996).
- **Minor validations.** Sometimes children simply want their presence to be acknowledged and validated. When playing, children often look to see if their parents are watching. Likewise, in public situations such as parks and sporting events, children often look to ensure that the parent is paying attention. When the parent is looking and waves, or otherwise indicates interest, the child can relax and continue in her activities. If the parent is always engaged in other activities or never responds to the child, she may interpret this lack of involvement as being meaningful.
- **Interest.** When a child approaches his parents, there is an expectation that the parent has some interest in what he is saying. If the parent consistently brushes

off the child, he will internalize messages of disinterest and withdraw. If the parent is overinterested and does not balance the adult and child worlds (e.g., drops everything just to listen to minor disclosures), the child may experience feelings of omnipotence and become controlling of the parent's attention.

*Behavioral Elements*   Access is an active function. Consequently, parents must exhibit behaviors that make access possible and reinforcing to the child. Family practitioners seek to understand how the parent and child engage in behaviors that initiate and promote access. If the parent is consistently isolated, this can interfere with child access. Similarly, if the parent consistently intrudes on the child's space, the access function will interfere with the development of child autonomy. The following behavioral issues are considered when assessing the access function:

- **Responding to expressed needs.** When children express dismay or a need for parental intervention (e.g., crying), most parents drop what they are doing and go to the child. This response conveys messages of importance to the child. When parents are nearby and fail to respond, the child will internalize messages of rejection or nonimportance.
- **Proximity maintenance.** Some parents seem to automatically relocate themselves in order to observe their children when in public places. Similarly, children often try to maintain proximity to the parent. Such efforts maintain a proximal distance that allows them to access each other if needs arise. In the home, such actions frequently involve the placement of play and work areas so children can be monitored while the parent performs tasks.
- **Seeking out.** When parents and children are distant from each other for a period of time, seeking-out behavior often occurs. When the parent feels that the child has been gone too long, the parent may phone about, trying to ensure the child's well-being. Children often engage in similar behavior. As with many behaviors, a balanced approach seems best to ensure that the parent is neither rejecting nor intrusive.
- **Reentry rituals.** Frequently, contact rituals occur between parents and children. Such rituals include such things as providing snacks after school, bathing after weekend visitation, or other rituals that accentuate the relationship importance when the child reenters the family after being away.

## Making the Assessment

When assessing the parental functions, the family practitioner considers how each adult authority figure in the family performs each area of functioning. When reviewing how each parent figure functions, you may first want to review how the parental functioning affects the loveable-limitable circle of child outcomes. The messages and responses of each parent within the different functions will form a pattern of messages directed toward the child. The nature of the pattern and the energy coming from the parent will have important implications for the child's development.

The nature of the messages directed toward the child raises concerns about how the child will begin to internalize self-statements. If the messages directed from parent figures are predominantly negative (e.g., you can't do anything right, you are bad, what do you want now, etc.), the sense of being loveable will be critically compromised. Messages that the child is competent and valued will have the opposite effect. Family practitioners search through the messages to determine the balance between negative and positive messages.

The second area of concern is the energy directed at the child. Some parents occupy an embattled position in relation to the child and invest a great deal of energy trying to control him. This energy is directed from the parental functions in such a way that the parental influence impinges on the child's sphere. In such situations, it is common for the child to fight back in a way, trying to create space for his own autonomy.

In an embattled position, the parents are frequently controlling toward the child and favor coercive and negative disciplinary strategies. Guidance functions are frequently negative and involve the parent yelling at the child. Nurturance functions are often overlooked in favor of parenting functions that provide opportunities to control the child. When a parent engages in this type of functioning, concerns about abusive interactions arise because the parent is putting his needs to control above the child's needs to develop. Exchanges are often power struggles, and the child will frequently become either very hostile or depressed.

A second common configuration is the disengaged parent. In this configuration the parent is focused primarily on her own needs, seldom attending to the child's needs. Depressed or addicted parents are examples of such a parenting style. In such situations, the child receives very little input from the parent and is left to his own devices. Such children are often found wandering around the neighborhood. Sometimes other parents start to fulfill the functions; but at other times, the child learns to survive with minimal parental input.

When there are two parent figures in the family, there can be splits between them; each parent adopts a different style of performing the parental functions. If the child is lucky, a balance is struck so that each parent's strengths compensate for the weaknesses of the other. Problems can also arise when no parent has strengths in certain areas of functioning. In such situations, practitioners may see a need to engage other adults to fulfill those functions or work with the family to enhance parental functioning.

# The Risk Assessment Framework

Although the family is generally presented as a place of safety, that assumption is often false. Spouse abuse, child abuse, and sexual abuse frequently cause families to be a place of danger for family members. The multiple forms of family violence require all family practitioners to develop skills in identifying potential risks. You cannot escape the need to assess risk and dangerousness when working with families. This need is elevated if you work in a setting where violence is expected (e.g., agencies dealing with domestic violence or child abuse). There is an expectation that family practitioners will be able to predict violence based on client background. Failure to develop and use such skills can result in legal action and lawsuits (Kermani & Drob, 1987; Milner & Campbell, 1995; Sonkin, 1986).

The demand to assess risk is easy to understand, but risk assessment is at best a difficult task. Risk assessment is complex because there are so many forms of family violence and so many purposes for assessment (Douglas & Ogloff, 2003; English & Pecora, 1994; Milner & Campbell, 1995). Assessing sexual abuse risk, child abuse risk, and spouse abuse risks are all different skills. Consequently, you must master multiple variations of the assessment skill. Compounding the assessment issues are the moral and emotional issues inherent in working with violence and abuse (Maden, 2003). Clinicians often are focused on family enhancement goals. When issues of risk and violence arise, role conflicts frequently occur. Consequently, risk assessment is still an unrefined skill in the area of family practice (Douglas & Ogloff, 2003).

There are many systems for assessing risk in the family. Each risk assessment system has strengths and weaknesses. All systems of risk assessment have problems because violent behavior is usually infrequent, and its timing hard is to predict (Hall, Catlin, Boissevain, & Westgate, 1984; Megargee, 1976; Monahan, 1981, 1984). A second prediction problem occurs due to the many illusionary correlations that, although associated with violence, do not help predict risk (Megargee, 1976; Monahan, 1981). Finally, the practitioner must consider many elements of risk, including the target of abuse, severity of abuse, treatment effects, and shifts to lesser types of abuse (Craig, Browne, & Stringer, 2003; Sjoestedt & Grann, 2002)

## Actuarial Approaches to Risk Assessment

Many researchers recommend an actuarial approach to risk assessment. An actuarial approach uses known correlates of risk considered together as the preferred method of predicting risk (Monahan, 2002, 2003). Such approaches use gender, age, income, and other methods for assessing violence risk. The predictive model is typically built on years of data identifying demographics and other variables that appear strongly associated with the violence. Actuarial approaches have been very effective in predicting people likely to violate others (Barbaree, Seto, Langton, & Peacock, 2001; Monahan, 2002, 2003; Sjoestedt & Grann, 2002).

Although this method is considered the best approach to risk assessment, it has some limitations in clinical practice. The first limitation is the use of static factors such as gender and background (Craig et al., 2003). Because these factors are not amenable to change during treatment, it is not possible to monitor changes in risk levels. Actuarial approaches also fail to identify when people will be violent. Rather, there is an indication that they are likely to abuse; but the current risk levels cannot be determined (Webster, Hucker, & Bloom, 2002). A final drawback is that the practitioner cannot assess the type or level of violence that is likely to be used (Barbaree et al., 2001).

The strength of an actuarial approach appears to be in identifying people who are likely to re-abuse (Craig et al., 2003). If the purpose of your assessment is to make this determination—for example, when making discharge decisions or altering treatment plans—an actuarial approach may be appropriate. Actuarial assessments may provide important information during intake if risk profiles lead to distinct treatment approaches and clinical decisions (Monahan, 2002; Szmukler, 2003; Webster et al., 2002).

In general clinical practice, the lack of refinement associated with actuarial approaches often requires it to be supplemented with alternative assessment methods. In clinical practice, professionals want more refined information about risk. Important decisions are often based on knowledge of lesser types of abuse, other problems or issues in the situation, and shifts in the risk profile (Sjoestedt & Grann, 2002; Webster et al., 2002). It is thus important to combine the actuarial approach to risk assessment with more clinical approaches (Doyle & Dolan, 2002).

## Psychometric Methods of Risk Assessment

A second type of risk assessment approach uses psychometric tests. These measures are quite promising and have proven useful in assessing violence risk in various forms of family violence (Barbaree et al., 2001; Campbell, Sharps, & Glass, 2001; Milner, 1995). Psychometric measures usually have a limited number of questions, most often with a very specific focus (Winick & Kenny, 2001). For example, one form may assess whether a person is apt to become violent; another form may assess whether the person is likely to use lethal violence. The measures can yield a specific number that can be contrasted with cutting scores to identify the level of risk.

The utility of psychometric methods is strong when you have access to an appropriate measure. Appropriateness is an important consideration when using psychometric risk assessments (Campbell et al., 2001). Appropriateness includes the following considerations:

- ◆ **Reliability and validity.** A risk assessment must be reliable and valid. Low reliability or validity will make results difficult to interpret and interfere with good clinical decisions. Reliability should be greater than .80 for clinical work, and construct and predictive validity should be established.
- ◆ **Focus.** There must be a focus on the specific type of risk you seek to assess. Measures provide information only on a specific area of functioning (e.g., a measure of dangerousness does not indicate risk for sexual violence).
- ◆ **Ease of use and interpretation.** Some measures require specific educational backgrounds or are very difficult to administer and score. Such measures cannot be easily used clinically, because you may need to involve other people.
- ◆ **Sensitivity.** If you are using measures to assess outcomes or changes during treatment, the measure must have sufficient sensitivity to pick up changes during treatment without being unduly influenced by the content of treatment.
- ◆ **Honesty.** If you are using a self-report measure, the inclusion of a lie, distortion, or social desirability scale is important to ensure that the client's responses are honest.

If these conditions are met, psychometric measures can be an important element of risk assessment. They can confirm clinical hunches and yield important information for clinical intervention.

Appropriate measures can yield critical information, but family practitioners must integrate the information with their ongoing clinical knowledge (Wald & Woolverton, 1990). Specific measures cannot account for additional clinical features of the case, so you must avoid total reliance on specific measures (Maden, 2003; Winick & Kenny, 2001). Although some clinicians resist including psychometric measures as part of their practice, such measures can be an important adjunct. Psychometric methods can also supplement actuarial approaches. It is important to remember, however, the limitations of the information.

An important limitation to remember when using risk assessment instruments is that the questions included on the form limit the focus. Consequently, you will achieve limited results that are not a comprehensive view of the situation. This focus presents a clinical double bind. On the one hand, clinicians receive focused information that limits confusion based on irrelevant information. On the other hand, practitioners receive data informing them about only one aspect of a complex situation. Additional forms or data collection methods are often necessary to get enough information to make clinical decisions.

## Clinical Approaches to Risk Assessment

Actuarial and psychometric methods of risk assessment are invaluable, but family practitioners must integrate these methods with a clinical approach to practice. The role of a family practitioner is to help families to overcome problems rather than simply identify risks. The practitioner role is critical to understanding the use and implementation of the risk analysis (Doyle & Dolan, 2002; English & Pecora, 1994). Indicators of risk emerge through an ongoing, change-focused exchange with family members (Elbogen, 2002). This clinical context does not easily allow for shifting into pencil-and-paper assessments. Rather, the clinician must identify risk cues and then negotiate the focus of a session to include a more specific risk assessment.

The challenge for clinically focused risk assessment is to identify appropriate indicators of risk so that further assessment may occur. Such assessment may include the other methods, or it may involve only the clinical information. In this section we examine a clinically based system of assessing risk based on the current research on family violence and violent behavior. This framework uses the response system framework that has been described in earlier chapters.

This model of risk assessment also focuses on two dimensions of risk: immediacy (how likely violence is to occur soon) and lethality or dangerousness (how likely the person is to use severe violence). See Table 5.2. Each of these two dimensions can be rated as either high or low. In interaction with the violent individual or family members, the practitioner will hear themes in the family situation that create a concern about the current level of risk. When reflecting on the inherent risk to family members, family practitioners can use this framework of indicators to identify the level of immediacy and dangerousness in the situation. Although Table 5.2 organizes many indicators into high and low ranges of concern, the following indicators are important when considering risk in a clinical setting.

## TABLE 5.2
### Two-Dimensional Domestic Violence Risk Indicators

| High Lethality/High Immediacy | |
|---|---|
| **Affect** | **Action** |
| ◆ Feels powerless or hopeless; nothing to lose | ◆ Has used weapons to control |
| ◆ Experiences nihilistic panic | ◆ Has violated other family members |
| ◆ Feels emotionally victimized by woman | ◆ Increased physical channeling |
| ◆ Feels shamed by woman's actions or statements | ◆ Frequent and unsuccessful attempts to control |
| | ◆ Past severe violence |
| **Thinking** | **Interaction** |
| ◆ Malefic attributions regarding woman | ◆ Makes explicit threats with details of lethal acts |
| ◆ Personalizes the meaning of the woman's actions | ◆ Threatens family members concurrent with woman |
| ◆ Visualizes lethal acts against the woman | ◆ Withdrawal or loss of supports |
| ◆ Ruminates on the meaning of the woman's actions | ◆ Diminished influence over life |
| | ◆ Seeks out like-thinking people |

| High Lethality/Low Immediacy | |
|---|---|
| **Affect** | **Action** |
| ◆ Expresses love for partner | ◆ Relaxed body language versus physical channeling of stress |
| ◆ Can identify some hope for relationship | ◆ Few threatening acts |
| ◆ Feels guilty about how he has treated the partner | ◆ Long time since violence used |
| ◆ Can break negative moods | ◆ Positive (other-versus self-focused) actions |
| ◆ Identifies positive elements to life | ◆ No access to weapons |
| **Thinking** | **Interaction** |
| ◆ Balanced (positive versus negative) attributions | ◆ Positive support network |
| ◆ Cognitively mediates impulses | ◆ Mediating relationship tension |
| ◆ Low personalizing, catastrophizing, and rumination | ◆ No current use of death threats |
| ◆ Able to shift focus away from negative affect and events | ◆ Low use of coercion to control the partner |

| Low Lethality/High Immediacy | |
|---|---|
| **Affect** | **Action** |
| ◆ Feels inadequate, powerless, helpless, jealous, put down (etc.) | ◆ Never uses weapons to control |
| ◆ Needs nurture or validation from partner | ◆ Physically channels stress |
| ◆ Feels overwhelmed by events | ◆ Uses symbolic forms of violence |
| | ◆ Explosive with and controlling of the woman |
| | ◆ Sullen, inactive, and withdrawn |
| **Thinking** | **Interaction** |
| ◆ Blames the woman for affect | ◆ Accusatory and jealous themes |
| ◆ Denies risk of violence through focus on desired outcomes externalizing onto woman | ◆ Reacts to the woman's actions |
| ◆ Ruminates on negative event or affect | ◆ Uses threats to try controlling the woman |
| ◆ Does not identify or accept options for action | ◆ Escalation of tension in interactions |
| | ◆ Demanding, negative, and hostile |

| Low Lethality/Low Immediacy | |
|---|---|
| **Affect** | **Action** |
| ◆ Low personalized affect | ◆ Low or no channeling of stress |
| ◆ Rapid recovery from volatile affect | ◆ Often helpful and willing to engage in activities |
| ◆ Lack of extreme affective reactions | ◆ Fulfills obligations to work, self, and others |
| ◆ Often denies affect in the situation | |
| **Thinking** | **Interaction** |
| ◆ Accepts situations rather than attributing personalized meaning | ◆ Can engage in give and take without struggles |
| ◆ Ruminates less on negative events | ◆ Often gives in too much or remains unassertive |
| ◆ Rational abilities more pronounced | ◆ May cater to the woman or at least consider her needs |
| | ◆ Can be very open and friendly |

In assessing risk from a clinical position, the family practitioner must identify and capture the meaning associated with indicators of risk. In the following sections we identify specific indicators drawn from clinical practice and the family violence research. The indicators are organized according to immediacy and dangerousness. Notice that there are processing system and action system indicators. The processing system indicators include thinking and feeling, whereas the action system indicators include behavior and interaction. When monitoring for these indicators, you often must listen carefully. If an indicator appears present, explore the theme fully to understand the nature of the potential risk.

## Indicators of High Immediacy

Several response patterns appear to indicate that a family member is priming for, or potentially building up to, a volatile state. Most often, indicators are embedded in how the potentially violent person reacts to events. These indicators should serve as red flags indicating that someone is potentially volatile. In the assessment phase, explore each indicator that appears present; try to gain a sense of the potential risk. If risk seems substantiated, shift efforts to de-escalating the situation or arranging for safety. Consider the following cues that can emerge in a family or individual session.

*Processing Indicators*   The first set of indicators focuses on the potentially violent family member's emotional reactions and thinking patterns. Thinking and feeling are often central to violence risk. You need to understand the thinking and internal experience of the violent person. Cognitive-affective patterns can cause a violent individual to externalize and then amplify her emotions. As emotional states become amplified and rationalized, the risk of violence becomes greater. We will examine this escalation pattern after looking at the indicators. The violence pattern often begins with feeling reactions. Consider the following affective responses as indicators of potential risk.

- ◆ **Shame.** Violence is often associated with perceived slights and attacks on the self-concept feelings of being "shamed" (Dutton et al., 1995; Menninger, 1993). Researchers have found that negative and unstable self-concepts are associated with violence (Ragg, 2001). If a client makes statements indicating that someone in the family has caused him great shame, increased concern for safety is warranted.
- ◆ **Powerlessness.** When a violent individual feels powerless, efforts to control family members may increase (Gelles & Straus, 1979; Straus, 1973). Increased power needs and low assertion skills seem to elevate risk (Coleman & Straus, 1986; Dutton & Strachan, 1987).
- ◆ **Discounting.** When the behavior of family members causes the violent person to feel discounted (e.g., like they don't matter or don't exist), anger is likely to result and escalate (Menninger, 1993).

- ◆ **Inadequacy.** One of the highest-risk times is when the relationship with the other family member is clearly impervious to the violent family member's control efforts (Dutton, 1988; Dutton & Strachan, 1987; Edleson & Gruszinski, 1988; Gondolf, 1987; Hart, 1984; Prince & Arias, 1994; Ptacek, 1984). This is most pronounced during power struggles and other exchanges, wherein the violent individual invests heavily in controlling the outcome in an exchange with other family members.

- ◆ **Hostility.** Hostility and malefic attributions are associated with an escalation of problems (Dutton, 1986; Dutton & Browning, 1987; Dutton & Strachan, 1987; Murphy & O'Leary, 1989; Rosenbaum & O'Leary, 1981). Verbal hostility and malefic attributions frequently precede violence (Athens, 1977, 1980).

- ◆ **Emotional agitation.** Research findings indicate that as emotions become agitated, rationality decreases (Dutton & Browning, 1988; Goldfried & Sobocinski, 1975). If the violent individual is both irrational and externally focused, risk is heightened (Eisikovits, Edleson, Guttmann, & Sela-Amit, 1991).

The emotional state of the potentially violent family member is accompanied by thinking patterns that escalate the situation. These thinking patterns tend to externalize responsibility for the feeling and then justify reactions. Listen for the following themes when assessing a situation where a family member may be at risk of violence:

- ◆ **Paranoid thinking.** Jealous or paranoid thoughts (e.g., "she wants to leave me," "my child is out to get me") can indicate increased risk (Roy, 1982). Higher levels of controlling behaviors can help predict actively violent relationships (Ragg, 1998).

- ◆ **Polarized thinking.** Actively violent people often respond to situations with all-or-nothing propositions (Bedrosian, 1982). This lack of a middle ground is problematic because it removes the potential for negotiation, cognitive mediation, and compromise.

- ◆ **Obsessive thinking or ruminating.** It is not unusual for violent people to adopt obsessive thinking patterns. As people become obsessive, they begin to filter out and disregard thoughts and alternatives that can de-escalate the situation. This behavior further erodes rationality (Dutton & Browning, 1988).

- ◆ **Cognitive distortion.** As situations escalate, violent people often become less rational (Bedrosian, 1982). Cycles of personalizing, catastophizing, and overgeneralizing the impact of a family member's behavior are common forms of distortion that fuel the importance of negative events and violent behavior.

*Behavioral and Interactive Indicators*   The second set of immediacy indicators focuses on behavior and interaction that may indicate increased risk. Family practitioners may observe or hear these dynamics described by family members. You will often hear of the behavior and interaction, and this becomes the flag that risk may be evident. When you hear these indicators, try to explore the processing systems that occurred before the behaviors. This pattern of exploration is useful because violent people are more likely to shut down during behavioral exploration, but they desperately want their feelings validated.

◆ **Use of threats.** Verbal violence, psychological violence, and threats are commonly used to control family members (Edleson, Eisikovits, & Gottman, 1985; Maiuro, Cahn, & Vitaliano, 1986). Such behaviors escalate prior to the use of violence (Murphy & O'Leary, 1989).

◆ **Overcontrol.** There is a strong association between violence risk and attempts to control the victim (Goldsmith, 1990; Prince & Arias, 1994). In situations where control cannot be maintained, risk tends to increase (Bernard & Bernard, 1984; Dutton & Browning, 1988).

◆ **Substance use or abuse.** Irrational and violent behaviors are exacerbated by the use of alcohol and other mind-altering substances (Edleson & Gruszinski, 1988; Okun, 1986). Several studies find a strong association between alcohol abuse, hostility, and violent incidents (Davies, 1985; Finn, 1985; Hastings & Hamberger, 1988; Oriel & Fleming, 1998; Renson, Adams, & Tinklenberg, 1978; Slade, Daniel, & Heisler, 1991; Sonkin, Martin, & Walker, 1985). Substance abuse intensifies the level of need, increases the obsessive position in relation to problems, and lowers the inhibition to use violence (Bushman & Cooper, 1990; Hastings & Hamberger, 1988; Sonkin et al., 1985).

## Indicators of Potential Dangerousness

Concurrent with cognitive emotional patterns suggesting that violence may be imminent, some thinking patterns can indicate a propensity for more severe forms of violence. Although no thinking pattern is a direct predictor, some thinking patterns allow the family member to justify highly abusive acts. Professionals in the domestic violence field have identified the following four thinking patterns as possibly indicating lethal types of risk.

1. **Malefic attributions.** Malefic attributions justify the use of severe violence by diminishing the victim's humanity or value. Basically, the violator identifies responses in the other that he considers inexcusable and then uses these responses as a platform for casting the other person as evil. This thinking pattern becomes a justification for extreme retaliation (Athens, 1977, 1980).

2. **Omnipotent disregard for legal limits.** When the family member maintains an attitude of total disregard for laws, conventions, and societal sanctions, there is a clear message that she does not acknowledge any limits on her

behavior (Andrews, 1989; Kropp, Hart, Webster, & Eaves, 1994). Such feelings of omnipotence often translate into high-risk behavior.

3. **Attitudes of ownership and objectification.** If the family member treats others as possessions rather than as people, he overrides many cognitive structures that inhibit the use of severe violence. He ceases to view family members as people with rights; he sees any actions against the other family members not as violations but rather as an extension of his privilege (Campbell et al., 2001).

4. **Cognitive degeneration.** In extreme situations, family members can become so emotionally agitated that cognitive functions are overwhelmed. This can become dangerous because cognitive mediation of violent impulses becomes unlikely. Thoughts of suicide, a common example of this level of degeneration, indicate very high risk (Stawar, 1996).

Along with the four processing indicators of dangerousness, there are five behavioral indicators suggesting that a family member may be at risk of using very severe forms of violence. If you hear about these types of behavior, you should raise concerns about the level of violence possible. Although the threat may not be imminent, you should be concerned about the potential for very severe violence. These five behaviors are as follows:

1. **Stalking.** Professionals in the field consider stalking behavior as an indicator of serious risk (Brewster, 2003; McCann, 2001; Meloy, 1997). This behavior is more common in marital situations after separation, but any time a family member begins following someone and using clandestine methods of tracking people, you should be worried about how far the behavior may extend. Risk goes up when stalking is combined with use of threats and there has been a past relationship with the potential victim (Brewster, 2003; Rosenfeld & Harmon, 2002).

2. **Public use of violence.** Typically, family members seek to hide their violence from people external to the family (Sonkin et al., 1985). Inherent in hiding violence, there is an attempt to maintain a public image of nonviolence. When a family member feels free to violate others in public, this inhibition is not present, suggesting that the person has very few mechanisms limiting the use of violence. People with a pattern of violating others in full public view should be considered high risk for severe forms of violence.

3. **Use of weapons.** A family member who has used weapons against a person in the past should be considered dangerous. This consideration should be acute if she has ready access to weapons (Campbell et al., 2001).

4. **Past patterns of violence.** The family member's past patterns of violence are important in understanding the level of risk. If the family member has engaged in impulsive violent behavior with people in and outside of the family, the risk of severe violence is elevated (Grann & Wedin, 2002). This includes violence against animals. If the family member has seriously harmed or killed a pet, the risk for severe violence is very high.

5. **Threats.** Threats indicate that a person is prepared to use violence. When a family member uses threats, pay attention to the content of the threat. If a family member describes the details of his violence when threatening other people, risk should be elevated. The details of the threat operate like a plan in evaluating suicide risk. The existence of a plan suggests that the family member has considered and visualized the violent act and is prepared to use violence.

## Assessing the Emergence of Risk

In family practice, your role makes risk assessment an ongoing rather than a static process. At times you will be called on to conduct an assessment with recommendations; but mostly, you are working with the risk situation on an ongoing basis and trying to help the family members change. Consequently, the family practitioner is mandated to ensure safety while still attempting to keep family members engaged in the change effort (Szmukler, 2003). Because you are constantly seeking to reduce the risk, the process of risk assessment is different from that used for a static assessment (Borum & Reddy, 2001).

Even when dangerousness is high, immediacy may be low, rendering the current level of risk somewhat low. The indicators of risk just described tend to vacillate depending on the family situation. A framework is needed to understand how the risk progresses and changes. The flowchart in Figure 5.8 depicts a cognitive-affective model for understanding the priming of the violence. Notice how the indicators present in this model allow you to identify the current level of risk depending on the current processing indicators. Using this model can provide a method for identifying how immediate the risk is at a specific time.

When using the model in Figure 5.8, consider the risk moderate if the family member is externalizing his feelings and blaming others. This would suggest that he is holding others responsible for his emotional state. If there are indicators that the family member is amplifying his emotions, risk will be moderate to high, depending on your knowledge of the family patterns. The risk elevation is due to the family member's entry into rumination. This is a critical point. If the rumination involves deflecting attempts to engage the person in problem solving or cognitive mediation, the immediate risk is very high, and safety planning should become a priority.

Concurrent with using the model in Figure 5.8, practitioners need a systematic approach to identifying the prognosis for ongoing risk (Borum & Reddy, 2001; Elbogen, 2002). Such assessment builds on how the family members respond to the indicators and interact on an ongoing basis. If there are ongoing family patterns that keep emotions externalized, risk will be a continuing concern. This risk elevates if the violent family member retains thinking and behavioral patterns that help her to avoid taking self-responsibility (Borum & Reddy, 2001; Campbell et al., 2001). The risk increases if indicators of dangerousness are present, because the use of violence is patterned behavior.

**Figure 5.8** Cognitive-Emotional Processing and Violence

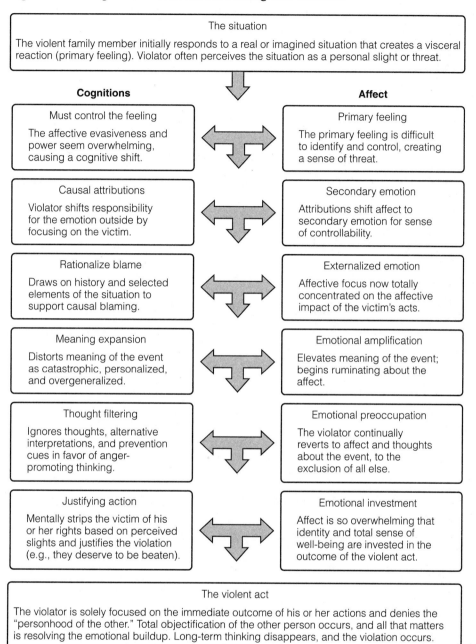

**The situation**

The violent family member initially responds to a real or imagined situation that creates a visceral reaction (primary feeling). Violator often perceives the situation as a personal slight or threat.

**Cognitions**                                              **Affect**

**Must control the feeling**

The affective evasiveness and power seem overwhelming, causing a cognitive shift.

**Primary feeling**

The primary feeling is difficult to identify and control, creating a sense of threat.

**Causal attributions**

Violator shifts responsibility for the emotion outside by focusing on the victim.

**Secondary emotion**

Attributions shift affect to secondary emotion for sense of controllability.

**Rationalize blame**

Draws on history and selected elements of the situation to support causal blaming.

**Externalized emotion**

Affective focus now totally concentrated on the affective impact of the victim's acts.

**Meaning expansion**

Distorts meaning of the event as catastrophic, personalized, and overgeneralized.

**Emotional amplification**

Elevates meaning of the event; begins ruminating about the affect.

**Thought filtering**

Ignores thoughts, alternative interpretations, and prevention cues in favor of anger-promoting thinking.

**Emotional preoccupation**

The violator continually reverts to affect and thoughts about the event, to the exclusion of all else.

**Justifying action**

Mentally strips the victim of his or her rights based on perceived slights and justifies the violation (e.g., they deserve to be beaten).

**Emotional investment**

Affect is so overwhelming that identity and total sense of well-being are invested in the outcome of the violent act.

**The violent act**

The violator is solely focused on the immediate outcome of his or her actions and denies the "personhood of the other." Total objectification of the other person occurs, and all that matters is resolving the emotional buildup. Long-term thinking disappears, and the violation occurs.

◆ **EXERCISE 5.3   RISK ASSESSMENT**

You are working in a family counseling agency when a male client phones, needing an emergency session. He seems very depressed on the phone, so you give him your next opening. When he comes in for the session, he seems more sullen than sad. As you talk with him, he says he thinks his wife is going to leave him. He expresses anger that she has found another man and wants to move out. As you explore the situation, it

Structuring the Family Exploration

becomes evident that this man's wife has not said she is leaving, nor has she announced that she is having an affair. When you question him, he responds, "She doesn't have to say anything. A man just knows when something is up. She is not looking me in the eye, and she is always on the phone. When I come in the room, her voice changes and she hangs up soon after." He is very emphatic that his wife is having an affair and is planning to leave. You engage him in the following exchange.

*THERAPIST:* So, have you talked to her about your suspicions?

*MALE:* She would only lie about it. I have to catch them in the act.

*THERAPIST:* It seems like it is taking over your life.

*MALE:* That's a good way to put it. I can't think about anything else. Just her and him.

*THERAPIST:* . . . if there is a him.

*MALE:* Oh . . . there's a him alright; and when I catch them, they will learn it is not right.

*THERAPIST:* You are not going to do anything stupid, are you?

*MALE:* No, they are the stupid ones. They need a good lesson.

*THERAPIST:* I am concerned that you are getting all bent out of shape, and there is still no proof that she is planning to leave.

*MALE:* She is up to something . . . you know we have wedding vows, and they are very serious.

*THERAPIST:* I can tell you are thinking a lot about this. How is this affecting your work?

*MALE:* I can't work. I have been phoning in sick. I can't do anything.

Based on your exchanges with this man, you are concerned about the risk to his wife. Identify the themes and content that make you think there is elevated risk. Identify themes based on the four response systems (thinking, feeling, behavior, and interaction). List as many risk identifiers as possible for each area.

   1.  Thinking themes:

2. Feeling themes:

3. Interaction themes:

4. Behavior themes:

## Summary

Family practitioners use many frameworks and models to help organize the gathering and processing of information. In this chapter we looked at four models that can be used when making a family assessment. Each framework focuses on different family elements because family practitioners must have several frameworks or models in their repertoire to help with different areas of family assessment. The frameworks presented in this chapter provide some models for common clinical concerns. As a practitioner, you will need to continue adding new models to your repertoire and expand your abilities to assess new areas of family functioning.

# Critical Content

1. Different elements of the family have different frameworks for organizing and making sense of the family information.
2. The genogram is useful for gathering and tracking multigenerational information and family system development. It uses symbols, lines, and notes to organize information.
3. The four-cell model is useful for tracking and assessing the development of the adult relationship. This model takes a cognitive-behavioral approach to organizing information.
4. The parental functions model organizes information into the parental functions and assesses how the parents are functioning. This model builds on information contained in Chapters 3 and 4.
5. The risk assessment model guides practitioners in using different indicators to assess the current level of risk and dangerousness.
6. All of the models simply organize knowledge in a manner that allows family practitioners to easily draw clinical conclusions.

# Suggested Readings

Borum, R., & Reddy, M. (2001). Assessing violence risk in Tarasoff situations: A fact-based model of inquiry. *Behavioral Sciences and the Law, 19*, 375–385.

McGoldrick, M., Gerson, R., & Shellenberger, S. (1999). *Genograms: Assessment and intervention* (2nd ed.). New York: Norton.

Milner, J. S., & Campbell, J. C. (1995). Prediction issues for practitioners. In J. C. Campbell (Ed.), *Assessing dangerousness: Violence by sexual offenders, batterers, and child abusers* (pp. 20–40). Thousand Oaks, CA: Sage.

## Chapter 6

# Moving From Assessment to Treatment

In the first two chapters of this section, we explored the data collection aspects of family assessments. By now you will have gained some insight into methods for collecting and organizing information for assessment purposes. In this chapter we examine information on how to frame and present the assessment information as a written assessment and how to build on the assessment to develop a treatment contract.

## Theoretical Grounding

This chapter is largely atheoretical. Building on all of the models reviewed in earlier chapters, here we consider general guidelines for completing a formal assessment and building a treatment plan. Some theoretical models—such as narrative, constructivist, and solution-focused approaches to treatment—rarely use a formalized assessment because the treatment direction tends to emerge during the family-therapist interaction. Other models—such as structural (Minuchin, 1974), (trans)intergenerational family systems (Bowen, 1978), and cognitive-behavioral—more often will spend time organizing thinking into a formal assessment process. When developing a preferred approach to family treatment, you will find that the perceived value of a formal assessment shifts depending on your eventual theoretical approach.

Although the clinical utility of a formal assessment shifts according to theories, you will most often do so because agencies and funding sources expect some sort of formal assessment. Requirements for these assessments are likely to change, depending on the organizational expectations. Typically, organizational expectations for formal assessment serve the organization by meeting accreditation, decision-making, or program needs. The clinical utility of such assessments vacillates depending on how organizational needs are balanced with clinical needs.

As a family practitioner, you may conduct assessments for family court systems. These assessments have very rigorous requirements. The rigor in a court-related requirement stems from the adversarial nature of the court system. Very often there are opposing lawyers in a court system, and seldom do opposing lawyers agree on the merits of any assessment. You must thus frame the assessment in a way that leaves little ground for argument. In this chapter we examine a model that will not only survive family court scrutiny but also contain clinically relevant information. The materials are consequently pragmatic rather than theoretically driven. Theory becomes important when you are drawing inferences and making recommendations; but largely, formal assessments must conform to the expectations of the organizations funding the assessment.

## Toward Formalizing the Assessment

Developing a formal assessment from the data you have collected involves four steps, in which you are organizing and drawing inferences from the family information. These steps require you to use both theory and knowledge, in concert with the family, to develop an understanding of the family situation. From this understanding, the family and practitioner can develop a direction for change.

1. Identifying critical themes in the data
2. Attributing meaning to the array of themes
3. Inferring potential solutions
4. Developing goals and planning intervention

Although each step in the assessment process is linked and blended with the others, in this chapter we will explore each phase separately.

## Identifying Critical Data Themes

During data collection, the family practitioner faces a quagmire of relationships, individual and shared histories, beliefs, misunderstandings, standardized scale scores, and other information about the family situation. The breadth and depth of the information can be overwhelming. Consequently, the practitioner explores aspects of the situation with the family in order to identify important themes.

In this first step, you and the family members begin to distinguish potentially meaningful information from superfluous information. This step requires you to maintain a naïve position with the family, picking up on information that appears important (based on knowledge and theories) and exploring the potential importance with the family. Information, events, and issues that achieve mutual importance are highlighted for further reflection and consideration as you gather more information.

In the decision-making process about what constitutes meaningful data, you must be aware of your cultural, personal, and professional biases. Such biases can lead you to label information as meaningful based on semiconscious processes. Common sources of bias are visceral reactions and predetermined frameworks.

◆ **Visceral reactions.** Many family practitioners attribute meaning to elements of the family story for which they have affective responses or visceral reactions. Frequently, such reactions originate in practitioner responses to aspects of the family that create subjective bias in the worker. Such bias can cause a practitioner to misattribute meaning. The resulting assessment is based on the practitioner biases rather than on family events and needs. For example, a therapist was hired to conduct a custody assessment on a Native American child. The child's Caucasian grandparents were seeking custody. The biological (teenage) mother was living on a reservation, and she was living with multiple relatives. Her mother was concerned about the grandparents because of potential abuse. They met with the therapist and shared their history. The therapist reacted to the mother living with multiple relatives and referred to the family as chaotic. The therapist recommended placing the child with the grandparents because they had a more structured family life.

◆ **Predetermined frameworks.** Some practitioners have predetermined systems of assessment that govern what is considered meaningful and what is not considered important. These frameworks may include formal intake and assessment protocols determined by the agency, standardized systems of assessing, and/or assessments based on available services. The practitioner follows the protocols with a minimum of critical thinking and reflection. The protocols often miss important elements, resulting in faulty assessments. For example, a practitioner was instructed to assess mental functioning and American Psychiatric Association *Diagnostic and Statistical Manual of Mental Disorders (DSM)* criteria with every family using standardized measures. The worker followed these instructions for every family, yielding recommendations focused on maternal mental health and child disorders. When the guardian's office approached a supervisor about an assessment when the practitioner was on vacation, the supervisor read the assessment on file and informed the guardian that the mother was depressed and the child appeared to be oppositional. The guardian's office asked some questions about the child's danger to others, but no information was on file. The guardian expressed concern about this lack of information, because the child had been setting buildings on fire. The supervisor continued to review the file but found no mention of fire setting in the assessment report.

When reviewing information and identifying meaningful information, you must also balance your expertise and knowledge with the lived expertise of the family members. Practitioners bring to this equation critical thinking skills, theoretical understandings, and past practice. The family brings their lived experience, knowledge of the family situation, and their own theoretical understandings. Each party (worker and family) will raise observations and concerns to see how the other responds. Over repeated explorations, you and the family will identify critical elements in the situation that are promoting family problems.

# Attributing Meaning to the Array of Themes

Critical themes and elements identified by the practitioner and family initially have few connections to each other and almost stand alone as elements of the problem. After identifying these elements, the family practitioner must work with the family to infer meaning and connections in the information (Rober, 2002). It is only by attributing meaning that a deeper understanding of the family situation can be achieved.

To attribute meaning, you and the family will build on the traces of information to organize the information into a package that has explanatory power. You contribute to this organization by bringing in theory and knowledge that can help explain the family situation. The family members consider potential explanations and compare them to their experience in the family. If the potential explanations fit the lived experience, the meaning is retained. Piece by piece, meaning is attributed to the critical elements in the situation and a model of explanation is built. Two steps are inherent in the attribution process:

1. Organizing the information
2. Generalizing the meaning to the family situation

## Organizing the Information

In family practice, you will use your knowledge to help the family members organize the information into a coherent picture. Family members often experience problems in a fragmented manner. When working with the family to build an image of the problem, you will take the fragmented elements and help the family draw connections. As connections and organization are achieved, the family story starts to become clearer. Here are some typical methods of organizing data:

- ◆ **Chronological organization** (e.g., start with dating relationship and move to the present). This is a good method of organizing the data when the assessment involves a lot of historical information. By including a timeline, you can help family members start to see the milestones and events as associated to the current problem.
- ◆ **Organizing into known subsystems** (e.g., parental, spousal, and sibling subsystems). Subsystem organization is useful when you are assessing a complex system that may become confusing if each subsystem is not addressed individually.
- ◆ **Organizing into narrative elements** (e.g., protagonist, antagonist, symbolic meaning). Such organization often works best when you are assessing

an individual (or a less complex system) and historical information is not being used to understand the situation.

The interactive development of meaning is clinically important during the assessment phase. However, sometimes the service system requires a different type of organization. In situations where family practitioners are required to produce written assessment reports, the mutual meaning achieved with the family members often must be adjusted to fit the external assessment criteria.

- ◆ **Organizing into diagnostic criteria** (e.g., *DSM* criteria). When the funding demands, or when you are working in a medical setting, it is common to organize the material into the different *DSM* axis categories.
- ◆ **Organizing into predetermined domains** (e.g., subscales on the tests). Often the methods used in the assessment have an inherent organization that can be used to organize and describe the findings.
- ◆ **Organizing into theoretical domains** (e.g., subsystem functioning). Many practitioners organize their inner thinking according to theoretical constructs such as subsystem functioning. These constructs lend themselves well to written reporting.

Although these organizational systems appear separate and distinct, many workers combine the types of organization. For example, you might want to organize the raw data of a family assessment using a historical framework (individual development leads to dating, followed by marriage and family formation, and then the problem situation). If standardized tests are used, you can organize the data into the domains predetermined by the tests selected. The assessment write-up may then be organized according to subsystem functioning.

It is useful to consider the written and externally dictated assessment report as something different from the interactive assessment. In the interactive assessment, the practitioner and family collaborate on meaning. In the written assessment, the practitioner becomes the expert in the family situation. When engaging in the written assessment report, ensure that the content reflects the interactive meanings that have been attributed. Significant divergence can create problems in the helping relationship.

## Generalizing the Meaning

After you have identified critical elements, attributed meaning, and organized the data elements, it is important to tease out a dynamic understanding of the family problems. This involves reflection; think about the different data elements and how they might fit with the problem situation. As you reflect on the possible linkages between the findings and the problem, consider different interpretations and configurations as you attempt to find the most plausible explanation of how the problem situation emerged in the life of the family.

As you and the family members engage in the mental rigors of drawing inferences from the family data, many elements of the family situation must be integrated into the understanding to ensure that the family's situation is understood within its social environment. Here are some important elements to integrate:

- **Integration of contextual variables** (e.g., influence of poverty, addiction, grief). Problems do not occur in a vacuum; you must consider the social, cultural, racial, historical, and relational elements that may influence the situation.
- **Integration of theory** (e.g., attachment theory, trauma theory, narrative). When you are using a theoretical base, elements of the theory become integrated with the data at points in the assessment to produce a dynamic understanding of what may be occurring in the family situation.
- **Integration of empirical findings and knowledge base** (e.g., training, research, and journal articles you have read on the subject). As with theoretical integration, when you are current in your reading, new information from journals and other professional literature becomes influential in drawing inferences about the data.
- **Integration of political processes** (e.g., agency mandate interpretations, community pressures). Just as you integrate bias, you also often integrate agency politics and protocols. For example, if the agency insists on using the *DSM* procedures, many data elements will not be considered in the interpretation. Such integration can become political when agencies subscribe to specific ideologies, or when community events (e.g., school shootings) have sensitized agency personnel to specific issues. These biases should also be reviewed and addressed.

Inherent in generalizing the information to develop an understanding of the family situation, an explanation of the family problems should develop. The family data, perspectives, and your own critical thinking should all converge to explain the nature of the presenting problems. The emerging definition of the family situation should explain what precipitates and contributes to the family problems.

While generating an explanation of the family problems, you must avoid service-related temptation. Avoid the temptation to resort to status quo or rote responses. In many agencies, multiple clients all receive the same services regardless of the assessment (e.g., parent training groups). In such circumstances, assessments may become history-taking exercises rather than opportunities to work with the family members to establish an understanding of what needs to change. A second outcome in service-focused settings is categorizing problems according to available services rather than family needs (e.g., the person needs anger control treatment).

## Inferring Potential Solutions

As an image of the family problems emerges, a sense of direction begins to develop. Direction should flow from the explanation inferred from the family information. As you explain the family situation, potential solutions should become evident. If you are working in a purely clinical role, the direction will prompt intervention. In other settings, you are expected to make recommendations in a formal assessment report.

Regardless, the assessment should advance the practitioner's and the family's understanding to the point that both know what must occur to correct the situation.

Intervention direction is usually fairly abstract. Contracting later organizes this direction into goals and objectives. You seldom need to be specific in an assessment report, because the assessment is a document explaining the situation rather than a document outlining a plan. The assessment, however, must be able to ground the eventual service contract by providing a rationale for all of the interventions to follow.

At this point in the assessment, it is important to avoid the pitfalls associated with service-based (rather than family-based) thinking. Some workers will simply list a number of referrals at this point rather than describing what the family needs to accomplish. Here are some examples of problematic direction statements:

◆ Making vague categorical statements (e.g., learn parenting skills) rather than identifying specific areas for change (e.g., increase consistency in providing discipline).

◆ Identifying services without first identifying what the family needs to accomplish (e.g., needs substance abuse treatment rather than needs to decrease drinking).

◆ Relying on solutions that are easy and readily available even if they won't actually help the family resolve its situation (e.g., attending AA although the family was referred due to child abuse).

You must be clear about specific changes needed in the family to correct the situation. Such changes typically will involve a family accomplishment that can be described. If the direction statement does not provide for an observable change in family behaviors or interactions, then the direction for change is likely to be vague or incomplete. When you attempt to build on such statements through treatment plans or interventions, their lack of clarity may pose problems.

# Elements of the Assessment Report

After achieving a clear explanation of the problem and ensuring the direction for change, you will often be required to prepare an assessment report. When writing an assessment report, you must structure it so that people can easily read and understand the family situation. In this section we examine report elements and consider suggestions for organizing the family material. Typically, practitioners use section titles to help organize the assessment. Report structures change according to the practitioner's role and organizational protocols. The following section headings are common to many assessments.

1. **Background or Presenting Request.** Describe the background for the assessment, including events precipitating the assessment, the purpose of the assessment, and the anticipated outcomes of the assessment.
2. **Assessment Procedures**
   ◆ Outline the assessment procedures used (e.g., scales, who attended interviews, observational opportunities, third-party informants).

◆ Also include a paragraph on how the family responded to the assessment procedures. Example considerations: Were they hesitant or easy to engage? Did they complain? Did they try to verbally influence you to believe certain things? If you used a lie scale or social desirability measure, what were your findings? How do all these considerations affect the validity of the statement?

3. **History**
    ◆ Writing the history section can be difficult because there is often a lot of information to organize. Frequently, families also present information in an unorganized manner. It is useful to use frameworks for organizing this information both during the interview and in the report.
    ◆ One method of organizing historical information is to use the beginning, middle, and end framework. Divide the history into three sections: (a) the early period before any problems existed, (b) the period when problems were developing or becoming evident, and (c) the current state of the problem. This analysis will change from situation to situation, but organizing your thinking according to three distinct periods of time can keep you from getting lost in the details.

4. **Findings**
    ◆ At this point in the report, you will introduce the critical information gleaned through the assessment procedures. Often you will integrate a group of findings that seem to conceptually fit together. For example, with a couple having difficulty with arguments, you might write, "There were elevated problem-solving scores for both Bob and Velma on the Couples Interactional Style Inventory. These elevated scores indicate that both Bob and Velma tend to avoid problems rather than attempting to table problems for resolution. This finding is consistent with their backgrounds. Bob and Velma's families of origin were both very volatile. Bob and Velma both described learning to avoid problems as very young children."
    ◆ With the findings associated with interviews and observations, you may also want to use frameworks for organizing the information.
       (a) For couples, you might try the four-cell model outlined in Chapter 5. This framework organizes background information, biological information, processing systems, and action systems for each person. You can then extrapolate from each model and develop the model for the current relationship.
       (b) For families, you can organize the information according to family subsystems and functions (e.g., parental functions include nurturing, accessibility, guidance, and discipline).

5. **Assessment**
    ◆ In the assessment section, you build on the findings to develop an explanation of the problem. This section references the important findings and ties them together into a coherent picture of the family problem. For example, "Bob and Velma currently do not have a model for

problem solving. Based on their backgrounds, each developed methods of avoiding problems. This works for a short time, but tension eventually escalates and causes volatile arguments."

◆ You will use the findings to generate hypotheses about the family situation. This section requires clear thinking about the situation. Often the challenge to this section is avoiding jumble and jargon. It is useful to make short clear statements and then ground them in the data that led to the conclusion. Grounding statements in the findings is important because it protects the conclusions if the assessment is challenged.

6. **Recommendations.** Recommendations build on the assessment, making suggestions about what will need to change in order to rectify the problem. The recommendations provide the foundation for goals and objectives. Avoid listing services that the families should receive because services are part of a treatment plan rather than an assessment. For example, "The couple needs to develop a system for solving problems and settling differences. Currently, no system is in place other than yelling and blaming each other. The cycle of arguing can be interrupted through acquiring skills such as tabling, exploring, and selecting and implementing solutions. Couple counseling is recommended to help them to improve their problem solving."

## Sample Family Assessment

In this section, we will examine an example of a family assessment. When reading this example, notice how the general assessment areas were applied to a situation where there is no clinical expectation of change, but rather an assessment of capacity for a court proceeding. Even with this focus, the background, findings, and recommendations are clearly followed. Notice also that the assessment needed to integrate cultural elements from Native American culture.

---

*Family Members:*  Ms. Nancy Greenbird, Mr. Steve Greenbird, Ms. Magena Jones, and Ms. Leah Jones

*Background to the Assessment:*  This assessment was commissioned by the Tribal Office of the Turtle Point Reservation to determine whether the home of Nancy Greenbird and her husband Steve is an appropriate setting for raising the preschool child known as Leah Jones. The family is currently engaged in a custody dispute with Ms. Jones's in-laws, Tom and Frances Smyth. Reportedly, the Smyths, the nonnative paternal grandparents, want sole custody of Leah and have petitioned, stating that the Greenbird home is not an appropriate setting to raise Leah.

The specific assessment questions to be answered are:

1. Is the Greenbird home an appropriate setting for raising Leah?
2. How is the child functioning in the Greenbird family?
3. Are the present arrangements potentially harmful to Leah's development?

*Assessment Procedures:*  This assessment was conducted using the following procedures:

1. A psychometric assessment of family of origin influences, current personality, and current family situation using the Parental Acceptance and Rejection Questionnaire and the Personality Assessment Questionnaires.
2. A parent-child observation session with Nancy Greenbird, Magena Jones, and Leah Jones. Observations occurred through use of a play therapy setting during a conjoint interview with the adult women.
3. An interview with the co-parental team of Nancy Greenbird and Steve Greenbird.
4. Two interviews with Nancy Greenbird and Magena Jones.
5. One home visit to the Greenbird home to observe family functioning and assess the family environment.
6. Telephone interviews with professionals who have observed family members in interaction. These professionals were selected based on their level of training and expertise to judge parental behavior concurrent with their past observations of family interaction in nonagency settings. Two informants were selected according to the criteria:
   ◆ Mr. Cecil Adams of the Child Abuse Prevention Program of Turtle Point Tribal Office
   ◆ Beverley Strong of the Parent-Child Program of Turtle Point Tribal Office and leader of the NEW START early language development program

*Background:*  Leah was born to Magena Jones (age 17) and her boyfriend Tom Smyth (age 20) on January 7, 2000. The Greenbird family reported that after Leah was born, Magena Jones and Tom Smyth lived with the Smyth family for about three days, until which time Magena's incision became infected and she returned to her mother's home to ensure proper care. Magena recounted that the move home was difficult for Ms. Smyth as she had reportedly assumed she would be raising the infant as her own child.

After the move back to Ms. Greenbird's home, Magena and Leah maintained weekly contact with the Smyth family, often staying at the Smyth home on weekends. While staying at the Smyth home, Magena reported that she and Tom Smyth maintained the primary caregiving roles but Ms. Smyth was usually in the home. Magena further reported that Mr. Smyth was often absent and quite uninvolved with the child.

After Magena and Tom ceased romantic relations, contact with the Smyths became sporadic until the death of Magena's grandfather. Around the time of the death and funeral, the Smyth family was asked to care for the child. Upon picking up the child after being cared for by the Smyths, Ms. Greenbird noted changes. First, Ms. Greenbird noted that Leah fought the removal of her clothing when it was time for a diaper change. The second change noted by Ms. Greenbird was a rash near Leah's vagina. A third change was Leah rubbing toys against her vagina. While these changes were noted, they were not immediately interpreted as meaningful until the next day, when Mr. Smyth picked up the child and Leah began stiffening her body and resisting when being placed in the car seat. These changes caused the family to stop visits with the Smyths. When visitation was terminated, the grandparents (Smyths) petitioned the court for full custody of Leah.

*Assessment of Primary Parent Figures:* In assessing the Greenbird family, this assessment focuses on more than one parent figure to reflect the full caregiving system. Consequently, Mr. and Ms. Greenbird and Magena are included as parental caregivers.

*Ms. Nancy Greenbird* Ms. Greenbird reports that she was raised in a most difficult environment with both parents active alcoholics. Ms. Greenbird further reported that the parents used to sell bootleg alcohol out of the home, resulting in a steady flow of drunken people in the home. In this early period of her life, Ms. Greenbird reported that her older brother had fondled her genitals. She further reported witnessing domestic and child abuse in the home. For about a two-year period during middle childhood, Ms. Greenbird was removed from the parental home and placed in the foster system.

As Ms. Greenbird aged, she drank heavily. At that time, Ms. Greenbird reportedly made poor choices in cohabitation partners, living first with a drug abuser and then with an alcoholic. These men reportedly did not attend well to family matters and were at times volatile. After marrying Steve Greenbird, Nancy began to grapple with her personal history. In the eighteen years the couple has been together, she reports that she has stopped drinking and adopted new coping strategies. She has now achieved more than nine years of sobriety, completed educational upgrading, and taken several courses on child development.

While making changes in her life, Ms. Greenbird relied heavily on the Tribal elders, Native American spiritual leaders, and other tribal-focused counseling services. Ms. Greenbird and third-party informants report that she has worked very hard to overcome any impact of her family of origin. She has taken part in traditional healing circles and has worked intensely with a sexual assault counselor at Turtle Point. Ms. Greenbird has become involved with helping parents and children through the Parent-Child Program at Turtle Point (NEW START early language development program). This program focuses on using the parent to promote language development in young children. Ms. Greenbird reportedly participated in the group that adapted the program for First Nations Peoples. The program leader, Ms. Beverley Strong, described Ms. Greenbird as the "ideal parent" in the program. Ms. Strong reported that she had observed positive, happy, and relaxed interactions with Leah. Ms. Strong added that Ms. Greenbird was a punctual, responsible, and highly motivated parent.

Ms. Strong reported that both she and the officials of the NEW START program were so impressed by Ms. Greenbird's interactions with Leah that they selected the parent and child to be part of an instructional video. Ms. Strong reportedly had contacted Ms. Smyth to have Leah brought to the taping because the Smyth family had access on the day of taping. Reportedly, Ms. Smyth began an involved discussion of custody rights and obligations and would not bring Leah to be part of the production.

When Ms. Greenbird arrived, she reportedly operated as an assistant rather than a model. Ms. Greenbird has been asked to assist the next time the NEW START program is offered.

This author's direct observations of Ms. Greenbird found stable affective bonds between all parental figures and Leah. When the issue of the custody battle was raised, Ms. Greenbird's eyes welled up slightly with tears, but she was able to regain control of her emotions if allowed a moment to collect herself. When speaking of her own victimization experience (a single incident with her brother), she remained calm and direct in her expression. However, when speaking of children being victimized or when talking of her desire to keep children from being harmed, her eyes would well up. These were the only moments of emotional fluctuation noted in the interviews.

The psychometric assessment of Ms. Greenbird included: (1) the Parental Acceptance and Rejection Questionnaire to assess the nature of Ms. Greenbird's relationship with both of her parents; (2) the Personality Assessment Questionnaire to assess the impact of her parental relationships on her personality development; (3) the Parental Acceptance and Rejection Questionnaire focused on her own parental functioning to assess whether her personal history has affected her parenting abilities.

Ms. Greenbird's responses on the Parental Acceptance and Rejection Questionnaires about her parents indicated a lack of warmth and heightened neglect in her family of origin. This finding was most significant with her father, with an absence of warmth and heightened neglect being above the average range. Paternal ratings in the area of aggression were heightened but within the normal range. Ms. Greenbird's mother, however, scored within the normal range.

Because there was some question that Ms. Greenbird's personal history might be interfering with her current adjustment, the Trauma Symptom Inventory was also administered. This instrument includes three validity scales, all of which indicated no attempts to malinger or create favorable impressions. The Trauma Symptom Inventory contains ten clinical scales measuring trauma reactions in the respondent. In each of the scales, Ms. Greenbird scored in the range of emotional health. Clinical problems are indicated when T scores exceed a value of 65. In all of the clinical scales, Ms. Greenbird's T scores ranged between 39 and 51, suggesting an absence of post-traumatic effects from her personal history. The findings of little impact from personal history were supported by findings on the Personality Assessment Questionnaire, which found Ms. Greenbird to be either in or above the normal range of functioning on all scales.

The psychometric assessment of Ms. Greenbird's parental functioning occurred through both a self-report and an assessment of her by Magena. These reports provided measures of (1) warmth, (2) aggression and hostility, (3) neglect and indifference, and (4) rejection. Both the self-report and report by Magena placed Ms. Greenbird in or above normal ranges of functioning. The same pattern of responses was evident between the two respondents, with many values being almost the same. These findings suggest that Ms. Greenbird's parental functioning is unimpaired.

The evidence from psychometrics, direct observations, and observations from third-party reports lead this assessor to conclude that Ms. Greenbird is unimpaired in her parental and personal roles. She does have some areas of sensitivity regarding maltreatment of children, and at times these areas tend to cause some tearful moments. There is no indication of functional impairment in the parental role.

*Mr. Steve Greenbird*   Like his wife, Mr. Greenbird came from a somewhat difficult family background. His father was alcoholic and at times quite volatile. Mr. Greenbird also drank heavily during his late adolescence and early adult years. Mr. Greenbird worked hard to overcome any adversity experienced during his childhood. In regaining control over his own life, Mr. Greenbird has become very involved in his culture. He has become recognized for his contributions to his community. Cub Scout troops continually approach him to instruct youth in native culture and environmental concerns. He works at the Turtle Point First Nations Heritage Center and volunteers in many roles to assist with cultural events and ensure community pride.

Mr. Greenbird completed the Parental Acceptance and Rejection Questionnaire on both of his parents. This instrument measures the levels of warmth, anger and hostility, neglect and indifference, and rejection experienced in his relationship with both parents. Mr. Greenbird's responses on the measures indicated poor paternal modeling of warmth and affection from his father, but all other areas for both parents fell within normal ranges. Mr. Greenbird's responses regarding his mother indicated no significant problems in the mother-child relationship.

The lack of paternal warmth appears to have had some impact on Mr. Greenbird. His responses on the Personality Assessment Questionnaire indicated a slightly depressed score on Emotional Reactivity. This score was still in the normal range, and Mr. Greenbird scored better than normal in all other areas, but normal in emotional reactivity. This suggests that he may be somewhat uncomfortable with identifying, formulating, and communicating his emotional responses to specific events. This finding should be interpreted with caution given the absence of American Indian norms.

Direct observations did indicate some slowness in emotional reactivity with Mr. Greenbird. These observations came when the assessor required him to complete the questionnaires. Although Mr. Greenbird complied with the requests without question, he appeared to be disturbed by the nature of the activities, which he indicated by avoiding eye contact and giving short answers. After being encouraged to discuss his feelings, he did so in a direct and honest manner. These exchanges were interpreted as indicating an ability to discuss his reactions to events but with some hesitation about initiation of emotionally laden conversations.

Mr. Cecil Adams reported that he has observed Mr. Greenbird in many roles on the reserve. His observations of Mr. Greenbird are consistent with the above findings. Mr. Adams describes Mr. Greenbird as a man who derives significant strength from his culture and from his accomplishments in the community. He further describes Mr. Greenbird as someone who does not immediately express feelings verbally. Mr. Adams stressed that even though verbal expression was not immediate, Mr. Greenbird was clearly able to process his feelings through work, music, and cultural activities. In this processing, if someone opens the door for a discussion of his feelings, he described Mr. Greenbird as open and able to discuss his internal states.

Although psychometric results and observations suggest some affective discomfort, Magena's assessment of Mr. Greenbird on the Parental Acceptance and Rejection Questionnaire did not indicate any difficulties in the parenting dimensions. Rather, Mr. Greenbird was rated as above average in all areas. This suggests that he is able to respond with acceptance, warmth, and calmness in his parental roles. Based on the findings and observations, it appears that Mr. Greenbird is not immediate in his expression of feelings; but this has little impact on his parental role. He is described and was observed to be amply responsive to the children and able to engage at an emotional level as required by the situation.

*Magena Jones*  Magena was born from the union between Ms. Greenbird and a previous partner. Magena has experienced only Steve Greenbird as a father figure, and she has no recollection of her biological father. Magena was reportedly a bright child and an independent thinker. As Magena moved into puberty, her quest for independence was at times challenging for Mr. and Ms. Greenbird. The Greenbird family adhered to strict behavioral rules and would seek out the children and retrieve them from friends' homes if there was a concern that drinking or other prohibited behaviors might be occurring. Magena tended to resist the strict rules, but Mr. and Ms. Greenbird were consistent in their enforcement of limits.

At the age of 12, Magena met Tom Smyth at a friend's home. Tom was 15 years old at the time, and Magena found she was attracted to the young man. When they were both at a dance at the Moose Lodge, the two of them reportedly began a dating relationship. The dating activities during this period most often involved the consumption of drugs and alcohol to the point of intoxication. Magena reported that there was frequent conflict between Mr. Greenbird and herself due to his disapproval of her dating an older male. Magena was apparently staying out late and would often stay at Tom's home after "partying" together. Magena reported that Mr. Greenbird wanted her to break off the relationship and stop seeing Tom Smyth.

Magena recounted that she and Tom did not want to break off the relationship, so Tom asked his mother if Magena could live with the Smyth family. Ms. Smyth agreed that Magena could live in the Smyth home. Reportedly there was no discussion with the Greenbird family in making this decision. Magena stated that she moved in with the Smyths at the age of 12 and stayed with them for about six months. Initially Tom slept on the couch and Magena slept in Tom's room. After a period of time, both Tom and Magena slept in Tom's bedroom.

Magena reported stress and tension while living in the Smyth home. Apparently Tom had a somewhat volatile relationship with Ms. Smyth and would often storm out of the house when she attempted to curb or control his behavior. At one point Magena was told to move back with her family as a punishment to Tom. Magena reported that Tom had vandalized some vehicles and broken into a friend's apartment, stealing some valuables. In response to this misbehavior, Magena was not allowed to live with Tom for a period of time.

The relationship between Tom and Magena was reportedly volatile, and after the fall term at school, Magena arranged to return home. Although many rules were restated upon her return home, Magena and Tom continued their pattern of substance abuse and contact. Near the end of her 13th year, Magena became pregnant. Fearing that Mr. Greenbird would phone the police on Tom, she kept the pregnancy secret until the seventh month. Mr. Greenbird reported that he was very angry when Magena's pregnancy was disclosed and wanted to have Tom arrested for intercourse with a minor. Magena and Ms. Greenbird resisted this action, and no report was made to the authorities.

After the birth of Leah, Magena reported that there was stress with Ms. Smyth concerning differences in parenting beliefs. Magena reported that she and Tom shared the parenting responsibilities when in the Smyth home; however, Ms. Smyth would often criticize their parenting actions even though Magena was acting as instructed in parenting class. For example, Ms. Smyth reportedly told Magena to constantly feed the child even when the child was refusing to eat.

Magena and Ms. Greenbird completed the Personality Assessment Questionnaire on Magena, assessing Magena on the dimensions of anger and hostility, dependence, negative self-esteem, negative self-adequacy, emotional unresponsiveness, emotional instability, and negative worldview. No apparent problems were noted in any of these dimensions; Magena's scores clearly fell in ranges indicating either normal or above normal emotional health. It should be noted in these findings that Ms. Greenbird's scores for Magena indicated more problem proneness than Magena's self-report did. In particular, Ms. Greenbird scored Magena as less healthy than self-reported in areas of hostility and emotional stability. This difference notwithstanding, Magena scored in the normal range of functioning on both self and maternal reports. Particular areas of strength appeared to be self-conception in the areas of positive esteem and adequacy. Magena also completed the Parental Acceptance and Rejection Questionnaire on her own parental style. Again, no problems were noted.

Magena Jones presents as a young teenage mother struggling with achieving a balance between her responsibilities as a parent and her developmental needs. This creates some inconsistencies in her life; at times she will pursue activities with her friends and live away from the Greenbird home, and at other times she will act very responsible and live at home. Currently, Magena is living in the Greenbird home. Overall, Magena appears to be a good student and very capable in her studies. She has reportedly achieved strong grades except for the period when she was living in the Smyth home. Magena reported that she was achieving failing grades during this period, but her grades improved to about an "A" average upon returning home.

As a parent figure, Magena appears to assure that Leah is cared for even when she is attending to social needs appropriate for her age. Many times Magena counts on Ms. Greenbird and other family members to care for Leah. Magena also will often take Leah with her and her friends, providing there will be no risk to the child. Both third-party respondents reported seeing Magena taking Leah to community events. Their observations at these times are that Magena is attentive to the child's needs even though she is attending the events with friends. The Greenbirds also report that Magena does not bring Leah into settings where "partying" might create an atmosphere that could be undesirable for a child of Leah's age.

*Assessment of Family Functioning:* To assure healthy emotional and physical development, parent figures need to (1) provide nurturing, (2) be geographically and emotionally accessible, (3) provide the child with guidance, and (4) use discipline to help the child learn to live within acceptable limits. These four functions provide a base that promotes a sense of positive self-worth concurrent with the ability to adhere to societal standards and limits. This portion of the assessment focuses on how the primary caregivers and the family environment perform nurturing-accessibility and guidance-discipline functions.

*Nurturing and Accessibility Functions*   The Greenbird family exhibits several strengths in the area of child nurturing. Direct observation indicates that there is a clear and responsive attachment between Leah and the three parenting figures. This is indicated by Leah's eye contact, lack of hesitation with the caregivers, and differential use of caregivers to meet her emotional needs. Attachment is also indicated in the way that caregivers attend to her needs without hesitation. For example, in the playroom, Leah expressed fear about the male "punch dummy." This therapeutic aid, which looks somewhat like a large, bald, expressionless figure, created discomfort for Leah. She summoned Magena and told her that the figure made her scared. Without hesitation, Magena removed the dummy and then followed up by asking the child if removing the figure helped. Ms. Greenbird was equally attentive when called by Leah.

In observing Leah with all three parent figures, she appeared to use them differentially to meet her needs, often turning to them for comfort when first introduced into the play setting and when this author arrived at the home. Every time Leah approached a parent figure, he or she would attend to the child even though they were in adult conversation. While in the home, Ms. Greenbird's older children were equally attentive to Leah.

The observational findings were consistent with findings derived from the parent functioning measures. The Parental Acceptance and Rejection Questionnaire measured warmth and affection, aggression and hostility, negativity and indifference, and undifferentiated rejection between parent and child. Mr. and Ms. Greenbird completed the questionnaire, as did Magena Jones. In reviewing the results, no problems were noted in any area. Rather, strengths were found, with all parent figures supplying Leah with a responsive and nurturing environment.

Further evidence of strengths in this area was supplied by the third-party reports. Both informants had observed the family members with their children in natural settings. Mr. Cecil Adams spoke of both parents' attentiveness to the children. He reported that both Mr. and Ms. Greenbird would often bring the children with them and involve them in many aspects of their lives. Ms. Beverley Strong spoke at length of how Ms. Greenbird maintained a positive and responsive approach to encouraging Leah to develop language and other developmentally appropriate skills. Both Mr. and Ms. Greenbird were described as providing high levels of warmth, acceptance, and responsiveness. Magena was less commonly observed in interaction with Leah, but comments were made that she tended to take the baby out with her often rather than leaving her with alternate caregivers.

The model of caregiving in the Greenbird family is strongly influenced by Chippewa culture. Parental roles are not limited by the nuclear structure inherent in Caucasian family roles. Rather, multiple caregiving agents work in concert with each other to assure a broad range of nurturing options and highly accessible caregiving options. Although Ms. and Mr. Greenbird act as the primary parent figures, Magena and an Aunt Glenna also occupy caregiving functions. This report has been able to directly access only three of the caregivers in the caregiving system, but they are the caregivers who have the most influence. Other caregivers live within about 100 feet of the family home and are reportedly involved in ensuring a responsive and available system. Within the native culture, the caregiving system appears to be strong in its ability to nurture and respond to children.

*Guidance and Discipline Functions*   Guidance and discipline functions also seem to occur within the native framework. Mr. Greenbird's interactions with this author stressed responsibility for the environment, obligation to community, and pride in the children's native heritage. One third-party informant, Mr. Cecil Adams, reported that this was a consistent message given to the children. Reportedly, Mr. Greenbird has encouraged the older children to participate in cultural activities and operate a radio show on the native station.

Ms. Greenbird was observed promoting areas of behavioral and developmental guidance. In the playroom her interactions with Leah were consistently accompanied with explanations of why actions were taken. For example, as she dressed the child to go, she explained that they needed to go so she could get her rest. This type of interaction was ongoing, spoken in a calm voice, and positive in orientation. Such interactions can help the child to internalize limits and healthy patterns of living. Ms. Beverley Strong of the NEW START program reported similar patterns of interaction in helping Leah engage in the developmental activities of the program. Both Mr. and Ms. Greenbird appear to be cognizant of the potential dangers in the Turtle Point environment. They adopt strict codes of behavior for the children and maintain them with consistency. This includes behavioral codes as well as restricting the people with whom the children can associate.

In general, the family situation at the Greenbird home appears to provide a solid base for child development. The family structure is heavily influenced by the Chippewa culture with a network of caregivers who are responsive to Leah. This network of caregivers is cohesive, with a strong native value base and a celebration of native heritage. Such a value base can be instrumental in helping Leah to form a positive sense of self-worth and capacity. Testing of family members indicates that positive self-worth is consistent among the family members. The family system also appears to provide adequate limits and guidance functions to promote responsible behavior patterns. Rules are clear and appear to be consistently enforced.

*Assessment of Leah in the Current Situation:*   At this interviewer's first meeting with Leah, she appeared to be a bright and pleasant child while being held in Ms. Greenbird's arms. Upon entering the interview situation, however, she seemed quite nervous. She did not respond readily to this interviewer. Several attempts were made to engage Leah verbally, but she would not respond to verbal prompts. There was no misbehavior in her lack of responsiveness. Rather, Leah would stay close to Mr. Greenbird and Magena and would not verbalize directly to the interviewer. She did, however, respond readily to Ms. Greenbird and Magena.

This same pattern of nervousness was noted during home visits, even though Leah acknowledged that she remembered the interviewer. When this pattern was explored with Ms. Greenbird and Magena, they stated that Leah tended to be somewhat nervous around males. They stated that this included Mr. Greenbird; however, when this interviewer first entered the family home, Leah sought to be picked up by Mr. Greenbird. It is possible that as this male entered the setting, she experienced Mr. Greenbird as a source of safety.

Leah also displayed some anxiety regarding a punch dummy in the play therapy room. This dummy stands about five feet tall and has a white canvas body and head. Leah was so unnerved by the dummy that she summoned Magena into the room and told her that "he is scaring me." The dummy looks clearly male in its natural form, due to an apparent baldness and an absence of identifiable female traits. Leah could not settle at all until the dummy was removed.

Leah appeared to be attached to both Ms. Greenbird and Magena, and although nervousness was present, she showed no hesitation in approaching Mr. Greenbird. While in the playroom, Leah would call out for both Ms. Greenbird and Magena separately, seeming to have a differential preference for who was to respond. At one point, Ms. Greenbird started to respond; this resulted in a second call for Magena.

Aside from the apparent fear of males, Leah appears to be developing well. Her tendency to call for caregivers was clear, and there was no hesitation in her voice. It might be concluded that she vocalizes her requests with a full expectation that her needs will be met. She also is able to maintain eye contact with parent figures without looking down or breaking her glance. This can also be interpreted as indicative of personal confidence in the relationship.

Ms. Beverley Strong of the NEW START program also observed Leah's sense of esteem and confidence. Ms. Strong stated that Leah is a happy and confident child who responds well to the positive approach observed with Ms. Greenbird. Leah was described as spontaneous in her interaction. Ms. Strong also explained that Leah was developing well in her language skills.

The current system of passing Leah back and forth between two families seems to be more protective of the grandparent rights than Leah's rights. Leah is a three-year-old child and cannot assert her own rights in the face of the emotional intensity reported at the adult level. She is currently being bounced from one day at the Greenbird home and a native system of caregiving to a different family system the next day. This practice cannot promote secure development. It is important that she be able to form a positive sense of identity. It is unlikely that drastic living changes and perpetual conflict can accomplish this task. In this task, there must be sensitivity to Leah's clear native features. It will be important that wherever she lives, her heritage can be celebrated and normalized. Positive identities cannot be formed if this child simply feels different. She must feel special. Feelings of being special might be difficult in a setting that fails to value her native ancestry.

Based on the information gleaned though the above assessment procedures, this interviewer concludes that the Greenbird family is clearly an appropriate setting for raising this child. Strengths are noted in the individual, parental, family, and cultural levels. Concerns about parental stability appear to be largely unfounded, given the native family structure and healing that has occurred among the caregivers.

---

In this assessment, you can observe the factual nature of describing data in the early stages of the assessment. Notice that most information is provided either in a descriptive form or with qualifiers such as *reportedly*. These methods of data presentation protect practitioners from challenges if the assessment should be used in court. After the data presentation, you can also observe the use of theory and cultural information to make sense of the data. In this assessment, parenting functions (described in Chapter 2) provided a framework that was adjusted using the culture ring (described in Chapter 3).

## ◆ EXERCISE 6.1   FORMAL ASSESSMENT ELEMENTS

Three critical skills are associated with documenting the formal assessment: presenting data, drawing inference, and developing direction. For this exercise you will use the information generated in Exercise 5.2 (the four-cell model exercise on assessing relationships), which you completed in Chapter 5 for the assessment information. Different aspects of the formal assessment will require you to draw on specific information.

1. **Presenting historical information.** Using the information in the environment cell, describe your family (who was in the family). After describing the family, outline the power structures and rules around which the family was organized. Make sure you try to use quotes, qualifying statements (e.g., *reportedly*), and are as descriptive and factual as possible.

2. **Presenting belief-behavior systems.** Describe one of your most critical belief systems, values, or codes of living. Begin by describing the family dynamic that promoted the belief (be descriptive). Then outline how the dynamic influenced your beliefs and values. Finally, describe how this dynamic leads to behaviors or interactive patterns. Again, be sure to keep

the description either descriptive or qualified. Also ensure that your description of current thinking and behaviors is linked to the family influences.

3. **Making an inferential assessment statement.** Based on your inherited beliefs and behaviors and those of the partner you used during Exercise 5.2, select a set of beliefs and behaviors that seem to conflict, and infer how these contributed to the demise of the relationship. Be sure to start with a statement such as, "It appears that core value differences may have contributed to the relationship breakdown." Next describe the belief for yourself, and then describe the partner's belief. After these descriptions, outline how they conflicted and discuss the problematic outcomes.

## Developing Treatment Goals

In the sample family assessment presented earlier, the report ended at the recommendation phase. In an ongoing clinical situation, the assessment outlines the situation in a way that leads to measurable goals and objectives. The goals emerge from the assessment by identifying exactly what must change for the problem situation to be resolved.

Developing treatment goals involves complex thinking. After developing a clear understanding of the problem through the assessment, the practitioner must identify critical elements that must change to alleviate the family problem. The elements that must change will involve processing (how people think and feel) and actions (what people say and do). The practitioner and family carefully consider the elements to identify common themes. It is the common themes underlying the problem elements that provide the goals for change. As such, the goals extend the direction outlined in the recommendations and begin to describe concrete plans for change.

## Formulating Goal Statements

Goal statements provide a clear marker that, when accomplished, will improve the family situation (Armstrong, 1997). The concept of family accomplishment is critical when formulating goals because it keeps the focus on family-level changes (Armstrong, 1997; Ellis, 2003b; Stewart, 1997). Many workers confuse goals and services. Such workers present services as a goal (e.g., the father needs anger management training). This is common in case management types of jobs, where the worker wants to find other people to help the family. However, locating services is the worker's goal rather than the family goal.

Another problem associated with goal statements is a lack of clarity. Many times a vague or unfocused statement is used in place of a strong goal statement (Armstrong, 1997). Vague or unfocused statements do not provide a direction or vision for the changes that need to occur. A strong goal statement will have the following six features:

1. The change is a family accomplishment altering how family members function within the situation (Ellis, 1993).
2. The change has a direction for change that allows observation, for example, increase or decrease the frequency, severity, or duration (Armstrong, 1997; Ellis, 2003b).
3. There is the potential for measuring and verifying that the goal has been accomplished (Ellis, 2003b; Stewart, 1997).
4. The change goal is realistic for the family and can be accomplished given their circumstance (Sills & Wide, 1997; Van Audenhove & Vertommen, 2000).
5. The goal is adequate for solving the presenting problem (Ellis, 2003b).
6. The goal lends itself to establishing clear objectives that can achieve the overall goal (Stewart, 1997; White, 2002).

Table 6.1 contrasts different goal statements. All of the goal statements focus on the same couple, so you can easily compare the different statements. The problems with different statements are also listed in Table 6.1, so you can understand why the different goal elements were not achieved. When reviewing the table, observe how a strong goal statement leads the couple to a very clear and measurable venture. You can evaluate success and identify when the goal is accomplished.

An adequate goal statement provides a strong indication of what will be accomplished through service. When families sign off on a contract agreeing to such a goal, they should know the focus of therapy, the direction for change, and how to know when the goal is accomplished. Such a goal not only provides vision for the family, but is ethically grounded by providing informed consent about the focus of service.

**TABLE 6.1**
**Weak and Adequate Goal Statements**

|  | Weak—Vague | Weak—Unfocused | Weak—Service Oriented | Adequate |
|---|---|---|---|---|
| Goal Statement | The couple needs to learn to get along better. | The couple needs help with their communication skills. | The couple needs an anger control group. | The couple will decrease their arguing from three times daily to once per week. |
| Problem | Nothing is defined enough to know what actions and interactions must change. | There is no direction for change and just a broad category of skills to focus the change. | There is no direction or accomplishment. If they show up once, the goal is met. | No problems—this statement (a) is an accomplishment, (b) has direction for change, and (c) is measurable. |

## Establishing Objectives

Although goals can give family members a sense of what to expect, they do not specify what must occur in order to achieve the outcomes. This gives rise to the need for objectives. Just as goals identify the direction of the assessment, objectives divide the goal into smaller tasks that when accomplished will achieve the goal (White, 2002). Objectives are nested in the goals. The goals are nested in the assessment. The assessment, in turn, is nested in the presenting problems. This logical flow must exist for the contract to truly address the presenting problem.

In setting objectives, you must be true to the assessment and goal statement by breaking down intervention direction to the most concrete level. For example, if you want to decrease fighting, the task of identifying objectives will include looking at the pattern of fighting identified in the assessment. From the pattern, you can begin to break down the elements that might promote fighting and those that can be changed. Possible objectives might be to interrupt automatic patterns, to decrease taking other people's comments personally, to develop a system of problem solving, and to make other concrete efforts that will decrease fighting. Note that some elements might not be available to change. For example, if the couple fights because they cannot pay their bills and you cannot influence their finances, increasing money is not a realistic objective. However, you can develop objectives around how the couple deals with situations out of their control or with their money management skills.

To establish the objectives for each goal, consider what needs to happen to ensure that the goal is accomplished. Objectives often focus on skill development (e.g., learn problem-solving skills, learn how to interrupt escalation, identify problems before they begin, identify "buttons," take control of buttons, etc.). The assumption is that skills deficits maintain the problem situation, so the objectives (skills) can rectify the situation.

There are often many objectives, because you will identify several elements that seem to contribute to the problem.

In writing up objectives, it is important to ensure that the following three elements are present:

1. The goal is broken into component tasks that, if achieved, can accomplish the goal outcome (e.g., if the goal is to stop fighting, the tasks might be to learn time-out strategies, follow a problem-solving format, develop check-in procedures to address problems before they become too large, etc.).
2. The tasks are concrete achievements, each related to the others (in the first element, you can see that each objective represents a piece that can contribute to the success of the goal and that builds on the other objectives).
3. The objectives logically lead to techniques or methods that can help accomplish the objective.

## Additional Contracted Elements

Based on the goals and objectives, workers must consider methods that will be used to accomplish the changes in the family system. Some service contracts also spell out the methods to be used in accomplishing the family goals. In direct service, this might include spelling out the configuration of meetings (e.g., individual sessions, couple sessions, group sessions, home visits, etc.) that will be used to accomplish various objectives and goals.

It is in a case management situation that the services will be included. Notice the difference that is implied by including the service as a method rather than as a goal. Identifying the service as a method nests it within a specific objective and goal. It is implicit that the service will help the family toward a specified accomplishment. The worker can then follow up with the family members after they have attended the service to monitor objective and goal achievements.

Some contracts will limit the number of sessions or weeks according to the different goals and objectives. This can be useful in keeping people focused, but some workers also find it limiting because it does not allow for a lot of divergences. If you work in a setting that enforces limits on the numbers of sessions or weeks, the importance of clear, achievable goals is accentuated.

A final contracted element is monitoring. Goals and objectives are useful only when they are monitored. You must be able to review progress toward goals so that accountable service can be assured (Stewart, 1997). With measurable goals, you can periodically take a measure of progress (e.g., "over the past two weeks, how often have you fought?"). Such monitoring should occur at regular intervals, so that the pace of change can be observed and treatment can be altered accordingly. Such monitoring can also be used for documenting outcomes. Some agencies document how many goals are achieved or partially achieved to demonstrate service effectiveness. On an individual worker level, such measurement also provides invaluable feedback for guiding professional development.

## Sample Plan of Care

The following sample contract is modeled after a contracting system used in a child and family therapy agency. This contract contains all of the elements discussed in this section. Notice how the goals and objectives work together to outline exactly what the family members can expect while they are in service. The explicit nature of the contract also focuses the intervention. Notice how reasons for referral lead to an update. The update, in turn, provides a rationale for goal setting. Notice also how the goal statements are clear statements of a family accomplishment that provide a foundation for identifying objectives.

Agency settings will have different expectations of the treatment plan or contract. In some settings, all of the contractual elements will be required; other situations may require only a few. Regardless of the written expectations, it is useful to negotiate all of the elements with the family members so expectations are clear. Family members should have input into the goals, just as they have had input throughout the assessment process (Van Audenhove & Vertommen, 2000).

---

### Sample Treatment Plan

---

Date: 2/15/06

Client/Family: Woods, Diane

Child's Date of Birth: 6/22/92

Client No.: 5908                                    Counselor: Mark Ragg

---

Projected Discharge Date: 6/15/04

---

| Reasons for Referral: | Present Status: |
|---|---|
| Diane and her mother are in frequent power struggles that escalate to the point of screaming, yelling, and physical fighting when Diane is asked to perform chores. | Still a problem |

---

**Interdisciplinary & Agency Involvements:**
CPS has been involved for about six months. Worker: John Dole
Diane sees a counselor in the school system around attendance issues. Worker: Jan Fuentes

---

**Current Understanding:**
The power struggles tend to occur whenever mother instructs Diane to complete her chores. Diane rolls her eyes and sighs, which causes mother to increase her volume to gain compliance. The two escalate volume and verbal attacks, which can lead to violent exchanges. There has been no substantiated abuse, but pushing and shoving occurs at least once per week. Often father is in the home watching television or meeting with an intern. When the situation escalates, he comes into the room and

tells mother to back off and keep things calm. Mother then leaves the room and Diane goes back to what she was doing before the argument.

| | |
|---|---|
| **Family Goal(s):** | 1. To decrease the frequency of arguments between Diane and her mother |
| | 2. To decrease the severity of the arguments between Diane and her mother |

| | |
|---|---|
| **Objective(s):** | 1. To develop positive exchanges between Diane and mother |
| | 2. To develop cuing methods to identify and preempt arguments |
| | 3. To identify "hot buttons" and affective states that promote the arguments |
| | 4. To develop methods for expressing and discussing feelings that underlie the anger |
| | 5. To implement a time-out procedure to de-escalate arguments |
| | 6. To increase parental cohesion and support |
| | 7. To increase paternal functioning in discipline |
| | 8. To develop a system of reinforcing task completion |
| | 9. To develop acceptable options for venting anger |

| | |
|---|---|
| **Method:** | Parental meetings with Mr. and Ms. Woods |
| | Full family meetings on alternate weeks |

| | |
|---|---|
| **Time Frame:** | Weekly meetings for the first eight weeks |
| | Meetings every other week for the remainder of the time period until anticipated termination in June |

**Tasks for Client/Family:**

All family members will attend meetings as outlined above.
All family members will complete tasks as outlined in meetings.

**Tasks for Therapist:**

Therapist will conduct parental and family sessions as outlined.
Therapist will construct and follow up on tasks.
Therapist will be available for one midweek telephone consult for each family member if needed.
Therapist will maintain telephone contact with school counselor and CPS worker.

**Tasks for Others:**

CPS worker will monitor the level of fighting and risk in the home.
School counselor will monitor Diane's reactions to family work.

**Evaluation Procedure:**

Frequency of fights will decrease from four per day to one per week.

Severity of fights will decrease from weekly physical contact to no physical contact in the final two months of service.

**Family Participation:** The following client/family members agree to implement this treatment plan.

_____Diane_____ , _____Mother_____ , _____Father_____ ,

**Additional Participants:** In addition to the client/family members agreeing to participate in this treatment plan, the following people agree to participate according to the roles and tasks outlined above.

_____John Dole_____ , _____Jan Fuentes_____ ,

**Attendance:** It is required that all client/family attend all scheduled sessions with the therapist. If two sessions in a row are missed without advance notification (24 hours) or if attendance is below 80% of the scheduled appointments, the case will be reviewed and may be terminated. This is necessary due to the high demand for service. Client/family members can expect that the counselor will also make every effort to attend appointments and avoid changing or missing appointments. If the counselor fails to meet this expectation, any client/family member can request a review of the case with a supervisor.

**Active Participation:** People engaged in the therapy process must be active participants. This means that issues are discussed openly in therapy and all homework assignments are completed as discussed. Furthermore, there will be no alteration of treatment decisions without discussion between the therapist and client/family. Client/family members can expect the counselor to actively participate and to remain focused on these contracted goals. If the counselor fails to participate as agreed, any client/family member can request a review of the case with a supervisor.

**Task Completion:** Client/family members and therapist all agree to complete the tasks outlined in this contract. If either party fails to complete their agreed tasks, the case will be reviewed with a supervisor so a decision can be made concerning continued treatment. Client/family members can also expect the counselor and others to complete agreed tasks. If this is not evident, any client/family member can request a review of the case with a supervisor.

**Date of Plan of Care Review:** April 15, 2004

**Signatures/Date:**

_____

Notice in the plan of care that there are only two goals. Each goal is specific to a single behavior, making the expected change very clear. The goals are somewhat abstract but have a clear and observable direction for change. The changes will also represent a family accomplishment. The two goals produce nine objectives. When reviewing the objectives, you will be able to identify how achieving the objectives should meet the goals. The objectives also provide a focus for the work. After working with the family to identify each objective, you should have a very clear sense of what they need to accomplish in order to meet their goals. Finally, details of the work are outlined—who will attend, who will provide support, and the nature of contacts—so that the family knows exactly what to expect.

The write-up of the assessment and the contract form the basis for the family service provision. Although the formats of assessments and contracts are likely to change across agencies, there will be similarities in how information is organized and used to guide intervention. This is very important in family practice, because families are often the focus of services. In agency practice, there must be an organized system of understanding and planning work with these complex systems.

## ◆ EXERCISE 6.2   GOAL SETTING

Based on the elements of strong goal statements, read and critique the goals statements listed below. For each goal statement, identify the problems with the statement. After identifying the problems, write a new goal statement that meets the criteria for a strong goal statement.

1. Bob and Fred are going to change how they solve problems.

   a. What is wrong with this goal statement?

   b. Write a new goal statement that meets the requirements of a strong goal statement.

2. Thelma will attend anger management classes.

   a. What is wrong with this goal statement?

b. Write a new goal statement that meets the requirements of a strong goal statement.

3. Fiona will improve her parenting skills.

a. What is wrong with this goal statement?

b. Write a new goal statement that meets the requirements of a strong goal statement.

4. Tom will enhance his ability to listen.

a. What is wrong with this goal statement?

b. Write a new goal statement that meets the requirements of a strong goal statement.

_____

# Summary

The information gathered during the exploration process must be organized so that a treatment direction emerges. Family practitioners work collaboratively with the family members to identify important milestones, events, and information to explain the family situation. From the negotiated meaning, the family practitioner and family arrive at an understanding of the family problems and a direction for intervention. The understanding and general direction are often documented as an assessment report. The direction is refined by negotiating a treatment contract including goals, objectives, and expectations.

# Critical Content

1. Information must be sorted and organized to make it easier to understand.
2. As the information is organized, the practitioner and family select the important elements and attribute meaning to the events and milestones.
3. As meaning is attributed to the different information elements, an image of what is causing the family problems emerges. This image is highlighted by the practitioner and validated by the family members.
4. The assessment takes the understanding and organizes data so the problems can be explained. The explanation should provide a sense of what must change.
5. The direction for change is included as part of the assessment, but must be further elaborated to identify goals and objectives.
6. Goals must fit specific criteria to be clinically useful. The practitioner must negotiate with the family to identify specific goals and objectives.
7. Goals and objectives form a contract that outlines what will occur during family service.

# Suggested Readings

Armstrong, P. (1997). Assessment and accountability. In S. Palmer & G. McMahon (Eds.), *Client assessment* (pp. 115–133). Thousand Oaks, CA: Sage.

Ellis, A. (2003). Helping people get better rather than merely feel better. *Journal of Rational-Emotive & Cognitive Behavior Therapy, 21,* 169–182.

Lew, A., & Bettner, B. L. (1999). Establishing a family goal. *Journal of Individual Psychology, 55,* 105–108.

Van Audenhove, C., & Vertommen, H. (2000). A negotiation approach to intake and treatment choice. *Journal of Psychotherapy Integration, 10,* 287–299.

## SECTION III

# BUILDING THE WORKING ALLIANCE

In this section of the text, we explore the critical skills associated with engaging family members and starting the change process. Although this section follows the information about assessment (Section II), the engagement processes occur simultaneously with assessment. Section III follows the assessment discussions because the first two sections of the book involve frequent use of theories, knowledge, and thinking. In Sections III through V of this book, we focus primarily on interpersonal skills.

Section III contains three chapters that range from having initial contacts with the family to launching into change-focused work. In Chapter 7 we explore issues of inclusion and initial engagement. In family-based practice, you often must ensure that specific family members are included in service. Such inclusion is not easy, because family members are differentially motivated to begin treatment. In Chapter 7 we examine the critical issues and skills needed for helping family members enter the treatment setting.

Chapter 8 builds on the initial engagement skills. Even when the family practitioner negotiates successful entry into treatment, many family members will feign motivation and may even undermine progress. The skills and strategies explored in Chapter 8 are focused on deepening the engagement of all family members to achieve a common direction for change. These skills should coincide with the contracting skills discussed in Chapter 6.

The final chapter in this section, Chapter 9, builds on engagement strategies to motivate family members to change. Even when families have agreed on change goals, many will avoid changing because the current situation has benefits and pay-offs. In Chapter 9 we explore positioning skills and strategies that can enhance motivation and neutralize counter-change elements in the family situation. These three chapters provide a skill and strategy foundation for the change-focused chapters presented later, in Section IV of this text.

## Chapter 7

# Preliminary Engagement With Family Members

In the flow of treatment, the chapters in Section III actually deal with methods that coincide with the assessment chapters described in Section II; thus, you will experience a "disconnect" in the flow of the book. It is impossible to present simultaneously occurring events in text, because ideas must flow in a linear manner. In this book, the chapters on assessment information are presented first because they build on the "Thinking Family" section. However, in practice you will be using all of the interpersonal skills described here in Section III throughout assessment and exploration because exploration, assessment, and engagement begin at the same time. Although these skills cannot be separated in actual practice, when studying them, we can examine them one by one.

Engaging families is a unique challenge. Therapists must attend to individuals within the family system concurrent with the needs of the system to achieve full engagement in service. Many pitfalls and traps that can occur as you approach the family at the beginning of service. It is very common for one family member to decline participation. It is equally common to have a family member elect to withdraw from service after very few sessions. These events underscore the engagement challenges with families. In this chapter, we explore some of the challenges and strategies for maximizing engagement success.

# Theoretical Grounding

Although most family models consider engagement a critical stage of treatment, very few models focus on engagement issues as part of their treatment approach. Most family models advocate engaging the entire family system in treatment to ensure that all members are equally invested in the changes (Ackerman, 1970; Minuchin, 1974; Stoolmiller, Duncan, Bank, & Patterson, 1993). However, family members often do not embrace treatment and are not equally engaged in the treatment process (Miller & McLeod, 2001).

Issues of engagement have not been widely embraced at the level of family models. Although some researchers compared psychoanalytic and structural models as affecting engagement, they found that the most critical issue in engaging families was cultural sensitivity and competence (Szapocznik et al., 1988). In recent years, using postmodern approaches—notably narrative, multisystemic, and constructivist models—researchers have begun to explore methods of maximizing family member engagement in treatment (Donohue, Azrin, Lawson, Friedlander, Teicher, & Rindsberg, 1998; Henggeler, Peckrel, Brondino, & Crouch, 1996). These approaches prioritize developing a partnership with the family by allowing family members to define their situation (Gold & Morris, 2003; White & Epston, 1990). The therapist must work from, and affirm, the family's systems of attribution in order to successfully engage them in treatment. Table 7.1 provides chapter concepts, theoretical links, and recommended readings to help you understand the theories that promote a focused engagement process.

# The Challenges of Engagement

The family practitioner needs to approach family problems the way a tap dancer approaches performing in a minefield—watchfully. Areas that may seem to be simple bumps in the terrain can explode with catastrophic results if nudged the wrong way. In working with a family, you cannot trust simple definitions or potential solutions, because problems are often very complex. Each family member will have a different story to tell; yet concurrently, all of the stories will have shared elements. These differences among family members come from the following four features of families:

1. Family members have histories together that will alter their experiences of the problem situation. At the time of engagement, you will not have a full understanding of how history has caused a buildup of emotional energy in different areas of family functioning (Terry, 2002).
2. Family systems often organize around particular problem areas so that the system can continue to function despite the problem (Bowen, 1978). This is an adaptive function that is often hidden at the time of engagement. Family members may be unaware of or feel unsafe about such adaptations. Consequently, you may not be privy to important elements of the situation until a safe working alliance is established with the family you are treating.
3. Depending on his or her position in the systemic adaptation, each member of the family system has different responses (processing and action systems). You cannot assume that the responses experienced by one member

**TABLE 7.1**
**Chapter Concepts, Theoretical Models, and Sources**

| Chapter Concepts | Theoretical Models | Recommended Readings |
|---|---|---|
| Tailor treatment to the family needs. | Narrative model<br>Postmodern and constructivist models<br>Solution-focused model | Goldenberg & Goldenberg, Chapters 13, 14<br>Horne, Chapters 8, 18<br>Nichols & Schwartz, Chapters 11, 12, 13, 14, 16 |
| Balance the power in the therapist role. | Adlerian model<br>Narrative model<br>Postmodern and constructivist models<br>Solution-focused model | Goldenberg & Goldenberg, Chapters 13, 14<br>Horne, Chapters 8, 13, 18<br>Nichols & Schwartz, Chapters 11, 12, 13, 14, 16 |
| Select family members most invested in the problem. | Narrative model<br>Postmodern and constructivist models<br>Solution-focused model | Goldenberg & Goldenberg, Chapters 13, 14<br>Horne, Chapters 8, 18<br>Nichols & Schwartz, Chapters 11, 12, 13, 14, 16 |
| Understand the family perspectives. | Adlerian model<br>Narrative model<br>Postmodern and constructivist models<br>Solution-focused model | Goldenberg & Goldenberg, Chapters 13, 14<br>Horne, Chapters 8, 13, 18<br>Nichols & Schwartz, Chapters 11, 12, 13, 14, 16 |
| Validate the family members. | Adlerian model<br>Narrative model<br>Postmodern and constructivist models<br>Solution-focused model | Goldenberg & Goldenberg, Chapters 13, 14<br>Horne, Chapters 8, 13, 18<br>Nichols & Schwartz, Chapters 11, 12, 13, 14, 16 |

coincide with those of other family members. Consequently, you must ensure that each member is individually open to engagement (Terry, 2002).

4. Response system differences will produce disparate investments in problem maintenance, problem definition, and potential solutions. As their therapist, you must be aware of people's hidden agendas and investments so that true common ground can be established among the family members.

In exploring the four features of families, the astute reader will discover that you must respond to dynamics at the individual as well as system level to ensure that family members engage in service. Tuning in at the individual level must include some understanding of how the individuals and their concerns fit with the larger system. Concurrently, aspects of the larger system influence individual concerns.

Two levels of engagement are observed with families. The first is tentative engagement, which occurs when family members agree to try service. Such trials are but testing the water, with family members reserving judgment on how they will become involved. Whether the family members will remain in service depends on how the family practitioner manages the tentative stage. If family members survive this initial stage, they may achieve the second level of engagement—investment in the working alliance. This deeper level of engagement is the ultimate goal, because family members are not likely to work toward change without being engaged at this level. Because there are unique challenges at each level of engagement, we will discuss the two levels separately.

# Level 1: Tentative Engagement

Tentative engagement is the first challenge of service. The family practitioner must get the right people involved in the service. This can be a challenging task, because some family members may not identify a problem and will decline involvement. Their decision inhibits the therapist's ability to help clients achieve their goals. Tentative engagement has two phases: (a) the therapist must get people to attend the sessions or meetings, and (b) the therapist must help family members to identify a reason for continued participation.

## Getting People to the Session

The first challenge is to actually get family members to meet with the family practitioner. This is a difficult challenge, because each family member will have different responses to the thought of entering service. The practitioner must support each family member as he or she makes the decision to enter service while concurrently providing information to maximize the likelihood that each member will attend (Flaskas, 1997). This phase of tentative engagement tends to occur over three related steps:

1. Tuning in to the family members
2. Selecting the mode of invitation
3. Facilitating initial interest

*Tuning In (Shulman, 2006)*    The first step in getting people to the session is tuning in to each family member's possible experience as he or she makes the decision to attend sessions. Tuning in requires the practitioner to reflect critically on what it might be like for each specific person to be asked to participate in family-based counseling. When tuning in to the different family members, you will try to consider each person's potential concerns that might interfere with attending sessions. Here are some common issues that emerge when engaging various family members:

- **Issues of blame.** Some family members fear that they will be blamed for the family problems (Furlong & Young, 1996).
- **Issues of guilt.** Some family members know they have done things that make the family situation worse (Flaskas, 1997).
- **Issues of exclusion.** Family members may worry that their position will be ignored or discounted (Flaskas, 1997).
- **Issues of pressure.** Family members are sometimes concerned that the practitioner will take the side of other people or gang up on them to change (Flaskas, 1997).
- **Issues of culture.** Some cultural, ethnic, or racial groups are less willing to engage in therapy because there are cultural implications (Jackson-Gilfort,

**TABLE 7.2**
**Situation Blocks to Entering Family Treatment**

| Feeling | Action |
|---|---|
| ◆ Given how the referral occurred, what anxieties can be considered normal? | ◆ What behaviors has each member engaged in that could be difficult to explore? |
| ◆ What feelings do most people feel when entering your service? | ◆ What evasive tactics might be expected of each member? |
| **Thinking** | **Interaction and Relationship** |
| ◆ How might each person interpret the referral differently? | ◆ How might each person interpret the presenting problem? |
| ◆ What is the nature of interactions and relationships in the family? | ◆ How might the relationships promote or inhibit a smooth entry into service? |

Liddle, Tejeda, & Dakof, 2001; Santisteban, Szapocznik, Perez-Vidal, Kurtines, Murray, & LaPerriere, 1996).

Along with these common concerns, the family practitioner uses available information about the family situation to gain a sense of the probable concerns for each person. The family file often includes details of the referral discussion, data collected in previous contacts with the family, and any data provided by others. You will reflect on this information to consider how the different family members might respond to the thought of entering service. Table 7.2 uses the response system framework to identify some potential blockages based on the family situation.

In Table 7.2, notice that when a family is referred for service, the family members respond in different ways. Some will welcome entry into service and are likely to be looking for an ally in the practitioner. Others are likely to be neutral or may see themselves as removed from the family situation. Still other family members will not want to enter service.

*Selecting the Mode of Invitation*    Armed with this sensitivity to the individual members, the practitioner must approach the family members to encourage participation. Although you will seldom approach every family member, you must often approach critical individuals. Selecting the critical individuals involves two judgments. First, you will try to identify family members who are interactively or behaviorally involved in the family situation. Such individuals are most critical to problem resolution. Typically you will invite all family members involved at this level. The second judgment is to identify family members affected by the family situation but not necessarily actively involved. These family members may need to be included at some point.

After critical individuals are identified, you must attempt to engage them in services. This step can be challenging, because these people frequently are not motivated to enter treatment. Most often, only one person approaches the family practitioner, so that family member and the practitioner must approach the other family members. Here are several methods for contacting family members to engage them in service:

◆ **Delegation.** Some practitioners expect the referring family member to motivate the other family members to attend the session. This method is easy;

but it is not always effective, because the referring member often has the greatest investment in therapy and the others are more likely to be reticent. They are also likely to view the referring member's rationale for entering service as self-serving.

◆ **Coached delegation.** Some practitioners explore with the referring family member how they will approach the other family members. The practitioner can then help the referring family member think through, and plan for, the responses of others. This approach is superior to delegation but still leaves the presentation of rationale to the referring family member.

◆ **Written invitation.** Some family practitioners send letters to family members to introduce themselves and their service (Coles, 1995). Writing a letter provides an opportunity to control how the presentation occurs with each family member and allows you to address probable questions about what will occur during treatment.

◆ **Third-party invitation.** Some practitioners work through concerned significant others to convince specific family members to enter service (Meyers, Smith, & Miller, 1998). This approach has some ethical issues to resolve regarding disclosing information, but it can be effective when some family members are already engaged but a single family member refuses participation. In such situations, you can work with the other family members and their network to try to convince someone that service can improve his situation.

◆ **Telephone invitation.** To encourage a family member to consider entering service, you may find it necessary to discuss your services in a telephone conversation. During this exchange, the family member will have an initial experience of you as the practitioner and an opportunity to understand what will be required of her if she elects to participate.

◆ **Individual engagement meetings.** Some practitioners meet individually with critical family members before attempting a family group session (Slesnick, Meyers, Meade, & Segelken, 2000). This approach gives each family member a unique engagement experience. After the practitioner–family member relationships are formed, you can broaden the services scope to include more family members.

◆ **Home visit or community-based meeting.** Sometimes it is useful to engage with family members in the community or in their home, where they feel most comfortable (Cunningham & Henggeler, 1999). This approach sidesteps some of the pragmatic problems associated with arranging for transportation and entering a clinical environment.

## Facilitating Initial Interest

After selecting an approach method, you must begin the engagement process with the family member. In the early discussions, the family member must begin to believe that there is a benefit to entering service (Becker, Hogue, & Liddle, 2002). He must also begin to believe that he can relate to you as the practitioner (Sargent, 2001). If you can facilitate these two outcomes during the initial discussion, the likelihood of engagement is enhanced. To promote family member engagement, four tasks must be accomplished during the initial discussion:

1. **Validate the client experience.** When reaching out to family members to engage them in service, you must disarm the potential negative energy that could keep them away. This task typically requires that you validate the clients' experience so they feel understood during the discussion about service (Flaskas, 1997). Until their fears and concerns are validated, clients are unlikely to be open about coming into service.

2. **Resolve perceived risks.** During the tuning-in process, the family practitioner identifies probable concerns and anxieties associated with service. In the discussion with the family member, you will attempt to resolve these concerns as well as to minimize the perceived risk. You must assure each family member that he will be valued and respected while also remaining realistic about the types of exchanges that are likely during treatment (Becker et al., 2002; Sargent, 2001).

3. **Identify unique contributions.** Knowing that each family member has a unique perspective, and having tuned into the client experience, you now have information to use in identifying a unique contribution that each family member can bring to service. Your acknowledgment of this contribution must be grounded in the client's sense of her situation rather than being patronizing. The family practitioner builds on positive energy by exploring the client perspective, validating the perspective, and demonstrating how such a perspective is needed for success. You must be able to take what the client expresses and build on it so she feels that she has something to contribute.

4. **Create interest.** All family members will want to believe that there is something in it for them as they engage in service (Becker et al., 2002; Sargent, 2001). If family members feel they are entering service to benefit somebody else, long-term engagement will be difficult to achieve (Allgood & Crane, 1991). The family practitioner must help the family member identify some personally meaningful outcome. This task builds on your tuning-in efforts when you identified the likely experience of each critical person. Through interaction with each family member, you can explore and build on that member's perspectives to identify some potentially beneficial outcomes.

The tentative engagement phases of tuning in, selecting an approach, and facilitating interest work in concert to help family members make the decision to enter service. These skills can help to get the critical people into the first group session. This first step of engagement is critical for the eventual success of treatment. If people enter services with a sense of hopefulness and a belief that they may benefit, they may approach treatment with a positive energy. This is the ideal situation. If some family members remain skeptical, you must continue to validate, resolve perceived risks, value the unique contributions, and help members find a reason to continue.

# ◆ EXERCISE 7.1 TUNING IN AND PITCHING TREATMENT

You are working in a child guidance clinic and have just met a young man named Corey (age 14), who was referred by his mother due to fighting at home and school. Corey and his two brothers live with his mother Brenda and her live-in boyfriend, Carl. Carl moved in about 18 months ago. This was six months after Corey's father died. Even though Corey's father often abused him and his mother, the death was sudden, and Corey has been withdrawn and sullen since the death. In the home, Corey has become verbally abusive to his mother and is violent to his younger brothers. Corey appears to like Carl at times; but when Carl intervenes to curb Corey's violence and verbal aggression, their relationship becomes strained. Corey is not very cooperative in the meeting, but does share some information about the family. In this sharing, it is clear that Corey's mother, Brenda, has very little power to discipline Corey.

1. Who would you like to include in service?

2. How would you invite these family members to come in for the next meeting?

3. What might Brenda's concerns be about entering service?

4. What would you need to address to help her feel comfortable coming into service?

5. What unique contributions would Brenda bring to sessions?

6. What exactly would you say to Brenda when you called to invite her to attend the next session?

7. What might Carl's concerns be about entering service?

8. What would you need to address to help Carl feel comfortable about coming into service?

9. What unique contributions would Carl bring to family sessions?

10. What exactly would you say to Carl when you called to invite him to attend the next session?

11. What exactly would you say to other people (if you elect to include others) when you invited them to enter service?

# Level 2: Building Investment in the Working Alliance

After you have gained an initial commitment to attend family sessions, the next engagement challenge is to get family members to identify a reason for continuing in treatment. This commitment is built through the experience that each family member has with you, the practitioner. If they feel comfortable and safe in their interactions with you, they are more likely to continue in treatment. Here are three critical tasks for building investment:

1. Affirming individuals to build a family focus
2. Establishing an atmosphere for work
3. Developing a sense of purpose

## Affirming Individuals to Build Family Focus

When family members enter their first session with you, do not expect everyone to be unified in their expectations. Most often there are multiple individual expectations, concerns, and fears about the helping situation. These initial concerns can cause any family member to withdraw from treatment unless he or she feels that his or her concerns have been resolved. As the therapist, you must help each family member resolve any concerns so that he or she can relax and participate fully in treatment (Anderson, 1985; Lever & Gmeiner, 2000). The themes of thinking, feeling, interaction and relationship, and action are often expressed in the family members' concerns.

*Thinking Themes*    Thinking and interpretation issues are paramount as people enter service. Family members have lived with aspects of the problem and often have their own thoughts about what is happening. As family members enter service, they reflect on the situation and want to make sure that other people's opinions will not be more highly valued than their own opinions. Defining the problem is a critical concern, because the problem definition will lead to the eventual solution. Consequently, as each member enters service, he or she reflects on the following questions:

◆ How does the definition of the problem fit with (or implicate) me?
◆ Will my perspective be validated or dismissed by the therapist (and others)?
◆ Do I have a reason to continue participating?

*Feeling Themes*    As they enter service, family members experience some typical feelings. Having anxiety about what will occur is commonplace. Family members often are aware that they have some stake in the problems and may worry that they will be held solely responsible. They also fear having their position dismissed or treated as irrelevant. In situations where abuse or noxious behavior has occurred, family members may experience shame based on secrets or behaviors that they would rather not discuss. These fears and anxieties often surface through the following types of questions:

- ◆ Will people be blaming me for problems in the family?
- ◆ Will I be supported when things get rough?
- ◆ Will this do any good, or will it just be a bunch of emotionally charged talk?

*Interaction and Relationship Themes*   Because family relationships have rich and emotionally invested histories, relationship themes and interaction concerns are important as each family member enters service. Family members may retain visions of past or feared interactions and project these visions into the helping relationship. It is not unusual for one member of the family to express concerns that the therapist is going to start telling him what to do. This is especially common when working with parent-child difficulties. Therapists need to model an interactive tone that can answer the following types of concerns:

- ◆ Will people take sides against me and try to gang up on me?
- ◆ Will the therapist tell me what to do?
- ◆ Will the therapist help my family listen to what I have to say?

*Action Themes*   Family members often have concerns about what actions will occur due to service. Concerns may focus on what the individual may have to do as a result of entering service. This theme is very common when you are dealing with marital problems, or with older teens when issues of autonomy are evident in the presenting problem. Frequent concerns also focus on what will occur during family sessions. You are advised to address these concerns early in service, so that family members can relax and open up. Here are some frequent types of questions expressing these concerns:

- ◆ What changes will I have to make?
- ◆ What will we do during the sessions?
- ◆ What will the therapist expect of me?

The family's multiple individual concerns and perspectives present the initial challenge for the family practitioner. You must establish a foundation and sense of common purpose so that everyone in the family can identify a reason for continuing in service (Anderson, 1985; Terry, 2002). All family members must be invested in changing the family situation. Without such an alliance, therapeutic outcomes are likely to be compromised, and family members are less likely to continue in service (Jordan, 2003). At this early stage of treatment, you must accomplish two critical tasks. You must (a) establish a working atmosphere that is comfortable for all family members (Lever & Gmeiner, 2000) and (b) develop a sense of common purpose among the family members.

## Establishing an Atmosphere for Work

To facilitate this deepening of the initial interest in service, the family practitioner must create an atmosphere of affirmation, collaboration, and respect (Barnard &

Kuehl, 1995; Patalano, 1997). If family members have a positive and hopeful experience, they are likely to engage more fully in service; conversely, negative experiences may result in the members' withdrawal (Anderson, 1985; Boland, 1993; Lever & Gmeiner, 2000; Patalano, 1997).

In family practice, you will build the initial work atmosphere using two skills. These skills build on the tuning-in skills already discussed in this chapter. It is important for you to be open to every family member's different concerns and perspectives. Each person must feel that you are listening and understanding his or her unique perspective. You can accomplish this task by using three critical skills: making an opening statement, neutralizing divisive issues, and validating perspectives.

*Making an Opening Statement (Shulman, 2006)*   When family members enter service, they experience both individual concerns and overlapping concerns. The family practitioner, through early conversations, seeks to tune into the experiences of each member and identify both individual and overlapping concerns. Many of the individual concerns guided the initial invitations into service. At this time of building common ground and a working atmosphere, you will shift the focus to the family members' shared or overlapping concerns. It is very important to have a sense of what critical concerns (described earlier) are likely to be shared by two or more family members.

After tuning into these important concerns, you must quickly reflect on and identify which concerns must be addressed immediately in order to set a positive working atmosphere. The concerns identified as most critical for people in the family become the basis of your opening statement.

An opening statement is the transition the therapist uses to move from the initial small talk (e.g., offering coffee, introducing the services) to the initial focused discussion. Many family practitioners lose the opportunity to use this powerful moment to set the stage for work by throwing the ball immediately to the family, asking questions such as, "What brings you here today?" Although this question is okay, you can have a stronger impact if you first "set the table" by making a statement that can help different family members feel affirmed and understood.

---

**CASE EXAMPLE**

A family practitioner meets with a new family. Right after they are seated and she has introduced the services, the therapist says, "I want to take this opportunity to share some of my thoughts about what will occur today. I know that many people don't know what to expect and may even fear that I am going to make them do or say things they will later regret. Some people worry that I am going to take sides or try to tell them what to do. I want to assure you that this is not my plan for you today. I want to first spend time listening to your understandings of your family situation and then see how we can work together to make your family as strong as it can be. I want to start by asking each of you to share your perceptions about the family's purpose of coming here to see me."

---

Notice in this opening statement that the therapist puts on the table some of the common (and likely shared) concerns in a way that can cause family members to feel understood, affirmed, and normal in their reactions. When the baton passes to each of the family members for their response, some of their initial concerns are likely to be resolved. This resolution will in turn influence the content of their responses. Such initial statements also give family members an experience of the practitioner that sets a tone for the ensuing discussions.

*Neutralizing Divisive Issues*   As family members begin to share their stories, you will often find divisive issues. These hot topics often involve one family member blaming another or holding others responsible for her emotional state. It is useful to neutralize the power of divisive issues until you have established common ground and direction. To diminish the power of divisive topics, family practitioners use two common strategies: (a) postpone or minimize discussion of divisive topics until the common ground is established, and (b) shift the focus of conversation to avoid externalized discussions.

1. **Postponing or minimizing discussion.** It is not unusual for family members to want to get hot topics on the table immediately, but you may initially want to table hot topics until ground rules and mutually accepted commonalities provide a foundation for work. If family practitioners get into hot topics too quickly and begin intervention before the working alliance is set, family members may drop out of service (Anderson, 1985; Lever & Gmeiner, 2000). Although it is important to deal with conflict eventually in treatment, initially you may want to say, for example, "I know this is important to you, and I want to make sure we get to it. But right now I think we need to hear what everyone has to say." However, do not rely on this as your only response, because people will eventually feel that their concerns are being invalidated (Anderson, 1985).

2. **Shifting focus.** As family members tell their stories, you must be careful to avoid externalized presentations. Externalized presentations include family members blaming each other for their problems, expecting other people to change, and other mechanisms that shift the focus away from the person who is speaking. Such presentation styles are a minefield for therapists as family members begin to tell their stories, because the externalized statements of one person often result in externalized defensive statements in other family members. One method of shifting the externalized statements is to reflect the person's processing (feelings or thinking) rather than the action themes in the family member's statement.

---

## CASE EXAMPLE

Fred, a 27-year-old husband, is talking about a difficulty with his partner Doris since he recently entered a job training program. This excerpt is taken from the first couple session. At the beginning of the session, Fred looks angry and Doris is avoiding eye contact. The therapist picks up on this and begins the following sequence.

*THERAPIST:* Fred, you look upset about something.

*FRED:* Damn right, I have a right to be upset. And she knows why too.

*DORIS:* Well if you would just help around the house, I wouldn't have to ask you to help me.

*FRED:* Well fine, then. I'll just quit school and be your slave.

*THERAPIST:* Fred, I am going to interrupt here. I know you guys fight like this at home, but we need to try something different.

*FRED:* Fine.

*THERAPIST:* Fred, what do you think Doris is upset about? (*Trying to validate Doris so she will de-escalate*)

*FRED:* That I am not doing any chores.

*THERAPIST:* What chores are you not doing? (*Reinforcing a shift to talking about self rather than Doris*)

*FRED:* Dishes, vacuuming, and the paper route.

*THERAPIST:* Did you do those before you started in the job training program?

*FRED:* Yeah, but I can't do them now because I have homework.

*THERAPIST:* So when you went into the job training program, more time pressures were put on you?

*FRED:* Yeah.

---

At the beginning of this excerpt, notice the escalation that was inherent in the externalized exchange between Fred and Doris. Both people are focused on the other person and blame their emotional states on each other. The therapist moves into the discussion by negotiating doing something different and then begins to shift the use of language by attending to how the questions are framed. He begins with a perspective-taking question to validate Doris's position and then begins to explore the situation with Fred. The questions used with Fred are designed to start him talking about himself rather than remaining externalized.

As you can see, this early engagement involves activity focused on interrupting automatic conflict cycles caused by the different perspectives and validating the multiple positions in the family. You must be careful when validating the members because other members may feel that you are taking sides. This is always a difficult issue early in family practice because family members will seek to engage the practitioner as an ally against the others in the family. Frequently, you will use circular questioning and reflecting strategies to move from validating one family member to engaging with the next, so that every person feels validated.

*Validating Multiple Perspectives* After the opening statement, family practitioners encourage each person to share his or her perspectives. The working alliance is enhanced as the therapist listens to, and validates, each person's story (Lever &

Gmeiner, 2000). At this early juncture in treatment, it is important to ensure that people feel that their expressions of concern are valued. Reflection skills and statements of appreciation are commonly used to ensure that each person feels heard and appreciated.

The family practitioner invites each family member to share his or her story. As each person talks, the practitioner encourages and protects her disclosure. If other family members try to correct, take over, or otherwise interrupt, you must set the tone by affirming that everyone has his or her own opinion, and then encourage the family member to complete her story. This early stage of treatment requires the practitioner to have skills for attending to the multiple perspectives within families. To help hone these skills, a framework for multiple perspectives is helpful.

When a family enters service, there are many perspectives and experiences of the problem. Typically, one family member's feelings precipitate the referral. This person's perspective will be very different from other family members' perspectives on the problem. In practice, you will have one primary and several secondary perspectives on the problem. You must understand how each person's perspective leads to a unique definition of the family problems.

◆ **Primary felt perspective.** It is important to identify whose feelings drove the referral, and how that person defines the problem. This perspective is referred to as the *primary felt perspective* (Ragg, 2001). The term is used to identify the person whose feelings and perspective are primary in the initial problem definition. Although the term *primary felt perspective* sounds complicated, just remember that *primary* = first, *felt* = feelings, and *perspective* = view of the problem. Consequently, you must find out whose feelings initiated the referral and learn that person's view of the problem.

◆ **Secondary felt perspective.** You cannot stop at the primary (or first) understanding without alienating the rest of the family members. Every family member has a unique perspective on the problem. To ensure all family members that you have heard and understood their perspective, it is important to explore the alternate problem definitions. The other family members' definitions and feelings about the problem are referred to as *secondary felt perspectives*. These perspectives are different from those of the person who initiated the referral.

The family practitioner tunes into each perspective to draw out the unique problem definitions of each family member. As the problem definitions are described, you will validate the perspective of each member without dismissing or invalidating the perspectives of other family members. This task is very challenging, because different members often are defensive when first entering service. You must ensure that each person experiences you as valuing his or her perspective.

The following considerations are useful when you are attempting to engage members with different perspectives:

◆ **Engaging system members with the primary felt perspective.** When a family member is feeling that there is a problem in the family, she is motivated to enter treatment and solve what she perceives to be the problem. However, not all in the system are in a position to define the problem for service.

Consequently, it is often the people with some power who get to make the contact and assume the primary problem perspective. These members are often easy to engage, but they may be expecting you to be an ally in their quest for specific changes.

- **Engaging system members with the secondary felt perspective.** The family practitioner must move from the primary perspective to then explore the other perspectives in the family. This task requires that you give permission for all family members to have their own perspective. You then explore the position of each family member. As the family members tell their story, you will seek overlaps that can encompass both the primary and secondary perspectives. For example, in a family where there are high levels of noncompliance with a child, the parent (primary) will likely want the child to comply with requests. The child (secondary) will want the parent to stop "bugging" him. An overlapping definition might be that there are a lot of arguments and hassles in the family that people want to decrease.
- **Engaging systems for which an external system has the primary problem perspective.** Sometimes the family members who enter treatment are engaging because someone outside of the family is insisting that they get service. Engaging clients systems where some external body is defining the problem can be difficult, because everyone in the family has a secondary felt perspective and the practitioner runs the risk of becoming a puppet for the external force. In such situations, you might attempt to engage the family in allowing you to mediate the external relationship. Alternatively, you might attend to the secondary perspectives, trying to help the family members find a reason to continue in treatment.

Some therapists deal with the externalized force by defining the problem in such a way that the external person provides a motivating force. For example, in a situation where the teacher is upset with the child, a therapist might define the situation that the teacher is making judgments and demands of the family. Based on this definition, you can help the parent and child to team up to "outsmart" the teacher so she will leave them alone.

The need for multiple validations requires practitioners to strategically choose one member as a starting point and then move to others in a very focused and purposeful manner. The order of interaction is often strategic, because as the practitioner you can influence the family according to whom they speak to first, second, and so on. Some of the thinking involved in selecting the order of interaction is as follows:

- **Shifting from the primary felt perspective.** Often the first person to make contact has presented her perspective. Practitioners often want to invite other family members to share their perspectives early in service before turning focus to the initial contact person. For example, "Mary, I have heard some of your concerns, so I am going to start off by asking Bob what he thinks about Sue going off to school in Alaska."
- **Engaging the reluctant member.** If one member seems reluctant to enter service, you may want to speak with him first to create an experience of

acceptance early in service. For example, "Frank, often people come in here a little concerned about what is going to happen. Some even think that I might gang up with other family members and take sides against them. I think it is generally uncomfortable because people don't know what is going to happen. Would you like me to explain what is likely to occur today?"

◆ **Disempowering polarities.** If the situation bringing a family into service is volatile, family members may be locked into polarized positions. You may want to avoid reinforcing a polarized position and may invite someone in a more neutral position to talk about the family situation first. For example, "Katy, I know your mom and dad disagree on how to respond when you get into trouble. What do you think they should do to help you stay out of trouble at school?"

◆ **Disrupting apparent coalitions.** When family members are forming coalitions against another member, you may want to reinforce the person outside the coalition in order to disrupt the balance in the family. For example, "Mom, I know these kids sometimes set it up so you can't get control of them. Which one of your children benefits most when you lose control?"

## ◆ EXERCISE 7.2   TOWARD THE WORKING RELATIONSHIP: IDENTIFYING AREAS FOR EXPLORATION

This exercise continues from Exercise 7.1, when you selected family members to include in treatment. In this exercise, you continue the tuning in based on interactions occurring among the family members. When Corey and his family come in for the first family session, they all appear angry and defensive. Corey's mother, Brenda, begins by lecturing him on how he needs to pay attention to other people's needs in the family. She implies that his behavior is the core problem in the family and that he should change to make other people's lives better. Corey's brother Tim has accompanied the family upon his mother's insistence. Tim adds comments in support when Brenda makes her points. This causes Corey to verbally counterattack the brother. The counterattacks are primarily verbal, but they feel like they might escalate if you were not present. Brenda's boyfriend, Carl, sits quietly but watches carefully and nods silently when Corey's mother makes statements about the family needing to get along and stop fighting so much.

1. What do you think Corey's experience is as the family comes into service?

2. What do you think Brenda's hopes are as her family enters service?

3. What might Brenda's anxieties be about entering service?

4. What does Tim's agenda appear to be as he enters service?

5. What in Tim's contributions must you be careful about?

6. What is your sense of Carl's experience as the family enters service?

7. What can you infer about the relationship and interaction system of these people?

8. What divisive topic(s) will you try to avoid when engaging this family?

9. Who will you focus on as you try to engage the family?

10. Write down exactly what you would say as an opening statement to try to address the concerns, hopes, anxieties, and so forth while at the same time setting the table in order to avoid divisive topics at the beginning of treatment.

---

# Developing a Sense of Purpose

After establishing an atmosphere in which all family members feel that they will be respected, you must develop a sense of purpose so that every member will identify a reason to continue with treatment. The challenge is to create a purpose that not only allows each individual to identify a reason to continue but also has enough commonality to create mutual goals. Ironically, the common concerns usually emerge from family members' individual experiences of the family situation. As each family member shares his or her experiences of the situation, the therapist monitors for themes that can provide a common direction for everybody.

Many areas of commonality require you to tune in to overlapping themes and concerns. Two basic areas of possible commonality provide opportunities for identifying common ground: (a) experiences associated with service and (b) shared family processes.

## Building on Perspective Overlaps

As a family practitioner, you will want to maintain a sense of purpose as you begin listening to the family members' stories. This sense of purpose stems from the family's request for service. As each person's story and perspectives are shared, the purpose is used to integrate overlapping aspects of each story to create common ground. As the common ground is built, a cumulative sense of purpose evolves. This sense of purpose is altered as each person's perspectives are integrated, promoting a shared ownership of the direction.

Even when family members have multiple perspectives about the problem situation, you can identify overlaps that provide common ground for engagement. Track the themes in the perspectives of different family members to identify common ground upon which goals can be established. This task involves listening to the different perspectives and identifying how they can be rephrased to promote collaboration. It also involves identifying the response system themes within each perspective and monitoring for overlaps.

## CASE EXAMPLE

The following case excerpt is taken from a first session with a family referred by the mother due to conflict with her son. After a very messy divorce three years ago, the family has just added a new father figure. To diminish the harassment from her ex-husband the mother moved the family to a different town, and they are living in a low-rent district. Santos, her son, was nine when he entered the new school and did not adjust well. Because the mother has referred the family for service, the therapist begins his exploration with her. After making the opening statement and covering the initial orientation to service, the therapist engages the family in the following exchange.

*THERAPIST:* Christina (mother), you asked for this meeting hoping that it would help you with something. What is the most important thing that you are hoping to accomplish?

*CHRISTINA:* Santos. Santos has me at the end of my rope. Maria listens and does her schoolwork without complaining, but every time I ask Santos something, he goes off on me.

*THERAPIST:* That sounds difficult, like you have run out of things to try.

*CHRISTINA:* Yes; I don't know what to do, but we cannot have a family that keeps acting like this.

*THERAPIST:* It is painful to feel powerless in a family. Santos (*12-year-old son*), what kind of power do you feel in the family?

*SANTOS:* I have no power.

*THERAPIST:* Funny, you sounded so powerful when your mother spoke. How is it that you feel like you have no power?

*SANTOS:* Nobody cares about me. They only look at the bad things I do. That is all they care about.

*THERAPIST:* So you have no power to make them see the good things about you.

*SANTOS:* Yeah, they just won't do it.

*THERAPIST:* You haven't found a way to get them to see that part of you yet?

*SANTOS:* Yeah.

*THERAPIST:* What about you, Maria? (*10-year-old daughter*) Are you the person with all the power in this family?

MARIA: No. But I don't get into trouble all the time either. Not like Santos. He is the reason we have to come here.

THERAPIST: You sound unhappy about coming here today.

MARIA: Yes. I don't see why I should come. If Santos would just behave, I wouldn't have to come here.

THERAPIST: You sound like you don't want to be here. How is it that you decided to come?

MARIA: Mom told me I had to.

THERAPIST: . . . and you always do what you are told?

MARIA: Yes.

THERAPIST: Even when you don't want to?

MARIA: Right.

THERAPIST: So even though you try hard to be good, you don't have much power either. Is that right?

MARIA: Right.

THERAPIST: So mom feels powerless, Santos feels powerless, and Maria feels powerless in this family. Juan (*father*), how do you feel about your power?

JUAN: I have no power. I joined the family about three years ago and can't do anything.

THERAPIST: What kinds of things do you want to do?

JUAN: I have always wanted kids. I would love to teach Santos how to hunt and play ball, but there is always too much fighting to have fun. Maria is a good kid and I am trying to do things with her.

THERAPIST: Sounds like you feel on the outside looking in.

JUAN: Yes. I don't feel like I can do anything to make things better. Just support Christina when she is fighting with Santos.

THERAPIST: It sounds like people feel a bit disconnected from each other. Even though people want more positive relationships, nobody feels that they have enough power to make it happen. Is that right?

ALL: Yes.

---

In the example, you can see many of the skills described earlier. First, the therapist set the tone by soliciting and validating multiple perspectives on the family. In soliciting perspectives, the therapist seeks to keep the discussion internalized. Notice how the therapist's responses to externalized statements force the family members to focus on their internal processes or their own behavior. This helps to focus each person so his or her themes and potential overlaps can be highlighted.

Through the example, the therapist builds on themes produced first by the mother and then tracks them with each family member. At the end, the therapist highlights the overlaps between the themes to illustrate the family members' common

**T A B L E 7.3**
**Identifying Overlapping Themes From Family Members**

|  | Expressed Concerns | Themes | Overlapping Themes |
|---|---|---|---|
| Father | Wants to play with Santos<br>Feels he cannot influence the family<br>Feels like an outsider | Desires more positive interaction<br>Feels powerless<br>Does not feel connected | Disconnection<br>Powerlessness<br>Wanting positive interaction (overlap with Santos) |
| Mother | Feels at the end of her rope with Santos<br>Has little parental authority with Santos<br>In comparison, Santos is the bad child and Maria the good child | Desires more compliance<br>Feels powerless<br>Does not feel connected to Santos | Disconnection<br>Powerlessness |
| Son | Feels that others look only at his bad behavior<br>Feels that others are against him | Wants more positive interaction<br>Feels powerless<br>Feels disconnected | Disconnection<br>Powerlessness<br>Wants positive interaction (overlap with Juan) |
| Daughter | Feels different from Santos<br>Tries to be the good child<br>Does things she does not want to do because she is asked | Feels disconnected from Santos<br>Feels powerless<br>Feels she is the good child | Disconnection<br>Powerlessness |

ground. In this process, the therapist listened to what each person had to say (keeping discussions internal), used themes from one person to build common ground with the next, and then summarized the common ground. This process is laid out in Table 7.3. In reviewing the table, you can see how each family member produces themes that can be overlapped with one or more members. Everyone has themes of powerlessness and a lack of connection. Santos and the father also have themes of wanting increased positive interactions.

## Framing the Situation to Promote Collaboration

In framing the response to the members of the client system, therapists will want to select observations and frames that will build on shared experiences and goals among the system members. Such therapist statements affirm the positions of different members and promote collaboration toward goals. Here are some methods used to maximize commonalties:

◆ **Frame the situation as enhancing shared purpose.** Collaboration toward change works best when there is a fit with the goals of everybody within the system.

- ◆ **Create win-win situations.** Try to create situations where all involved come out looking good or get some benefit from the collaboration.
- ◆ **Identify partners.** Try to identify other people who are interested in the change, will benefit from the change, or are willing to work toward the change.
- ◆ **Use shared experiences to provide examples.** When talking to someone in a larger system, try to use examples he or she already knows. That person will feel affirmed by such examples.

## CASE EXAMPLE

A mother, Tanika, has referred her son, Randy, new husband, DaJuan, and herself for service. Tanika states that her son is out of control and no longer listens to her. Reportedly, there have been many arguments in which she asks Randy to do something but he refuses. His refusal leads to an argument, and eventually DaJuan enters the fray to support the Tanika. Randy then claims they are ganging up on him and runs away. When he returns (up to two days later), people will not talk about the problems. The therapist wants to get the different perspectives out on the table, so he begins with Tanika.

*THERAPIST:* Tanika, you were the one who made the call to meet with me. What drove you to the point that you wanted someone like me to be helping the family?

*TANIKA:* I can't stand it anymore. No matter what I say, Randy never listens to me. He just won't let me be the mother anymore.

*THERAPIST:* How long have you been concerned about this?

*TANIKA:* About two years now.

*THERAPIST:* What else happened about two years ago?

*TANIKA:* My first husband died, and then about one year later I met DaJuan.

*THERAPIST:* Randy, I have heard your mother's experience of when the problems began in your family. Usually young men like you have a different experience of what is causing problems in the home. How would you describe the problems?

*RANDY:* There is no problem really. Dad died and then there was nobody lording over me. I don't see a problem.

*THERAPIST:* What do you mean by lording over you?

*RANDY:* Dad would always make me do things even if I didn't want. He said he was the man of the house and I had to do what he said.

*THERAPIST:* He sounds pretty powerful.

*RANDY:* I'll say; everyone was afraid of him. Even Mom.

*THERAPIST:* Ms. Smith, what made your first husband so frightening?

*TANIKA:* He could be pretty violent if you didn't do what he said.

*THERAPIST:* So did he keep Randy in line?

*TANIKA:* Yes.

*THERAPIST:* Did he keep you in line too?

*TANIKA:* Yes.

*THERAPIST:* So when he died, the force that could make you and Randy do things you didn't want to do disappeared?

*TANIKA:* I guess you could say that.

*THERAPIST:* It seems that the force that helped you to get Randy to do things also disappeared.

*TANIKA:* Definitely.

*THERAPIST:* DaJuan, you just joined this family about one year ago. What have you noticed about this problem?

*DAJUAN:* I don't know what to make of it. Randy, he is just a normal kid, but sometimes she wants him to do things that he doesn't want to do. When that happens, things get pretty crazy.

*THERAPIST:* How crazy do they get?

*DAJUAN:* Well. She tells him what to do and he refuses. Then she tries to talk him into it and he argues back. Eventually they start yelling at each other. I step in just to make the yelling stop. I hate yelling.

*THERAPIST:* Does anyone in the family like yelling?

*DAJUAN:* No. We all hate it when things get this way.

*TANIKA:* I'll say.

*THERAPIST:* Randy, do you hate this too?

*RANDY:* I hate it, but I don't want people making me do what I don't want. I had enough of that with Dad.

*TANIKA:* Don't you think I hate it too? You weren't the only one he used to hit.

*THERAPIST:* It sounds like nobody in this family likes the conflict. Is that right?

*TANIKA:* I hate it.

*DAJUAN:* I can't stand it.

*RANDY:* I hate it, but I can't let people push me around.

*THERAPIST:* Sounds like you made yourself a promise that nobody else would ever treat you like your father.

*RANDY:* Yeah.

*THERAPIST:* Ms. Smith, I get the sense that you made a similar promise to yourself.

*TANIKA:* Yes. I made a promise that nobody would ever push me around again.

*THERAPIST:* So nobody wants to be pushed around, but nobody seems to know what to do when people want different things. Is that what is happening?

In this example, you can see that each person begins with a very different perspective on the problem. As the therapist explores each perspective, common ground is highlighted so direction can be established. As commonalities are noted, the therapist reflects them to the family.

These and other strategies form a foundation of strategy and thinking that guides family practitioners at the early stages of engagement. After you have created an experience in all of the family members that helps them to become more comfortable and willing to invest, the preliminary engagement is complete. You can then progress with interactive engagement.


#### ◆ EXERCISE 7.3   TOWARD BUILDING A SENSE OF PURPOSE

As your session with Corey and his family continues, the following exchange occurs. As the family is talking, you are trying to identify common ground among the members. You are scanning the themes in the family's discussions, trying to find themes at different levels (action, relationships, thinking, and feeling) that you can tap into to build common ground and a sense of purpose.

> *BRENDA:* Corey has always been a problem. When he gets upset, he doesn't express it like normal kids; he clams up and then later explodes. He takes things out on everyone else, and I have had enough of it. Why can't we get along like a normal family?
>
> *COREY:* Normal . . . yeah, right.
>
> *TIM:* Corey . . . NORMAL. (*giggles*)
>
> *COREY:* Get lost, Tim.
>
> *BRENDA:* Leave Tim alone. He knows what you need to do.
>
> *COREY:* Like you don't have anything to do with it. You are no angel.
>
> *BRENDA:* I don't take it out on people like you do.
>
> *COREY:* At least I care . . .
>
> *TIM:* Hah . . .
>
> *BRENDA:* When you treat people like you have been treating us, don't try to tell me that you care.
>
> *COREY:* I care a lot more than you. You don't know the first thing about caring.
>
> *BRENDA:* I most certainly do. I spend all my time doing nothing but caring for you, your brothers, and Carl. I need someone to start caring about me.
>
> *TIM:* Yeah.
>
> *BRENDA:* Why should I do all the caring?
>
> *COREY:* You don't do any caring.
>
> *CARL:* Hey, That's enough. Let's just try to get along.
>
> *COREY:* Nobody asked you. You just always take mom's side anyway.

1.  In this exchange, use the response system framework to identify the critical elements for the different family members. For each person, write elements for each response system. You will need to infer some possible themes based on content themes, level of interaction, type of interaction, and so forth.

| Behavior Themes | Cognition and Belief Themes |
|---|---|
| Brenda | Brenda |
| Corey | Corey |
| Tim | Tim |
| Carl | Carl |
| **Interaction and Relationship Themes** | **Feeling and Affect Themes** |
| Brenda | Brenda |
| Corey | Corey |
| Tim | Tim |
| Carl | Carl |

2.  Based on the themes and elements found for the different family members, identify one overlapping theme that can provide a foundation for common ground.

3. Identify additional themes (based on this exchange and previous exercises) that you must avoid until you have established enough common ground for a working relationship.

4. How can the common theme be used to develop a new definition to the family problems?

5. Write exactly what you would say to the family to reframe and redefine the situation for them.

## Summary

Preliminary engagement involves the practitioner skills and actions that will get family members into, and comfortable with, treatment. The practitioner identifies the critical family members (and others) who will maximize success if involved. When skillfully approached, these people should agree to meet with the practitioner. After entry into treatment, the practitioner establishes an atmosphere and sense of purpose that will promote continued attendance. Preliminary engagement is referred to as *preliminary* because it provides the human foundation for work.

The human foundation is necessary, but not sufficient, to organize the family members in a focused change effort. Other levels of engagement are needed to ensure that the family is ready and willing to work. In Chapter 8 we explore interactive engagement, during which the sense of common purpose is expanded into energy that can be directed for change. In Chapter 9 we explore positioning strategies that deepen engagement to enhance family members' willingness to change. These three chapters of Section III work in concert to provide the skills and strategies for preparing families for entry into service and readiness for change.

## Critical Content

1. Family members do not view the family problems the same way.
2. Some family members are motivated to change, and others are content with the current situation.
3. Similarly, some family members ideally should be part of therapy while others may need only minimal participation.
4. Practitioners must tune into every family member to be invited into treatment in order to identify their perspectives and experience in the situation.
5. Practitioners use their sensitivity to identify unique contributions and perspectives for each family member that may motivate participation.
6. When people enter treatment, the practitioner creates an atmosphere that supports disclosure and validates the positions of the various family members.
7. The practitioner listens to each person's story, tracking individual themes that can be used to enhance continued attendance and common purpose.
8. The practitioner provides a new frame, or understanding of the situation, that captures individual concerns while also giving family members a sense of common purpose.

## Suggested Readings

Lever, H., & Gmeiner, A. (2000). Families leaving therapy after one or two sessions: A multiple descriptive case study. *Contemporary Family Therapy: An International Journal, 22,* 39–65.

Patalano, F. (1997). Developing the working alliance in marital therapy: A psychodynamic perspective. *Contemporary Family Therapy: An International Journal, 19,* 497–505.

Sargent, J. (2001). Variations in family composition: Implications for family therapy. *Child & Adolescent Psychiatric Clinics of North America, 10,* 577–599.

Chapter 8

# Interactive Engagement With Family Members

After family members have entered service and the family practitioner has started developing a working alliance, the engagement challenge shifts to helping all family members broaden their focus to the family and contextual level (Mirkin & Beib, 1999; Weber, 2001). Such expansion of focus allows family members to identify and exchange information about a shared problem. This task can be difficult, because the multiple perspectives and experiences of the problem can quickly interfere with developing a shared vision. Practitioners must be very active during this phase of engagement to avoid alienating family members and/or failing to develop common ground. In this chapter, we explore the challenges of and techniques for helping the family to develop a unified direction for change.

## Working With Family Energy During Interactive Engagement

When families enter service, the family energy is often very divisive and negative (Newell, 1999). This divisive negativity maintains family problems by setting up automatic systems of interpreting and reacting to the other members of the family. Often coalitions and alliances have been formed that reinforce people's automatic responses. In the family, people are watchful of the others and tend to be entrenched in their own perspectives on the problem. This stance presents challenges to interactive engagement.

**Figure 8.1** Initial Family Energy Patterns

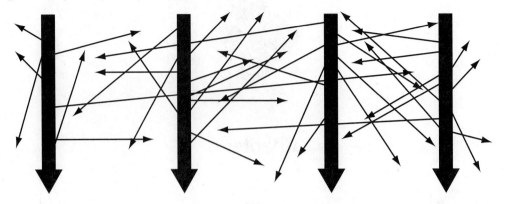

Notice in Figure 8.1 that the family energy is scattered and without unified direction at this beginning point in service.

In Figure 8.1, the large arrows pointing downward indicate family members moving forward in time. The smaller arrows pointing in many directions indicate the mental and emotional energy generated by the individual family members. Notice that the energy generated by the individual members points away from the individual. Very often, the energy is directed toward other family members, at people outside of the family, or otherwise deflected from the individual. This pattern indicates externalization in the family.

Externalization often presents the first challenge to engagement. Family members typically view other people as causing problems and frequently locate the family's problems in other family members (Stratton, 2003b). This type of energy makes family members afraid of being blamed for the family problems and very quick to shift responsibility from themselves and onto another person (Furlong & Young, 1996). There is often a belief that the family problems would be solved if other people would change, but little realization that everyone needs to assume some responsibility for solving the family problems.

Problem-focused interactions in the family tend to shift into past-focused arguments and other minutiae that cannot be controlled or influenced by the family members. The focus is usually on other people's actions or inactions and how those affect others in the family. Attempts to solve problems often generate automatic defensive reactions as family members deflect perceived blame and rationalize their own actions. Family members are frequently unwilling to be vulnerable with each other for fear of being criticized or attacked.

The family energy at this early point in treatment interferes with developing common ground and shared goals. Family members tend to be in isolated camps where they can best defend themselves from the judgments and perceived attacks by other family members. As a therapist, you must work to move family members from these divisive positions to more unified positions in order to help the family achieve changes and improved problem-solving capacities (Friedlander, Heatherington,

Johnson, & Skowron, 1994; Phillips, Munt, Drury, Skoklosa, Spink, & Chapman, 1997; Stratton, 2003a).

Therapists help families redirect the family energy through four basic stages of interactive engagement. Each of these stages provides a platform upon which the next stage is built:

1. Blocking automatic patterns of reacting
2. Neutralizing negative energy
3. Building common ground
4. Developing a foundation for change

In this chapter, each of these stages is described separately. We also discuss each stage in relation to each of the others, to best indicate how family practitioners can redirect and reshape the divisive energies of families as they enter service.

# Blocking Automatic Patterns of Reacting

During the first phase of interactive engagement, the family practitioner must move the family members from their externalized positions so they can talk about themselves rather than talking about other people (Boland, 1993). In this phase, you must explore the different experiences of members without triggering the automatic defensive reactions. In effect, you are seeking to identify attempts by family members to deflect energy away from themselves; you are then trying to loop it back so that each member begins to share information about himself or herself rather than about other people in the family (see Figure 8.2).

To redirect family energy away from automatic defensive reactions, the practitioner commonly employs these four strategies:

1. Interrupting automatic patterns of responding
2. Shifting focus from others to oneself

**Figure 8.2**  Redirecting Family Energies

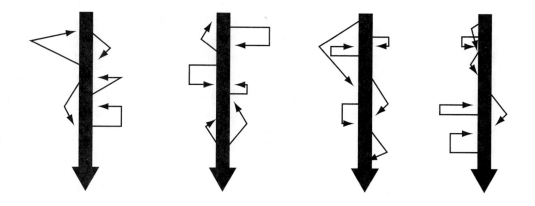

3. Shifting focus from action to processing systems
4. Validating experiences and perspectives

## Interrupting Automatic Responses

One of your first tasks as the therapist is to block the automatic systems of responding and fighting among the family members. As part of an assessment strategy, you may want to observe a family's pattern of escalation or fighting; but when moving toward work, you will want to develop new methods of interacting that help to prevent family members from fighting and attacking each other. The following strategies are frequently used to interrupt the automatic patterns of families:

◆ **Interruption** (Amatea & Sherrard, 1991; Ellis, 2003a). Many practitioners will verbally interrupt arguments or automatic responses immediately when they are starting. By making statements such as, "I suspect this is how arguments start at home. Let's try something new as long as you are here with me," you can redirect the energy away from automatic responses and begin influencing family interactions.

◆ **Tabling forward.** When the family has hot issues or topics that are more likely to generate automatic reactions, you can acknowledge the importance of the issue, but have the family wait before addressing the problem. This allows for the building of cohesion and reframing before potentially volatile content is addressed.

◆ **Disallowing specific interactions.** If specific issues or interactions are disruptive to the family, you may use your initial power to prohibit those interactions during the course of treatment (Brown, 2000). For example, if one member has had an affair, many practitioners make the family member promise to cease all contact with the other person as long as he or she in treatment. Such a move blocks automatic interactions that accompany suspicions or desires associated with the affair.

◆ **Controlling the process.** Frequently, family practitioners take active control over the sequencing and content of discussions. By instructing people to share or interact, you can control the focus and nature of the interaction and block the family's automatic responding patterns (Johnson, 1993).

◆ **Decreasing tension.** Practitioners often make a statement that diminishes tension when they feel that a family member may be priming herself for an automatic reaction. Small jokes or observations can make people laugh at themselves rather than shifting into the more serious responses that accompany the automatic reactions.

◆ **Addressing blame** (Furlong & Young, 1996). Practitioners often must identify, label, and discuss how blame is used in the family. After identifying the family's blaming processes, you can label them as they emerge and help the family find other ways of responding to each other.

## Internalizing the Focus

Concurrent with interrupting automatic responses, family practitioners use communication techniques to preempt externalized patterns. Questions that require family members to report on their own experiences, perspective-taking questions, and personalizing probes (e.g., "and what did you think that meant about you?") all can direct a family member's focus to himself and away from other people. Such strategies are most useful when people appear to be externalizing, because they immediately shift the focus away from others and back to the individual. Here are three common strategies for shifting the focus:

1. **Redirection.** When using redirection, you will directly instruct family members to report on themselves rather than on other people. Redirection must be carefully used to ensure that the family member does not feel that his position is being invalidated. For example, "Dad, I know that John's behavior is important to you. I am really interested in how you respond when he does those things." Notice in this example how the focus is shifted after the importance of the father's last statement is validated.

2. **Self-report questions.** A subtle shift in focus can be accomplished by targeting the question more specifically to the family member who is externalizing. For example, "When John does that, what do you do in response?" Notice that the same shift is achieved with no setup sentence. The practitioner simply picks up what the family member put on the table and builds the new focus into the next question.

3. **Perspective focusing.** Sometimes you will want to target the question, so that a family member must respond from his unique perspective. In this type of question, you set up the question by identifying the specific perspective the respondent is to use for his answer. For example, "Dad, from your perspective as the person who is responsible for helping John learn responsibility, how have your strategies been working?" Notice how the setup sentence for this question focuses the nature of the response. This setup line not only requires the father to self-report, it requires the father to respond to a very specific question.

## Shifting From Action to Processing Systems

When family members focus on action systems, there is a higher likelihood of triggering an automatic response because of the behavioral and interactive focus. It is also easier to externalize, because family members are much better observers of each other's behavior than their own. Family practitioners often shift focus to peoples' processing systems to prevent externalization. Practitioners frequently pick up on the affective and thinking themes to highlight the internal realities. It is not easy to externalize when talking about feelings. Although some family members may attempt to shift focus to what others do to cause the feeling, you can shift focus back to exploring the feeling and cause the family member to talk more about him- or herself.

By using the processing system focus, you can easily sidestep defensive reactions because people are talking only about their internal experiences. If other family members become offended, you can de-escalate the situation by reminding the family that people are talking about their own feelings and beliefs. Intrinsically, each person is the expert on his or her own experience. Notice how both the questioning strategies mentioned earlier and the redirection in this section refocus the individual's attention to internal rather than external elements of the situation. This effect is depicted in Figure 8.2 by the energy arrows turning back toward the individuals in the family. There are two techniques for achieving this shift in focus:

1. **Shift to feeling.** The therapist can sidestep blame and defensiveness by shifting the family member's focus to his affective processes. You can accomplish this shift by asking basic questions (e.g., "What are the feelings that start to emerge when John doesn't follow through on his chores?") You can also use setup lines, such as, "Dad, you sound frustrated when you describe John's behavior. What is the feeling underlying that frustration?" When you are shifting to feelings, it is useful to focus on the primary feelings (e.g., powerlessness, helplessness, hopelessness, shame, etc.) rather than the secondary emotions (anger, frustration, hurt).

2. **Shift to thinking.** An alternative to a feeling focus is to shift the focus to the family member's thinking. This includes the beliefs and interpretations underlying his responses to the other family members. You can easily pick up on any action or interaction, shifting the focus to interpretations of the situation or the fit with their beliefs. For example, "Dad, having John follow the rules seems important to you. What do you think will happen if he continues in the current direction?"

## Validating Experiences and Perspectives

A fourth strategy for interrupting the automatic responses is to validate each family member's perspective. In tracking the patterns of arguments, you will find that many arguments involve each person seeking to have her own position validated. People often persist until they feel their point is validated. You can sidestep this common pattern by validating the perspectives shared by each family member (Johnson & Greenberg, 1988).

When family members assume defensive postures, the practitioner can validate their affect and normalize the reaction in the family context. Validation interrupts the buildup of energy that might otherwise fuel one of the automatic responses (Elliott, Watson, Goldman, & Greenberg, 2004a; Farber & Lane, 2002). In making this validation, you can stress the need for difference and invite family members to work on different ways of dealing with their internal experience. As different positions are validated in the family, its members can see a possibility for multiple perspectives to coexist. Here are some common validation strategies:

◆ **Validating underlying feelings** (Zinner, 1997; Greenberg, 1999). Regardless of the behavior or interactions in the family, you can usually validate people on the affective level. Even when someone misinterprets the situation, you can summarize his thinking and validate his feelings based on what he believes might be happening. For example, if a husband believes his wife is having an affair, you can say, "It is natural to have those feelings if you think your wife is having an affair . . . and it is very difficult to shake those feelings if you don't know for sure."

◆ **Validating internal experience.** People's internal experiences evolve from a blend of emotion and attribution (Greenberg & Pascual-Leone, 1997). The attribution of meaning is used to help the person take control of a powerful emotional experience (Elliott et al., 2004b). When people feel that these internal realities are being discounted or ignored, they often become reactive with others. You must often validate these internal experiences to interrupt reactivity and automatic responses (Elliott et al., 2004a). For example, when working with a parent from a very punitive background, you might respond, "Mom, it seems that following rules has been very important in your life. The fact that Juanita does not follow your rules is almost intolerable because it is something that you would never consider doing as a child."

◆ **Using exception-focused questions** (Melidonis & Bry, 1995). Therapists often use exception questions to validate family members who are the focus of all-encompassing or limiting family statements. If family members make statements including the words *always, never,* or other absolutes, you can use exception questions to soften the statement and validate the focal family member without actively challenging the statement. For example, when a mother states, "I hate it . . . Juanita never comes home on time . . . I feel like I should never let her out," you can reply, "This sounds serious; has there ever been a time when Juanita came home at curfew?"

◆ **Stressing nonblaming perspectives** (Zinner, 1997). When family members make negative and externalized statements, you can often encourage other family members who may have a more conciliatory or reflective position on the situation to share their thoughts and observations. By shifting focus, and stressing the kinder position, you can block some of the automatic family negativity. For example, "Mom, you are angry that Juanita doesn't follow the curfew rules. How do other people in the family make sense out of this problem?" If a family member offers an explanation that has the hope of compromise or common ground, you can explore that position and then reapproach the mother to revise her position slightly.

When using the different strategies for blocking automatic and negative responses, practitioners often employ several methods successively to respond to the interaction and processing of the family members. Often, you will cycle through the tasks of blocking reactions and developing exploration. During these cycles, family members will engage in frequent automatic or externalized responses.

## CASE EXAMPLE

This example is taken from a session focused on the parents' (Fran and Tom) management of their young adolescent daughter, Nancy. Notice how the therapist first blocks the automatic reactions and then redirects the energy back to the individuals in the family.

*THERAPIST:* Mom, you spoke as if Nancy never follows your instructions.

*FRAN:* Well, she never does . . .

*NANCY:* That is bull.

*FRAN:* Well, you don't.

*NANCY:* I certainly do. Last week I tidied my room.

*TOM:* That was after we told you that you couldn't go out until it was done.

*NANCY:* I still did it. She said never . . .

*THERAPIST:* I am going to interrupt you right now. I know this is important, but I think this is how you argue at home. I want to try some new ways of solving problems while we are in the room together.

*FRAN:* But she never listens to me . . .

*THERAPIST:* Sounds like you feel pretty powerless in this situation.

*FRAN:* I do. No matter what I try, she just won't listen.

*THERAPIST:* What do you do with your feelings of powerlessness?

*FRAN:* I get angry.

*THERAPIST:* Does that help?

*FRAN:* No . . . we just fight and I get more powerless.

*THERAPIST:* Nancy, I thought I heard powerlessness in your voice too. What do you feel powerless about in the family?

*NANCY:* Everything. No matter what I do, it is not good enough. They are always on me about what I should be doing and how I never do things right.

*THERAPIST:* And what do you do with your feelings of powerlessness?

*NANCY:* I try to ignore them.

*THERAPIST:* Ignore the feelings or your parents?

*NANCY:* (slight laugh) Both.

*THERAPIST:* Does this work?

*NANCY:* No. Nothing changes.

*THERAPIST:* Dad, it seems that both mom and Nancy feel pretty powerless in this situation. What do you feel as these arguments evolve?

*TOM:* I feel . . . oh, here we go again.

*THERAPIST:* So those are the thoughts going through your head?

*TOM:* Yes. We go through the same thing all of the time. If Nancy and Fran would just get along, we would have a normal family.

*THERAPIST:* So from your position observing this situation, what is the feeling that lies underneath these thoughts?

*TOM:* I guess it would be powerless.

---

# Neutralizing Negative Energy

As family members share their experiences (rather than tell tales of others' evil acts), the therapist explores the details. This elaboration allows family members to gain comfort in disclosing their perspectives while providing potential information for building common ground. While still avoiding the divisive issues at this point, you will want to provide reflections and frames that shift family interpretations in a positive direction.

## Positive Illumination

While people are sharing their perspectives, the practitioner reaches for positive or neutral interpretations (Farber & Lane, 2002; Friedlander, Heatherington, & Marrs, 2000; Robbins, Alexander, & Turner, 2000). After a family member shares her story, you can highlight a positive element of the story. Often these positive elements are current or past intentions, or evidence of caring. Whenever opportunities emerge, highlight the positive elements in each person's story. Your strategy of positive illumination will begin to counterbalance the negative energy that has tainted the family's stories in the past (Bowling, Kearney, Lumadue, & St. Germain, 2002; Friedlander et al., 2000).

While stressing positive or neutral interpretations of people's intentions and affect, you will track the positive elements in all family members, seeking common feelings and intentions. Make a mental note of these themes, and seek to elicit more examples of the positive themes. As the themes emerge, encourage family members to elaborate on the positive indicators. The interventions and strategies discussed next are common during this phase.

## Continued Validation

The therapist must continue to validate the processing and perspectives of each family member. In practice, you will frequently accompany continued validation with your own reflections on the positive or neutral elements inherent in the family member's experience. This strategy starts to shift the family members' assumptions of negative intent that may be causing their defensive reactions. Second, as you reinforce and validate the members' internal perspectives, they will begin to generalize and contextualize their observations. This situation occurs as a result of circular exploration, during which you ask each family member to share stories, observations, and experiences that can promote positive interpretations.

For example, when a parent mentions that she wants the best for her child, you might observe, "It seems that multiple members want the best for the others in the family, but they are often misunderstood." This statement affirms the feelings not only of the member who is sharing but also of others in the family. This type of reflection also creates a neutral foundation that can support positive reframing of the situation.

## Identifying Overlapping Themes

As family members share their perspectives and experiences, the family practitioner has them expand on and elaborate their experience. Such expansion allows you to identify elements that can be used to highlight the positive or neutral elements in the family member's story. Eventually, all family members have shared multiple perspectives, all of which have been validated and identified as having positive elements. The use of multiple elements allows others to relax the patterns of negative interpretation that maintain the problems.

As the family stories, observations, and experiences are shared and neutralized, you will mentally track the story themes, thinking themes, and affective themes that overlap among the family members. Repeated themes across the membership offer some potential for developing common ground. Near the end of this stage, you will highlight the common themes for the family members so that they can identify the shared neutral elements in the situation.

## Cycling Back to Neutral Territory

The family energy during the cycling phase is expansive, often shifting from stage to stage as family members flip back and forth from calmly telling their stories to experiencing externalized and automatic exchanges. You must continually block the automatic processes, refocus the family members, and facilitate disclosures that can be shifted into a more positive frame. Each time through this process, you are highlighting more neutral or potentially positive shared feelings or thoughts upon which common ground can be built.

Each time you cycle through the process, you also take the energy associated with each disclosure and help family members expand on it (different examples, themes, variations). You can then help the family members see elements that they all have in common. This process is depicted in Figure 8.3 by the different line patterns shown for the different family members. Notice that although family members do not necessarily have the same patterns, some common patterns can be identified. The neutral, or positive, areas of potential identification are shared and highlighted by the therapist so that family members can begin viewing each other in a slightly different manner.

**Figure 8.3**   Highlighting Common and Neutral Themes

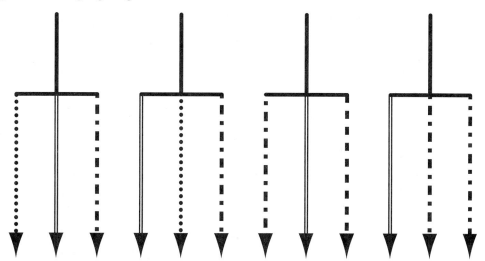

---

## CASE EXAMPLE

The following sequence is taken from the same session used to illustrate blocking strategies in the first case example. In this segment, observe how the therapist continually reframes people's intent and meaning to a neutral or positive interpretation. Also notice how the therapist highlights common elements without openly informing the family members that they have motivations in common.

*THERAPIST:* These themes of powerlessness suggest to me that people in this family are working very hard. Mom, what are you working hard to achieve?

*FRAN:* I want her to know how to succeed. If she doesn't follow the rules, she can't get ahead.

*THERAPIST:* So by reminding her of the rules all the time, you are trying to help her become a successful adult?

*FRAN:* Yes. She can't succeed if she just does what she wants . . .

*NANCY:* I do follow rules . . . you just don't see it.

*THERAPIST:* Nancy, it sounds like you have given the importance of rules some thought as well.

*NANCY:* Yes.

*THERAPIST:* What are your thoughts on the rules needed to succeed?

*NANCY:* I know I have to do things. You have to go to work on time and do what you are told, but you also have to be able to think. You won't succeed if people don't let you make decisions.

*THERAPIST:* So you are trying to learn several skills that you need for success, following rules, and thinking.

*NANCY:* Yes.

*THERAPIST:* Mom, do you agree that thinking is also an important skill?

*FRAN:* Yes, but that doesn't mean she can break all of the rules.

*THERAPIST:* You are right. There needs to be a balance, doesn't there?

*FRAN:* Yes . . . and I think she should start with following the rules at home.

*THERAPIST:* It can be quite frustrating when someone is thinking when you want them to just do what they are told.

*FRAN:* You can say that again.

*THERAPIST:* I bet it is frustrating for Nancy to have someone expect compliance when she is working on thinking too.

*NANCY:* Yeah.

*THERAPIST:* Dad, when you see both of these people working hard on developing the skills for success, do you ever see times when one is trying to develop one skill and the other is focused on something else?

*TOM:* They are always focused on something else. They are never together.

*THERAPIST:* This must be frustrating for everyone in the family.

---

### ◆ EXERCISE 8.1  BLOCKING AUTOMATIC REACTIONS AND NEUTRALIZING ENERGY

This exercise continues the work from Chapter 7 (the Corey case). As you may remember, in this family Corey is the 14-year-old son who is aggressive, Tim is his younger brother, Brenda is the mother, and Carl is her live-in boyfriend of 18 months. We are continuing with this case because you have already done the preliminary work. In this exercise, you will focus on the interactive skills needed to block automatic reactions and neutralize the emotional energy. The interaction picks up immediately after your reframing of the family problem, with Brenda saying, "It is not just everyone wants to feel that others care. Corey needs to learn to care."

1. Write a statement that can block this automatic reaction.

As the discussion continues, the following exchange occurs:

COREY: I don't know why we even try, nobody cares about me.

BRENDA: That's because you don't care about others. Why should we care?

COREY: See. You don't care.

BRENDA: I didn't say we don't care, I said "why should we care," because you don't care.

TIM: We shouldn't care.

COREY: Screw you, you little twirp. I'll show you caring.

BRENDA: See. This is why nobody cares about you.

COREY: See . . . you said it again. You don't care.

2. You want to interrupt this pattern of automatic reactions. What can you do?

3. Make a statement that can punctuate the interaction so you can begin interrupting the exchange.

4. To begin neutralizing the energy in the room, you want to slow things down and get people focused on their processing. Select one family member and ask a question that can start them exploring how they process situations.

5. Where would you try to take this discussion?

6. Use a circular questioning strategy to help others to begin their own processing. Write the question you would use to help the next person to start this exploration.


7. Why did you focus on this person?


8. Write a statement that can affirm Brenda without challenging the perspectives of the others in the family.


9. Write a statement that can affirm Corey without challenging the perspectives of the others in the family.


10. You have now begun the internal exploration and shifted people away from their externalized focus (reread the earlier exchange and notice how most statements included a "you" focus). Use a reframe to again redefine the family situation in a way that affirms all of the family members' internal perspectives.


---


# Building Common Ground

Establishing common ground gives family members direction and goals (Lown & Britton, 1991; Sholevar & Schwoeri, 2003). Consequently, as family practitioners neutralize the negative energy, they begin to reflect on common themes that emerge through the family stories. Through the commonalities, the practitioner helps the family decide on important themes that can promote shared purpose. Typically, two or three themes are identified and highlighted to build the common ground among the family members. These common themes often focus on beliefs, motivations, and feelings because the abstract nature of these processes allows the practitioner to identify potential commonalities.


## Closing Gaps Between Family Members

During this stage of engagement, the therapist uses two ongoing styles of interaction to reinforce the commonalities among the family members. First, you will highlight and frequently point out similarities and overlaps among the family members.

Second, you will attempt to decrease the power of differences so the commonalities can become more pronounced. When highlighting similarities, family practitioners often use the following strategies:

◆ Pointing out similarities in people's stories
◆ When people make divisive statements, reflecting the common ground and overlaps rather than highlighting the divisiveness
◆ Identifying feeling states that appear shared by all within the family system
◆ Framing individual feelings as family-level feelings
◆ Drawing out validations from other people that they also experience the same feelings

When responding to differences that might promote divisiveness, you must allow for individual experiences while still highlighting the commonalities among the members. This is accomplished by validating the feelings or thoughts of the individual coupled with reflecting on shared feelings or beliefs that are similar to the individual position. You are thus balancing the individual investments with shared experience. When this technique is successful, you can preempt the family's divisive processes while highlighting shared themes.

At times family members may persist in bringing up divisive issues. In such situations, you must interrupt the automatic processes while encouraging the family members to move toward new patterns of interaction. To strengthen common themes, actively highlight and elaborate on the neutral or potentially positive shared experiences. Figure 8.4 shows common themes as thicker lines and individual themes as thinner lines.

**Figure 8.4** Development and Strengthening of Common Themes

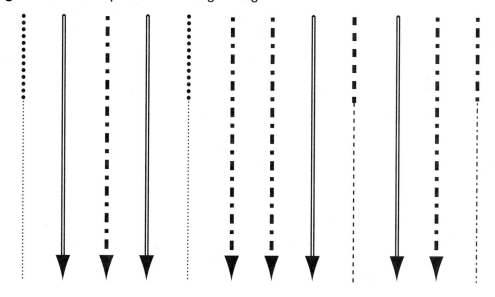

## CASE EXAMPLE

The following dialogue is from the same session used earlier to illustrate other stages of interactive engagement. In these exchanges, notice how the therapist highlights common ground and attempts to build more commonalities among the family members.

*THERAPIST:* Fran, I notice that both you and Nancy are concerned about building the skills for success. Is that surprising to you?

*FRAN:* Yes. I didn't think she cared.

*THERAPIST:* Now that you know she cares, can you see times where both of you were working on building skills for success but the efforts just didn't jibe?

*FRAN:* I think so. Tom, what do you think?

*TOM:* I think she has. But you never talk to each other about it. You just butt heads.

*THERAPIST:* (*to Tom*) Do you think they are both working hard on the same thing but aren't really coordinating with each other?

*TOM:* Yes.

*THERAPIST:* What do you think the important skills are?

*TOM:* Thinking is important, following rules, being responsible, and getting along with others.

*THERAPIST:* So you see the skills they have been working on as important and also identify other important skills.

*TOM:* Yes. Especially getting along with others. We fight and argue way too much.

*NANCY:* That's for sure.

*FRAN:* Well, if she would listen to me, we would get along . . .

*THERAPIST:* I am going to interrupt you right there. I know that you have been working hard on solutions and want to keep that energy going. Do you agree with the skills for success that Tom just talked about?

*FRAN:* Yes. I think they are all important.

*THERAPIST:* Ask Nancy how she feels about the list of skills.

*FRAN:* (*looks at Nancy*) Well?

*NANCY:* They are okay, but I am not going to kiss anyone's ass.

*THERAPIST:* I promise you that nobody is asking you to kiss their ass. I am just interested in how people feel about the full list of skills, because so far you have had your favorite and your parents have focused on another skill area. It seems that there are many important skills.

*NANCY:* They all look important. But they have to get along with me, too.

*THERAPIST:* You are right. Everyone needs to find ways to get along.

# Developing a Foundation for Change

After highlighting and strengthening the family members' common themes, the practitioner begins to build intervention direction by reframing the commonalities as shared needs and wants. Individual members are coaxed to acknowledge the shared healthy needs and hopes. This stage of interactive engagement occurs through the following three interventions and strategies:

1. **Building on future hopes.** As individual family members express their hopes, you will generalize individual hopes to the family level. You can then guide family members in visualizing the outcomes they would like to see for the family.
2. **Capitalizing on noble or irrefutable positions.** You will highlight undeniable or noble positions that no family member can refute (e.g., nobody wants Nancy to get hurt). Because nobody can argue against these positions, they act to bind family members into collaborating.
3. **Capitalizing on shared human needs.** In the family sessions, you will identify human needs that are common to all members (e.g., need for validation, need for love) and integrate the family's needs into these universal needs. This strategy tends to normalize people's desires and needs.

## Highlighting Shared Needs and Desires

The family practitioner integrates common ground into family needs and desires, channeling the family's emotional energy into limited but shared needs. You will focus individual positions into these shared needs and hopes common to all family members. This technique reduces the energy investment from several themes to a limited number of central themes. Focus emerges as the number of needs reduce. Notice in Figure 8.5 how the common themes merge to form two identifiable goals.

Shared needs and desires become the foundation for a new problem definition that builds on the shared themes while simultaneously validating individual experiences. This balance between the shared and individual perspectives creates a definition of the family situation that all can buy into. As family members buy into the new definition, they begin to let go of the old self-serving definitions. Engagement deepens as the new definition is endorsed.

## Developing a Shared Problem Definition

To achieve a new definition, the practitioner and family members explore possible explanations of the family problems using the shared needs and desires. The new definitions must fit the lived experience of the family members. Some therapists develop the new definition without family collaboration (Jankowski & Ivey, 2001), but increasingly it is recommended that the new problem definition be developed through

**Figure 8.5**  Limiting the Common Needs

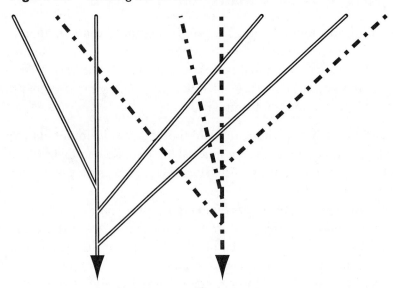

discussion and collaboration with family members (Hawley & Weisz, 2003; Tyron & Winograd, 2002). When family members feel that they are involved in the new definition, engagement and outcomes can be enhanced (Hawley & Weisz, 2003; Stewart, Valentine, & Amundson, 1991; Tyron & Winograd, 2002).

When developing the family's new problem definition, you must ensure that the family members experience hopefulness and safety. *Hopefulness* provides a belief that the family situation can be improved. *Safety* refers to definitions that prevent scapegoating and continued blame. As you explore the needs and potential definitions with the family, monitor the hopefulness and safety themes. If a proposed definition violates either consideration, continue exploring until a suitable understanding can be developed. In developing the new definition, it is useful to maintain a positive or strength-based focus.

## Identifying Direction for Change

In identifying the direction for change, the family practitioner begins to focus energy into one or two shared elements that fit within the new problem definition (see Figure 8.6). As energy is focused, a direction develops. In Figure 8.6 you can see how the number of needs can be reduced to a couple of overarching directions that can help the family to accomplish its goals. These goals capture the spirit of the multiple needs and desires identified in earlier steps. The family energy now becomes focused and has direction. This direction becomes the foundation for establishing family goals.

The final phase of direction introduces the concept of change. Based on the problem definition, you will help family members to explore what will need to

**Figure 8.6**  Development of Direction

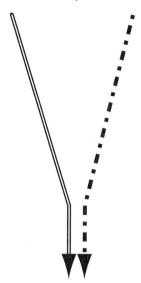

change. Such discussions move the family members toward goal setting and establishing objectives. At this point, you will build on the new problem definition by using the following three strategies:

1. **Identify what changes are needed to resolve the problems as newly defined.** Help the family to explore the new definition of the family problems and identify changes that could help resolve the current challenges. As in earlier stages, it is helpful to keep the focus on the family level rather than identifying individual changes, to avoid the defensive reactions.
2. **Identify what new family processes are needed to achieve the change.** Given that you have initially focused changes so they do not rely on individual-level change, help the family explore new processes that would help members meet their shared needs in the family. At this point, it is helpful to identify new types of interaction rather than identifying what not to do.
3. **Commit to work together to achieve the changes.** Solicit a commitment from all family members to work together to achieve the changes. Highlight and explore the positive outcomes associated with the changes for each member.

---

## CASE EXAMPLE

This example builds on the case examples used to illustrate the first three stages of interactive engagement. In this segment, observe how the direction evolves from the discussions of individual and family needs.

*THERAPIST:*  I am impressed with how much people want Nancy to succeed. Tom, what are the things that you find yourself doing to help her build the skills to success?

*TOM:* I try to pay for opportunities like teams and clubs that will help her develop skills. I know that she thinks they are fun things to do, but I see them as opportunities.

*THERAPIST:* Nancy, did you know that these activities were learning opportunities?

*NANCY:* No. I like to play soccer; I just want to play and like the people I play with.

*THERAPIST:* Does it surprise you to know that your father sees this as an investment in your future?

*NANCY:* A little.

*THERAPIST:* What do you see your mom doing to promote your being successful?

*NANCY:* She nags me and lectures me when I do something wrong.

*THERAPIST:* Do you think she likes these arguments, or is she doing these things to help you learn?

*NANCY:* I don't think she likes them.

*FRAN:* (*laughs*)

*THERAPIST:* Mom, you seem to agree with Nancy.

*FRAN:* I sure do. I wouldn't fight with her so much if I didn't care.

*THERAPIST:* Funny how fighting is often a statement of how much someone cares.

*FRAN:* Funny or sad, I don't know which one.

*THERAPIST:* It seems that everyone wants the best for Nancy, but things are not well coordinated. Kind of like everyone is working on things without talking to each other.

*TOM:* At least not without yelling.

*THERAPIST:* Sounds like you would like a calmer approach.

*TOM:* That is for sure.

*THERAPIST:* Is that something that everyone wants?

*ALL:* Yes.

*THERAPIST:* I am also struck that along with being loud and conflictual, you have missed out on some of the skills that you listed. I only hear you focusing on following rules, thinking, and some focus on getting along with others. What has happened on the responsibility skills?

*FRAN:* Well . . . we give her chores, but that ends up in arguments.

*TOM:* It is like more of the same.

*THERAPIST:* It sounds like you are trying to sneak in some responsibility, but you end up taking responsibility to make sure things get done.

*FRAN:* That is for sure.

*THERAPIST:* This seems similar to the other skills. A kind of backdoor approach without a lot of discussion and collaboration.

*TOM:* As compared to yelling and confrontation.

*THERAPIST:* Something like that. Is this something that people want to change?

*NANCY:* I want to change it.

*FRAN:* Me, too.

---

## ◆ EXERCISE 8.2  BUILDING COMMON GROUND

In your work with Corey's family, you have managed to neutralize the energy to the point that the automatic reactions are occurring less frequently. You are now ready to start building common ground. This exercise builds on your reframe, and it assumes that your reframe builds on the family's themes about caring. You want to use these themes to build common ground among the members as well as a sense of purpose. Remember, so far with this family, you have affirmed people individually but have not pointed out how everyone is really saying the same thing. Begin this process by describing your observation that everyone in the family is basically making the same argument. Make sure you are very descriptive. After describing your observation, get the family members to disclose what they need emotionally in the family.

1. First, make your observation.


2. Now, ask Brenda to describe to you what she needs in order to feel that people care.


3. In response to your question, Brenda replies, "I want people to listen to me when I tell them what I need rather than attacking me." You notice that Corey has been saying something similar, and you want to get him to discover the commonality between him and his mother. Describe an observation you have made about Corey, and use it to focus a question about his needs.


4. Corey stops slightly and thinks for a second; then he replies, "Nobody listens to me, they just accuse me of being a jerk." You notice he is shifting back to externalizing and want to get him to describe his internal experience.

Quickly respond to him with a question that will refocus him on his internal needs.

5. Corey responds, "I feel that nobody listens to me or cares at all." You sense that you are on the right track, but you want him to continue before people pick up on the embedded externalizing at the end of his statement. Follow up with another question that will get him focused on his internal needs.


6. Corey replies, "I just need people to hear what I say without it becoming an argument or an accusation that I am the asshole. I need to be heard too." You want to follow up this statement to support Corey's internalized exploration; ask a question (or make a reflection) that can continue this work.


7. You finally have Corey outlining how he wants to be heard without fighting. You know that this theme is very similar to Brenda's statement. You want to pull in others to solidify the common ground. Engage Carl in the exploration to highlight the common ground that he will likely have observed between Brenda and Corey.


8. Carl replies, "I think that both Corey and Brenda want to feel that they are being listened to when they talk." You want to include Carl in this need to expand the common ground; ask him about his needs.


9. Carl now identifies that he has similar needs when he talks with other family members. It is now time for Tim to be included; write your question to Tim that can include him in the common ground.


10. As Tim validates that he has similar needs to the others, you have established common ground among the members. Make a summary statement that can highlight the common ground.

11. Now take the common ground and redefine the problem in a way that infers a goal for treatment. Make sure the goal statement has a clear direction but is still abstract enough to gain broad acceptance from the family members.

---

Astute readers will have noticed that this exercise has brought you full circle to the goal-setting discussion in Chapter 6. Notice also how the exploration of common ground and other engagement activities yields important assessment information. As the exploration occurs through engagement, you will glean critical information that is reflected upon to form the understanding of family needs and treatment direction. At the end of engagement, the initial assessment is typically complete, and a treatment direction is achieved. The term *initial assessment* is used because you are constantly gathering additional information that influences your understanding of the family situation. This means that assessment is a dynamic rather than static event. Even after completing a formal assessment, you will always be adjusting clinical understanding as you continue working with the family to explore and adjust the understanding of the family situation.

## Summary

The four basic stages of interactive engagement, although discussed in a linear fashion in this chapter, cycle throughout the early stages of treatment. Family therapists often have to block the automatic patterns, move to promoting self-directed interaction, and then employ positive reframing. This stage will extend into the change-focused treatment, because families have many hot issues that can trigger the automatic reactions. Ideally, these cycles become easier as the therapist's working relationship with the family becomes more strongly established.

By the end of the interactive stage of family engagement, the therapist should have all important family members attending and sharing openly in the sessions. Defensive reactions should be minimal because the family members will have a shared sense of purpose and a definition of the problems that focuses on family-level change rather than individual change. This definition should lay a foundation for goals and objectives.

Although the focus at this point is on family-level change, every family member should have a strong sense that he or she will not be able to remain the same and count on others to change. Each person should understand that all family members will have different interactions and experiences as treatment progresses. While the therapist and family explore these demands, the hopefulness of the new problem definition must be strong enough to sustain motivation. This is why the individual needs and wants are a central element of the new definition.

Figure 8.7 illustrates the flow of the interactive engagement process and briefly describes the therapist's general strategies. Review this figure to understand the ideal flow of family energy as the therapist attempts to shape the family goals and treatment direction.

**Figure 8.7**  Phases of Family Engagement

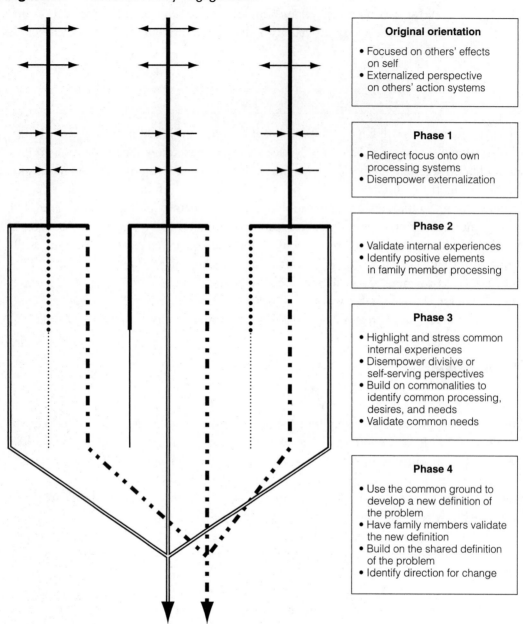

**Original orientation**
- Focused on others' effects on self
- Externalized perspective on others' action systems

**Phase 1**
- Redirect focus onto own processing systems
- Disempower externalization

**Phase 2**
- Validate internal experiences
- Identify positive elements in family member processing

**Phase 3**
- Highlight and stress common internal experiences
- Disempower divisive or self-serving perspectives
- Build on commonalities to identify common processing, desires, and needs
- Validate common needs

**Phase 4**
- Use the common ground to develop a new definition of the problem
- Have family members validate the new definition
- Build on the shared definition of the problem
- Identify direction for change

# Critical Content

1. After preliminary engagement, the family practitioner must deepen the engagement so all family members are interacting with a focus on shared family goals.
2. Interactive engagement occurs through four stages of therapist activity.

3. In the first stage of therapist activity, the practitioner blocks the automatic responses of the family members.

4. In the second stage, the practitioner tries to shift the emotional energy from negative to neutral or positive.

5. In the third stage, the family practitioner builds common ground among the concerns and perspectives of the family members.

6. Finally, the family practitioner uses the commonalities among the family members to negotiate a limited number of goals with the family members.

7. These four steps repeat and cycle, especially during the early stages of treatment.

## Suggested Readings

Friedlander, M. L., Heatherington, L., & Marrs, A. L. (2000). Responding to blame in family therapy. *American Journal of Family Therapy, 28,* 133–146.

Robbins, M. S., Alexander, J. F., & Turner, C. W. (2000). Disrupting defensive family interactions in family therapy with delinquent adolescents. *Journal of Family Psychology, 14,* 688–701.

Sholevar, G. P., & Schwoeri, L. D. (2003). Techniques of family therapy. In G. P. Sholevar (Ed.), *Textbook of family and couples therapy: Clinical applications* (pp. 225–250). Washington, DC: American Psychiatric Publishing.

Tyron, G. S., & Winograd, G. (2002). Goal consensus and collaboration. In J. C. Norcross (Ed.), *Psychotherapy relationships that work: Therapist contributions and responsiveness to patients* (pp. 109–125). London: Oxford University Press.

## Chapter 9

# Positioning Families for Change

The initial phases of engagement (preliminary and interactive) help family members make the decision to attend and actively participate in treatment. Although these are necessary preconditions for effective work, attendance and participation do not guarantee that family members will be willing to make the necessary changes. Many family members attend sessions and share their story, but when it comes to making changes, their motivation can begin to wane if not nurtured by the family practitioner.

## Theoretical Grounding

The concepts in this chapter are very strongly influenced by four theoretical schools. All of the theoretical models are related to each other and are often referred to as *brief therapy*. The models emerged over several years, beginning with the strategic model and emerging into the constructivist or narrative model. The differences between these models are often very subtle; the strategic model often is slightly more focused on action systems, and the solution-focused, narrative, and constructivist models are focused on how meaning is attributed. All theoretical models are useful to explore and understand, because the concepts employed in these models are highly influential in the family therapy field today.

To achieve the best grounding, you may want to examine the writings recommended in Table I.1 of the Introduction. These sources include some of the primary

**TABLE 9.1**
**Chapter Concepts, Theoretical Models, and Sources**

| Chapter Concepts | Theoretical Models | Suggested Reading |
| --- | --- | --- |
| Capturing motivating affect to facilitate change | Solution-focused model<br>Strategic model | Goldenberg & Goldenberg, Chapters 11, 13<br>Horne, Chapters 7, 9<br>Nichols & Schwartz, Chapters 12, 13 |
| Developing two visions: status quo versus change | Narrative model<br>Constructivist model | Goldenberg & Goldenberg, Chapters 13, 14<br>Horne, Chapters 8, 9<br>Nichols & Schwartz, Chapters 12, 13 |
| Using the tension between visions to generate change-focused energy | Narrative model<br>Constructivist model | Goldenberg & Goldenberg, Chapters 13, 14<br>Horne, Chapters 8, 9<br>Nichols & Schwartz, Chapters 12, 13 |

authors in the family practice field. For a briefer exploration, you can explore the sources presented in Table 9.1. Again, the sources in this table are limited to the following widely available textbooks:

◆ *The Essentials of Family Therapy* (2nd ed.), by M. P. Nichols & R. C. Schwartz, 2005, Boston: Allyn & Bacon.
◆ *Family Counseling and Therapy* (3rd ed.), by A. M. Horne, 2000, Pacific Grove, CA: Brooks/Cole.
◆ *Family Therapy: An Overview* (6th ed.), by I. Goldenberg & H. Goldenberg, 2004, Pacific Grove, CA: Brooks/Cole.

# Toward Positioning for Change

Family practitioners often refer to positioning skills as *double description* or *paradoxes* (White, 1986; de Shazer & Nunnally, 1991). In this chapter, *positioning* refers to the skills and strategies practitioners use to set the stage for change. Positioning helps family members to focus energy for change by creating a paradox (Guilfoyle, 2002; Huat, 1994). Most positioning strategies involve helping family members view the current situation in contrast to an alternate way of being. Thus a positioning strategy produces some tension between two visions of possibility (White, 1986). The juxtaposition of the two visions can tip the balance of competing forces (change-promoting versus change-hindering) in favor of change.

The concept of positioning evolves from the strategic family therapy literature (Bross, 1982). Strategic therapists viewed the therapist as actively involved in shaping the change effort. More recently, narrative theorists have refined the thinking on positioning. In this chapter, we will explore several common positioning strategies as well as the critical elements and strategies of positioning.

# Understanding Homeostasis

Positioning is best understood after first grasping the concept of homeostasis. The term *homeostasis* initially came from physics and was transposed into the behavioral sciences when von Bertalanffy (1968) promoted general systems theory as a paradigm whereby human problems could be understood. The homeostasis concept was advanced through the work of Gregory Bateson (1972) as he and his colleagues attempted to understand why families resisted change. In this chapter, we will sidestep the complexities of a full theoretical discussion, but it is important to be respectful of homeostasis and the counterchange forces whenever you attempt to help family members change.

*Homeostasis* refers to the energy-balancing mechanism in the family that keeps the system stable (Ariel, Carel, Tyano, & Dell, 1984). Homeostasis tends to operate in opposition to change-driven forces in the family. When forces begin to press for reorganization and change in the family system, homeostasis emerges (Goldstein, 1989). Homeostasis counterbalances the change forces to protect family members from the chaos associated with the loss of stability or predictability.

Homeostatic effects are evident in the fear and anxiety that often occurs when people find they must change. Even with family members who are initially motivated for change, the counterchange forces can be formidable (Adams, 2003). These counterchange forces may include habit, addictions, relationship payoffs, avoidance of feelings, interference of others, and a host of forces that are invested in maintaining the problem situation. When family practitioners attempt to create change without addressing the counter-work forces, change is often short lived because family members quickly return to pretreatment patterns.

Fortunately, families have internal mechanisms that enable change and adaptation. These internal mechanisms include problem solving, decision making, and goal setting. Notice that these family mechanisms for change all involve viewing a current situation and then constructing an alternative vision for a goal. These natural energies in the family are activated during positioning. At its most basic level, positioning helps the family members critically explore the current situation while simultaneously assessing an alternative vision for the family.

# Working With Motivating Affect

Although the basic assumptions of positioning are simple, positioning strategies can seem complex because they must tap into the family's motivations and healthy change mechanisms. Critical elements of positioning are in the family's power rather than a tool under the therapist's control, making the skills and strategy more difficult to apply. As the therapist, you must consequently begin by tuning in to the family members to learn how their belief systems operate (White, 1983). Here are four critical elements to find during the tuning-in process:

1. What feeling states motivate people in the family?

2. What in the current situation feeds the motivation of the different members?
3. What do people feel is missing in the current situation, and how do these gaps dovetail with the motivating feelings?
4. How do the missing elements combine to form a vision of what might be?

As you glean an understanding of these elements, you will discover important clues about how the family can best change. Some of these elements will have emerged during the assessment stage, but when positioning, you must listen from a different perspective. In assessment, you listen to the family story with the intent of understanding how the problems evolved and what the problem elements mean to the family members. As you listen to the family during positioning, you are interested in how people in the family become motivated to take action. This information becomes the critical understanding at this point in the treatment process.

## Feelings That Motivate Change

When you are listening for motivating feelings, it is useful to distinguish between the primary feelings and secondary emotions. The term *primary feeling* refers to feelings that occur at a visceral or pure level rather than feelings that are transformed through thinking. Feelings such as hopelessness, powerlessness, inadequacy, shame, joy, and so forth are all primary feelings. Notice that each of these feeling states has no direction or implicit focus for controlling the feeling. This makes the feelings difficult to control and manage. When experiencing a primary feeling, people can only make peace with and seek to understand the feeling. We cannot control or easily deflect the feeling. Many people struggle to cover up or make their primary feelings more controllable (Anderson & Leitner, 1996; Elliott, Watson, Goldman, & Greenberg, 2004a). In the attempt to control primary feelings, we often generate secondary emotions.

*Secondary emotions* are transformed feelings. The transformation occurs as we combine thinking and feeling to make the feelings state appear more manageable. Secondary emotions cannot exist without the presence of a primary feeling; this is why they are referred to as secondary. The term *emotion* is used to infer that a cognitive or thought process is also associated with the feeling. Emotions such as guilt, anger, frustration, and infatuation are all examples of secondary emotions.

Notice how each secondary emotion has a direction that allows us to externalize responsibility for the feeling. This externalization feature of secondary emotions creates the illusion that the primary feeling can be controlled (Elliott et al., 2004a). For example, if a woman is feeling powerless (e.g., she is late for work; people ahead are driving slowly; she cannot make up any time), she can shift the feeling from powerlessness to anger by blaming other drivers for the situation. In essence, the locus of control for the feeling has shifted outside of her to an external source. This externalization of the primary feeling makes it seem easier to handle, because the woman can now target someone else for causing the feeling.

## Recognizing Feelings and Emotions

Practitioners must listen intently to family members, for their story holds the clues to the solution (de Shazer, 1993, 1997). When you are listening to the family to learn how feelings motivate behavior, it is important to understand both the primary feeling and the secondary emotion. The primary feeling provides the energy for motivation. The secondary emotion indicates how the family member tends to process his feelings. If certain feelings promote anger, you may want to avoid using these feelings when positioning the family for change. It is most helpful to identify the primary feelings and secondary emotions that spur the family members to take action. Such feelings can become your ally in the change effort.

When you identify the primary feeling that motivates each family member, you will find that negative feelings are most obvious. You will often want to avoid dwelling on the negative feelings when working with family members, because doing so seems to pull people back into a problem focus. It is important to understand that every primary feeling has a positive counterpart (for example, the negative feeling of inadequacy is counterbalanced by mastery, shame is balanced by pride, etc.). When you try to use the feeling to motivate family members, it is helpful to identify the positive pole so it can be stressed. This approach is discussed later in the chapter, when we explore how to ally with the motivating affect.

## ◆ EXERCISE 9.1   POSITIONING FAMILY MEMBERS FOR CHANGE

You are working with a couple, Roland and Melissa, who are entering treatment because of their frequent arguments. Melissa shares that she is very unhappy and feels that Roland often judges her harshly. She reports that he tends to become verbally abusive when she says anything that can be construed as criticism. Even something as simple as asking him if he bought Halloween candy while he was out results in a counterattack. She reports that when they start the pattern of suggestion or question and counterattack, she presses him to see her point and seeks affirmation that her points and positions are valid. Roland says that Melissa is unreasonable and relentless when she is in an argument. Roland states that she follows him from room to room during an argument, and he sometimes has to lock himself in the bathroom for up to two hours to evade her pressure. Melissa states that the solution can be very simple if he will only admit when she is right. Roland argues that she is attacking him, and he will not agree that she is right.

Melissa comes from a family background full of physical, sexual, and emotional abuse perpetrated by her mother. When she was a child, her father was seldom around and would always tell the kids to "get along" with their mother when he left. Even when they told him about the abuse, he did nothing except tell them to get along with her. Roland comes from a family that was not physically abusive. His father was also seldom around, because he was active in community organizations. Roland's father was the main disciplinarian and had very high standards of conduct and performance. If Roland did not live up to his father's expectations, his father belittled him and chastised him, often in public. When Roland was a child, his father often belittled him in front of his teammates if he made mistakes while playing sports. Roland eventually quit all organized sports, even though he was a good athlete (according to Melissa).

Early in treatment, Roland and Melissa had the following exchange:

*ROLAND:* I don't know why you always have to find fault. It is like you are just waiting for me to make a mistake so you can point it out to me.

*MELISSA:* I'm waiting for you to screw up. I don't think so. You never see anything that I do right. Even if a million people told you I was right, you wouldn't believe it.

*ROLAND:* At least I don't follow you around just waiting.

*MELISSA:* No. You just assume I'm wrong and you are right. You never admit it when I am right.

*ROLAND:* Yeah . . . so you can rub my face in it.

*MELISSA:* I never rub your face in anything.

*ROLAND:* Then why do you follow me around just to gloat that you are right and I am wrong?

1. In the exchange, you notice some assumptions each person is making about the other. List the assumption each person is making about the other person.

2. Consider each assumption, and then identify which emotion (beneath the assumption) seems to be fueling the problem.

3. Review the emotion you identified. If the emotion is a secondary emotion (e.g., anger, frustration, guilt, etc.) identify a primary feeling that may be the foundation for the secondary emotion (remember that secondary emotions contain thinking elements that allow the feeling to be externalized). List the primary feeling for each family member.

4. Review the primary feelings that you identified. Most primary feelings have a positive and a negative pole. If the primary feelings you have identified are negative, identify a positive pole for each.

5. How might you use each of the positive primary feelings to help motivate change?

---

# Developing Two Visions: Change Versus Nonchange

Given the family homeostasis, practitioners appreciate that family members experience two simultaneous desires—one to stay the same, and the other to change (Giardino, Giardino, MacLaren, & Burg, 1994; Goldstein, 1989). Both desires exist simultaneously within each family member, but they seldom experience both desires at the same time. In practice, you cannot assume that all family members are consistently tuned into the same vision of change. Rather, you must attend to conflicted visions and feelings associated with change. These visions are at opposite ends of a continuum of current and possible family situations:

| | | |
|---|---|---|
| What is missing | versus | What could be |
| What must be given up | versus | What will be gained |

## Identifying the Visions

While tuning into the affective processes that can promote motivation, you will be listening intently to how these conflicting visions and feelings occur with each family member. In the assessment and engagement discussions, family members share what is missing for them in the current situation. Concurrently, they share information about the changes they would like to see in the family. You will be tracking these themes (what is missing and what could be) and starting to build two mental images: the current and possible situations (de Shazer & Nunnally, 1991).

As the images start to build, your critical thinking skills and the family discussions will start to illuminate the vision of what each family member must give up to achieve change. Such illumination emerges from the family discussions that indicate the benefits in the current situation. It must always be noted that situations continue over time only because there are payoffs for the people involved. These payoffs and benefits will become a problem if they remain ignored. Consequently, you must consider both the costs and benefits of change for each family member.

Family members' discussions of the current situation should give you valuable information about the benefits each person derives from the current problems along with the costs that they experience. The stories will be replete with winners and losers in many situations. These stories will give you some sense of how each person might be affected by change. The family practitioner pays close attention to the possible differential impact of change. Positioning will focus primarily on family members who have the most to lose if changes occur.

During the exploration, you will find two visions that fit for the family members. Each vision must be balanced according to costs and benefits. The first vision is the status quo vision, which includes the positive and negative outcomes that each family member will experience if he or she remains the same. The second vision includes the positive outcomes and costs that are associated with successful change.

## Assessing the Balance

When listening to the family stories, practitioners seek to understand the feelings, beliefs, relationships, and potential action choices that produce payoffs and maintain the problem (White, 1983, 1993). As you begin to understand the family's potential payoffs and change-hindering forces, you can acquire a balanced view of the true forces at play in attempting to facilitate change.

A useful method of documenting the change and counterchange forces is the *force field analysis*, developed by Kurt Lewin (1948). This method uses an energy metaphor to illuminate how some forces restrain change while others simultaneously attempt to promote change. The force field analysis is an attempt to list the elements on each side of the problem in order to identify the forces that are pushing in each direction.

To help understand the change and counterchange forces, you will find it useful to consider some of the payoffs inherent in the family system. The following is a partial list of potential payoffs that can inhibit change-focused action. These change-inhibiting elements can be inserted on one side of a force field analysis (see Figure 9.1).

◆ Other family members who benefit from or have an investment in the problem (e.g., I am a good child because you are bad)
◆ Problems occurring in response to another's actions (e.g., you have been volatile and I can play the victim)

**Figure 9.1** Force Field Analysis

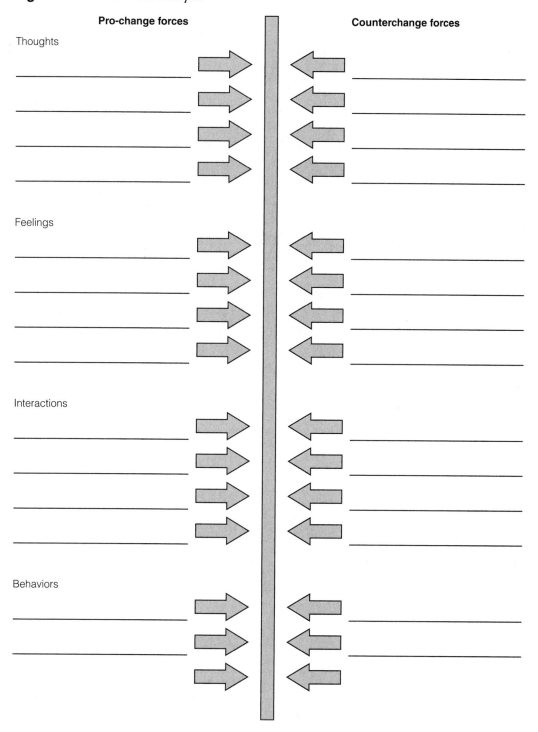

◆ Getting one's way through behavioral means (e.g., anger, pouting, etc.)
◆ Getting away with behaviors rather than being responsible (e.g., can drink all night, leave dishes around, blame others, etc.)
◆ Family members catering to another (e.g., I am volatile and others walk on eggshells around me, which gives me power)

- Instant catharsis (e.g., it feels good to blow up and get it over with rather than holding in or having to deal with tension)
- Highly reinforcing behaviors and problem behavior that yields its own reward (e.g., addiction, emotional catharsis)
- Belief systems that justify or rationalize the problem behavior (e.g., beliefs that tension must be avoided)
- Feelings that have a long association with past adaptive responses (e.g., soiled-goods feelings due to abuse, fears)
- Feelings experienced as enormous, overwhelming, or potentially dangerous and tending to breed avoidance reactions (e.g., avoiding tension, avoiding disappointing others)

## ◆ EXERCISE 9.2   CHANGE AND COUNTERCHANGE FORCES

Consider the case of Roland and Melissa from Exercise 9.1, and identify what each person will have to give up (or will lose or what costs might be evident) if the problems in their relationship are to be resolved. Identify costs in each of the processing system areas (behavior, interaction, thinking, and feeling).

1.  The costs to Roland will be:
    a. Interactions


    b. Behaviors


    c. Thinking patterns and beliefs


    d. Feelings

2. The costs to Melissa will be:
    a. Interactions


    b. Behaviors


    c. Thinking patterns and beliefs


    d. Feelings


Now identify what each person will gain if the problem is resolved.
    3. Roland will gain:
        a. Interactions


        b. Behaviors


        c. Thinking patterns and beliefs


        d. Feelings


    4. Melissa will gain:
        a. Interactions


        b. Behaviors

c. Thinking patterns and beliefs

d. Feelings

# Positioning Family Members for Change

As the practitioner considers the forces on each side of the field analysis, a picture of how the problem is maintained emerges. This balanced picture is important because both sets of energy will be activated when working toward change (Giardino et al., 1994). In practice, you can better set up the change effort by first trying to neutralize the family's counterchange energy while simultaneously increasing the pro-change energy.

As the family members' payoffs, desires, and needs become clear, you can mentally map out the linkages between the two visions and the affect of family members. Eventually you have a clear idea of problems in the current status, desired outcomes, and potential inhibitors to change. As these elements crystallize, you can reflect on the two visions, motivating affect, and elements to overcome to maximize the change efforts.

Tuning into the family motivations, visions, and inhibitors is but the first skill associated with positioning. Family practitioners also require refined thinking and interpersonal skills to repackage the family information and communicate it back to the family in a way that focuses the family's adaptive energies. In repackaging the family feelings and visions, you will engage the family in a focused exchange to harness the family's adaptive energy. This energy becomes a foundation for change-focused intervention. Here are the three interpersonal worker skills required for positioning:

1. Allying with the motivating feelings
2. Communicating the dual visions
3. Juxtaposing the visions to maximize tension

## Allying With Motivating Feelings

The first step of positioning is to ally yourself with the motivating feelings of the family members. Most family practitioners intuitively partner with affect. You can often sense what is important to the family members and use family thinking and affective patterns to keep the family's change motivation kindled. When described step-by-step, this intuitive process may appear complex; but as you examine the steps and skills, try to reflect on how you use these skills in relationships and in practice without thinking too hard about them. It is best to learn how you naturally use such skills and then harness your natural ability rather than trying to force yourself into a mold.

Alliance skills most often flow from your comfort in identifying and responding to feelings. This does not mean that you need to explore and have long discussions about affect. Rather, you need to notice feelings and be able to work with people's affective states. Most people do this on a regular basis; in practice, you need to be aware of how this recognition is occurring so you can use your ability with purpose.

When working with feeling states, you must understand the polarities of affect. Many feelings exist in polarized pairs. In this pairing, one feeling is pervasively negative, but it is paired with another feeling that is equally positive. If you are aware of the pairing, you can tap into either feeling to influence the family member. For example, if a family member is highly sensitive to feelings of inadequacy, you can access motivating affect by focusing on the positive feeling of proficiency. Notice in Figure 9.2 how the polarized pairs include both negative and positive feelings that you can stress in positioning for change.

When working through a family member's motivating affect, you are often appealing to the positive pole. This focus is particularly pronounced when conceptualizing the vision of what is possible. This approach can be particularly powerful if the opposite, negative pole is embedded in the current situation. For example, if a family member is motivated by reactions to powerlessness, you can stress increased influence

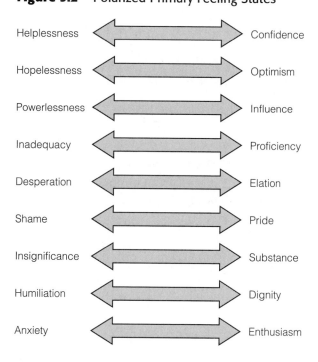

**Figure 9.2** Polarized Primary Feeling States

| | |
|---|---|
| Helplessness | Confidence |
| Hopelessness | Optimism |
| Powerlessness | Influence |
| Inadequacy | Proficiency |
| Desperation | Elation |
| Shame | Pride |
| Insignificance | Substance |
| Humiliation | Dignity |
| Anxiety | Enthusiasm |

in relationships as a by-product of change when discussing the alternative vision for the family. Concurrently, you can highlight powerlessness as a central element in the current situation.

## Communicating the Dual Visions

After identifying the affective poles in the family members' motivation system, you will develop the dual visions out of the family's descriptions of current and possible family situations. This double description provides a paradox for the family that can enhance the change potential (de Shazer & Nunnally, 1991; White, 1986). You will tie the affective polarities to the dual visions by allowing the negative pole to exist in the current situation while the positive pole is embedded in the alternative situation; the two poles thus function much like the antagonist and protagonist in psychodrama (Leveton, 1991).

When communicating the dual visions, you can either facilitate their emergence in interaction with the family or present them as an icebreaker for family discussion. If you want to have the two visions emerge through family discussion, you will make frequent reflections and summary comments to highlight each vision. If adopting an icebreaker approach, you will present the two visions to the family in a way that allows further exploration and discussion. Either way, you are seeking to establish both visions as a central focus for discussion. In the discussion, you need to ensure that the motivating affect is stressed through details and points of emphasis. These details and points of emphasis must be powerful enough to tip the balance of change and counterchange forces in the family.

As you communicate these dual visions to the family you will want to ensure that affective, cognitive, and behavioral elements are included in the descriptions, so that the family members can envision both alternatives at once. This can be a complex discussion with the family members, but it may be as simple as embedding a suggestion into a question. The important element is that you present both the current situation and alternative (new) situation in close succession, so that the family members can consider them together (Lobovits & Freeman, 1997).

---

**CASE EXAMPLE**

A family practitioner made the following statement to a man in treatment for spousal abuse. In this complex presentation, notice how the worker lays out the payoffs associated with both visions while stressing the man's anxiety and insecurity in the current relationship.

> I know that there are benefits you get from the current relationship with your wife. Right now she cannot question you, because she is afraid of you. She gives in to whatever she thinks you want, just to avoid hassles, and she will cater to you to make sure that you don't hit her. You have a lot of power in the relationship. Even though we both know that you don't have a right to all of this power, it must be nice to be able to control family members and have them cater to you. If you

decide not to change, you will keep this power; and if you do change, much of your power will be lost. However, the cost of this power is that you never know if your partner does things because she likes you or because she is afraid of you because your power comes from her fear. I know that many times you want to know that she loves you and she wants to be with you because of her love. You can never really know this unless you change. If you stop some of your controlling and violent ways in the relationship, your partner will be able to experience you in a different manner. You can be someone who gives in once in a while and lets her set some of her own priorities; through sharing her growth and encouraging her to be a whole person, you can be a much fuller part of her life and learn that she will stay with you because of the positive shared experiences. However, you must be brave enough to change to really experience this kind of relationship. Ultimately, the choice is yours.

## Juxtaposing Visions

As the two visions are articulated and explored, tension between the two directions (change versus nonchange) is created. The tension is inherent in the combination of change-focused versus counterchange forces. When the tension elevates, adherence to the status quo vision tends to loosen as family members consider the alternative (Giardino et al., 1994; Vaughn, 2000). Given that the two visions cannot coexist, family members must abandon one vision while endorsing the other (Huat, 1994).

The elevation of tension can have a powerful impact. The impact largely flows from the credibility of the description. Credibility stems from accurate presentations of both visions. In family practice, this requires you to accurately reflect both the positive and negative elements of each vision. When family members hear the current situation described, they feel affirmed and understood. When you describe the second vision, family members can transfer that credibility to the description of what is possible.

The emergent tension can disrupt the family homeostasis, because it can no longer operate outside the family's conscious considerations (White, 1993). Family members are encouraged to explore and consider both polar images as they begin thinking about change. Typically, you will first explore the current situation. This can be an interactive exploration that highlights the positive and negative elements in the situation or a descriptive sharing of the practitioner's observations. Regardless of how you develop the status quo vision, you must be sure to explore the drawbacks as well as the payoffs of the current situation.

After developing the status quo vision, you can begin exploring or laying out the alternative vision. In this phase of tension elevation, you will explore the benefits and costs of change. Although you may often wish to stress the benefits of change, it is important to provide a balanced exploration of what is involved in changing. This requires acknowledgment of the costs associated with change. Family members need to make an informed decision if they are going to select the alternative vision (Gross, 1994;

White, 1993). When the family members have all of the information and are empowered to choose, tension between the two options is at its greatest.

In presenting and exploring the two visions, an important element is to ensure that the family is involved in creating and assessing both options (Joyce-Becker, 1996; Vaughn, 2000). The partnership, the credibility of both visions, and the empowering of family members to choose are all critical elements for loosening tightly held beliefs and behavior patterns (Vaughn, 2000; White, 1993).

As the family members consider the two visions, they are placed in a position where they must abandon one in favor of the other. At this point the therapist actively explores the meaning of adopting either vision to ensure that the family members understand the meaning of change. As the family members develop a commitment to the change vision, you must help them identify how the changes will affect each person. It is sometimes useful to explore the change ramifications with each person so that all members of the family articulate a commitment to change.

# Strategies of Positioning

There are two basic strategies of positioning. The first is *punctuated positioning*, during which the family practitioner focuses significant time and energy on developing the two visions. The term *punctuated* is used because the flow of interaction is paused as you develop and explore the two visions. This type of positioning often occurs near the end of the engagement phase, when the practitioner is poised to move into change-focused intervention and wants to focus the energy so that everyone in the family is prepared to make changes.

The second type of positioning is *interactive positioning*. Interactive positioning strategies most often occur interactively during change-focused intervention. In interactive positioning, the practitioner briefly refocuses family members in a change-focused direction as part of the ongoing discussion with the family. Such strategies often occur seamlessly in the interaction through questions and reflections.

In the rest of this chapter, we will explore both types of positioning. First, we consider the mechanisms and strategies of punctuated positioning, which are illustrated with case examples. Following the exploration of punctuated positioning, interactive positioning strategies are described and illustrated. It is important to develop skills in both types of positioning because each type of positioning achieves different goals. Punctuated positioning provides an opportunity to stop and reflect about change, whereas interactive positioning is used as a nudge toward change during ongoing therapist-family exchanges.

## Punctuated Positioning

Many punctuated positioning strategies can be used with family members. Some strategies focus on providing visions of alternative behaviors and interactions; others focus on family beliefs. In the earlier example, the family practitioner selected a focus on the client's internal processing and emotional experiences. To disrupt how the current situation is understood or processed by the family, you will stress thinking and feeling in the alternative vision. Likewise, if you want to create visions of alternative behaviors and transactions, you will focus on action systems. In this section, we explore two approaches to punctuated positioning: action system strategies and processing system strategies.

*Action System Strategies*   As a practitioner, you will often want to promote family openness to new behaviors, interactions, and ways of relating. Consequently, you will focus the tension by juxtaposing the current problematic actions with a new vision of behavior and interaction. These strategies are referred to as *action system strategies* because the desired outcome is to enhance the behavioral and interactive change potential in the family. Two common action system positioning strategies are found in the clinical practice and professional literature:

1. Strategies highlighting past behaviors and interactions
2. Strategies that uncover alternative visions

*Highlighting Past Behaviors and Interactions*   An increasingly popular positioning strategy involves exploring past patterns of healthy responding to provide a vision of what the family might do differently. This strategy is a staple in strength-based and solution-focused approaches. This strategy is very affirming, because you will start by exploring the current situation and then shift to examples of family success. Family members identify and have the opportunity to build on past successes. Three specific strategies used in these approaches include identifying unique or exceptional outcomes, identifying the relative influence the family member has over the problem situation, and using scaling questions to identify progress and direction.

- ◆ **Highlighting exceptions and unique outcomes** (Weiner-Davis, de Shazer, & Gingerich, 1987; White, 1993, 1986). In using exceptional outcomes, you will explore the family situation and then explore times when the problem could have emerged but was circumvented by the family members (Carr, 1998; Milne, Edwards, & Murchie, 2001). First, you explore the typical outcomes and problem sequence to establish the status quo vision. After exploring this vision, you refocus the family members on unique outcomes or incidents when the problem should have emerged but did not. In this exploration, you go over the details of what people were doing differently at those times. The exploration builds on the unique outcomes to develop a new vision of how the current situation could be different.

---

## CASE EXAMPLE

A couple enters marital counseling because they are having difficulty with sexual relations. The woman reports that she has Crohn's disease, making intercourse painful. The therapist explores how each partner is approaching foreplay and intercourse, asking many questions about the thinking and feelings that emerge before the actual intercourse. The therapist then asks about when they have had intercourse and the woman felt no pain. They begin talking about several times when they have succeeded in pleasurable intercourse. The therapist again begins exploring the thinking, affect, and interactions surrounding successful attempts. She instructs the couple to keep thinking about these times and to try something different before the next session. In the next session, the couple explains to the therapist that stress seems to be a factor in the unsuccessful attempts to have pleasurable intercourse. The therapist again focuses on the successful attempts, asking the couple about how they might manage stress differently. After discussing many details leading up to the sexual act, the couple develops a plan for future lovemaking. About one year later, the therapist received a card announcing that the couple was pregnant and "things are much better now."

---

◆ **Using relative influence strategies** (White, 1986). Relative influence exploration follows a similar pattern to the unique outcomes approach. In this technique, the practitioner explores the impact or influence of the problem on the family members. In this initial exploration, you will spend time understanding how the problem is affecting different family members and how they are responding to this effect. In shifting to the alternative vision, you will turn the focus from the problem's influence on the family members to their influence on the problem. This second vision of the situation presents the family members as having control and power over the problem situation. As the family members describe areas of influence, they inadvertently describe an alternative vision.

---

## CASE EXAMPLE

Two parents enter treatment because of child disciplinary problems. The parents initially describe their child, a boy, as being out of control. They talk about bedtime routines and the multiple arguments arising whenever they ask their son to perform chores or follow rules. The therapist asks, "How is this problem influencing your lives?" In response, the parents speak of giving up going to friends, having to attend multiple meetings at school, arguing and fighting, and many adjustments. The therapist has the parents explore the extent to which the problem influences them in all areas of their lives. Again the parents reveal a long list of areas, including their intimacy, work, and other areas of functioning. The therapist then asks, "Tell me about the influence you have over this problem." The parents at first look puzzled, so the therapist states, "There are times that you influence the problem; let's start with one time." The parents then start talking about times when they are successful with their son. The exploration continues with a focus on the thinking, beliefs, affect, and interactions during those times. These parental elements are then explored in detail in the problem situations. The parents begin to identify how their tone and attitude often are different when their approach to the son yields arguments. The therapist encourages the parents to continue reflecting on the power they have in this situation. In successive sessions, the parents identify many areas that are under their control and begin making changes in their approach.

---

◆ **Using scaling questions** (Cade & O'Hanlon, 1993). Family practitioners use scaling questions to ask the family members to identify where they currently stand in relation to the two visions. The practitioner begins by asking the family to envision a scale with 1 being the status quo or problem vision and 10 (or some other higher number) being the vision of change. The practitioner then asks the family members to identify where they are on that continuum of change at the current time. Such questions help family members identify progress that they have made toward change while simultaneously orienting the family members in the direction of change.

---

## CASE EXAMPLE

A mother enters treatment because she has been lashing out at her children. Exploration identifies that she is struggling with the differentiation that occurs as children become adolescents and feels rejected because they no longer need her input. When she feels rejected by her children, she loses control and becomes verbally abusive with them. She is most uncomfortable with this change in their relationship and enters treatment to gain control. A vision of the problem is achieved in the early exploration, and a second vision emerges as goals are set. Occasionally, the therapist uses scaling questions as a check-in system. He says to the woman, "I want you to picture a scale where the number 1 means there has been no change and you are still lashing out at your daughter, and the number 10 means that you are in control of your lashing out and able to relate to your daughter's independence without feeling rejected. Based on how you are feeling and responding today, where would you be on that scale?" This use of the scaling question affirms the two visions while affirming progress toward the woman's goals.

---

In the techniques just described, the family members are led by the practitioner from an initial exploration of the problem situation into an exploration of elements that can be used to promote change. This duality provides visions of both sides of the problem situation in a way that enhances change-promoting energy. Through such exploration, you can easily move into change-focused work by helping the family members apply their undeniable strengths.

*Uncovering Alternative Visions*   A second action-system positioning strategy is to develop the alternative vision by identifying options in the problem situation. In such strategies, you will first explore the status quo situation. In shifting to the alternative vision, you then refocus the family members on action alternatives. Common strategies include creating dilemmas, exploring alternative paths, and using miracle questions.

◆   **Creating dilemmas.** In creating a dilemma for the family, the practitioner wants to guide the clients through their ambivalence about change. The originator of this approach, Michael White (1986), invites family members to explore and debate the reasons that they should not change, presenting the status quo as a viable option. The practitioner explores the benefits and seductive elements of not changing, helping the family members to seriously consider the nonchange option. The practitioner then has the family explore the costs of staying the same and the benefits of change. The practitioner remains neutral in the debates and seeks to have the client seriously consider both perspectives. The struggle between the two options is presented as a dilemma for the family members that only they can resolve.

---

### CASE EXAMPLE

A husband enters treatment because his wife is threatening to leave him. When he describes his situation, it becomes evident that he is very jealous and controlling. He speaks of his anxieties that his wife will find another man more attractive than him and he will lose her. As he describes the current situation, he outlines how he uses tension, anger, and money to limit his wife's ability to be with her friends or go out. He rationalizes that if she stays home, she will not meet another man and will stay with him. The practitioner says:

> I see a real dilemma for you. You can continue using resources, anger, and even nasty types of behavior to keep your wife in the home. You are a big guy, and you seem to be threatening enough to make her stay in. You can continue doing this, almost keeping her captive in the home to try to ease your anxiety. It has kept her in, but your anxiety never seems to go away, because you never know if she is with you because of her fear or because she wants to remain with you. Based on her recent discussions with you, it appears that even without another man, she may leave. Your continued use of these strategies will seem to take her in that direction. Another alternative is to relax your attempts to keep her home. Allow her to have friends, and make home a place where she can relax rather than feel captive. Your anxiety

about her leaving will probably remain; but if she stays, you will know that she is with you because you are the person she wants. This is a real dilemma. What are your thoughts about how you might resolve it?

---

◆ **Exploring alternative possibilities** (Milne et al., 2001). This technique involves first exploring the status quo vision. In this exploration, the practitioner focuses on the anticipated outcomes of the interactions and behaviors. As these goals are described and elaborated, the practitioner stresses how well the behaviors achieve the anticipated outcomes. This exploration highlights the futility inherent in the current position. After the initial exploration of the status quo, the practitioner guides the family members on other methods for achieving the goals. As other methods are explored, the practitioner helps the family assess each new option.

---

## CASE EXAMPLE

A couple enters treatment due to frequent arguments. The woman has precipitated the referral, complaining that her husband was perpetually coming home late from work. The woman expresses anger that when her husband was building his business, she was left at home alone with young children. She states that she is still left alone, because he works late almost every night. In exploring the situation, the woman explains that she becomes angry and argues with her husband whenever he is late. The husband outlines how he often loses track of time; and when he notices he is late, he stays very late because he is already in trouble. The practitioner explores how each person's reaction escalates the other person's. The practitioner then begins exploring alternative methods for ensuring that the husband can come home earlier. The couple begins listing alternatives and agrees to try some new options.

---

◆ **Using miracle questions** (de Shazer, 1985). Another brief strategy is the miracle question. In this technique, the practitioner uses an elaborate setup to prompt the family into reflecting on an alternative vision. The setup tends to include two important features: (a) The practitioner asks the family to pretend that a miracle has occurred; and (b) the practitioner introduces the idea that the miracle occurred outside of the family's awareness. Based on this setup, the practitioner asks the family members what they might see occurring to help them identify that the miracle has happened. From the family's answers and ensuing discussion, the practitioner helps the family develop the alternative vision. Questions are very detail focused and draw out descriptions of actions, interactions, thoughts, and feelings that would lead to awareness that the problem is gone. The level of description solicited from the clients provides the alternative vision of change.

---

## CASE EXAMPLE

A family enters treatment because the children are unhappy about their mother's remarriage. The children resist the stepfather's authority and he, in turn, tends to pressure and harp on the children. Often the mother becomes triangulated and feels she must protect the children from the husband while also protecting the husband from the children. The therapist wants to highlight an alternative picture and chooses the following miracle question: "I want you to think that in the middle of the night there is a flash and a soft sound. At the very moment that this flash and sound occur, a miracle happens and this problem is magically solved. However, you are all sleeping when it happens. Even those of you who hear the sound do not know that the problem is solved. Now the next morning, you get up as normal and start your daily routines. As you go about your day, what exactly do you notice that tells you that the problem is solved?" The mother talks mostly about internal changes, whereas the husband and children outline behavioral changes. A full exploration of an alternative vision is made possible.

---

*Processing System Strategies*   The action system strategies stress alternative visions of behavior or interactions to enhance change-producing energy. Such positioning strategies can converge with the initial motivation of family members to enhance the potential for change. In practice, you will often wish to focus on the family's tightly held beliefs and processing to develop enough maneuvering room to introduce the notion of change (Joyce-Becker, 1996; Vaughn, 2000; White, 1983). Processing system strategies attempt to create tension at the thinking and feeling levels to disrupt entrenched systems of processing that may inhibit change. Here are two types of strategy commonly used by workers:

1. Generating change-focused energy by modulating affect
2. Generating change-focused energy by altering attributions

*Modulating Affect*   At times, the practitioner wants to alter the affective experience of the family by introducing an alternative affect rather than a behavioral vision. This strategy is most frequently used when family members are ambivalent about change or at risk of changing too rapidly. In such situations, the practitioner seeks to slow down the process so that family members can gain emotional focus before trying to change. Practitioners engage family members in an emotionally focused exchange to allow a second affective vision to emerge and crystallize. Popular strategies include restraining change and the "shaggy dog."

♦ **Restraining change** (de Shazer & Molnar, 1984; Fish, 1997). To interrupt the clients' tendency to change too quickly (and thus shallowly), workers often side with the counter-work forces to restrain family members from changing. Workers enact such restraining strategies by verbally cautioning the clients to move slowly so they can better observe, assess, and learn about their situation (de Shazer & Molnar, 1984). Such actions often have a paradoxical effect of amplifying the motivating energy. In extreme situations, workers may even prescribe problems or relapses. Such activities allow the ambivalence to be accentuated and brought under conscious control. Change energies can concurrently be allowed to develop while the focus is on not changing.

## CASE EXAMPLE

A single mother and her two children enter therapy because her son is getting into trouble at school and in the community. In the initial exploration, the practitioner determines that the son is identified as the bad child in the family because he is loud and demanding. The daughter, who tends to whine, is identified as the good child. The mother finds the after-school period of the day most stressful because she is preparing dinner and the children are whining and demanding. The mother yells at the son because he is the hardest to ignore, and the evening is filled with tension. The family members cannot identify any patterns in the situation; so the therapist informs them that this problem seems to be very important, and it would be unfair to try interventions without first understanding the family. She consequently asks the family members to practice their behaviors every evening from 4:00 to 5:00 and write down their observations. They practice the behaviors in the office and are then expected to use them daily. When the family returns for its next session, the therapist helps them identify the daily and relationship patterns. She also recommends that they continue the pattern until they can identify an alternative that will work for the family. In the next session, the family members state that they did not complete the homework; instead, each family member identifies some different behaviors they are trying.

♦ **The shaggy dog strategy.** A common restraint strategy is referred to as the *shaggy dog* (Cade & O'Hanlon, 1993; Madanes, Keim, & Smelser, 1995; Otani, 1989). This strategy is useful when the practitioner expects resistance or high levels of ambivalence from the family. When using the shaggy dog strategy, you will state that you know of a solution, but the time isn't right to use it. Typically, you will imply that the family is not yet ready for the change strategy because it is very demanding and suggest that family members need to learn more about the problem. You then instruct the family to continue learning about the problem. This strategy is often used in successive sessions, each time identifying that there is a solution while concurrently restraining the family from change. After several repetitions of this strategy, family members have gained new motivation to try the change strategy. You can then gain a commitment to try the change strategy.

---

## CASE EXAMPLE

A couple enters therapy because of frequent arguing. In the initial exploration, a pattern of verbal assault is noted in which the husband frequently berates, puts down, and humiliates his wife. Although there is no physical abuse, the level of emotional and verbal abuse is causing the wife to fight back and consider leaving. The payoffs for the husband are very strong, because the woman tends to cater to him. Neither person is happy in the marriage, but the distress is not strong enough to prompt changes, especially for the husband. The therapist wants to use a contingency contract intervention, but is not sure that the husband will comply. The therapist is also concerned that the wife does not have enough personal power to monitor compliance. The therapist consequently states that there is an intervention that would likely work, but the couple is not ready to try it. The therapist makes this statement again during the next session, causing the couple to argue that they are ready. The therapist responds, "I know you want to try the intervention, but it will require you to both do things that will be unwelcome and uncomfortable. I don't think we are at a point where you will follow through. For this to work, you must agree to do certain things that you won't want to do; and I can't tell you what they are until you guarantee that you will do them. Let's wait until we know we are ready." During the next session, the couple makes the guarantees, and the therapist proceeds with the intervention.

---

*Altering Attributions*   Family members tend to experience life with either an internalized or externalized locus of control. An *internalized* locus of control is associated with an individual's beliefs that he can influence life events. Family members with an externalized locus of control deflect responsibility to external sources and feel controlled by external forces. Some people internalize aspects of a problem and feel that the cause of the problem is inherent in their personality. In such situations, they want to shift the stigma to an external source. Likewise, when a family member is *externalized*, she often wants to enhance internalizing attributions. Common strategies for achieving this switch are externalizing symptoms, personification, and reframing.

◆   **Externalizing the symptom.** This approach has been advanced in the work of Michael White (1984). When using this positioning strategy, the practitioner and family member first explore current conceptualizations of the problem. In listening to the client story, the practitioner pays particular attention to the causal links, meanings, and attributions made by the client. After gaining an understanding of how the client understands the problem, the practitioner externally reframes the symptom. This shift moves the sense of ownership of the symptom and allows the client to experience the symptomatic behavior as some external enemy rather than a loathed part of their personality. This shift in perspective alters the focus of change, so the worker and client are collaborating to overcome the external problem rather than trying to change the individual.

---

## CASE EXAMPLE

A lesbian couple enters treatment due to frequent arguments. The initial exploration indicates a pattern wherein each person at times takes the comments or behaviors of the other personally and begins escalating an argument. Each woman refers to the other as insensitive and uncaring. The escalation continues until the person who initiated the argument feels validated. Both partners have abusive backgrounds: One has a history of physical, emotional, and sexual abuse and the other has a history of psychological abuse through shaming. In discussions, the therapist observes reactivity in both partners whenever criticism is provided by the other. The therapist externalizes the reactions by suggesting, "It seems like both of you have a little creature hiding in the shadows. Every once in a while you are talking with each other and this creature jumps onto your shoulder and starts whispering in your ear. Donna, I notice that he whispers things like 'You can't trust her. She doesn't like you. She really hates you'; and Frances, I notice messages like 'You are inadequate. You can't do anything right' whispered in your ear." The couple explores these messages and agrees that they are the themes of their self-talk. The therapist then suggests that it will be important to learn more about these little animals; he asks the couple to reflect on the animals and find their name. The next week, each woman says she has named her animal after the parent who was most abusive to her. The quest of treatment becomes helping the couple to outsmart these abusive animals.

---

◆ **Personification.** Sometimes people disempower themselves by making introjected statements and by viewing themselves from another person's critical position. Family practitioners can often identify that a family member is judging himself by adopting someone else's judgments or views. When such perspective borrowing occurs, the therapist can externalize the judgments by helping him attach an identity to the judgment. As the judgment is personified, it is easier for the family member to adopt a new perspective on the situation.

## CASE EXAMPLE

Antoine is very volatile and becomes verbally aggressive when his partner Gwen says things that could be interpreted as critical. The therapist, who knows that Antoine has a long history of severe criticism by his mother, notices themes suggesting that Antoine experiences criticism as an extension of his mother's influence. When he receives criticism during a session and the therapist notices an emotional reaction, she asks Antoine to close his eyes and visualize the person who is judging him. Antoine immediately states that it is Gwen. The worker suggests that maybe Gwen is using someone else's eyes; she asks Antoine to focus only on the eyes and then share whose eyes he is seeing. Antoine states that they are his mother's eyes. The therapist then develops an image of the mother leaping out from the shadows onto Antoine's back and whispering negative statements in his ear when he and Gwen have difficult discussions. The therapist suggests that the mother is controlling him by robbing his power and setting up a fight with Gwen. This image became useful in helping Antoine separate his sensitivities to criticisms from the intended messages of his partner.

◆ **Reframing the meaning.** Family therapists have used reframing strategies for many years. Such strategies became popular with the strategic therapy movement (Adams, 2003) and have been expanded by the narrative therapists (Fish, 1997). In reframing, the worker first explores the current belief systems that guide interpretation. In this initial exploration, the practitioner pays particular attention to the beliefs, events, and cast of characters involved in the problem situation. The practitioner then identifies alternate meanings that fit the characters and circumstance but lead the family toward change-permitting interpretations. The worker then shares the alternative meaning, using the same elements and details and changing only the interpretation of the situation.

## CASE EXAMPLE

A family enters treatment, complaining that the children often get out of control. The parents punish the children, but long-term changes have not been evident. In the initial exploration, it appears that the children become loud and argue with each other when the parents are stressed and busy. Frequently, the behaviors emerge when the parents are running late for work in the morning or having to hurry through dinner because of other obligations. The therapist highlights the elements (stress, limited time, lack of attention to the children) and offers the following interpretation for the family: "It seems to me that the children are like a stress barometer in your family. When you (parents) are off of a balanced schedule, the children start to wind up. They are almost like the canary in the mineshaft. As they start to become loud, you are running out of time and energy." The parents agree that this seems to be occurring and start looking at the children's behavior as reflecting their emotional state rather than as a problem inherent in the children.

---

### ◆ EXERCISE 9.3   USING THE TWO VISIONS

In Exercise 9.1, you identified motivating affect for both Roland and Melissa. In Exercise 9.2, you identified what each person will gain and lose if the problem is resolved. In this exercise, you will use that information to develop and present dual visions for the couple.

1. Using the information you already have, present a dilemma to Roland. Begin with some sort of statement, such as "This must be a real quandary for you," and then lay out a summary of what he will have to give up and what he will gain. After laying out the two sides of the dilemma, establish it as a challenge that he must resolve.

2. Using a miracle question format, set up and ask a question of Melissa that will help her visualize how her life would be different if the problem were resolved.

3. Using the unique outcomes (or exceptional situation) questioning strategy, have Roland describe the times that he could have reacted in a counter-attack mode with Melissa when he felt criticized, but he did not.

4. Both Roland and Melissa have backgrounds that likely caused them to internalize difficult messages when they tried to make sense of things during their childhood. Consequently, you want to externalize the negative messages that seem to fuel the difficult emotions. Using the strategy of either externalizing the symptom or personification, make a statement that will challenge the couple to shift these elements to an external focus

(you may want to review the examples and descriptions before attempting this).

5. Reframe the meaning in the problem situation so that Roland's mastery needs and Melissa's validation needs can coexist through the new definition of the problem.

## Interactive Positioning

In interactive positioning, the two visions have already been established for the family members. Frequently, punctuated positioning has already occurred; but the family members may momentarily be losing focus. In such situations, you will seek to refocus the family member toward change. Interactive positioning achieves focus without stopping the interactive flow. Rather, it builds on the client's last statement while incorporating small challenges or refocusing statements that cause the family members to think more critically about the situation.

The practitioner's interactive positioning responses take what the family members have put on the table and extend the story line to create critical thinking and focus. The interactive nature of this style of positioning allows you to redirect family members toward change in a natural manner. The positioning occurs through the questions and reflections you offer in response to family statements. These responses usually contain three elements:

1. The practitioner affirms the family member's statement.
2. After the affirmation, the practitioner adds a thought or observation that introduces information not reflected in the family member's statement.
3. The practitioner poses a question that causes the family member to respond based on integrating the new information.

Following are response strategies that illustrate some of the interactive positioning alternatives.

◆ **Reflecting logical outcomes.** Logical outcomes tend to be used when the family members have not fully identified the potential costs or outcomes inherent in their position. The practitioner begins by acknowledging the family member's position and then extends the position to a logical outcome. The practitioner then prompts the family for a response that must use the logical outcome.

---

### CASE EXAMPLE

An abusive parent is upset with his son for throwing rocks through a neighbor's window and says, "I should just throw rocks at him. That will teach him." The practitioner wants to reorient the parent to the work toward nonviolence and responds, "While that can ease the embarrassment, taking your child to the emergency room after the rock bashes in his head might create some new challenges. Any thoughts on what else you might do?"

---

◆ **Reflecting ambivalence.** Family members often have tendencies to rush solutions by ignoring payoffs in the status quo. Another tendency is to engage in change efforts that are unlikely to succeed. In such situations, family members fail to fully appreciate the costs of change and set up potential failures. When such tendencies emerge in treatment, practitioners often slow down the change effort by reflecting the ambivalence in the situation.

In such responses, the practitioner first affirms the family position and then cautions the clients to move slowly so they can explore some of the reasons they may not want to change.

## CASE EXAMPLE

A 15-year-old woman enters treatment because her mother has sent her to live with relatives after a volatile argument. There have been many arguments due to an anxiety disorder that causes the mother to accuse the daughter of using drugs and engaging in sexual activity. In the most recent argument, the mother has tried to restrain the daughter from going out with her friends. The daughter is referred for treatment because of her pain and anger about the mother. Shortly after entering treatment, the young woman visits her mother during the winter break. During the visit, there is no arguing, so the mother tells her daughter she can move back home. The young woman consequently announces to the therapist, "Things have blown over now, so I am going to move back in with my mother." The therapist responds, "Sounds like the visit went well. It seems like part of you wants to believe that your mother has changed. Tell me about the other part of you that is afraid to believe in the change."

◆ **Incorporating new knowledge.** Sometimes family members make decisions based on old patterns of thinking rather than including changes developed in the treatment context. When a practitioner notices that a family is basing decisions on old patterns, he seeks to challenge the family members to revise their responses based on the new information. The practitioner consequently affirms an element of the family statement and then reminds the family members about the new information developed in treatment. He then poses a question that requires the family members to integrate the new information into their decision making.

## CASE EXAMPLE

A family enters treatment to focus on more effective discipline. The parents both have different models and expectations of the children, which allows the children to pit one parent against the other and undermine cohesive co-parenting. In a family session, the eldest daughter makes a statement indicating that she is going to a party at a senior's house on the weekend. Upon hearing the statement, the mother appears stern, and she looks at her husband. The worker, suspecting that the old pattern is emerging again, says, "Felicia, I know you want to go to the party, and you have used your skills to get permission. Now, given what you now know about the family from our work together, what do you need to do right now to ensure that your permission is really legitimate?"

♦ **Embedding options** (Penn, 1982; Tomm, 1987b). Family members sometimes struggle to identify a viable direction that seems obvious to the therapist. In such situations, practitioners do not want to tell family members what to do; but they do want to help focus the family members' thinking. To achieve this focus, practitioners can embed a suggestion in a question or reflection. As the practitioner asks the question or summarizes, she presents the alternative vision to the client without directly suggesting it. Rather, she puts the idea on the table in a way that requires the clients to reflect on the alternative but be in control of how they adopt the suggestion.

## CASE EXAMPLE

A woman enters treatment because her lesbian partner is thinking of leaving the relationship. She speaks at length about misunderstandings and differences about how each partner handles stress. She is very distraught about the idea that her partner may leave over issues that are nothing but misperceptions. It is obvious that neither partner has discussed the nature of their differences. At one point the young woman says, "I just think it is stupid. Gail always thinks I am angry, but I am not. She just can't tell the difference." The therapist responds, "When you discuss the differences with her, what is her reaction?"

♦ **Embedding hypotheses** (Penn, 1982; Tomm, 1987b). The same strategy can be used for offering alternative understandings to family members. In this adaptation of the preceding technique, the family practitioner introduces an alternate vision by embedding a new meaning or hypothesis in her response. Again, the practitioner can embed the hypothesis in a question or use a reflective response.

## CASE EXAMPLE

A couple enters treatment due to frequent arguments. In the initial exploration, they describe a pattern of tension buildup, arguments, and then closeness. The practitioner suspects that there is no mechanism for problem solving in the relationship, so differences remain unresolved until an argument occurs. She hypothesizes that this is why the couple experiences closeness after a fight. The therapist asks, "Do you notice that after a fight the two of you seem to feel closer? How is it that you use fighting to bring yourselves closer to each other?"

---

◆ **Perspective taking** (Penn, 1982; Tomm, 1987b). When family members are locked into their own perspective, practitioners often use perspective-taking strategies to help each understand the other's position. In this strategy, the status quo vision is the polarized rigidity, and the alternative vision is the other person's understanding. Perspective taking is frequently used when one person adopts a strong position and is oblivious to the perspectives of other people. The practitioner encourages the "stuck" family member to state the alternative position in order to promote self-reflection and openness. This strategy can involve perspective-taking questions, role-reversal activities, and other methods of promoting perspective adoption.

---

## CASE EXAMPLE

A couple attends a session looking very upset. When this observation is shared, they begin arguing about sources of stress in the home. The husband is very upset and angry that he is being accused of not helping out. The conflict is escalating and becoming irrational. The therapist, wanting to shift energy toward more fruitful problem solving, asks the husband, "Frank, what is it that Delores feels you should be doing around the house?" Frank then starts outlining the chores he should be performing and freely admits that he has stopped doing these chores. Delores remains silent during this exchange because Frank is presenting her argument. The therapist's perspective-taking question allowed the tension to decrease to the level where rational problem solving could occur.

---

## ◆ EXERCISE 9.4   INTERACTIVE POSITIONING

In your continuing work with Roland and Melissa, you come across several situations where their motivation and focus have started to slip. Use interactive positioning skills to help them with the following situations.

1. You are in a session with Roland and Melissa, and the topic of parenting comes up. Melissa indicates that Roland is quite harsh and says that she wishes he would be a little more lenient with their son. Roland begins to

counterattack. Describe your observation of the escalation to Roland and use a logical outcomes strategy to help him regain his focus.

2. In the sessions, you have been able to help Roland understand that Melissa's experiences were always denied when she was growing up. You are also able to help Melissa understand that Roland is prone to feeling inadequate when he feels criticized, especially if the criticism seems overwhelming and continuous. In one session, Melissa begins to criticize Roland and pressure him for validation of her perspective. Using a perspective-taking strategy, make a statement to Melissa that will help her understand Roland's perspective.

3. In today's session, both Roland and Melissa seem on edge and are highly critical of each other. You get the sense that Melissa is feeling a need for validation, and for some reason, Roland is withholding the validation. Use an embedded hypothesis question to start positioning the couple to change the interaction.

4. The hypothesis seems to have been partially effective, but Roland appears to be struggling with changing his responses to Melissa. Use a question with embedded options to help him focus.

5. Although the embedded options seemed to help initially, Roland still seems reticent to validate Melissa. You want to reflect his ambivalence to change, so that you can highlight once again the rewards and costs associated with resolving the relationship problems. Use a reflecting ambivalence strategy to spur Roland toward validating Melissa.

# Summary

Positioning is important but limited in scope. The importance of positioning stems from the foundation it provides for creating change. This foundation contains four important elements. First, the juxtaposition of two visions that can both fit into the family realities threatens the family beliefs that support the status quo. Without loosening these belief structures and interactions, enabling lasting change will be difficult. Change-focused interventions can build on the openness that accompanies this loosening.

The second element is the provision of a new vision. In the dual visions, the family members can explore and adopt the second vision for directing their change. As family members discover strengths and options, they are in a better position to exercise control over their situation (White, 1984, 1986). Each person has an opportunity to envision himself or herself differently in the family situation. Such visions provide a blueprint for the necessary changes.

A third critical element of positioning is the exploration that emerges between the family and therapist. Through this exploration, the practitioner gleans an appreciation for the counterchange forces in the family. As the family gains full knowledge of these forces, they are empowered to take more complete control of their situation (White, 1993). Seldom do families openly acknowledge and address the counterchange forces that keep problems in place. Having engaged in such assessment, the family is better prepared to control its members' own resistance (Goldstein, 1989).

The final element of positioning is the deepening of family engagement. As the family members explore the conflicting forces and corresponding visions for the family, motivation for change deepens. Family members will not only be more open to engaging in change-focused intervention but also able to focus their energy on achieving change.

These elements provide the foundation for change-focused intervention. Notice in this language that the scope of positioning is presented as a precondition rather than as the impetus for ongoing change. In practice, you must build on this foundation with other strategies to help families achieve their visions (de Shazer & Nunnally, 1991). Doing so requires family practitioners to be skilled in intervention strategies that can alter the family behaviors, interactions, beliefs, and affective processes. These intervention strategies are explored in the upcoming section.

Although positioning provides a foundation, do not assume that the foundation requires no further attention once established. Positioning strategies are used repeatedly during treatment, because family members and their change motivations will fluctuate throughout treatment. You will begin positioning early in service, but you will often need to use some positioning strategies throughout treatment to set up change interventions and adjust the working alliance. You are likely to use interactive positioning quite frequently; however, because of the time and energy involved in the punctuated positioning strategies, you will use them less.

# Critical Content

1. *Positioning* refers to a class of strategies for addressing homeostatic and counter-change processes in the family.
2. Positioning builds on the feelings that motivate each family member. The therapist works through the positive pole of the family members' primary feelings.
3. Positioning relies on two visions, or a double description of the family situation. The first vision is status quo; the second is an alternative vision for the family members.
4. The two visions cannot coexist in the family, and they create tension that helps to loosen up the family's rigid beliefs and actions.
5. There are two types of positioning: punctuated (self-contained events during treatment) and interactive (occurring in the ongoing exchanges with family members).
6. There are many strategies for creating and exploring the two visions with family members.
7. Positioning is often necessary at different times to adjust the helping relationship and to refocus the family on change.

# Suggested Readings

de Shazer, S., & Nunnally, E. (1991). The mysterious affair of paradoxes and loops. In G. R. Weeks (Ed.), *Promoting change through paradoxical therapy* (pp. 252–270). Philadelphia: Brunner/Mazel.

Joyce-Becker, J. (1996). The dominoes fall: Attending to stability. *Journal of Systemic Therapies, 15,* 80–91.

White, M. (1986). Negative explanation, restraint, and double description: A template for family therapy. *Family Process, 25,* 169–184.

White, M. (1993). Deconstruction and therapy. In S. G. Gilligan & R. Price (Eds.), *Therapeutic conversations* (pp. 22–61). New York: Norton.

## SECTION IV

# CHANGE-FOCUSED INTERVENTION

Throughout Section IV, we will examine the skills and strategies for creating change in the family. Chapters 10 and 11 are an exploration of direct strategies of change. Direct change strategies are compliance based and rely on a solid working relationship with family members. The direct change strategies are followed in Chapter 12 by an exploration of indirect strategies for change.

In Chapter 10 of this section, we explore four basic types of direct strategies for influencing family action systems. First, we look at actor-model strategies and consider the assumptions of role-playing and modeling behaviors. We then turn to a discussion of teacher-coach strategies, which are more intrusive. After considering specific teacher-coach strategies and their assumptions, we examine several behavior interruption strategies, which help to interrupt the pattern of problem behaviors. Finally, we discuss weight-shifting strategies and look at some examples.

In Chapter 11, we explore direct change strategies for influencing family processing systems. The focus of this chapter is on strategies for altering beliefs, interpretations, and feelings. We begin by examining strategies that highlight cognitive and emotional processes in the family. Then we consider slightly more directive strategies for challenging family belief systems. Finally, we look at some strategies for altering the internal-external and positive-negative dimensions of people's experience.

In Chapter 12, we explore indirect change strategies. We begin by considering the strengths and challenges of internal resource activation strategies such as visualization and metaphoric interventions. Then we examine methods of working indirectly through people in the family environment, and look at some examples of negotiating roles with potential support people.

## Chapter 10

# Direct Change Strategies for Influencing Family Action Systems

In earlier chapters we explored the assessment and understanding of family action systems. It is not enough just to understand family behaviors and interactions; the family practitioner must be able to help families make important changes in how their members act and relate to each other. In this chapter, we focus on strategies and skills for helping families with such changes. Building on the concept of positioning families for action system changes as described in earlier chapters, here you will learn specific strategies for creating change in the family system.

## Theoretical Grounding

Although there are multiple theoretical models in family treatment, some models of promoting family change have a stronger emphasis on behavior and interaction. These models also may seek to change thinking or affective elements, but they often do so by first trying to change the behaviors or interactions in the family. It is often assumed that as the behaviors change, the feeling and thinking will follow. Consequently, the family practitioner begins with the behavioral or interactive focus. You will often find it useful to start with behavioral types of change, because the interventions can be less intrusive. However, if the family member has feelings such as guilt or shame attached to the behaviors, you may be wiser to start with the thinking or affect.

**T A B L E 10.1**
**Chapter Concepts, Theoretical Models, and Sources**

| Chapter Concepts | Theoretical Models | Recommended Readings |
|---|---|---|
| Modeling skills and behaviors can promote change. | Behavioral model Cognitive-behavioral model | Becvar & Becvar, Chapter 12<br>Goldenberg & Goldenberg, Chapter 12<br>Horne, Chapter 15<br>Nichols & Schwartz, Chapter 10 |
| Role-playing builds skills. | Behavioral model Cognitive-behavioral model | Becvar & Becvar, Chapter 12<br>Goldenberg & Goldenberg, Chapter 12<br>Horne, Chapter 15<br>Nichols & Schwartz, Chapter 10 |
| Family members often need to be coached in new interactions. | Behavioral model Cognitive-behavioral model Strategic model Structural model Communication (human validation) model | Becvar & Becvar, Chapters 9, 10, 11, 12<br>Goldenberg & Goldenberg, Chapters 9, 10, 11, 12<br>Horne, Chapters 4, 6, 7, 15<br>Nichols & Schwartz, Chapters 6, 7, 10 |
| Interrupting habitual or learned behavior patterns allows room for change. | Behavioral model Cognitive-behavioral model Strategic model | Becvar & Becvar, Chapters 11, 12<br>Goldenberg & Goldenberg, Chapters 9, 10, 11, 12<br>Horne, Chapters 6, 7, 15<br>Nichols & Schwartz, Chapters 6, 7, 10 |
| Tipping the balance between work and counter-work forces promotes change. | Behavioral model Cognitive-behavioral model Strategic model | Becvar & Becvar, Chapters 11, 12<br>Goldenberg & Goldenberg, Chapters 9, 10, 11, 12<br>Horne, Chapters 6, 7, 15<br>Nichols & Schwartz, Chapters 6, 7, 10 |

Table 10.1 presents the theoretical models that focus most strongly on behavior and interactive changes. As in previous chapters, this table provides some of the critical chapter concepts along with the theoretical models that support these concepts. Five theoretical models tend to focus on action system change as an avenue of first attention. The strategic model focuses on a directive approach to having family members try different behaviors and interactions. This approach is directive, because the therapist using it tells family members exactly what to do. Behavioral and cognitive-behavioral models adopt more of a teaching approach or use modeling types of strategies along with finding methods for enhancing or restraining the work and counter-work forces described in Chapter 9.

As you explore the chapter concepts, it is useful to remember that many roles, behaviors, and behavioral constraints have a cultural element. Nurturing, disciplinary, access, and guidance functions in the family will change from culture to culture. It is important to consider the cultural scripts and constraints before identifying a behavior or interaction as a primary target for change. The culture ring introduced in Chapter 3 can be useful when you are considering family behaviors or interactions for change. This is an especially sensitive area when you are working with family role performance.

The theoretical models introduced in Chapter 10 are discussed in the following easy-to-find textbooks:

- *The Essentials of Family Therapy* (2nd ed.), by M. P. Nichols & R. C. Schwartz, 2005, Boston: Allyn & Bacon.
- *Family Counseling and Therapy* (3rd ed.), by A. M. Horne, 2000, Pacific Grove, CA: Brooks/Cole.
- *Family Therapy: An Overview* (6th ed.), by I. Goldenberg & H. Goldenberg, 2004, Pacific Grove, CA: Brooks/Cole.
- *Family Therapy: A Systemic Integration* (5th ed.), by D. S. Becvar & R. J. Becvar, 2003, Boston: Allyn & Bacon.

# Changing Action Systems

The professional literature includes many different strategies, each grounded in a theoretical approach to treatment. When you are looking for change strategies, this array of strategies can confusing, because the multiple approaches are all touted as being distinct and different. In this chapter, we will seek to sift through the differences to find commonalities among the different approaches to treatment. Within these commonalities are the important skills you need to become an effective family practitioner.

In the literature, four types of strategy appear to be commonly used by practitioners when trying to influence action systems. Each of these strategies involves different skill combinations for influencing the family's actions and interactions:

1. Actor-model strategies
2. Educator-coach strategies
3. Behavior interruption strategies
4. Weight-shifting strategies

Each of these strategic categories contains important assumptions and skills. Family practitioners must understand these requirements when applying the strategy. In the following sections, we outline some important assumptions and then explore specific interventions within each strategic category. This approach will give you not only an understanding about applying each type of strategy but also the particulars of using the different interventions to promote change.

# Actor-Model Strategies

In one of the most common behavior change strategies, the therapist functions as an actor or model to help family members learn new behaviors and interactions. To use this type of intervention strategy, you must be well versed in the goal behaviors because you will be demonstrating the skills that your clients are learning. The interventions included in this category usually rely on the family members first observing the family practitioner and then electing to adopt the observed skills and behaviors. It is then expected that the family members will continue to use the skills in their life situation. As a therapist, you have no control over how the family applies the skills, or even whether they elect to emulate your behaviors.

The first critical assumption regarding interventions in this category is that the family members have sufficient cognitive skills to identify a particular skill when the therapist demonstrates it. If this assumption is not met, it is unlikely that the family members will understand what they are learning. Concurrent with the assumption of ability is an assumption of motivation. Family members must be sufficiently motivated to take the skills they observe in treatment and generalize them to the home situation. The final critical assumption is the existence of a positive working alliance. If the family members do not like the therapist, or do not feel the therapist is credible, they are not likely to emulate the practitioner or generalize the skills to the home situation.

If these three assumptions are met, actor-model strategies can be very effective. They are concrete and provide family members with a clear demonstration of specific skills. If adopted by the family, actor-model strategies can enhance current skill levels. Two common actor-model interventions are modeling and role-playing.

## Modeling Interventions

Family members who have not been exposed to effective behavior models in the past are typically unaware of how to perform certain behaviors. In such cases, the family practitioner may tune into the family members' needs and find opportunities to engage in the appropriate behavior as a model. When you engage in the goal behavior, family members can see the performance and effects of that behavior. Most often, you will model the behavior subtly, so the family members can observe and then integrate aspects of the behavior without prompting or coaching. This strategy is often used to help family members acquire new skills (Sundel & Sundel, 1999; Uhlemann & Koehn, 1989).

The modeling intervention has two sets of prerequisites. First, you must establish active engagement with the family members; they should feel open and willing to explore alternatives while working with you. In this activity, the working relationship should be focused so that family members know which skills or behaviors they are trying to develop. Concurrently, the helping relationship must be sufficiently positive to motivate the family members to emulate the behaviors you are modeling. If the relationship is strained or negative, use of this strategy may cause family members to reject the modeled behaviors.

The second set of prerequisites includes the focus and timing of the intervention. Modeling cannot be forced. Consequently, it must occur within a fairly natural exchange with the family members. If you try to structure the modeling, it often seems like instruction. This approach disempowers the family members, who may then feel that you are setting up the situation to show them what to do. Thus it is sometimes better to capitalize on natural situations. For that reason, modeling is often an intervention of choice in many in-home or family-based interventions.

## Role-Playing Interventions

Role-playing interventions are useful for practicing new behaviors. Many readers will have used role-playing in developing their basic practice skills. This is a strong learning strategy because it can be highly effective (Froehle, Robinson, & Kurpius, 1983). Role-playing is common in many behavioral and psychodramatic approaches to serving family members (Wiener, 1999).

A critical assumption with role-playing is that the practitioner has created sufficient engagement with the family members. It is also assumed that you can help family members feel safe and supported as they try out new behaviors. When learning new behaviors, family members may feel awkward and will tend to make mistakes. You must engage the family members in such a way that they will not feel judged when attempting the new skills. If this level of comfort is achieved, role-playing provides a risk-free environment to practice the new skills.

A second critical skill when using role-playing is *tuning in*. In role-playing, the practice of tuning in is not limited to the family members' experience; it also extends to other people in the family members' situation. In your practice, this expansion of the tuning-in skill allows you to adopt the complementary role to that of the family members. Tuning in thus allows a realistic portrayal of the other roles. If you attempt to role-play a skill, but do not portray the other people in a manner consistent with actual situations, the family is likely to discredit your role-playing.

After the role-playing, you will often use questioning and reflecting skills to explore how the family members experienced the skill and to help them determine how to apply the skill to their life situation. This aspect of role-playing is an important step in helping the family members generalize the skill to the situations where it will be applied. In this exploration, you often must identify events or elements of the situation that will challenge the family's ability to apply the new skill.

### ◆ EXERCISE 10.1 ACTOR–MODEL STRATEGIES

You are a worker in an agency contracted with the Child Welfare Agency to work with parents. You have been working with an abusive parent (Mike) in trying to improve his parenting skills. This man (age 42) does not feel he needs help with parenting skills and very much resents your coming into his home. Even though the children (ages 10 and 13) are quite open with you, Mike is reluctant to work with you and disagrees with your goals. The family is in very poor financial condition, and Mike is often at risk of losing the apartment he is renting. He says that he needs help finding a job so he will not be stressed out, but your supervisor has informed you that he needs to improve his parenting. She suggests that you go in and model effective parenting with the children when they are there for a visit.

1. What is the prognosis that your supervisor's strategy will work?

2. Would role-playing be more effective? Why?

3. What would you need to do with Mike to improve the effectiveness of a modeling or role-playing strategy?

---

# Educator-Coach Strategies

When using educator-coach strategies, family practitioners become very active in shaping family member responses. The practitioner constantly interacts with the family members to help them think through and carry out new behaviors and interactions. *Educator-coach strategies* are central to many intervention approaches, including "in-home" intervention, problem-solving interventions, psychoeducational interventions, and many interactive interventions such as marriage counseling.

The educator-coach set of strategies requires high levels of self-awareness, thinking, questioning, and reflecting. Having this skill set allows you to serve as an educator and coach, actively helping family members acquire and apply new skills. There is a high level of power in the practitioner role when using these strategies. Because coaches and teachers must often resort to telling people how to perform certain tasks and functions, you are at constant risk of slipping into this power position when working with families. The ideal is to let family members explore and decide rather than follow your direction.

## Maintaining Family Empowerment Through "CARE"

With the practitioner so actively involved in shaping family responses to different situations, it is important to have guidelines to protect the family from undue influence. The acronym *CARE* symbolizes the following important guidelines, to which behavioral-focused efforts should attend when trying to alter a client's behavior:

♦ **Client led.** The family members must be able to choose whether they will engage in the intervention (Tokar, Hardin, Adams, & Brandel, 1996). Such a choice should be negotiated as the intervention develops. As the work of the session is concluding, you might say, "You know, we could strengthen this skill if you did some practice at home. Are you interested in a couple of practice exercises?" Without being called on to make the choice, the family members are not fully involved in the decision to engage in the task. They may feel that they must answer to, or perform for, the therapist.

◆ **Allied.** The change effort must stem from the working alliance you have established with the family. This requires a clear connection to the goals of service (Hay & Kinnier, 1998; Scheel, Seaman, Roach, Mulling, & Mahoney, 1999). If there is no connection, the family members are not likely to complete the task because it does not make sense according to the goals.

◆ **Realistic.** The intervention must fit with the family member's personality and values (Tokar et al., 1996). It makes no sense to ask people to do things that are foreign to their way of living. Concurrently, the intervention must reflect the realities of family life (Scheel et al., 1999). If you do not tune into the family's pressures, demands, and life circumstances, the tasks assigned are likely to be ineffective or even frustrating to the family members.

◆ **Enhancement.** Action system interventions must enhance the family's current situation and increase its members' control over the situation (Tokar et al., 1996). Consequently, tasks and active interventions should focus on expanding the family members' mastery in their life situations. To be successful, the tasks should be achievable and doable. In your practice, you must carefully avoid setting up family members to fail.

## Using Educator-Coach Strategies

The direct influence strategies associated with the education and coaching roles of therapists often involve helping families acquire new skills. When using active coaching strategies, it is important that you clearly negotiate their use with the families by following the CARE criteria, after you are sure that using directive strategies will not threaten the working alliance. Five very common educator-coach interventions are used when helping families to change behavior and interactions:

1. Problem-solving interventions
2. Option evaluations
3. Skill development interventions
4. Homework and task assignments
5. Coaching in new behaviors

*Problem-Solving Interventions*  Often, the adult family members have not been exposed to effective problem solving in their families of origin. Consequently, it is common for families to enter treatment for help in the area of problem solving. When families have not developed the ability to get problem situations on the table for discussion, the family practitioner often must help structure problem-solving efforts to help them develop a pattern of addressing family problems (Bell & Eyberg, 2002; Shriver, 1998).

Structured problem-solving models are common. The number of steps and labels change from model to model, but there tends to be common movement in structuring the problem situation. Common themes tend to be as follows:

- Defining or acknowledging the problem
- Exploring possible solutions
- Selecting a solution
- Implementing the solution (Bedell & Lennox, 1997; Sundel & Sundel, 1999)

A basic problem-solving structure is useful for families, because they can take the steps and apply them to multiple situations. Although this linear model of solving problems may seem simple, it has existed for decades. In situations where families have no system for solving problems, you may find it useful to help them learn a model that they can apply when problem solving breaks down.

In structuring the problem-solving sequence, the family practitioner is directive, keeping family members working on the problem one step at a time. In this chapter, we consider a five-step model based on the work of Louis Lowy (1976) and Grace Coyle (1962): defining the problem, listing potential solutions, reviewing options, developing a plan, and evaluating success.

1. **Defining the problem.** Often families have poorly defined problems. One of the most common problems is that different family members will have divergent definitions of the problem. Consequently, each is attempting to achieve different goals. If more than one problem is on the table, problem solving is confounded because no solution can solve both problems simultaneously. When two problem definitions occur simultaneously, the practitioner must help the family achieve a single problem focus. Failure to separate problems results in complications during later steps.

---

## CASE EXAMPLE

A couple enters a session in the midst of a major argument. The family dog has died, and the mother is advocating buying another pet. The father argues against the purchase, claiming that he is far too busy to care for another dog. He claims that the walking, feeding, and cleanup will fall on him. The mother claims that the children are devastated by the loss and need another pet. Clearly, there are two problems on the table. The father is trying to solve the problem of his children not taking responsibility for their chores. The mother is trying to solve the problem of her children experiencing a significant loss. Given these two distinct problems, it is impossible to find any common ground to resolve either one. The therapist separates the problems, so that each one can be addressed separately.

---

2. **Listing potential solutions.** A common difficulty with problem solving is that people move through this stage too quickly. Often family members have preselected solutions that they pressure others to adopt rather than openly exploring all of the potential solutions. The practitioner must keep families focused on generating solutions rather than criticizing other people's ideas. Practitioners must encourage families to be creative and even silly when generating ideas, so they do not censor the ideas coming forth. It is important to stay focused on generating several options before analyzing each one.

## CASE EXAMPLE

A couple enters treatment because the husband tends to work late and does not contact his wife to advise her of his schedule. The definition of the problem is that the husband often becomes preoccupied in his work and loses track of time. This definition provides criteria for potential solutions. All solutions must meet the criteria of "helping the husband to become more sensitive to his wife's needs for information." After a clear definition is achieved, the couple begins exploring options. The wife immediately states that he should just remember (if he cares). The therapist jots down "just remember," and adds that expressions of caring might be a problem to consider later, but the current solutions need to focus on helping him remember. The therapist then encourages the couple to generate more solutions. Some solutions include putting a clock in the workspace, tuning a radio to a station that announces times frequently, and other logical solutions. Because the couple is being encouraged to generate novel solutions, the wife suggests that an electrode can be implanted into her husband's rectum. This idea, which lightens the discussion, is duly recorded by the therapist. In all, the couple generates 15 possible solutions—many of them humorous.

3. **Reviewing options.** Once a list of solutions has been developed, each option can be reviewed to determine what will be required. You must assess not only what resources are needed, but how realistic the resources might be, given the family's constraints. You must also try to assess any unintended consequences that might occur. Based on the review, inappropriate options are ruled out or altered. Options that seem promising are left in the option pool. This process usually involves the therapist crossing off some options and changing the wording on others. After assessing the list with the family, you will read the remaining options and conduct a second review to determine which options are most promising.

**CASE EXAMPLE**

As the session described in the previous example continues, the couple discusses options such as the radio, and just remembering, and decides that those would not be effective options given the husband's work situation. He works as a mechanic—a job that is very task focused. The machinery often makes radios hard to hear, and the nature of the work often requires extensive, focused attention. These two suggestions are thus considered weak. The electrode idea is changed rather than rejected. It would be difficult to find a doctor to perform the operation, and the couple cannot guarantee enough funds (or patient compliance) to use the idea as originally conceived. They also explore the idea of having the husband keep a vibrating beeper in his pants pocket. This and the clock become very viable options.

4. **Developing a plan.** From the options reviewed, family members decide on the most viable options and fit them into a plan. At this stage, family members plan how they will implement the solutions in order to solve the problem. In the discussions, family members agree to the changes each person will make. These changes are spelled out, along with resources and actions needed to implement the plan. This step often needs to be detailed, and it is most effective if everyone involved in the problem situation can have designated changes in the plan.

**CASE EXAMPLE**

Continuing with the preceding case example, the beeper (aka the electrode) and the clocks seem to be desirable options. In exploring the use of the clocks, the couple decides that they will be placed in the shop to help the husband remember to call. They discuss in detail where to place the clocks in the workspace so that they will be most visible to him. The couple also does some research to find a type of clock that will draw his attention. The husband commits to noting the time; he agrees that if it appears he might be late, he will call his wife immediately. The wife also needs an alternative to ruminating about possible lateness. Consequently, it is decided that the husband will buy a vibrating beeper. If he is more than 20 minutes late, she will beep him, and he will immediately call to update her on his schedule. After planning how to make these options work, both agree to try the plan.

5. **Evaluating success.** Evaluating the outcome of a plan is often the most forgotten stage in problem solving. It is important for families to be able to

determine what changes they will observe when the plan has been successful. Once they have determined how success will look, it is useful to set a date for reviewing the plan. In scheduling a review, assessing the outcomes and adjusting the plan are important topics of exploration.

---

**CASE EXAMPLE**

The couple in the preceding example decides that the arguments about his not caring should be greatly decreased if the plan works. The couple estimates the current level of arguing and determines that the arguments will decrease to once per week if their plan succeeds. They then review the list of options to determine what they might do if the goal is not achieved. The couple commits to the review and leaves to implement the plan.

---

*Option Evaluations*  In a strategy similar to problem solving, practitioners often engage in helping families assess and select options without engaging in the more structured problem-solving process. This approach is common when families are able to define and understand their situation, but cannot see that they have many options. The need for option exploration often is associated with families feeling overwhelmed by the situation. In such an experience, families get bogged down in the details of the problem and lose their awareness that options exist.

The practitioner can work with families to identify and implement new options by exploring the situation and helping them to evaluate alternative actions. Frequently, you will help families focus on similar situations from the past to generate potential solutions. You will also probe in a directive manner to identify options that may be difficult for the families to see. After identifying several options, you will use reflection and questions to help the families decide which option might be best in the given situation. The CARE criteria can be used to help families decide which option might be best for their situation.

---

**CASE EXAMPLE**

A young man enters service, upset that his wife has asked for a divorce. He states that he cannot cope and is at risk of losing his job. He has phoned in sick several times and is distracted at work. As he tells his story, he mentions that this is his second marriage. The therapist then shifts the focus to explore how the young man had dealt with the previous marital breakdown. He describes his story, stressing that he had been working out more and channeled his stress physically. The therapist also explores other times when there has been tremendous stress in his life. The man speaks of

---

receiving support from team members (on a softball team) and getting satisfaction from taking personal development courses at a community college. The therapist then asks the man which of these options might work in his present situation. The young man verbalizes thoughts that he can start working out again. The therapist supports the decision and helps him plan how to focus his workouts for the maximum benefit.

---

*Skill Development Interventions*   Frequently, families lack important skills because the parents inherited family models that lacked these very same skills. In such situations, family practitioners must help the family members identify and acquire desirable skills (Diamond & Liddle, 1999). In many situations, practitioners refer such clients to psychoeducational groups that teach the skills. Although this approach is expedient for the worker, many of the programs do not individualize programs enough for families and fail to develop effective partnerships with family members. In many situations the families are fragmented, with parents attending one type of group and the children attending some other form of treatment.

Family skills training programs are effective in this limited scope, but they are not ideal for all families (Spoth & Redmond, 1996). Often, the practitioner must integrate skill education with other forms of family treatment (Hinton, Sheperis, & Sims, 2003; Miller, Meyers, & Tonigan, 1999). Family practitioners need methods for working with full family systems in order to develop family skills (Dumas, Blechman, & Prinz, 1992). In particular, approaches that maximize collaboration with the family, rather than limiting family influence, are recommended (Cantwell & Holmes, 1994).

A critical feature of family-based skill development is therapist-family collaboration (Hansen, Litzelman, & Salter, 2002; Liberman & Liberman, 2003). As part of this collaboration, you will follow the family lead by exploring family situations to find new and novel approaches (Jacobs & Wachs, 2002). In the exploration, you will provide information, clarify communication, and support family problem-solving efforts (Liberman & Liberman, 2003). By adopting a questioning and exploratory approach, you can help families to develop skills without having to tell them what to do; the family learns to explore its own solutions (Jacobs & Wachs, 2002). Ideally, this work occurs in the family's natural environment to enhance generalization and integration (Hansen et al., 2002).

---

**CASE EXAMPLE**

A father is struggling with his adolescent daughter's individuation. He is very strict with her and feels that he must protect her from the world's multiple dangers. Because the daughter wants more freedom, their conflict leads to frequent arguments and groundings. In the early exploration, it becomes clear that the father was allowed to run free as a youth, receiving no parental guidance or discipline. He ran into trouble with the law and ended up in training school. The therapist concludes that he has no model for parenting an adolescent, so is relying on his adolescent history to guide his parenting. The therapist begins questioning the father about what he thinks he needed as a teen. The father begins with a focus on a firm hand; but with deeper questioning, he is able to identify that family closeness and guidance were lacking in his life as a youth. These lacks become the foundation for skill development as the therapist explores behaviors that the man would have appreciated in his father. Piece by piece, the father is able to identify and practice several skills that he feels were missing in his development.

---

*Homework and Task Assignments*   When families are learning new behaviors, it is important that they also be able to practice in real-life settings. Many workers have these families commit to using their new skills between meetings, so that at the next session they can discuss the results of their practice (Hay & Kinnier, 1998; Hecker & Deacon, 1998; Reid, 1997). In prescribing such tasks, you must match the homework very carefully to the in-session content and treatment goals. Consider assigning subtasks or component skills that build a foundation for success. For example, if you are attempting to build assertive behavior in a mother who tends to be passive, her homework might center on being assertive with a stranger and then move through friendships before she practices with family members.

In using homework and tasks, engagement is a necessary skill. Many practitioners assign homework but are not able to help the families feel that the task is necessary. Families consequently do not complete the homework. Poor follow-through can become problematic, because you must explore the family members' noncompliance without chastising or engaging in power struggles. Such problems are averted if both you and the family members are equally engaged in developing the task or the homework (Reid, 1997). The following criteria can be helpful in developing homework and tasks.

- ◆ **Ensure that the family members are fully engaged in the change process.** The goals and working relationship must make sense for the members and be responding to their felt problem (primary, secondary, etc.). This assurance provides an emotional investment for the families in the outcome.
- ◆ **Ensure that the task is a logical outgrowth of the current session.** The task or homework should be highly consistent with the content and work that was completed in the current meeting with the family. If a task is based on previous meetings or anticipated future meetings, family members have no immediate experience to help them understand the purpose of the assignment.
- ◆ **Ensure that the task maintains a clear focus on one of the family action systems associated with the problem situation.** Typically, either the acting or the interacting system is highlighted for focus.
- ◆ **Ensure that the task fits the CARE acronym.** With tasks, as with any behavior change, CARE remains an important consideration.
- ◆ **Ensure that you follow up on the task in the next meeting.** When you assign a task, it is important to explore the application in the next meeting. This

provides a context for the task within the ongoing work and helps to focus the next meeting. If you do not follow up on the task, future assignments may be viewed as irrelevant.

---

**CASE EXAMPLE**

A family enters treatment because the three sons often engage in physical fighting. During the initial exploration, the family outlines how the boys' biological father (now deceased) had been very violent and abusive. Since the father's death, the mother has not been able to effectively discipline the boys, because they respond only to coercive strategies of discipline. In the therapy room, the practitioner helps the family practice alternative methods of discipline and problem solving. To help the family generalize the new skill, he prepares problem-solving worksheets and asks the family to practice solving minor problems every evening after supper.

---

*Coaching in New Behaviors*   When working with behaviors and interactions, the practitioner often functions as a coach to help the family develop new skills (Bell & Eyberg, 2002; Shriver, 1998; Sundel & Sundel, 1999). In this coaching role, the practitioner frequently shares observations about skill performance to help the families shape their responses. If the skills require adjustment, the practitioner often uses reflection and questioning to explore methods for better achieving the desired outcomes. At times, the worker may incorporate actor-modeling strategies or embed suggestions to help families to identify alternative skills (Goodstone & Diamante, 1998; Guerin, Fogarty, Fay, & Kautto, 1996).

When coaching a family, you will often want to observe and intervene during actual skill applications (Bedell & Lennox, 1997). You can then stop the interaction and help the families use the new skills. This is a common use of instructive skills in practice, during which you will coach parents, children, or marital partners in their interactions. Coaching is a common approach for building skills in client systems of any size (Diedrich, 1996; Katz & Miller, 1996; Witherspoon & White, 1996). Coaching requires both you and the family members to be engaged in the work. As you become actively involved in the family interaction, the families must be open to the activity lest they feel that you are interfering or criticizing.

---

**CASE EXAMPLE**

A single father and his adolescent son attend treatment because the son is defiant and refuses to follow any rules. The son is currently on probation for underage drinking. In the initial exploration, it is apparent that the father has never taken a firm stand with the child and is rarely able to use guilt or persuasion effectively when the child becomes defiant. The son is into staying out all night and drinking with older youth. The father wants to exert influence but cannot take an effective stance. The therapist supports the father in confronting the youth and using the power of the probation to make a stand. The father takes the lead in the room, and the therapist remains behind a one-way mirror. Whenever the father begins to falter, the therapist phones into the room and offers feedback and suggestions. The father is able to assume the stance that if the youth does not obey curfew rules, he will take action to have the probation breached.

---

## ◆ EXERCISE 10.2 EDUCATOR-COACH STRATEGIES

You are continuing to work with Roland and Melissa (from exercises in Chapter 9). When they come in for a recent session, they have obviously been arguing. They explain that the argument is about their son, Theo. They have made a deal with him that he needs to maintain a B average at school before being allowed to go to Florida during spring break with a friend and his family. Theo now has only a B⁻ average in school, so Roland maintains that he should not go to Florida. Melissa, on the other hand, argues that Theo was in grief during the examination period because his aunt (her sister) had died near the end of the semester. Melissa maintains that Theo did not ask for leniency from the teachers for compassionate reasons, even though he and his aunt were very close. Melissa advocates lessening the standard due to Theo's grief. She continues, explaining that Theo is hurting and is in serious grief and the trip will help distract him from his loss. Roland argues that Theo needs to learn responsibility, and this is an opportunity for him to learn. He argues that life lessons are important, and there will be other losses. Theo needs to handle life's pressures and still be able to perform according to the promises that he makes. Ronald and Melissa are unable to resolve the argument.

1. What appears to be the couple's difficulty in the first stage of problem solving? (Make sure you identify specifics about problem definitions, etc.)

2. You want to help the couple generate more options. First, identify four possible options that they have not yet considered.

3. Write what you would say to them to introduce an option exploration strategy. (Make sure you do not invalidate their current positions.)

4. When Roland and Melissa begin listing options, they start arguing about which option is best. You decide to coach them in problem solving. What will you need to do first?

5. What will you say to introduce the need for this couple to try a different problem-solving approach?

6. What homework might you encourage for the couple?

# Behavior Interruption Strategies

Problematic behaviors often occur automatically with family members, making these behaviors very difficult to change. Thus the family practitioner frequently must intervene to block these automatic patterns by using *behavior interruption strategies*. This type of strategy assumes that the behaviors or interactions are habitual and operate outside of the family's conscious control. The goal of the strategy is to increase the family's control and awareness of the behaviors.

Behavior interruption strategies require high levels of motivation and compliance from family members, because they must follow specific procedures. Practitioners typically position families to ensure that all members will engage in the assigned interactions and tasks. Concurrent with compliance, family members must have sufficient self-control to respond appropriately when the strategies are used. If compliance or ability is questionable, you may want to use other strategies. Here are five common examples of interruption strategies:

1. Time-out strategies
2. Cuing strategies
3. Scheduling strategies
4. Pattern interruption strategies
5. Incompatible alternatives

## Time-Out Strategies

Time-out strategies are designed to interrupt escalating tensions, creating an opportunity for self-reflection and refocusing (Veenstra & Scott, 1993). Typically, time-out is implemented early in the escalation process, when the behavior or interaction is beginning to escalate. The rationale for time-out argues that when people take a break from a difficult situation and reflect on how they are handling the situation, they can reenter the situation with a clearer head and increase their chances of successfully resolving differences.

When you assign parents the task of using time-out procedures with children, you will usually work with the parents to ensure that they remain calm and in control when implementing the procedure. Typically, time limits ensure that the length of time-out is reasonable. You will also warn the parents about their child's likely testing behaviors. By rehearsing and practicing before implementing the procedure with children, parents can optimize their opportunity for success. A final critical feature of the time-out strategy is for the parent to reengage with the child afterward to discuss the situation.

For adults, time-out is often self-imposed, to break an escalating pattern or situation. Typically, in practice you will instruct the adults to say "Time-out" when they believe the situation is escalating. It is expected that each person will honor the time-out suggestion and take a reasonable break. The adults are expected to resume the discussion after calming themselves and reflecting on the situation.

**T A B L E 10.2**
**Legitimate and Politicized Use of Time-Out Strategies**

| Legitimate Uses of Time-Out | Politicized Uses of Time-Out |
|---|---|
| ◆ Gaining control of emotional buildup so rational intercourse can resume | ◆ Escaping the discussion to avoid losing the argument |
| ◆ Stopping escalating processes to preempt abusive exchanges | ◆ Blocking the other person from presenting his or her argument |
| ◆ Reflecting on the other person's position so it can be duly considered | ◆ Stopping the exchange of ideas and thoughts |
| ◆ Ensuring self-control | ◆ Controlling the other person |

One person's ability to end a discussion with the expectation that the others must comply can become a problem in some families. This is a powerful weapon for silencing the other person and is sometimes misused in this fashion. You must be careful to instruct the families on legitimate versus political uses of time-out. Table 10.2 presents common uses and abuses of the time-out procedure.

## Cuing Strategies

Another strategy for interrupting automatic responses is cuing. You may want to use cuing strategies to help families know when the situation is escalating or when problems might occur. With cuing strategies, you can work with family members to identify escalation milestones and indicators (i.e., cues) that will help them understand when a situation may become problematic (Margolin, 1979). You can then coach the family in how to respond to the cues. Many therapists develop a behavioral protocol, so that once a family acknowledges the cue, its members will engage in behaviors or interactions designed to interrupt further progression of the problem.

Two types of cues are frequently used. *Internal cues* are used by an individual to help himself become aware, and gain control of, his responses. Internal cues are usually body sensation, thinking, or self-observation cues. It is expected that the individual will self-identify the cue and then follow the prescribed behavioral response. The second type of cue is an *interactive cue*, which can be identified by anyone in the family situation. This type of cue frequently relies on code words, which communicate to the other people in the situation that a problematic dynamic may be operating.

---

### CASE EXAMPLE

A couple is attending marriage counseling to decrease their escalating arguments. During the positioning, each person externalizes his or her self-talk that promotes angry and volatile reactions. The female partner identifies her self-talk as her mother, and the male partner names his self-talk "Beelzebub." As the couple is working toward increasing their control over the arguing, the therapist asks them to identify quick phrases or words that can help them identify when the self-talk is promoting escalation. Each decides that they will simply state that "mother" or "Beelzebub" is in the room. The therapist then helps the couple practice responses to the statements so they can interrupt the escalation.

## Scheduling Strategies

Family problems frequently start to interfere with daily living. When this occurs, family members begin to feel that they have no control over the situation. As you work with families in such situations, you can interrupt the problem by having the family members schedule the problem (Madanes, 1980). The assumption in this strategy is that small changes in the pattern of the problem will result in larger changes. A benefit of this strategy, if the family can successfully schedule spending time on the problem, is that they have already exerted some control.

In scheduling the problem, you will help the family members identify a time during their day when they can engage in the problem. Once they identify a time, you can work with the family members to structure their interaction so they can experience the "problem" under their own control. Because you are asking the family to engage in the behavior only at certain times, their compliance is important. Motivated families are usually able to follow the therapist's directives, but ambivalent or involuntary families are less open to the activity. Careful positioning is an important element in this type of intervention.

### CASE EXAMPLE

A couple attending marriage counseling has a habit of continually complaining and "sniping" at each other. This pattern often leads to arguments and fights in public or when they are out with friends. The couple wants to decrease this behavior, so the therapist suggests that they schedule time to express their displeasures. The therapist notes that complaining appears to be important to each of them and suggests that the problem might be the forum in which they present their complaints. The therapist has the couple book 30 minutes per day to meet and review their complaints. In the 30 minutes, each partner is instructed to present a list of all grievances. The therapist stresses that airing these grievances is important, so asks them to schedule 15 minutes each. One by one, each partner is to read his or her list of grievances, and the other partner will apologize for each one. After 15 minutes, the couple will change position so each partner has a full 15 minutes to express grievances. After two weeks of scheduling these grievance sessions, the couple returns to the therapist and argues against continuing the exercise because most of the grievances are very small and petty.

## Pattern Interruption Strategies

Family practitioners often want to introduce small changes in the pattern of the problem. Such small changes start to disrupt the family's behavioral and cognitive rituals surrounding the problem (Gross, 1994; White, 1994). Small changes are often ideal because they begin the unraveling of the pattern but are concurrently achievable for the family (de Shazer & Molnar, 1984). Many pattern interruption strategies are described in the literature, and all have the common thread of creating a small change to disrupt the behavior and family response patterns. Through exploration and collaboration with family members, you will find creative possibilities emerging that can be both effective and enjoyable. Consider the following minor changes and reflect on the possibilities.

◆ **Incorporate additional behaviors.** For example, add a ritual or have each person stand when talking.
◆ **Change the setting.** For example, go to the park or change rooms.
◆ **Change the arrangement.** For example, have a couple hold hands; or have them change the timing of the behavior (e.g., if they usually fight before dinner, have them try to arrange their fights for after dinner time).
◆ **Change the interaction.** For example, include an additional person, or have the participants whisper.
◆ **Incorporate incompatible behaviors.** For example, add a role such as handing out snacks or behaving in a way that interferes with the problem.

The pattern interruption strategy requires you to tune into the pattern of the problem to understand how the behavior evolves. With this understanding, you can collaborate with family members to identify a small change that can be introduced into the problem pattern. You can then encourage the family to make this small change. Spend subsequent sessions in helping the family to explore the new patterns and integrate new minor changes.

---

### CASE EXAMPLE

A lesbian couple, Wanda and Erica, enters treatment because one of the partners is contemplating leaving the relationship. Erica identifies the problem as Wanda's anger. Erica complains that Wanda is "as loud as an opera singer" day in and day out. Erica often becomes defensive when Wanda speaks to her and tends to start yelling. Wanda reports that her voice is naturally loud, and she cannot control the volume. As the exploration continues, it becomes evident that Erica gets defensive only when Wanda is asking her to do something or giving her a suggestion. As the situation is further explored, the phrase "opera singer" comes up again. The therapist adopts the theme and asks if Erica will still get defensive if Wanda is singing like an opera star rather than talking loudly. Erica giggles and says, "No. It would even be funny. You should hear her sing." The couple then explores the possibility of making this small change. Wanda agrees to start requests and suggestions by singing, "Erica . . . I have something to say to you." She will then continue to sing the suggestions. In the next session, both women are laughing and mimicking Wanda's singing.

---

# Weight-Shifting Strategies

In many cases, family practitioners must seek to directly influence the balance between change-focused and counterchange forces in the client situation. *Weight-shifting strategies* are a class of intervention strategies that attempt to accomplish such shifts in balance. There are two basic approaches to weight-shifting strategies. First, you can tip the balance of forces toward change by adding weight to the pro-change elements. Alternatively, you can neutralize the power of the counterchange elements. In applying a weight-shifting strategy, you will consider the change versus counterchange forces and strategically apply weight to shift their balance.

Weighting strategies are variants of the operant conditioning techniques of positive and negative reinforcement. Operant conditioning provides consequences for specific behaviors. The consequences may be positive or negative (Latham, 1996). When employing this type of strategy, you will explore the antecedents of the behavior and rewards or outcomes from the behavior. You can then develop a plan to disrupt the reward cycle. When exploring the following applications of operant conditioning, notice how the positive and negative themes emerge from the different techniques. The following five strategies are common weighting approaches:

1. Contingency contracting
2. Establishing ordeals
3. Pairing stimuli
4. Behavioral contracting
5. Reinforcing behavior

## Contingency Contracting

*Contingency contracts* involve the family practitioner arranging for some outcome to occur based on change-oriented results (de Risi & Butz, 1975). In its essence, this type of strategy is an extension of the positive and negative reinforcement. However, contingency contracts are formalized through a contracted agreement between the therapist and the family. In using contingency contracts, you must first have a family that is willing to negotiate and follow the contract. This requires careful positioning, engagement, and motivation.

The first precondition for success is ensuring highly motivating outcomes in the contract. While negotiating the contract, you must identify specific outcomes that are highly enticing for the family members. To provide extra motivation, you can couple highly enticing outcomes with powerful deterrents. If you incorporate deterrents, they too must have sufficient influence to motivate family members.

After identifying and negotiating these outcomes with the family, you can then formalize the outcomes in a contract. Ideally, you will include a blend of different outcomes and deterrents in the plan. In the written contract, you will document detailed descriptions of each outcome and how they will evolve. Here are some possible outcome categories:

◆ **Relational outcomes.** For example, writing a letter of confrontation that will be mailed, or arranging a second honeymoon
◆ **Monetary outcomes.** For example, setting up an escrow account that either will revert to the family member or be dispersed in some other way depending on results
◆ **Values-based outcomes.** For example, donating money to a despised political action group, or having the individual reward himself with a cultural outing
◆ **Affective outcomes.** For example, ensuring that an individual can engage in activities that bring pleasure, or that she has to visit someone despised

When negotiating a contingency contract, the therapist meets with the family (and possibly others) to identify and quantify the behaviors that must change. It is important to have very specific behavior and a system for reliably monitoring progress. If the behavior is nebulous, or you cannot reliably determine the emergence of the behavior, this strategy will not work. When you have identified very clear behaviors, you can pair the outcomes and behaviors. The following are common elements of a contingency contract:

◆ Establishing an interim outcome each time the behavior occurs (e.g., putting money in an escrow account)
◆ Establishing a goal level and a time frame for reviewing outcomes (e.g., in three months, swearing will decrease to once every other week)
◆ Attaching a positive outcome to the successful achievement of the outcome (e.g., if the swearing is at the goal level when the contract is reviewed, all of the money is yours)
◆ Attaching a contingency cost to problem maintenance (e.g., if the swearing is not at the goal level, the money in the escrow account will be distributed to the people who have to listen to the swearing)

The power of this type of intervention is directly proportional to the enticement or deterrent value of the outcomes (Madanes, 1994). You must frequently tap into powerful feelings or desires when negotiating rewards and punishments with the family. As you listen for appropriate outcomes, pay attention to dearly held values and priorities in the family member's life. The family member's expressed values and priorities provide clues as to what contingencies might work best.

## CASE EXAMPLE

A young mother refers herself for treatment because she has struck her son. The mother reports that she had been abused as a child and does not want to hit her child ever again. She also speaks of wanting to curb her verbal abuse. As the therapist explores her situation, it appears that the woman is lashing out at her children daily. Her history is one of being exposed to violence as both a witness and a victim while being raised by two alcoholic parents. The woman hates her father, but has resolved some feelings about her mother. Her verbal and physical violence remind her of her father. The therapist wants to set a deterrent in place and elects to use contingency contracting to help curb the woman's difficult behaviors. After the therapist has conducted a lengthy "shaggy dog" positioning strategy, the woman agrees to a contingency contract. She will use an escrow account and deposit $5.00 every time she lashes out at her children. As part of the contract, she agrees that by the end of six months, her lashing out will decrease to once every other month. If she achieves this goal, all of the money in the account is hers to spend as she wishes. If she does not achieve the goal, she will send the money to her father. The woman follows the agreement and gains control of her lashing out within one month.

## Establishing Ordeals

In family practice, you may frequently want to make it more difficult for a family to keep its problems than to change them (Haley, 1987). *Establishing ordeals* is one method that therapists use to intensify the cost of problem retention. To create ordeal strategies, you will attach tasks or protocols to the problem situation in order to increase the energy that a family must invest to avoid changing. These strategies work best with motivated people who will commit to completing the tasks recommended. It is assumed that each time the problem behavior occurs, the ordeal will be completed. This strategy is not likely to succeed if family members are only minimally engaged or unmotivated to change. Positioning and monitoring for motivation are important to avoid illusionary compliance or lack of follow-through.

### CASE EXAMPLE

A family enters treatment with a pattern of constant complaining about each other. Even in therapy sessions, the parents enter complaining about the children, and vice versa. The therapist explains that he is very interested in the complaints but cannot understand what is really happening. He then asks the family to use some complaint forms that he has devised. The family members agree to list all of their complaints on the supplied forms. The therapist further stresses that he cannot properly discuss a problem unless it is carefully documented. The family returns home, and during the next week the members dutifully complete their forms as instructed. They return to the counseling session with completed forms, which the therapist reviews with them quite matter-of-factly. He then gives the family a very large stack of forms for the next week. When the family returns the next week, only three forms have been completed.

## Pairing Stimuli

Family practitioners frequently want to neutralize the counterchange forces by tainting critical payoffs (Madanes, 1990). This strategy is most helpful if the problem behavior is rewarding in some way to the family member. When faced with powerful rewards, the practitioner can taint them slightly by having a negative experience follow the payoff in quick succession. *Pairing stimuli* involves the practitioner and family member identifying an action that can interfere with the positive elements of the problem. The practitioner then positions the family to agree to engage in the new behavior every time the problematic behavior is used. This begins to bring a negative association to the behavior that an individual is trying to change.

Like many of the action system strategies, this technique requires a high level of openness and compliance from the family members. They must first be open to discussing potential stimuli with the therapist. They must also follow up on the agreement to consistently pair the behaviors. If the family is inconsistent or overstates the potential impact of the pairing, no change will occur. However, if the therapist selects stimuli with sufficient power and the family consistently follows through on the exercise, the payoff will lose some of its appeal.

---

### CASE EXAMPLE

A woman refers herself because she has hit her daughter and wants stop before she becomes abusive. This woman had been severely abused as a child and hates her father. Her father is still an alcoholic and counts on the woman for emotional support. The therapist wants to pair the woman's feelings of hate with the feelings and thoughts that promote her abusiveness. Consequently, the therapist has the woman agree that anytime she lashes out at her daughter, she will phone her father that night. After following this procedure for a while, the woman knows that if she loses control with her daughter, she will have to phone her father. This pairing eventually interrupts the cycle and allows the woman to get control of the sequence that supported the abusive interactions.

---

## Behavioral Contracting

The final behavior interruption strategy is known as *behavioral contracting* (de Risi & Butz, 1975). This is a very collaborative technique whereby the therapist and family members negotiate an agreement for two or more family members to engage in different behaviors (Fraser, Hawkins, & Howard, 1988). This strategy requires at least two family members, each of whom must identify behaviors in the other that they would like to see changed. If both members are not invested in the behavior change of the other, change is unlikely, because there is not enough benefit for them to justify the discomfort of changing. Critical elements of behavioral contracts are as follows:

- Identifying specific behaviors (in the other) that each party in the contract wants changed
- Negotiating how each behavior needs to change among the family members
- Ensuring that each person has a stake or investment in the other person's change
- Ensuring that each person is willing to make the change according to the contract

If elements are lacking, change is unlikely. Most readers have observed situations in which contracts have been used, but the family members fail to follow through. This failure usually occurs when the family members feel the process was not collaborative. In such situations, people will agree to contracts to please the practitioner. You must be careful to build the contract collaboratively, in order to maximize success in any behavioral contracting strategy (Strong, 2000).

## Reinforcing Behavior

Some family practitioners seek to weight the change and counterchange forces by finding rewards or penalties that can change the balance of the forces (Falloon, 1988; Wahler, 1980). *Positive reinforcement* is the term commonly used for rewards. Therapists work with the family to identify outcomes that can enhance the members' motivation to change (Falloon, 1988). Therapists also attempt to find ways to remove potential rewards from the situation, so that status quo behaviors will be less rewarding.

◆ **EXERCISE 10.3   USING BEHAVIOR INTERRUPTION AND WEIGHT-SHIFTING STRATEGIES**

Your work with Roland and Melissa is progressing; however, lately they have been starting to regress. Melissa has started following Roland around the house, seeking validation, and Roland has become a little more critical than he has been for the past month or so. You want to implement some strategies for interrupting their patterns and making them less appealing.

1. First you focus on Melissa. You want her to be able to identify when she needs validation before she starts following Roland around the house. Select a strategy that can help her identify when the problem is about to occur and indicate your rationale for selecting this strategy.

2. What exactly will you say to Melissa to implement this strategy?

3. You want to add some act or event to the situation, so that Melissa can interrupt herself before getting to the point where she follows Roland around the house. Select a strategy that can help her interrupt her standard pattern of behavior.

4. Now focus on Roland. He has become somewhat critical of Melissa. You want to make it more difficult for him to continue criticizing her. Select a strategy that will start to shift the weight of staying the same. Outline how you would use this strategy with Roland.

5. What exactly would you say to Roland to introduce the use of this strategy?

6. You also want to introduce some reinforcement for changing. Suggest a positive reinforcer that might work for Melissa and Roland together, and indicate why this reinforcer might work.

7. Develop a negative reinforcement that can help motivate Melissa to change. Write about how you would implement this strategy.

8. Develop a negative reinforcement that can help Roland to change. Write about how you would implement this strategy.

9. How would you develop the reinforcements into a behavioral contract? Explain exactly how the contract would read for this couple to stop Melissa's pressing for validation and Roland's criticism.

# Summary

The action system strategies described in this chapter are all direct interventions in which the family practitioner is engaged in compliance-based activity. The practitioner is implicitly asking family members to try new behaviors and interactions so they can increase their mastery of the family situation and decrease the influence of problems. Such interventions can be effective if the family members meet the assumptions of the strategy, are well positioned, and are motivated to change.

With the level of activity and the focus on change, it is critical that the therapist work within the family's goals and tolerances. Controlling, manipulating, and instructing family members are not desirable approaches (Strong, 2000). Collaboration and relational influence will promote a strong partnership even when working toward behavior change. This outcome requires the therapist to explore the situation fully with the family members and share the requirements of a strategy when interventions are forming.

Any strategy that erodes the family's control over its situation should be resisted. Even if you have strategies that consistently work, it is important to retain the family partnership to avoid disrupting the working alliance. Increased competence and control are the clear measure of success with families. There are always going to be influence strategies that promote increased competence and control. There will also be strategies that undermine the family's sense of control. Whenever you elect to engage the families in an activity, assignment, or task, always use the CARE acronym to ensure that the families are not being disempowered by the intervention.

# Critical Content

1. Family practitioners often help families to change behaviors and interactions.
2. Although there are multiple interventions, there are four common types of intervention strategy.

3. The four types of intervention strategy include actor-model, educator-coach, behavior interruption, and weight-shifting.
4. Actor-model strategies are the least direct and require a strong therapist-family relationship.
5. Teacher-coach strategies are more direct and active strategies in which the therapist provides feedback to improve family functioning.
6. Behavioral interruption strategies involve blocking or altering the pattern of family problems.
7. Weight-shifting strategies involve the therapist using activities and influence to disrupt the balance between change and counterchange strategies.
8. All strategies require therapist-family collaboration.

## Suggested Readings

de Shazer, S., & Molnar, A. (1984). Four useful interventions in brief family therapy. *Journal of Marital & Family Therapy, 10,* 297–304.

Hay, C. E., & Kinnier, R. T. (1998). Homework in counseling. *Journal of Mental Health Counseling, 20,* 122–132.

Strong, T. (2000). Collaborative influence. *Australian & New Zealand Journal of Family Therapy, 21,* 144–148.

White, M. (1994). Ritual of inclusion: An approach to extreme uncontrolled behavior in children and young adolescents. *Journal of Child & Youth Care, 9,* 51–64.

## Chapter 11

# Direct Change Strategies for Influencing Family Processing Systems

Whereas the action system strategies described in Chapter 10 can be very effective in facilitating change, many problems have underlying beliefs and affective responses that require intervention at the processing system level. Many problems are deeply entrenched in the way that family members interpret situations (Epston, White, & Murray, 1992). Consequently, family practitioners must develop skills for intervening with family processing systems. This requires practitioners to be able to identify, explore, and influence family beliefs and affective responses.

## Theoretical Grounding

The assumption underlying cognitive-affective interventions is that the root of family problem maintenance can be found in the interpretations and visceral reactions of family members (Alexander, Jameson, Newell, & Gunderson, 1996; de Shazer, 1997; White, 1983). Even when family members are trying to change the problem, tightly held beliefs and corresponding behaviors often serve to entrench the problem more deeply in the family rather than remedy the situation (White, 1984, 1986). Family practitioners seek to decrease emotionality and rigid thinking in relation to problem situations to help family members find new ways to approach the problem (Alexander et al., 1996; Place, Reynolds, Cousins, & O'Neill, 2002). Even family intervention models heavily associated with behavioral change are embracing the need to work

**TABLE 11.1**
**Chapter Concepts, Theoretical Models, and Sources**

| Chapter Concepts | Theoretical Model(s) | Recommended Reading |
|---|---|---|
| Highlighting underlying processes and adaptations | Psychodynamic models<br>Rational-emotive model<br>Cognitive-behavioral model<br>Intergenerational models | Becvar & Becvar, Chapters 6, 12<br>Goldenberg & Goldenberg, Chapters 6, 8, 12<br>Horne, Chapters 11, 16<br>Nichols & Schwartz, Chapters 8, 9, 10 |
| Interrupting the underlying processes | Symbolic experiential model<br>Narrative model<br>Human validation model (Satir)<br>Solution-focused (brief) model | Becvar & Becvar, Chapter 13<br>Goldenberg & Goldenberg, Chapter 7<br>Horne, Chapters 4, 5, 8, 9<br>Nichols & Schwartz, Chapters 5, 8, 9 |
| Changing attribution systems | Narrative and constructionist models (postmodern)<br>Cognitive and cognitive-behavioral models<br>Reality therapy model<br>Rational-emotive model<br>Solution-focused (brief) model | Becvar & Becvar, Chapters 12, 13<br>Goldenberg & Goldenberg, Chapters 11, 12, 13, 14<br>Horne, Chapters 8, 9, 14, 16<br>Nichols & Schwartz, Chapters 10, 12, 13 |
| Working with emotional reactions | Psychodynamic models<br>Gestalt model<br>Human validation-communications model (Satir)<br>Rational-emotive model<br>Symbolic experiential model | Becvar & Becvar, Chapters 10, 12<br>Goldenberg & Goldenberg, Chapters 6, 7, 8<br>Horne, Chapters 4, 5, 11, 16<br>Nichols & Schwartz, Chapters 5, 8, 9 |

with family belief systems (Duncan, 1992). Practitioners must often address feelings and thinking before shifting a focus to behavior change (de Shazer, 1997).

Many theoretical approaches focus on family processing. Table 11.1 presents a partial list of popular theories. This table identifies some of the critical chapter concepts, theoretical models associated with the practice skill, and sources you can consult to expand your theoretical knowledge. When reviewing the table, you will see that each skill or chapter concept has links to more than one theoretical approach. To enhance your thinking associated with family practice, additional reading about the nuances and theoretical understandings may be helpful. Theoretical models underlying the concepts in this chapter can be found in the following easy-to-find textbooks:

◆ *The Essentials of Family Therapy* (2nd ed.), by M. P. Nichols & R. C. Schwartz, 2005, Boston: Allyn & Bacon.

◆ *Family Counseling and Therapy* (3rd ed.), by A. M. Horne, 2000, Pacific Grove, CA: Brooks/Cole.

◆ *Family Therapy: An Overview* (6th ed.), by I. Goldenberg & H. Goldenberg, 2004, Pacific Grove, CA: Brooks/Cole.

◆ *Family Therapy: A Systemic Integration* (5th ed.), by D. S. Becvar & R. J. Becvar, 2003, Boston: Allyn & Bacon.

In reviewing Table 11.1, you will observe that many models use similar interventions. In applying the model-specific thinking of the different approaches, the family practitioner must be able to influence beliefs and affective processes. Here are four practitioner skills used when working with family processing systems:

1. Identifying processing themes and patterns
2. Highlighting the processing themes and patterns
3. Influencing the processing themes and patterns
4. Altering the experience of events

Typically, you will use all four skills when helping a family change its systems of processing situations or events. The skills logically follow each other: noting a process, bringing it to the family's attention, and working with the family to alter how its members process situations. Within each skill set are several component skills and strategies used by family practitioners.

# Identifying Processing Themes and Patterns

In family practice, you cannot effectively help families change their processing systems without first identifying the processing elements that underlie problem situations. You must be able to tease out family rules, thinking patterns, and feelings while exploring the family situation. This critical first step is often the most difficult skill for new family practitioners, because it involves a combination of focused exploration, observation, and critical thinking skills.

The focused exploration elements of this skill require that the practitioner be able to guide the family discussion. You must influence the topics of discussion so that family members will provide processing-level information. The response system framework (Ragg, 2001) is useful in focusing the exploration. Because this framework has been discussed earlier in this text, it is only briefly summarized here. The response system framework suggests that problems occur in how people respond to situations. In their responses are two systems of responding (processing and action), each with two subsystems. During exploration, you will shift the focus from one subsystem to the next to ensure that all elements are covered during the discussion.

1. Processing systems
   ◆ The thinking and beliefs of the family members
   ◆ The feelings and affective reactions of the family members
2. Action systems
   ◆ The behaviors of the family members
   ◆ The interactions and relationships among the family members

As exploration and discussion occur with the family, the family practitioner tracks the interaction patterns and themes that might indicate underlying processing problems. These are sometimes referred to as *mystery themes* (Ragg, 2001) because when the family members are discussing an issue, the practitioner will sense that there is more to the situation than meets the eye. Frequently such situations occur when a family member injects additional meaning or emotion into the situation, thus causing processing-related problems. Four common patterns or themes can be observed in family interaction:

1. Shifts in focus
2. Repeated themes
3. Reaction intensity
4. Cognitive distortion

## Shifts in Focus

During exploration, family members often shift focus either away from or toward a subject, even though there appears to be no logical link. Such shifts may indicate a subject that has particular meaning or affective power in the family. Family practitioners follow the interaction patterns of families for sudden shifts, knowing that hidden meaning or emotion is associated with such shifts.

---

**CASE EXAMPLE**

A mother is describing her childhood and discloses that the children in her family had to drink powdered milk and eat margarine, but the parents had whole milk and butter. She immediately shifts to explain that the parents worked hard and the double standard was justified. Later, when discussing discipline, she shares that her mom had a temper and then immediately adds that she had never seen her yell or act inappropriately. The practitioner picks up on these shifts and begins to explore the subtle family rules about criticizing parents.

---

## Repeated Themes

In a manner similar to shifts in focus, family members will often revert to specific themes that have power in the family. As the themes are repeated, the family practitioner can identify that the theme has particular power, at least for the family member who produces the theme. Sometimes it is just one family member who produces the theme. In such situations, the family member often has had experiences that create the additional meaning. In your family practice, it is important to explore these individual differences so they can be negotiated with the other family members. At other times, the theme is common to all family members; in such situations, a shared experience may be creating the additional power in the theme. It is often important to explore the events that create the additional power to increase the family's ability to master the past event.

**CASE EXAMPLE**

A father refers his family due to an "unruly" adolescent daughter. As the family explores the situation, the therapist finds that the child's behavior is not excessive. However, the father repeatedly talks about her "disrespect" toward him. As the themes of respect are explored, it becomes apparent that the father was raised in an environment where he could never express an opinion without being punished. His parents referred to respect during the punishment. Because the daughter is individuating from the parents, her statements of independence are experienced as threatening to the father, who is referring to them as disrespectful.

## Reaction Intensity

Often a family member will react to situations in a manner that is inconsistent with objective reality. At times, family members may overreact (e.g., severe punishment for talking back to the parent); at other times, they may underreact (e.g., no punishment for playing in traffic). When a reaction does not seem to fit the situation, it is often a sign of additional meaning or emotion attached to the situation. Family practitioners often select such reactions for further exploration.

**CASE EXAMPLE**

A family refers for treatment because the father is unhappy and considering a separation. As the family describes the problems, it becomes clear that any disorder in the home (e.g., clothes not picked up, homework left on the table) will result in an immediate angry reaction by the father, including yelling and punishment. As the situation is explored, it becomes clear that the father feels very uncomfortable when his physical environment is not perfect.

## Cognitive Distortion

Occasionally, a family member's beliefs about an event or situation are not supported by the objective facts of the situation. When this occurs, the family member extends or amplifies some aspect of the exchange or situation in a way that distorts the perceived meaning. Common patterns of distortion include personalizing, catastrophizing, and overgeneralizing. Family practitioners often cue into such distortions because they tend to be central in family problems.

## CASE EXAMPLE

A couple enters treatment due to frequent arguments. As the pattern of arguing is explored, the family practitioner notes that whenever any criticism is offered, the woman reacts immediately with responses such as, "Well, if I'm not good enough for you," and begins a counterattack. Such reactions often lead to arguments and hurt feelings.

---

When considering family processing, you must be careful about cultural elements. Remember that in Chapter 3, we examined several cultural elements that will influence gender, religious, role-related, and general beliefs that are strongly held by the family. Concurrently, several cultural elements influence the amount of time, resources, and supports available for the family. Before you identify any belief of emotional reaction as problematic, it is first important to consider the cultural elements that may be influencing the family members.

## ◆ EXERCISE 11.1  IDENTIFYING UNDERLYING PROCESSING ELEMENTS

You are a worker in a battered women's shelter, and you are working with a 17-year-old battered woman. This woman came into the shelter after some horrendous abuse—her boyfriend almost killed her. After she came into the shelter, her boyfriend found her and has started seeing her again. He is very apologetic and has promised not to hurt her again. He cries frequently when they speak and talks of how he cannot live without her and how much he needs her. She is considering returning to live with him. When she talks with you, she outlines how he has been under pressure for awhile due to being laid off from his job. She also stresses that he really loves her and is very sorry. Although you try to warn her about the risks for her safety, she denies the risks, claiming that he really loves her and has promised not to hit her again.

1. Identify the battered woman's potential beliefs about responsibility.

2. Identify the woman's potential beliefs about relationships.

3. Identify potential emotional triggers that seem to be influencing the woman's thinking.

You are working with a couple. The husband is a businessman who sells and fixes farm equipment. The wife is a stay-at-home mother. When the couple first comes in, they explain that the husband was very involved in setting up the business at the time of their daughter's birth. He worked for up to 16 hours per day, throughout the wife's pregnancy and the early years of their child's life. He now has a stable business but is often late getting home. His tardiness coming home from work is often the subject of arguments. You witness the following exchange while the couple discusses his lateness.

*HUSBAND:* It is not like I am running around on her. I am working for the family.

*WIFE:* I am not saying you are running around. I just want you home. I spend all day taking care of Julie and making supper, and then you just show up when you feel like it.

*HUSBAND:* I try to come home on time; but when I am fixing a tractor, things come up and it sometimes takes longer.

*WIFE:* You are your own boss. That is what you wanted. So just send yourself home at the end of work.

*HUSBAND:* It is not that easy. People need their equipment, especially during harvest. I have to try to get it done right away.

*WIFE:* So you cater to them but not to me?

*HUSBAND:* If I don't get things fixed, they will go somewhere else; then we won't have any money.

*WIFE:* But you seem to care more about them than you do about me and Julie. Where do we fit in? Maybe we should go somewhere too, so we will start to matter in your life.

*HUSBAND:* You know you matter. I built this business up for both of us. It allows us to have a good life.

*WIFE:* I don't consider being home alone a *good* life. I married you because I wanted a husband.

*HUSBAND:* I try to get home. I want to be with you, it is just that some days I can't.

4. In the couple's exchange, what appears to be the wife's critical interpretation that leads her to become upset?

5. What underlying emotional element seems to fuel the wife's interpretations?

6. Identify a potential historical element that fuels the couple's emotions and ensuing interpretations.

7. What is the husband's interpretation of why he has to stay late?

8. How do the interpretations conflict or not allow room for a common understanding?

# Highlighting Processing Themes and Patterns

After identifying a family's processing themes and patterns, the family practitioner must put these themes and patterns on the table so they can be explored and resolved (Greenberg & Johnson, 1988). Frequently, affective and attributive processes are not fully conscious to family members, so you will want to respond in a way that highlights the processes and allows for further exploration. The assumption behind this type of strategy is that when the family members are aware of their unconscious processes, they will be better able to control the situation. Four common family patterns and issues require highlighting.

1. **Emotional and cognitive patterns.** Often the emotional energy in a problem situation is diffuse, shifting from situation to situation through emotional reactivity. Family practitioners observe the patterns of reactivity, tuning into the emotional experience of family members. During this tuning-in process, you will be looking for patterns and common themes across situations to identify the critical emotional and cognitive processes.

2. **Patterns of past adaptation.** Sometimes you will notice a cognitive-affective pattern that appears to be based on a family member's personal history. Although the family may have adapted to the individual's interpretive patterns, its members cannot master the situation until the historical issues stop holding the family hostage. As their family practitioner, you will often want to bring past adaptations into the family member's conscious awareness to enhance their ability to control the situation.

3. **Hidden investments.** Family practitioners are often confronted with family members who have an investment in maintaining the family problems. Family roles such as scapegoat, rescuer, good child, and hero all derive power and privileges from the family problems. Such roles promote investment in the family problems. This investment is common in families that identify one child as bad and another as good. A similar pattern of investment can occur when past events cause invested emotional reactions in family members. For example, past slights may hurt the feelings of a family member. As his hurt feelings prevail, he may begin to ruminate about the situation and generate thinking about the situation (e.g., believe he is a victim) that promotes additional investment in the original slight. It is very difficult to resolve the past events when a family member is heavily invested in the affective experience (Barnett & Youngberg, 2004; Rotter, 2001)

4. **Rules and injunctions.** Some family members operate on rules and injunctions that do not fit their current situation. Most often, these rules evolved as part of their upbringing or early experiences and have been carried into the family without conscious thought. When rules and injunctions operate outside the awareness of people within the family system, it is problematic because no rationale or logic is attached to the injunction. Problems occur when people within the system interact with others who do not adhere to

the same injunctions, because people within the system often expect others to subscribe to the same rules or standards. People consequently become intolerant of differences or behaviors that threaten the rule.

## Critical Skills for Highlighting

After identifying a processing theme, the family practitioner responds to the family in a way that will put the processing on the table so it can be explored and resolved. Four steps are involved in this type of communication:

1. **Observe the process or pattern** (e.g., tension in the air or sequences of behavior). For example, the practitioner notices avoidance of talk and eye contact between two people.
2. **Describe the observation or reflect on the process.** For example, the practitioner shares the observation, "I notice that neither one of you is looking the other in the face."
3. **Engage others to explore the process.** For example, the practitioner asks, "What is going on between you two?"
4. **Access the thinking or affective elements.** For example, the practitioner asks, "When she acts this way, what do you think it says about you?"

Notice that two critical interpersonal skills are used in the highlighting process: describing and reflecting. *Describing* involves recapturing the details that the practitioner observes and stating them objectively to the family. The critical feature in using this skill is to be very descriptive (e.g., "I noticed the volume in your voice became louder when . . . ") rather than sharing conclusions about what is observed (e.g., "you became upset when . . . " or "you started to yell when . . . "). *Reflecting* involves restating the meaning, emotion, or critical content contained in the client statement.

## Critical Description Skills

To get the internal processes (thinking and feeling) on the table for family exploration, the family practitioner often must rely on describing what is observed in family members to introduce the existence of processing-related issues. The practitioner thus must be able to verbally list observations for the family. Three common types of observation need to be described:

1. Interpersonal indicators of the processing
2. Nonverbal (behavioral) indicators of the processing
3. Attribution sequences that indicate processing

*Describing Interpersonal Indicators*   Often in family practice, you will identify a processing-related issue by listening to the exchanges among the family members. As family members interact, you will observe tension, defensive reactions, and other phenomena. Patterns of interactive reactions can indicate that one family member experiences situations differently from the others. You can also identify interactive indicators via repeated interaction themes. When observing such phenomena, you can describe your observations so that family member(s) can explore the underlying thinking or feeling (e.g., "Rick, last time when we were together, Maxine asked you to change how you dealt with the kids, and you stated that she was meddling and should leave you alone. Today, I noticed that when she asked you to call her if you are going to be late home from work, you again stated that she is meddling. Does it always feel like meddling when she asks you to do something differently?")

---

## CASE EXAMPLE

A family enters treatment at a child guidance clinic with the presenting complaint that the son is aggressive. As they explore the situation, the worker notes a family pattern emerging in which the son (Mark) is labeled as "bad" and the daughter (Doris) is labeled as "good." These designated roles have both children locked in, so that neither child is acknowledged for behavior outside of his or her designated position. The worker shares this observation by saying, "I have noticed something fascinating. I hear stories about Mark and Doris's behaviors and see that they both do similar things. In the session I have noticed that when Mark becomes upset, he becomes loud and asks people to change how they treat him. His voice becomes quite demanding. When Doris becomes upset she also becomes loud, but talks about how people are unfair. Her voice almost becomes whiny at times. Is there something in how each child responds when they are upset that causes them to appear good or bad?"

---

If the feeling or belief appears historical, you can trace the reactions back in time by asking exploratory questions (e.g., "Have you always felt this way?" "When did you first start believing this?" "This rule sounds like an important one for you; who helped you learn this rule?"). As the family members disclose the linkages between their current processing patterns and their historical experiences, you can identify the important affective, relational, and thinking elements of the past adaptation. You can then reflect these elements to the family in order to illuminate how they are contributing to the current situation.

---

## CASE EXAMPLE

A woman enters treatment because she is unhappy in her family relationships. When describing her situation, she informs the therapist that her family has no respect for her wishes. She also discloses many beliefs that this is her fault, and she should not expect anything different. The therapist, suspecting a past adaptation, begins to explore the historical roots of feeling that one does not have a right to respect. In the exploration, the woman describes several relationships in which men have treated her poorly. The woman states that she deserved this type of treatment because she was not a good partner. Eventually, the woman describes a sexually abusive relationship with her father. The therapist notes that she is not connecting the abusiveness of her past with her resignation to the current relationship situations. The worker, wanting to bring the connection out so the woman can see the similarities, says, "You say your husband belittles you and makes you feel bad about yourself. Interesting how you say very similar things about your father." The woman thinks for a moment and then acknowledges the similarities. The worker then asks, "On a scale of 1 to 10, with 1 being no connection and 10 being a total connection, how much of your taking crap in your current relationships is connected to the lack of power and abuse in your relationship with your father?" The woman pauses thoughtfully and responds, "I would say about nine." The therapist and woman are then able to explore the nature of her past adjustments and disentangle them from her current relationships.

---

*Describing Nonverbal Indicators*   Often the reactions that indicate an underlying belief or emotional reaction are not shared verbally; rather, they are expressed through nonverbal behavior. In such situations, you will pick up on the nonverbal expression and describe what you have observed to ensure that the reactions can be explored (e.g., "Roberto, I noticed your eyes rolled back into your head when Marcia stated that she wanted to visit her mother. What are your feelings about this visit?")

---

**CASE EXAMPLE**

A couple (Steve and Francine) enters treatment due to frequent arguments. In the early exploration the focus of their arguments is unclear; but as time goes on, the therapist notices that whenever Steve becomes assertive in the sessions, Francine immediately casts her eyes downward and angrily counters his assertions. A pattern of tuning into feelings, anger, and counterattack is evident, regardless of the topic. In observing the pattern, the therapist can see that any time Francine senses that Steve is attempting to assert control, she reacts angrily. The therapist draws on several examples and describes the pattern of responding, saying, "Francine, I have noticed that three weeks ago when Steve suggested using flour in the gravy once in a while because that is how his mother used to make gravy, you became very angry at the suggestion. Last week when he told you he wanted to go boating on the weekend, you became angry and told him he was not to plan your time for you. Now today, Steve suggested a trip to London; and again

I see you expressing anger that he is trying to control you. Have there been times in your life when people took control of you in abusive ways?" Francine hesitates and then shares that an uncle had been sexually abusive toward her. She adds that she has always fought control attempts since that time. The therapist thus expands the treatment focus to include Francine's abuse issues along with the marital issues.

---

*Describing Attribution Sequences*   In a similar fashion to observing interaction sequences and nonverbal responses, family practitioners often track sequences of meaning attribution to understand underlying issues. When a family member consistently interprets events, an underlying belief or emotional response may exist. Given that the pattern of attribution operates over a series of situations, description is frequently the skill needed to put the pattern on the table.

---

## CASE EXAMPLE

A couple has been struggling with low morale for several years. The morale problem tends to be named different things at different times. At one point, they called it a lack of motivation. Months later, they referred to the problem as feeling vulnerable. Later, they accused each other of being unsupportive. Finally, the problem definition reverted to a lack of trust. The couple has made several attempts to deal with the labeled issues, but the problem continues. As the couple enters treatment, they describe the different feelings experienced over the past years. The therapist highlights the pattern of metamorphosis and begins to explore the affect and beliefs associated with each definition. In each definition, the couple describes feeling listless, taken for granted, and unfulfilled. Both partners believe that the other should be attending more closely to their needs, and they want to rekindle the feelings of closeness they experienced earlier in the relationship. The definitions of the problem shifted when these feelings and expectations gave rise to arguments. The content of the argument provided the new definition. The therapist observes, "You have talked with me about several problems including trust, a lack of support, and a lack of motivation to do things together. Inside each problem, you feel the same way and believe the same things. Could it be that you have one problem that goes by many names?" As the couple begins exploring this possibility, they describe how nothing is ever resolved. Rather, they would have an argument and based on their discussion, they would define the situation in a new way. The couple then would adopt the new definition and act as if it were a new problem. The worker is then able to help the couple identify a central issue that remains unresolved.

---

## Critical Reflecting Skills

Although sequences of behavior and attribution require description so that thinking and emotional issues can be placed on the table, sometimes the therapist can simply use reflective skills to capture important emotional and cognitive content. *Reflection* involves restating or summarizing critical elements of the family member's statements. Reflection is most useful when the meaning or emotion is clearly embedded in the content of the family's interaction. Notice in the preceding section that family members most often were not aware of the emotional or attribution-based issues. Consequently, the therapist had to be very descriptive in highlighting the issue for discussion. When a family member is more aware of the underlying issues, the therapist can reflect on what has been stated (sharing conclusions) to stimulate further exploration. Two reflective skills are commonly used to begin the exploration of family processing systems:

1. Reflecting the emotion in the situation
2. Reflecting the meaning in the situation

When using reflective skills, you will look for themes in the family discussions that indicate either underlying belief systems or emotional responses. The themes guide you to identify either an emotion or a meaning in the interaction that appears critical for understanding the family situation. You can then reflect on the theme to highlight the issue for further discussion. You can use the same reflective skill to capture either underlying meaning (interpretations) or underlying feeling states. In either use of the skill, you will reflect the processing theme to the family so that together you can explore the situation in more detail.

---

**CASE EXAMPLE**

A homosexual couple, Thomas and David, enters treatment because their frequent arguing is causing ongoing tension in the relationship. Both of the men are self-employed in professional fields, affording them maximum flexibility in their work lives. At home, however, they have many arguments about being on time. In the early exploration, Thomas states that David is often late. The therapist responds, "David seems to have a different approach to time. I notice that time is very important to you, and it seems important to you that people be on time. Can you tell me more about how you approach time?" Thomas begins to discuss his family background and explains that he was always expected to be on time. He adds that his mother used to accuse people of not caring if they were late. This leads to a discussion of David's family, which had no time-related rules. Through this exploration, Thomas is able to see that being on time was an inherited rule for him, but David was raised by different rules.

---

Chapter 11

## ◆ EXERCISE 11.2   HIGHLIGHTING FAMILY PROCESSING

This exercise is a continuation of the same situation used in Exercise 11.1 (repeated here). You are working with a couple. The husband is a businessman who sells and fixes farm equipment. The wife is a stay-at-home mother. When they first came in, they explained that the husband was very involved in setting up the business at the time of their daughter's birth. He spent up to 16 hours per day working throughout the pregnancy and the early years of the child's life. He now has a stable business but is often late home. His tardiness in coming home from work is often the subject of arguments. You witness the following exchange when they are discussing his lateness.

> *HUSBAND:* It is not like I am running around on her. I am working for the family.
>
> *WIFE:* I am not saying you are running around. I just want you home. I spend all day taking care of Julie and making supper, and then you just show up when you feel like it.
>
> *HUSBAND:* I try to come home on time; but when I am fixing a tractor, things come up and it sometimes takes longer.
>
> *WIFE:* You are your own boss. That is what you wanted. So just send yourself home at the end of work.
>
> *HUSBAND:* It is not that easy. People need their equipment, especially during harvest. I have to try to get it done right away.
>
> *WIFE:* So you cater to them but not to me?
>
> *HUSBAND:* If I don't get things fixed, they will go somewhere else; then we won't have any money.
>
> *WIFE:* But you seem to care more about them than you do about me and Julie. Where do we fit in? Maybe we should go somewhere too, so we will start to matter in your life.
>
> *HUSBAND:* You know you matter. I built this business up for both of us. It allows us to have a good life.
>
> *WIFE:* I don't consider being home alone a *good* life. I married you because I wanted a husband.
>
> *HUSBAND:* I try to get home. I want to be with you; it is just that some days I can't.

1. Describe the pattern of the wife's attributions (try to describe two or more statements that she has made) that indicate the critical beliefs that fuel the problem. Make sure you describe them in statement form, just as you would describe them to her during a session.

2. Provide a reflective statement that captures the emotion in the wife's experience.

3. Provide a reflective statement that captures the core belief in the wife's experience.

4. Provide a reflective statement that captures the husband's emotional experience.

5. Provide a reflective statement that includes the historical element (from the time of pregnancy and childbirth).

## Challenging Current Systems of Processing

In problem situations, strongly held beliefs or reactions may surround the problem behaviors. These beliefs frequently solidify the problem, making it more difficult to change (Alexander et al., 1996; de Shazer, 1997; White, 1983). At times, simply highlighting the beliefs or emotions will increase awareness and allow the family to resolve underlying conflicts. At other times, the therapist must actively seek to neutralize the power of the beliefs and emotions so that the corresponding behaviors will be amenable to change. In this section we explore some strategies that can be used for challenging and neutralizing problem-maintaining belief systems.

The strategies explored throughout this section are based on the assumption that a person's interpretation and definition of a situation will dictate subsequent behavior. When such beliefs lead to problematic behavior, the beliefs must be challenged so the family members can rethink their situation and engage in alternate behaviors. When challenging family processing systems, family practitioners often use one of two general strategies. Practitioners either challenge the processing system or seek to alter the family experience of events.

The first type of strategy involves the family practitioner actively challenging the way a family member interprets or responds to a situation. When using this type of strategy, you will begin by identifying the underlying processing and then highlighting it for further exploration. When it becomes evident that simple highlighting will not alter the underlying processing of the situation, you may elect to introduce information to the family that will alter the belief or emotion. The following five strategies are common when challenging a family member's reactions:

1. Reconstructing beliefs
2. Overgeneralizing the belief
3. Amplifying the belief
4. Cognitive restructuring
5. Direct challenges

## Reconstructing Beliefs

Many adult family members operate on strongly held beliefs that they formed as young children (Claridge, 1992). Problems emerge when these beliefs are applied in adult situations where they do not apply. This dynamic is common with adults who were abused as children. Emotional, psychological, physical, and sexual abuse act to create adaptive beliefs in children (Cohen & Mannarino, 2002; Runyon & Kenny, 2002). For example, it is very difficult for young children to perceive the parent as bad, so they often develop self-blame (Quas, Goodman, & Jones, 2003). Later in life, these childhood adaptations frequently lead to adult problems.

In situations where outdated beliefs are creating problems, family practitioners often seek to reconstruct the belief to fit the new realities. During the reconstruction process, you and the family member work together to identify the underlying elements that led to the initial adaptation. As you explore each element, the individual strips away her childhood attributions to deconstruct the belief. You can then reconstruct the situation from an adult perspective. This allows you and the family member to incorporate adult-level understandings. The assumption of reconstructing belief systems is that when the adult realities are incorporated into the belief, the adult can relinquish the childhood attributions that have been maintained for many years.

---

### CASE EXAMPLE

Pam, an adult survivor of childhood sexual abuse, enters a battered women's shelter. When meeting with her practitioner, Pam expresses a belief that something is wrong with her and that she deserves the abuse. The worker has tried other methods of challenging her belief; but Pam is not able to let go. The practitioner asks her to visit a local preschool and observe the children playing. She is instructed to identify a child the same age that she was at the onset of the abuse. The practitioner asks Pam to take notes when observing the child. The focus of Pam's note taking is to list all the reasons that child deserves to be abused. After observing the child during recess, Pam returns to the practitioner with a blank sheet of paper. She states that there are no reasons that a child deserves to be abused. The practitioner and Pam then begin exploring the nature of abuse. This allows them to deconstruct Pam's abuse and rethink her beliefs about responsibility.

## Overgeneralizing Beliefs

A family member frequently may retain a belief in a limited context. The contextual limitations allow the belief to appear rational, even though the logic may be flawed. In such situations, the family member draws on limited experiences and events to support the belief and does not look beyond this narrow range of data. In the family setting, the person with the rigid beliefs often vehemently argues his position and then obfuscates when other family members attempt to introduce conflicting data.

In such situations, family practitioners often wish to challenge the family member by extending the discussion beyond his limited range of supporting materials. In this extension, the practitioner generalizes the belief to the point where the lack of logic is apparent. Generalization often extends the logic across everyone within a category (e.g., "Do you mean that no woman can be trusted? Not even your mother? Is it possible that there is one trustworthy woman in the world?"). You can also extend the reasoning across logical categories (e.g., "You tell me you don't want your daughter dating. Right now, she is 17 and will be going away to college next year. At what age should she start learning about boys?")

You must be careful in using this strategy, because it is often experienced as a direct challenge to personal beliefs. You must be well tuned into the family members so that you can monitor their reactions. It is important to explore the belief after the intervention, so that you can discuss the history and functions of the belief and help the family to construct new, more growth-enhancing beliefs.

---

**CASE EXAMPLE**

A couple enters treatment because the wife is thinking of leaving. In the initial exploration, the woman describes her husband as controlling. She reports that he has followed her when she is out with her friends. The husband explains that he needs to control his wife's drinking behavior, "because I am a man." The worker responds, "You mean to tell me that just because you have a penis, you have to follow her around to make sure she doesn't get drunk? I am a male, too; do you think I should be doing this?" Seeing the absurdity of his belief, the husband starts to recant his statement. He is initially sheepish, but is eventually able to explore how he uses this belief to justify his controlling behaviors. The therapist then encourages him to explore his underlying anxiety and helps him to see his real reasons for controlling his wife.

---

## Amplifying Beliefs

At times, a family member uses a belief as a launching point into a prepared tirade or speech. The family treats the belief as a given, and there is no attempt to argue or support. Often this pattern emerges when a family member is feeling hopeless or powerless. To try to control her underlying feeling, she exaggerates an element of the situation to justify the belief. You can identify this process when she uses absolute words, like *every, all, never,* and *always*. The belief and overgeneralization are used to justify behaviors or interactions that are not logically justifiable.

When beliefs are used this way in a family, the practitioner often seeks to defuse the belief so the underlying feelings and family interactions can be addressed. You will first tune into this use of language and then attempt to engage the family member in an exploration of the processing that underlies the statement. This involves strong tuning-in and engagement skills as well as critical thinking about the validity of the family statement.

---

### CASE EXAMPLE

A Child Protective Services worker is meeting with a father. This man complains, "These kids are so lazy, they never do anything around the house." Before he can launch into his prepared soliloquy, the worker responds and engages the father in the following discussion.

*WORKER:* They never do anything. I am very concerned about the slothfulness of your children.

*FATHER:* Yeah . . . they are lazy.

*WORKER:* No . . . I believe this is far worse than lazy. You told me that they do absolutely nothing around the house. I have worked with some lazy children in the past, but never anything quite so drastic.

*FATHER:* Well they are pretty bad . . .

*WORKER:* To do absolutely nothing . . . I think we might need to do something quite drastic. How can you stand it?

*FATHER:* Well, it is not really nothing . . . they cook and babysit their brother, but they never clean their room or do chores when I ask them.

*WORKER:* So, they are more disobedient than lazy.

*FATHER:* Yeah . . . they are disobedient. I tell them to do things, and they say they will; but when I come home from the club, nothing is done. No matter what I do . . . yell, punish them, anything, it doesn't change.

*WORKER:* You sounded exasperated.

*FATHER:* I don't know what to do.

*WORKER:* When you feel helpless like this, is that when you tend to get very negative about your kids?

*FATHER:* I try so hard, but it just doesn't work.

*WORKER:* So the more negative wording you use, the more helpless you feel?

*FATHER:* Yeah . . . I think that is it.

*WORKER:* Well, we can't have you feeling this helpless; we got to get some handle on these kids.

*FATHER:* Uh-huh.

*WORKER:* I am going to try to tease out three things with your kids. Kind of like putting different types of fish into buckets. Some of their behavior will be normal . . . they are teens, right?

*FATHER:* Right.

*WORKER:* . . . and some of their behavior will be based on their being able to get away with things, and I think some will be because of their personality. I think if we can start to figure out how much of their behavior goes into each bucket, then we can find some direction.

---

## Cognitive Restructuring

Often the family practitioner wants to directly challenge the beliefs and meaning systems of family members. *Cognitive restructuring* provides a direct challenge, first by breaking down the belief into its component parts. You can then help the family member tune into one of the elements. After the family member identifies the element, you will add a construct, experience, or mental image that can maximize her control of the belief. The core assumption of this type of strategy is that by increasing control over the belief, she gains control over her behavior in the situation. Here are a few of the many methods of cognitive restructuring:

◆ **Identify self-talk** (Lazarus, 1997). The practitioner helps the family member identify the internal messages that fuel the belief. After identifying the messages, the practitioner helps the family member select new messages that will help him change his behaviors.

◆ **Link thoughts and body sensations** (Clark, 1986). The practitioner helps the client tune into her thinking during the problem situation. The practitioner then helps her identify her body sensations when the thinking occurs. The body sensations are used as clues that the thinking is operational.

◆ **Use an emotional thermometer** (Lazarus, 1997). The practitioner helps the family member tune into his emotions. The practitioner then uses an image such as a thermometer to help him identify emotional changes.

◆ **Link images** (Lazarus, 1997). The practitioner helps the family member tune into her affective pattern and concurrent thinking. The practitioner then helps her use calming images to help her manage the emotional agitation.

## CASE EXAMPLE

A family enters treatment because of frequent father-son (14-year-old) conflict. As the initial exploration proceeds, the father begins to express anger about his son, Anthony. As the feelings of anger are explored with the family, it appears that the father is often upset because Anthony will not listen to him. The father tends to tell Anthony what to do and then becomes angry if the he does not comply. The father explains, "I only want the best for Anthony, but he just doesn't care." In the exploration, Anthony explains that he wants to make his own decisions. He further shares that he feels smothered and inadequate when his father starts telling him what to do. His father responds that he never had a good relationship with his own father and wants to be a good dad. He reports that his father was never around and just didn't care about him. Now, when Anthony rejects his gestures of caring, he feels inadequate. The therapist picks up on the theme of inadequacy and shares an image of a button. When presenting this image, the therapist says, "I see that you two have something in common that seems to contribute to this problem. Dad, you are trying hard to be a good dad; but when things start to make you feel inadequate, your button gets pushed and you start to pressure Anthony. I also see that you, Anthony, have a similar button. When your dad tries to help you, it sometimes makes you feel inadequate. When that happens, you withdraw from your father. I see that each of your buttons is sure to push the other person's buttons." The family picks up on the button image and expands on how each tends to work. The therapist then says, "The buttons seem to get charged and ready whenever the two of you are not listening to each other . . . when you are listening only to your own needs. Perhaps the feelings of inadequacy can be used to identify when one of you is not listening."

## Direct Challenges

At times, family practitioners become more active in challenging family beliefs. This most often occurs when the logic or rationale for the belief is not likely to withstand scrutiny. When using these strategies, you will explore the situation with the family member and then begin questioning the application of the belief to the details of the situation.

- ◆ **Disputing** (Ellis & Dryden, 1997). The therapist questions the validity of family members' beliefs.
- ◆ **Hindsight bias analysis** (Kubany, 1998). The therapist explores the bias and possible distortions associated with hindsight.
- ◆ **Responsibility analysis** (Kubany, 1998). The therapist challenges the family members' responsibility-related attributions.
- ◆ **Laddering and inference chaining** (Dryden, 1989; Neenan & Dryden, 1999). The therapist uses successive questions to trace the multiple inferences

contained in the belief. The therapist then explores these inferences with the family member, and links the inferences to the family member's emotional experience and problem patterns.

---

**CASE EXAMPLE**

A couple attends premarital counseling because the female partner is having second thoughts about getting married. When exploring the hesitancy, the woman explains that her fiancé is too laid back and does not seem responsible. The therapist feels that some irrational beliefs are inherent in this position and begins laddering. The following exchange ensues.

*THERAPIST:* How is it a problem if someone is not responsible?

*WOMAN:* You have to be responsible. People need to count on you.

*THERAPIST:* . . . and if you aren't responsible?

*WOMAN:* . . . then they can't count on you.

*THERAPIST:* So what if they can't count on you?

*WOMAN:* Then you let them down.

*THERAPIST:* . . . and if you let them down, what does that mean about you?

*WOMAN:* It means you are worthless.

*THERAPIST:* . . . and if you are worthless.

*WOMAN:* Then you may as well not exist.

At this point the woman stops and looks at the therapist, stating that her mother used to harp on her to be responsible. If she was not responsible, her mother would ignore her and act as if she were not there.

---

# Altering the Experience of Events

In most of this chapter, we have explored interventions into family belief systems. Although these strategies are useful, some problems are nested in how a family member experiences his situation. People's experiences and beliefs are indelibly connected because their affective experience of an event is immediately processed to generate interpretations. Often, a feeling or visceral response underlies a family member's interpretations of the event (de Shazer, 1997). When feeling responses are strong, beliefs provide a bridge between the affective realm and actions. In family practice, you must be able to identify and intervene with affective experiences concurrent with family member beliefs.

Affective experiences are often difficult to identify, because you must infer feelings from articulated thoughts and behaviors. Consequently, you must begin by tuning into the processes that underlie the family members' thinking and behavior. After identifying the underlying affect, you can explore the family members' affective experiences in order to identify how the family pairs affect and thinking to process its experience. As you achieve an understanding of the family's emotional processes, you will find it is useful to share this information with the family. Such sharing validates the internal experience of the family members while concurrently allowing them to correct any misunderstanding. After ensuring an accurate understanding, you can repackage the information to start altering the experience. Most often, you will seek to alter the meaning so that family interpretations result in enhanced control over the affect.

---

## CASE EXAMPLE

A couple is attending treatment due to frequent volatile arguments. At the beginning of a session, the husband describes how he had "lost it" with his partner on the weekend. The worker explores the story with the couple. In the exploration, it appears that the husband had a visceral reaction when the wife was leaving to go out with a friend. Apparently, the couple had just enjoyed a wonderful time together at the lake. As they arrived home, he wanted to enjoy more positive time together; but she wanted to go out and party with a friend. He was lying on the floor and she went to her car to leave. Suddenly he found himself running to the car, opening the door, and yelling. She then left in the car and did not return for several days. In exploring the story, the worker is able to tune into the family feelings of wanting the positive time and desperation when that could not occur. She reflects this understanding so the man can feel understood. She then restates the process, with the following change: "Seems like when you really want something and you find it won't happen, you try so hard to make it happen that you guarantee that it won't . . . kind of like taking a gun and blowing a big hole in your foot. Then it takes forever to even have a good day again." The couple latches onto the new meaning and begins exploring methods of dealing with his feelings without "putting another hole in his foot."

---

Two dimensions are commonly involved in affective experiences. Each of the dimensions is polarized. One dimension focuses on internal versus external polarity, and the other focuses on the positive versus negative polar experience. Often when you are working with family members' experiences, the focus is either on altering the internal-external sense of control or the positive-negative meaning. In the preceding case example, you can identify both polarities. The first polarity is present in the husband's wanting to control something external. The second is his quest to maintain a positive feeling.

## Influencing Internal and External Dimensions

Externalization is the most common problem in the internal versus external polarity. *Externalization* occurs when an individual feels that other people and events control critical elements in his or her life. Externalization is associated with family problems such as controlling and volatile behaviors (Bhatia & Sanford, 1978; Rouse, 1984; Wiehe, 1986) and marital dissatisfaction (Doherty, 1981). When family members exhibit problems with externalization, practitioners often try to increase their internalized locus of control. Here are several common strategies for promoting shifts in the internal versus external polarity:

◆ Analyzing responsibility
◆ Teasing out primary feelings
◆ Identifying spheres of control
◆ Framing and reframing situations

*Analyzing Responsibility (Lazarus, 1997)* In many problem situations, family members adopt a position of defensive externalization (Lazarus, 1997). This is common in situations where a family member is oppressive and/or violent with others. The defensive externalization, while initially implemented as a protective mechanism, maintains the problem as the family member blames others while denying his own responsibility (Bowen, Madill, & Stratton, 2002). The family member often argues that he is a victim in the situation, even though behaviorally, he victimizes others (Adams, 1990).

You will frequently be required to confront this externalized position so that an externalized family member can reconceptualize the situation in a way that allows internalized responsibility. This shift is necessary to engage that family member in change efforts. Without the shift, he will have an ongoing expectation that others should change to ease the burden on him.

When working with heavily externalized and potentially abusive family members, you must first consider safety issues. This requires you to conduct a risk assessment. If there is risk to other family members, it is not wise to work with potential victims in the same room as potential perpetrators of violence (Jory, Anderson, & Greer, 1997). Consequently, you may want to separate the family members to ensure safety. Even when risk is low, you will want to monitor reactions and engage the family in safety planning (O'Leary, 2002).

After ensuring safety, you must tune into the affective issues underlying the externalization and blaming (Bolton et al., 2003). You can then work with the family member to develop alternative attributions that will help him to better manage his feelings. Such work involves an exploration of his internal experiences while deflecting efforts to shift focus to other family members and events. This is often difficult work, because heavily externalized family members are often unskilled in exploring affective material (Bolton et al., 2003). The following strategies can be useful in shifting externalized family members to an internal focus.

◆ **Disallow provocation.** It is common for people who have responded in an oppressive manner to describe their behavior as a reaction to someone else. The oppression or violation is somehow construed as a justified action based on the provocation. By tuning into the client's feelings when delivering the provocation argument, you will enable her to acknowledge the feelings while concurrently isolating her behavior from the behaviors of other people. You can then help the family member identify elements that are her responsibility. When exploring her behavior and thinking, you will continually redirect the locus of control to undermine her provocation excuses.

◆ **Segregate reasons and excuses.** When a heavily externalized family member evades responsibility by shifting blame through excuses, you can respond to his excuse making by first acknowledging the stresses and feelings inherent in the situation. After affirming his affect, you will redirect the focus to his behavior and interactions and to his underlying choices. The concept of choice is important, because decisions are made in light of the situation. Given that decisions are made, free will is involved. This free will is the foundation that allows you to relabel the excuses as reasons. As responsibility for the choices is established, you can help the family member assume responsibility for his behaviors and outcomes.

◆ **Disentangle multiple motivations.** Very often, when a family member engages in difficult behavior, she begins with an altruistic motivation and then integrates self-serving motivations. When issues of responsibility emerge, the family member responds in a self-righteous manner, identifying the altruistic motivation as a reason that she should not be responsible. In such situations, you can validate the noble nature of the initial motivation. Then you will explore the situation with the family member to identify her additional motivations. As the full array of motivation is identified, you can neutralize the self-righteous position and refocus on the behaviors and outcomes. Problematic behaviors can then be paired with non-altruistic motivations for promoting responsibility.

---

## CASE EXAMPLE

A therapist is seeing a woman who has been physically abusive to her children. In the early stages of service, the woman continually states that her children are horrible and she "has to hit them to make them listen." The therapist, who wants to enhance responsibility taking, responds to the woman in the following exchange.

*THERAPIST:* So when you get upset and hit them, it is because they are so bad and you are trying to teach them to be good.

*MOTHER:* Yeah . . . they can be so impossible.

*THERAPIST:* If I was watching them, what kind of behavior would I see when they are being bad?

*MOTHER:* They are disrespectful to people and don't listen when you tell them to do things.

*THERAPIST:* . . . and when they are disrespectful and don't listen, what is so bad about that?

*MOTHER:* Well, kids should listen to their parents and do what they are told. I couldn't get away with the crap they are doing when I was a kid. Kids need to pay heed.

*THERAPIST:* When kids don't pay heed, what does it say about the parent?

*MOTHER:* It says they aren't doing their job.

*THERAPIST:* Many parents don't do their job, what is so bad about that?

*MOTHER:* If you are not doing your job, you are worthless.

*THERAPIST:* . . . and if your children are respectful and obedient, then that means that you are doing your job and are worth something?

*MOTHER:* (*pauses*) Yeah . . . I guess it does.

*THERAPIST:* This parenting sounds really complicated with you trying to control their behavior, but at the same time their behavior controlling whether or not you are worthwhile.

*MOTHER:* I don't know what to think anymore. It was simple before I came in here. If it was good enough for me, it is good enough for my kids, but now I'm confused (starting to sound angry).

*THERAPIST:* It is confusing, from the sound of it . . . do you want to try figure out how the confusion gets so powerful?

---

In the example, you can see how different methods of shifting responsibility back to the mother can be accomplished without tension-filled confrontation. The therapist disallows provocation basically by reflecting the larger meaning to the mother and exploring her experience of the situation. The therapist is able to engage the mother in exploration and then use combinations of skills to tease out the second motivation. This alters the woman's experience of the situation, allowing the therapist to reinforce self-responsibility.

***Teasing Out Primary Feelings*** Many times, a family member reacts to situations at an emotional level, but does not identify her internal experience (Bolton et al., 2003). Rather, she focuses on the behavior and perceived intent of other people. Her externalized position hinders solutions, because she expects the changes in others to create changes in her emotional state. This externalization hinders change, because the source of the solution is outside of her control. Consequently, efforts to empower her to deal more effectively with the situation fail, because she does not believe she needs to change. As her family practitioner, you may want to shift the focus from the behaviors of others to her internal affective states.

You can begin the refocusing by tuning into the woman's internal experience of the situation (de Shazer, 1997). This requires looking below secondary emotions such as anger to identify the more vulnerable primary feelings such as powerlessness, helplessness, and inadequacy. After identifying her affective experience, you must begin to explore her feelings. This involves focusing questions on how she is processing the situation. The shift away from behaviors and into internal experiences causes her to refocus on herself. With this shift of perspective, you encourage the family member to speak only about her perceptions and feelings rather than what she perceives the other person means or wants from her.

---

**CASE EXAMPLE**

A mother refers her daughter for treatment because the child is noncompliant. Fairly early in treatment, the mother maintains that she wants the practitioner to talk with the child, explaining, "I have done everything I can do. She just won't change, so see what you can do with her." The therapist says he will explore situations and help the mother and child find potential solutions; but the mother will not change her approach. She states her feeling that it is the daughter who needs to change. The therapist, who is concerned about the mother's externalization, starts exploring her feelings of helplessness and powerlessness. The mother responds as the therapist continually validates her feelings. The therapist begins exploring the mother's need to control these feelings rather than entrusting them to her daughter. The mother begins to identify ways that she can respond differently to protect her feelings.

---

*Identifying Spheres of Control*   When people struggle with issues of internal versus external control, it is sometimes useful to help them sort out how much control or influence they can expect in a given situation. Very often, a family member operates with an assumption that he should be able to control other people or events. When control is not forthcoming, he may become angry and engage in coercive behaviors in a futile attempt to expand his ability to control.

The problem associated with control attempts is that no one can realistically expect to control other people. However, when a family member does not understand this limitation, control-based dynamics often lead to tension and coercion in the family. Control-based dynamics are common in battering, child abuse, depression, and burnout. Consequently, family practitioners often wish to neutralize the power of control expectations in the family.

The *spheres of control strategy* is used to help family members understand the limits to their control. This understanding is accomplished by considering three concentric circles, as illustrated in Figure 11.1. The center (and smallest) circle is the sphere of control. This area refers only to the client's actions, words, feelings, and thoughts. It is often useful to draw a small circle for family members to help them visualize how little control they actually have in a situation.

**Figure 11.1** Spheres of Control

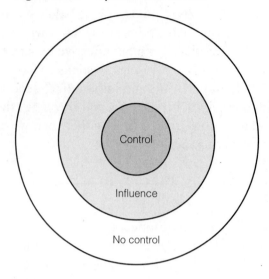

After exploring with your clients how each of us can control only our own actions and processing, you can then draw the largest circle. In describing this sphere of no control, you can explain that most of life is outside of our ability to control. Explore this sphere with family members to help them identify the many elements of the situation that they cannot control. You can label these elements in the circle to reinforce that no one can realistically expect to control important elements.

After exploring what family members can and cannot control, draw the middle circle and identify it as the sphere of influence. In this sphere, family members can use what they say and do to provide enticements, logic, and relationships to influence people and events in the sphere of no control. You can graphically represent this by drawing arrows from labels in the sphere of no control to the sphere of influence. It is often useful to explore current family member strategies of influence. While exploring how well the current methods are working, you can identify the family's need to rethink the current approach. You can then use the sphere of influence to guide exploration into possible new strategies of influence.

---

## CASE EXAMPLE

A father enters treatment to work on his expressions of anger with his children. Early in treatment, he describes being very angry that his son went to school without a proper jacket when it was cold out. He describes telling him that it was cold outside as the son left for school, and says he was angry that the boy did not wear his winter coat. The therapist draws the sphere of control and explores the limits of the father's control over his children. The therapist then moves to the sphere of no control. The father outlines several examples of futile attempts to help his son do the right thing. The therapist validates the father's feelings of helplessness and frustration then explores the typical influence strategies he uses. While outlining the strategies, the therapist helps the father identify his beliefs that he should be able to control the child. As he explores these beliefs, the father is able to identify how they promote frustration because they are not realistic. After this exploration, the therapist and father begin to explore the sphere of influence. In this exploration, the father expresses frustration because none of his strategies are working. The therapist helps him outline different methods of influence that may work better.

---

*Framing and Reframing Experiences*   As families approach situations, they do so with a predetermined mind-set that controls how they interpret and respond (Barker, 1994; Coyne, 1985). The mind-set is often referred to as a *frame*. The frame that family members put on a problem situation contributes to the problem by organizing the family's understanding and interactions (Coyne, 1985). Practitioners often seek to change the frame used by family members to promote new interpretations that better allow for change (Barker, 1994). This strategy for changing the family's interpretive system is referred to as *reframing*. Reframing strategies are very useful when dealing with issues of externalization, defensiveness, and blame (Eckstein, 1997; Morris, Alexander, & Turner, 1991; Robbins et al., 2000).

Families often pay attention to selected elements in a situation and use these elements to build the initial frame. When using reframing, you will first tune into these elements of the initial frame to discover how the family members link their interpretations to situational events (Coyne, 1985). You will also tune into other elements of the situation that may be able to shift thinking if included in a new definition. During this tuning-in process, you must assess how rigidly the family adheres to the initial definition and how the different elements promote such adherence (Coyne, 1985).

After identifying critical elements in the initial frame, you can mentally construct a new definition or frame. This new frame must include the critical elements of the situation, but change the meaning attributed to the elements (Coyne, 1985). The new frame must also fit the situation better than the initial frame. Often the improved fit can be achieved by including elements overlooked by the family in the initial frame. After mentally constructing the reframe, you can propose the new definition to the family. If the family adopts the new frame, old behaviors associated with the old definition will become redundant and amenable to change. As reframes are adopted by the family, many problems may be averted (Miller & Osmunson, 1989). We will consider two common reframing strategies used when working with issues of externalization.

1. **Reframe the power in a situation.** When a family member sees others as more powerful than herself, she may project some of her own power onto the other person. The practitioner often attempts to help family members reclaim their projected power by using one of two common reframing strategies. First, you can reframe the situation to reflect that the family member is giving her power away. Use this reframe when you notice that she is trying to please others. The second common reframe is that others are robbing her

power. Use this strategy when you determine that others have undermined the client's sense of empowerment.

2. **Reframe the responsibility in a situation.** Often, a specific family member is identified as responsible (or not responsible) in the initial frame. Sometimes this frame is used to deflect responsibility onto someone else; at other times, the frame maintains coalitions and role structures. When the responsibility attributions maintain the problem or inhibit change, you will attempt to shift the meaning systems by reframing the situation. Reframes often seek to broaden the responsibility attributions so that more family members are included in the problem definition. For example, when a situation is seen as one child causing the problems in the family, you can redefine the problem to indicate that the child needs a different approach that the family has not yet learned. A second type of reframe is to loosen the responsibility beliefs by creating a definition that defies clear responsibility. For example, you might say, "I know that Shawna is loud and active in the mornings, and this seems to be at its worst when you are rushing around. Could she be acting like a stress barometer for the family?" A third common reframe is to move responsibility to an individual family member. For example, with a mother who believes that she needs to love (not discipline) her child, you might say, "One of the toughest acts of love you will ever need to perform is to discipline Felicia."

## Influencing Positive and Negative Dimensions

The second critical theme in exploring how family members experience situations is the positive-negative polarity. Family members frequently stress negative interpretations of events, themselves, and others. These negative interpretations promote problems when they become a fixed lens that filters out positive intentions, attributes, solutions, and outcomes. In such situations the family practitioner often seeks to change the interpretation so that family members can experience themselves as stronger or more competent. Here are four common intervention strategies that can help influence the positive-negative polarities in a family:

1. Positive reframing
2. Solution focusing
3. Strength finding
4. Strength coupling

*Positive Reframing*   Family members often organize their attributions of meaning into a frame that highlights the positive or negative aspects of the situation (Barker, 1994; Coyne, 1985). This behavior can present problems when the direction of emotional energy is unable to incorporate a balanced view of the situation (Alexander et al., 1996). Concurrently, family members often experience negative events that cast an emotional pall on the family. In both types of family situation, positive reframing can be an effective strategy for neutralizing negative affect and restoring balance (Friedlander et al., 2000; Larson, 1998). Although the mechanisms of positive reframing are the same as those described earlier, the use of positive reframing has important implications when working with issues of negativity in the family (Kraft, Claiborn, & Dowd, 1985; Robbins, Alexander, Newell, & Turner, 1996).

When using positive reframing, you tune into the family situation to identify the critical elements for constructing the frame. You can then construct positive interpretations and propose them to the family members. The new frame must be acceptable to the family and fit the reality of its members' situation rather than attempting to talk the family members out of their feelings. When you propose a positive reframe, use the same facts as those in the initial frame, but select positive attributions to replace the initial negative meanings.

---

## CASE EXAMPLE

A worker at a battered women's shelter is meeting with a woman who was abused as a child and is now in her second abusive dating relationship. The woman interprets herself as somehow deficient because she seems to gravitate toward abusive people. She is also upset that she has never taken action to leave the people who were abusing her. She says, "I must be sick to keep staying in these messed-up relationships." The worker responds with a positive reframe: "I know that you often stay in relationships that are not good for you. I am impressed with how hard you work on your relationships. Many people would give up, but I see you as being so adept at love that you will try everything before you throw in the towel. I prefer the word *rare* rather than sick to describe you, because your level of commitment is rare."

---

*Solution Focusing*    Frequently when families enter treatment, they expect the therapist to assume the position of expert and tell them what to do about their problem. This expectation shifts the family members' focus away from their inherent resources and leaves them trapped in a problem-focused identity. The family practitioner typically wants to start an immediate shift in the family's position by focusing the family members on their own resources and capacity for solutions (de Shazer, 1988). This strategy is based on an assumption that families already have the capacity for change and that it is the therapist's job to help them tune into their capacities (de Shazer, 1988; Hoyt & Berg, 1998).

*Solution focusing* is a redirection strategy whereby the family, typically focused on the problem, is redirected to explore potential solutions (de Shazer, 1988; Gale & Newfield, 1992). The focus on solutions is also a change for workers, who traditionally have been trained in strategies for which in-depth diagnosis has been considered necessary. Solution-focused intervention shifts from the negative focus to exploring family capacities and resources (Hoyt & Berg, 1998). This strategy occurs through five different phases:

1. The practitioner must validate the desires and direction of the family members (Friedman & Lipchik, 1999). Such validation sets the relationship and direction for change.
2. The practitioner then begins exploring for times when the problem could have occurred but did not (exceptions).
3. As exceptions are identified, the practitioner guides the exploration into identifying the differences between the exceptions and the problem events (Molnar & de Shazer, 1987).
4. The practitioner explores the family's resources and capacities that are used during the exceptions to the problem (Hoyt & Berg, 1998).
5. The practitioner shifts focus to the future and begins exploring what the family will do differently next time similar situations arise (de Shazer, 1988; Hoyt & Berg, 1998).

---

## CASE EXAMPLE

A family consisting of two gay male parents, a 14-year-old daughter, and a 10-year-old son enters treatment due to the daughter's poor performance at school. In the past year, the daughter's grades have dropped from A's to C's. The daughter has also been suspended for arguing with teachers. In the early exploration, the parents describe the daughter as always being high-strung, but say they have managed the problem until the past year. The therapist acknowledges their current struggle and then says, "It sounds like Marie (daughter) sometimes does well. Tell me about a time when she was functioning well in school." The parents outline how Marie was able to balance sports and academics during the fall semester of the previous year. The therapist begins exploring how Marie managed things differently that semester. The focus is eventually broadened to include how the parents were able to help Marie stay on track. The son is also included as an observer of the differences he noticed between the two times. The family is able to identify how the parents helped Marie structure her time. As the details are explored, the parents begin to identify tasks that they are no longer performing. As this information emerges, the therapist begins asking about changes they might make in the next few weeks based on what has worked in the past. The parents begin talking with Marie about changes that she can expect.

---

*Strength Finding*   Solution focusing seeks to mobilize family resources based on past solutions. Another approach focused on family resources is the strengths perspective. Like solution focusing, *strength finding* focuses on family resources. However, the focus is slightly broader, encompassing multiple areas of family strength and resilience (de Jong & Miller, 1995; Saleebey, 1996). The strengths perspective focuses on finding opportunities to highlight, illustrate, and use family strengths. It is assumed that all families have strengths evidenced in their adaptation and survival (Wolin & Wolin, 1993). It is also assumed that identifying these areas of strength will enable family members to feel less defeated and to apply their resources toward mastering their situation.

When using a strengths approach, you will explore the family story. During the exploration, pay close attention to themes of adaptation, resilience, and effective coping (Saleebey, 1996, 2001). As opportunities are presented, you can describe or reflect these observations to the family. When the family members revert to positions of helplessness, help them recall the areas of strength and highlight them for the family to encourage mastery. Try to continually reference areas of strength as the family works toward its goals.

One caution associated with the strength-finding approach is to keep all strengths, not just positive strengths, in focus (Saleebey, 1996). Some practitioners become confused and try to shift the family focus to positive elements. This is not the spirit of a strength-finding approach. Some strengths are positive, but often strengths can be perceived as negative. Take, for example, an adolescent who enters treatment and refuses to open up. The adolescent's behavior is not positive, but there is an inherent strength in her protective silence.

## CASE EXAMPLE

A family enters treatment for help with a daughter who was sexually abused. The family had initially been treated by a practitioner who was problem focused; believing that the family was at high risk for neglect, he was seeing the family frequently. When the new practitioner assumes the case, she reads the file and notes a pattern wherein the family brings in a problem, explores the problem, and then gets some advice from the practitioner. The next week, they arrive with a new problem. It appears that no changes are generalized beyond the session, and the daughter is becoming very resentful about treatment. When the new practitioner meets with the family, she adopts a strengths perspective and maintains a strict focus on areas of functioning where the daughter is doing well. The parents are informed that if they want to discuss problems, they will need to book a separate meeting without the daughter present. Within three months, remarkable changes are noted in the child's behavior. The case is closed shortly afterward.

*Strength Coupling*   Some family members resist acknowledging strengths. Often such resistance is predicated on experiences that create feelings of negative self-worth. In such situations, the practitioner may seek to be less direct when introducing the family strengths. It is assumed that an indirect approach to sharing strengths can be used to avoid the family's normal resistive mechanisms. When you highlight the strength through a quick reference, the family members can incorporate the message with no efforts to dismiss or rationalize the statement of strength.

*Strength coupling* is an approach that allows the therapist to introduce the strength to the family by making offhand comments rather than conducting an extended exchange. When using strength coupling, you will pair family members with social symbols that metaphorically indicate strength (Madanes, 1990). Typically, you will use strength coupling in a reflective manner to ensure that the family strength is included in your comment.

---

**CASE EXAMPLE**

A mother enters treatment due to frequent conflict with her adolescent daughter. The mother has a long history of childhood physical abuse and often feels inadequate. The daughter is a very successful student and typically makes the mother feel inadequate during arguments. In sessions, the practitioner attempts to highlight strengths; but the mother tends to explain away the therapist's observations. In discussions about arguments both with the daughter and at work, the mother demonstrates an ability to see through situations. The mother is also skilled at articulating issues. The therapist starts sharing comments about these skills by stating that the mother is like a lawyer. At first these comments are slipped into the discussions. When the mother becomes comfortable with the comments, the therapist begins expanding on them by adding observations about her skills.

---

#### ◆ EXERCISE 11.3   CHALLENGING BELIEFS

You are a working with Jeanine, a depressed mother. Jeanine was sexually abused as an eight-year-old child. She told her teacher, and her father was apprehended, causing the family to lose his income; they ended up moving into a housing project. Jeanine believes that she is responsible for the problems in her family. Because of this belief, she maintains a steady sense of low self-worth that culminates in depressive episodes. When she is depressed, Jeanine sits on the couch for days and does nothing to help the children. When they ask for things, she starts crying; and they then go to the neighbors. The neighbors have contacted Child Protective Services, and the children are in custody. Your job is to help Jeanine become more active. You believe her low self-worth and cognitions are important in the problem, and you want to change her thinking about the past abuse. Jeanine says, "I don't know why I even try. I am always screwing up. I messed up my family by having my dad taken away, and now I am doing it again. What's the use?"

1. You want to respond to Jeanine in a way that starts to challenge her feelings of responsibility. To start with a response that can prompt a responsibility analysis, what exactly would you say?

2. In the space below, draw the circles for the spheres of control. In the sphere of control, enter the elements of the situation that Jeanine as a young girl would have in the abusive situation. Next, enter the elements in the sphere of influence and the sphere of no control.

3. Now, write the statement that you would make to Jeanine to start reconstructing her beliefs about her level of control in the abusive situation.

4.  How would you follow this up with Jeanine to continue the meaning recon-
    struction process?

5.  Write a reframing statement to challenge Jeanine's belief that she is the per-
    son who destroyed her family. Try to use a positive reframe that will fit her
    situation.

## Summary

Throughout this chapter, we have explored specific strategies and techniques to help
identify methods for influencing family member processing systems. Notice that no
single intervention is powerful enough to shift long-standing beliefs. As a family practitioner, you will need to use different iterations of these strategies repeatedly to
begin the slow process of change. One aspect that makes change slow involves the
contextual elements that influence beliefs. Some beliefs and feelings will be stronger
or more pronounced in certain relationships. When the family has contact with different people, the amplitude of the potential problems will increase. Consequently, you
must be prepared to revisit critical issues as relationships and other contextual elements come into play. You may also need to involve critical relationships in the clinical work to ensure that the context can be addressed simultaneously with the belief
systems.

# Critical Content

1. Beliefs and affect frequently underlie problematic behaviors and interactions.
2. Family practitioners must often alter thinking and feeling patterns to create changes. These changes provide a foundation for behavioral change.
3. Four different strategies are used for altering thinking and feeling processes in the family: identifying processing themes and patterns, highlighting cognitive-affective processing, challenging family cognitions, and altering the experience of the situation.
4. Highlighting strategies seek to make underlying beliefs, past adaptations, and affective processes conscious for the family. It is assumed that knowledge of these processes will enable change.
5. Challenging cognitions involves highlighting processes while including alternative visions that can fit the situation better than the initial belief. Practitioners directly challenge family beliefs.
6. Changing the experience of the situation focuses on two areas of experience: the internal-external dimension and the positive-negative dimension.
7. Each type of processing system strategy employs many different adaptations and techniques to help family members gain mastery of their situation.
8. All strategies use exploratory skills to prevent the practitioner from assuming a position of being expert on the family dynamics. The family must be allowed to remain the expert in its own situation.

# Suggested Readings

Alexander, J. F., Jameson, P. B., Newell, R. M., & Gunderson, D. (1996). Changing cognitive schemas: A necessary antecedent to changing behaviors in dysfunctional families? In K. S. Dobson & K. D. Craig (Eds.), *Advances in cognitive-behavioral therapy* (Vol. 2, pp. 174–192). Thousand Oaks, CA: Sage.

Hoyt, M. F., & Berg, I. K. (1998). Solution-focused couple therapy: Helping clients construct self-fulfilling realities. In M. F. Hoyt (Ed.), *The handbook of constructive therapies: Innovative approaches from leading practitioners* (pp. 314–340). San Francisco: Jossey-Bass.

Robbins, M. S., Alexander, J. F., & Turner, C. W. (2000). Disrupting defensive family interactions in family therapy with delinquent adolescents. *Journal of Family Psychology, 14,* 688–701.

## Chapter 12

# Influencing Family Members Through Indirect Strategies of Change

The first two chapters of this section focus on intervention strategies in which family practitioners assume an active and at times directive role in helping family members change. In Chapter 10 we explored direct interventions focused on action systems, and in Chapter 11 we explored direct interventions with processing systems. All of these strategies are based on an assumption of a strong and focused working alliance. Without such an alliance, the client compliance needed in many strategies will be missing and result in failed intervention.

## Theoretical Grounding

Indirect methods of influence in family therapy have been strongly associated with the strategic model of practice. However, there are different schools of thought within the strategic model of practice. The Milan school focuses heavily on the use of language. The American schools of strategic practice were influenced by Milton Erikson's work in clinical hypnosis. These strategic models, the Washington school (Jay Haley and Chloe Madanes) and the Mental Research Institute (MRI), tend to focus more on indirect methods of influence.

In traditional family practice textbooks, it is difficult to find complete information from these theorists because most of their publications are in trade books rather than textbooks. You may want to explore *Handbook of Family Therapy*, edited by A. S. Gunman and D. P. Kniskern (Vol. 2, New York: Brunner/Mazel, 1991), to find a comprehensive resource with chapters devoted to different indirect strategies. Another valuable source is *A Brief Guide to Brief Therapy*, by B. Cade and W. H. O'Hanlon (New York: Norton, 1993). If your school library has these books, you will find they contain valuable information about the concepts presented in this chapter. You can find brief information about the American schools of strategic practice in the following textbooks:

◆ *Family Counseling and Therapy* (3rd ed.), by A. M. Horne, 2000, Pacific Grove, CA: Brooks/Cole.
◆ *Family Therapy: An Overview* (6th ed.), by I. Goldenberg & H. Goldenberg, 2004, Pacific Grove, CA: Brooks/Cole.

# Using Indirect Methods of Influence

When the working alliance is tenuous, or the practitioner is not in a position to exert direct influence, indirect intervention strategies are useful for helping families master their situations. The indirect strategies we explore in this chapter exert a diffuse influence on family members. Because the influence is indirect, practitioners must believe that the family members have the capacity and resources to master their situation. The practitioner's task is then to help the family members activate their capacities for change. Such activation occurs through the process of creating experiences and planting seeds designed to help family members discover their own capacities and resources.

There are two common types of indirect change strategies. The first involves indirect resource activation. This type of strategy is similar to the past strategies where the therapist and family members meet and explore situations. However, the therapist selects indirect responses to initiate subtle changes. The second type of strategy involves intervention into the holding environment. This requires the therapist to broaden the scope of treatment and begin to involve additional people in the change effort. Both are considered indirect, because the influence on the family members is circuitous.

# Indirect Resource Activation

When using the strategy of *indirect resource activation*, the family practitioner attempts to sidestep the rational defenses of family members by stimulating the nondominant side of the brain. Typically, the nondominant brain hemisphere is more accepting of input without rationalizing or cognitively filtering out information provided by the therapist (de Shazer, 1980). Concurrently, emotions are processed in the nondominant hemisphere so indirect techniques may have a more powerful emotional impact (Campbell, 1982; Tucker, 1981). This effect occurs because the right side of the brain (in right-handed individuals) tends to take in holistic images and pictures as an entire pattern, or *gestalt*. The left side of the brain is then engaged to make sense of the input. Indirect strategies are thus different from logic, which is processed on the dominant side of the brain (Bradshaw & Nettleton, 1981; Myers, 1982; Tucker, 1981; Walker, 1980).

With indirect resource activation, family members are in control of how they interpret and use the therapist's input (Lankton & Lankton, 1983; Lankton, 2002).

The goal is to make comments, create experiences, or share information that will cause the family members to critically reflect on their situation. The nature of such reflection dictates the ensuing changes (or lack of change). Interventions may generate unanticipated changes because of the limited therapist control. The practitioner must have faith in the family's resources when using this type of strategy.

Indirect strategies require strong interactive engagement, because these strategies often involve exercises and activities that may not make logical sense (Lankton, 2001). The practitioner frequently asks family members to close their eyes, breathe deeply, visualize, and/or follow a string of verbal instructions. Most clients will not engage in such exercises unless they trust the practitioner.

Indirect strategies of influence require the practitioner to first tune into the family situation to identify strengths, resources, and patterns in the family situation. The practitioner then uses this knowledge to identify how the elements, themes, and patterns might be used to promote change. Finally, the practitioner must plan a statement, experience, or story that can activate the family resources. Activation usually involves creating a powerful experience in the session that will cause the family members to reflect and eventually apply their thinking to the family situation. In this section we consider five common indirect strategies:

1. Meaning attribution exercises
2. Visualization and guided imagery
3. Analogies and metaphors
4. Storytelling
5. Symbolic expressions

## Meaning Attribution Exercises

Many people turn to others to find meaning and purpose in their lives. This can become a problem in family practice, because such people may pressure other members of their family to provide a sense of meaning that can realistically come only from within themselves (Haley, 1973; Lankton, Lankton, & Matthews, 1991). As a family practitioner, you will often want to activate a family member's internal resources for generating his own meaning. Frequently, this is a projective exercise requiring him to reflect on some situation, event, or item and to generate a personalized meaning from the exercise (Haley, 1973). There are three basic steps in creating such an exercise.

1. Create a safe atmosphere for the family member to engage in the exercise. This often requires a solid rationale for the behavior and presenting the situation as a form of play. The play framework is useful because people will often engage in new, awkward, and/or novel activities under the guise of play when they would turn down participation under other definitions (Winnicott, 1971).
2. Provide a situation or concrete opportunity (e.g., object) and give explicit instructions guiding the family member to explore the opportunity and learn from it. Inherent in the opportunity, the family member is instructed to experience the situation and apply the experience to himself.

3. Invite the family member to reflect on the meaning he has attributed and learn from how the new meaning applies to his life situation. This element helps the family member generalize beyond the specific exercise.

As a family member begins to generate meaning from within himself, he will generate untapped new resources. When you notice he is trying to revert to externalized meaning generations, you can draw on such experiences to remind him that he has the capacity to understand situations without needing others to frame his experience for him. As the family member becomes increasingly accustomed to looking inward for answers, relationships begin to change in the family.

---

**CASE EXAMPLE**

A very intelligent but emotionally awkward medical practitioner enters treatment because he and his wife are becoming distant and he feels at risk of losing her. In the early exploration, he shares how he often counts on his wife to respond to his needs and to family situations in a way that helps him feel better about himself. He waits for her to comment on actions he takes to improve his looks (haircuts, new clothes, etc.) and follows her lead to make his final judgments about the value of his actions. His wife complains that she feels smothered in the relationship. The therapist, knowing that this man is both externalized and intellectually oriented, asks him to go alone on a nature hike. The therapist describes a path in a nearby wildlife area and tells the man to follow the path to a specific landmark, where he is to sit (on a log) until he discovers the real reason that he was told to be there. The next weekend, the man follows the instructions. When he returns for the next session, he describes sitting on the log for about 10 minutes and then seeing a small bird. He describes reaching out, expecting the bird to land on his hand; but explains that as he extended his arm, the bird became frightened and left. He says that through this activity, he learned that he has very unrealistic expectations of other people. The therapist then helps him explore how these unrealistic expectations influence his behavior (reaching out), the results (scaring off the bird), and his experience (disappointment). After sharing these new insights, the therapist helps the man apply the new knowledge to his marital situation.

---

## Visualization and Guided Imagery

*Visualization* strategies can focus on either action or processing systems. When focusing on interaction and behavior, you will often create an experience to help clients visualize themselves mastering their situation. This experience frequently involves clients visualizing situations in which the problem could occur and then being guided through successful avoidance of the problem (McConaghy, Blaszczynski, Armstrong, & Kidson, 1989). Visualization is a forward-thinking exercise that requires the therapist to tune into the family members' problematic patterns, engage them in the exercise, and then coach them through the visualization. Through visualization, the family members can foresee potential problems and identify alternate paths. When using the strategy to influence processing systems, you will often focus on conflicting values or important decisions. The visualization is used to help the family members reach into themselves for advice on resolving the family situation.

Visualization and guided imagery techniques require the therapist to have a clear, well-prepared image or script. You will begin by helping the family members relax and then move the story to a point where they can seek information within themselves (Barrios & Singer, 1981; Winder, 1996). *Guided imagery* requires you to first tune into the clients to determine the symbols and themes that appear to be important. You can then develop these themes into a story or visualized scene in which the clients will most likely be able to access their internal resources (Hoffman, 1983).

After developing the image or story, you must implement the guided image with the clients. This process most often begins with relaxation (Heikkinen, 1989; Hoffman, 1983). Relaxation strategies often use breathing and progressive relaxation to achieve a more susceptible state. At that point, you can guide the family members by sharing the story line. The story often culminates in an opportunity to access internal resources or confront specific issues. After this culminating moment, you can bring the family members back to the present time by having them refocus on their breathing. When the family members are reoriented to the present time and place, you will instruct them to open their eyes (Heikkinen, 1989; Lankton & Lankton, 1989; Laselle & Russell, 1993).

## CASE EXAMPLE

A woman (Collette) is struggling with the decision of whether to place her severely disabled, 12-year-old child in a group home or to keep the child in the home with her. Collette works full time, is divorced with no support from her partner, and is very depressed as a result of caring for this child. Her child is in a wheelchair, has no verbal or self-care skills, and basically operates at the level of an infant. Although the therapist has tried several methods to help her resolve the decision, Collette cannot resolve her ambivalence. The therapist elects to use the following image. After having Collette tune into her breathing for about one minute, he then begins describing a scene in which Collette climbs up a large hill toward a Greek-looking temple. To deepen Collette's engagement in the scene, the therapist describes all aspects of the climb and includes descriptions that involve all the senses (sight, smell, feeling, hearing, etc.). The therapist relates that upon reaching the temple, Collette is greeted by a wise-looking woman who is sitting in the temple. Collette is guided through the step of asking the woman how to proceed. The therapist then has the woman answer

Collette silently. The woman advises Collette not to share this answer, to be secure in the answer because it has come from the wisest part of her soul. The therapist then guides Collette back to the room and ends the exercise. Collette, who never discusses the advice, puts her child on the waiting list the next week.

---

Guided imagery strategies can be useful for many types of problems. For example, you can use guided imagery in helping family members to access old memories or trauma (Roland, 1993). If you use guided imagery in this way, be aware that debriefing the experience is essential. In debriefing, you will use primarily exploratory questions and reflecting strategies to help the clients make sense of the past event, revisit how they have adapted, and then try to integrate the events into current life.

## Analogies and Metaphors

Metaphoric communication can be a very powerful method of intervention with family members (Lankton, 2002). This style of communication is often safer with hesitant families, because you can use it to access difficult topics such as past abuse (Miller, 1998; Winder, 1996). Although resorting to metaphoric communication gives you a tool for influencing families that might otherwise be unresponsive, a metaphor does require interpretation. This is where you will lose influence, because the family members ultimately assign the meaning to the metaphor (Paulson, 1996).

When using metaphors to provide indirect suggestions, you will first tune into the patterns inherent in the family situation. You can then tune into similar patterns and motivations in other situations. When considering the similar situations, you will select a theme or story that is parallel, but not identical, to the family situation.

After identifying a parallel situation, you construct a statement, story, or exercise to explore the parallel situation with the family. While exploring the parallel situation and stressing specific elements, you are exerting an indirect influence on family members (Boone & Bowman, 1997; de Shazer, 1980; Zeig, 1980). Then, when the family members reflect on the parallel situation, they begin to apply the parallel discussion and experience to their current situation (Paulson, 1996). Solutions to the current situation emerge through this application. Here are three types of metaphor frequently used by family practitioners:

1. Client-generated metaphors
2. Therapist-constructed metaphors
3. Concrete metaphors

*Client-Generated Metaphors*   Client-generated metaphors emerge from the client's description of her situation (Hoffman, 1983). Listening closely to your client's use of language, you will select symbols that have some power in her life (Gladding, 1984; Kopp & Craw, 1998; Sims & Whynot, 1997). These symbols are then used in your response. For example, when a family member states that she feels like a doormat, you can explore the parallels with the family member (e.g., doormats protect important elements in the home, are viewed as expendable, get left out, etc.).

---

## CASE EXAMPLE

A husband (Enrique) going though separation is talking about how difficult the changes are in his life. In describing the enormity of the changes, he says it is like climbing a mountain. The therapist picks up the analogy, exploring the details of climbing up and over a mountain. She talks about how when climbing, a person needs to carefully pick hand- and toeholds and balance attention between long-term direction and finding the next toehold. With Enrique, she also explores the dangers of looking back. The discussion has a calming effect. Enrique then begins to identify toeholds (things he needs to do right away). The therapist explores these tasks and then asks Enrique about direction. When he looks puzzled, the therapist says, "I want you to look ahead and identify a path that seems to have a lot of hand- and toeholds." Enrique hesitates and says, "I haven't been doing that because I am hoping to get stuck on a ledge. I really want her to rescue me." The therapist then asks, "You know your wife better than I. When she discovers that you put yourself on a ledge, is she the type of woman who will come running?" Enrique replies, "Maybe . . ." The therapist then responds, "Are you willing to be hung out on a ledge taking that type of gamble?" Enrique indicates that this behavior is not wise and reorients himself to begin identifying some direction for rebuilding his life.

---

*Therapist-Constructed Metaphors*   Therapist-constructed metaphors involve the therapist developing a metaphor or story that parallels the client situation (Lankton, 2002). You will introduce the parallel situation, often stressing specific themes to challenge the family members or provide new alternatives (Donnelly & Dumas, 1997; Wenger, 1982). There are many methods for introducing a metaphor to the family members. Many therapists use themselves to provide metaphors by sharing personal experiences, past events, and dreams. Other approaches include embedding metaphors in visualization exercises, constructed stories, and talking about other people in similar situations.

---

## CASE EXAMPLE

A family enters treatment because the father abuses his eldest son when drunk. Although the family attended treatment as outlined in the probation order, the father has never taken treatment seriously (in eight months of treatment). He continues to drink, brag about fooling the police, and undermine the mother's authority with the sons. After trying multiple direct approaches, the therapist selects a metaphoric strategy. The metaphor is designed with a hope that the father will start to critically assess his behavior. When the family comes into the session, the therapist addresses the youngest son: "David, I had a dream about you. It was really strange, because you weren't you. In my dream you were actually this female client I used to have. Her father used to sit in his room above the homeless shelter, drinking and looking at the people on the street and talking about how he was so superior to them. He just didn't know that people in the town laughed at him and saw him for exactly what he was. I couldn't believe it when you turned into her during this dream. I hope you will stay out of my dreams in the future." About three days after the session, the mother phones the therapist, telling him that she and the children have moved out of the home and will not move back in until the father changes.

---

*Concrete Metaphors*   In family practice, you can create metaphoric experiences by using objects to parallel the client situation (Murray & Rotter, 2002). In creating concrete metaphors, you first tune into the family situation and then select physical objects that can provide a parallel experience. You can then introduce the objects into the session to underscore the parallel themes (Satir, 1988; Murray & Rotter, 2002). Concrete metaphors are most useful when a physical property such as weight, elasticity, texture, or visceral experience parallels some aspect of the client situation. You can also use concrete aids, such as a labyrinth to parallel the complicated paths that families must sometimes walk (Peel, 2004).

---

## CASE EXAMPLE

A couple, Walker and Gloria, enters treatment to get help in dealing with their frequent arguments. Due to the pattern of arguments, the therapist is seeing each person separately. Early in treatment, the therapist notes that the themes of the couple's arguments repeated. He explores this idea with Gloria, who explains that she does not want to forgive her partner for these transgressions. The therapist jokes with her that they are her rocks that she keeps with her to throw when she needs them. Gloria laughingly agrees. The therapist then has Gloria list the transgressions and assess the size of rock associated with each transgression. Gloria describes about seven transgressions of varying sizes. The therapist asks her to go to the beach on the weekend and find seven rocks that will fit her specifications. Gloria brings them in for the next session. The therapist has written descriptions of each transgression, and he asks Gloria to wrap them around the rocks. He then asks Gloria to carry them with her for the next week. In the follow-up session, the therapist and Gloria explore the level of energy needed to carry these rocks. She then starts to consider which transgressions she can forgive.

---

## Storytelling Techniques

Similar to metaphoric interventions, storytelling interventions often operate through parallel situations. Storytelling strategies can be particularly useful when children and youth are involved in the family sessions (Darou, 1992; Lawson, 1987; Scorzelli & Gold, 1999). Here we distinguish between therapist stories and family stories. Therapist-generated stories fall mainly under the earlier discussion of metaphors and analogies. In this section we explore other methods for using stories with a family. The following uses of storytelling involve family members actively expressing aspects of their situation by developing or telling stories.

The increased level of client activity in storytelling techniques demands a slightly different skill set in the therapist. The most important skill is engagement, for unless the clients are comfortable, they will not be willing to participate in the exercise. You must also be able to enter the story at times, in order to stress certain themes or bring resolution to issues. Here are three common uses of storytelling when working with families:

1. **Develop thematic stories.** Engage family members in developing stories during the family session.
2. **Elicit family stories.** Elicit specific stories from family members during the session.
3. **Assign storytelling homework.** Assign storytelling or reading as homework assignments as an adjunct to the session work.

*Developing Thematic Stories*  Therapists often ask family members to develop stories about specific themes. First you will tune into the themes inherent in the family struggles. Based on the themes in the family situation, you will ask the family to create a story based on the theme. Then you will instruct the family on the story creation process and introduce the content area for the story. Here are some different structures that can be used during the storytelling:

- **Collaborative stories.** Ask the family to collaborate in developing a story. All of the family members are expected to have input, but they must combine their efforts to develop a single story.
- **Turns.** Ask each family member to each develop his or her own story. After the stories are developed independently, they are shared with the family as a group.
- **Rounds.** Have each family member take turns adding to the story. The family is typically seated in a circle, and each person adds to the story. The therapist controls how long each person contributes to the story by signaling when the next person is to take his or her turn.

- ◆ **Cartooning.** Mix art with storytelling and ask the family to develop a cartoon strip (Bergin, 1998).
- ◆ **Written stories.** Have the members create the story or write letters (Penn & Frankfurt, 1994).

As the family members share their stories, you will explore the material to find the power and symbols embedded in the story (Penn & Frankfurt, 1994). You can then use these story elements to influence the family. Here are just a few common strategies for influencing your clients:

- ◆ **Revise the story's ending.** The family members tell a complete story. The therapist then retells the story, making specific alterations, or invites another family member to suggest revisions.
- ◆ **Challenge the storyteller.** The family members tell the story as instructed by the therapist. The therapist then makes comments about the story, stressing specific themes and possibly challenging other themes.
- ◆ **Conduct a debriefing.** The family members share the story. The therapist then explores the themes and symbols from the story with the family members.

---

## CASE EXAMPLE

A family is attending treatment because of parent-child conflict. One area of conflict involves allowing the daughters to date. The mother is supportive of dating, but the father is overprotective. The therapist asks each family member to write a story about the 14-year-old daughter's upcoming first date. The daughter writes a romanticized story about being treated well and being taken out for a nice meal before the dance. The mother's story has a similar story line but portrays the male as being much clumsier. The father's story focuses on the male trying to steal a kiss and pressuring the daughter to have sex. As each person reads his or her story, the therapist engages the family in an exploration of how realistic the story might be and how to handle situations outlined in the story. The therapist then says to the daughter, "I know the stories are make-believe, but what have you learned that you can apply to your upcoming date?" The daughter reflects on each story. Then the therapist asks the same question of both parents.

---

*Eliciting Family Stories*   Many therapists will ask family members to share stories from their own lives. Sometimes, as family members are talking, you will sense a story and then ask family members to disclose their experiences. At other times, you may have information about family members and ask them to share specific stories that can advance goal achievement.

**CASE EXAMPLE**

A family enters treatment due to conflict between an adolescent son and his father. During a session, the father starts cautioning the son about getting into trouble at school and getting a reputation. The son responds from an assumption that the father does not understand. The therapist turns to the father and asks, "Dad, is there a story in there somewhere?" The father pauses and says, "Yes." The therapist then asks the father to share his story. The father shares a story of how he and a friend always acted tough and picked on weaker children at school. Two outcomes of the father's story were being ostracized by his peers and scrutinized by the teachers. As the therapist explores these elements with the father, the son sits silently. Although he still does not admit his father understands, his behaviors at school change in the next month.

*Assigning Storytelling Homework* Sometimes therapists assign storytelling homework. Through such assignments, you can single out dyads in the family for story-reading homework to strengthen the relationship (Barrett-Kruse, 2000; Correa, Gonzalez, & Weber, 1991). You can further strengthen the impact by prescribing which stories are to be read. You may also want to prescribe the telling of specific family stories. In using this variant of storytelling, you will consider the impact of the storyteller, the designated recipient, and the content themes when planning the intervention.

**CASE EXAMPLE**

A family enters treatment because their four-year-old boy, Colin, is very clingy and demanding of his mother's time. Whenever the father hugs or gets close to the mother (Maureen), Colin tries to squeeze between them. The therapist, noticing that Maureen is about six months pregnant, asks if she has concerns about how Colin will react to the baby. Maureen states that she is concerned, so the therapist asks her to read a book to Colin every night at bedtime. The therapist then gives her a book to read. It is a "Berenstain Bears" book about a pregnant mother bear that is getting her son ready for the birth of a new cub. Maureen takes the book home and begins reading it to Colin. At the next session, Maureen reports that while they are reading the book, Colin asks many questions about the upcoming baby.

## Symbolic Expressive Interventions

The strategies we have just explored are primarily verbal in nature. These techniques thus are best reserved for family members with language skills. Symbolic expressive strategies do not assume that clients have advanced verbal and language skills (Rotter & Bush,

2000). These strategies include play and art as media for expressing and resolving family difficulties (Allen & Crandall, 1986; Jordan, 2001; Sweeney & Rocha, 2000; Ulak & Cummings, 1997). Play and art techniques promote increased creativity and spontaneity among the family members (Christensen & Thorngren, 2000; Harvey, 2003) and can be used to build family skills through more creative interactions (Johnson, Franklin, Hall, & Prieto, 2000).

There are many models and strategies of play- and art-based intervention. They all attempt to promote symbolic expression as a means of resolving problems (Kaduson & Schaefer, 1997). To achieve this end as a therapist, you must first create a safe atmosphere that is distinct from the verbal therapy setting (Wiener & Cantor, 2003). Include toys and materials in this setting that can help the family engage and symbolically communicate the family problems (Botkin, 2000; Carey, 2001; Rotter & Bush, 2000). Although specialized materials and equipment can vary, most play therapists insist on including dolls, puppets, sand play (in a tray or sand box), figurines (people and animals), play-dough, varied drawing materials, and equipment for aggressive expression such as punching bags or bop dolls (Botkin, 2000; Carey, 2001; Harvey, 2003; Rotter & Bush, 2000).

In using symbolically expressive media, you must have very strong engagement and tuning-in skills. The engagement skills increase clients' comfort and self-expression in the setting. If you are using a directive style of play- or art-based intervention, you will also use your engagement skills to help the clients shift between activities at different points during their time together. Tuning-in skills are imperative for teasing out the symbolic meaning in the different expressions. Finally, you will use reflection skills to bring out the meaning of the clients' behaviors as they express themselves in the room. Your self-awareness and self-control are also important, because the clients' expressiveness frequently can become impulsive and almost out of control. Except for safety issues, you should allow your clients the maximum expressiveness.

Several family applications may be used with play therapy and expressive techniques. The centrality of the play and artistic techniques varies across the different methods. Some methods use play primarily for assessment (Burns, 1987; Jordan, 2001), inclusion, and adjunct treatment to supplement family work (Carns, English, Juling, & Carns, 2003; Johnson et al., 2000). Many therapists are using play therapy techniques with the full family on a regular basis. Here are some family applications:

- **Parent-child play therapy.** When there are relationship problems between a parent and child, you can engage the dyad in play therapy to encourage working on the relationship issues (Carns et al., 2003; Johnson et al., 2000).

- **Integration of play into the interactive family session.** You can have play materials in the family therapy room and use play techniques such as puppet work, dolls, art, and other expressive techniques during the family session. This technique, often viewed as a critical way of including younger children in the session, gives you an opportunity to focus on issues in the parent-child relationship (Botkin, 2000; Rotter & Bush, 2000).

- **Full-family play therapy.** You can hold family sessions in a play therapy setting, creating an opportunity for all members of the family to engage in play techniques. This technique requires a large dedicated space and a therapist willing to coach the family in playing together concurrent with reflecting and interpreting the symbolic expressions of the family (Carey, 2001; Harvey, 2003). You will find this strategy most effective when you are working with child problems that are a symptom of family-level dynamics (Hardaway, 2000).

◆ **Family improvisation work.** A variant of full family play therapy, family improvisation work calls for using improvisation exercises with the family members. These exercises often allow the family members to interact while pretending to be someone else. The family-level communication and relationship problems will surface in improvisation problems and can be corrected as an improvisation problem rather than a relational problem (Harvey, 2000; Wiener & Cantor, 2003).

◆ **Games.** You can incorporate board games and other gamelike activities into the family session, or you can include the game as part of the family homework. Games can promote focused interaction (such as prescribing a water-gun fight to promote playfulness) or build specific skills, such as identifying feelings (Cron, 2000).

## CASE EXAMPLE

A four-year-old child has witnessed his mother being raped and held hostage at knifepoint by his father all night. His mother escaped and called the police, and the father was arrested. Later the father feigned suicide and was taken to a psychiatric hospital, from which he escaped. The child and his mother are engaged in play-oriented intervention. When the child enters the playroom, he immediately gathers together every item that represents a weapon and places them in a pile. He then puts his mother in a safe corner and puts the male therapist in the opposite corner. He then pretends to tie up the male therapist and break his feet so he cannot escape. The child repeats this sequence of activity every time he comes in for service. Each time, the therapist reflects what he anticipates the child's inner experience is for each act (e.g., "you want to make sure I don't escape," "it seems that you don't feel safe with anyone having weapons," and "you want to make sure your mother is safe."). After about three sessions, the mother begins to engage with the child while the therapist continues to reflect and coach the mother from his corner. One week, the therapist asks the mother to gather the weapons and play out the safety ritual. As she starts, the son tries to intervene; but the mother explains that she is the parent and needs to protect her son. The child begins to relax after this point in treatment and becomes more attentive to his mother. After repeating this theme in subsequent sessions, the mother eventually decides the therapist is safe to have in the room. The child allows this and is very relaxed. The therapist then focuses on helping the child and parent engage in spontaneous play.

## ◆ EXERCISE 12.1   INTERNAL RESOURCE ACTIVATION

You are working with a lesbian couple on the brink of a relationship breakdown. In this relationship, Rhonda, who has grown up in a violent and abusive home environment, has a volatile temper and often pressures and escalates tension when she feels her needs are not being met in the relationship. Francine comes from a family that avoids tension. Family members would sometimes sulk or become silent, but there was no active coercion among the members. Francine claims that she cannot stand Rhonda's behavior, and that she will have to leave the relationship for her emotional health. Both women are potters and enjoy working with clay. They run a pottery studio and are members of a potters' guild that is largely comprised of gay and lesbian members. Because of the women's artistic nature, you want to tap into their creativity to help them understand their differences.

1. Knowing that both women work with clay and both have a potter's wheel, develop a metaphor for each of them that uses working with clay to parallel how they are trying mold the relationship. Make this metaphor verbal, based on how a potter needs to work with clay. The themes to include are Rhonda's pressuring to get what she wants and Francine's tendency to withdraw from tension. Describe a separate metaphor for each woman. Start each metaphor with a statement such as, "Rhonda, I want you to picture yourself trying to turn a pot."

2. Knowing that these women were instrumental in establishing the potters' guild, what could you ask them to begin eliciting stories in which their natural approaches to tension could emerge as areas of strength? Formulate a question for each woman that could have her begin telling a story that would build an appreciation of the other person.

3. Knowing that both women work with clay, are struggling with issues of difference in their relationship, and need to reflect on themselves differently, what meaning-generating activity might help them to reflect on themselves? Try to include both women in an activity associated with clay or sculpture making that can result in their looking at either the process or the product of the activity to find some learning about themselves. Write the details of an activity that would help them, and explain how you would use the activity in therapy.

# Working Through Others in the Family Environment

Every family has external people who are intimately involved in the family processes. At times, such people keep the family stable. For example, single parents often have friends who fulfill many of the spousal support functions. This is a functional arrangement providing the parent adult exchanges and emotional support that would not exist without the external relationship. Whenever one of the family functions is lacking, it is not unusual for family members to reach outside the family boundary to find someone who can fulfill the function.

When these people in the family environment inadvertently maintain problem patterns, family practitioners must expand their focus to include them. Sometimes external people provide a holding environment for family problems. Problem maintenance can occur through these people's actions or lack of action. Family practitioners often seek to alter the holding environment by removing impediments and increasing the probability for change.

Sometimes family practitioners seek to involve external people to supplement the family functions. If family functions are not being met within the family system, you may want to look for someone in the natural family environment to perform roles to enhance family functioning. This is common when situations overwhelm the family or when the family does not have enough resources (e.g., people) to perform family functions.

Intervention at the family environment level requires you to break with the traditional models of office-based therapy as you become more involved in the family's life space. Practitioners use three common types of intervention when working with the family environment: changing the responding system, engaging supports, and negotiating room for change. Each strategy focuses on people, systems, and situations external to the family members attending active treatment.

## Changing Responding Systems

Changing the responding system is a common strategy, because it is based on the behaviorist systems of positive and negative reinforcement. In this type of strategy, the practitioner attempts to tip the balance of forces toward change by altering the environmental influences on the problem. The assumption is that the environment maintains the problem, and client behaviors will change after the responding environment is altered (Patterson, Reid, Jones, & Conger, 1975). Two types of intervention commonly used in changing the responding system are enlisting change partners and decreasing change inhibitors.

*Enlisting Change Partners*   You will often want to increase the family's capacity for change. This type of intervention occurs first by identifying environmental relationships and situations that are highly motivating. Such identification often occurs through listening to family stories about important relationships and situations. While listening to the family stories, you will keep mental notes regarding important people and activities for the family.

When family motivation wanes, or people in the family require additional capacity to master the changes, you will find that the information about motivating people and activities can become useful. When seeking to increase change capacity, you can begin by exploring the external relationships to find a potential role for helping the family members to achieve their goals. There are two common uses of such relationships:

1. **Supplement functions and needs.** In many families, there are functions or needs that are not fulfilled. In such situations, you can employ environmental relationships to supplement the family members.

---

**CASE EXAMPLE**

A family enters treatment to work on child behavior problems. After several sessions, it appears that parental mental health and disability concerns are limiting their capacity for nurturing and guidance. The therapist learns that the daughter has a positive relationship with an aunt and negotiates the family's permission to engage the aunt in the treatment. The therapist contacts the aunt and encourages her relationship with the daughter. The aunt increases contact and begins including the daughter in trips and family functions. The girl's behavior problems begin to decrease at school as her aunt's positive influence takes effect.

---

2. **Shift the balance.** In situations where the change and counterchange forces are at a stalemate, you may seek to shift the balance by bringing in additional people. These people can increase the rewards or costs associated with the problem. This often requires you to engage the external person into a specific role. Often you will want the external person to react strongly to the behaviors of family members. This can be a positive or negative reaction, depending on the situation.

---

## CASE EXAMPLE

A family enters treatment because their adolescent son, Robert, has been harassing an old girlfriend. The parents have very little influence on Robert, and most of their attempts to influence him have failed. Robert maintains that his girlfriend still loves him, but other people are causing her to stay aloof. The therapist finds that the girlfriend is ready to report Robert to the police and wants to stop his behavior using less intrusive means. The therapist consequently engages an older brother, Steve, who is no longer living in the home. Steve has a good relationship with Robert, but the two have infrequent contact. Steve meets with the therapist and agrees to increase contact with Robert, but only when he is not harassing his ex-girlfriend. Steve also informs Robert that he will cease all contact if Robert continues to phone his old girlfriend.

---

Notice in both examples that the therapist employs people naturally in the family environment to alter the holding environment. Such relationships are part of the natural family environment. However, without an invitation, these potentially powerful forces for change remain untapped and unfocused. The act of engagement is simple because such people are already involved in the family situation.

*Decreasing Change Inhibitors*   Sometimes people in the family environment are vested in the family problems and work behind the scenes to interfere with the family's goals. Most often, such people are meeting personal needs by interacting with the family and will act to maintain their interactions. They tend to be oblivious to their role in the family problems and frequently see themselves as trying to help. You must often engage such people so their efforts to help can coordinate with the family treatment.

When confronted with external people who are invested in the problem situation, the family practitioner often must identify the role of these external people and engage them to alter their investment. Engaging external people follows a process similar to that of engaging family members. Three important steps are as follows:

1. Tuning into the external person's experience and functions in the family situation

2. Exploring and expanding on the external person's perspective on the family situation

3. Finding common ground between the family goals and the position of the external person

---

**CASE EXAMPLE**

A couple enters treatment due to frequent arguments. As treatment progresses, it becomes obvious that most of the marital tension is about the wife's mother. The husband complains that his mother-in-law interferes in the marriage, while the wife views her mother as a support. When tracing the history of the problem, the therapist finds that early in the marriage, the husband started his own business. To get the business started, he had to work long hours. Rather than sit at home alone, the wife would visit her mother every evening. Now that the business is established, the husband is home more often, but the wife and mother have a pattern of daily contact. The husband resents his wife's attention toward her mother, and arguments have ensued. As the husband pressures the wife to spend more time at home, she decreases contact with her mother, who then misses her daughter and begins pressuring for more contact. The wife is triangulated between her mother and husband. The therapist includes the mother in a few sessions, explaining that the wife has conflicted loyalties that need resolution. The mother, who immediately wants to decrease her daughter's anguish, works with the husband to decrease the pressures being placed on her daughter.

---

## Engaging Supports

To be successful in changing situations, individuals often need strong support systems. When families lack adequate support systems, change can be difficult. A poor support system is a factor in family violence, parenting problems, marital distress, and many areas of mental health. Therapists often must intervene in the family's environment to ensure that there are enough supports for them to succeed. Here are a few of the multiple types of support that are necessary for success (Leavy, 1983; Medalie, 1985; Van der Poel, 1993):

- **Emotional support.** People who can listen to the client, understand his situation, provide encouragement, and celebrate his successes
- **Instrumental support.** People who can offer concrete types of help, such as money, rides, shelter, and so forth
- **Informational support.** People who can provide important information to the client so that she can make the right connections and actions
- **Appraisal support.** People who can give honest feedback to the client on how he is performing and acting

Optimally, families will have many people to draw on for these types of support. Problems can occur if there are not enough support people for a family. Family members can access support people from multiple sources (Ceballo & McLoyd, 2002; Cohen & Willis, 1985). Typically, there are several sources for drawing family support (Rook & Ituarte, 1999). The impact on family members will vary according to the types of support provided (Malecki & Demaray, 2003; McColl & Friedland, 1993). Here are four sources of support:

1. **Kinship supports.** The support people are relatives or others in the client's system (e.g., in-laws, aunts and uncles, foster parents, cousins).
2. **Peer supports.** The support people are friends, neighbors, co-therapists, and/or other people who are part of the client's life situation (e.g., friends, neighbors, gangs).
3. **Informal support systems.** The support people are members of organized groups (e.g., choirs, AA, clubs, teams, big brothers, etc.).
4. **Formal support systems.** The support people are paid or enlisted (e.g., volunteers) to provide support (e.g., social workers, therapists, mentors, family support workers).

When working with client support systems, you must first assess the adequacy of the support system. This can be accomplished by constructing a matrix and then placing the types of support along the left side of the matrix and the support people across the top (see Figure 12.1). Although there are only four sources of support and

**Figure 12.1**   Support System Assessment Matrix

|  | Kinship supports | Peer supports | Informal supports | Formal supports |
|---|---|---|---|---|
| Emotional support |  |  |  |  |
| Instrumental support |  |  |  |  |
| Informational support |  |  |  |  |
| Appraisal support |  |  |  |  |

providers of support in the matrix, you can use a matrix like this to assess most types of support networks. By listing available supports in the cells, you can easily assess the adequacy of the client support system. If there are many gaps, you may find it necessary to try to enlist additional support people.

Concurrent with the family's sources of support, you must be concerned with other people's willingness and capacity to provide adequate support for family members (Shumaker & Brownell, 1984). When you finds gaps in the support system, or discover that people providing support are ill equipped or unwilling to support the client, you will need to explore the client's life situation to identify alternate supports. Therapists must be skilled at engaging others to assure that additional supports can be arranged. This often requires creative thinking on your part, because you must consider all types of people as potential supports.

Many practitioners struggle with identifying peer and informal supports. Although such sources of support are often evident in the family members' stories, many therapists do not consider approaching peers and kin for ongoing support. This decision is often due to value differences between the therapist and the potential supports. Sometimes potential sources of support have criminal histories, or their past roles with the family cause therapists to overlook their potential as a support person. Consequently, most therapists focus on formal supports and programs while ignoring the friends, relatives, and informal systems available to the client. Therapists must put their biases aside and identify people who can be supportive.

## Negotiating Room for Change

Concurrent with engaging support systems, therapists must often negotiate with support people to make change possible for family members. There are frequently people whose actions and interactions interfere with the family's ability to make changes. When this occurs, you must intervene and negotiate flexibility for the family.

This external negotiation function is often tricky for therapists, because they are at risk of triangulation between the family and external others. When external people are inflexible, you must attempt either to change their responses or to work with the family in helping them find alternate ways of meeting their goals. When working directly with community supports, you often must engage quickly, find common ground between the family and the other person, and use the common ground to create change. Success is often contingent on the ability to find fertile common ground between the family and the other person.

When the family appears to be triangulating or manipulating, you must be very careful. Sometimes family members will try to get you to convince others to make accommodations for reasons other than supporting goal-oriented changes. Be wary of such attempts. The following three cautions can help you to avoid manipulative situations:

1. **Focus on the family's true needs.** You often must challenge the family members when they begin presenting a desire for others in the environment to

change. Such discussions can be an attempt to avoid responsibility in order to gain concessions from others through your influence.

2. **Avoid "if-then" situations.** If the family members are making their changes contingent on the other person changing or complying with their will, manipulation is likely. You should focus on the manipulation rather than on negotiating the change.

3. **Beware status quo motivations.** If the family members are attempting to restore elements of their situation to a prior state (e.g., have an estranged spouse return), you must avoid becoming an ambassador for reinstating the status quo.

## ◆ EXERCISE 12.2 INDIRECT INTERVENTION THROUGH THE ENVIRONMENT

You are a family-based worker. This family was referred to you because of mother-daughter fighting. The family came into service because a neighbor called the police during a fight. There is no substantiated abuse, but the intake worker wants to refer the family for prevention purposes. There is a mother (37), a father (39), and a daughter (15).

The mother, Betty, works at a local hospital as a dietary aid. She works part-time, is a member of the hospital auxiliary, and is active in the local women's baseball league. Betty complains that every time she tries to tell her daughter Tana something, she rolls her eyes, sighs, and states that she already knows. When Betty persists with her point, the discussion escalates into a major fight. The daughter, Tana, is becoming more disobedient. The mother thinks she is sexually active because she is staying out late at night with her friend Marie. Marie has been in residential care and was a significant problem in the neighborhood in the past. Betty dislikes Marie and wants Tana to stay away from her.

The father, Tom, is a factory worker. He was Betty's high school sweetheart, and they started their family immediately after graduation. Tom was lucky to get a job at the local auto manufacturing plant. He now has good seniority and can get lots of overtime. He is the union steward in his unit and is very popular with the men. They often call him for advice and invite him to participate in several activities, such as ball tournaments and bowling. Tom is also a member of the Kiwanis Club. Financially, things are pretty good; but in the past two years, things have become stressful at home. When Tom gets home, Betty and Tana are often fighting. The fights appear constant at times, so Tom responds by yelling at both of them and then leaving the home to spend time with his friends.

Tana is doing well at school but seems strong willed at home. She has a decent grade point average and is a member of the swim team and volleyball team. She was voted the most improved swimmer last year, and she helped the coach with a children's team during the summer. Tana is popular with her peers and considered a youth leader.

1. In this family situation, to decrease some of the conflict, you will first want to change how some of the family members respond to situations. Starting with Betty (mother), what response would you recommend that she change to decrease the tension and conflict with Tana?

2. How would you approach Betty about this matter, so that she doesn't feel you are taking sides? Write exactly what you would say.

3. When you focus on Tom, what responses might he change to help the situation?

4. How would you approach him about this change (what exactly would you say)?

5. Use the support matrix to identify potential supports for each person.

a. Betty:

|  | Kin | Friends | Informal | Formal |
|---|---|---|---|---|
| Emotional |  |  |  |  |
| Informational |  |  |  |  |
| Instrumental |  |  |  |  |
| Appraisal |  |  |  |  |

b. Tom:

|  | Kin | Friends | Informal | Formal |
|---|---|---|---|---|
| Emotional |  |  |  |  |
| Informational |  |  |  |  |
| Instrumental |  |  |  |  |
| Appraisal |  |  |  |  |

c. Tana:

| | Kin | Friends | Informal | Formal |
|---|---|---|---|---|
| Emotional | | | | |
| Informational | | | | |
| Instrumental | | | | |
| Appraisal | | | | |

6. How would you use each of these supports?
   a. With Betty:

   b. With Tom:

c. With Tana:

7. What area of support seems to be most lacking?
   a. For Betty:

   b. For Tom:

   c. For Tana:

---

## Summary

When direct methods of intervention lose effectiveness, family practitioners must find indirect ways to achieve the family goals. Indirect methods involve two general approaches. One is to use indirect methods to activate the resources inherent inside the family. These methods often involve using right-brain methods to stimulate alternative ways of thinking and approaching the family situation. Such methods are often creative and fun for the therapist, but may lose precision because the therapist has less control over how the family interprets the therapist's input. The second method is to activate external resources that can help family members achieve their goals. External resources are most often the support people and others who are intimately involved with the family.

# Critical Content

1. Therapists need indirect methods to activate internal and external resources when the family needs stimulation beyond the direct methods of change.
2. There are two types of indirect methods: activating internal resources and activating external resources.
3. Internal resource activation uses primarily visual techniques such as visualization, metaphors, storytelling, and symbolic expression. These techniques stimulate family thinking without using traditional logic.
4. External resource activation uses relationships and people in the family environment to remove blocks to change and increase family motivation.

# Suggested Readings

Boone, R. K., & Bowman, V. E. (1997). Therapeutic metaphors: Gateways to understanding. *International Journal for the Advancement of Counseling, 19,* 313–327.

Kopp, R. R., & Craw, M. J. (1998). Metaphoric language, metaphoric cognition, and cognitive therapy. *Psychotherapy, 35,* 306–311.

Sims, P. A., & Whynot, C. A. (1997). Hearing metaphor: An approach to working with family-generated metaphor. *Family Process, 36,* 341–355.

Wiener, D. J. (1999). Rehearsals for growth: Applying improvisational theater games to relationship therapy. In D. J. Wiener (Ed.), *Beyond talk therapy: Using movement and expressive techniques in clinical practice* (pp. 165–180). Washington, DC: American Psychological Association.

## SECTION V

# WORKING WITH MULTIPROBLEM AND HIGH-RISK FAMILIES

In this final section of the text, we explore the challenges and potential treatment options with families identified as high-risk or multiproblem. Such families are often difficult to assist, because they are not easily influenced by traditional family treatment methods. Environmental and family history concerns often create pressures and stresses that require new and innovative methods of family practice.

Section V is divided into three chapters. Chapter 13 is an exploration of the challenges associated with high-risk and multiproblem families. In the chapter, we explore two continua that contribute to family problems. In the first continuum, family resources, we examine resources such as income, support, and marketable skills in light of their impact on the family. In the second continuum, adaptive challenges, we discuss issues of parental history in their family of origin, mental illness and/or disability, and substance abuse. We also consider some dynamics that interfere with traditional treatment and identify promising treatment approaches.

Chapter 14 of this section is an exploration of the multiagency challenges associated with treating high-risk and multiproblem families. In this chapter, we examine organizational barriers to effectiveness and consider some suggestions on how to mitigate interagency differences. We also look at issues of referral failure and poor client follow-up, along with suggestions on how to maximize referral effectiveness. We also explore and illustrate the skills and strategies needed for supporting family members and other professionals when working as part of a community team.

Chapter 15, the final chapter in the text, is an exploration of support-focused interventions. In this chapter we focus on three types of intervention. We discuss mutual-aid-oriented group work, along with methods for maximizing the mutual aid among the group members. This discussion is followed by a section exploring in-home interventions. The dynamics and challenges of in-home work are described. In the final section, we explore community-based programming whereby practitioners deliver service either through host agencies or through partnerships with volunteers.

## Chapter 13

# Challenges and Promise

Most family practitioners will eventually work with families that are considered high risk or multiproblem. Such families are frequently overrepresented in the social service systems; but they are actually underserved, because they do not respond well to traditional intervention methods. Because these families often exhibit multiple needs, they commonly are referred to many different services. Thus family practitioners must work with the family in conjunction with many other professionals. Such service situations are likely to contribute to family stress and frequently yield ineffective results.

## Theoretical Grounding

In this chapter we explore family situations in which multiple stresses and internal family dynamics overload the family's ability to manage. These families are often called *multiproblem* or *high-risk families*. The presence of multiple problems and stressors yields situations that exceed the explanatory capacity of most family theories. Consequently, in this chapter, and the remaining chapters in the text, we will approach this service situation from an ecological systems perspective. Table 13.1 contains critical chapter concepts associated with this theoretical model and recommends

**T A B L E  13.1**
**Chapter Concepts, Theoretical Models, and Sources**

| Chapter Concepts | Theoretical Models | Recommended Reading |
| --- | --- | --- |
| A lack of supports and resources in the social environment creates stress for families. | Ecological systems model | Franklin & Jordan, Chapter 8<br>Janzen & Harris, Chapters 10, 11, 13, 14, 16<br>Kilpatrick & Holland, Chapters 2, 5<br>Nichols & Schwartz, Chapter 11<br>Whitelaw Downs et al., Chapter 3 |
| Social pressures such as racism, sexism, and other discriminatory practices contribute to low resources. | Ecological systems model | Franklin & Jordan, Chapters 10, 11, 12, 13<br>Janzen & Harris, Chapters 7, 9, 10,<br>Kilpatrick & Holland, Chapter 13<br>Nichols & Schwartz, Chapter 11 |
| Some family dysfunctions such as alcoholism and violence are passed from generation to generation. | Intergenerational model | Goldenberg & Goldenberg, Chapter 8<br>Janzen & Harris, Chapters 13, 14<br>Kilpatrick & Holland, Chapter 1 |
| Genetic and health problems are associated with low resources and family stress. | Ecological systems model | Janzen & Harris, Chapters 11, 12<br>Kilpatrick & Holland, Chapter 3 |
| Stresses and intergenerational problems affect family structures. | Ecological systems model | Janzen & Harris, Chapters 6, 8<br>Kilpatrick & Holland, Chapter 3 |
| Traditional family treatment models are challenged when families have resource, support, and intergenerational problems. | Ecological systems model<br>Empowerment model | Janzen & Harris, Chapters 2, 17<br>Kilpatrick & Holland, Chapter 3 |

additional reading that can help you to further understand these concepts. The readings are contained in the following easy-to-find textbooks:

- *Child Welfare and Family Services: Policies and Practice* (7th ed.), by S. Whitelaw Downs, E. Moore, E. J. McFadden, S. Michaud, & L. B. Costin, 2004, Boston: Allyn & Bacon.
- *The Essentials of Family Therapy* (2nd ed.), by M. P. Nichols & R. C. Schwartz, 2005, Boston: Allyn & Bacon.
- *Family Practice—Brief Systems Methods for Social Work* (1st ed.), by C. Franklin & C. Jordan, 1999, Pacific Grove, CA: Brooks/Cole.
- *Family Therapy: An Overview* (6th ed.), by I. Goldenberg & H. Goldenberg, 2004, Pacific Grove, CA: Brooks/Cole.
- *Family Treatment in Social Work Practice*, by C. Janzen & O. Harris, 1997, Pacific Grove, CA: Brooks/Cole.
- *Working with Families: An Integrative Model by Level of Need* (3rd ed.), by A. C. Kilpatrick & T. P. Holland, 2003, Boston: Allyn & Bacon.

# Toward Helping Multiproblem and High-Risk Families

Whereas multiproblem or high-risk families exhibit varied needs and areas of risk, two dimensions seem to contribute to family-related problems: family resources and adaptive challenges. The term *family resources* refers to the family properties that promote or hinder the family's ability to survive and prosper. If resources are low, family energy must be diverted into basic maintenance functions. If resources are high, basic functions are met, allowing family energy to be invested in other pursuits. The term *adaptive challenges* refers to elements in the family environment or history that interfere with optimal family functioning. Such elements require family members to adapt to such influences, which threaten stability and the family's ability to focus on task accomplishment. To truly understand the challenges inherent in serving such families, it is important to understand the contribution of each dimension.

## Challenges to Family Resources

All families have internal resources that help them navigate and negotiate with the environment. Higher levels of resources often permit families to be mobile because they can generate options in their environment. Lower resources often result in the family feeling stuck in situations and may result in learned helplessness. Three resource considerations tend to influence multiproblem and high-risk families. These considerations tend to be correlated, but are worth considering separately:

1. Educational achievement and marketable skills
2. Financial resources
3. Available supports

### Educational Achievement and Marketable Skills

Educational achievement is a necessary prerequisite for job entry, job mobility, and career advancement (Garman, Hammann, Hoodak, Fiume, Manino-Corse, & Wise, 2000; Mitra, 2000; Smart & Pascarella, 1986). Higher levels of education are associated with advanced cognitive skills such as problem solving, mediation, and self-efficacy (Mitra, 2000). Concurrently, lower levels of education are associated with job dissatisfaction, poor job stability, and poor job performance (van der Linde, 2000).

Many families considered multiproblem or high risk have lower levels of education. Some parents in such families have learning or neurological problems that have interfered with their ability to complete their education. In rural areas or areas underserved by social and psychological services, such parents often went undiagnosed as children; thus their school system did not meet any special learning needs they may have had (Schulman, 1986). As children, such parents would have experienced repeated failures, judgments, and stigma as they tried to succeed in a system designed for children with no special needs (Heyman, Swain, Gillman, Handyside, & Newman,

1997). Such children typically left school early to take jobs in factories and other settings that did not insist on the completion of high school (Fergusson & Woodward, 2000). In such situations, a difficult relationship may exist between the parent and the school system now serving their children.

In family practice, you will often see parents whose children are having difficulty in the school system. When parents have lower levels of education (for whatever reason), there is frequently some tension between the family and the school (Dempsey, 1994). Such tension involves issues of feeling judged, unrealistic expectations placed on the family, and conflicting priorities between the parents and the school system. If the parent had difficulties in school as a child, she may feel incompetent and inadequate when she deals with the school system. These remnants from childhood are very active whenever the parent must deal with the educational system. If teachers or other professionals in the school consider the parent to be contributing to the child's problems, these feelings of inadequacy and powerlessness can result in angry reactions, devaluation of education, and/or withdrawal.

Educational achievement of the parents is associated with emotional problems and volatility in the family (Elmer, 1977; Goldstein & Rosenbaum, 1985; Polansky, Gaudin, Anmous, & Davis, 1985). Many parenting functions require cognitive agility and mediation that may be underdeveloped without education. Education is also instrumental in helping families escape poverty (Long & Vaillant, 1984). Most jobs in today's economy are highly technical. Consequently, employability in jobs paying more than poverty wages requires education and training (Nichols-Casebolt & McClure, 1989). Parents who have low levels of education are often relegated to entry-level positions and cannot access better-paying and more fulfilling jobs.

## Financial Resources

As just mentioned, many parents who have low educational achievement can access only entry-level jobs. Such underpaid positions promote stress as parents parcel out meager earnings trying to meet all of the family's financial obligations. Here are a few of the parents' multiple financial stressors:

◆ Needing to work more than one job to make ends meet
◆ Living in subsidized or substandard housing
◆ Having to rely on credit or charity to respond to emergent needs
◆ Trying to stretch family resources to meet multiple demands

These stressors and the lack of opportunity associated with poverty create stress in the family (Dohrenwend & Dohrenwend, 1981; Gibbs, 1984; Lorion & Felner, 1986). Over time, the repeated stressors cause the parents to feel they cannot influence the events in their life (Eron & Peterson, 1982; Lorion & Felner, 1986). This feeling creates learned helplessness and a reactive rather than proactive approach to living (Dohrenwend & Dohrenwend, 1981; Eron & Peterson, 1982; Ross, Mirowsky, & Cockerham, 1983).

The combination of stress and adjustment places children at high risk for emotional and behavioral problems (Gibbs, 1984; Wolfe, 1987; Elder, Conger, Foster, & Ardelt, 1992). This is partially due to the stigmatized social environment and lack of opportunity. This is also due to the relationship of poverty to child maltreatment (Jones & McCurdy, 1992; Vondra, Barnett, & Cicchetti, 1990; Wolock & Horowitz, 1979). The stress can at times contribute to parental venting and overreactions to children's demands and behaviors.

## Available Supports

Many multiproblem and high-risk families have limited external supports. In Chapter 12 we looked at four types of support: emotional, instrumental, informational, and appraisal. These supports are critical for family success. Most families garner support from friends and neighbors, family members, and many informal groups such as clubs. Many multiproblem families are uninvolved with informal support groups. Frequently, family, friends, and neighbors have their own stresses and challenges inhibiting support provision. As a result, such families typically must rely on formal support systems such as agencies.

When support is low, problems often develop in families. Research indicates that many child psychological problems are associated with low levels of support (Dumas & Wahler, 1983; Wahler, 1980; Wolfe, 1987). Low social support is also associated with child maltreatment and other forms of family violence (Gaudin & Pollane, 1983; Maluccio, 1989; Seagull, 1987; Tracy, 1990; Wahler, 1980; Zuravin, 1989).

In therapeutic outcome studies, social support interacts with personality to predict treatment success across multiple intervention methods and problems (Gaston, Marmar, Thompson, & Gallagher, 1988; Krantz & Moos, 1988). Families with very little support often succumb to environmental pressures because they cannot respond. Adaptive responses tend to require emotional and cognitive agility in family members. When people must respond to multiple environmental demands with no help or replenishment, their emotional and cognitive agility wanes.

# Challenges of Adaptation

Along with resource-related problems, multiproblem and high-risk families often have adaptive challenges that compromise family functioning. These adaptive challenges form a second continuum inherent in high-risk and multiproblem families. This continuum presents two types of adaptive challenges that influence family functioning. First, there are adaptive challenges that stem from parental backgrounds. These are commonly related to the parenting and home environment in the parent's families of origin. The second type of adaptive challenge stems from current parental functioning. Both types of adaptive challenge influence family functioning and the prognosis for change (Fraser, Pecora, & Haapala, 1991). Here are five common adaptive challenges:

1. Intergenerational family violence
2. Domestic violence
3. Ineffective parenting and socialization
4. Parental substance abuse
5. Mental illness or disability

## Intergenerational Family Violence

Violence in the family can have a devastating impact on all family members. If parents grew up in family systems where there were high levels of violence, they are likely to have made many adaptations that will influence their current family. Some children emerge from such family environments well adjusted, but the dynamics of violent families often require children to make extreme adaptations. These adaptations can lead to the following challenges with parents who grew up in such settings:

◆ **Coercive parenting.** Some parents will be desensitized to the impact of coercive exchanges and use them because they appear effective as a means for control (Bandura, 1973; Kalmuss, 1984; McCord, 1988).

◆ **Adjustment problems.** Some parents exposed to violence as children may exhibit internalizing (e.g., depression, anxiety) or externalizing (e.g., aggression, overreacting) adjustment problems (David, Steele, Forehand, & Armistead, 1996; Kolbo, Blakely, & Engleman, 1996; Lorenz, Hoven, Andrews, & Bird, 1995).

◆ **Developmental compromises.** Some parents exposed to violence as children have compromised cognitive skills and belief systems that promote overreactions to family situations (Bradley et al., 1989; Polansky et al., 1985).

Concurrent with the preceding adaptive challenges, exposure to family violence requires adaptation due to elevated stress and low levels of emotional support. The early environments of violent individuals do not often reflect parental celebration of the child's inherent traits. Rather, they are typified by tension, emotional rejection, and unresponsiveness (Menninger, 1993). Children are frequently exposed to negative perceptions and negative parent-child interactions (Jouriles, Barling, & O'Leary, 1987; Webster-Stratton, 1989).

Children from such conflict-prone homes seek support, are demanding of attention, and become hostile when their needs are ignored (Camras et al., 1990; Dadds, 1987; Donovan & Leavitt, 1989; Kolko, Kazdin, Thomas, & Day, 1993; Olson, Bates, & Bayles, 1990; Firestone, 1987; Frankel & Bates, 1990; Park & Waters, 1989; Robertson & Simons, 1989). When children from such environments eventually become parents, they often have adaptive patterns that interfere with effective parenting.

# Domestic Violence

There are many forms of domestic violence, but the most common form is adult male to adult female violence in the spousal relationship. Given this tendency, in this section we will explore the dynamics and adaptations associated with this form of violence in the family. Living in a family with domestic violence requires all family members to adapt to the behavior of the batterer. Such adaptation is critical, because batterers are very controlling of family members. Inherent in the controlling behavior, men who batter are often attempting to restore feelings of mastery or decrease insecurity (Murphy, Meyer, & O'Leary, 1994; Stets, 1995). Inherent in this need for control, the batterer often expects others to compensate for his own negative self-concepts and lowered self-esteem (Goldstein & Rosenbaum, 1985; Murphy et al., 1994). As a result, many batterers pressure others to reassure them and cater to their emotional needs (Bernard & Bernard, 1983, 1984; Gondolf, 1985a; Hale, Zimostrad, Duckworth, & Nicholas, 1988; Hastings & Hamberger, 1988).

Although the male who assaults family members is controlling, his internal sense is often one of being controlled by external forces (Bern, 1985; Eisikovits, Edleson, Guttmann, & Sela-Amit, 1991). He thus does not tend to assume responsibility for his own actions and blames others for his feelings and behaviors (Bernard & Bernard, 1984; Dutton, 1986). This externalized position results in high levels of reassurance seeking, dependency on the female partner, and sensitivity to criticism (Bernard & Bernard, 1983, 1984; Gondolf, 1985a; Hale et al., 1988; Hastings & Hamberger, 1988; Lystad, 1975; Murphy et al., 1994). Such dependence and reassurance seeking often increase tension in the spousal relationship (Murphy et al., 1994; Potthoff, Holahan, & Joiner, 1995).

The externalized needs of the batterer set him up to be dependent on a source that can never truly accommodate his needs (because they are internal needs). Consequently, many batterers rate the responses of their wives as low in caring (Langhinrichsen-Rohling, Smutzler, & Vivian, 1994). Such males often use tension to achieve the caring response that they need. This escalation of tension is important because the risk of violence increases when the batterer perceives his externalized demands as not being met (Bernard & Bernard, 1984; Dutton & Browning, 1988; Dutton, Fehr, & McEwan, 1982; Dutton & Strachan, 1987; Gondolf, 1985a, 1985b). Such perceptions are not always accurate, given that batterers are likely to misread and overreact to situations (Bedrosian, 1982; Berkowitz, 1990; Murphy & O'Leary, 1989).

The demanding nature of this family dynamic is compounded by the indirect manner in which batterers express their demands. The communication patterns of batterers are indirect and unassertive (Allen, Calsyn, Fehrenbach, & Benton, 1989; Dutton, 1986; Dutton & Browning, 1988; Dutton & Strachan, 1987; Maiuro, Cahn, & Vitaliano, 1986; Vivian & O'Leary, 1987). This pattern could be expected because emotional dependency and assertion are negatively correlated (Assor & Aldor, 1993). Consequently, the male batterer has unspoken expectations that the woman will attend to his needs (Lystad, 1975). The batterer justifies these unspoken expectations through societal beliefs that women should attend to relationship needs (Saunders, Lynch, Grayson, & Linz, 1987; Smith, 1990). Unmet needs, consequently, are interpreted as her failure (Lystad, 1975).

*Maternal Adaptation*   Given the dynamic just described, women living with a batterer are often placed in a position where they must leave or adapt. The decision to adapt rather than leave is based on many dynamics:

◆ Batterers are highly passionate and cater to the woman when their needs are perceived as met.

◆ Many batterers are not violent all the time, making it difficult to attribute cause and effect to the violence.

◆ Many battered women have been abused as children (or exposed to family violence), thus compromising their ability to take a firm stand with the batterer (Downs & Miller, 1998; Weaver & Clum, 1996).

◆ Batterers often diminish the competence and worth of their female partners, making it hard for them to take a firm stand (Aguilar & Nightingale, 1994; Weingourt, 1996).

In many of the scenarios just described, the woman in the violent home is not in a strong position to enforce an end to the violence. This situation leaves her in a position where she must adapt.

To survive the domestic violence, the abused partner often develops thinking patterns designed to make the relationship appear more tenable (Dutton & Painter, 1983). Some studies have found that battered women deny the seriousness of their abuse by focusing on the positive elements of their situation (Herbert, Silver, & Ellard, 1991). This pattern is more common when the abuse is infrequent, with poorly developed patterns of abuse, thus allowing the woman to retain a hopeful perspective on the partner (Follingstad, Laughlin, Polek, Rutledge, & Hause, 1991; Kemp, Green, Hovanitz, & Rawlings, 1995).

In a pattern similar to assuming a positive focus, battered women also shift responsibility away from the batterer to excuse him from full responsibility (Follingstad et al., 1991). It is theorized that by focusing on elements outside of the abuser's control, the woman can deny the intent to do harm and rationalize her experience (Ferraro & Johnson, 1983). Such externalization of responsibility helps to maintain her commitment to the relationship (Mills & Malley-Morrison, 1998). An extreme form of externalized responsibility is self-blame. Self-blame allows the woman to experience some hope that she can control the abuse by seeking elements within her control that are associated with the battering (Langford, 1996). Guilt and self-blame tend to be most prevalent when the woman has little social support (Barnett, Martinez, & Keyson, 1996).

The combined effects of abuse, trauma, and disempowerment can severely undermine the battered woman's parenting ability (Stanley & Penhale, 1999). Such effects have an indirect impact on the child because the mother, when traumatized and abused, becomes less available to respond to the child (Bilinkoff, 1995; Findlater & Kelly, 1999). Many professionals are beginning to focus on the need to enhance the parenting roles of the battered woman (Findlater & Kelly, 1999; Jouriles, McDonald, Stephens, Norwood, Spillerm, & Ware, 1998). Such an intervention will empower the woman in her personal and family relationships while increasing positive family interactions that mitigate the psychological damage to the child witnesses of spouse abuse (Magen, 1999; Stanley & Penhale, 1999; Stephens, 1999).

*Child Adaptation*   Just as women must adapt to the violence, so do children. Although this adaptation varies depending on the age of exposure, many children develop a tendency to view the control of situations as being in the hands of powerful others (Bryant & Trokel, 1976; Howes & Markman, 1989; Joseph, Yule, & Williams, 1993; Koestner, Franz, & Weinberger, 1990; Rankin, 1991; Robertson & Simons, 1989). Consequently, children are often in a position where they experience no choice but to accommodate the adults in the family. Through this accommodation, the child often has a father who is too involved in his own needs to be an effective parent and a mother who is too undermined to be effective.

Children must also adapt to the negative exchanges in the family. Such exchanges compromise the child's social and emotional functioning (Boyum & Parke, 1995; Jouriles et al., 1987). As the children adapt, they are more likely to rationalize and adopt the use of violent problem-solving strategies (Cantrell, MacIntyre, Sharkey, & Thompson, 1995; Boldizar, Perry, & Perry, 1989; Breslin, Riggs, O'Leary, & Arias, 1990). Assertion, on the other hand, may cause parental anger (Kalmuss, 1984; McCord, 1988). Children from such violent homes often develop internalizing problems such as depression and anxiety along with externalizing problems such as aggression (David et al., 1996; Kolbo et al., 1996; O'Keefe, 1994, 1996; Wolfe, Jaffe, Wilson, & Zak, 1985).

*Family-Level Adaptation*   The literature provides very clear and specific evidence that the family is affected by the male parent often underfunctioning in his parental role while concurrently placing demands on the family members. When his demands are not met, he often uses verbal and physical violence. Domestic violence tends to be primarily adult male to adult female abuse (compromising maternal functioning), but at times the children are also at risk of being assaulted. Clearly, this is not a safe environment.

At the family level, two adaptations are evident. First, the abuse and threats that occur in the home cause all family members to become hypervigilant to tension in the family. After a violent incident, the male partner often experiences internal tension as he repositions the female partner into her need-fulfilling roles through promises and bribes (Sonkin, Martin, & Walker, 1985; Walker, 1979). After she is repositioned, the family members tend to actively ignore or dismiss minor problems in an attempt to keep tension low (Walker, 1979). In time, tension rises to the point where volatile expressions are likely. This ignore-and-explode cycle becomes the family system for managing tension in the home.

The adaptations used to control tension inhibit effective problem solving in the family. Minor problems are ignored, because the act of identifying problems and exploring solutions increases interpersonal tension. The male's lack of assertiveness, dependency, and tendency to overreact to perceived slights also inhibits entry into problem-solving exchanges. Consequently, all family members learn to avoid problem solving. Even if the violence ceases, the adaptations of family members require support and skill-building interventions to re-empower the mother, manage tension, and instill problem-solving capacities in the family.

## Ineffective Parenting and Socialization

The third parental background challenge involves problematic behaviors and belief systems inherited from a person's parents. Many parents in high-risk and multiproblem families inherit rigid and unrealistic expectations of their children (Rothery & Cameron, 1985). Such beliefs often preclude age-appropriate expectations, placing unrealistic behavioral demands on the child or misinterpreting developmental limits as intentional misbehavior (Heap, 1991; Acton & During, 1992).

When parents were raised in unresponsive or negative environments, they adapt to their family background by creating interpretations and beliefs to convince themselves that their upbringing was adequate. These beliefs normalize the family background, setting the stage for a continued pattern in the adults' own parenting. These inherited beliefs and parenting behaviors often compromise the parenting functions. The following patterns are common when children from dysfunctional backgrounds become parents:

- ◆ **Discipline functions** may become extreme, reflecting patterns of neglect or coercion. Neglectful parents do not note misbehavior until it interferes with parental desires or activities (Kagan & Schlosberg, 1989). Coercive parents are often negative and forceful (Conger & Patterson, 1995; Kochanska, 1995). Potentially injurious discipline strategies are difficult to challenge, particularly if the parent received that form of discipline during childhood without defining her parents' behavior as abusive (Bower & Knutson, 1996).
- ◆ **Guidance functions** may become blaming and negative rather than engaging in positive learning exchanges (Mash & Johnson, 1990; Whipple & Webster-Stratton, 1991). This promotes negative and externalized systems of childhood coping (Kolko et al., 1993; Wolfe, 1987).
- ◆ **Accessibility functions** may be compromised as parents become self-absorbed and fail to tune into child needs. Children must then become demanding to ensure their needs are met (Camras et al., 1990; Dadds, 1987; Donovan & Leavitt, 1989; Olson et al., 1990). The negativity in this pattern can result in parenting responses that diminish child self-worth (Kolko et al., 1993). Other parents may become anxious and intrusive, compromising child attachment and promoting aggressive child reactions (Lyons-Ruth, 1996; Nachmias, Gunnar, Mangelsdorf, Parritz, & Buss, 1996).
- ◆ **Nurturing functions** may become negative. This pattern can compromise child development (Boyum & Parke, 1995). Concurrently, if parents are self-absorbed, they are less likely to identify and attend to the child's emotional needs.

---

## CASE EXAMPLE

A family enters treatment because of conflict in the family. The family consists of a divorced mother, her son, and her male partner of three years, Rick. Rick is a successful businessman who provides well for the family and is very involved with the son. The source of conflict is about the use of corporal discipline. The mother tends to argue that her child should not be physically punished. Rick, who advocates spanking as a form of punishment, has spanked Nathan on several occasions. When the situation is explored, Rick argues that he was spanked frequently as a child and he turned out okay. He further argues that the spanking was instrumental in helping him learn right from wrong, and then states, "If it is good enough for me, it is good enough for Nathan." When the mother argues against physical punishment, Rick counters that the son is manipulating the mother, and suggests that he was doing so on purpose.

---

In this example, notice how Rick rationalizes his childhood disciplinary experiences. Even though some parenting functions seemed strong, the discipline function was seriously compromised and was at risk of becoming negative. It is not unusual for a parent to rationalize and justify personal experiences and repeat the patterns with their own children. It is difficult to argue against their logical position, because the parent's justifications are combined with denial of harm and loyalty to their own parents.

## Mental Illness and/or Disability

Many family practitioners assume that disability and/or mental illness render parents as unfit (Benjet, Azar, & Kuersten-Hogan, 2003; Feldman & Case, 1999). This assumption may be common, but it is not necessarily true. Although parents with mental illness or disabilities have clear adaptive challenges, many parents can perform parenting functions and work well with children, especially if they understand the nature of their adaptive challenges and have compensatory plans to ensure that the children's needs are met (Thomas & Kalucy, 2003). This point is important, because the impact of an illness or disability is not constant. Because symptoms and skill requirements shift from situation to situation, it is important to be aware of the potential compromises to parenting functions so you can help the family plan for problematic situations.

 ◆ **Discipline functions** may be compromised because the disability or illness may impair the parent's ability to identify risk and take safety precautions for the child (Llewellyn, McConnell, Honey, Mayes, & Russo, 2003).
 ◆ **Guidance functions** may become compromised because the disability or illness interferes with the parent's logical abilities. These functions are also impaired if the parent is not sensitive to the impact of her illness or disability on the child (Mullick, Miller, & Jacobsen, 2001; Thomas & Kalucy, 2003).
 ◆ **Access functions** may be compromised during hospitalizations or times when the parent is unable to respond due to the illness or disability (Bassett, Lampe, & Lloyd, 1999; Feldman & Case, 1999).

◆ **Nurturing functions** may become compromised when the illness or disability diminishes parental skills or causes the parent to misunderstand the nature of the child's needs (Benjet et al., 2003; Llewellyn et al., 2003). Many parents have also had a long history of traumas and negative experiences associated with the illness that may at times interfere with parental responding (Mowbray, Schwartz, Bybee, Spang, Rueda-Riedle, & Oyserman, 2000)

Parents with mental illness or disabilities can be effective and committed parents when the impact of their disability or illness is understood and mediated (Bassett et al., 1999). This often requires additional supports such as group programs (McGaha, 2002), self-help materials (Feldman & Case, 1999), and ongoing supports (Bassett et al., 1999; Mowbray, Oyserman, & Bybee, 2000). The family practitioner should not automatically assume that there are problems, but should ensure that the impact of the disability or illness is understood and a central part of the treatment planning (Mowbray, Oyserman, Bybee, & MacFarlane, 2002; Thomas & Kalucy, 2003).

## Parental Substance Abuse

When a family member is addicted to mind- or behavior-altering substances, the condition is often considered a family-level disease (Steinglass & Moyer, 1977). Addiction is considered a family disease because family patterns, roles, and rituals change as family members adapt. Such adaptation by the individual family members acts to maintain the addictive problem and promote the intergenerational transmission of the addiction (Sholevar & Schwoeri, 2003).

Parental substance abuse disrupts all aspects of family functioning (Jacob & Krahn, 1988; Liepman, Nirenberg, Doolittle, Begin, Broffman, & Babich, 1989). Findings indicate that substance abuse is associated with family violence and child neglect (Davies, 1985; Dunn, Tarter, Mezzich, Vanyukov, Kirsci, & Kirillova, 2002). Further, there is some indication that substance abuse promotes emotional, behavioral, and academic problems in the child (Conners et al., 2003; Kroll, Stock, & James, 1985; Mayes & Truman, 2002). Parental substance abuse is thus a serious concern for family practitioners.

Substance abuse disrupts all of the parenting functions. When a parent is impaired, he often neglects to perform critical parenting tasks (Dunn et al., 2002). Routines become disrupted, and the children are often left to fend for themselves. The addicted parent often is preoccupied with setting up opportunities to abuse the substance when not impaired, thus inhibiting the psychological energy available for parenting. Once impaired, the parent often ignores the parenting functions due to incapacitation (Conners et al., 2003; Dunn et al., 2002). The impact on parental functioning is often profound.

◆ **Nurturing functions** become impaired as the parent shifts focus away from caring for the child (e.g., feeding, bathing, tucking into bed) and toward the pleasures of inebriation (Dunn et al., 2002).

- **Access functions** become impaired as the parent stops noticing and attending to the children's needs. Often the parent is oblivious to the children's activities and whereabouts (Dunn et al., 2002).
- **Discipline functions** become impaired as the parent's judgment about right and wrong becomes suspect. Parents may overreact to minor situations and underreact to problems (Conners et al., 2003).
- **Guidance functions** become impaired as the parent's thinking becomes less exact and logic erodes due to the inebriation (Mayes & Truman, 2002).

## CASE EXAMPLE

At the beginning of a group program for children from high-risk families, the children are invited to share the best and worst things that happened during the week. A 13-year-old boy states that the best thing was that he was allowed to stay up until three in the morning the night before. As the group starts exploring his situation, it becomes clear that his parents were drinking in the kitchen and he was watching television in the living room. The parents failed to feed him and did not put him to bed. He finally became bored at about three in the morning and went to bed himself. At the end of the exploration, the boy states, "I said that was the best thing in my week, but it was really the worst."

In response to the compromised parental functions, family members must adapt. The most commonly identified family adaptation is the assumption of addiction-related roles to compensate for the addicted family member. Such roles are necessary because the substance abuser is often unable to fulfill her family functions. Concurrently, the family needs to control information about the substance abuse. Most family roles function to either compensate for the family member's impairment or prevent outsiders from identifying the family problem. As family members adapt to the new roles, they become invested and develop a codependent relationship whereby their adaptive behaviors enable and may even promote continued substance abuse (Scaturo, Hayes, Sagula, & Waltre, 2000). Here are some of the most common roles:

- **Enabler.** This family member saves the substance abuser from the consequences of her addiction by assuming caretaking functions with the substance abuser and covering up the impact of the substance abuse.
- **Hero.** This family member excels in some area of life (sports or school) to create the illusion that the family is successful.
- **Scapegoat.** This family member displays many unacceptable behaviors, drawing attention away from the substance abuse and providing someone to blame for family problems.
- **Mascot.** This family member is funny and jovial. Often very popular, the mascot distracts people from the family problems and substance abuse.

◆ **Lost child.** This family member never causes trouble and maintains a very low profile in the family, so he is seldom even noticed (Ackerman, 1987; Black, 1981).

Maintenance of such family roles distorts the emotional development and relationships of the family members (Black, 1981; Fendrich, Warner, & Weissman, 1990; Wekesser, 1994; Veronie & Fruehstorfer, 2001; Ziter, 1988). Problems emerge because the family members, once locked into their roles, cannot individuate from the family system (Room, 1996). Consequently, children from substance-abusing homes tend to experience low self-esteem, loneliness, guilt, helplessness, and fear of abandonment (Berger, 1993; Silverstein, 1990). Behavior problems are common; however, the behavior problems are also associated with the quality of the marriage in the substance-abusing home (Benzies, Harrison, & Magill-Evans, 1998). In homes where there is evidence of parental warmth and involvement, there tend to fewer child-related problems (Alford, 1998).

Children in substance-abusing homes also experience social problems because they never know how impaired the parent may be at any given time. Consequently, children often isolate themselves from peers and find reasons not to bring their friends home (Silverstein, 1990). This begins to affect the children's social development because they do not develop some of the give-and-take skills associated with hosting friends and having sleepovers.

Family-based treatment is a critical element of effective substance abuse intervention (Heath & Stanton, 1998; Sholevar & Schwoeri, 2003). Many professionals adopt a multisystemic approach to treatment, with individual or group treatment focused on stopping the substance abuse and family therapy to help all family members adjust their roles and enabling behaviors (Center for Substance Abuse Treatment, 2004). The readjustment of roles is critical because the children lose their roles when the substance abuse ceases (Bepko & Krestan, 1985). Multifamily groups and family psychoeducational groups are commonly used in place of family therapy (Center for Substance Abuse Treatment, 2004).

Substance abuse and domestic violence are often related. As such, many families will be affected by both extreme situations, causing multiple adaptations that interfere with family member functioning. When working with such situations, the family practitioner is often challenged by the past adaptations and family dynamics that promote the ongoing problems (Willett, Ayoub, & Robinson, 1991; Mohr, Beutler, Shoham-Solomon, Bergan, Kaszniak, & Yost, 1990). To mediate the impact of these factors on the family, you must often incorporate additional supports and services. You may also have to work in the family environment in order to help change the family adaptations (Gruber, Fleetwood, & Herring, 2001; Moore & Finkelstein, 2001; Richter & Bammer, 2000). Four steps are commonly used to guide intervention with such families:

1. **Deal directly with the difficult behavior.** This step often requires encouraging or insisting on treatment for the behaviors that are driving the adaptation. You cannot provide long-term effective (change-focused) intervention if the behavior continues to require ongoing adaptation.

2. **Deal with the adaptive responses to the difficult behaviors.** The second step of intervention is to help family members identify the adaptations that were made at the individual and family levels to allow them to coexist with the problematic behavior. After identifying and labeling such adaptations, you can begin to explore methods for interrupting these automatic responses.

3. **Develop new skills and behaviors to replace the past adaptive behaviors.** Remember that the past adaptations served functions in the family and that ceasing the adaptive behaviors will leave important functions unfulfilled if the family members do not replace them with new behaviors and skills.

4. **Build on new adaptations to promote healthy family relationships.** After the family has interrupted and built new adaptive behaviors, you can help them identify and build on family strengths so they can feel better about the family and develop new strengths.

## ◆ EXERCISE 13.1   UNDERSTANDING MULTIPLE STRESSORS

You are a social worker in a child guidance clinic located in a small city. The city has hit rough times lately, with high unemployment due to factory shutdowns and a drought that is affecting farms in the area. You are one of the few in your graduating class to get a job. You work in an attractive office setting, located at the end of a wide driveway near the edge of town. At the entrance of the building (about five years old) is a very large foyer; at its far ends are groups of overstuffed chairs that comprise waiting areas. The foyer is well lit through a large skylight that brightens up the art and sculpture carefully set around the space. Curving around the back area of the foyer is a ceramic tile reception counter about 30 feet long. Counseling offices are furnished with oak desks, matching shelves, and a computer table for working as well as with a couch and one chair for seating clients. The setting also has three large boardrooms, viewing rooms, and a play therapy room.

The intake procedures for your agency involve several steps. First the client (or client's parent) phones the agency requesting a referral. During this call, the secretary takes the referral information and then has an intake counselor call back to determine the nature of the concern. In this phone conversation, the intake worker explores the problem and then asks a series of questions to determine if the child might be at risk to self or others. If the client is at risk, an appointment is booked right away. If not, the secretary sends the family a package of standardized questionnaires to be completed. Once the family returns these questionnaires, an intake appointment is booked. Currently, the team is booking six months ahead. When the appointment comes due, the intake worker updates information, conducts a social history, and informs the client that they will be placed on a waiting list to be disposed to an ongoing counselor. Clients on this list will wait about three to six months before seeing the ongoing counselor. When the time for the family to meet with the counselor is near, the intake worker and the psychometrist review the information and write reports explaining to the counselor what he or she should do to serve the family. The counselor is then given the file and can contact the family to make an appointment.

You are an ongoing counselor preparing to meet a new client. A 15-year-old young woman is currently in foster care, but was living with her mother until recently when they had a physical fight. The mother has made the referral to ask for help in the parent-child conflict. When talking with the intake worker on the phone, she discloses the physical fighting. The intake worker consequently contacts Child Protective Services. Since that contact, the child has been living in foster care to ensure her safety. The child protection agency wants the family to get help before placing the child back into the home. The child is in frequent conflict in foster care, and both mother and child dislike the Child Protective Services worker.

As you look into the file, there is ample information. On the left side of the file is the intake form that was completed by the receptionist when the client first came. This form indicates that a lot of parent-child conflict has occurred, leading to the referral. Behind the intake form is the series of testing questionnaires that the mother completed and mailed to the agency before an intake appointment was booked. These questionnaires are accompanied by an analysis of the testing results by the psychometrist and treatment recommendations. These recommendations indicate that the mother is a concerned and caring woman who is struggling with her 15-year-old daughter. The assessment report further indicates that the teen might have some form of conduct disorder and recommends parent-child counseling to strengthen the mother's ability to control the child.

On the right side of the file is a two-page assessment from the intake worker. This report explains that the family has just moved to the community from a larger city. They lived in the larger city until the mother left her husband due to infidelity. He was reportedly a heavy drinker who tended to stay out all night, usually with a woman whom he met in the bar. He was often abusive to the mother, but apparently had never harmed the children. Mother stayed in the relationship regardless of the abuse. She grew up in an alcoholic and abusive home. She has stated to the intake worker that she knows how to make a relationship work, but when he (her husband) started seeing other women, it told her that she was the only one working on things.

After the mother decided to leave, the father moved in with another woman and ceased his contact with the family. The family moved to this small town because the mother wants to be closer to her family. Mother and daughter initially lived with mother's parents and two brothers in a three-bedroom home. This arrangement lasted for about three months while the mother was trying to get established. While mother and daughter were living in this setting, a lot of drinking and drug use went on because the grandparents and brothers are still actively abusing substances. The mother finally got a job at McDonald's and was able to move into a subsidized apartment. The parent-child conflict was common while living with the extended family but did not escalate. The conflict got out of control when the family moved into its own apartment. You are now preparing to meet with the family.

In this case, there are multiple problems and elements that contribute to the family situation.

1. Identify the intergenerational problems that are evident in the family situation.

2. Identify the resource problems that are evident in the family situation.

3. What elements in the current family situation (excluding extended family and resources) contribute to the family situation?

---

# Challenges to Traditional Treatment Approaches

Family resources and adaptive challenges form two continua that challenge the effectiveness of traditional treatment methods. Families with low resources are difficult to treat through traditional methods because they frequently miss sessions and terminate treatment before achieving their goals (Berrigan & Garfield, 1981; Rosenblatt & Mayer, 1972; Weighill, Hodge, & Peck, 1983). Such families often refer again when problems resurface. Families with low resources may have so many pressures that they shift attention to other priorities when tension is relieved (Brill & Storrow, 1960).

Many researchers working with families low on resources argue that the most effective interventions also focus on easing environmental pressures (Dohrenwend & Dohrenwend, 1981; Maluccio, 1989; Rivara, 1985; Wood, 1978; Gomes-Swartz, Hadley, & Strupp, 1978). This involves helping families to navigate predictable crises within the environment rather than attempting to cure dysfunction (Layzer & Goodson, 1992; Lorion & Felner, 1986; Maluccio, 1989; Rothery & Cameron, 1985). Traditional office-based treatment may be detrimental because it implies that clients can control their life situation (Home & Darveau-Fournier, 1990). This message can diminish self-esteem and increase family stress.

Traditional treatment methods are also ineffective for families exhibiting adaptive challenges. Parents with difficult backgrounds, active mental illness symptoms, and/or current substance abuse problems are not often in a position to benefit from office-based treatment. The assumption that an individual can go to a therapist for one hour each week and have an experience that will mitigate past abuse or current adaptive challenges is unrealistic. Such a person needs multidimensional treatment to effectively influence the individual and family issues associated with the adaptive functions. The assumptions of office-based treatment listed below demonstrate the lack of fit for multiproblem families (Keithly, Samples, & Strupp, 1980; Luborsky, Chandler, Auerbach, Cohun, & Achrach, 1971; Moras & Strupp, 1982; Staples & Sloane, 1970; Sloane, Staples, Cristal, Yorkston, & Whipple, 1975).

- ◆ **Acute onset of focal problems.** The problems brought to treatment should be recent rather than chronic. The problems should also be easy to identify, measure, and crystallize into goals (e.g., depressive reactions to marital separation).
- ◆ **Adequate previous adjustment.** Before the onset of the problem, it is expected that the client was functioning adequately. Treatment either restores adequate functioning or enhances previous functioning.
- ◆ **Good relational capacity.** The client should have enough relational abilities to focus treatment and perform treatment tasks and assignments. Interpersonal dependency and distortion interfere with this ability.
- ◆ **High initial motivation.** The client must be willing to work to change because responsibility is placed on him during treatment. If he is not motivated, he will not complete assignments.

These criteria for successful office-based treatment suggest that effectiveness is enhanced when there are no chronic stressors in the family. Furthermore, it is expected that clients have personal and social resources that can be mobilized in response to the problem (Resnick, 1985; Spaid & Fraser, 1991). These assumptions and preconditions do not apply to families considered multiproblem or high risk (Sarason, 1984). Problems in high-risk and multiproblem families have both environmental and personal elements that render casework and psychoeducational approaches ineffective (Daro, 1988; Howing, Wodarski, Gaudin, & Kurtz, 1989; Layzer & Goodson, 1992; Mann & McDermott, 1983; Rothery & Cameron, 1985).

Researchers working with this population caution practitioners about the concept of cure when working with high-risk and multiproblem families (Daro, 1988; Layzer & Goodson, 1992; Rothery & Cameron, 1985). Rather, many experts suggest that practitioners focus on extending the number and length of safe periods in the family rather than on expecting permanently improved functioning (Layzer & Goodson, 1992).

# Promising Approaches to Treatment

Families with low resources and multiple problems require direct and practical input about specific family situations (Howing et al., 1989; Lengua, Roosa, Schupak-Neuberg, Michaels, Berg, & Wechsler, 1992; Lorion 1973; Love, Kaswan, & Bugental, 1972; Rothery & Cameron, 1985). Such input can either occur within the context of an ongoing relationship or involve very brief intervention. Researchers have noted that one-session counseling can be effective with this population (Bloom, 1984; Malan, Heath, Bacal, & Balfour, 1975).

A critical element of treatment with families identified as high risk and multiproblem is immediate access (Green, Power, Steinbook, & Gaines, 1981; Howing et al., 1989; Rothery & Cameron, 1985). This availability of service is important due to the reactive nature of these families. If families have to wait long periods for service or navigate complicated intake procedures, success is highly unlikely.

Researchers and clinicians have identified promising approaches for working with high-risk and multiproblem families. As part of most approaches, the family practitioner addresses chronic environmental and personal stressors concurrent with focusing on family functioning (Daro, 1988; Dumas, 1984). Frequently, effective treatment is multidimensional and fashioned around the family's needs rather than taking single or prefabricated approaches to treatment (Howing et al., 1989). Here are three promising approaches:

1. **Group treatment.** Group programs that provide support and creative programming (rather than education) can be helpful (Lutzker, 1990; Rothery & Cameron, 1985; Tremblay et al., 1991).
2. **In-home support and family preservation.** Moving practitioners out of the office and into the family environment can be helpful. In moving into the family environment, the practitioner also assumes more support provision and advocacy functions (LeCroy, 1992; Rothery & Cameron, 1985; Seagull, 1987; Spaid & Fraser, 1991; Tracy, 1990).
3. **Multisystemic treatment.** Practitioners must be able to work with multiple support people. Such supports can be formal systems but should also include informal people from the family environment (Sheidow & Woodford, 2003).

## Group Treatment

Group treatment is a promising mode of intervention, especially when a broader family focus is maintained (e.g., including children at some level or using multiple family groups (Graziano & Mills, 1992; Kirchenbaum 1979; Lutzker, 1990; Tremblay et al.,

1991). Effectiveness can be further enhanced if the group is supplemented with in-home and/or environmental intervention (Wolfe, Sandler, & Kaufman, 1981; Daro, 1988; Dumas, 1984). Group services increase social support (Barber, 1992; Herrera & Sanchez, 1980; Szykula & Fleischman, 1985). Feedback from group participants indicates that the ideal group provides some information but also includes time for informal sharing of practical issues (Home & Darveau-Fournier, 1990). Other parent feedback suggests that mutual aid and self-direction are important elements of the group programming (Home & Darveau-Fournier, 1990; Lengua et al., 1992; Rothery & Cameron, 1985).

Children's groups are promising because children in high-risk families often respond better to peers than to adults (Fantuzzo, Jurecic, Stovall, Hightower, Goins, & Schachtel, 1988). Many of these children exhibit social deficits and aggression that are best served in a group format (Graziano & Mills, 1992). Through the group, children from these families increase self-control, responsibility, self-esteem, cognitive organization, and nonaggressive problem solving (Graziano & Mills, 1992). Group programs associated with preschools have been highly successful with young children (Cicchetti, Toth, & Hennessy, 1989; Crittenden, 1989; Culp, Little, Letts, & Lawrence, 1991; Jason, DeAmicus, & Carter, 1978).

## In-Home Support

In-home programming has proven helpful with many high-risk and multiproblem families. This approach has been most helpful for parents of young children who themselves experienced difficult childhoods (Beckwith, 1988). The key element of such treatment is providing support that is based on the client's expressed needs rather than on a preset curriculum (Beckwith, 1988). In-home support enhances the potential for change because the practitioner intervenes with problems in their context (Tracy, 1990; Green et al., 1981). Concurrently, engaging all family members is often easier because meetings are in the family home (Hodges & Blythe, 1992; Green et al., 1981; Rzepnicki, 1991). Working with the whole family within the problem context aids generalization, because there is no need to translate office-based advice back to nonclinical situations.

Often the official focus of in-home intervention is parent-child relationships. Practitioners frequently use coaching interventions to help family members respond differently to specific situations. However, while in the home, the in-home practitioner may find that many other types of problems emerge, providing opportunities for concrete and direct input as the in-home practitioner helps family members solve other basic problems of living. This support decreases stress and hopelessness in the family and can prevent parent-child conflicts.

## Multisystemic Treatment

The multiple needs of high-risk and multiproblem families often require strengthening their relationships with the systems and people in their environment (Sheidow & Woodford, 2003). Several interventions fall into the broad category of multiple systems.

Each intervention model tends to focus on specific problems. The following intervention methods all attempt to strengthen relationships between the family members and available supports in the family environment:

- Multisystemic therapy
- Wraparound services
- Family group decision making
- Family conferencing

The premise of multisystemic therapies is that families are often poorly connected to the people and systems in their lives (Burns, Schoenwald, Burchard, Faw, & Santos, 2000). The therapist works with the family in their home environment to help strengthen their ties with potential supports. The support systems can be formal (e.g., agency services) or informal. When working with the family, the practitioner mediates and facilitates collaboration among the various support systems. Such approaches have been very effective in working with juvenile delinquents, substance abusers, and other problems that result in a high-risk or multiproblem designation (Henggeler & Lee, 2003). All family functions can be improved through multisystemic approaches (Huey, Henggeler, Brondino, & Pickrel, 2000).

## Summary

When working with families designated as high risk or multiproblem, therapists must expand their approaches to compensate for environmental challenges. Families that have very few resources (money, education and skills, supports) often do not benefit from office-based family therapy, because environmental demands are too high. Parental histories, illness or disabilities, and substance abuse can also render traditional treatment approaches ineffective. Family practitioners must change their approach when working with such families. Three family treatment approaches show promise for working with high-risk and multiproblem families: multisystemic, in-home, and group approaches. In the next two chapters, we will explore some of the strategies and skills needed when adopting these environmentally focused therapy strategies.

## Critical Content

1. High-risk and multiproblem families do not often benefit from traditional treatment. They often drop out before meeting goals.
2. Two continua interfere with treatment: (a) a continuum of resources and (b) a continuum of adaptive challenges.
3. The continuum of resources refers to income, education and marketable skills, and supports. Lower levels of any of these resources can interfere with treatment effectiveness.
4. The continuum of adaptive challenges includes parental background (exposure to violence, ineffective parenting) and illness or disabilities (substance

abuse, mental illness). These elements can interfere with treatment effectiveness.

5. The family practitioner must adapt to the multiple needs of families when working with high-risk and multiproblem families.

## Suggested Readings

Burns, B. J., Schoenwald, S. K., Burchard, J. D., Faw, L., & Santos, A. B. (2000). Comprehensive community-based interventions for youth with severe emotional disorders: Multisystemic therapy and the wraparound process. *Journal of Child & Family Studies, 9,* 283–314.

Eamon, M. K., & Venkararaman, M. (2003). Implementing parent management training in the context of poverty. *American Journal of Family Therapy, 31,* 281–293.

Sheidow, A. J., & Woodford, M. S. (2003). Multisystemic therapy: An empirically supported, home-based family therapy approach. *The Family Journal: Counseling & Therapy for Couples & Families, 11,* 257–263.

## Chapter 14

# Multiagency Work

In this chapter we will build on the ecosystemic model discussed in Chapter 13 to highlight promising intervention approaches for families who have low levels of resources concurrent with internal family problems. When families have multiple stresses and problems, multiple systems are often impinging on the family. Family practitioners must be skilled in navigating the complex support systems as part of practice when working with high-risk and multiproblem families.

## Theoretical Grounding

The concepts in this chapter are based on the ecosystemic model and empowerment theory, as well as empirical findings. We explore these concepts to suggest several promising interventions and identify critical skills for working with the multiple impinging systems. Table 14.1 presents some chapter concepts, theoretical models, and possible sources of additional information. The following textbooks have additional information for understanding the chapter concepts:

- ◆ *Child Welfare and Family Services: Policies and Practice* (7th ed.), by S. Whitelaw Downs, E. Moore, E. J. McFadden, S. Michaud, & L. B. Costin, 2004, Boston: Allyn & Bacon.
- ◆ *Family Practice—Brief Systems Methods for Social Work* (1st ed.), by C. Franklin & C. Jordan, 1999, Pacific Grove, CA: Brooks/Cole.

**TABLE 14.1**
**Chapter Concepts, Theoretical Models, and Sources**

| Chapter Concepts | Theoretical Models | Recommended Reading |
|---|---|---|
| Office-based practice is often ineffective with multiproblem families requiring different approaches. | Ecological systems model | Franklin & Jordan, Chapter 8 Janzen & Harris, Chapters 6, 10, 11, 13, 14 Kilpatrick & Holland, Chapters 3, 5 Whitelaw Downs et al., Chapters 3, 8 |
| When working with multiproblem families, the family practitioner needs to work with multiple systems and agencies. | Ecological systems model | Franklin & Jordan, Chapter 8 Janzen & Harris, Chapter 17 Kilpatrick & Holland, Chapters 3, 6 |
| Understanding agency policies and procedures is critical for supporting multiproblem families. | Ecological systems model Empowerment model | Franklin & Jordan, Chapters 13, 14 Janzen & Harris, Chapter 17 Kilpatrick & Holland, Chapter 3 |
| Family professionals often need to advocate for families and support them in their dealings with formal systems. | Ecological systems model Empowerment model | Franklin & Jordan, Chapters 13, 14 Janzen & Harris, Chapter 17 Whitelaw Downs et al., Chapters 8, 12 |

◆ *Family Treatment in Social Work Practice,* by C. Janzen & O. Harris, 1997, Pacific Grove, CA: Brooks/Cole.

◆ *Working with Families: An Integrative Model by Level of Need* (3rd ed.), by A. C. Kilpatrick & T. P. Holland, 2003, Boston: Allyn & Bacon.

# Understanding Systemic Family Stresses

The multiplicity of family needs existing in high-risk and multiproblem families typically requires the family to be involved with multiple services and supports (Altshuler, 2003; Hinshaw & DeLeon, 1995). Often family members have several appointments with different services throughout the month. Although these services are intended as a source of family support, families often experience them as a source of stress (Ziemba, 2001). Families must prioritize time and energy, and they frequently must attend to other pressing issues, such as monetary shortages and problems with other systems (Smith, 2000). These emergent issues frequently gain a higher priority, causing family members to miss appointments (Altman, 1993; Rothery & Cameron, 1990). Agencies, however, react to missed appointments by pressuring the family to be more committed, or they will threaten some sanction such as withdrawing services. This pressure can greatly elevate the family stress levels.

## CASE EXAMPLE

A woman named Cecilia and her two children have recently left her abusive husband and entered a battered women's shelter. Although the violence to Cecilia has been ongoing, her partner recently began hitting the children, causing Children's Protective Services (CPS) to become involved. The CPS practitioner recommended the shelter and referred Cecilia for parent skills training. Cecilia was with her partner for 10 years, and they have two male children. The eldest child, Manny, is nine years old and has a severe learning disability and ADD/HD. These conditions have caused Manny to have many social and behavioral problems. The school has him in tutoring and is planning to enter him in special education programming. The second child, Andre, is 18 months old and small for his age. He is being tested for cystic fibrosis and for failure to thrive. A public health nurse has been assigned to the family to help with his development.

The CPS practitioner helped Cecilia access child counseling through the community mental health program; she also referred Manny to Big Brothers. The family was lucky because a new program to help children who have been victimized was being formed, and the family received a big brother right away. Cecilia was also able to receive adult mental health services, because she was diagnosed as depressed. This condition may have some connection to past abuse and growing up in an alcoholic home. Cecilia attends Al-Anon every week.

Very recently, Cecilia has been seeing her husband again. He has begun substance abuse programming and has entered the violence abatement program at a local agency. With the potential for reconciliation, the CPS practitioner has become more actively involved and has charged the father with child abuse. The shelter staff strongly encourages Cecilia to continue in her support groups and places the children on a waiting list for upcoming children's groups.

Although each service has a rationale and a supportive function, this family currently has the following services involved:

| | |
|---|---|
| Women's shelter group | Tutoring program |
| Children of violence group | Big Brother |
| Children's Protective Services | Public health nurse |
| Al-Anon | Parenting program |
| Substance abuse services | Probation officer |
| Children's mental health | Violence abatement program |
| Adult mental health | Lawyer |
| School | Court |

**TABLE 14.2**
**Service System Messages and Approaches**

| | Mission | Frequent Problem Definition | Frequent Solutions |
|---|---|---|---|
| Women's shelter group | Strengthen and protect the woman. | Men are abusers, women are victims. | Leave the partner, lay charges. |
| Children of violence group | Help the child understand and cope. | Violence against the mother is harming the child. | Teach child safety skills, responsibility, and coping. |
| Children's Protective Services | Protect the child. | Adults are abusers and children are victims. | Remove child, change adult behavior. |
| Al-Anon | Support members of alcoholic families. | People enable alcoholics to continue. | Stop enabling behaviors, support each other. |
| Substance abuse services | Help alcoholic stop. | Substance abuse is an illness. | Help individual take control. |
| Children's mental health | Promote optimal child development. | Child adaptation is compromised. | Change parental functioning, support child. |
| Adult mental health | Optimize individual adult functioning. | Adult has mental illness. | Support adult to optimize functioning. |
| School | Help child learn. | Child has a disorder or parental dysfunction. | Provide special classes and additional supports. |
| Tutoring program | Help child learn. | Child has disability or problem. | Provide specific help with learning. |
| Big Brother | Support child. | Child needs same-sex relationship. | Provide social and supportive activities. |
| Public health nurse | Optimize child development. | Child is ill and environment needs help. | Train in caregiving. |
| Parenting program | Teach parent skills. | Parents have skill deficits. | Teach skills. |
| Probation officer | Monitor criminals. | Dad is criminal. | |
| Violence abatement program | Decrease male violence against women. | Dad has thinking and behavior problems. | Enroll in psychoeducational groups. |
| Lawyer | Defend father. | Dad needs protection from court. | Provide advocacy and strategic referrals. |
| Court | Administer justice. | Assess whether law was broken. | Hear arguments and judge. |

As you can see by this example, the array of supports involved with a family can become overwhelming. Although no practitioner wants to overburden family members, stress occurs inadvertently because family members must balance meetings and attempt to integrate input from the different service providers. The input from each service system will have ideological and mission-related biases that present conflicting definitions of the family problems and ideal solutions.

Table 14.2 is a matrix of the different messages that may converge on the family from the preceding example. Although its format does not reflect the complexity of the services, the table does reflect some of the bottom-line messages and approaches to the family members. Notice how the different definitions and approaches often contradict each other. Similarly, the solutions can result in multiple and incompatible sets of recommendations. As family members attempt to manage these messages and divergent approaches, confusion and stress are the likely results.

Family practitioners are well aware of this confusion and stress, because they must also manage the different messages. Most family practitioners have experienced frustration emerging from other professionals overlooking family needs or taking action that is disruptive to the family. It is often said that it is not the clients, but the agencies and systems, that cause practitioner burnout. For practitioners working with multiproblem families, this old adage is often put to the test. In reviewing Table 14.2, you will notice that the identified client changes from service to service. Some services identify the mother, some the father, and some the child as the client. Very few services adopt a family focus.

The multiple services and perspectives involved with formal supports require family practitioners to develop specific sets of skill when working with high-risk and multiproblem family systems (Schlosberg & Kagan, 1988; Smith, 2000). These skills have four basic domains:

1. Formal support services to ensure that family–service provider connections are successful
2. Collaborative support functions with family members and service providers
3. Case-specific advocacy within the array of formal services
4. Class advocacy to address shared problems experienced by the families

## Formal Support Services

To help manage the family's multiple demands and potential confusion, family practitioners often develop a family-based plan of care. Although contracts and plans of care are discussed in Chapter 6, planning when a family is engaged with multiple service providers is a more complex type of service plan. When you are helping high-risk and multiproblem family systems, the plan of care often involves coordinating and integrating the multiple services so that each service makes a specific contribution to the family plan (Henggeler, Melton, & Smith, 1992; Lyon & Kouloumpos-Lenares, 1987). Thus you have an unmistakable case management function when working with this type of family system. You cannot expect to achieve change with this type of family without taking a multisystems approach to service (Suarez, Smokowski, & Wodarski, 1996).

For less stressed family systems, you can engage additional services simply by suggesting that the family contact the supplementary service and then allowing the family to follow up. For multiproblem and high-risk families, making a referral to other services requires you to carefully consider the family and the helping system. You will often need to become very active in helping the family members and the formal services make a successful connection (Ziemba, 2001). Two important considerations influence the referral process: the level of autonomy and the level of fit.

## The Level of Autonomy

Not all family members are able to follow up on a referral without support. Five aspects of the referral situation have the potential to interfere with the family member's ability to follow up on a referral to a formal support system. These situational aspects can result in failed referrals.

1. **Limitations.** Some family members may have developmental or cognitive limitations that inhibit autonomous action and interfere with referral follow-up.
2. **Learned helplessness.** Past negative experiences with organizations can predispose family members to learned helplessness that leads to referral abandonment if family members sense potential problems.
3. **Emotional reactivity.** Entry protocols often require repetitive sharing of sensitive information, causing emotional reactivity and the potential abandonment of the referral.
4. **Pragmatic challenges.** Geographic access may be difficult or create an ordeal (such as multiple bus transfers) that can cause a family member to abandon the referral.
5. **Emergent priorities.** Shifts in the emergent family stresses may cause other issues to be prioritized, resulting in abandonment of the referral.

## The Level of Fit

If the fit is not obvious between the family member and the formal support to which they are referred, the referral can fail. This lack of fit can compound issues of autonomy because programs of low fit are unlikely to generate high levels of motivation when the family member has to follow through on the referral. The following aspects of program fit can interfere with a successful referral.

- **Narrow mandates.** Some professionals have a narrow interpretation of organizational mandates. When talking to such practitioners, family members are challenged to match their situation to the narrow interpretation. Matching the situation to the program requires cognitive sophistication and abstract thinking in the family member.
- **Partial responses.** Some programs respond only to one aspect of the family member's situation. If the aspect that fits the service is not a priority for the family member on the day she follows up, the referral may fail because the available services do not fit the current need.
- **Redundant processes.** Clients entering most formal service agencies are expected to tell their story. High-risk and multiproblem family members have told and retold their stories many times. Having to retell their stories can lead to resentment and cause family members to question the fit when they find they must repeat this process.
- **Buzzwords.** Referral sources listen for specific buzzwords for screening referrals. If the family member cannot identify or comfortably use the buzzwords, the referral may fail.

- **Agency protocols.** If programs have a lot of paperwork or bureaucratic hoops involved in accessing service, family members may abandon the referral, feeling that it is a waste of time. This situation is a higher risk when the benefits of the service are not clear to the family member.
- **Standardized services.** Some programs are predetermined and cover skills or content already mastered by the family member. In such situations, he may feel insulted by the program focus and abandon the referral.

This list is not exhaustive, but it is clear that the challenges are common in many referral situations. It is easy for practitioners to overlook these challenges because they are endemic in the way that service systems operate with clients. Family members, however, find the challenges to be confusing, irritating, and possibly intrusive. Practitioners must consequently be prepared to help the family members cope with the challenges to service fit that exist in any referral situation.

As illustrated in the preceding list, many issues can interfere with a successful referral. Family members may require active support to overcome some of the potential problems. Family practitioners must be willing and able to help the family members address the problems and actively facilitate the referral process. Six family practice skills are needed to facilitate new system engagement with multiproblem or high-risk family members:

1. **Exploring potential roadblocks.** When you are promoting a referral with family members, it is useful to predict potential roadblocks to success and discuss them with the family. Roadblocks can be internal or external. Internal roadblocks are associated with affective or thinking-based responses in the family members. Here are some affective roadblocks:
   - **Feelings of blame or responsibility.** A family member feels that she is being singled out as the cause of family problems.
   - **Feelings of shame.** A family member feels ashamed of the behaviors that prompt the referral.
   - **Feelings of inadequacy.** A family member feels inadequate or feels that he can't measure up because he needs the new service.
   - **Affective fluctuations.** Family feelings fluctuate, possibly changing members' motivation to follow up on the referral.
   - **Approach and avoidance responses.** A family member may be reticent or shy and hesitate to meet the new practitioner.

   Here are some thinking-based internal roadblocks:
   - **Win-lose framing.** A family member believes that her accepting a new service means that someone else wins.
   - **Judgment sensitivity.** Past or current experiences cause a family member to believe that others might judge him harshly.
   - **Devaluation.** A family member is likely to devalue the new service or the potential benefit that the service might bring to the family.

   External roadblocks include such issues as transportation difficulties, agency protocols, and scheduling. It is useful to anticipate any potential roadblocks and explore them with the family member. Such exploration helps the family member to plan for the roadblock and prepare a solution in advance.

2. **Exploring the family member's capacity for follow-up.** Sometimes disability or learned helplessness can interfere with the family member following up on the referral. If the member is not able to autonomously follow-up on the referral, you may need to assume a more active role in supporting the initial connection with the new service.

3. **Clarifying roles for self and the family member.** As the referral proceeds, the client will need to take specific actions; and as the practitioner, you may have corresponding tasks to support the referral. By summarizing and clarifying the different roles that people will take in making and following up on the referral, you can develop shared responsibility with your client.

4. **Mediating and supporting initial contacts.** It is often helpful for the practitioner to phone the referral source or even attend the initial session with the family member. This is especially important when there are significant potential roadblocks. If you make telephone contact, it is often useful to have the family member in the office. She can then hear what is being shared and can take the phone and have an initial experience with the new practitioner. When attending the initial contact session, you often need to begin by discussing progress being made with the family and family strengths. You can then outline how the new practitioner can supplement and support the ongoing progress.

5. **Following up with both family and service providers.** After completing the referral, you must often phone or meet with the new practitioner and/or family members. In the follow-up, you can explore and intervene to deal with any potential problems before they interfere with the new service.

6. **Using strength-focused framing.** When they enter services, families often feel that the professionals involved are focusing on their weaknesses. Because the family is being referred to a new service, this interpretation is usually quite accurate. To mitigate the impact of the family interpretations, you need to operate within a strength-based framework. This involves affirming the current situation by identifying the strengths that the family members are already using. From this foundation of strength, the new service must fit with the family's strengths and enhance what they are already doing. If family members cannot see the new service as an enhancement of their current efforts, they will likely see the new service as an indication that they are failing. This belief promotes a sense of poor fit.

When making a referral, consider both the autonomy and fit to determine the necessary level of practitioner activity. In some situations, you must be prepared to work closely with both the family and the other professionals to ensure that a collaborative team is formed to help the family (Altshuler, 2003; Henggeler et al., 1992; Hinshaw & DeLeon, 1995; Shepard & Carlson, 2003). Table 14.3 captures some of the demands that different configurations place on practitioners. As you examine the table, notice that each cell requires different types of activity from the practitioner.

**TABLE 14.3**
**Autonomy and Fit Implications for Practitioner Activity**

| High Autonomy/High Fit | High Autonomy/Low Fit |
|---|---|
| ◆ Help the youth identify the need, what the program offers, and how to access.<br><br>◆ It is often the youth's option whether the practitioner makes the referral or just provides information.<br><br>◆ Practitioner occupies a standby position to help with issues identified by the youth. | ◆ Help the youth identify the need, what the program has to offer, and explore options.<br><br>◆ If no other options, help the youth think through the potential benefits.<br><br>◆ Help the youth identify how they must present (buzzwords, concerns, etc.) to maximize success.<br><br>◆ Practitioner occupies a consultant role. |
| Low Autonomy/High Fit | Low Autonomy/Low Fit |
| ◆ Help the youth identify the needs and what the program has to offer.<br><br>◆ Partner with the youth to make the referral (either practitioner makes referral or helps the youth make initial contact).<br><br>◆ Remain involved as potential advocate if the referral stalls. | ◆ Help the youth identify the needs and what the program has to offer.<br><br>◆ Make the referral contact and explain the situation.<br><br>◆ Accompany the youth to initial meeting, acting as mediator and advocate.<br><br>◆ Monitor the situation and act as advocate for the youth if problems occur. |

Also notice in Table 14.3 that professional roles range from support person to advocate. In this range of roles, three specific functions are associated with helping families to deal with formal systems. These include the collaborative support function, the case advocacy function, and the class advocacy function.

# Collaborative Support Functions With Multiple Helping Systems

The primary feature of the collaborative support function is mediating the multiple differences between the systems of helping and the family system. Through this function, the family practitioner must partner with and support both the family and the other professionals. Each group needs to feel that the practitioner remains available and is not just dumping the family on the other service (Altshuler, 2003; Schlosberg & Kagan, 1988). Although the family practitioner occupies a supportive position with both the other practitioners and the family, the nature of the work changes slightly with each constituency.

## Collaborative Support With Other Professionals

When partnering with other professionals or services, the family practitioner must clarify how the new service fits into the current array of services helping the family. Sometimes this occurs briefly over the phone; at other times, it may require meetings or case conferences to ensure that everyone understands the family situation and goals. Three critical areas are explored at this point in treatment.

1. **Clarify the family needs and fit with the services.** The practitioner speaks with the other professionals, so that each person can identify how his services can best meet the family's needs. Ideally, the family needs provide an organizing framework that allows each professional to identify her specific role in an array of services.

2. **Clarify roles and responsibilities.** As each professional identifies how his services can assist the family, parameters must be developed so everybody understands their areas of influence, their goals, and how their work will intersect with others. Failure to clarify such domains of influence can result in interagency or interprofessional politics.

3. **Clarify communication needs.** When partnering with other professionals, the practitioner needs to understand the communication needs of each service provider. Some professionals need to be informed of critical events, while others may not need to know all areas of family functioning. By clarifying communication needs, you will further clarify how the services will work together.

After making the initial clarifications, the family practitioner often plays a special role with the other service providers because of the whole-family focus. Other service providers often work with subsystems or individuals within the family. Doing so can distort their view of other family members due to side taking, mandate limitations, limited perspectives, family politics, or other mechanisms of distortion. Frequently, you must provide a broader perspective with other professionals and mediate the inherent conflicts that come from more individualized perspectives. This requires ongoing contact through which reframing and coordination of activities can occur.

Concurrent with the potential misunderstandings that may evolve among the multiple service providers, family members may also have difficulties with the professionals involved. It is worth remembering that the mandates governing professional activities all have implications for how different family members are perceived. Family members may react to such perceptions. Family members may also react to the nature of services, professional interactions, protocols, and other service elements. You must monitor for difficult interactions and mediate the relationships between the family members and the service providers. In such situations, early intervention is best, and it requires constant monitoring and attention to shifts in the family–service provider relationships.

Frequently, family practitioners must contact service providers to reorient them to the agreements and roles outlined during the initial referral. It is often difficult for service providers to remain in these narrow roles. Consequently, advice and influence attempts may expand beyond agreed directions. Although such expansion is often well meaning, it can interfere with the services that others are providing. Similarly, professionals may cut back on the services provided to the family. Again, as the family practitioner you must measure such changes against the original agreements and ensure that the array of services continues to meet the family needs.

## CASE EXAMPLE

A family practitioner is seeking to focus the work of a family. The family consists of a mother, her live-in partner, and three adolescent sons. The mother's ex-husband was very violent, which resulted in the sons' using violence as their primary mode of problem solving. Child Protective Services (CPS) and an in-home support program are also involved with the family. The problem with focus appears to stem from conflicting messages between the CPS practitioner and the other practitioners. The in-home program and the family practitioner are trying to decrease the violence in the home; the CPS practitioner is focusing on multiple areas of family functioning and giving directives about how the family should respond. To bring focus, the family practitioner arranges a meeting with the parents, the CPS practitioner, and the in-home practitioner. At the meeting, the practitioner guides the "team" through the most pressing problems in the family and then tries to orient everyone to clear goals. Upon achieving better focus for the work, the family practitioner asks each person to identify how he or she can best serve the family goals. Through this discussion, each service provider begins to clarify their roles with the family. The professionals then start to negotiate how they can work effectively toward these goals.

## Collaborative Support With Family Members

Many practitioners, upon hearing the word *support*, associate it with low levels of activity. This vision of support is far from true. Often the act of supporting people involves confronting and cajoling family members to help them make the best of the available services. Frequently, support equates to problem solving. Many families, because of resource and adaptive challenges, are hypervigilant to issues of caring, coercion, and control. When family members experience a practitioner in another setting who is unresponsive, they may become angry and respond in ways that can undermine the referral. Consequently, part of the supportive function is to help family members deal more effectively with such professionals.

Three intervention tools can help you to sort through challenging situations with family members:

1. De-escalation
2. Stages of problem solving
3. Spheres of control

These tools help to structure the family members' thinking in difficult situations so they can prevent volatile responses when confronted with problems.

*De-escalation*   De-escalation involves exploring or debriefing a situation in a way that shifts the emotional energy from volatile to benign. This movement from volatile to calm sets the stage for using problem solving or the spheres of control. A family member cannot use such tools when he is emotionally agitated, because the tools are cognitive in nature. When he is heavily invested in his emotions, rumination interferes with logical processing (Dutton & Browning, 1988). Consequently, the deescalation is needed to provide a foundation for the individual to use cognitive or logical procedures.

Four common steps are involved in de-escalation. Most people proceed through these steps in a very intuitive manner, learned through repeated de-escalation attempts. In this section, we will break down the steps of de-escalation and consider each one separately. When reading these steps, reflect on how you have used each one in different ways in your own practice.

1. **Explore.** The first step requires the practitioner to begin exploring the situation. In the exploration, you will gather some details about the story. Frequently, these details are external in focus (e.g., the family member talks about what other people are doing), so you will consciously begin to shift the focus from action to processing systems. This causes the family member to begin talking more about herself and avoids a focus that might escalate emotional reactivity. Note that a focus on people's behaviors may escalate negative emotions, so be sure to direct discussion away from behavior and interaction by focusing on thinking.

2. **Validate.** As the shift occurs from action to processing, the family member is likely to express emotional content. At this time, you will validate her internal experiences and emotions that logically stem from the interpretations that she has shared with you. Note that when people are feeling something, they will often persist until they feel that their experience is acknowledged. Given this typical pattern, it is critical for you to validate the family member's emotional experience. When validating her emotional experience, make sure that you focus on the primary feeling (e.g., powerlessness, hopelessness, inadequacy) rather than secondary emotions such as anger. If you focus on secondary emotions, her emotional agitation is likely to persist because secondary emotions tend to be externalized.

3. **Shift.** As feelings are validated, they often lose some of their power. This is because the shift back to the primary feeling brings an internalized focus. The family member can no longer focus attention on the other people and begins to share her more vulnerable and softer feelings. As she expresses such feelings, you can then shift the focus from emotion to thinking by asking her about family member interpretations and beliefs. You will then use frameworks and meanings to access the underlying beliefs that fuel her emotion. These beliefs are then highlighted and explored to make them more conscious.

4. **Set a new frame.** As the family member's thinking is expressed, you can begin to alter its meaning by making minor changes in her frameworks and interpretations. Express to her some potential alternate interpretations or frames that fit the situation but sidestep the personalized or exaggerated

meanings she has attributed. Create frames that will allow her to increase self-control. These frames provide the foundation for engaging the family member in problem solving or using the spheres of control.

---

## CASE EXAMPLE

A family practitioner is meeting with a grandmother who lives with her two teenage daughters and one of their children. Child Protective Services (CPS) is involved with the family and has just threatened to remove the grandchild because the grandmother and the child's mother have been fighting with each other. The grandmother is very irate; continually focusing on how the CPS practitioner is uncaring, she cannot think effectively. The grandmother makes use of numerous swear words and angry statements as she describes the exchange with the CPS practitioner. The family practitioner listens to the grandmother and validates her feelings: "It is difficult when people with a lot of power don't understand what is happening in the family and start threatening you." The grandmother agrees. The practitioner then explores the feelings that the grandmother is experiencing underneath the anger. Eventually, they identify the feeling of powerlessness. The practitioner then starts exploring the sense of powerlessness in the grandmother as she explains that she is trying hard to raise her daughters and grandchild, but the adolescents are often disrespectful and unruly. She elevates her emotion again as she speaks of getting no support from the professionals who should be helping her. The practitioner then reflects, "It seems that you are working as hard as you can and desperately need someone on your side, but don't know how to get them to support you." The grandmother nods and asks, "How can I get her (CPS practitioner) to see my side?" The practitioner then starts exploring how the grandmother is trying to engage supports and suggests some new options that may be more effective.

---

Notice in this example that the grandmother first enters the session feeling very angry and maintains an externalized focus. When her perspective is validated, some of the externalization and anger allow the practitioner to focus on the feelings underneath. After the underlying feeling is identified, a new definition of the problem is developed. This new definition allows the grandmother to move into problem solving.

*Stages of Problem Solving*   There is general consensus that problem solving occurs over a series of stages. Some argue that there are as few as two stages (Polanyi, 1957); others have identified up to 14 (Ives, 1977–1978). The most common model involves five problem-solving stages that have been around since the turn of the last century.

Because we discussed these stages at length in Chapter 10, they are summarized for application in this chapter. The five stages of problem solving are as follows:

1. Define the problem.
2. Generate options or potential solutions.
3. Consider each option.
4. Develop a plan.
5. Evaluate the outcome.

Each stage involves common challenges. Frequently, multiproblem families, due to their adaptive challenges, have not inherited effective models of problem solving. Consequently, you will likely have to help the family members sidestep these challenges and develop new skills in problem solving. Next we briefly consider some common problem-solving challenges.

1. **Defining the problem.** Coming up with a single definition of the problem is sometimes a struggle. In many situations, more than one problem is being debated. For example, a family member may be upset because he feels disrespected while the practitioner is focusing on noncompliance with program requirements. In such situations no problem solving can occur, because you and he are not approaching the same problem. You will often have to help separate the different problems so that they can be tackled one at a time. In coaching family members, you are frequently debriefing situations and asking many questions to get at the family members' definition of the problem. If another person involved in the problem situation is present, you can engage the two people in a parallel process; if more than one problem exists, you can acknowledge this fact and help people set one problem aside so that they can solve each problem separately.

2. **Generating options.** The biggest challenge to generating options is staying with the generation processes. People tend to grab a quick solution and immediately try to implement it. If more than one person is involved, each person may select a different option; a power struggle then ensues as each person advocates for his or her chosen solution. When generating options it is best to identify several options that might work. In working with problem-solving skills, you may have to persist in identifying more options because people will tend to cut this process short. They may also shoot down options as you suggest them. Practitioners often need to block their clients' tendency to criticize options during this stage and promote the idea of generating a list of several choices. Sometimes the best solutions come out only after the most obvious options have been listed.

3. **Considering options.** If you have successfully generated a strong list of options, this stage should present few challenges. Basically, during this stage you and your client will explore each option to determine what will be required if the option is chosen. You may also need to help him identify potential consequences associated with the option. For example, cursing out a practitioner is always an option; however, what might happen next time he wants to ask the practitioner for special considerations? By the end of this

stage, you and he will have explored each option and listed its outcomes and requirements.

4. **Developing a plan.** Based on the discussion in the preceding stage, the family member will have identified options that are more and less desirable. At this time, you will help him to cross out options that he does not want to pursue. Let this be his choice, because he may want to keep some fallback options. After crossing out the undesirable options, he can observe his current options and decide how he wants to proceed. The biggest challenge for practitioners at this stage is to allow the family member to make his own decisions and avoid prompting him toward practitioner-endorsed choices.

5. **Evaluating the outcomes.** As the family member finishes the problem-solving task, it is worth exploring what should be different if the solutions work. This allows him to consider possible contingencies and adjust the plan. This stage is important because many aspects of the situation are outside of the family's control. Sometimes a plan B may be needed to address contingencies.

---

### CASE EXAMPLE

This example is a continuation of the preceding case. In the same session, the family practitioner and grandmother are starting into problem solving. When the grandmother accepts the new definition of the problem, they begin to explore options. In the case situation, the family practitioner helps the grandmother to identify several options for engaging the CPS practitioner as a support. Some of the options include having the grandmother (a) complain to a supervisor, (b) ask for a new practitioner, (c) phone the practitioner to calmly explain her position (combined with apologizing for swearing at the practitioner), and (d) write the practitioner a letter. After exploring each option, the grandmother decides to phone the practitioner. The family practitioner and grandmother then spend some time planning the conversation and discussing what should be different if the option is working.

---

*Spheres of Control*   A final useful framework when supporting families is referred to as *spheres of control*. Although we explored this framework in Chapter 11 on changing processing systems, we will briefly discuss it here to consider its application with high-risk and multiproblem families. Like the problem-solving technique, the spheres of control can be used to help families debrief or understand a situation. In your family practice, you will tend to adopt a coaching type of role while guiding the family in applying the framework.

When using this framework, you will start at the center, drawing the sphere of control, because it contains everything the family members can control in the situation—what they say, do, think, and feel. It is sometimes good to advise the family members of this limitation, because they often believe that they should have more control than is realistic. You may find it useful to draw this sphere to show family members how small it is (see Figure 14.1). In reviewing Figure 14.1, notice that the circle is deliberately made small; the letters *T, F, S,* and *D* in the circle depict what the family thinks, feels, says, and does.

When you are exploring the sphere of control with family members, it is useful to help them understand that on a good day, they will have control over only these four things. On rotten days, they will lose control of at least one of these parts of their life. Playing with examples of those days can be useful if family members are not prone to taking things personally.

After exploring the sphere of control, you can shift the family's focus to the sphere of no control. For now, this sphere occupies the rest of the page or whiteboard on which you drew the initial sphere; but for impact, you may want to draw a very large circle that encompasses most of the free space outside the sphere of control (see Figure 14.2). Most family members are well acquainted with the reality that much of

**Figure 14.1**   The Sphere of Control

**Figure 14.2**   Imposing the Sphere of No Control

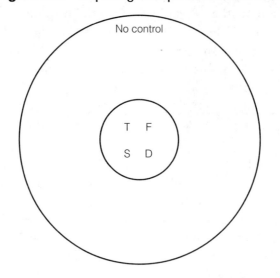

**Figure 14.3**  Including the Sphere of Influence

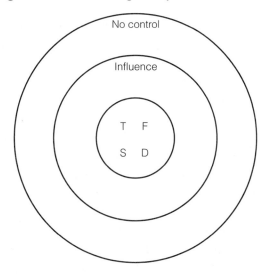

their life is beyond their ability to control, so advising them of this fact will be consistent with their experience. You can then have them look at the situation and identify elements in their current situation that fit into the sphere of no control.

After the family members have identified aspects of the situation that are outside of their control, you can introduce the sphere of influence. Draw this circle inside the sphere of no control, around the sphere of control (see Figure 14.3). After drawing this sphere, help the family members identify how their actions and statements can create some influence over people and events in the current situation that are currently outside of their control. Again, this is a good time to use examples of how the family members have influenced outcomes in the past. As they identify strategies for influencing aspects of the situation, the work becomes very similar to generating options during problem solving. You can then take the family members' ideas for influence and begin to build a plan for resolving the family situation.

---

### CASE EXAMPLE

In the case of the grandmother explored earlier, the spheres of control framework could be used. By first identifying elements of the situation that she can control, the grandmother will focus on the things that she says, does, thinks, and feels. She will then recognize that the CPS practitioner is outside of her control. This frame can help the grandmother see that she cannot control the practitioner's responses. The grandmother will then use the sphere of influence to identify how she is currently influencing the CPS practitioner and explore different options for influencing the practitioner (similar to stage 2 of problem solving).

---

## ◆ EXERCISE 14.1   SUPPORT FUNCTIONS

You are employed in a child and family therapy agency and are working with a three-generational family involving Kenyata (mother and grandmother), Magena (15-year-old daughter), and Danielle (Magena's two-year-old daughter). The family referred themselves due to frequent arguments that have escalated into physical confrontations between Magena and her mother. Child Protective Services (CPS) is involved with the family and has been threatening to take the toddler out of the home because of the fighting. The family moved to town about three years ago, after Magena's father died of cancer. Reportedly, she was alone in the room with him at the time of his death. The family lives in subsidized housing because there is currently no work in Kenyata's field. She is consequently receiving assistance. Last December, Magena's older sister also died of cancer.

When Kenyata phoned to refer the family for treatment, it was after a severe verbal fight during which Magena had yelled, "Well, I may as well kill myself then!" When the intake worker heard of this threat, she immediately booked the family for a crisis session. During the crisis session, it was reported that Magena was not eating well. Based on the lack of eating and potential for suicide, the intake worker arranged for Magena to be brought into the psychiatric unit for observation. While in the unit, Magena was angry and reportedly attacked a social worker when she informed Magena that she would need to go to an out-of-town hospital for the eating disorder assessment.

You are the family's full-time family worker. The case is new, and you are meeting with the family for the fifth time. When the family enters the office, both Kenyata and Magena are very angry; Jodee (the CPS worker) has threatened to take the baby away because Magena is not following the plan to attend school. The family reports that they swore at Jodee and stormed out, stating that they needed to meet with you. When they first enter your office, the two women are very loud and angry. Kenyata states, "Jodee has no right to try to take Danielle. She is such a bitch. I can't believe she has the nerve to even try. We sure told her, though!"

1. You need to de-escalate the family and move them toward problem solving. Begin with a statement that will encourage the exploration.


2. Your question yields the following information.

*KENYATA:* She just wants to get her own way. That's what she wants.

*THERAPIST:* So it feels like she is trying to control you.

*KENYATA:* Damn right. You don't pull a kid just because the mother isn't going to school.

*THERAPIST:* She told you that is why she was thinking of taking Danielle.

*MAGENA:* I haven't been feeling well, and I am so far behind now because they stuck me in the hospital.

*KENYATA:* She said that we weren't following the plan so she can't attest to Danielle's safety.

*THERAPIST:* So is she planning to take you to court?

*KENYATA:* She said she was going to.

*THERAPIST:* What did the judge say when you went to court last time?

*KENYATA:* He said she didn't have enough to take Danielle.

*THERAPIST:* What would need to be present for her to have enough to take Danielle?

*KENYATA:* There would have to be violence.

*MAGENA:* We haven't been fighting at all lately. There is no violence.

*THERAPIST:* So what do you think Jodee might say?

*KENYATA:* She could lie about us and say there was violence.

*THERAPIST:* So you feel pretty powerless and vulnerable when it comes to her.

*KENYATA:* Damn right. She is a witch.

3. You notice that the family members are always on the edge of escalating their anger, so you want to validate some aspects of their perspective. Make a statement to the family members that can validate some element of their experience.

   a. First, make a statement to validate Kenyata's experience.

   b. Now, make a statement to validate Magena's experience.

4. Now identify a new (reframed) understanding of the situation that can build on the validation but shift some of the emotion of meaning.

5. Based on the reframing, what would be a new definition of the problem occurring between the family and Jodee?

6. What elements of the situation are clearly outside of Kenyata and Magena's control?

7. What elements of the situation are within their sphere of control?

8. What elements of the situation are within their sphere of influence?

## Case Advocacy

The second function involved in helping families who are involved with multiple service systems is case advocacy. The need for such advocacy emerges when collaboration and support efforts fail to yield family–service system relationships that can help the family (Ezell, 2001). Sometimes service systems are reticent to provide services for families due to issues of poor fit or agency protocols that block an effective referral. In such situations, the collaborative and supportive role, with its assumptions that everyone is working together on behalf of the family, loses effectiveness. In these situations, the family practitioner often must apply pressure to other practitioners, agencies, or systems to ensure that they become responsive to the family. This application of pressure for a single family is referred to as *case advocacy* (Ezell, 2001; Schneider & Lester, 2001).

Case advocacy is a critical function when the family practitioner must respond to issues of service denial, respectful treatment, or unethical practitioner behavior. A critical difference between the support and advocate roles is a shift in focus from family needs to family rights. The shift to a rights-related focus allows the practitioner to be more direct and confrontational. Such approaches are often a last resort because they may erode a collaborative relationship. When collaboration has not worked, the priority of achieving reasonable scrutiny and judgment replaces the need for collaboration.

The shift in priority from collaboration to advocacy requires practitioners to move beyond the front-line relationships, because scrutiny occurs at the higher levels of the chain of command. Consequently, practitioners seek to access and bring scrutiny from people in positions of power (Ezell, 2001). Typically, you will start one position above the position at which the problem appears to exist and continue to bring scrutiny until the family's rights are honored. If the problem starts with a front-line practitioner, your advocacy will likely begin with that person's supervisor; but it may proceed through itinerant rights offices and directors, and it may eventually engage funding sources or external advocates depending on the outcomes at each level.

Often when advocating a case, you will use grievance or appeal procedures to trigger the scrutiny from higher levels within the organization. Almost every agency or service that receives state or federal funding will have an appeals procedure. Typically you will, step-by-step, exhaust all internal avenues of appeal before going outside the organization. Although it is possible to go outside the organization immediately, doing so often breeds resentment that can interfere with later collaboration on other cases. Once outside the organizational structure, you can focus on advocacy groups (e.g., juvenile rights attorneys, ombudsman offices), funding sources, or news media to bring the required scrutiny.

When you advocate on behalf of a family, tension will increase in the service system. Tension increases for several reasons:

◆ Tension escalates whenever someone identifies a problem and puts it on the table to be addressed.
◆ Tension escalates when one professional disagrees with the decisions or positions of another professional.
◆ Tension escalates whenever a concern is raised to the level of a person's supervisors or superiors in an organization.
◆ Tension escalates whenever someone is being held accountable for errors in judgment or misguided action.
◆ Tension escalates when a person's professional conduct is called into public scrutiny.
◆ Tension escalates when issues of ethical conduct are raised with professionals and service providers.

Although each professional individual action just listed will create tension, in advocacy situations you will often engage in more than one advocacy behavior. You should consequently expect tension to occur at least between yourself and the other practitioner(s) involved in the situation. Because tension may lead to scrutiny of you as well as the others involved in the situation, bear in mind these five cautions when acting as an advocate:

1. **Keep client rights the focal issue.** Make sure to build all of your arguments on the organizational mandates and associated rights. If you vary too much from the family's rights and organizational obligations, you may come across as a malcontent.

2. **Create a documentation trail.** Try to use e-mail, letters, and faxes as much as possible because you can use them to start a documentation file. Having paper trails tends to force a response because you can use them to hold people accountable for their actions—or lack of action. A paper trail also protects you because it documents what you have said and how you have said it.

3. **Maintain a rational focus.** As tension increases, people sometimes become less rational. Be sure to remain calm and focused. Lapses into anger can undermine your credibility and allow people to dismiss the family's rights and legitimate concerns.

4. **Support client self-empowerment.** Encourage the family members to take as much action as they can handle. With disempowered families, this ability will vary greatly. However, keep the family members as involved as possible. If the family is not visible at some level, people may suggest that this is your issue rather than the family's.

5. **Maximize the potential for success.** It is noble to go for ideal solutions, but remember that a fallback position may be necessary. Work with the family members to identify more than one acceptable outcome. You may also want to keep the organizational realities in mind when pushing for solutions, so that you can tailor your advocacy toward resolutions you know the organization can deliver.

When you are functioning as a case advocate, it is helpful to have support people. When tension is high, your support systems can provide an outlet for emotions and help you to maintain perspective. Ideally, the support system will include supervisors and other professionals in your agency. However, sometimes family practitioners must select support people from outside of the service system. In such situations, it is important to disguise information and events to protect the identity of the family members and professionals involved in the situation.

## CASE EXAMPLE

A teen mother and her infant have just left foster care (against the desires of their caseworker). They approach a family practitioner in the children's mental health agency for help. When exploring the family situation, the practitioner discovers that the family has no food stamps or medical insurance, because the social service agency has redirected benefits based on the mother being in care. Further exploration indicates that even though the infant was still in the young mother's care while in foster care, all benefits had been shifted to CPS. The family practitioner helps the mother call her assistance worker to ask for things to be changed immediately, but the other professional states that it will be at least three months before changes can be made. In response, the family practitioner works with the mother to draft a letter to the supervisor at the family assistance agency. The letter outlines that the infant has never been out of the mother's care and asks for special dispensation to restore benefits. The supervisor responds to the family practitioner and arranges for an alternate system of meeting the family's needs while the benefits are being redressed.

---

### ◆ EXERCISE 14.2   CASE ADVOCACY

Continuing the previous case example, Kenyata (mother and grandmother) and Magena (teenage mother) have continued to have difficulty with Jodee (CPS worker). Magena is forced into foster care because Jodee says that she will take them to court and have Danielle (two years old) removed if they do not comply. Magena consequently agrees to enter care with Danielle and is placed in a foster home in another county. The foster care agency is contracted with CPS, but is independent of the CPS system. It has a separate management system and board of directors. Magena is upset because she cannot see her mother or her friends. She also states that people at the foster home have been listening in on her phone conversations, looking through her belongings, and watering down Danielle's formula. She states that she has told Jodee about these problems, but nothing has been done. When Kenyata phones Jodee, Jodee says that the foster home is a good home. Jodee adds that if Kenyata and Magena continue to slander the foster parents, she will probably have to place Magena and Danielle in different homes. Kenyata is asking for your advice on how to get Jodee to respond.

1. First, identify the client rights that are being violated by the foster parents.

2. Identify the client rights being violated by Jodee.

3. Given the rights that are being violated, identify people (roles) inside the CPS system whom Kenyata could approach about the violations.

4. Identify people (roles) in the foster care system who could help Kenyata resolve her complaints.

5. Knowing the systems in your area, what external bodies are available for monitoring such problems and ensuring the system is accountable?

6. How would you help Kenyata and Magena advocate against the system? Begin by helping them to frame the problem (rights), and then outline a strategy that can empower them in the situation.

## Class Advocacy

The third function involved in helping families engaged with multiple service systems is class advocacy. The use of the word *class* may be confusing due to its legalistic background. In this context, *class advocacy* indicates that the practitioner is advocating on behalf of a group (or class) of families whose rights are not being adequately served (Ezell, 2001; Schneider & Lester, 2001). In its most legalistic form, class advocacy can include class action suits. Only lawyers can carry out such actions. Family practitioners tend to perform less formal acts of class advocacy.

Many family practitioners shy away from class advocacy and leave it up to lawyers, macro social workers, and other policy-oriented professionals. Practitioners often feel that it is not their job, or that they do not have enough influence to make a difference. This view is unfortunate, because front-line practitioners are the first people to be aware of unmet needs and practitioner violations. On the front line, the practitioner is confronted with service gaps, partially fulfilled mandates, and agencies creating the illusion of service rather than actually attending to the rights and needs of clients. Most practitioners want to be able to influence these situations, but feel that the system will not be responsive.

When important issues do rise to the level of decision makers, it is usually because front-line practitioners have been talking about the issues for a long time. Very few service gaps are addressed without first being identified by practitioners at the front-line level. It seems that the service system has two realities. First is the reality of front-line practitioners, who must deal with the gaps and inconsistencies of service delivery. In this reality, practitioners feel disempowered and helpless as they try to make the system more responsive to clients. The second reality is that of administrators and policy developers, who have power to make a difference but often lack good information about what is happening on the client level. Because of the two realities, it takes a very long time for client needs to drift up to the level of administrators and policy makers.

Class advocacy is the method that effectively transmits information from the front-line levels of service to the decision-making levels. Class advocacy systematically gathers information, builds consensus about what is needed, compares client realities to policy intents, and promotes change for clients (Ezell, 2001; Schneider & Lester, 2001). Class advocacy involves four stages, and front-line practitioners can be involved in each of them.

1. **Identify the issue.** Class advocacy begins when a front-line practitioner, in partnership with a client, identifies that services are not adequately meeting the needs or rights of clients. This awareness usually begins with a single client, but through observation and discussion with other practitioners and clients, it becomes evident that a gap exists for several clients who have something in common. The common bond may be based on ability (such as developmental or mental disabilities), age, culture, race, sex, or other identifiers forming a group that is not being adequately served.

2. **Build critical consensus.** After becoming aware that some need or right is being violated within the system, the practitioner needs to explore how widespread the problem is. This usually involves talking to other clients, family members, practitioners, community partners, and agency personnel to determine whether others have noticed this need. As she talks about the problem, the practitioner attempts to engage people at each level of the service system, so that a diverse group of people can promote the necessary

**Figure 14.4** Movement Toward Consensus

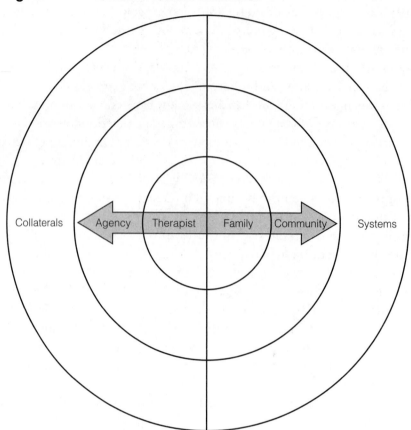

change. The pattern of seeking consensus and support tends to fan out from the practitioner and client levels to involve increasing numbers of people (see Figure 14.4).

3. **Involve administration.** After a need, violation, or gap is identified and ratified by other people, the practitioner is obligated to raise the concerns to agency or system administration. Meetings, documentation, and the chain of command within the agency all provide mechanisms for getting good information transmitted to upper management. The practitioner must be strategic about which managers become involved in the advocacy. Typically, she will want to begin one level above where the problem is occurring. For example, if problems are occurring in how practitioners are interpreting a policy, advocacy is likely to begin at the supervisory level. The practitioner may want to book a group meeting with the manager so concerns can be discussed from multiple perspectives. The practitioner should not be surprised if the manager includes other people at the administrative levels. She must plan for this and make sure the numbers are fairly equal. Here are five principles for advocating at this level:

◆ Keep a paper trail.

◆ Always send copies to management at the next highest levels.

- Keep client rights central in the discussions.
- Try to focus on solving the issue rather than blaming people.
- Involve groups of diverse people as much as possible.

Ideally, advocacy at this level involves partnering with management to plan for new ways to meet the emerging need. This goal can often be accomplished when class advocacy is with one's agency. This ideal, however, is not always the case. Sometimes management is not open to identifying problems. This can be uncomfortable when the family practitioner is advocating against her own agency. In such situations, it is helpful to involve people from other agencies so they can be more visibly active. The practitioner can then appear to be brokering feedback and concerns that exist in the community.

4. **Broaden the level of attention.** It is frequently useful to go beyond the immediate agency involved in the advocacy effort to ensure that solutions are attentive to multiple perspectives. Other agencies often need input into the solutions and can be powerful partners in pushing for change. Professional groups, advocacy organizations, funders, and other groups also can help identify options and monitor for the adequacy of change. Here are some of the potential partners in change:

   - **Other agencies and services.** Many agencies have a stake in the outcome. Try to involve coordinating bodies, collateral agencies, and other organizations that are frequently in partnership with the service.
   - **Media.** The practitioner can involve newspapers, television, and radio media in covering the issue or the solutions. This does not have to be a negative or investigative involvement. The media can become involved in covering the issue (e.g., lack of services for addicted youth). Reporters will typically approach agency management for comment on the issue.
   - **Funding sources.** Funding bodies have a stake in ensuring that the money they are providing is meeting the spirit of their agreements with community agencies. They are always interested in gaps and wrinkles in how services are delivered, and they can sometimes help develop resources and programs to resolve the needs. If agencies are underserving their populations, funding bodies can also enforce accountability.
   - **Government agencies.** Government agencies such as the Children's Bureau at the Department of Health and Human Services (http://www.acf.hhs.gov/programs/cb/) or their funded centers, such as the Center for Youth Services (http://www.nrcys.ou.edu/), can provide support through advice and connections to funding sources or bodies that can help elevate the need to higher levels. These bodies are funded to help communities ensure adequate services for specific populations. The centers can also provide training and expert commentary. The practitioner can highlight scrutiny by engaging center staff to provide community training on a specific issue with multiple community partners and invite the media to cover the community training.

- ♦ **Advocacy groups.** There are often advocacy groups such as the ombudsman's office, juvenile rights projects, or other bodies with the sole purpose of protecting youth rights. Such groups can be involved in advocacy efforts. Such groups are very effective because they are aware of the policies and rights at a more sophisticated level than that of front-line staff. When an advocacy group's expertise in rights is combined with staff expertise on client needs, a strong advocacy effort can be mounted.
- ♦ **Politicians.** Sometimes people holding political office can be engaged in an advocacy effort. Many politicians have a fondness for certain populations or issues and are willing to take a public stand. Politicians can also be instrumental in arranging for funding for projects or services. The practitioner may want to research the interests and positions of the different political representatives in the community.

It takes a long time to build an effective class advocacy effort, so do not be dismayed if movement is slow. Every time a new person is engaged in the effort, it takes time for them to build passion for the issue. Be patient, and remember that it took awhile for the issue to emerge as important at the front line. Everybody needs time to arrive at his or her own decision.

Just as case advocacy creates tension, class advocacy can become very tense because the practitioner is often highlighting how current services are failing to meet their mandates. Such information may not be welcomed by the leaders of the social service organizations involved. Organizational leaders can be very powerful, and you must be careful of backlashes and defensive counterattacks. Tension will also emerge because you often must engage diverse allies in the effort. The diversity will yield multiple perspectives and make it difficult to generate unified action. The following four elements supplement the suggestions for case advocacy to help survive the stresses and strains of class advocacy.

1. **Work with a diverse group of advocates.** Include clients, family members, and practitioners from your own and other agencies. Different people can use different strategies. This helps spread out the stress, avoid personal vulnerability, and share the work.
2. **Maintain the client rights focus.** Nobody can attack a practitioner for promoting services that clients have a right to expect. Even if feathers get ruffled, most people involved will agree on client rights issues. Remain calmly grounded in the issue of client rights so you can avoid regressions into personal attacks and accusations.
3. **Maintain documentation.** Ensure that decisions, actions, and outcomes are documented. Scrutiny increases at each level of the advocacy effort, and tension may increase with each level of scrutiny, so you can expect to defend your advocacy position. Documentation helps to protect advocates against counterattacks if tension escalates.
4. **Use a support network.** Make sure that you have people open to discussing the situation who can provide advice, information, appraisal, and emotional support. If tension escalates, you will need a safe place to vent. This is

important given that you must remain calm when engaged in the actual advocacy efforts.

---

## CASE EXAMPLE

Three families who are living in a rural county have developmentally disabled children. Recently, the parents of the three families approached Angelica, a local practitioner because they are concerned that a government-funded integrated preschool in the center of the county is being closed. The government supervisor states that the new plan is to bus the children to a larger center for day programming. The parents are concerned that their preschool children, all of whom have severe disabilities, are going to be on a bus with regular schoolchildren for up to two hours per day. Angelica meets with the parents and township politicians (administrators of the preschool program) to identify the issues. The parents work with the practitioner to identify other parents and other stakeholders (administrators, workers, politicians) who are willing to take a stand. The group contacts the government supervisor to arrange a town hall meeting with the supervisor and local government officials. Angelica helps the parents identify media personalities who would be interested in covering the story. The meeting is tense and involves the parents and other local people challenging the decision. The government supervisor maintains his position and states that the government is funding the program and needs to curtail expenses. The press is critical of the government for its position and starts public scrutiny of the developments. The parents know of a politician in the neighboring county who has a disabled sister. They contact the politician, who agrees to challenge the minister of social services during a question-and-answer period in the legislature. This questioning leads to heated phone calls to the local government offices. Eventually, two integrated daycare centers are developed in the rural areas of the county, leading to an exemplary program. This whole process took about 10 months and resulted in high levels of scrutiny for the practitioner. The government officials contacted Angelica's executive director and other agency directors, criticizing her and casting dispersions on her agenda. Fortunately, Angelica kept the client issues central and engaged the parents in many of the advocacy tasks.

---

## ◆ EXERCISE 14.3   CLASS ADVOCACY

Continuing the previous case, you have been talking with other family practitioners about Magena's situation and have found that there are no resources for teen parents in your community. Many of them have to drop out of school because no day-care spaces are available. Because there are also service gaps around helping them with parenting skills, most teenage mothers must live either isolated in the community or with their parents. In almost every teen parent case, there have been problems with school and ensuring adequate supports. You believe you have identified an unmet need in your community and want to promote some additional services (or ways of serving) for teen parents.

1. First, you decide to build some consensus around the issue by having a brief meeting of other professionals. Identify some important professionals to invite to the meeting.

2. After the professional meeting, it was suggested that consumers should be involved. How will you accomplish this?

3. The consensus among the professionals and the consumers is that the young women need some supports to be able to complete their education. They also need some less formal supports for sharing parenting ideas and discussing their situation. Knowing your community and the services available, identify some critical administrators to involve in the planning.

4. To increase the community scrutiny of the issue, what additional resources might you involve so more people could support the initiative?

## Summary

It is easy to identify the difficult balancing act involved when working with multi-problem families when multiple services are involved. Family-focused practitioners must attend to these multiple needs and perspectives to ensure that the needs of all family members can be met by the array of services. The family practitioner must also ensure that the integrity of the family boundaries is maintained. These tasks are not always easy and require the practitioner to assume roles to supplement the clinical roles explored in the early chapters of this text.

Some practitioners will feel awkward when assuming the new roles and may interpret the new functions as a burden or unworthy of a clinician. This is a natural reaction to the imposition of new and difficult expectations. In most situations, however, it is the family practitioner who is best suited to assuming these roles. In many situations other professionals have more limited mandates and perspectives. This allows them to focus on individuals rather than the full family functioning. Family practitioners are less prone to this kind of individualistic thinking and are better suited for attending to the multiple perspectives. The strong clinical skills that help the family practitioner negotiate with the family members are vital to negotiating with multiple professionals.

Family practitioners must be prepared to support families in many areas of functioning, including advocating for the family's rights. To refrain from performing advocacy functions while a family's rights are being violated is a disservice to the family and indirectly supports the rights violations. With multiproblem and high-risk families, rights violations are more common because the service systems are not designed to provide effective service for this type of family. As a family practitioner, you cannot escape these new family practice roles when working with such challenging case situations.

## Critical Content

1. In working with multiple services, the family practitioner must adopt new roles. These include support and advocacy roles.

2. The supportive role requires the practitioner to negotiate how his role overlaps and dovetails with those of other professionals.
3. The supportive role requires the practitioner to help family members more effectively deal with the other service providers, including helping them de-escalate and solve problems in the service system.
4. The case advocacy role requires the practitioner to take a stand when other service systems are not responding to family needs.
5. The class advocacy function requires the family practitioner to address service gaps and problems that affect multiple families.

## Suggested Readings

Henggeler, S. W., Melton, G. B., & Smith, L. A. (1992). Family preservation using multisystemic therapy: An effective alternative to incarcerating serious juvenile offenders. *Journal of Consulting & Clinical Psychology, 60,* 953–961.

Smith, J. M. (2000). Psychotherapy with people stressed by poverty. In A. Sabo & L. Havens (Eds.), *The real world guide to psychotherapy practice* (pp. 71–92). Cambridge, MA: Harvard University Press.

Suarez, K., Smokowski, P., & Wodarski, J. S. (1996). The process of intervention with multiproblem families: Theoretical and practice guidelines. *Family Therapy, 23,* 117–144.

Ziemba, S. J. (2001). Therapy with families in poverty: Application of feminist family therapy principles. *Journal of Feminist Family Therapy, 12,* 205–237.

## Chapter 15

# Support-Focused Intervention

In the first two chapters of Section V, we explored the challenges associated with high-risk and multiproblem families and practitioner skills associated with multiple agency work. In Chapter 13 we identified group work, in-home work, and multiple-systems work as promising interventions. In Chapter 14 we explored practitioner skills associated with multiagency work. In this chapter, we will expand on the previous discussions by exploring important skills and strategies for engaging informal support people.

## Theoretical Grounding

This final chapter in the textbook is an exploration of support-based interventions that build on ecosystemic thinking. As in Chapter 14, in this chapter we focus on the supports that can be established to help multiproblem families achieve equilibrium in their environment. Table 15.1 presents some chapter concepts, theoretical models, and possible sources for of additional information. Here are the texts recommended for additional reading:

- ◆ *Child Welfare and Family Services: Policies and Practice* (7th ed.), by S. Whitelaw Downs, E. Moore, E. J. McFadden, S. Michaud, & L. B. Costin, 2004, Boston: Allyn & Bacon.
- ◆ *Family Practice—Brief Systems Methods for Social Work* (1st ed.), by C. Franklin & C. Jordan, 1999, Pacific Grove, CA: Brooks/Cole.

**TABLE 15.1**
**Chapter Concepts, Theoretical Models, and Sources**

| Chapter Concepts | Theoretical Models | Recommended Reading |
|---|---|---|
| Many informal supports are available through cultural, kin, and community systems. | Ecological systems model | Franklin & Jordan, Chapters 6, 10<br>Janzen & Harris, Chapter 10<br>Kilpatrick & Holland, Chapter 13 |
| Working in the family home and environment is often more effective with multiproblem families. | Ecological systems model | Franklin & Jordan, Chapter 8<br>Janzen & Harris, Chapters 8, 10, 12<br>Kilpatrick & Holland, Chapters 2, 13<br>Whitelaw Downs et al., Chapter 8 |
| Multiple family groups and support groups can be effective in helping multiproblem families. | Ecological systems model | Kilpatrick & Holland, Chapter 5 |

◆ *Family Treatment in Social Work Practice,* by C. Janzen & O. Harris, 1997, Pacific Grove, CA: Brooks/Cole.

◆ *Working With Families: An Integrative Model by Level of Need* (3rd ed.), by A. C. Kilpatrick & T. P. Holland, 2003, Boston: Allyn & Bacon.

# Support-Based Interventions

Promising interventions such as group work, wraparound services, and family conferencing and decision making all seek to engage natural helpers who can provide support to the family. This approach to family service is quite different from office-based clinical practice because the practitioner begins to work less as a clinician and more as a facilitator of aid. Practitioners must develop new skills because therapy is delivered through a network of relationships rather than directly with the family. In this chapter we explore some of the critical skills associated with this type of work.

# Principles for Intervention

In support-focused intervention with multiproblem and high-risk families, there are three guiding principles. These principles are based on the clinical and research findings on working with such families:

1. Maintain a family focus.
2. Maximize support and mutual aid.
3. Avoid traditional interventions.

## Maintaining a Family Focus

In your work with high-risk and multiproblem families, it is important to avoid an individual focus. Although one person in the family may appear to be central to the problem behavior (e.g., an addicted parent), all family members adapt to the individual. To ensure comprehensive treatment of such families, you must consider not only the individual but also the adaptations of the family (Brown, 1993; Kendall & Grove, 1988). As you work with parents to alter negative or unresponsive behaviors, the children often may act out, setting the stage for coercive cycles (Gara, Rosenberg, & Herzog, 1996; Lyons-Ruth, 1996).

Intervention with high-risk parents normally focuses on listening to the parental story, highlighting behavior and interaction patterns, restructuring cognitive processes, building skills, and coaching in alternate behavior (George, 1996). When working with children, you will seek to promote positive self-concepts while promoting respect for limits and rights of others. Self-concept is slower to change, because it is built through experience. This means that intervention must build experiences of success for the parent and child.

Maintaining a family focus is sometimes difficult. The first challenge is typically the nature of individual problems in the family. When one family member is abusive or engages in irresponsible behavior, it is tempting for the practitioner to revert to individual thinking. The second challenge is accessing both parents and children for intervention (Bogenschneider, 1996). If the parent has learning problems or disabilities or is living in a disadvantaged circumstance, the challenge intensifies because such conditions inhibit generalization of treatment effects (Dohrenwend & Dohrenwend, 1981; Eron & Peterson, 1982; Gibbs, 1984; Lorion, 1973; Lorion & Felner, 1986; Ross, Mirowsky, & Cockerham, 1985).

## Maximizing Support and Mutual Aid

Social support is critical for both the child and the parent. At the child level, research finds that children who have supportive relationships with alternate figures exhibit less emotional and psychological harm than nonsupported children do (Grizenko & Pawliuk, 1994). Adults who experienced support are also more able to break the intergenerational transmission of violence (Amato, 1986; Dubow & Tisak, 1989; Egeland, Jacobvitz, & Srouge, 1988; Farrington, Gallagher, Morley, St. Ledger, & West, 1988; Grizenko & Pawliuk, 1994; Gullette, 1987; Koestner, Franz, & Weinberger, 1990; Lackey & Williams, 1995; Litty, Kowalski, & Minor, 1996; Milich & Landau, 1984).

At the parent level, the parent's mental health is directly and positively related to the level of support she receives (Barratt, Roach, Morgan, & Colbert, 1996). Research has consistently found that parents at risk of abusing their children tend to have kin-dominated, but unsupportive, social support systems (Lacharite, Ethier, & Couture, 1995; Spoth & Redmond, 1996; Tracy, 1990). In outcome studies, social support interacts with personality to predict success (Krantz & Moos, 1988). Lack of social support is also correlated with child psychopathology and child maltreatment (Dumas & Wahler, 1983; Maluccio, 1989; Seagull, 1987; Tracy, 1990; Wahler, 1980; Wolfe, 1987; Zuravin, 1989).

## Avoiding Traditional Responses

Many practitioners turn to office-based family casework and psychoeducational groups as an approach of first resort when working with high-risk families. Case managers typically promote parent skills training and counseling as soon as high-risk families enter service. This approach usually involves referrals to multiple traditional services. Unfortunately, the traditional approaches are often ineffective (Rothery & Cameron, 1985). In addition, the use of multiple services tends to fragment the family and result in more confusion than assistance.

There are promising nontraditional interventions that can maintain a family focus while maximizing mutual aid and support. In the following section we explore the use of group work, in-home work, and community-based programming. These intervention strategies appear most promising when working with high-risk and multiproblem families.

# Using Group Work Methods

Group programming can provide effective intervention with adults and children from high-risk and multiproblem families. Many researchers recommend group work for children because they often respond better to peers than to adults (Fantuzzo et al., 1988). Concurrently, children in high-risk homes often develop social problems. Such problems can be effectively addressed through group intervention (Graziano & Mills, 1992). Group programming can help children to increase self-control, responsibility, self-esteem, cognitive organization, and nonaggressive problem solving (Graziano & Mills, 1992). Such programming is effective even with young children (Cicchetti, Toth, & Hennessy, 1991; Crittenden, 1989; Culp, Little, Letts, & Lawrence, 1991; Jason, DeAmicus, & Carter, 1978).

Table 15.2 contains a list of skills frequently developed through group programs. Feedback from participants indicates that the ideal group provides not only information but also time for informal sharing around practical issues (Home & Darveau-Fournier, 1990). Other parent feedback suggests that mutual aid and self-direction are important elements of a group program (Acton & During, 1992; Home & Darveau-Fournier, 1990; Lengua, Roosa, Schupak-Neuberg, Michaels, & Berg et al., 1992; Rothery & Cameron, 1985).

When planning a group program, you must consider the focus and membership of the group. Programs with a primary focus on parents are able to decrease the parent's reactivity to child behavior, but have little impact on child behavior problems (Acton & During, 1992; Whipple & Wilson, 1996). Consequently, many recommend that both parents and children be involved in the group program (Bogenschneider, 1996; Graziano & Mills, 1992; Kirchenbaum, 1979; Lengua et al., 1992; Lutzker, 1990; Tremblay, McCord, Boileau, Charlebois, & Gagnon et al., 1991; Whipple & Wilson, 1996). Influencing fathers is also problematic because fathers are more difficult to influence than mothers (Spoth & Redmond, 1996).

Group programs also have pragmatic barriers that prevent families from engaging in the program. The most common barrier is the timing of the program (Spoth &

**T A B L E  15.2**
**Family Skills Training Program Foci**

| Focus | Member | Skill Sets |
|---|---|---|
| Establishing group rapport | Parent | ◆ Accepting parents as a component in treatment |
| | Child | ◆ Establishing rules and systems of working together |
| Developing monitoring skills | Parent | ◆ Increasing attending behaviors, assessing danger, responding to child during check-in |
| | Child | ◆ Checking in with parents |
| Parental leadership | Parent | ◆ Making decisions and withstanding challenges |
| | Child | ◆ Complying with parental decisions, appropriate expression of input |
| Challenging assumptions or models | Parent | ◆ Exploring own attachment and parental models coming from own childhood |
| | Child | ◆ Looking at current family model of functioning |
| Increasing positive interaction | Parent | ◆ Neutralizing negativity, use of positive reinforcement, appropriate use of praise |
| | Child | ◆ Building motivation to respond to positive reinforcers, highlighting strengths |
| Listening and empathic responding | Parent | ◆ Hearing the child without hearing criticism, understanding normal child life |
| | Child | ◆ Identifying and verbalizing feelings, basic social skills |
| Decreasing coercive parenting | Parent | ◆ Developing alternate forms of using power, using alternate discipline strategies |
| | Child | ◆ Avoiding power struggles and escalation of stress |
| Problem solving | Parent | ◆ Model of identification, exploration, and decision making about problems |
| | Child | ◆ Peer problem solving in the group |
| Communication of feelings | Parent | ◆ Identifying and verbalizing feelings |
| | Child | ◆ Identifying and verbalizing feelings |
| Anger control | Parent | ◆ Cognitive restructuring, impulse control |
| | Child | ◆ Aggression options, challenge cognitions |

Note: Adapted from Acton & During, 1992; Barber, 1992; Gaudin, Polansky, Kilpatrick, & Shilton, 1996; Herrera & Sanchez, 1980; Horne, 1974; Lengua et al., 1992; McInnis-Dittrich, 1996; Szykula & Fleischman, 1985; Thomas, 1996; Tolan & McKay, 1996; Tremblay et al., 1991.

Redmond, 1996; Spoth, Redmond, Hockaday, & Chung, 1996; Tolan & McKay, 1996). Often, family members are not able to consistently coordinate their available time with the timing of the program. Additional pragmatic issues include travel, child care, and language barriers (Tolan & McKay, 1996; Spoth et al., 1996). When planning a group program, you must resolve such access issues to prevent inconveniencing parents.

A common family-related barrier is the family's beliefs about the service being provided. Many families have negative relationships with helping organizations. They express confidentiality concerns and tend to minimize the family problems to control their relationship with formal helpers (Spoth & Redmond, 1996; Spoth et al., 1996). Do not expect families to welcome an invitation to join a group. You must find ways of structuring programs so that families feel they will benefit from the program. For example, you might name the group "Surviving Your Adolescent" rather than "Parent Skills Training." Here are four principles worth following when you develop a group for high-risk and multiproblem families:

1. Avoid teaching and promoting complex concepts.
2. Ensure that materials are culturally sensitive.
3. Build discussions from the issues that parents bring to the group.
4. Maximize support and mutual aid among the group members.

Inherent in these four principles is the idea that you must avoid replicating the family members' past educational experiences, in which a professional lectures and tells people what to do. Many high-risk parents are sensitive to judgments and power dynamics with helping professionals. Consequently, the guiding principles promote a group-based, rather than content-based, approach to group programming. This technique requires practitioners to tune into the group members' current situations and help them resolve their immediate concerns. You can wrap content around the issues by inserting information into the group discussions, as long as you avoid assuming expertise regarding the family's problems.

A group-based approach requires you to develop interaction and mutual aid among the parents, children, and/or families in the group. This environment is accomplished by focusing on two dimensions of the group: the structure and the interpersonal processes. The group structure focuses on the activities and direction for the group. The interpersonal processes focus on how the group members interact and support each other. To ensure that the program actively involves the group members in exploring and resolving situations, you must attend to both of these group dimensions.

## Developing the Group Structure

The group structure involves establishing meeting patterns so group members know what to expect when they attend group sessions. If you are seeking to maximize mutual aid and support among group members, avoid assuming too much power or responsibility when establishing these patterns. Provide a structure that allows group members to have influence while still experiencing direction toward goal achievement.

Developing the group structure begins with a consideration of who to include in the group. A first step is to identify some parameters for inclusion. Sometimes you will want to limit the types of problems in a group to family dynamics (e.g., exposure to violence, parenting adolescents); at other times, you may want to broaden group membership. Consider also how the people will interact with and experience other group members. In making these decisions, you will seek to ensure that group members have experiences and desires in common. It is often useful to meet with each group member ahead of time to explore his or her goals and outline the basic expectations of group membership (Hannah, 2000).

After the people have entered the group, you must develop the group structure by guiding the discussion among the members. Three critical tasks are involved:

1. Establishing group goals
2. Establishing group expectations
3. Establishing group decision making

*Establishing Group Goals*   Having goals is a critical feature of a group program. Groups without goals cannot gel; they remain an assembly of individuals rather than a cohesive group. As members come into a group, they are seeking to understand the goals and purpose of the group (Kurland & Salmon, 1998). This becomes the reason for attending and the measuring stick for success. Thus it is important that the goals become central early in the group, so that members can make clear decisions about attending. If people do not see the purpose at the first meeting, they are unlikely to attend or commit to the program. The purpose should have direction but also be flexible, so that the group members can influence the direction as the group progresses (Kurland & Salmon, 1998). The following practitioner activities help to establish the goals and purpose of the group:

1. **Contracting.** Group members need to agree on how they will treat each other in the group. In early group sessions, it is important to discuss how people will act toward each other and treat information. Out of the discussion, agreements should be reached about these issues:
   - *Confidentiality.* Decide whether it is permissible to talk about group members and content with people outside of group. In this discussion, issues of mandatory reporting to Child Protective Services should be discussed so the group knows the limits of the contract.
   - *Responsibility.* Explore how members need to take care of themselves in the group by not sharing information that they don't want other people to know.
   - *Leader role.* Explore with the members how they want the leader to intervene and what the members would like the leader to bring to group (e.g., activities, games, snack). It is also useful to discuss how the leader should intervene with conflict and difficult behavior so the group might be preserved (note that evicting children does not preserve the group and sets up dangerous precedents).

2. **Group agenda setting.** Allowing group members to have input into the focus of the group meetings provides shared ownership and investment in the group. The practitioner actively seeks input into what each session will cover. This task can be accomplished by building on group discussions, summarizing themes at the end of each meeting, and using these themes to identify a focus for the next session. Summarizing and building direction based on group discussions at the end of sessions provides time for planning between meetings. You can then ratify the decision at the beginning of the next meeting to allow for emergent issues to be expressed.

3. **Group structure setting.** Group members should have input into the use of activities in the group. This activity often requires you to present multiple options, so that the group can choose from them.

*Establishing Group Expectations*    Given the variety of people and needs in a group, there are many roles that people can occupy (Zastrow, 1990). Some roles are useful, and some can hinder the work of a group. For people to get the most help out of a group, it is important for them to be able to explore many new roles. Consequently, practitioners have expectations of how people will enter the group and work with others (Hannah, 2000). These practitioner expectations must coincide with and adjust to member expectations to ensure that the group functions well (Steinberg, 1999). It is also important for you to provide parameters that allow members to feel safe. The following practitioner activities help to clarify expectations.

- ◆ **Establish consensual norms.** To ensure group-level agreement, it is helpful to promote consensual agreement when discussing the group rules and expectations. This activity requires full discussions among members. It also requires you to engage group members in responding to deviant or potentially problematic behaviors and interactions. To develop a consensual system, leaders must fight the temptation to have members vote. A vote works against cohesion by creating two groups—one that wins and one that loses.
- ◆ **Appreciate roles.** When members contribute to the group, it is useful to describe what you observe and express appreciation for each member's contribution. Expressions of appreciation validate member contributions and model positive behavior that can eventually establish norms in the group.
- ◆ **Solicit input.** Early in the group, it is important for the leader to survey or solicit input from every member when making a decision. Even nonverbal members can agree or disagree by nodding their heads. This sets the norms for input and begins resolving some of the control questions common to members.

*Establishing Group Decision Making*    Participatory patterns of group decision making are critical for goal accomplishment and comfort in the group (Ramey, 1993; Saulnier, 2003). Anyone who has attended group functions where control shifted from meeting to meeting knows the frustration of not having established patterns. The nature of the pattern is also important. If decision making is in the control of the leader, members will not invest at the same level as when they have significant input. You must engage the group members in making decisions without letting the group lose focus. The following practitioner activities help to establish decision-making patterns in the group.

- ◆ **Defer to the group.** Typically, when issues arise in a group, leaders feel compelled to take responsibility for the solution. However, if the leader fights this impulse and solicits solutions from the group members, interaction can be greatly enhanced. As the group mobilizes to solve issues that arise, members use their skills and strengths in service of the group. This effort creates investment and helps members extend their competence.
- ◆ **Summarize and clarify.** When group decision making and problem solving occur, you often must summarize discussions to help clarify issues for the group. This serves to refocus group energy on the decision or problem.
- ◆ **Ratify decisions.** As a decision is made, sometimes portions of the group appear to be somewhat unsure or may seem lost in the process. At these times, it is important to ask members to affirm their decision so the group can move on. You can accomplish this by first stating the decision that appears to be achieved and then soliciting affirmation from the group members.

## Establishing Interpersonal Processes

The second element of group-focused programming is the interpersonal processes. When working with the interpersonal processes in the group, the practitioner focuses on the nature and patterns of interaction among the group members. Interaction is frequently shallow and guarded early in the group, but a deepening of content occurs over time (Bienstock & Videka-Sherman, 1989). In focusing on interpersonal processes, you will be helping members to form relationships and engage in helpful discussions.

Your primary practitioner task is to get group members talking to each other rather than through you. Group members frequently tend to view the practitioner as a teacher. When members adopt this perspective, they ask questions and seek your advice. You need to redirect the questions and advice seeking back to the group to promote discussion and mutual aid. As interaction develops among the members, you can promote sharing to deepen the intermember relationships. Here are three common activities that help to establish the interpersonal processes:

1. Ensuring acceptance
2. Building relationships
3. Establishing an interactive flow

*Ensuring Acceptance*   People enter a group with anxiety about how they will be treated by the other members. Members want to ensure that they fit with, and are accepted by, the other group members (Abrams, 2000). If a group member cannot find a fit or feels as if others do not accept her, she will quickly leave the group. However, if the group member believes she is important to the other group members, she will continue attending and participating in the group. The following practitioner behaviors help to promote intermember acceptance.

- ◆ **Normalize.** When people experience feelings, they tend to withdraw and focus on their internal experience. This turning inward interrupts their connection to others and often makes them feel that they are somehow different from the others. Practitioners frequently use normalization to reinforce that a group member's experience is shared broadly. For example, if people appear anxious in the early group meetings and do not speak much, you might say, "I find first group meetings kind of scary and awkward, because when people don't know each other they don't know what to say . . . Does anyone else find that?"
- ◆ **Stress commonalities.** When people believe that they have something in common with other group members, they are more accepting. In practice, you can promote the sense of commonality by highlighting feelings, values and beliefs, and experiences that members share. You can also solicit commonalities after a member has made a statement by asking the group, "Does anyone else ever feel this way?" As the other members begin sharing similar feelings or experiences, the group's common bonds and acceptance can be elevated.
- ◆ **Neutralize strong affect.** When group members express strong affect in the group, there is a risk that others may withdraw. This risk is highest early in the group, when the members are still tentative in their engagement. You can respond to strong affect by reframing or softening the expression. For example, if a member is angry with his children, you may want to stress the underlying primary feeling. You can then solicit sharing about similar feelings from the other members.

*Building Relationships*   After group members begin to feel that they are accepted by the group, they focus on getting to know the other people. As group members listen to each other, they form impressions. If impressions are favorable, the members form positive relationships. You will seek to elicit information that will allow the members to form such impressions. Often this activity involves creating opportunities for the members to talk and share. As the members disclose elements of their situations, the depth of information increases and relationships form. As people feel connected to each other, they become more motivated to continue with the group. The following activities are often used to deepen the intermember relationships.

- ◆ **Elicit disclosures.** To promote mutual aid, group members need to start disclosing and sharing feedback with each other. Practitioners often use exercises to promote initial sharing. Typically, the initial sharing is safe information because group members may be unwilling to risk. Over time, the personal nature of the disclosures can be elevated. In practice, you will often seek to balance personal, situational, and safe information to form well-rounded impressions.
- ◆ **Build subgroups.** To build slightly deeper relationships, leaders often have members discuss situations in dyads or in smaller groups. As the smaller collections of members meet with each other, they have an opportunity to share in a more personal context. Getting to know one or two other people in more depth can promote comfort and a willingness to continue with the group.

*Establishing Interaction*   Unless the members share information, group programs will fail. Every member must discuss his or her situation with the others. Concurrently, every member must listen and pay attention to other members when they are sharing. Early in the group, you will want to encourage discussion and sharing. Monitor who is talking, and seek to engage all members in the group exchanges. The following practitioner strategies help to promote sharing among the group members:

- ◆ **Invite participation.** Early in the group and in a consistent manner, group members must be invited to participate. Statements such as "Does anyone else have any thoughts on that?" "What do you guys think about that?" and "Ask the group if anyone can give you a suggestion" are typical invitation lines. This strategy may be awkward at first, because people are used to deferring to the authority figure for answers. This is particularly true early in a children's group, because the children typically tend to view the group leader as a teacher.

- ◆ **Use gossip hooks.** You can usually start group sharing by generalizing from one member's statements to hook others into a discussion. Using "gossip hooks" involves commenting on one member's statement to another member to get them involved in discussing the first disclosure. For example, if one member complains about his child, the group leader can expand the discussion by saying to another member, "It seems that John is frustrated with his son's behavior. You know something about that feeling, don't you?"

- ◆ **Make the rounds.** The use of "rounds" is a strategy that sequentially solicits input from everybody in the group. The leader begins by soliciting feedback or sharing from a group member and then proceeds person by person around the circle. Rounds are often used to promote sharing on a specific issue, or when there seems to be a problem in the group that requires every member to have input.

## ◆ EXERCISE 15.1   GROUP INTERVENTION

You are contracted with the child protection agency to work with high-risk families. These families are all living in a local housing project and have been identified by workers as possibly abusive and severe in their discipline. The past worker prepared a program that teaches parents about normal development of children and what can be expected at the different stages of child development. The program also instructs parents in positive ways to shape behavior at these different stages of development.

1. What do you see as the problems inherent in the program that is provided for you?

2. Before you meet with these parents, what will you arrange to make it easier for them to attend the group?

3. What kind of programming will you try to set up for these families?

4. When you approach the individual family members to invite them into the group, what will you say to them to entice them into joining as you introduce the group?

5. Write down what you will say to these parents as your opening statement.

6. How will you get the parents talking to each other (activities, exercises, etc.)?

7. One of the parents looks at you early in the group and says, "How can you help us? Our kids are a handful and we're living in a hellhole; what can you do?" Respond to this parent in a way that can promote mutual aid among the group members.

# In-Home Work With Families

The in-home model of intervention has a long history in family services. This model predates the use of settlement houses and the later development of agencies. As social services became more clinically focused, the use of home visiting was abandoned in favor of the more professional trappings supplied through agency-based intervention. Recent research has indicated that in-home work may be more suitable than agency-based treatment for high-risk and multiproblem families (Hodges & Blythe, 1992; Johnson & Clancy, 1991).

The in-home model improves the prognosis for change because the practitioner is working in the natural family setting. This change in location preempts the family members' need to generalize discussions from the clinical setting to their home situation (Fraser, Pecora, & Haapala, 1991; Rothery & Cameron, 1985). Here are several programs currently using an in-home model of service delivery:

◆ **Special services at home.** This program offers behavioral and developmental programming for people who are developmentally delayed. Programming occurs in the clients' home and community. The goals of such programs involve behavior change and skill development.

◆ **Infant stimulation.** These programs involve bringing developmental therapists into the family home to provide gross motor, fine motor, and other developmental programs designed to enhance infant development. The population served is most often infants exhibiting a developmental lag or parents who do not possess the personal resources to provide a stimulating environment. Parents are trained in the procedures so programming may be intensified. The goals of the program are to rectify the observed developmental delays or to increase the level of parental interaction, which can promote development.

◆ **Family preservation.** These programs involve sending family therapists into the family home for about five hours per week. Therapists carry a caseload of about four families and work intensively for short periods of time. The goal of such programs is usually to prevent imminent placement of the child. Consequently, either the child or adult behavior is sufficiently out of control to be considered a risk.

♦ **Public health programs.** Several public health programs provide professional services in the client's home. These include infant care programs and self-care during convalescence. The goals of such programs are to improve the general level of health by increasing health-care activities.

Compared with office-based models of intervention, the in-home model has significant promise for working with parents coming from multiproblem families (Cherniss & Herzog, 1996; Spaid & Fraser, 1991). In-home support helps such parents understand the normal expectations and strains associated with parenting. Most stressors reported by parents of infants and toddlers are normal developmental changes that are misunderstood by the parent. Whining, refusal to eat, noncompliance unless threatened, and anger when the child does not get her own way commonly prompt families to want help with parenting (O'Brien, 1996).

For parents raised in impoverished and/or multiproblem families, needs increase because there is no model of normal development in the parent's experience (Fraser et al., 1991; Heap, 1991). Consequently, the parent has distorted beliefs of both self and the child (Gara et al., 1996). In such families the in-home worker first has to nurture the parents, to generate experiences that they can then use to enhance the parent-child relationship (Bogenschneider, 1996; Gara et al., 1996). The practitioner then promotes an understanding of normal child behavior, addresses chronic stressors, and creates positive parent-child experiences (Cherniss & Herzog, 1996; Daro, 1988; Dumas, 1984; Luster, Perlstadt, McKinnery, Sims, & Juang, 1996; Rivara, 1985).

Program comparisons indicate that in-home family intervention can improve mother-infant attachment (Barnard, Magyary, Sumner, Booth, Mitchell, & Spieker, 1988; Jacobson & Frye, 1991; Lyons-Ruth, Connell, Grunebaum, & Botein, 1990; Van den Boom, 1991; van Ijzendoorn, Juffer, & Duyvesteyn, 1995). Along with improved attachment, studies have found that disadvantaged adolescent mothers who receive in-home support are more attentive and verbally involved with their children (Cherniss & Herzog, 1996; Luster et al., 1996).

In-home intervention does not have to involve long-term intervention. Limited in-home intervention has been found to create early improvements in the parent-child relationship (Cherniss & Herzog, 1996). A recent meta-analysis found that short-term in-home intervention can be more effective than longer-term treatment in improving parent-child attachment (van Ijzendoorn et al., 1995). Clinical and research findings indicate that the following nine program elements are essential for creating a successful in-home intervention program:

1. It is best to start working with the parents as early as possible, ideally before or shortly after their child's birth.
2. Visit frequently enough to get to know the family and establish trust, so they will display potentially problematic interactions before problems form.
3. Develop a therapeutic relationship with the parents so you can nurture them and help them feel better and more positive about themselves.
4. Monitor for signs of maltreatment, and intervene early.

5. Model effective parenting in a natural way without being critical or lecturing the parents (they will be hypersensitive to criticism if they have been abused).

6. Provide concrete services (such as help with transportation, housing, toys, budgeting, etc.) so the parents can better organize and enjoy their lives.

7. Never lose sight of the child's needs, even though the parents are primary at the intervention level.

8. Include the fathers or boyfriends in the intervention, because they are a large part of the natural family interaction.

9. Tailor activities to the family's needs rather than working from a structured program model.

This list is derived from the accumulated findings in the following articles: Beckwith, 1988; Fraser et al., 1991; Gara et al., 1996; Goldstein, Keller, & Erne, 1985; Green, Power, Steinbook, & Gaines, 1981; Howing, Wodarski, Gaudin, & Kurtz, 1989; Leventhal, 1996; Resnick, 1985; Schmitt, 1980; Spaid & Fraser, 1991; Willett, Ayoub, & Robinson, 1991.

When working in the family home, you will find many differences in how treatment proceeds. First, you will find that the power relationship shifts. When you are in a family's home, the family has more control. They are the ones offering coffee, and they can ask you to leave if you make them angry. Family members can also leave the room during the session and never return. These possibilities require that you negotiate participation expectations very early in treatment. Discuss all of the possible evasive maneuvers, so that all family members know what to expect during the sessions. A detailed plan of care can be useful to outline what each family member agrees to when beginning treatment.

A second difference you will observe when working in a family home is the increase in interruptions and distractions. Family members are used to living under certain conditions, so you may find the television blaring and people walking in during the session. It is often useful to limit the background noise during sessions, to alleviate the chaos. However, you must remember that the family members will be using their new skills amid the chaos. Interruptions by family and friends should be discussed. Some friends may turn out to be allies, while others can be a very negative influence on sessions. You may need to discuss the different friends and talk about how to proceed if they enter the home or call during sessions.

A third difference when working in the family home is the environment. Sometimes the home will be unkempt and perhaps dirty. You will need to develop tolerances to such environments rather than expecting family members to live up to external standards of housekeeping. If environmental chaos appears to influence the family problems, you may end up helping the family to reorganize or clean. The discussions and bonding that can occur during this concrete work can make a difference in the treatment relationship. However, be careful when engaging in such tasks because the family may feel judged if a practitioner suggests housecleaning. It is best if the issue emerges naturally in the conversation.

When working on behavior change or skill acquisition, you will most often rely on the actor-model and teacher-coach strategies to help the family develop skills. Be careful to ensure that you have met the assumptions of each strategy. The most important assumptions are engagement and motivation. For treatment to be effective, you must work hard to build a positive relationship with the family members. If you are not welcome in the family home, it is unlikely that modeling will be effective. Many of the action system and processing system strategies can be used in the home as long as you have met the intervention assumptions.

Much of the work in the home involves providing support. Many families are very stressed, and family members need opportunities to talk about their pressures. The practitioner listens and often tries to reconstruct beliefs and interpretations of events to mitigate the stress. In these practitioner responses, it is important to identify and build on the strengths of the family members. You must also be prepared to advocate and mediate relationships with other people and systems to minimize the family stress.

## Community-Based Family Interventions

A new and creative direction for family-based practice is working with community partners to provide family services in nontraditional settings. Family practice has been provided in settings such as immigrant organizations, jails, band offices on Indian reservations, schools, and recovery clinics. Stressed families are often in contact with such settings, which provide a natural environment for assisting families. Nontraditional settings often have the added benefit of allowing the practitioner to sidestep cumbersome intake procedures commonly used in clinical settings. Families consequently have expedited access to practitioners in a setting that is less stigmatizing than those in clinical agencies.

A benefit of working in a community setting is that you can access families before significant problems develop. For example, a very effective strategy is to provide conjoint parent-child counseling through preschool settings (Miller & Prinz, 1990; Rae Grant, 1994; Tuma, 1989). In settings such as schools, you can work simultaneously with teachers, parents, and children (Tremblay et al., 1991). This move into the community adds an additional dimension, because you can then work with others who affect the family as part of the treatment. Such interventions have been effective in strengthening parent-school cooperation and curbing aggressive behavior (Kumpfer, Alvarado, Tait, & Turner, 2002).

There are two models for community-based delivery of family intervention. First, a family practitioner (or team) works directly with families in the community setting. Typically this involves the practitioner operating as a guest in the community setting. Most often, the practitioner does not have an office; he must enter the foreign setting, provide the service, and then return to his home agency. The second model is working through community partners to provide the service. This approach often uses past clients and/or paraprofessionals to supplement service.

## Working Through Host Settings

When you work through a host setting, you are perpetually a guest in the setting. There is no permanent office space, and you are on-site only at the time of service delivery. You will consequently yield no bureaucratic influence in the setting and must rely on being viewed as a valued expert by others in the setting.

The power shift associated with delivering service through a host setting can be awkward. If you are perceived as providing a valuable service, people in the host setting will welcome and cater to you. However, priorities can change quickly in the host setting, depending on new emergent needs. Such shifts can result in devaluing the service, and changes in the host agency, and may interfere with service delivery. For example, a practitioner was providing parent-youth groups in a high school setting. After establishing the groups, she was told that a teacher's committee wanted the meeting room. When she arrived for group, the practitioner found that the room was no longer available. The group ended up meeting in the parking lot.

When providing service through a host setting, you must clarify your expectations about the setting as well as with the families. During meetings with the host, you must negotiate and formalize issues of space and privacy before beginning service, to avoid mix-ups. If you are not on-site to troubleshoot changes and potential disruptions, a firm agreement before starting can help prevent potential problems. In the preservice agreement with the host, you should discuss these issues:

- ◆ **Space.** You will need adequate space to provide the service.
- ◆ **Privacy.** Family members must be able to talk without being overheard.
- ◆ **Practitioner access.** You will frequently need identification, keys, or permission to enter the setting. You may also have to arrange access protocols before service can begin.
- ◆ **Client access.** Family members need a method for getting to the service and communicating with you, the practitioner. For example, in jail a guard must bring the parents to group.
- ◆ **Timing.** The space needs to be ready not only before the service begins but also for a period after the end of service, so that you have time for tidying up and having discussions with family members.
- ◆ **Host expectations.** Clarify reports, informal consultations, tidying up, and other possible expectations that the host may have of you.

Even with clearly negotiated protocols and expectations, the practitioner must also attend to informal relationships in the host setting. You will find it useful to meet people within the host setting to explain the services you are providing and to answer any questions that might arise. If people in the host setting ask for advice on client situations, you can elevate their expert status by helping them think through their cases in an informal consultation. If you can achieve respect from the people in the host setting, interference with service is less likely to occur.

## Working Through Community-Based Partners

The second model of community-based family work involves using volunteers, peer counselors, or paraprofessionals to supplement or provide the primary intervention. Such programs often seek to decrease family dependence on formal helping systems by implementing peer supports (Tuma, 1989). Community-based programs are often provided after clinical interventions to ensure that a family's difficult clinical issues have been addressed before using the less intrusive approaches (McInnis-Dittrich, 1996).

The use of peers and mentors is particularly useful if a family member has difficulties that cause her to be identifiably different from the rest of the population. For example, learning disabled children respond well to peer approaches (Rawson & Cassady, 1995). Similarly, addicted parents and pregnant teens benefit from peer approaches to support (Sherman, Sanders, & Banks, 1998). One benefit of using peers is that the shared history provides instant credibility and a sense that the helper will understand (Hill, 2001). You can use peer volunteers as one-to-one supports or as part of a group or team (Johnson & Johnson, 1995). Some clinicians are beginning to use peers as part of a reflecting team to highlight issues and provide gentle confrontation (Selekman, 1995).

Using paraprofessionals or nonclinical professionals as an adjunct to therapy can also be useful. You can train teachers to work differently with high-risk children (Simon, Ginsburg, & Byrne, 1993). Similarly, shelter staff, clergy, health aides, and others can all be trained to extend therapeutic services to families (Davis, Spurr, Cox, Lynch, von Roenne, & Hahn, 1997; Grant, Henley, & Kean, 2001; Stanley et al., 2001). Most often, the paraprofessionals are adjunctive to clinical services. You will work closely with the paraprofessional helpers to extend treatment into the community setting. Frequently, the paraprofessional works with the family members in the home or community settings to help generalize and integrate clinical changes (Davis et al., 1997; Stanley et al., 2001).

When you are using any type of supplemental partners in the provision of family services, certain criteria will promote success. You cannot just have people meeting with families on an ad hoc basis; instead, you must include the paraprofessionals and volunteers as part of a team. As team members, the support people must ensure that the following conditions are met:

◆ **Frequent contact.** Support partners must meet with family members frequently to ensure that a solid helping relationship develops.
◆ **Ready access.** Support partners must be available for the family members so they can be reached during critical periods in the family life.
◆ **Specific responding skills.** Support partners must be trained to respond to family situations in a therapeutic rather than ad hoc manner.
◆ **Commitment.** Support partners must be prepared to continue working with family members even if their relationship becomes strained at times. Family members cannot be repeatedly rejected.
◆ **Accepting attitude.** Support partners must accept, rather than negatively judge, the family members and be willing to work collaboratively with the family.

Family practitioners working with community-based partners must develop new skills and abilities as their role is greatly expanded (Leitch & Thomas, 1999). You must be able to recruit and prepare support partners for effective work with family members. You must also be able to integrate the community partner into a well-conceived plan of care that includes multiple elements, all working together to improve the family system (Morison, Bromfield, & Cameron, 2003). Here are some of the new skills needed by family practitioners:

◆ **Program planning.** The practitioner must be able to conceptualize and plan a program that includes clinical and support partner elements operating under unifying goals.

◆ **Training.** The practitioner must be able to train support partners to understand and respond effectively to family situations.

◆ **Supervising.** The practitioner must be willing and able to meet with support partners and explore their relationship with the family members. The practitioner must also provide suggestions and additional education to ensure that the support partner is providing adequate service.

◆ **Supporting.** The practitioner must support the community partner concurrently with the family so that each participant feels understood and replenished.

◆ **Supplementing.** The practitioner must provide services that supplement and complement the work of the support partner.

## Summary

High-risk and multiproblem families need support to help them manage the multiple stresses in their lives. The family practitioner often uses innovative service delivery methods to provide such support. Family practitioners must have the ability to work with multiple family members in a group format to promote structured peer support. Group intervention requires facilitative skills for helping members to interact and provide each other with mutual aid. Family practitioners must also be able to work in the family home to ensure generalization of skills to the home environment. When working in family homes, the family practitioner must learn to work within the less clinical environment. A third practice innovation involves working in community settings, providing services through either host organizations or community partners. Skills in all three areas are important when working with high-risk and multiproblem families.

## Critical Content

1. High-risk and multiproblem families do not respond well to office-based treatment or psychoeducational groups. In family practice, you must adapt your practice skills to work effectively with these families.

2. When adapting your approach, it is important to maintain a family focus, maximize mutual aid, and use innovative interventions.
3. Three promising interventions include group interventions, in-home interventions, and community-based interventions.
4. Group intervention using mutual aid and peer support is a potentially effective model for intervention. When facilitating groups, you must attend to structural and interpersonal processes to ensure that mutual aid is developed.
5. In-home work requires you to adapt and work within the family environment. Because this type of work provides less practitioner power, you must collaborate more closely with the family.
6. Community-based work requires you to work closely with host organizations, volunteers, and paraprofessionals to provide an integrated approach to treatment.

## Suggested Readings

Gruber, K. J., Fleetwood, T. W., & Herring, M. W. (2001). In-home continuing care services for substance-affected families: The Bridges Program. *Social Work, 46,* 267–277.

McKay, M. M., Gonzales, J. J., Stone, S., Ryland, D., & Kohner, K. (1995). Multiple family therapy groups: A responsive intervention model for inner city families. *Social Work with Groups, 18,* 41–56.

Selekman, M. D. (1995). Rap music with wisdom: Peer reflecting teams with tough adolescents. In S. Friedman (Ed.), *The reflecting team in action: Collaborative practice in family therapy* (pp. 205–219). New York: Guilford.

Thomas, V., McCollum, E. E., & Snyder, W. (1999). Beyond the clinic: In-home therapy with Head Start families. *Journal of Marital and Family Therapy, 25,* 177–189.

# References

Abrams, B. (2000). Finding common ground in a conflict resolution group for boys. *Social Work with Groups, 23*, 55–69.

Ackerman, N. (1970). Child participation in family therapy. *Family Process, 9*, 403–410.

Ackerman, R. J. (1987). *Same house, different homes: Why adult children of alcoholics are not all the same.* Deerfield Beach, FL: Health Communications.

Acton, R. G., & During, S. M. (1992). Preliminary results of aggression management training for aggressive parents. *Journal of Interpersonal Violence, 7*, 410–417.

Adams, D. (1990). Identifying the assaultive husband in court: You be the judge. *Response to the Victimization of Women & Children, 13*, 13–16.

Adams, J. (2003). Milan systemic therapy. In L. L. Hecker & J. L. Wetchler (Eds.), *An introduction to marriage and family therapy* (pp. 123–147). Binghamton, NY: Haworth Press.

Adams, J. F. (1997). Questions as interventions in therapeutic conversation. *Journal of Family Psychotherapy, 8*, 17–35.

Aguilar, R. J., & Nightingale, N. N. (1994). The impact of specific battering experiences on the self-esteem of abused women. *Journal of Family Violence, 9*, 35–45.

Albert, S., Amgott, T., Krakow, M., & Marcus, H. (1979). Children's bedtime rituals as a prototype rite of safe passage. *Journal of Psychological Anthropology, 2*, 85–105.

Alexander, J. F., Jameson, P. B., Newell, R. M., & Gunderson, D. (1996). Changing cognitive schemas: A necessary antecedent to changing behaviors in dysfunctional families? In K. S. Dobson & K. D. Craig (Eds.), *Advances in cognitive-behavioral therapy* (Vol. 2, pp. 174–192). Thousand Oaks, CA: Sage.

Alford, K. M. (1998). Family roles, alcoholism, and family dysfunction. *Journal of Mental Health Counseling, 20*, 250–260.

Allcorn, S. (1995). Understanding organizational culture as the quality of workplace subjectivity. *Human Relations, 48*, 73–96.

Allcorn, S., & Diamond, M. A. (1997). *Managing people during stressful times: The psychologically defensive workplace.* Westport, CT: Quorum.

Allen, J., & Crandall, J. (1986). The rosebush: A visualization strategy. *Elementary School Guidance & Counseling, 21,* 44–51.

Allen, J. G., Gabbard, G. O., Newsom, G. E., & Coyne, L. (1990). Detecting patterns of change in patients' collaboration within individual psychotherapy sessions. *Psychotherapy, 27,* 522–530.

Allen, K., Calsyn, D. A., Fehrenbach, P. A., & Benton, G. (1989). A study of the interpersonal behaviors of male batterers. *Journal of Interpersonal Violence, 4,* 79–89.

Allgood, S. M., & Crane, D. R. (1991). Predicting marital therapy dropouts. *Journal of Marital & Family Therapy, 17,* 73–79.

Altman, N. (1993). Psychoanalysis and the urban poor. *Psychoanalytic Dialogues, 3,* 29–49.

Altshuler, S. J. (2003). From barriers to successful collaboration: Public schools and child welfare working together. *Social Work, 48,* 52–63.

Amatea, E. S., & Sherrard, P. A. (1991). When students cannot or will not change their behavior: Using brief strategic intervention in the school. *Journal of Counseling & Development, 69,* 341–344.

Amato, P. R. (1986). Marital conflict, the parent-child relationship, and child self-esteem. *Family Relations, 35,* 403–410.

Anderson, N. B., & Armstead, C. A. (1995). Toward understanding the association of socioeconomic status and health: A new challenge for the biopsychosocial approach. *Psychosomatic Medicine, 57,* 213–225.

Anderson, S. A. (1985). Dropping out of marriage and family therapy: Intervention strategies and spouses' perceptions. *American Journal of Family Therapy, 13,* 39–54.

Anderson, T., & Leitner, L. M. (1996). Symptomatology and the use of affect constructs to influence value and behavior constructs. *Journal of Counseling Psychology, 43,* 77–83.

Andrews, J. D. (1989). Integrating visions of reality: Interpersonal diagnosis and the existential vision. *American Psychologist, 44,* 803–817.

Aponte, H. J. (1994). *Bread and spirit: Therapy with the new poor.* New York: Norton.

Archer, S. L. (1985). Identity and the choice of social roles. *New Directions for Child Development, 30,* 79–99.

Ariel, S., Carel, C. A., Tyano, S., & Dell, P. F. (1984). A formal explication of the concept of family homeostasis. *Journal of Marital & Family Therapy, 10,* 337–349.

Armstrong, P. (1997). Assessment and accountability. In S. Palmer & G. McMahon (Eds.), *Client assessment* (pp. 115–133). Thousand Oaks, CA: Sage.

Assor, A., & Aldor, R. (1993). Motivational similarity and interpersonal evaluations: The role of ambiguity, self-derogation, and emotion. *Journal of Personality, 61,* 111–131.

Athens, L. H. (1977). Violent crime: A symbolic interactionist study. *Symbolic Interaction, 1,* 56–69.

Athens, L. H. (1980). *Violent criminal acts and actors: A symbolic interactionist study.* Boston: Routledge & Kegan Paul.

Bagarozzi, D. A., & Anderson, S. A. (1989). *Personal, marital, and family myths: Theoretical formulations and clinical strategies.* New York: Norton.

Bandura, A. (1973). *Aggression: A social learning analysis.* Oxford, England: Prentice-Hall.

Barbaree, H. E., Seto, M. C., Langton, C. M., & Peacock, E. J. (2001). Evaluating the predictive accuracy of six risk assessment instruments for adult sex offenders. *Criminal Justice & Behavior, 28,* 490–521.

Barber, J. G. (1992). Evaluating parent education groups: Effects on sense of competence and social isolation. *Research on Social Work Practice, 2,* 28–38.

Barker, P. (1994). Reframing: The essence of psychotherapy? In J. K. Zeig (Ed.), *Ericksonian methods: The essence of the story* (pp. 211–223). Philadelphia: Brunner/Mazel.

Barnard, C. P., & Kuehl, B. P. (1995). Ongoing evaluation: In-session procedures for enhancing the working alliance and therapy effectiveness. *American Journal of Family Therapy, 23,* 161–172.

Barnard, K. E., Magyary, D., Sumner, G., Booth, C. L., Mitchell, S. K., & Spieker, S. (1988). Prevention of parenting alterations for women with low social support. *Psychiatry, 51,* 248–253.

Barnett, J. K., & Youngberg, C. (2004). Forgiveness as a ritual in couples therapy. *Family Journal: Counseling & Therapy for Couples & Families, 12,* 14–20.

Barnett, M. A., Quackenbush, S. W., & Sinisi, C. S. (1996). Factors affecting children's, adolescents', and young adults' perceptions of parental discipline. *Journal of Genetic Psychology, 157,* 411–424.

Barnett, O. W., Martinez, T. E., & Keyson, M. (1996). The relationship between violence, social support, and self blame in battered women. *Journal of Interpersonal Violence, 11,* 221–233.

Barratt, M. S., Roach, M. A., Morgan, K. M., & Colbert, K. K. (1996). Adjustment to motherhood by single adolescents. *Family Relations, 45,* 209–215.

Barrett-Kruse, C. (2000). Strengthening the mother-daughter relationship through bibliotherapy and storytelling. *TCA Journal, 28,* 111–113.

Barrios, M. V., & Singer, J. L. (1981). The treatment of creative blocks: A comparison of waking imagery, hypnotic dream, and rational discussion techniques. *Imagination, Cognition, & Personality, 1*, 89–109.

Bassett, H., Lampe, J., & Lloyd, C. (1999). Parenting: Experiences and feelings of parents with a mental illness. *Journal of Mental Health, 8*, 597–604.

Bateson, G. (1972). *Steps to an ecology of the mind.* New York: Ballantine.

Beavers, W. R., & Hampson, R. B. (1990). *Successful families: Assessment and intervention.* New York: Norton.

Becker, D., Hogue, A., & Liddle, H. A. (2002). Methods of engagement in family-based preventive intervention. *Child & Adolescent Social Work Journal, 19*, 163–179.

Beckwith, L. (1988). Intervention with disadvantaged parents of sick preterm infants. *Psychiatry: Journal for the Study of Interpersonal Processes, 51*, 242–247.

Beckwith, L., & Cohen, S. E. (1989). Maternal responsiveness with preterm infants and later competency. *New Directions for Child Development, 43*, 75–87.

Bedell, J. R., & Lennox, S. S. (1997). *Handbook for communication and problem-solving skills training: A cognitive-behavioral approach.* New York: Wiley.

Bedrosian, R. C. (1982). Treatment of marital violence. In J. C. Hansen (Ed.), *Clinical approaches to family violence* (pp. 119–138). Rockville, MD: Aspen.

Bell, S. K., & Eyberg, S. M. (2002). Parent-child interaction therapy: A dyadic intervention for the treatment of young children with conduct problems. In L. VandeCreek (Ed.), *Innovations in clinical practice: A source book* (Vol. 20, pp. 57–74). Sarasota, FL: Professional Resource Press.

Benjet, C., Azar, S. T., & Kuersten-Hogan, R. (2003). Evaluating the parental fitness of psychiatrically diagnosed individuals: Advocating a functional-contextual analysis of parenting. *Journal of Family Psychology, 17*, 238–251.

Benzies, K. M., Harrison, M. J., & Magill-Evans, J. (1998). Impact of marital quality and parent-infant interaction on preschool behavior problems. *Public Health Nursing, 15*, 35–43.

Bepko, C., & Krestan, J. A. (1985). *The responsibility trap: A blueprint for treatment of the alcoholic family.* New York: Free Press.

Berg, J. H., & McQuinn, R. D. (1986). Attraction and exchange in continuing and noncontinuing dating relationships. *Journal of Personality and Social Psychology, 50*, 942–952.

Berger, G. (1993). *Alcoholism and the family.* New York: Franklin Watts.

Bergin, K. (1998). A picture in mind: A reflection on a cartoon as a metaphor for relationship counseling. *Journal of Client Studies, 4*, 223–225.

Berg-Nielsen, T. S., Vikan, A., & Dahl, A. A. (2002). Parenting related to child and parental psychopathology: A descriptive review of the literature. *Clinical Child Psychology & Psychiatry, 7*, 529–552.

Berkowitz, L. (1990). On the formation and regulation of anger and aggression: A cognitive neoassociational analysis. *American Psychologist, 45*, 494–503.

Berlin, S. B. (1996). Constructivism and the environment: A cognitive-integration perspective for social work practice. *Families in Society, 77*, 326–335.

Bern, E. H. (1985). Domestic violence: Some theoretical issues related to criminal behavior. *Journal of Applied Social Sciences, 9*, 136–147.

Bernard, J. L., & Bernard, M. L., (1984). The abusive male seeking treatment: Jekyll and Hyde. *Family Relations, 33*, 543–547.

Bernard, M. L., & Bernard, J. L. (1983). Violent intimacy: The family as a model for love relationships. *Family Relations, 32*, 283–286.

Berrigan, L. P., & Garfield, S. L. (1981). Relationship of missed psychotherapy appointments to premature termination and social class. *British Journal of Clinical Psychology, 20*, 239–242.

Bertram, H. (2000). Life course dynamics and the development of new relations between generations. In L. J. Crockett & R. K. Silberseisen (Eds.), *Negotiating adolescence in times of social change* (pp. 157–177). New York: Cambridge University Press.

Betancourt, H., & Lopez, S. R. (1995). The study of culture, ethnicity, and race in American psychology. In N. R. Goldberger & J. B. Veroff (Eds.), *The culture and psychology reader* (pp. 87–107). New York: New York University Press.

Bhatia, K., & Sanford, G. (1978). Role of locus of control in frustration-produced aggression. *Journal of Consulting & Clinical Psychology, 46*, 364–365.

Bienstock, C. R., & Videka-Sherman, L. (1989). Process analysis of a therapeutic support group for single parent mothers: Implications for practice. *Social Work with Groups, 12*, 43–61.

References    

Bilinkoff, J. (1995). Empowering battered women as mothers. In E. Peled, P. G. Jaffe, & J. L. Edleson (Eds.), *Ending the cycle of violence: Community responses to children of battered women* (pp. 97–120). Newbury Park, CA: Sage.

Bing, E. (1970). The conjoint family drawing. *Family Process, 9,* 173–194.

Biringen, Z. (1990). Direct observation of maternal sensitivity and dyadic interactions in the home: Relations to maternal thinking. *Developmental Psychology, 26,* 278–284.

Bischoff, M. M., & Tracey, T. J. G. (1996). Client resistance as predicted by therapist behavior: A study of sequential dependence. *Journal of Counseling Psychology, 42,* 487–495.

Bitter, J. R. (2004). Two approaches to counseling a parent alone: Toward a Gestalt-Adlerian integration. *Family Journal: Counseling & Therapy for Couples & Families, 12,* 358–367.

Black, C. (1981). Innocent bystanders at risk: The children of alcoholics. *Alcoholism: The National Magazine, 1,* 22–26.

Blanton, P. W., & Vandergriff-Avery, M. (2001). Marital therapy and marital power: Constructing narratives of relational and positional power. *Contemporary Family Therapy: An International Journal, 23,* 295–308.

Bloom, B. L. (1984). Community mental health training: A personal view. *American Journal of Community Psychology, 12,* 217–226.

Bluhm, C., Widger, T. A., & Miele, G. M. (1990). Interpersonal complementarity and individual differences. *Journal of Personality and Social Psychology, 58,* 464–471.

Bogenschneider, K. (1996). An ecological risk/protective theory for building prevention programs, policies, and community capacity to support youth. *Family Relations, 45,* 127–138.

Bograd, M. (1986). A feminist examination of family therapy: What is women's place? *Women and Therapy, 5,* 95–106.

Boland, C. (1993). Child behaviour management programs: Avoiding parental drop-out. *Australian & New Zealand Journal of Family Therapy, 14,* 168–170.

Boldizar, J. P., Perry, D. G., & Perry, L. C. (1989). Outcome values and aggression. *Child Development, 60,* 571–579.

Bolton, C., Calam, R., Barrowclough, C., Peters, S., Roberts, J., Wearden, A., et al. (2003). Expressed emotion, attributions and depression in mothers of children with problem behavior. *Journal of Child Psychology & Psychiatry & Allied Disciplines, 44,* 242–254.

Boone, R. K., & Bowman, V. E. (1997). Therapeutic metaphors: Gateways to understanding. *International Journal for the Advancement of Counseling, 19,* 313–327.

Borum, R., & Reddy, M. (2001). Assessing violence risk in Tarasoff situations: A fact-based model of inquiry. *Behavioral Sciences and the Law, 19,* 375–385.

Botkin, D. R. (2000). Family play therapy: A creative approach to including young children in family therapy. *Journal of Systemic Therapy, 19,* 31–42.

Boverie, P. E. (1991). Human systems consultant: Using family therapy in organizations. *Family Therapy, 18,* 61–71.

Bowen, C., Madill, A., & Stratton, P. (2002). Parental accounts of blaming within the family: A dialectical model for understanding blame in systemic therapy. *Journal of Marital & Family Therapy, 28,* 129–144.

Bowen, M. (1974). Toward the differentiation of self in one's family of origin. In E. Andres & J. Lorio (Eds.), *Georgetown family symposium* (Vol. 1). Washington, DC: Georgetown University Medical Center, Department of Psychiatry.

Bowen, M. (1978). *Family therapy in clinical practice.* New York: Aronson.

Bower, M. E., & Knutson, J. F. (1996). Attitudes toward physical discipline as a function of disciplinary history and self-labeling as physically abused. *Child Abuse & Neglect, 20,* 689–699.

Bowling, S. W., Kearney, L. K., Lumadue, C. A., & St. Germain, N. R. (2002). Considering justice: An exploratory study of family therapy with adolescents. *Journal of Marital & Family Therapy, 28,* 213–223.

Boyum, L. A., & Parke, R. D. (1995). The role of family emotional expressiveness in the development of children's social competence. *Journal of Marriage & the Family, 57,* 593–608.

Bradbury, T. N., & Fincham, F. D. (1992). Attributions and behavior in marital interaction. *Journal of Personality and Social Psychology, 63,* 613–628.

Bradley, R. H., Caldwell, B. M., Rock, S. L., Ramey, C. T., Barnard, K. E., Gray, C., et al., (1989). Home environment and cognitive development in the first three years of life: A collaborative study involving six sites and three ethnic groups in North America. *Developmental Psychology, 25,* 217–235.

Bradshaw, J. L., & Nettleton, N. C. (1981). The nature of hemispheric specialization in man. *Behavioral & Brain Sciences, 4,* 51–91.

Bredehoft, D. J. (2001). The framework for life-span family life education revisited and revised. *Family Journal: Counseling & Therapy for Couples & Families, 9*, 134–139.

Breslin, F. C., Riggs, D., O'Leary, K. D., & Arias, I. (1990). Family precursors: Expected and actual consequences of dating aggression. *Journal of Interpersonal Violence, 5*, 247–258.

Brewster, M. P. (2003). *Stalking: Psychology, risk factors, interventions, and law.* Kingston, NJ: Civic Research Institute.

Brill, N. Q., & Storrow, H. A. (1960). Social class and psychiatric treatment. *Archives of General Psychiatry, 3*, 340–344.

Bross, A. (1982). *Family therapy: A recursive model of strategic practice.* Toronto: Methuen Press.

Brown, C. H. (1993). Analyzing preventive trials with generalized additive models. *American Journal of Community Psychology, 21*, 635–664.

Brown, E. (2000). Working with marital affairs: Learning from the Clinton triangles. In L. Vandercreek & T. L. Jackson (Eds.), *Innovations in clinical practice: A source book* (Vol. 18, pp. 471–478). Sarasota, FL: Professional Resource Press.

Brown, J. (1997). Circular questioning: An introductory guide. *Australian & New Zealand Journal of Family Therapy, 18*, 109–114.

Brown, J. D., & Dutton, K. A. (1995). The thrill of victory, the complexity of defeat: Self-esteem and people's emotional reactions to success and failure. *Journal of Personality and Social Psychology, 68*, 712–722.

Bryant, B. K., & Trokel, J. F. (1976). Personal history of psychological stress related to locus of control orientation among college women. *Journal of Consulting and Clinical Psychology, 44*, 266–271.

Burkett, L. (1991). Parenting behaviors of women sexually abused as children in their families of origin. *Family Process, 30*, 421–434.

Burns, B. J., Schoenwald, S. K., Burchard, J. D., Faw, L., & Santos, A. B. (2000). Comprehensive community-based interventions for youth with severe emotional disorders: Multisystemic therapy and the wrap-around process. *Journal of Child & Family Studies, 9*, 283–314.

Burns, R. C. (1987). *Kinetic-house-tree-person drawings (K-H-T-P): An interpretative manual.* Philadelphia: Brunner/Mazel.

Bushman, B. J., & Cooper, M. M. (1990). Effects of alcohol on human aggression. *Psychological Bulletin, 107*, 341–354.

Buss, D. M., & Barnes, M. (1986). Preferences in human mate selection. *Journal of Personality and Social Psychology, 50*, 559–570.

Byng-Hall, J. (1988). Scripts and legends in families and family therapy. *Family Process, 27*, 167–179.

Cade, B., & O'Hanlon, W. H. (1993). *A brief guide to brief therapy.* New York: Norton.

Campbell, J. C., Sharps, P., & Glass, N. (2001). Risk assessment for intimate partner homicide. In G-F. Pinard & L. Pagani (Eds.), *Clinical assessment of dangerousness: Empirical contributions* (pp. 136–157). New York: Cambridge University Press.

Campbell, R. (1982). The lateralization of emotion: A critical review. *International Journal of Psychology 17*, 211–229.

Camras, L. A., Ribordy, S., Hill, J., Martino, S., Sachs, V., Spaccarelli, V., et al. (1990). Maternal facial behavior and the recognition and production of emotional expression by maltreated and nonmaltreated children. *Developmental Psychology, 26*, 304–312.

Cantrell, P. J., MacIntyre, D. I., Sharkey, K. J., & Thompson, V. (1995). Violence in the marital dyad as a predictor of violence in the peer relationships of older adolescents/young adults. *Violence & Victims, 10*, 35–41.

Cantwell, P., & Holmes, S. (1994). Social construction: A paradigm shift for systemic therapy and training. *Australian & New Zealand Journal of Family Therapy, 15*, 17–26.

Carey, L. (2001). Family sandplay therapy. In H. G. Kaduson & C. E. Schaefer (Eds.), *101 more favorite play therapy techniques* (pp. 317–322). Northvale, NJ: Jason Aronson.

Carich, M. S., & Spilman, K. (2004). Basic principles of intervention. *Family Journal: Counseling & Therapy for Couples & Families, 12*, 405–410.

Carns, M. R., English, R., Juling, L., & Carns, A. (2003). An approach to treatment of attachment issues in the adult and child subsystems through the use of thematic play therapy in conjunction with couples therapy. In P. Erdman & T. Caffery (Eds.), *Attachment and family systems: Conceptual, empirical, and therapeutic relatedness* (pp. 213–223). New York: Brunner/Routledge.

Carpenter, D. (1996). Constructivism and social work treatment. In F. J. Turner (Ed.), *Social work treatment: Interlocking theoretical approaches* (4th ed., pp. 146–167). New York: Free Press.

Carr, A. (1998). Michael White's narrative therapy. *Contemporary Family Therapy: An International Journal, 20*, 485–503.

Carter, E., & McGoldrick, M. (2005). *The expanded family life cycle* (3rd ed.). Boston: Allyn & Bacon.

Caspi, A., & Herbener, E. S. (1990). Continuity and change: Assortative marriage and consistency of personality in adulthood. *Journal of Personality and Social Psychology, 58*, 250–258.

Ceballo, R., & McLoyd, V. C. (2002). Social support and parenting in poor, dangerous neighborhoods. *Child Development, 73*, 1310–1321.

Center for Substance Abuse Treatment. (2004). *Substance abuse treatment and family therapy.* Rockville, MD: Substance Abuse and Mental Health Services Administration.

Cherniss, C., & Herzog, E. (1996). Impact of home-based family therapy on maternal and child outcomes in disadvantaged adolescent mothers. *Family Relations, 45*, 72–79.

Christensen, T. M., & Thorngren, J. M. (2000). Integrating play in family therapy: An interview with Eliana Gil, Ph.D. *Family Journal: Counseling & Therapy for Couples & Families, 8*, 91–100.

Cicchetti, D., Toth, S. L., & Hennessy, K. (1989). Research on the consequences of child maltreatment and its application to educational settings. *Topics in Early Childhood Education, 9*, 32–55.

Claridge, K. E. (1992). Reconstructing memories of abuse: A theory-based approach. *Psychotherapy: Theory, Research, Practice, Training, 29*, 243–252.

Clark, D. M. (1986). A cognitive approach to panic. *Behaviour Research and Therapy, 24*, 461–470.

Cohen, J. A., & Mannarino, A. P. (2002). Addressing attributions in treating abused children. *Child Maltreatment: Journal of the American Professional Society on the Abuse of Children, 7*, 82–86.

Cohen, S., & Willis, T. (1985). Stress, social support, and the buffering hypothesis. *Psychological Bulletin, 98*, 310–357.

Coleman, D. H., & Straus, M. A. (1986). Marital power, conflict, and violence in a nationally representative sample of American couples. *Violence & Victims, 1*, 141–157.

Coles, D. (1995). A pilot use of letters to clients before the initial session. *Australian & New Zealand Journal of Family Therapy, 16*, 209–213.

Conger, R. D., & Patterson, G. R. (1995). It takes two to replicate: A mediational model for the impact of parents' stress on adolescent adjustment. *Child Development, 66*, 80–97.

Connell, G. M., Mitten, T. J., & Whitaker, C. A. (1993). Reshaping family symbols: A symbolic-experiential perspective. *Journal of Marital & Family Therapy, 19*, 243–251.

Conners, N. A., Bradley, R. H., Mansell, L. W., Liu, J. Y., Roberts, T. J., Burgdorf, K., et al. (2003). Children of mothers with serious substance abuse problems: An accumulation of risks. *American Journal of Drug & Alcohol Abuse, 29*, 743–758.

Correa, J. E., Gonzalez, O. B., & Weber, M. S. (1991). Storytelling in families with children: A therapeutic approach to learning problems. *Contemporary Family Therapy: An International Journal, 13*, 33–59.

Cox, R. P., & Anderson, H. (2003). Family assessment tools. In R. P. Cox (Ed.), *Health-related counseling with families of diverse cultures: Family, health, and cultural competencies* (pp. 145–167). Westport, CT: Greenwood Press.

Coyle, G. L. (1962). Concepts relevant to helping the family as a group. *Social Casework, 43*, 343.

Coyne, J. C. (1985). Toward a theory of frames and reframing: The social nature of frames. *Journal of Marital & Family Therapy, 11*, 337–344.

Craig, L. A., Browne, K. D., & Stringer, I. (2003). Risk scales and factors predictive of sexual offense recidivism. *Trauma Violence & Abuse, 4*, 45–69.

Crittenden, P. M. (1989). Teaching maltreated children in the preschool. *Topics in Early Childhood Education, 9*, 16–32.

Cron, E. A. (2000). The feeling word game: A tool for both teaching and therapy. *Family Journal: Counseling & Therapy for Couples & Families, 8*, 402–405.

Culp, R. E., Little, V., Letts, D., & Lawrence, H. (1991). Maltreated children's self-concept: Effects of a comprehensive treatment program. *American Journal of Orthopsychiatry, 61*, 114–121.

Cunningham, P. B., & Henggeler, S. W. (1999). Engaging multiproblem families in treatment: Lessons learned throughout the development of multisystemic therapy. *Family Process, 38*, 265–286.

Dadds, M. R. (1987). Families and the origins of child behavior problems. *Family Process, 26*, 341–357.

Dadds, M. R., & Salmon, K. (2003). Punishment insensitivity and parenting: Temperament and learning as interacting risks for antisocial behavior. *Clinical Child & Family Psychology Review, 6*, 69–86.

Daro, D. (1988). *Confronting child abuse: Research for effective program design.* New York: Free Press.

Darou, W. G. (1992). An intervention with an adolescent incest victim/abuser. *Canadian Journal of Counselling, 26*, 152–156.

David, C., Steele, R., Forehand, R., & Armistead, L. (1996). The role of family conflict and marital conflict in adolescent functioning. *Journal of Family Violence, 11*(1), 81–91.

Davies, J. (1985). The role of alcohol in family violence. *Dissertation Abstracts International, 45*(12B, Pt. 1), 3770.

Davis, H., Spurr, P., Cox, A., Lynch, M. A., von Roenne, A., & Hahn, K. (1997). A description and evaluation of a community child mental health service. *Clinical Child Psychology & Psychiatry, 2*, 221–238.

de Chateau, P. (1976). The influence of early contact on maternal and infant behavior in primiparae. *Birth in the Family Journal, 3*, 149–155.

de Jong, P., & Miller, S. D. (1995). How to interview for client strengths. *Social Work, 40*, 729–736.

Dempsey, I. (1994). Parent-school communication in special schools and support classes. *Issues in Special Education & Rehabilitation, 9*, 7–21.

Deren, S. (1975). An empirical evaluation of the validity of the Draw-A-Family Test. *Journal of Clinical Psychology, 31*, 542–546.

de Risi, W. J., & Butz, G. (1975). *Writing behavioral contracts: A case simulation practice manual.* Champaign, IL: Research Press.

de Shazer, S. (1980). Investigation of indirect symbolic suggestions. *American Journal of Clinical Hypnosis, 23*, 10–15.

de Shazer, S. (1982). *Patterns of brief family therapy.* New York: Guilford.

de Shazer, S. (1985). *Keys to solution in brief therapy.* New York: Norton.

de Shazer, S. (1988). *Clues: Investigating solutions in brief therapy.* New York: Norton.

de Shazer, S. (1993). Creative misunderstanding: There is no escape from language. In S. G. Gilligan & R. Price (Eds.), *Therapeutic conversations* (pp. 81–94). New York: Norton.

de Shazer, S. (1997). Some thoughts on language use in therapy. *Contemporary Family Therapy: An International Journal, 19*, 133–141.

de Shazer, S., & Molnar, A. (1984). Four useful interventions in brief family therapy. *Journal of Marital & Family Therapy, 10*, 297–304.

de Shazer, S., & Nunnally, E. (1991). The mysterious affair of paradoxes and loops. In G. R. Weeks (Ed.), *Promoting change through paradoxical therapy* (pp. 252–270). Philadelphia: Brunner/Mazel.

Devaux, F. (1995). Intergenerational transmission of cultural family patterns. *Family Therapy, 22*, 17–23.

Diamond, G. S., & Liddle, H. A. (1999). Transforming negative parent-adolescent interactions: From impasse to dialogue. *Family Process, 38*, 5–26.

Dickstein, S. (2002). Family routines and rituals—the importance of family functioning: Comment on the special section. *Journal of Family Psychology, 16*, 441–444.

Diedrich, R. C. (1996). An interactive approach to executive coaching. *Consulting Psychology Journal: Practice & Research, 48*, 61–66.

Dillard, C. K., & Protinsky, H. O. (1985). Emotional cut-off: A comparative analysis of clinical and non-clinical populations. *International Journal of Family Psychiatry, 6*, 339–349.

Dix, T., & Grusec, J. E. (1983). Parental influence techniques: An attributional analysis. *Child Development, 54*, 645–652.

Doherty, W. J. (1981). Locus of control differences and marital satisfaction. *Journal of Marriage & the Family, 43*, 369–377.

Dohrenwend, B. S., & Dohrenwend, B. P. (1981). Hypothesis about stress processes linking social class to various types of psychopathology. *American Journal of Community Psychology, 9*, 146–159.

Donnelly, C. M., & Dumas, J. E. (1997). Use of analogies in the therapeutic situations: An analogue study. *Psychotherapy, 34*, 124–132.

Donohue, B., Azrin, N., Lawson, H. Friedlander, J., Teicher, G., & Rindsberg, J. (1998). Improving initial session attendance of substance abusing and conduct disordered adolescents: A controlled study. *Journal of Child and Adolescent Substance Abuse, 8*, 1–13.

Donovan, J. M. (2004). *Short-term object relations couples therapy: The five-step model.* New York: Brunner/Mazel.

Donovan, W. L., & Leavitt, L. A. (1989). Maternal self-efficacy and infant attachment: Integrating physiology, perceptions, and behavior. *Child Development, 60*, 460–472.

Douglas, K. S., & Ogloff, J. R. P. (2003). Multiple facets of risk for violence: The impact of judgmental specificity on structured decisions about violence risk. *International Journal of Forensic Mental Health, 2*, 19–34.

Downs, W. R., & Miller, B. A. (1998). Relationships between experiences of parental violence during childhood and women's self-esteem. *Violence & Victims, 13*, 63–77.

Doyle, M., & Dolan, M. (2002). Violence risk assessment: Combining actuarial and clinical information to structure clinical judgments for the formulation and management of risk. *Journal of Psychiatric & Mental Health Nursing, 9,* 649–657.

Dozier, R. M., Hicks, M. W., & Cornille, T. A. (1998). The effect of Tomm's therapeutic questioning styles on the therapeutic alliance: A clinical analog study. *Family Process, 37,* 189–200.

Dryden, W. (1989). The use of chaining in rational-emotive therapy. *Journal of Rational-Emotive & Cognitive Behavior Therapy, 7,* 59–66.

Dubow, E. F., & Tisak, J. (1989). The relation between stressful life events and adjustment in elementary school children: The role of social support and social problem-solving skills. *Child Development, 60,* 1412–1423.

Duck, S. (1985). Attraction, acquaintance, filtering and communication—but not necessarily in that order. In F. Epting & A. W. Landfield (Eds.), *Anticipating personal construct theory* (pp. 87–94). Lincoln: University of Nebraska Press.

Duhl, F. J., Kantor, D., & Duhl, B. S. (1973). Learning, space and action in family therapy: A primer of sculpture. In D. A. Bloch (Ed.), *Techniques of family psychotherapy.* New York: Grune & Stratton.

Dumas, J. E. (1984). Indiscriminant mothering: Empirical findings and theoretical speculations. *Advances in Behavior Research and Therapy, 6,* 13–27.

Dumas, J. E., Blechman, E. A., & Prinz, R. J. (1992). Helping families with aggressive children and adolescents change. In R. D. Peters & R. J. McMahon (Eds.), *Aggression and violence throughout the life span* (pp. 126–154). Thousand Oaks, CA: Sage.

Dumas, J. E., & Wahler, R. G. (1983). Predictors of treatment outcome in parent training: Mother insularity and socioeconomic disadvantage. *Behavioral Assessment, 5,* 301–313.

Duncan, B. L. (1992). Strategic therapy, eclecticism, and the therapeutic relationship. *Journal of Marital & Family Therapy, 18,* 17–24.

Dunn, M. G., Tarter, R. E., Mezzich, A. C., Vanyukov, M., Kirsci, L., & Kirillova, G. (2002). Origins and consequences of child neglect in substance abuse families. *Clinical Psychology Review, 22,* 1063–1090.

Dutton, D. G. (1986). Wife assaulters' explanations of assault: The neutralization of self punishment. *Canadian Journal of Behavioural Sciences, 18,* 381–390.

Dutton, D. G. (1988). Profiling of wife assaulters: Preliminary evidence for a trimodal analysis. *Violence & Victims, 3,* 5–29.

Dutton, D. G., & Browning, J. J. (1987). Power struggles and intimacy anxieties as causative factors of violence in intimate relationships. In G. Russell (Ed.), *Violence in intimate relationships.* New York: Spectrum.

Dutton, D. G., & Browning, J. J. (1988). Concern for power, fear of intimacy, and aversive stimuli for wife abuse. In G. T. Hotaling, D. Finkelhor, J. T. Kilpatric, & M. Straus (Eds.), *New directions in family violence research* (pp. 163–175). Newbury Park, CA: Sage.

Dutton, D. G., Fehr, B., & McEwan, H. (1982). Severe wife battering as deindividuated violence. *Victimology: An International Journal, 7,* 13–23.

Dutton, D. G., & Painter, S. L. (1983). Traumatic bonding: The development of emotional attachments in battered women and other relationships of intermittent abuse. *Victimology: An International Journal, 6,* 139–155.

Dutton, D. G., & Strachan, C. E. (1987). Motivational needs for power and spouse-specific assertiveness in assaultive and nonassaultive men. *Violence & Victims, 2,* 145–156.

Dutton, D. G., van Ginkel, C., & Starzomski, A. (1995). The role of shame and guilt in the intergenerational transmission of abusiveness. *Violence & Victims, 10,* 121–131.

Eaker, D. G., & Walters, L. H. (2002). Adolescent satisfaction in family rituals and psychosocial development: A developmental systems theory perspective. *Journal of Family Psychology, 16,* 406–414.

Eckstein, D. (1997). Reframing as a specific interpretive counseling technique. *Individual Psychology: Journal of Adlerian Theory, Research & Practice, 53,* 418–428.

Edleson, J., Eisikovits, Z. C., & Gottman, E. (1985). Men who batter women: A critical review of the evidence. *Journal of Family Issues, 6,* 229–247.

Edleson, J. L., & Gruszinski, R. J. (1988). Treating men who batter: Four years of outcome from the domestic abuse project. *Journal of Social Service Research, 12,* 3–22.

Efron, D., & Rowe, W. S. (1987). *The strategic parenting manual.* London, ON: *Journal of Strategic and Systemic Therapies.*

Egeland, B., Jacobvitz, D., & Srouge, L. A. (1988). Breaking the cycle of abuse. *Child Development, 59,* 1080–1088.

Eisikovits, Z. C., Edleson, J. L., Guttmann, E., & Sela-Amit, M. (1991). Cognitive styles and socialized attitudes of men who batter: Where should we intervene? *Family Relations, 40,* 72–77.

Elbogen, E. B. (2002). The process of violence risk assessment: A review of descriptive research. *Aggression & Violent Behavior, 7,* 591–604.

Elder, G. H., Conger, R. D., Foster, E. M., & Ardelt, M. (1992). Families under economic pressure. *Journal of Family Issues, 13,* 5–37.

Elliott, R., Watson, J. C., Goldman, R. N., & Greenberg, L. S. (2004a). Accessing and allowing experiencing. In R. Elliott & J. Watson (Eds.), *Learning emotion-focused therapy: The process-experiential approach to change* (pp. 169–192). Washington, DC: American Psychological Association.

Elliott, R., Watson, J. C., Goldman, R. N., & Greenberg, L. S. (2004b). Reprocessing problematic experiences. In R. Elliott & J. Watson (Eds.), *Learning emotion-focused therapy: The process-experiential approach to change* (pp. 193–217). Washington, DC: American Psychological Association.

Ellis, A. (1993). The rational-emotive therapy (RET) approach to marriage and family therapy. *Family Journal: Counseling & Therapy for Couples & Families, 1,* 292–307.

Ellis, A. (2003a). The nature of disturbed marital interaction. *Journal of Rational-Emotive & Cognitive Behavior Therapy, 21,* 147–153.

Ellis, A. (2003b). Helping people get better rather than merely feel better. *Journal of Rational-Emotive & Cognitive Behavior Therapy, 21,* 169–182.

Ellis, A., & Dryden, W. (1997). *The practice of rational-emotive therapy* (2nd ed). New York: Springer.

Elmer, E. (1977). *Fragile families, troubled youth: The aftermath of infant trauma.* Pittsburgh: University of Pittsburgh Press.

English, D. J., & Pecora, P. J. (1994). Risk assessment as a practice method in child protective services. *Child Welfare, 73,* 451–473.

Epstein, N., Schlesinger, S. E., & Dryden, W. (1988). *Cognitive-behavioral therapy with families.* New York: Brunner/Mazel.

Epston, D., White, M., & Murray, K. (1992). A proposal for a re-authoring therapy: Rose's revisioning of her life and a commentary. In S. McNamee & K. J. Gergen, *Therapy as social construction* (pp. 96–115). Thousand Oaks, CA: Sage.

Eron, L. D., & Peterson, R. A. (1982). Abnormal behavior: Social approaches. *Annual Review, 33,* 231–264.

Ezell, M. (2001). *Advocacy in the human services.* Pacific Grove, CA: Brooks/Cole.

Fagan, R. (2002). What I learned in school today: Reflections on my training in marriage and family therapy. *Family Journal: Counseling & Therapy for Couples & Families, 10,* 262–268.

Falicov, C. J. (1998). *Latino families in therapy: A guide to multicultural practice.* New York: Guilford.

Falloon, I. R. H. (1988). *Handbook of behavioral family therapy.* New York: Guilford.

Fantuzzo, J. W., Jurecic, L., Stovall, A., Hightower, A. D., Goins, C., & Schachtel, D. (1988). Effects of adult and peer social initiations on the social behavior of withdrawn maltreated preschool children. *Journal of Consulting & Clinical Psychology, 56,* 34–39.

Farber, B. A., & Lane, J. S. (2002). Positive regard. In J. C. Norcross (Ed.), *Psychotherapy relationships that work: Therapist contributions and responsiveness to patients* (pp. 175–194). London: Oxford University Press.

Farrington, D. P., Gallagher, B., Morley, L., St. Ledger, R. J., & West, D. J., (1988). Are there any successful men from criminogenic backgrounds? *Psychiatry, 51,* 116–130.

Feeney, J. A., & Noller, P. (1990). Attachment style as a predictor of adult romantic relationships. *Journal of Personality and Social Psychology, 58,* 281–291.

Feldman, M. A., & Case, L. (1999). Teaching child-care and safety skills to parents with intellectual disabilities through self-learning. *Journal of Intellectual & Developmental Disability, 24,* 27–44.

Fendrich, M., Warner, V., & Weissman, M. M. (1990). Family risk factors, parental depression, and psychopathology in offspring. *Developmental Psychology, 26,* 40–50.

Ferguson, T. J., Stegge, J., Miller, E. R., & Olsen, M. E. (1999). Guilt, shame, and symptoms in children. *Developmental Psychology, 35,* 347–357.

Fergusson, D. M., & Woodward, L. J. (2000). Family socioeconomic status at birth and rates of university participation. *New Zealand Journal of Educational Studies, 35,* 25–36.

Ferraro, K. J., & Johnson, J. M. (1983). How women experience battering: The process of victimization. *Social Problems, 39,* 325–339.

Findlater, J. E., & Kelly, S. (1999). Child protective services and domestic violence. *Future of Children Special Issue: Domestic Violence and Children, 9,* 84–96.

Finkelhor, D. (1978). Psychological, cultural, and family factors in incest and family sexual abuse. *Journal of Marital & Family Therapy, 4,* 41–49.

Finn, J. (1985). Men's domestic violence treatment groups: A statewide survey. *Social Work with Groups, 8*, 81–94.

Firestone, R. W. (1987). Destructive effects of the fantasy bond in couple and family relationships. *Psychotherapy, 24*, 233–239.

Firestone, R. W., Firestone, L. A., & Catlett, J. (2003). Family relationships. In R. W. Firestone & L. A. Firestone (Eds.), *Creating a life of meaning and compassion: The wisdom of psychotherapy* (pp. 271–289). Washington, DC: American Psychological Association.

Fish, J. M. (1997). Paradox for complaints? Strategic thoughts about solution-focused therapy. *Journal of Systemic Therapies, 16*, 266–273.

Fishbein, H. D. (1982). The identified patient and stage of family development. *Journal of Marital & Family Therapy, 8*, 57–61.

Fiske, S. T. (1995). Controlling other people: The impact of power on stereotyping. In N. R. Goldberger & J. B. Veroff (Eds.), *The culture and psychology reader* (pp. 438–456). New York: New York University Press.

Flaskas, C. (1997). Engagement and the therapeutic relationship in systemic therapy. *Journal of Family Therapy, 19*, 263–282.

Follingstad, D. R., Laughlin, J. E., Polek, D. S., Rutledge, L. R., & Hause, E. S. (1991). Identification of patterns of wife abuse. *Journal of Interpersonal Violence, 6*, 187–204.

Forgatch, M. S. (1989). Patterns and outcome in family problem solving: The disrupting effect of negative emotion. *Journal of Marriage & the Family, 51*(1), 115–124.

Framo, J. L. (1992). *Family-of-origin therapy: An intergenerational approach.* New York: Brunner/Mazel.

Frank, E. D. (1983). Effects of parental disciplinary practices on characteristics of children: A review of the literature. *Southern Psychologist, 1*, 77–83.

Frankel, K. A., & Bates, J. E. (1990). Mother-toddler problem solving: Antecedents in attachment, home behavior, and temperament. *Child Development, 61*, 810–819.

Fraser, M. W., Hawkins, J. D., & Howard, M. O. (1988). Parent training for delinquency prevention. *Child & Youth Services, 11*, 93–125.

Fraser, M. W., Pecora, P. J., & Haapala, D. A. (1991). *Families in crisis: The impact of intensive family preservation services.* New York: DeGruyter.

French, J. R. P., & Raven, B. H. (1959). The bases of social power. In D. Cartwright (Ed.), *Studies in social power* (pp. 150–167). Ann Arbor, MI: Institute for Social Research.

Friedlander, M. L., Heatherington, L., Johnson, B., & Skowron, E. A. (1994). Sustaining engagement: A change event in family therapy. *Journal of Consulting Psychology, 41*, 438–448.

Friedlander, M. L., Heatherington, L., & Marrs, A. L. (2000). Responding to blame in family therapy. *American Journal of Family Therapy, 28*, 133–146.

Friedman, S. (1993). *The new language of change: Constructive collaboration in psychotherapy.* New York: Guilford.

Friedman, S., & Lipchik, E. (1999). A time-effective, solution-focused approach to couple therapy. In J. M. Donovan (Ed.), *Short-term couple therapy* (pp. 325–359). New York: Guilford.

Froehle, T. C., Robinson, S. E., & Kurpius, D. J. (1983). Enhancing the effects of modeling through role-play practice. *Counselor Education & Supervision, 22*, 197–206.

Furlong, M., & Young, J. (1996). Talking about blame. *Australian & New Zealand Journal of Family Therapy, 17*, 191–200.

Gale, J., & Newfield, N. (1992). A conversation analysis of a solution-focused marital therapy session. *Journal of Marital & Family Therapy, 18*, 153–165.

Gara, M. A., Rosenberg, S., & Herzog, E. P. (1996). The abused child as parent. *Child Abuse & Neglect, 20*, 797–807.

Garman, F., Hammann, S., Hoodak, G, Fiume, M., Manino-Corse, F., & Wise, S. (2000). Enhancing reading achievement: A collaborative, community-based intervention model. *Education—Special Issue: Career Issues in Education, 120*, 795–799.

Gaston, L., Marmar, C. R., Thompson, L. W., & Gallagher, D. (1988). Relation of patient pretreatment characteristics to the therapeutic alliance in diverse psychotherapies. *Journal of Consulting and Clinical Psychology, 56*, 483–489.

Gaudin, J. M. Jr., Polansky, N. A., Kilpatrick, A. C., & Shilton, P. (1996). Family functioning in neglectful families. *Child Abuse & Neglect, 20*, 363–377.

Gaudin, J. M., & Pollane, L. (1983). Social networks, stress, and child abuse. *Children & Youth Services Review, 5*, 91–102.

Geddes, M., & Medway. J. (1977). The symbolic drawing of family life space. *Family Process, 16*, 219–228.

Gelles, R. J., & Straus, M. A. (1979). Determinants of violence in the family: Toward a theoretical integration. In W. Burr (Ed.), *Contemporary theories about the family*. New York: Free Press.

George, C. (1996). A representational perspective of child abuse and prevention: Internal working models of attachment and caregiving. *Child Abuse & Neglect, 20*, 411–424.

Giardino, A. P., Giardino, E. R., MacLaren, C. F., & Burg, F. D. (1994). Managing change: A case study of implementing change in a clinical evaluation system. *Teaching & Learning in Medicine, 6*, 149–153.

Gibbs, J. T. (1984). Black adolescents and youth: An endangered species. *American Journal of Orthopsychiatry, 54*, 6–21.

Gladding, S. T. (1984). The metaphor as a counseling tool in group work. *Journal for Specialists in Group Work, 9*, 151–156.

Godwin, D. D., & Scanzoni, J. (1989). Couple consensus during marital joint decision-making: A context, process, outcome model. *Journal of Marriage & the Family, 51*, 943–956.

Gold, J. M., & Morris, G. M. (2003). Family resistance to counseling: The initial agenda for intergenerational and narrative approaches. *Family Journal: Counseling & Therapy for Couples & Families, 11*, 374–379.

Goldberg, J. A. (1990). Interrupting the discourse on interruptions: An analysis in terms of relationally neutral, power- and rapport-oriented acts. *Journal of Pragmatics, 14*, 883–903.

Goldfried, M. R., & & Sobocinski, D. (1975). Effect of irrational beliefs on emotional arousal. *Journal of Consulting & Clinical Psychology, 43*, 504–510.

Goldman, M., Gier, J. A., & Smith, D. E. (1981). *Journal of Social Psychology, 114*, 75–83.

Goldsmith, H. R. (1990). Men who abuse their spouses: An approach to assessing future risk. *Journal of Offender Counseling, Services & Rehabilitation, 15*, 45–56.

Goldstein, A. P., Keller, H., & Erne, D. (1985). *Changing the abusive parent*. Champaign, IL: Research Press.

Goldstein, D., & Rosenbaum, A. (1985). An evaluation of the self-esteem of maritally violent men. *Family Relations, 34*, 425–428.

Goldstein, J. (1989). The affirmative core of resistance to change. *Organizational Development Journal, 7*, 32–38.

Gomes-Swartz, B., Hadley, S. W., & Strupp, H. H. (1978). Individual psychotherapy and behavior research. *Annual Review of Psychology, 29*, 435–471.

Gondolf, E. W. (1985a). Fighting for control: A clinical assessment of men who batter. *Social Casework, 66*(1), 48–54.

Gondolf, E. W. (1985b). Anger and oppression in men who batter: Empiricist and feminist perspectives and their implications for research. *Victimology: An International Journal, 10*, 311–324.

Gondolf, E. W. (1987). Seeing through smoke and mirrors: A guide to batterer program evaluations. *Response, 10*, 16–19.

Goodstone, M. S., & Diamante, T. (1998). Organizational use of therapeutic change: Strengthening multisource feedback systems through interdisciplinary coaching. *Consulting Psychology Journal: Practice & Research, 50*, 152–163.

Gottlieb, G. (1991). Epigenetic systems view of human development. *Developmental Psychology, 27*, 33–34.

Grann, M., & Wedin, I. (2002). Risk factors for recidivism among spousal assault and spousal homicide offenders. *Psychology, Crime & Law, 8*, 5–23.

Grant, K. J., Henley, A., & Kean, A. M. (2001). The journey after the journey: Family counselling in the context of immigration and ethnic diversity. *Canadian Journal of Counselling, 35*, 89–100.

Graziano, A. M., & Mills, J. R. (1992). Treatment for abused children: When is a partial solution acceptable? *Child Abuse & Neglect, 16*, 217–228.

Green, A. H., Power, E., Steinbook, B., & Gaines, R. (1981). Factors associated with successful and unsuccessful intervention with child-abusive families. *Child Abuse & Neglect, 5*, 45–52.

Green, S. K., & Brown-Standridge, M. D. (1989). Inferring the relational system: Interactional therapy within a constructionist paradigm. *Family Therapy, 16*, 99–111.

Greenberg, L. S. (1999). Ideal psychotherapy research: A study of significant change processes. *Journal of Clinical Psychology, 55*, 1467–1480.

Greenberg, L. S., & Johnson, S. M. (1988). *Emotionally focused therapy for couples*. New York: Guilford.

Greenberg, L. S., & Pascual-Leone, J. (1997). Emotion in the creation of personal meaning. In M. J. Power & C. R. Brewin (Eds.), *The transformation of meaning in psychological therapies: Integrating theory and practice* (pp. 157–173). New York: Wiley.

Greenberg, L. S., Rice, L. N., & Elliott, R. K. (1996). *Facilitating emotional change: The moment-by-moment process*. New York: Guilford.

Grinker, R. R. Sr. (1971). Biomedical education on a system. *Archives of General Psychiatry, 24*, 291–297.

Grizenko, N., & Pawliuk, N. (1994). Risk and protective factors for disruptive behavior disorders in children. *American Journal of Orthopsychiatry, 64*, 534–544.

Gross, S. J. (1994). The process of change: Variations on a theme by Virginia Satir. *Journal of Humanistic Psychology, 34*, 87–110.

Gruber, K. J., Fleetwood, T. W., & Herring, M. W. (2001). In-home continuing care services for substance-affected families: The Bridges Program. *Social Work, 46*, 267–277.

Guerin, P. J. Jr., Fogarty, T. F., Fay, L. F., & Kautto, J. G. (1996). *Working with relationship triangles: The one-two-three of psychotherapy.* New York: Guilford.

Guilfoyle, M. (2002). Power, knowledge and resistance in therapy: Exploring links between discourse and materiality. *International Journal of Psychotherapy, 7*, 83–97.

Gullette, L. C. (1987). Children in maritally violent families: A look at family dynamics. *Youth and Society, 19*, 119–133.

Hale, G., Zimostrad, S., Duckworth, J., & Nicholas, D. (1988). Abusive partners: MMPI profiles of male batterers. *Journal of Mental Health Counseling, 10*, 214–224.

Haley, J. (1973). *Uncommon therapy: The psychiatric techniques of Milton H. Erickson, M.D.* New York: Norton.

Haley, J. (1987). *Problem-solving therapy* (2nd ed.). San Francisco: Jossey-Bass.

Hall, H. V., Catlin, E., Boissevain, A., & Westgate, J. (1984). Dangerous myths about predicting dangerousness (Part I). *American Journal of Forensic Psychology, 2*, 173–193.

Hannah, P. J. (2000). Preparing members for the expectations of social work with groups: An approach to the preparatory interview. *Social Work with Groups, 22*, 51–66.

Hansen, M., Litzelman, A., & Salter, B. R. (2002). Serious emotional disturbance: Working with families. In D. T. Marsh & M. A. Fristad (Eds.), *Handbook of serious emotional disturbance in children and adolescents* (pp. 375–391). New York: Wiley.

Hardaway, T. G. II (2000). Family play therapy and child psychiatry in an era of managed care. In H. G. Kaduson & C. D. Schaefer (Eds.), *Short-term play therapy for children* (pp. 256–265). New York: Guilford.

Hareven, T. (1986). Historical changes in the social construction of the life course. *Human Development, 29*, 171–180.

Hart, K. E. (1984). Anxiety management training and anger control for Type A individuals. *Journal of Behavior Therapy & Experimental Psychiatry, 15*, 133–139.

Harvey, S. (2000). Family dynamic play. In P. Lewis & D. R. Johnson (Eds.), *Current approaches in drama therapy* (pp. 379–409). Springfield, IL: Thomas.

Harvey, S. (2003). Dynamic family play with an adoptive family struggling with issues of grief, loss, and adjustment. In D. J. Wiener & L. K. Oxford (Eds.), *Action therapy with families and groups: Using creative arts improvisation in clinical practice* (pp. 19–43). Washington, DC: American Psychological Press.

Hastings, J. E., & Hamberger, L. K. (1988). Personality characteristics of spouse abusers: A controlled comparison. *Violence & Victims, 3*, 31–48.

Hawley, K. M., & Weisz, J. R. (2003). Child, parent and therapist (dis)agreement on target problems in outpatient therapy: The therapist's dilemma and its implications. *Journal of Consulting & Clinical Psychology, 7*, 62–70.

Hay, C. E., & Kinnier, R. T. (1998). Homework in counseling. *Journal of Mental Health Counseling, 20*, 122–132.

Heap, K. K. (1991). A predictive and follow-up study of abusive and neglectful families by case analysis. *Child Abuse & Neglect, 15*, 261–273.

Hearn, J., & Lawrence, M. (1985). Family sculpting: II. Some practical examples. *Journal of Family Therapy, 7*, 113–131.

Heath, A. W., & Stanton, M. D. (1998). Family-based treatment: Stages and outcomes. In R. J. Frances & S. I. Miller (Eds.), *Clinical textbook of addictive disorders* (2nd ed., pp. 496–520). New York: Guilford.

Hecker, L. L., & Deacon, S. A. (1998). *The therapist's notebook: Homework, handouts, and activities for use in psychotherapy.* New York: Haworth Press.

Heikkinen, C. A. (1989). Reorientation from altered states: Please, more carefully. *Journal of Counseling and Development, 67*, 520–521.

Helms, J. E. (1995). Why is there no study of cultural equivalence in standardized cognitive ability testing? In N. R. Goldberger & J. B. Veroff (Eds.), *The culture and psychology reader* (pp. 674–719). New York: New York University Press.

Henggeler, S. W., & Borduin, C. (1990). *Family therapy and beyond: A multisystemic approach to treating the behavior problems of children and adolescents.* Pacific Grove, CA: Brooks/Cole.

Henggeler, S. W., & Lee, T. (2003). Multisystemic treatment of serious clinical problems. In A. E. Kazdin (Ed.), *Evidence-based psychotherapies for children and adolescents* (pp. 301–322). New York: Guilford.

Henggeler, S. W., Melton, G. B., & Smith, L. A. (1992). Family preservation using multisystemic therapy: An effective alternative to incarcerating serious juvenile offenders. *Journal of Consulting & Clinical Psychology, 60*, 953–961.

Henggeler, S. W., Peckrel, S. G., Brondino, M. J., & Crouch, J. L. (1996). Eliminating (almost) treatment dropout of substance abusing or dependent delinquents through home-based multisystemic therapy. *American Journal of Psychiatry, 153*, 427–428.

Herbert, T. B., Silver, R. C., & Ellard, J. H. (1991). Coping with an abusive relationship: I. How and why do women stay? *Journal of Marriage & the Family, 53*, 311–325.

Hernandez, S. L. (1998). The emotional thermometer: Using family sculpting for emotional assessment. *Family Therapy, 25*, 121–128.

Herrera, A. E., & Sanchez, V. C. (1980). Prescriptive group psychotherapy: A successful application in the treatment of low income, Spanish-speaking clients. *Psychotherapy Theory, Research and Practice, 17*, 169–174.

Heyman, B., Swain, J., Gillman, M., Handyside, E. C., & Newman, W. (1997). Alone in the crowd: How adults cope with social networks problems. *Social Science & Medicine, 44*, 41–53.

Hill, A. (2001). "No one else could understand": Women's experiences of a support group run by and for mothers of sexually abused children. *British Journal of Social Work, 31*, 385–397.

Hinshaw, A. W., & DeLeon, P. H. (1995). Toward achieving multidisciplinary professional collaboration. *Professional Psychology: Research & Practice, 26*, 115–116.

Hinton, W. J., Sheperis, C., & Sims, P. (2003). Family-based approaches to juvenile delinquency: A review of the literature. *Family Journal: Counseling & Therapy for Couples & Families, 11*, 167–173.

Hodges, V. G., & Blythe, B. J. (1992). Improving service delivery to high-risk families: Home based practice. *Families in Society: The Journal of Contemporary Human Services, 73*, 259–265.

Hoffman, L. W. (1983). Imagery and metaphor in couples therapy. *Client Therapy, 10*, 141–155.

Hoffman, M. L. (1963). Parent discipline and the child's consideration for others. *Child Development, 34*, 573–588.

Home, A., & Darveau-Fournier, L. (1990). Facing the challenge of developing group services for high-risk families. *Group Work, 3*, 236–248.

Hooper, J. O., & Hooper, F. H. (1985). Family and individual developmental theories: Conceptual analysis and speculations. *Contributions to Human Development, 14*, 1–30.

Horne, A. M. (1974). Teaching parents a reinforcement program. *Elementary School Guidance and Counseling, 9*, 102–107.

Horne, A. M., & Van Dyke, B. (1983). Treatment and maintenance of social learning family therapy. *Behavior Therapy, 14*, 606–613.

Houle, J., & Kiely, M. C. (1984, March). Intimacy: A little understood stage of development. *Canada's Mental Health*, 7–11.

Howes, P., & Markman, H. J. (1989). Marital quality and child functioning: A longitudinal investigation. *Child Development, 60*, 1044–1051.

Howing, P. T., Wodarski, J. S., Gaudin, J. M., & Kurtz, P. D. (1989). Effective interventions to ameliorate the incidence of child maltreatment: The empirical base. *Social Work, 34*, 330–338.

Hoyt, M. F., & Berg, I. K. (1998). Solution-focused couple therapy: Helping clients construct self-fulfilling realities. In M. F. Hoyt (Ed.), *The handbook of constructive therapies: Innovative approaches from leading practitioners* (pp. 314–340). San Francisco: Jossey-Bass.

Huat, T. B. (1994). Therapeutic paradox: Its use and function in therapy in a predominantly Chinese society. In G. Davidson (Ed.), *Applying psychology: Lessons from Asia-Oceania* (pp. 61–81). Carlton, South VIC: Australian Psychological Society.

Hudson, P., & O'Hanlon, W. H. (1992). *Rewriting love stories: Brief marital therapy*. New York: Norton.

Huey, S. J. Jr., Henggeler, S. W., Brondino, M. J., & Pickrel, S. G. (2000). Mechanisms of change in multisystemic therapy: Reducing delinquent behavior through therapist adherence and improved family and peer functioning. *Journal of Consulting & Clinical Psychology, 68*, 451–467.

Irwin, E., & Malloy, E. (1975). Family puppet interview. *Family Process, 14*, 179–191.

Ives, K. H. (1977–1978). Steps in client problem solving. *Case Analysis, 1*, 65–77.

Jackson, D. D. (1957). The question of family homeostasis. *Psychiatric Quarterly Supplement, 31*, 79–90.

Jackson, D. D. (1959). Family interaction, family homeostasis, and some implications for conjoint family therapy. In J. Masserman (Ed.), *Individual and family dynamics*. New York: Grune & Stratton.

Jackson, D. D. (1965). Family rules: The marital quid pro quo. *Archives of General Psychiatry, 12*, 589–594.

Jackson-Gilfort, A., Liddle, H. A., Tejeda, M. J., & Dakof, G. A. (2001). Facilitating engagement of African American male adolescents in family therapy: A cultural theme process study. *Journal of Black Psychology, 27*, 321–340.

Jacob, T., & Krahn, G. L. (1988). Marital interactions of alcoholic couples: Comparison with depressed and nondistressed couples. *Journal of Consulting and Clinical Psychology, 56*, 73–79.

Jacobs, L., & Wachs, C. (2002). *Parent therapy: A relational alternative to working with children.* Northvale, NJ: Aronson.

Jacobson, S. W., & Frye, K. F. (1991). Effect of maternal social support on attachment: Experimental evidence. *Child Development, 62*, 572–582.

Jankowski, P. J., & Ivey, D. C. (2001). Problem definition in marital and family therapy: A qualitative study. *Contemporary Family Therapy: An International Journal, 23*, 419–439.

Jason, L. A., DeAmicus, L., & Carter, B. (1978). Prevention intervention for disadvantaged children. *Community Mental Health Journal, 14*, 272–278.

Johnson, B. D., Franklin, L. C., Hall, K., & Prieto, L. R. (2000). Parent training through play: Parent-child interaction therapy with a hyperactive child. *Family Journal: Counseling & Therapy for Couples & Families, 8*, 180–186.

Johnson, C. F. (1993). Detriangulation and conflict management in parent-adolescent relationships: A model. *Contemporary Family Therapy: An International Journal, 15*, 185–195.

Johnson, D. W., & Johnson, R. T. (1995). Teaching students to be peacemakers: Results of five years of research. *Peace & Conflict: Journal of Peace Psychology, 1*, 417–438.

Johnson, S. M., & Greenberg, L. S. (1988). Relating process to outcome in marital therapy. *Journal of Marital & Family Therapy, 14*, 175–183.

Johnson, W. L., & Clancy, T. (1991). Efficiency in behavior-changing social programs: The case of in-home child abuse prevention. *Administration in Social Work, 15*, 105–118.

Jones, E. D., & McCurdy, K. (1992). The links between types of maltreatment and demographic characteristics of children. *Child Abuse and Neglect, 16*, 201–215.

Jordan, K. (2001). Family art therapy: The joint family holiday drawing. *Family Journal: Counseling & Therapy for Couples & Families, 9*, 52–54.

Jordan, K. (2003). Relating therapeutic working alliance to therapy outcome. *Family Therapy, 30*, 95–108.

Jory, B., Anderson, D., & Greer, C. (1997). Intimate justice: Confronting issues of accountability, respect, and freedom in treatment for abuse and violence. *Journal of Marital & Family Therapy, 23*, 399–419.

Joseph, S., Yule, W., & Williams, R. (1993). Post-traumatic stress: Attributional aspects. *Journal of Traumatic Stress, 6*, 501–513.

Jouriles, E. N., Barling, J., & O'Leary, K. D. (1987). Predicting behavior problems in maritally violent families. *Journal of Abnormal Child Psychology, 15*, 165–173.

Jouriles, E. N., McDonald, R., Stephens, N., Norwood, W., Spillerm, L. C., & Ware, H. S. (1998). Breaking the cycle of violence: Helping families departing from battered women's shelters. In G. W. Holden & R. Geffner (Eds.), *Children exposed to marital violence: Theory, research, and applied issues* (pp. 337–369). Washington, DC: American Psychological Association.

Joyce-Becker, J. (1996). The dominoes fall: Attending to stability. *Journal of Systemic Therapies, 15*, 80–91.

Kaduson, H. G., & Schaefer, C. E. (1997). *101 favorite play therapy techniques.* Northvale, NJ: Aronson.

Kagan, R., & Schlosberg, S. (1989). *Families in perpetual crisis.* New York: Norton.

Kagan, S. L., & Weissbourd, B. (1994). Toward a new normative system of family support. In S. L. Kagan & B. Weissbourd (Eds.), *Putting families first: America's family support movement and the challenge of change* (pp. 473–490). San Francisco: Jossey-Bass.

Kalmuss, D. (1984). The intergenerational transmission of marital aggression. *Journal of Marriage & the Family, 46*, 11–19.

Katz, J. H., & Miller, G. A. (1996). Coaching leaders through culture change. *Consulting Psychology Journal: Practice and Research, 48*, 104–114.

Keithly, L. J., Samples, S. J., & Strupp, H. H. (1980). Patient motivation as a predictor of process and outcome in psychotherapy. *Psychotherapy and Psychosomatics, 33*, 7–97.

Kemp, A., Green, B. L., Hovanitz, C., & Rawlings, E. I. (1995). Incidence and correlates of posttraumatic stress disorder in battered women shelter and community samples. *Journal of Interpersonal Violence, 10*, 43–55.

Kendall, P. C., & Grove, W. (1988). Normative comparisons in therapy outcome. *Behavioral Assessment, 10*, 147–158.

Kermani, E. J., & Drob, S. L. (1987). Tarasoff decision: A decade later, the dilemma still faces psychotherapists. *American Journal of Psychotherapy, 41*(2), 271–285.

Kilpatrick, A. C., & Holland, T. P. (1999). *Working with families: An integrative model by level of need* (2nd ed.). Boston: Allyn & Bacon.

Kirchenbaum, D. S. (1979). Social competence intervention and evaluation in the inner city: Cincinnati's social skills development program. *Journal of Consulting & Clinical Psychology, 47,* 778–780.

Kochanska, G. (1995). Children's temperament, mother's discipline, and security of attachment: Multiple pathways to emerging internalization. *Child Development, 66,* 597–615.

Kochanska, G. (2002). Mutually responsive orientation between mothers and their young children: A context for the early development of conscience. *Current Directions in Psychological Science, 11,* 191–195.

Koestner, R., Franz, C., & Weinberger, J. (1990). The family origins of empathic concern: A 26-year longitudinal study. *Journal of Personality and Social Psychology, 58,* 709–717.

Kolbo, J. R., Blakely, E. H., & Engleman, D. (1996). Children who witness domestic violence: A review of empirical literature. *Journal of Interpersonal Violence, 11,* 281–293.

Kolko, D. J., Kazdin, A. E., Thomas, A. M., & Day, B. (1993). Heightened child physical abuse potential. Child, parent, and family dysfunction. *Journal of Interpersonal Violence, 8,* 169–192.

Kopp, R. R., & Craw, M. J. (1998). Metaphoric language, metaphoric cognition, and cognitive therapy. *Psychotherapy, 35,* 306–311.

Kraft, R. G., Claiborn, C. D., & Dowd, E. T. (1985). Effects of positive reframing and paradoxical directives in counseling for negative emotions. *Journal of Counseling Psychology, 32,* 617–621.

Krantz, S. E., & Moos, R. H. (1988). Risk factors at intake predict nonremission among depressed patients. *Journal of Consulting & Clinical Psychology, 56,* 437–458.

Kroll, P. D., Stock, D. F., & James, M. E. (1985). The behavior of adult alcoholic men abused as children. *Journal of Nervous and Mental Disease, 173,* 689–693.

Kropp, P. R., Hart, S. D., Webster, C. D., & Eaves, D. (1994). *Manual for the spousal assault risk assessment guide.* Vancouver, BC: British Columbia Institute on Family Violence.

Krysan, M., Moore, K. A., & Zill, N. (1990). *Identifying successful families: An overview of constructs and selected measures.* Washington, DC: Child Trends.

Kubany, E. S. (1998). Cognitive therapy for trauma-related guilt. In V. M. Follette & F. I. Ruzek (Eds.), *Cognitive-behavioral therapies for trauma* (pp. 124–161). New York: Guilford.

Kumpfer, K. L., Alvarado, R., Tait, C., & Turner, C. (2002). Effectiveness of school-based family and children's skills training for substance prevention among 6- to 8-year-old rural children. *Psychology of Addictive Behaviors, 16,* 65–71.

Kurland, R., & Salmon, R. (1998). Purpose: A misunderstood and misused keystone of group work practice. *Social Work with Groups, 2,* 5–17.

Lacharite, C., Ethier, L., & Couture, G. (1995). The influence of partner on parental stress of neglectful mothers. *Child Abuse Review, 5,* 18–33.

Lackey, C., & Williams, K. R. (1995). Social bonding and the cessation of partner violence across generations. *Journal of Marriage & the Family, 57,* 295–305.

Laird, J. (2000). Gender in lesbian relationships: Cultural, feminist, and constructionist reflections. *Journal of Marital & Family Therapy, 26,* 455–467.

Laird, J., & Green, R. J. (1996). *Lesbians and gays in couples and families: A handbook for therapists.* San Francisco: Jossey-Bass.

Langford, D. R. (1996). Predicting unpredictability: A model of women's processes of predicting battering men's violence. *Scholarly Inquiry for Nursing Practice, 10,* 371–385.

Langhinrichsen-Rohling, J., Smutzler, N., & Vivian, D. (1994). Positivity in marriage: The role of discord and physical aggression against wives. *Journal of Marriage & the Family, 56,* 69–79.

Lankton, C. H., & Lankton, S. R. (1989). *Tales of enchantment: Goal-oriented metaphors for adults and children in therapy.* New York: Brunner/Mazel.

Lankton, S. (2001). Ericksonian therapy. In R. Corsini (Ed.), *Handbook of innovative psychotherapy* (2nd ed., pp. 194–205). New York: Wiley.

Lankton, S. (2002). The use of therapeutic metaphor in social work. In A. Roberts & G. Greene (Eds.), *Social workers' desk reference* (pp. 385–391). New York: Oxford University Press.

Lankton, S., & Lankton, C. (1983). *The answer within: A clinical framework of Ericksonian hypnotherapy.* New York: Brunner/Mazel.

Lankton, S. R., Lankton, C. H., & Matthews, W. J. (1991). Ericksonian family therapy. In A. S. Gunman & D. P. Kniskern (Eds.), *Handbook of family therapy* (Vol. 2, pp. 239–283). New York: Brunner/Mazel.

Lansberg, I. (1988). Social categorization, entitlement, and justice in organizations: Contextual determinants and cognitive underpinnings. *Human Relations, 41,* 871–899.

Larson, E. (1998). Reframing the meaning of disability to families: The embrace of paradox. *Social Science & Medicine, 47,* 865–875.

Laselle, K. M., & Russell, T. T. (1993). To what extent are school counselors using meditation and relaxation techniques? *School Counselor, 40,* 178–183.

Latham, G. I. (1996). The making of a stable family. In J. R. Cautela & W. Ishaq (Eds.), *Contemporary issues in behavior therapy: Improving the human condition* (pp. 357–382). New York: Plenum Press.

Lawson, D. M. (1987). Using therapeutic stories in the counseling process. *Elementary School Guidance & Counseling, 22,* 134–142.

Layzer, J. I., & Goodson, B. D. (1992). Child abuse and neglect treatment demonstrations. *Children and Youth Services Review, 14,* 67–76.

Lazarus, A. A. (1997). Friends, images, and appropriate self-talk. *Psychotherapy in Private Practice, 16,* 29–32.

Leavy, R. L. (1983). Social support and psychological disorder: A review. *Journal of Community Psychology, 11,* 3–21.

LeCroy, C. W. (1992). Enhancing the delivery of effective mental health services to children. *Social Work, 37,* 225–231.

Leitch, M. L., & Thomas, V. (1999). The AAMFT–Head Start training partnership project: Enhancing MFT capacities beyond the family system. *Journal of Marital & Family Therapy, 25,* 141–154.

Lengua, L. J., Roosa, M. W., Schupak-Neuberg, E., Michaels, M. L., Berg, C. N., & Wechsler, L. F. (1992). Using focus groups to guide the development of a parenting program for difficult-to-reach, high-risk families. *Family Relations, 41,* 163–168.

Leventhal, J. M. (1996). Twenty years later: We do know how to prevent child abuse and neglect. *Child Abuse & Neglect, 20,* 647–653.

Lever, H., & Gmeiner, A. (2000). Families leaving therapy after one or two sessions: A multiple descriptive case study. *Contemporary Family Therapy: An International Journal, 22,* 39–65.

Leveton, E. (1991). The use of doubling to counter resistance in family and individual treatment. *Arts in Psychotherapy, 18,* 241–249.

Lewin, K. (1948). *Resolving social conflicts: Selected papers on group dynamics.* New York: Harper & Row.

Liberman, D. B., & Liberman, R. P. (2003). Involving families in rehabilitation through behavioral family management. *Psychiatric Services, 54,* 633–635.

Liddle, H. A., & Saba, G. W. (1982). Teaching family therapy at the introductory level: A conceptual model emphasizing a pattern which connects training and therapy. *Journal of Marital & Family Therapy, 6,* 63–72.

Liepman, M. R., Nirenberg, T. D., Doolittle, R. H., Begin, A. M., Broffman, T. E., & Babich, M. E. (1989). Family functioning of male alcoholics and their female partners during periods of drinking and abstinence. *Family Process, 28,* 239–249.

Link, B. G., & Phelan, J. (1995). Social conditions as fundamental causes of disease. *Journal of Health and Social Behavior* (Extra Issue), 80–94.

Litty, C. G., Kowalski, R., & Minor, S. (1996). Moderating effects of physical abuse and perceived social support on the potential to abuse. *Child Abuse & Neglect, 20,* 305–314.

Llewellyn, G., McConnell, D., Honey, A., Mayes, R., & Russo, D. (2003). Promoting health and home safety for children of parents with intellectual disability: A randomized controlled trial. *Research in Developmental Disabilities, 24,* 405–431.

Lobovits, D. H., & Freeman, J. C. (1997). Destination grump station—getting off the grump bus. In C. Smith & D. Nylund (Eds.), *Narrative therapies with children and adolescents* (pp. 174–194). New York: Guilford.

Long, J. V. F., & Vaillant, G. E. (1984). Natural history of male psychological health: XI. Escape from the underclass. *American Journal of Psychiatry, 141,* 341–346.

Lorenz, G., Hoven, C., Andrews, H. F., & Bird, H. (1995). Marital discord and psychiatric disorders in children and adolescents. *Journal of Child and Family Studies, 4,* 341–358.

Lorion, R. P. (1973). Socioeconomic status and traditional treatment approaches reconsidered. *Psychological Bulletin, 79,* 263–270.

Lorion, R. P., & Felner, R. D. (1986). Research on mental health interventions with the disadvantaged. In S. L. Garfield & A. E. Bergin (Eds.), *Handbook of psychotherapy and behavior change* (pp. 739–775). New York: Wiley.

Love, L. R., Kaswan, J., & Bugental, D. E. (1972). Differential effectiveness of three clinical interventions for different socioeconomic groupings. *Journal of Consulting and Clinical Psychology, 39*, 347–360.

Lowe, G., & Sibley, D. (1991). Boundary enforcement in the home environment and adolescent alcohol use. *Family Dynamics of Addiction Quarterly, 1*, 52–58.

Lown, N., & Britton, B. (1991). Engaging families through the letter writing technique. *Journal of Strategic & Systemic Therapies, 10*, 43–48.

Lowy, L. (1976). Decision-making and group work. In S. Bernstein (Ed.), *Explorations in group work* (pp. 107–136). Boston: Charles River Books.

Lu, L., & Lin, Y. Y. (1998). Family roles and happiness in adulthood. *Personality & Individual Differences, 25*, 195–207.

Luborsky, L., Chandler, M., Auerbach, A. H., Cohun, J., & Achrach, H. M. (1971). Factors influencing the outcome of psychotherapy: A review of the quantitative research. *Psychological Bulletin, 75*, 145–185.

Luster, T., Perlstadt, H., McKinnery, M., Sims, K., & Juang, L. (1996). The effects of a family support program and other factors on the home environments provided by adolescent mothers. *Family Relations, 45*, 255–264.

Lutzker, J. R. (1990). Project 12-ways: Treating child abuse and neglect from an eco-behavioral perspective. In R. F. Dangel & R. F. Polster (Eds.), *Parent training: Foundations of research and practice.* New York: Guilford.

Lyon, E., & Kouloumpos-Lenares, K. (1987). Clinician and state children's services worker collaboration in treating sexual abuse. *Child Welfare, 66*, 517–527.

Lyons-Ruth, K. (1996). Attachment relationships among children with aggressive behavior problems: The role of disorganized early attachment patterns. *Journal of Consulting & Clinical Psychology, 64*, 64–73.

Lyons-Ruth, K., Connell, D. B., Grunebaum, H. U., & Botein, S. (1990). Infants as social risks: Maternal depression and family support services as mediators of infant development and security of attachment. *Child Development, 61*, 85–98.

Lystad, M. H. (1975). Violence at home: A review of the literature. *American Journal of Orthopsychiatry, 45*, 239.

Madanes, C. (1980). Marital therapy when a symptom is presented by a spouse. *International Journal of Family Therapy, 2*, 120–136.

Madanes, C. (1981). *Strategic family therapy.* San Francisco: Jossey-Bass.

Madanes, C. (1984). *Behind the one-way mirror.* San Francisco: Jossey-Bass.

Madanes, C. (1990). *Sex, love, and violence: Strategies for transformation.* New York: Norton.

Madanes, C. (1994). *The secret meaning of money.* San Francisco: Jossey-Bass.

Madanes, C., Keim, J. P., & Smelser, D. (1995). *The violence of men: New techniques for working with abusive families: A therapy of social action.* Rockville, MD: Family Therapy Institute.

Maden, A. (2003). Standardized risk assessment: Why all the fuss? *Psychiatric Bulletin, 27*, 201–204.

Magen, R. H. (1999). In the best interests of battered women: Reconceptualizing allegations of failure to protect. *Child Maltreatment: Journal of the American Professional Society on the Abuse of Children, 4*, 127–135.

Maiuro, R. D., Cahn, T. S., & Vitaliano, P. P. (1986). Assertiveness deficits and hostility in domestically violent men. *Violence and Victims, 1*, 279–289.

Malan, D. H., Heath, E. S., Bacal, H. A., & Balfour, F. H. (1975). Psychodynamic changes in untreated neurotic patients: II. Apparently genuine improvements. *Archives of General Psychiatry, 32*, 110–126.

Malecki, C. K., & Demaray, M. K. (2003). What type of support do they need? Investigating student adjustment as related to emotional, informational, appraisal, and instrumental support. *School Psychology Quarterly, 18*, 231–252.

Maluccio, A. N. (1989). Research perspectives on social support systems for families and children. *Journal of Applied Social Sciences, 13*, 269–289.

Mann, E., & McDermott, J. F. (1983). Play therapy for victims of child abuse and neglect. In C. F. Schaefer & J. O'Conner (Eds.), *Handbook of play therapy* (pp. 283–309). New York: Wiley.

Margolin, G. (1979). Conjoint marital therapy to enhance anger management and reduce spouse abuse. *American Journal of Family Therapy, 7*, 13–23.

Mash, E. J., & Johnson, C. (1990). Determinants of parenting stress: Illustrations from families of hyperactive children and families of physically abused children. *Journal of Clinical Child Psychology, 19*, 313–328.

May, K. M. (2001). Theory: Does it matter? *Family Journal: Counseling & Therapy for Couples & Families, 9,* 37–38.

May, K. M. (2004). How do we teach family therapy theory? *Family Journal: Counseling & Therapy for Couples & Families, 12,* 275–277.

Mayadas, N. S., & Duehn, W. D. (1976). Children in gay families: An investigation of services. *Homosexual Counseling Journal, 3,* 70–83.

Mayes, L. C., & Truman, S. D. (2002). Substance abuse and parenting. In M. H. Bornstein (Ed.), *Handbook of parenting: Vol. 4. Social conditions and applied parenting* (2nd ed., pp. 329–359). Mahwah, NJ: Erlbaum.

Maynard, P. E. (1996). Teaching family therapy theory: Do something different. *American Journal of Family Therapy, 24,* 195–205.

McCann, J. T. (2001). The risk of violence. In J. T. McCann (Ed.), *Stalking in children and adolescents: The primitive bond* (pp. 145–176). Washington, DC: American Psychological Association.

McColl, M. A., & Friedland, J. (1993). Community social support intervention: Results of a randomized trial. *Canadian Journal of Rehabilitation, 7,* 28–30.

McCollum, V. J. C. (1997). Evolution of the African American family personality: Considerations for family therapy. *Journal of Multicultural Counseling & Development, 25,* 219–229.

McConaghy, N., Blaszczynski, A., Armstrong, M. S., & Kidson, W. (1989). Resistance to treatment of adolescent offenders. *Archives of Sexual Behavior, 18,* 97–107.

McCord, J. (1988). Parental behavior in the cycle of aggression. *Psychiatry, 51,* 14–23.

McCubbin, H. I., & Lavee, Y. (1986). Strengthening Army families: A family life cycle stage perspective. *Evaluation & Parogram Planning, 9,* 221–231.

McGaha, C. G. (2002). Development of parenting skills in individuals with an intellectual impairment: An epigenetic explanation. *Disability & Society, 17,* 81–91.

McGee, D. R. (2000). Constructive questions: How do therapeutic questions work? *Dissertation Abstracts International: Section B. The Sciences & Engineering, 60*(9-B), 4966.

McGoldrick, M. (1998). *Re-visioning family therapy: Race, culture, and gender in clinical practice.* New York: Guilford.

McGoldrick, M. (2003). Culture: A challenge to concepts of normality. In F. Walsh (Ed.), *Normal family processes: Growing diversity and complexity* (3rd ed., pp. 235–259). New York: Guilford.

McGoldrick, M., & Carter, B. (2001). Advances in coaching: Family therapy with one person. *Journal of Marital & Family Therapy, 27,* 281–300.

McGoldrick, M., & Gerson, R. (1985). *Genograms in family assessment.* New York: Norton.

McGoldrick, M., Gerson, R., & Shellenberger, S. (1999). *Genograms: Assessment and intervention* (2nd ed.). New York: Norton.

McGoldrick, M., Giordano, J., & Pearce, J. K. (1996). *Ethnicity and family therapy* (2nd ed.). New York: Guilford.

McInnis-Dittrich, K. (1996). Violence prevention: An ecological adaptation of systematic training for effective parenting. *Families in Society: The Journal of Contemporary Human Services, 77,* 414–422.

McWhirter, J. J., McWhirter, B. T., McWhirter, A. M., & McWhirter, E. J. (1994). High- and low-risk characteristics of youth: The five Cs of competency. *Elementary School Guidance & Counseling, 28,* 188–196.

Medalie, J. H. (1985). Stress, social support, coping, & adjustment. *Journal of Family Practice, 20,* 533–535.

Mederer, H. J., & Hill, R. (1983). Critical transitions over the family life span: Theory and research. *Marriage & Family Review, 6,* 39–60.

Megargee, E. I. (1976). The prediction of dangerous behavior. *Criminal Justice and Behavior, 3,* 3–22.

Melidonis, G. G., & Bry, B. H. (1995). Effects of therapist exceptions questions on blaming and positive statements in families with adolescent behavior problems. *Journal of Family Psychology, 9,* 451–457.

Meloy, J. R. (1997). The clinical risk management of stalking: "Someone is watching over me . . ." *American Journal of Psychotherapy, 51,* 174–184.

Menninger, W. W. (1993). Management of the aggressive and dangerous patient. *Bulletin of the Menninger Clinic, 57,* 208–217.

Meyers, R. J., Smith, J. E., & Miller, E. J. (1998). Working through the concerned significant other. In W. R. Miller & N. Heather (Eds.), *Treating addictive behaviors* (pp. 149–161). New York: Plenum.

Milich, R., & Landau, S. (1984). A comparison of the social status and social behavior of aggressive and aggressive/withdrawn boys. *Journal of Abnormal Child Psychology, 12,* 277–288.

Miller, C. S. (1984). Building self-control: Discipline for young children. *Young Children, 40,* 15–19.

Miller, G. E., & Prinz, R. J. (1990). Enhancement of social learning family interventions for childhood conduct disorder. *Psychological Bulletin, 108,* 291–307.

Miller, L. D., & McLeod, E. (2001). Children as participants in family therapy: Practice, research, and theoretical concerns. *Family Journal: Counseling & Therapy for Couples & Families, 9,* 375–383.

Miller, L. D., & Osmunson, S. (1989). Reframing. *Journal of Human Behavior & Learning, 6,* 32–38.

Miller, R. B. (1998). Metaphors for men in marital therapy. *Journal of Client Psychotherapy, 9,* 79–84.

Miller, W. R., Meyers, R. J., & Tonigan, J. S. (1999). Engaging the unmotivated in treatment for alcohol problems: A comparison of three strategies for intervention through family members. *Journal of Consulting & Clinical Psychology, 67,* 688–697.

Mills, D. M. (1984). A model for stepfamily development. *Family Relations, 33,* 365–372.

Mills, R. B., & Malley-Morrison, K. (1998). Emotional commitment, normative acceptability, and attributions for abusive partner behaviors. *Journal of Interpersonal Violence, 13,* 682–699.

Milne, J. M., Edwards, J. K., & Murchie, J. C. (2001). Family treatment of oppositional defiant disorder: Changing views and strength-based approaches. *Family Journal: Counseling & Therapy for Couples & Families, 9,* 17–28.

Milner, J. S. (1995). Physical child abuse assessment: Perpetrator evaluation. In J. C. Campbell (Ed.), *Assessing dangerousness: Violence by sexual offenders, batterers, and child abusers* (pp. 41–67). Thousand Oaks, CA: Sage.

Milner, J. S., & Campbell, J. C. (1995). Prediction issues for practitioners. In J. C. Campbell (Ed.), *Assessing dangerousness: Violence by sexual offenders, batterers, and child abusers* (pp. 20–40). Thousand Oaks, CA: Sage.

Minuchin, S. (1974). *Families and family therapy.* Cambridge, MA: Harvard University Press.

Minuchin, P., Colapinto, J., & Minuchin, S. (1998). *Working with families of the poor.* New York: Guilford.

Minuchin, S., & Fishman, H. C. (1981). *Family therapy techniques.* Cambridge, MA: Harvard University Press.

Mirkin, M. P., & Beib, P. (1999). Consciousness of context in relational couples therapy. *Journal of Feminist Family Therapy, 11,* 31–51.

Mitra, A. (2000). Cognitive skills and black-white wages in the United States labor market. *Journal of Socio-Economics, 29,* 389–401.

Mohr, D. C., Beutler, L. E., Shoham-Solomon, V., Bergan, J., Kaszniak, A. W., & Yost, E. B. (1990). Identification of patients at risk for nonresponse and negative outcome in psychotherapy. *Journal of Consulting and Clinical Psychology, 58,* 622–628.

Molnar, A., & de Shazer, S. (1987). Solution-focused therapy: Toward the identification of therapeutic tasks. *Journal of Marital & Family Therapy, 13,* 349–358.

Monahan, J. (1981). *Prediction of violent behavior: An assessment of clinical techniques.* Beverly Hills, CA: Sage.

Monahan, J. (1984). The prediction of violent behavior. *American Journal of Psychiatry, 141*(1), 10–15.

Monahan, J. (2002). The MacArthur studies of violence risk. *Criminal Behaviour & Mental Health, 12,* S67–S72.

Monahan, J. (2003). Violence risk assessment in American law. In P. J. Koppen & S. D. Penrod (Eds.), *Adversarial versus inquisitorial justice: Psychological perspectives on criminal justice systems* (pp. 81–89). New York: Kluwer Academic/Plenum.

Montague, J. (1996). Counseling families from diverse cultures: A nondeficit approach. *Journal of Multicultural Counseling and Development, 24,* 37–41.

Moore, J., & Finkelstein, N. (2001). Parenting services for families affected by substance abuse. *Child Welfare, 80,* 221–238.

Moras, K., & Strupp, H. H. (1982). Pretherapy interpersonal relations, patients' alliance, and outcome in brief therapy. *Archives of General Psychiatry, 39,* 405–409.

Morison, J. E., Bromfield, L. M., & Cameron, H. J. (2003). A therapeutic model for supporting families of children with a chronic illness or disability. *Child & Adolescent Mental Health, 8,* 125–130.

Morris, S. B., Alexander, J. F., & Turner, C. W. (1991). Do reattributions of delinquent behavior reduce blame? *Journal of Family Psychology, 5,* 192–203.

Mowbray, C. T., Oyserman, D., & Bybee, D. (2000). Mothers with serious mental illness. In F. J. Frese III (Ed.), *The role of organized psychology in treatment of the seriously mentally ill* (pp. 73–91). San Francisco: Jossey-Bass.

Mowbray, C., Oyserman, D., Bybee, D., & MacFarlane, P. (2002). Parenting of mothers with a serious mental illness: Differential effects of diagnosis, clinical history, and other mental health variables. *Social Work Research, 26,* 225–240.

Mowbray, C., Schwartz, S., Bybee, D., Spang, J., Rueda-Riedle, A., & Oyserman, D. (2000). Mothers with a mental illness: Stressors and resources for parenting and living. *Families in Society, 81,* 118–129.

Mullick, M., Miller, L. J., & Jacobsen, T. (2001). Insight into mental illness and child maltreatment risk among mothers with major psychiatric disorders. *Psychiatric Services, 52,* 488–492.

Murphy, C. M., Meyer, S., & O'Leary, K. D. (1994). Dependency characteristics of partner-assaultive men. *Journal of Abnormal Psychology, 103,* 729–735.

Murphy, C. M., & O'Leary, K. D. (1989). Psychological aggression predicts physical aggression in early marriage. *Journal of Consulting & Clinical Psychology, 57,* 579–582.

Murray, P. E., & Rotter, J. C. (2002). Creative counseling techniques for family therapists. *Family Journal: Counseling & Therapy for Couples & Families, 10,* 203–206.

Myers, J. T. (1982). Hemisphericity research: An overview with some implications for problem solving. *Journal of Creative Behavior, 16,* 197–211.

Nachmias, M., Gunnar, M., Mangelsdorf, S., Parritz, R. H., & Buss, K. (1996). Behavioral inhibition and stress reactivity: The moderating role of attachment security. *Child Development, 67,* 508–522.

Nagaraja, J. (1984). Non-compliance—a behavior disorder. *Child Psychiatric Quarterly, 17,* 127–132.

Napier, A., & Whitaker, C. A. (1978). *The family crucible.* New York: Harper & Row.

Neenan, M., & Dryden, W. (1999). When laddering and the downward arrow can be used as adjuncts to inference chaining in REBT assessment. *Journal of Rational-Emotive & Cognitive Behavior Therapy, 17,* 95–104.

Neimeyer, G., & Hall, A. G. (1988). Personal identity in disturbed relationships. In F. Fransella & L. Thomas (Eds.), *Experimenting with personal construct theory* (pp. 297–307). London: Routledge & Kegan Paul.

Neimeyer, G. J., & Hudson, J. E. (1985). Couple's constructs: Personal systems in marital satisfaction. In D. Bannister (Ed.), *Issues and approaches in personal construct theory* (pp. 127–141). London: Academic Press.

Neimeyer, R., & Neimeyer, G. (1985). Disturbed relationships: A personal construct view. In E. Button (Ed.), *Personal constructs and mental health theory, research, and practice* (pp. 195–223). Cambridge, MA: Brookline.

Newell, R. M. (1999). The role of negativity in the first session of family therapy with delinquent youth. *Dissertation Abstracts International, Section B: The Sciences & Engineering, 60*(3-B), 1311.

Nichols, M. P. (1987). *The self in the system.* New York: Brunner/Mazel.

Nichols, W. C., & Pace-Nichols, M. A. (1993). Developmental perspectives and family therapy: The marital life cycle. *Contemporary Family Therapy, 15,* 299–315.

Nichols-Casebolt, A. M., & McClure, J. (1989). Social work support for welfare reform: The latest surrender in the war on poverty. *Social Work, 34,* 77–80.

Nix, J. C. L. (1999). Addressing friendship transitions in early adulthood: An inductive examination of how individuals manage romantic relationships and close friendships simultaneously. *Dissertation Abstracts International: Section A. Humanities & Social Sciences, 60*(4-A), 0938.

O'Brien, M. (1996). Child-rearing difficulties reported by parents of infants and toddlers. *Journal of Paediatric Psychology, 21,* 433–446.

O'Connell, P. (1972). Developmental tasks of the family. *Smith College Studies in Social Work, 42,* 203–210.

O'Heron, C. A., & Orlofsky, J. L. (1990). Stereotypic and nonstereotypic sex role trait and behavior orientation, gender identity, and psychological adjustment. *Journal of Personality and Social Psychology, 58,* 134–143.

O'Keefe, M. (1994). Linking marital violence, mother-child/father-child aggression, and child behavior problems. *Journal of Family Violence, 9,* 63–78.

O'Keefe, M. (1996). The differential effects of family violence on adolescent adjustment. *Child and Adolescent Social Work Journal, 3,* 51–68.

Okun, L. (1986). *Woman abuse—facts replacing myths.* Albany, NY: SUNY.

O'Leary, K. D. (2002). Conjoint therapy for partners who engage in physically aggressive behavior: Rationale and research. *Journal of Aggression, Maltreatment, & Trauma, 5,* 145–164.

Olson, D. H. (1988). Family types, family stress, and family satisfaction: A family development perspective. In C. J. Falicov (Ed.), *Family transitions: Continuity and change over the life cycle* (pp. 55–79). New York: Guilford.

Olson, S. L., Bates, J. E., & Bayles, K. (1990). Early antecedents of childhood impulsivity: The role of parent-child interaction, cognitive competence, and temperament. *Journal of Abnormal Child Psychology, 18,* 317–334.

Oriel, K. A., & Fleming, M. F. (1998). Screening men for partner violence in a primary care setting: A new strategy for detecting domestic violence. *Journal of Family Practice, 46*, 493–498.

Otani, A. (1989). Resistance management techniques of Milton H. Erickson, M.D.: An application to nonhypnotic mental health counseling. *Journal of Mental Health Counseling, 1*, 325–334.

Palazzoli, M. S., Boscolo, L., Cecchin, G., & Prata, G. (1978). *Paradox and counter paradox.* New York: Jason Aronson.

Palazzoli, M. S., Boscolo, L., Cecchin, G., & Prata, G. (1980). The problem of the referring person. *Journal of Marital & Family Therapy, 6*, 3–9.

Papero, D. V. (1990). *Bowen family systems theory.* Boston: Allyn & Bacon.

Papp, P., & Imber-Black, E. (1996). Family themes: Transmission and transformation. *Family Process, 35*, 5–20.

Park, K. A., & Waters, E. (1989). Security of attachment and preschool friendships. *Child Development, 60*, 1076–1081.

Patalano, F. (1997). Developing the working alliance in marital therapy: A psychodynamic perspective. *Contemporary Family Therapy: An International Journal, 19*, 497–505.

Patterson, G. R. (1982). *Coercive family process.* Eugene, OR: Castalia.

Patterson, G. R., Reid, J. B., Jones, R. R., & Conger, R. E. (1975). *A social learning approach to family intervention: Vol. 1. Families with aggressive children.* Eugene, OR: Castalia.

Patton, M. Q. (1980). *Qualitative evaluation methods.* Beverly Hills, CA: Sage.

Paulson, B. L. (1996). Metaphors for change. *Journal of College Student Psychotherapy, 10*, 11–21.

Peel, J. M. (2004). The labyrinth: An innovative therapeutic tool for problem solving or achieving mental focus. *Family Journal: Counseling & Therapy for Couples & Families, 12*, 287–291.

Penn, P. (1982). Circular questioning. *Family Process, 21*, 267–280.

Penn, P. (1985). Feed-forward: Future questions, future maps. *Family Process, 24*, 299–310.

Penn, P., & Frankfurt, M. (1994). Creating a participant text: Writing, multiple voices, narrative multiplicity. *Client Process, 33*, 217–231.

Phillips, R., Munt, G., Drury, J., Stoklosa, M. A., Spink, J., & Chapman, J. (1997). Dropouts in family therapy. *Australian & New Zealand Journal of Family Therapy, 18*, 115–123.

Place, M., Reynolds, J., Cousins, A., & O'Neill, S. (2002). Developing a resilience package for vulnerable children. *Child & Adolescent Mental Health, 7*, 162–167.

Polansky, N. A., Gaudin, J. M., Anmous, P. W., & Davis, K. B. (1985). The psychological ecology of the neglectful family. *Social Service Review, 57*, 196–208.

Polanyi, M. (1957). Problem solving. *British Journal for the Philosophy of Science, 8*, 89–103.

Potthoff, J. G., Holahan, C. J., & Joiner, T. E. Jr. (1995). Reassurance seeking, stress generation, and depressive symptoms: An integrative model. *Journal of Personality & Social Psychology, 68*, 664–670.

Prince, J. E., & Arias, I. (1994). The role of perceived control and the desirability of control among abusive and nonabusive husbands. *American Journal of Family Therapy, 22*, 126–134.

Proudfit, C. L. (1984). The Ramsay family in Virginia Wolff's *To the Lighthouse:* A study of arrest at stage three of family development as delineated in Solomon's "A developmental, conceptual premise for family therapy." *Family Process, 23*, 334–335.

Ptacek, J. (1984). *Men who batter: Recent research.* Paper presented at the Second National Conference for Family Violence Researchers, University of New Hampshire, Durham, NH.

Quas, J. A., Goodman, G. S., & Jones, D. P. H. (2003). Predictors of attributions of self-blame and internalizing behavior problems in sexually abused children. *Journal of Child Psychology & Psychiatry & Allied Disciplines, 44*, 723–736.

Rae Grant, N. I. (1994). Preventive interventions for children and adolescents: Where are we now and how far have we come? *Canadian Journal of Community Mental Health, 13*, 17–36.

Ragg, D. M. (1998). *The life situations questionnaire: A measure of violence-priming behavior in wife assaulters.* Presented at the Family Violence Research Conference, Durham, NH.

Ragg, D. M. (2001). *Building effective helping skills: The foundation of generalist practice.* Newbury Park, MA: Allyn & Bacon.

Ramey, J. H. (1993). Group empowerment through learning formal decision making processes. *Social Work with Groups, 16*, 171–185.

Rand, M. L. (1995). As it was in the beginning: The significance of infant bonding in the development of self and relationships. *Journal of Child and Youth Care, 10*, 1–8.

Rankin, C. I. (1991). An examination of students' familial backgrounds, locus of control, and evaluations of self and others. *Journal of Social Behavior and Personality, 6*, 153–155.

Rawson, H. E., & Cassady, J. C. (1995). Effects of therapeutic intervention on self-concepts of children with learning disabilities. *Child & Adolescent Social Work Journal, 12,* 19–31.

Ray, R. D., Upson, J. D., & Henderson, B. J. (1977). A systems approach to behavior: III. Organismic pace and complexity in time-space fields. *Psychological Record, 27,* 649–682.

Reid, W. J. (1997). Research on task-centered practice. *Social Work Research, 21,* 132–137.

Reinhard, H. G. (1990). Depression and moral identity in adolescence. *International Journal of Child & Adolescent Psychiatry, 53,* 104–125.

Renson, G. J., Adams, J. E., & Tinklenberg, J. R. (1978). Buss-Durkee assessment and validation with violent versus nonviolent chronic alcohol abusers. *Journal of Consulting & Clinical Psychology, 46,* 360–361.

Resnick, G. (1985). Enhancing parental competencies for high-risk mothers: An evaluation of prevention effects. *Child Abuse and Neglect, 9,* 479–489.

Richlin-Klonsky, J., & Bengston, V. L. (1996). Pulling together, drifting apart: A longitudinal case study of a four-generation family. *Journal of Aging Studies, 10,* 255–279.

Richter, K. P., & Bammer, G. (2000). A hierarchy of strategies heroin-using mothers employ to reduce harm to their children. *Journal of Substance Abuse Treatment, 19,* 403–413.

Rivara, F. P. (1985). Physical abuse in children under two: A study of therapeutic outcomes. *Child Abuse and Neglect, 9,* 81–87.

Robbins, M. S., Alexander, J. F., Newell, R. M., & Turner, C. W. (1996). The immediate effect of reframing on client attitude in family therapy. *Journal of Family Psychology, 10,* 28–34.

Robbins, M. S., Alexander, J. F., & Turner, C. W. (2000). Disrupting defensive family interactions in family therapy with delinquent adolescents. *Journal of Family Psychology, 14,* 688–701.

Robbins, S. P. (1993). *Organizational behavior: Concepts, controversies, and applications* (6th ed.). Englewood Cliffs, NJ: Prentice Hall.

Rober, P. (2002). Constructive hypothesizing, dialogic understanding, and the therapist's inner conversation: Some ideas about knowing and not knowing in the family therapy session. *Journal of Marital & Family Therapy, 28,* 467–478.

Robertson, J. F., & Simons, R. L. (1989). Family factors, self-esteem, and adolescent depression. *Journal of Marriage & the Family, 51,* 125–138.

Robin, M. W. (1979). Life without father: A review of the literature. *International Journal of Group Tensions, 9,* 169–194.

Roland, C. B. (1993). Exploring childhood memories with adult survivors of sexual abuse: Concrete reconstruction and visualization techniques. *Journal of Mental Health Counseling, 15,* 363–372.

Rook, K. S., & Ituarte, P. H. G. (1999). Social control, social support, and companionship in older adults' family relationships and friendships. *Personal Relationships, 6,* 199–211.

Room, R. (1996). Patterns of family responses to alcohol and tobacco problems. *Drug & Alcohol Review, 15,* 171–181.

Rosenbaum, A., & O'Leary, K. D. (1981). Marital violence: Characteristics of abusive couples. *Journal of Consulting & Clinical Psychology, 49,* 63–71.

Rosenblatt, A., & Mayer, J. E. (1972). Help seeking for family problems: A survey of utilization and satisfaction. *American Journal of Psychiatry, 128,* 1136–1140.

Rosenfeld, B., & Harmon, H. (2002). Factors associated with violence in stalking and obsessional harassment cases. *Criminal Justice & Behavior, 29,* 671–691.

Ross, C. E., Mirowsky, J., & Cockerham, W. C. (1983). Social class, Mexican culture, and fatalism: Their effects on psychological distress. *American Journal of Community Psychology, 11,* 383–400.

Rothery, M., & Cameron, G. (1985). *Understanding family support in child welfare: A summary report.* Toronto: Ministry of Community and Social Services.

Rothery, M., & Cameron, G. (1990). *Child maltreatment: Expanding our concept of helping.* Hillsdale, NJ: Erlbaum.

Rotter, J. C. (2001). Letting go: Forgiveness in counseling. *Family Journal: Counseling & Therapy for Couples & Families, 9,* 174–177.

Rotter, J. C., & Bush, M. V. (2000). Play and family therapy. *Family Journal: Counseling & Therapy for Couples & Families, 8,* 172–176.

Rouse, L. P. (1984). Models, self-esteem, and locus of control as factors contributing to spouse abuse. *Victimology, 9,* 130–141.

Rowatt, W. C., Cunningham, M. R., & Druen, P. B. (1999). Lying to get a date: The effect of facial physical attractiveness on the willingness to deceive prospective dating partners. *Journal of Social & Personal Relationships, 16,* 209–223.

Roy, M. (1982). *The abusive partner: An analysis of domestic battering*. New York: Van Nostrand Reinhold.

Runyon, M. K., & Kenny, M. C. (2002). Relationship of attributional style, depression, and posttrauma distress among children who suffered physical or sexual abuse. *Child Maltreatment: Journal of the American Professional Society on the Abuse of Children, 7*, 254–264.

Rusbult, C. E., Johnson, D. J., & Morrow, G. D. (1986). Impact of couple patterns of problem solving on distress and nondistress in dating relationships. *Journal of Personality and Social Psychology, 50*, 744–753.

Rzepnicki, T. L. (1991). Enhancing the durability of intervention gains: A challenge for the 1990s. *Social Service Review, 65*, 92–109.

Saleebey, D. (1996). The strengths perspective in social work practice: Extensions and cautions. *Social Work, 41*, 296–305.

Saleebey, D. (2001). The diagnostic strengths manual? *Social Work, 46*, 183–187.

Santisteban, D. A., Szapocznik, J., Perez-Vidal, A., Kurtines, W. M., Murray, E. J., & LaPerriere, A. (1996). Efficacy of intervention for engaging youth and families into treatment and some variables that may contribute to differential effectiveness. *Journal of Family Psychology, 10*, 35–44.

Sarason, S. B. (1984). If it can be studied or developed, should it be? *American Psychologist, 39*, 477–485.

Sargent, J. (2001). Variations in family composition: Implications for family therapy. *Child & Adolescent Psychiatric Clinics of North America, 10*, 577–599.

Satir, V. M. (1964). *Conjoint family therapy*. Palo Alto, CA: Science and Behavior Books.

Satir, V. M. (1988). The tools of the therapist. In J. K. Zeig & S. R. Lankton (Eds.), *Developing Ericksonian therapy: State of the art* (pp. 513–523). Philadelphia: Taylor Francis.

Satir, V. M., & Baldwin, M. (1983). *Satir step-by-step: A guide to creating change in families*. Palo Alto, CA: Science & Behavior Books.

Satir, V. M., & Bitter, J. R. (1991). The therapist and family therapy: Satir's human validation process model. In A. M. Horne (Ed.), *Family counseling and therapy* (3rd ed., pp. 64–101). Belmont, CA: Wadsworth/Thompson Learning.

Saulnier, C. F. (2003). Goal-setting process: Supporting choice in a feminist group for women with alcohol problems. *Social Work with Groups, 26*, 47–68.

Saunders, D. G., Lynch, A. B., Grayson, M., & Linz, D. (1987). The inventory of beliefs about wife beating: The construction and initial validation of a measure of beliefs and attitudes. *Violence and Victims, 2*, 39–57.

Scannapieco, M., & Jackson, S. (1996). Kinship care: The African American response to family preservation. *Social Work, 41*, 190–196.

Scaturo, D. J., Hayes, T., Sagula, D., & Waltre, T. (2000). The concept of codependency and its context within family systems theory. *Family Therapy, 27*, 63–70.

Scheel, M. J., Seaman, S., Roach, K., Mulling, T., & Mahoney, K. B. (1999). Families' implementation of therapist recommendations predicted by families' perception of fit, difficulty of implementation, and therapist influence. *Journal of Counseling Psychology, 46*, 308–316.

Schlenker, B. R., & Trudeau, J. V. (1990). Impact of self-presentation on private self-beliefs: Effects of prior self-beliefs and misattribution. *Journal of Personality and Social Psychology, 58*, 22–32.

Schmitt, B. D. (1980). The prevention of child abuse and neglect: A review of the literature and recommendations for application. *Child Abuse & Neglect, 4*, 171–177.

Schlosberg, S. B., & Kagan, R. M. (1988). Practice strategies for engaging chronic multiproblem families. *Social Casework, 69*, 3–9.

Schneider, R. L., & Lester, L. (2001). *Social work advocacy—a new framework for action*. Pacific Grove, CA: Brooks/Cole.

Schulman, S. (1986). Facing the invisible handicap. *Psychology Today, 20*, 58–64.

Schumm, W. R. (2004). Response to Kirkpatrick (2004): Differential risk theory and lesbian parenthood. *Psychological Reports, 95*, 1203–1206.

Schwebel, A. I., & Fine, M. A. (1994). *Understanding and helping families: A cognitive behavioral approach*. Hillsdale, NJ: Erlbaum.

Scorzelli, J. F., & Gold, J. (1999). The mutual storytelling writing game. *Journal of Mental Health Counseling, 21*, 113–123.

Seagull, E. A. W. (1987). Social support and child maltreatment: A review of the literature. *Child Abuse & Neglect, 11*, 41–52.

Selekman, M. D. (1995). Rap music with wisdom: Peer reflecting teams with tough adolescents. In S. Friedman (Ed.), *The reflecting team in action: Collaborative practice in family therapy* (pp. 205–219). New York: Guilford.

Selvini-Palazzoli, M., Boscolo, L., Cecchin, G., & Prata, G. (1978). *Paradox and counter paradox*. New York: Jason Aronson.

Shapiro, E. R. (1988). Individual change and family development: Individuation as a family process. In C. J. Falicov (Ed.), *Family transitions: Continuity and change over the life cycle* (pp. 159–180). New York: Guilford.

Sheidow, A. J., & Woodford, M. S. (2003). Multisystemic therapy: An empirically supported, home-based family therapy approach. *Family Journal: Counseling & Therapy for Couples & Families, 11*, 257–263.

Shepard, J., & Carlson, J. S. (2003). An empirical evaluation of school-based prevention programs that involve parents. *Psychology in the Schools, 40*, 641–656.

Sherman, B. R., Sanders, L. M., & Banks, S. M. (1998). How did the SISTERS program work and what was its impact? In B. R. Sherman (Ed.), *Addiction and pregnancy: Empowering recovery through peer counseling* (pp. 147–166). Westport, CT: Praeger.

Shields, M. J., & Sparling, J. W. (1993). Fathers' play and touch behaviors with their three-month-old infants. *Physical & Occupational Therapy in Pediatrics, 13*, 39–59.

Sholevar, G. P., & Schwoeri, L. D. (2003). Techniques of family therapy. In G. P. Sholevar (Ed.), *Textbook of family and couples therapy: Clinical applications* (pp. 225–250). Washington, DC: American Psychiatric Publishing.

Shriver, M. D. (1998). Teaching parenting skills. In T. S. Watson & F. M. Gresham (Eds.), *Handbook of child behavior therapy* (pp. 165–182). New York: Plenum.

Shulman, L. (2006). *The skills of helping individuals, families, groups, and communities* (5th ed.). Pacific Grove, CA: Brooks/Cole.

Shumaker, S. A., & Brownell, A. (1984). Toward a theory of social support: Closing conceptual gaps. *Journal of Social Issues, 40*, 11–36.

Sigelman, C. K., & Adams, R. M. (1990). Family interactions in public: Parent-child distance and touching. *Journal of Nonverbal Behavior, 14*, 63–75.

Sills, C., & Wide, M. (1997). Making contracts with different personality types. In C. Sills (Ed.), *Contracts in counseling* (pp. 142–154). Thousand Oaks, CA: Sage.

Silverstein, H. (1990). *Alcoholism*. New York: Franklin Watts.

Simon, S. R., Ginsburg, E. H., & Byrne, B. (1993). *Partnership with practice: School-based, early intervention model for child abuse prevention*. Paper presented at the 39th APM Council on Social Work Education, New York, NY.

Simons, R. L., Whitbeck, L. B., Conger, R. D., & Chyi-In, W. (1991). Intergenerational transmission of harsh parenting. *Developmental Psychology, 27*, 159–171.

Sims, P. A., & Whynot, C. A. (1997). Hearing metaphor: An approach to working with family-generated metaphor. *Client Process, 36*, 341–355.

Sjoestedt, G., & Grann, M. (2002). Risk assessment: What is being predicted by actuarial prediction instruments? *International Journal of Forensic Mental Health, 1*, 179–183.

Skynner, A. C. R. (1976). *Systems of family and marital psychotherapy*. New York: Brunner/Mazel.

Slade, M., Daniel, L. J., & Heisler, C. J. (1991). Application of forensic toxicology to the problem of domestic violence. *Journal of Forensic Sciences, 36*, 708–713.

Slesnick, N., Meyers, R. J., Meade, M., & Segelken, D. H. (2000). Bleak and hopeless no more: Engagement of reluctant substance-abusing runaway youth and their families. *Journal of Substance Abuse Treatment, 19*, 215–222.

Sloane, R. B., Staples, F. R., Cristal, A. H., Yorkston, N. J., & Whipple, K. (1975). Short-term analytically oriented psychotherapy versus behavior therapy. *American Journal of Psychiatry, 132*, 373–377.

Smart, J. C., & Pascarella, E. T. (1986). Socioeconomic achievements of former college students. *Journal of Higher Education, 57*, 529–549.

Smith, J. M. (2000). Psychotherapy with people stressed by poverty. In A. Sabo & L. Havens (Eds.), *The real world guide to psychotherapy practice* (pp. 71–92). Cambridge, MA: Harvard University Press.

Smith, K. K., Kamistein, D. S., & Makadok, R. J. (1995). The health of the corporate body: Illness and organizational dynamics. *Journal of Applied Behavioral Science, 31*, 328–351.

Smith, M. D. (1990). Patriarchal ideology and wife beating: A test of a feminist hypothesis. *Violence and Victims, 5*, 257–273.

Snyder, J., & Brown, K. (1983). Oppositional behavior and noncompliance in preschool children: Environmental correlates and skills deficits. *Behavioral Assessment, 5*, 333–348.

Sonkin, D. J. (1986). Clairvoyance vs. common sense: Therapist's duty to warn and protect. *Violence & Victims, 1*(1), 7–22.

Sonkin, D. J., Martin, D., & Walker, L. E. A. (1985). *The male batterer: A treatment approach*. New York: Springer.

Spaid, W. M., & Fraser, M. (1991). The correlates of success/failure in brief and intensive family treatment: Implications for family preservation services. *Children and Youth Services Review, 13,* 77–99.

Spigelman, G., Spigelman, A., & Engelsson, I. L. (1992). An analysis of children's drawings: A comparison between children from divorce and non-divorce families. *Journal of Divorce and Remarriage, 18,* 31–54.

Spoth, R., & Redmond, C. (1996). A theory-based parent competency model incorporating intervention attendance effects. *Family Relations, 45,* 139–147.

Spoth, R., Redmond, C., Hockaday, C., & Chung, C. Y. (1996). Barriers to participation in family skills preventive interventions and their evaluations: A replication and extension. *Family Relations, 45,* 247–254.

Sprecher, S. (1988). Investment model, equity, and social support determinants of relationship commitment. *Social Psychology Quarterly, 51,* 318–328.

Stanley, N., & Penhale, B. (1999). The mental health problems of mothers experiencing the child protection system: Identifying needs and appropriate responses. *Child Abuse Review, 8,* 34–45.

Stanley, S. M., Markman, H. J., Prado, L. M., Olmos-Gallo, P. A., Tonelli, L., St. Peters, M., et al. (2001). Community-based premarital prevention: Clergy and lay leaders on the front lines. *Family Relations, 50,* 67–76.

Staples, F. R., & Sloane, R. B. (1970). The relation of speech patterns in psychotherapy to empathic ability, responsiveness to approval and disapproval. *Diseases of the Nervous System, 31,* 100–104.

Stawar, T. L. (1996). Suicidal and homicidal risk for respondents, petitioners, and family members in an injunction program for domestic violence. *Psychological Reports, 79,* 553–554.

Steinberg, D. M. (1999). The impact of time and place on mutual-aid practice with short-term groups. *Social Work with Groups, 22,* 101–118.

Steinglass, P., & Moyer, J. K. (1977). Assessing alcohol use in family life: A necessary but neglected area for clinical research. *Family Coordinator, 26,* 53–60.

Stephens, D. L. (1999). Battered women's views of their children. *Journal of Interpersonal Violence, 14,* 731–764.

Stets, J. (1995). Modelling control in relationships. *Journal of Marriage & the Family, 57,* 489–501.

Stevens, P. (2000). Practicing within our competence: New techniques create new dilemmas. *Family Journal: Counseling & Therapy for Couples & Families, 8,* 278–280.

Stewart, I. (1997). Outcome-focused contracts. In S. Palmer & G. McMahon (Eds.), *Client assessment* (pp. 79–93). Thousand Oaks, CA: Sage.

Stewart, K., Valentine, L., & Amundson, J. (1991). The battle for definition: The problem with (the problem). *Journal of Strategic & Systemic Therapies, 10,* 21–31.

Stoolmiller, M., Duncan, T., Bank, L., & Patterson, G. R. (1993). Some problems and solutions in the study of change: Significant patterns in client resistance. *Journal of Consulting & Clinical Psychology, 61,* 920–928.

Stratton, P. (2003a). Causal attributions during therapy: I. Responsibility and blame. *Journal of Family Therapy, 25,* 136–160.

Stratton, P. (2003b). Causal attributions during therapy: II. Reconstituted families and parental blaming. *Journal of Family Therapy, 25,* 161–180.

Straus, M. A. (1973). A general systems theory approach to a theory of violence between family members. *Social Science Information, 12,* 105–125.

Strong, T. (2000). Collaborative influence. *Australian & New Zealand Journal of Family Therapy, 21,* 144–148.

Suarez, K., Smokowski, P., & Wodarski, J. S. (1996). The process of intervention with multiproblem families: Theoretical and practice guidelines. *Family Therapy, 23,* 117–134.

Sue, D. W., & Sue, S. (1992). *Counseling the culturally different.* New York: Wiley.

Sundel, M., & Sundel, S. S. (1999). *Behavior change in the human services: An introduction to principles and applications* (4th ed.). Thousand Oaks, CA: Sage.

Sweeney, D. S., & Rocha, S. L. (2000). Using play therapy to assess family dynamics. In R. E. Watts (Ed.), *Techniques in marriage and family counseling* (Vol. 1, pp. 33–47). Alexandria, VA: American Counseling Association.

Sweeney, T. J. (1998). *Adlerian counseling: A practitioner's approach* (4th ed.). Philadelphia: Accelerated Development.

Szapocznik, J., Perez-Vidal, A., Brickman, A., Foote, F. H., Santisteban, D. A., Hervis, O., et al. (1988). Engaging adolescent drug abusers and their families in treatment: A strategic structural systems approach. *Journal of Consulting & Clinical Psychology, 56,* 552–557.

Szmukler, G. (2003). Risk assessment: "Numbers" and "values." *Psychiatric Bulletin, 27*, 205–207.

Szykula, S. A., & Fleischman, M. J. (1985). Reducing out-of-home placements of abused children: Two controlled field studies. *Child Abuse & Neglect, 9*, 277–283.

Tangney, J. P., & Dearing, R. L. (2002). *Shame and guilt.* New York: Guilford.

Teichman, Y. (1984). Cognitive family therapy. *British Journal of Cognitive Psychotherapy, 2*, 1–10.

Terry, D. S. (2002). The multiple therapeutic alliances in family therapy. *Dissertation Abstracts International: Section B. The Sciences & Engineering, 63*(5-B), 2607.

Teyber, E. (1989). *Interpersonal process in psychotherapy: A guide for clinical training* (2nd ed.). Pacific Grove, CA: Brooks/Cole.

Thomas, L., & Kalucy, R. (2003). Parents with mental illness: Lacking motivation to parent. *International Journal of Mental Health Nursing, 12*, 153–157.

Thomas, R. (1996). Reflective dialogue parent education design: Focus on parent development. *Family Relations, 45*, 189–200.

Thyer, B. A., & Myers, L. L. (1999). On science, antiscience, and the client's right to effective treatment. *Social Work, 44*, 501–504.

Tokar, D. M., Hardin, S. I., Adams, E. M., & Brandel, I. W. (1996). Families' expectations about counseling and perceptions of the working alliance. *Journal of College Student Psychotherapy, 11*, 9–26.

Tolan, P. H., & McKay, M. M. (1996). Preventing serious antisocial behavior in inner-city children: An empirically based family intervention program. *Family Relations, 45*, 148–155.

Tomm, K. (1987a). Interventive interviewing: I. Strategizing as a fourth guideline for the therapist. *Family Process, 26*, 3–13.

Tomm, K. (1987b). Interventive interviewing: II. Reflexive questioning as a means to enable self-healing. *Family Process, 26*, 167–183.

Tomm, K. (1988). Interventive interviewing: III. Intending to ask lineal, circular, strategic, or reflexive questions? *Family Process, 27*, 1–15.

Tracy, E. M. (1990). Identifying social support resources of at-risk families. *Social Work, 35*, 252–258.

Tremblay, R. E., McCord, J., Boileau, H., Charlebois, P., Gagnon, C., LeBlanc, M., et al. (1991). Can disruptive boys be helped to become competent? *Psychiatry, 54*, 148–161.

Triandis, H. C. (1995). The self and social behavior in differing cultural contexts. In N. R. Goldberger & J. B. Veroff (Eds.), *The culture and psychology reader* (pp. 326–365). New York: New York University Press.

Tucker, D. M. (1981). Lateral brain function, emotion, and conceptualization. *Psychological Bulletin, 89*, 19–46.

Tuma, J. M. (1989). Mental health services for children: The state of the art. *American Psychologist, 44*, 188–199.

Tyron, G. S., & Winograd, G. (2002). Goal consensus and collaboration. In J. C. Norcross (Ed.), *Psychotherapy relationships that work: Therapist contributions and responsiveness to patients* (pp. 109–125). London: Oxford University Press.

Uhlemann, M. R., & Koehn, C. V. (1989). Effects of covert and overt modeling on the communication of empathy. *Canadian Journal of Counselling, 23*, 372–381.

Ulak, B. J., & Cummings, A. L. (1997). Using client members' artistic expressions as metaphor in counselling: A pilot study. *Canadian Journal of Counselling, 31*, 305–316.

Van Audenhove, C., & Vertommen, H. (2000). A negotiation approach to intake and treatment choice. *Journal of Psychotherapy Integration, 10*, 287–299.

Van den Boom, D. (1991). Preventive intervention and the quality of mother-infant interaction and infant exploration in irritable infants. In W. Koops, H. Soppe, J. L. van der Linden, P. C. M. Molenaar, & J. J. F. Schroots (Eds.), *Developmental psychology behind the dykes: An outline of developmental psychological research in the Netherlands* (pp. 249–269). Delft, The Netherlands: Eburon.

van der Linde, C. H. (2000). The need for relevant workforce education for the 21st century. *Career Issues in Education, 120*, 696–702.

Van der Poel, M. G. (1993). Delineating personal support networks. *Social Networks, 15*, 49–70.

van Ijzendoorn, M. H., Juffer, F., & Duyvesteyn, M. G. C. (1995). Breaking the intergenerational cycle of insecure attachment: A review of the effects of attachment-based interventions on maternal sensitivity and infant security. *Journal of Child Psychology & Psychiatry, 36*, 225–248.

Vaughn, M. J. (2000). Creating "maneuvering room": A grounded theory of language and therapist influence in marriage and family therapy. *Dissertation Abstracts International: Section B. The Sciences & Engineering, 60*(11-B), 5796.

Veenstra, G. J., & Scott, C. G. (1993). A model for using time-out as an intervention technique with families. *Journal of Family Violence, 8*, 71–87.

Veronie, L., & Fruehstorfer, D. B. (2001). Gender, birth order, and family role identification among children of alcoholics. *Current Psychology: Developmental, Learning, Personality, Social, 20,* 53–67.

Vivian, D., & O'Leary, K. D. (1987). *Communication patterns in physically assaultive engaged couples.* Paper presented at the Third National Conference for Family Violence Researchers, Durham, NH.

von Bertalanffy, L. (1950). An outline of general systems theory. *British Journal of Philosophy of Science, 1,* 39–164.

von Bertalanffy, L. (1968). *General systems theory: Foundations, development, applications.* New York: George Braziller.

Vondra, J. I., Barnett, D., & Cicchetti, D. (1990). Self-concept, motivation, and competence among preschoolers from maltreating and comparison families. *Child Abuse & Neglect, 14,* 525–540.

Wahler, R. G. (1980). The insular mother: Her problem in parent-child treatment. *Journal of Applied Behavior Analysis, 46,* 341.

Wald, M. S., & Woolverton, M. (1990). Risk assessment: The emperor's new clothes. *Child Welfare, 69,* 483–511.

Waldman, F. (1999). Violence or discipline? Working with multicultural court-ordered clients. *Journal of Marital & Family Therapy, 25,* 503–515.

Walker, L. E. A. (1979). *Battered women.* New York: Harper & Row.

Walker, S. F. (1980). Lateralization of functions in the vertebrate brain: A review. *British Journal of Psychology, 71,* 329–367.

Walsh, F. (1996). *Spiritual resources in family therapy.* New York: Guilford.

Waring, E. M. (1990). Self-disclosure of personal constructs. *Family Process, 29,* 399–413.

Watanabe-Hammond, S. (1990). Family dances and the rhythms of intimacy. *Contemporary Family Therapy, 12,* 327–338.

Waterman, A. S. (1985). Identity in the context of adolescent psychology. *New Directions for Child Development, 30,* 5–24.

Watts, R. E. (2003). Adlerian therapy as a relational constructivist approach. *Family Journal: Counseling & Therapy for Couples & Families, 11,* 139–147.

Watzlawick, P., Beavin, J. H., & Jackson, D. D. (1967). *Pragmatics of human communication.* New York: Norton.

Watzlawick, P., Weakland, J., & Fisch, R. (1974). *Change: Principles of problem formation and problem resolution.* New York: Norton.

Weaver, H. N., & White, B. J. (1997). The Native American family circle: Roots of resiliency. *Journal of Family Social Work, 2,* 67–79.

Weaver, T. L., & Clum, G. A. (1996). Interpersonal violence: Expanding the search for long-term sequelae within a sample of battered women. *Journal of Traumatic Stress, 9,* 783–803.

Weber, T. T. (2001). Widening the lens: Engaging a family in transition. In S. H. McDaniel & D. D. Lusterman (Eds.), *Casebook for integrating family therapy: An ecosystemic approach* (pp. 141–155). Washington, DC: American Psychological Association.

Webster, C. D., Hucker, S. J., & Bloom, H. (2002). Transcending the actuarial versus clinical polemic in assessing risk for violence. *Criminal Justice & Behavior, 29,* 659–665.

Webster-Stratton, C. (1989). Mothers' and fathers' perceptions of child deviance: Roles of parent and child behaviors and parent adjustment. *Journal of Consulting & Clinical Psychology, 56,* 909–915.

Weighill, V. E., Hodge, J., & Peck, D. F. (1983). Keeping appointments with clinical psychologists. *British Journal of Clinical Psychology, 22,* 143–144.

Weiner-Davis, M., de Shazer, S., & Gingerich, W. J. (1987). Building on pretreatment change to construct the therapeutic solution: An exploratory study. *Journal of Marital & Family Therapy, 13,* 359–363.

Weingourt, R. (1996). Connection and disconnection in abusive relationships. *Perspectives in Psychiatric Care, 32,* 15–19.

Wekesser, C. (1994). *Alcoholism.* San Diego, CA: Greenhaven Press.

Wenger, C. (1982). The suitcase story: A therapeutic technique for children in out-of-home placement. *American Journal of Orthopsychiatry, 52,* 353–355.

Wheelan, S. A., McKeage, R. L., Verdi, A. F., Abraham, M., Krasick, C., & Johnston, F. (1994). Communication and developmental patterns in a system of interacting groups. In L. R. Frey (Ed.), *Group communication in context: Studies of natural groups* (pp. 153–178). Hillsdale, NJ: Erlbaum.

Whipple, E. E., & Webster-Stratton, C. (1991). The role of parental stress in physically abusive families. *Child Abuse & Neglect, 15,* 279–291.

Whipple, E. E., & Wilson, S. R. (1996). Evaluation of a parent education and support program for families at risk of physical child abuse. *Families in Society: The Journal of Contemporary Human Services, 77*, 227–239.

Whitaker, C. A. (1975). Psychotherapy of the absurd: With a special emphasis on the psychotherapy of aggression. *Family Process, 14*, 1–16.

Whitbeck, L. B., & Gecas, V. (1988). Value attributions and value transmission between parents and children. *Journal of Marriage & the Family, 50*, 829–840.

White, J., Leggett, J., & Beech, A. (1999). The incidence of self-harming behavior in the male population of a medium-secure psychiatric hospital. *Journal of Forensic Psychiatry, 10*, 59–68.

White, J. M. (1991). *Dynamics of family development: A theoretical perspective.* New York: Guilford.

White, M. (1983). Anorexia nervosa: A transgenerational system perspective. *Family Process, 22*, 255–273.

White, M. (1984). Pseudo-encopresis: From avalanche to victory, from vicious to virtuous cycles. *Family Systems Medicine, 2*, 150–160.

White, M. (1986). Negative explanation, restraint, and double description: A template for family therapy. *Family Process, 25*, 169–184.

White, M. (1993). Deconstruction and therapy. In S. G. Gilligan & R. Price (Eds.), *Therapeutic conversations* (pp. 22–61). New York: Norton.

White, M. (1994). Ritual of inclusion: An approach to extreme uncontrolled behavior in children and young adolescents. *Journal of Child & Youth Care, 9*, 51–64.

White, M., & Epston, D. (1990). *Narrative means to therapeutic ends.* New York: Norton.

White, V. E. (2002). Developing counseling objectives and empowering clients: A strength-based intervention. *Journal of Mental Health Counseling, 24*, 270–279.

Wicki, W. (2000). Social control, perceived control, and the family. In W. J. Perrig & A. Grob (Eds.), *Control of human behavior, mental processes, and consciousness: Essays in honor of the 60th birthday of August Flammer* (pp. 477–486). Mahwah, NJ: Lawrence Erlbaum Associates.

Wiehe, V. R. (1986). Empathy and locus of control in child abusers. *Journal of Social Science Research, 9*, 17–30.

Wiener, D. J. (1999). Rehearsals for growth: Applying improvisational theater games to relationship therapy. In D. J. Wiener (Ed.), *Beyond talk therapy: Using movement and expressive techniques in clinical practice* (pp. 165–180). Washington, DC: American Psychological Association.

Wiener, D. J., & Cantor, D. (2003). Improvisational play in couples therapy. In C. E. Schaefer (Ed.), *Play therapy with adults* (pp. 62–77). New York: Wiley.

Willett, J. B., Ayoub, C. C., & Robinson, D. (1991). Using growth modeling to examine systematic differences in growth: An example of change in the functioning of families at risk of maladaptive parenting. *Journal of Consulting & Clinical Psychology, 59*, 38–47.

Winder, J. H. (1996). Counseling adult male survivors of childhood sexual abuse: A review of treatment techniques. *Journal of Mental Health Counseling, 18*, 123–133.

Winick, C., & Kenny, M. (2001). Risk assessment in domestic violence. In D. S. Sandju (Ed.), *Faces of violence: Psychological correlates, concepts, and intervention strategies* (pp. 319–335). Hauppauge, NY: Nova Science Publishers.

Winnicott, D. W. (1971). *Playing and reality.* New York: Basic Books.

Witherspoon, R., & White, R. P. (1996). Executive coaching: A continuum of roles. *Consulting Psychology Journal: Practice & Research, 48*, 124–133.

Wolfe, D. A. (1987). *Child abuse: Implications for child development and psychopathology.* Newbury Park, CA: Sage.

Wolfe, D. A., Jaffe, P., Wilson, S. K., & Zak, L. (1985). Children of battered women: The relation of child behavior to family violence and maternal stress. *Journal of Consulting and Clinical Psychology, 53*, 657–665.

Wolfe, D. A., Sandler, J., & Kaufman, K. (1981). A competency-based parent training program for child abusers. *Journal of Consulting & Clinical Psychology, 49*, 633–640.

Wolin, S. J., & Wolin, S. (1993). *The resilient self: How survivors of troubled families rise above adversity.* New York: Villard.

Wolock, T., & Horowitz, B. (1979). Child maltreatment and maternal deprivation. *Social Services Review, 53*, 175–194.

Wood, K. M. (1978). Casework effectiveness: A new look at the research evidence. *Social Work, 23*, 437–458.

Wynne, L. C. (1984). The epigenesis of relational systems: A model for understanding family development. *Family Process, 23*, 297–318.

Yalom, I. D. (2002). *The gift of therapy: An open letter to a new generation of therapists and their patients.* New York: HarperCollins.

Zastrow, C. (1990). Starting and leading therapy groups: A beginner's guide. *Journal of Independent Social Work, 4,* 7–26.

Zeig, J. K. (1980). Symptom prescription and Ericksonian principles. *American Journal of Clinical Hypnosis, 23,* 16–22.

Ziemba, S. J. (2001). Therapy with families in poverty: Application of feminist family therapy principles. *Journal of Feminist Family Therapy, 12,* 205–237.

Zimmer-Gembeck, M. J. (2002). The development of romantic relationships and adaptations in the system of peer relationships. *Journal of Adolescent Health, 31,* 216–225.

Zinner, J. (1997). A journey from blame to empathy in a family assessment of a mother and her sons. *Psychiatry: Interpersonal & Biological Processes, 60,* 104–110.

Ziter, M. P. (1988). Treating alcoholic families: The resolution of boundary ambiguity. *Alcoholism Treatment Quarterly, 5,* 221–233.

Zuk, G. H. (1971). *Family therapy: A triadic-based approach.* New York: Behavioral Publications.

Zuravin, S. J. (1989). The ecology of child abuse and neglect: Review of the literature and presentation of data. *Violence & Victims, 4,* 101–130.

Zusman, M. E., & Knox, D. (1998). Relationship problems of casual and involved university students. *College Student Journal, 32,* 606–609.

# Index

**A**

Abstract mindedness, 73–74
Acceptance in groups, 455–456
Access functions, 32–33,
    62–65, 71
  assessment of, 155–158,
    188–189
  boundary management,
    64–65
  cultural influences on, 79–81
  ineffective parenting and, 402
  mental illness/disability
    and, 403
  substance abuse and, 405
  supportive functions,
    63–64, 80
  types of access, 62–63
Acquiescence, 13, 110
Acting out, 111
Action systems
  direct change strategies and,
    297–325
  observation of, 107, 112
  punctuated positioning and,
    275–280
  response system framework
    and, 35

  shifting to processing sys-
    tems from, 237–238
  *See also* Processing systems
Action themes, 215
Active support, 63
Actor-model strategies,
  299–302
  exercise on using, 301–302
  modeling interventions,
    300–301
  role-playing interventions, 301
Actuarial approaches to risk
  assessment, 160–161
Adaptative challenges, 397–409
  domestic violence, 399–401
  ineffective parenting and
    socialization, 402–403
  intergenerational family
    violence, 398
  mental illness and/or
    disability, 403–404
  parental substance abuse,
    404–407
Adjustment problems, 398
Adult relationships, 10–17
  attraction formation in,
    10–13

  boundary formation in,
    13–15
  relationship formalization in,
    15–17
Advocacy groups, 442
Advocacy support, 64
  case advocacy, 434–438
  class advocacy, 438–445
Affective channeling, 111
Affective elements
  access function and, 156–157
  altering experience of,
    348–360
  discipline function and, 148
  guidance function and,
    150–151
  internal vs. external,
    350–356
  modulation of, 96, 280–282
  nurturing function and,
    153–154
  observation of, 111–112
  outcomes based on, 318
  positive vs. negative,
    356–360
  potential roadblocks based
    on, 421

risk assessment and,
164–165, 168, 169
*See also* Emotions; Feelings
Affective processing questions,
101
Affect systems, 16
information yielded by, 95
questions related to, 101–102
Affiliation systems, 21–22
Agencies
level of fit with, 420–423
messages and approaches
of, 418
systemic family stresses and,
416–419
*See also* Multiagency work;
Service providers
Agenda setting, 454
Agitation, 110, 165
Alliance
family patterns of, 116
positioning skills of, 270–272
Aloofness, 107
Altering attributions, 282–285
externalizing symptoms for,
282–283
personification as means of,
283–284
reframing strategies for,
284–285
Altering experience of events,
348–360
internal vs. external
dimensions, 350–356
positive vs. negative
dimensions, 356–360
Ambivalence, 288–289
Amplifying
beliefs, 345–346
emotions, 112
Analogies and metaphors,
370–373
Anxiety
access function and, 157
developing tolerance for, 39
Appraisal support, 382
Art-based interventions, 376
Assessing families
assessment report and,
179–191
family genogram for,
130–136
formal assessments and,
174–192
four-cell model for, 130,
137–146

frameworks for organizing
and, 130
general guidelines for,
126–127
initial assessment in, 255
interview process for, 93–106
observation process for,
106–121
overview of techniques
for, 93
parental functions frame-
work for, 130, 147–159
procedures for, 179–180, 182
projective techniques for,
121–123
risk assessment framework
for, 130, 159–171
standardized questionnaires
for, 123–126
theories related to, 92,
129–130, 173
treatment goals and, 192–200
Assessment report, 179–191
elements included in,
179–181
sample family assessment,
181–191
Atmosphere, 22, 215–223
Attention, parental, 45, 156
Attraction formation, 10–13
Attributions
altering, 282–285
causal, 156
malefic, 166
meaning, 176–179, 367–368
responsibility, 108, 147
Attribution sequences, 339
Automatic reactions, 235–241
Autonomy
beliefs about, 153
guidance function and, 57
intimacy and, 31
referrals and, 420, 423
Avoidance patterns, 109

## B

Balanced setup, 96
Bateson, Gregory, 261
Battered women. *See* Domestic
violence
Behavior
access function and, 158
beliefs corresponding to, 142
developing tolerances for, 16
discipline function and, 149
guidance function and, 152

highlighting of past, 275–278
interruption of, 313–317
normative, 27, 100, 101, 147
nurturing function and, 155
reinforcement of, 321
risk assessment and, 165–166
Behavioral contracting, 320–321
Behavioral/developmental
programming, 459
Behavior interruption
strategies, 313–317
cuing strategies, 314–315
exercise on using, 321–324
pattern interruption
strategies, 316
scheduling strategies, 315
time-out strategies, 313–314
Behavior systems
information yielded by, 95
questioning strategies and,
99–100
response system framework
and, 35
Beliefs
amplifying, 345–346
autonomy, 153
challenging, 347–348,
360–362
cultural, 76–77
family-influenced, 22,
140–142
limit-oriented, 42
observing systems of,
108–110
overgeneralizing, 344
questions highlighting,
100–101
reconstructing, 343–344
role, 153
shared, 16
*See also* Values
Bias, sources of, 175
Biological influences, 138
Blame issues
addressing in families, 236
nonblaming perspective
and, 239
potential roadblocks and, 421
tuning in to, 208
Blocking automatic reactions,
235–241
case example of, 240–241
exercise on, 244–246
internalizing the focus, 237
interrupting automatic
responses, 236

Blocking automatic reactions, *(continued)*
  shifting from action to processing systems, 237–238
  validating experiences and perspectives, 238–239
Boundaries
  changes in, 19
  family-environment, 24
  formation of, 11, 13–15, 55–56
  generational, 24–25, 31
  management of, 23–26, 64–65, 114, 154
  permeability of, 23
  rules related to, 110
  subsystem, 25–26
Bowen, Murray, 130
Brain hemispheres, 366
*Brief Guide to Brief Therapy, A* (Cade & O'Hanlon), 366
Brief therapy, 259
Building common ground, 246–248
  case example of, 248
  closing family gaps in, 246–247
  exercise on, 253–255
Building investment, 214–223
  affirming family focus, 214–215
  creating an atmosphere for work, 215–221
  developing a sense of purpose, 223–231
  exercises on, 221–223, 229–231
Buzzwords, 420

**C**
CARE acronym, 302–303, 307, 309
Caregiving acts, 59, 60–61
Cartooning, 374
Case advocacy, 434–438
  cautions related to, 435
  exercise on, 437–438
  *See also* Class advocacy
Causal attributions, 156
Celebrating accomplishments, 154
Challenging processing systems, 342–348
  amplifying beliefs, 345–346
  cognitive restructuring, 346–348

exercise on, 360–362
  overgeneralizing beliefs, 344
  reconstructing beliefs, 343–344
Change
  counterchange vs., 266–270
  decreasing inhibitors to, 381–382
  developing foundation for, 249–253
  direct strategies for, 297–325, 327–363
  elements inhibiting, 266–268
  enlisting partners for, 380–381
  family development and, 18–20
  feelings that motivate, 262, 270–272
  identifying direction for, 250–251
  indirect strategies for, 365–390
  positioning families for, 259–294
  responding system, 380–382
  restraining, 281
  visions of, 265–270, 272–274
Charismatic power, 28
Checking-in routines, 65, 157
Child-identified rewards, 46
Children
  curbing violence in, 40
  domestic violence and, 401
  group treatment for, 412, 450
  social support and, 449
*Child Welfare and Family Services: Policies and Practice* (Downs et al.), 394, 415, 447
Chronological organization, 176
Circular questioning, 98
Class advocacy, 438–445
  exercise on, 443–445
  guidelines for, 442–443
  stages of, 439–442
  *See also* Case advocacy
Client-generated metaphors, 370–371
Client rights, 436, 442
Clinical approaches to risk assessment, 162–164
Coaching
  behavior change and, 310–311
  family engagement and, 210
  parental guidance and, 151

*See also* Educator-coach strategies
Coalitions
  disruption of, 221
  questions about, 99
Coercive parenting, 398
Coercive power, 27, 114
Cognitive degeneration, 167
Cognitive distortion, 165, 331–332
Cognitive influences
  access function and, 156
  family inheritance and, 140–142
  risk assessment and, 165, 166–167, 168, 169
  *See also* Thinking
Cognitive patterns, 335
Cognitive restructuring, 346–348
Cognitive sequencing questions, 100–101
Cognitive systems, 95
Cohesion-building outcomes, 44
Collaboration, 148, 226–229
Collaborative stories, 373
Collaborative support, 423–434
  exercise on, 432–434
  family members and, 425–431
  professionals and, 423–425
Collectivist cultures, 77–78, 80
Commonalities, 11–12, 456
Communication
  observing elements of, 115–116
  positioning skills and, 272–273
Community-based interventions, 462–465
  community-based partners and, 464–465
  engagement process and, 210
  host settings and, 463
Community influences, 140
Comparative questions, 100, 101
Concrete metaphors, 372–373
Confidentiality, 453
Conflict management, 16
Congruence patterns, 116
Consensual norms, 454
Consensus building, 439–440
Consequences, 47–48
Conservative religious families, 81–83
Constructed consequences, 47
Construct validity, 125

Content patterns, 115
Content validity, 125
Contextual change setup, 97
Contextual variables, 178
Contingency contracts,
    317–319
Contracts
    behavioral, 320–321
    contingency, 317–319
    group member, 453
    treatment, 195, 196–199
Contractual skills, 40
Control
    mechanisms of, 27, 114–115
    spheres of, 353–355, 429–431
Cooperation
    sibling, 33
    spousal, 30
Counterchange forces, 266–270
Crisis responses, 113
Criterion validity, 125
Cronbach's alpha, 124
Cuing strategies, 314–315
Cultural influences, 69–87
    access functions and, 79–81
    assessment of, 140
    attraction formation and, 12
    dimensions of culture and,
        72–73
    discipline functions and,
        73–74
    exercise on identifying,
        85–86
    family violence and, 83–84
    guidance functions and,
        74–77
    invisible cultures and, 81–83
    nurturing functions and,
        77–79
    parenting functions and,
        71–83
    theories related to, 69–70
    tuning in to, 208
Culture ring, 72–73
Cutting score scale, 125

**D**

Dances, family, 123
Dangerousness indicators,
    166–168
Data gathering
    general guidelines
        for, 126–127
    observation process
        for, 106–121
    projective techniques for,
        121–123

standardized questionnaires
    for, 123–126
Debriefing, 374
Decision-making patterns, 16
    family functioning and, 113
    group functioning and,
        454–455
De-escalation, 425–427
Default setting, 5
Defining problems, 249–250,
    304, 428
Delegation, 209–210
Dependence, 115
Description skills, 336–340
    attribution sequences and,
        339
    interpersonal indicators and,
        336–338
    nonverbal indicators and,
        338–339
Descriptive measures, 125–126
Desires, shared, 249
Devaluation, 421
Developmental compromises,
    398
Developmental stages/tasks,
    8–9
Developmental theories, 7–20
    adult relationships and,
        10–17
    core assumptions of, 7–9
    exercise on identifying,
        33–34
    family systems and, 17–20
    problems and resolutions in,
        9–10
*Diagnostic and Statistical Manual
    of Mental Disorders
    (DSM),* 175
Diagnostic criteria, 177
Differences
    cultural groups and, 75–76
    developing tolerance for, 39
    family management of,
        117–118
    parental guidance and, 53,
        75–76
    processing changes in, 20
Dilemmas, creating, 278–279
Direct change strategies
    action systems and, 297–325
    actor-model strategies,
        299–302
    altering experience of
        events, 348–360
    behavior interruption
        strategies, 313–317

challenging processing
    systems, 342–348
educator-coach strategies,
    302–312
highlighting processing
    themes/patterns, 335–342
identifying processing
    themes/patterns, 329–334
processing systems and,
    327–363
theories related to, 297–299,
    327–329
weight-shifting strategies,
    317–324
*See also* Indirect change
    strategies
Direct expression, 112
Direct feedback, 61–62
Directional assumption, 8
Direct questions, 97
Disabled parents, 403–404
Disallowing provocation, 351
Disciplinary strategies, 43–51
    induction, 50–51
    inscription, 44
    power assertion, 48–49
    reinforcement, 45–48
    social illumination, 50
    strategic discipline, 49
    triangulation, 43–44
    withdrawal-of-love, 44–45
Discipline functions, 32,
    42–51, 71
    assessment of, 147–149, 189
    cultural influences on,
        73–74
    disciplinary strategies and,
        43–51
    ineffective parenting and,
        402, 403
    mental illness/disability and,
        403
    substance abuse and, 405
    types of limits and, 42
Disclosures, 456
Discounting, 115, 164
Discriminant validity, 125
Disempowering polarities, 221
Disengaging, 115
Disputing beliefs, 347
Disruptive power, 28
Distortions, 116, 153, 165,
    331–332
Distraction, 111
Divergence patterns, 116
Divisive issues, 217–218
Documentation trail, 436, 442

Domestic violence, 399–401
  child adaptation to, 401
  cultural issues and, 83–84
  family-level adaptation to, 401
  maternal adaptation to, 400–401
  risk assessment of, 162, 163
  substance abuse and, 406
  *See also* Family violence
Dominance hierarchies, 110
Double description, 260
Dramatizing, 111–112
Draw-a-family strategy, 122

**E**
Economic resources, 81
Educational achievement, 395–396
Educator-coach strategies, 302–312
  CARE acronym and, 302–303
  coaching in new behaviors, 310–311
  exercise on using, 311–312
  homework and task assignments, 309–310
  option evaluations, 307–308
  problem-solving interventions, 303–307
  skill development interventions, 308–309
Embedded options/hypotheses, 290
Emotional support, 382
Emotions
  expression of, 111–112, 139, 141–142
  highlighting patterns of, 335
  identifying changes in, 346
  investment of, 148, 151, 154
  neutralizing in groups, 456
  parental availability and, 62–63
  recognizing feelings and, 263
  reserves of, 156
  risk assessment and, 164–165, 168, 169
  secondary, 112, 262
  *See also* Affective elements; Feelings
Empirical findings, 178
Empowerment-enhancing support, 63, 436
Enabler role, 405
Energy processes, 21–23
  neutralizing negative energy, 241–246

working with family energy, 233–235
Engagement
  atmosphere for work in, 215–223
  blocking automatic reactions in, 235–241, 244–246
  building investment in, 214–231
  challenges of, 206–208
  common ground in, 246–248, 253–255
  facilitating interest in, 210–211
  family energy and, 233–235
  family focus and, 214–215
  foundation for change in, 249–253
  homework/task assignment and, 309–310
  interactive, 233–257
  modes of invitation for, 209–210
  neutralizing negative energy in, 241–246
  parental functions and, 149, 151, 157
  positioning strategies and, 259–294
  preliminary, 205–232
  reluctant members and, 220–221
  sense of purpose in, 223–231
  tentative, 208–213
  theories related to, 206, 207, 259–260
  tuning-in phase of, 208–209
Environmental influences, 138–140
  *See also* Family environment
Epigenetic principle, 9
Escalation patterns, 116
*Essentials of Family Therapy, The* (Nichols & Schwartz), 4, 38, 92, 260, 299, 328, 394
Establishing ordeals, 319–320
Evaluation
  of new options, 307
  of parental functions, 65–67
  of problem-solving success, 306–307, 429
Exceptional outcomes, 275–276
Exception-focused questions, 239
Exchanges, 26–27
Exclusion issues, 208

Excuses vs. reasons, 351
Expanding perspectives, 51–53
Expectations
  cultural, 79
  group, 454
  role, 150
Experiences
  altering, 348–360
  reframing, 355–356
  shared, 227
  validating, 238–239
Expert power, 28
Exploring alternatives, 279
Exploring family situations, 93–106, 426
  *See also* Interviewing families
Expressive systems, 16
Expressive techniques, 376–377
Externalization, 234, 350–356
  *See also* Internal vs. external dimensions
Externalized locus of control, 282
Externalizing symptoms, 282–283
External resource activation, 379–389

**F**
Families
  collaborative support in, 425–431
  common ground in, 246–248
  four features of, 206–207
  interviewing members of, 93–106
  loyalty issues in, 147˙
  maintaining focus in, 449
  positioning for change, 259–294
  problem solving in, 138–139, 141
  skill development in, 308
*Family Counseling and Therapy* (Horne), 4, 38, 92, 260, 299, 328, 366
Family dances, 123
Family energy
  interactive engagement and, 233–235
  neutralizing negativity of, 241–246
  *See also* Energy processes
Family environment
  boundary of, 24
  change inhibitors in, 381–382

engaging supports in, 382–384

enlisting change partners in, 380–381

exercise on intervening in, 385–389

negotiating change in, 384–385

working with others in, 379–389

Family functioning
cultural influences on, 71–83

domestic violence and, 83–84

invisible cultures and, 81–83

*See also* Parental functions

Family genograms, 130–136
exercise on developing, 134–136

relationship lines used in, 134

Family metaphors, 123

Family practice
developmental theory of, 7–20

identifying theories in, 33–34

response system framework for, 34–35

systems theory of, 20–34

thinking related to, 4–6

*Family Practice–Brief Systems Methods for Social Work* (Franklin & Jordan), 394, 415, 447

Family preservation programs, 459

Family resources, 395–397
educational achievement and, 395–396

external supports and, 397

financial stressors and, 396–397

*See also* Resources

Family rituals, 16, 22–23, 108

Family roles
addiction-related, 405–406

beliefs about, 153

changes in, 19

expectations and, 79, 114

exploration of, 139, 141

Family rules, 109, 110, 138, 140–141

Family sculpting, 122

Family standards, 109, 138, 140–141

Family stories, 108–109, 374–375

Family systems, 17–20

*Family Therapy: An Overview* (Goldenberg & Goldenberg), 4, 38, 92, 260, 299, 328, 366, 394

*Family Therapy: A Systemic Integration* (Becvar & Becvar), 299, 328

*Family Treatment in Social Work Practice* (Janzen & Harris), 394, 416, 448

Family violence
cultural issues and, 83–84

intergenerational, 398

risk assessment of, 162, 163

substance abuse and, 406

*See also* Domestic violence

Feedback
direct, 61–62

indirect, 62

Feelings
change motivation and, 262, 270–272

engagement concerns and, 214–215

potential roadblocks based on, 421

recognizing emotions and, 263

response system framework and, 35

shifting focus to, 238

tuning in to primary, 352–353

validating underlying, 238–239

*See also* Affective elements; Emotions

Fictive kin, 24

Focus
family, 449

rational, 436

shifting, 217, 237–238, 330, 426

Follow-up process, 102–103

Force field analysis, 266–268

Formal assessments, 174–192
attributing meaning to themes in, 176–179

elements of assessment report in, 179–191

exercise on documenting, 191–192

identifying critical data themes in, 174–176

Formalization of relationships, 11, 15–17

Formal support systems, 383, 419–423
autonomy level and, 420, 423

level of fit and, 420–423

Four-cell assessment model, 130, 137–146
behavior and interactions in, 142

beliefs and cognitive influences in, 140–142

environmental influences in, 138–140

exercise on using, 145–146

finding rubs and gaps with, 142–144

genetic and biological influences in, 138

Framing process, 226–229, 355, 422, 426–427

Friendships, 56

Funding sources, 441

Future hopes, 249

Future orientation questions, 100

## G

Games, 377

Gaps, 143–144

Gay or lesbian families, 81–83

Gender roles, 79

Generalizing beliefs, 344

Generational boundaries, 24–25, 31

Genetic influences, 138

Genograms, 130–136
exercise on developing, 134–136

relationship lines used in, 134

Geographic access, 62

Gestalt, 366

Goals
contracted elements and, 195

establishing objectives for, 194–195

exercise on setting, 199–200

formulating statements for, 193–194

group programs and, 453–454

sample contract for, 196–199

Goal statements, 193–194

Gossip hooks, 457

Government agencies, 441

Group programs, 411–412, 450–459
agenda setting in, 454

decision making in, 454–455

Group programs *(continued)*
  establishing goals in,
    453–454
  exercise on, 457–459
  expectations related to, 454
  family-related barriers
    to, 452
  group structure in, 452–455
  interpersonal processes in,
    455–457
  skills developed through, 451
Guidance functions, 32,
    51–58, 71
  assessment of, 150–152, 189
  boundary development,
    55–56
  cultural influences on, 74–77
  expanding perspectives,
    51–53
  ineffective parenting and, 402
  internalizing limits, 57–58
  mental illness/disability
    and, 403
  problem solving, 53–55
  social role development,
    56–57
  substance abuse and, 405
Guided imagery strategies,
    369–370
Guilt issues, 208

**H**
*Handbook of Family Therapy*
    (Gunman & Kniskern), 365
Happiness, 39
Health-related outcomes, 44
Hero role, 405
Hidden investments, 335
Hierarchical systems
  acquiescence/dominance
    hierarchies, 110
  adaptive changes in, 19
  privilege hierarchies, 109
  rule hierarchies, 147
High immediacy indicators,
    164–166
Highlighting processing
    themes/patterns, 335–342
  description skills for, 336–340
  exercise on, 341–342
  reflecting skills for, 340
  steps involved in, 336
High-risk families. *See*
    Multiproblem or high-risk
    families
Hindsight bias analysis, 347

Home-based support, 411, 412,
    459–462
Homeostasis, 261
Home visits, 210
Homework
  criteria for assigning,
    309–310
  storytelling assignments as,
    375
Hopefulness, 250
Hostility, 165
Host settings, 463
Hypotheses, embedded, 290

**I**
Idealization, 13
Identifying processing
    themes/patterns, 329–334
  cognitive distortion, 331–332
  exercise on, 332–334
  reaction intensity, 331
  repeated themes, 330–331
  shifts in focus, 330
"If-then" situations, 385
Ignore and explode cycles,
    110–111
Illustrative examples setup, 97
Image management, 13
Impartiality, 151
Improvisation work, 377
Inadequacy, 165, 421
Indirect change strategies,
    365–390
  analogies and metaphors,
    370–373
  changing responding
    systems, 380–382
  engaging supports, 382–384
  exercises on, 378–379,
    385–389
  indirect resource activation,
    366–379
  meaning attribution
    exercises, 367–368
  negotiating room for change,
    384–385
  reasons for using, 366, 389
  storytelling techniques,
    373–375
  symbolic expressive
    interventions, 375–377
  theories related to, 365–366
  visualization and guided
    imagery, 368–370
  working through others,
    379–389

*See also* Direct change
    strategies
Indirect feedback, 62
Indirect resource activation,
    366–379
Individual engagement
    meetings, 210
Individualistic cultures,
    77–78, 80
Induction strategies, 50–51
Infant stimulation, 459
Inference chaining, 347–348
Informal support systems, 383
Informational support, 382
Inherited family models, 137–146
In-home support, 411, 412,
    459–462
Initial assessment, 255
Injunctions
  highlighting, 335–336
  questions about, 100
Inscription strategies, 44
Instrumental support, 382
Intensity of reactions, 331
Interactions
  access function and, 157–158
  discipline function and,
    148–149
  engagement concerns and,
    215
  group processes and,
    455–457
  guidance function and,
    151–152
  highlighting from the past,
    275–278
  nurturing function and,
    154–155
  risk assessment and, 165–166
Interaction sequence
    questioning, 99
Interaction systems
  changes related to, 18–19
  family patterns and, 29–30
  information yielded by, 95
  questioning strategies and,
    98–99
  response system framework
    and, 35
Interactive cues, 314
Interactive engagement,
    233–257
  blocking automatic reactions
    in, 235–241, 244–246
  building common ground in,
    246–248, 253–255

developing foundation for change in, 249–253
exercises on, 244–246, 253–255
neutralizing negative energy in, 241–246
overview of stages in, 235, 256
working with family energy during, 233–235
Interactive positioning, 274, 287–292
exercise on, 291–292
strategies of, 288–291
Intergenerational family violence, 398
Intermember exchanges/control, 26–28
Internal cues, 314
Internal experience
external experience vs., 350–356
shifting the focus to, 237
validation of, 239
Internalized locus of control, 282
Internalizing limits, 57–58
Internal resource activation, 366–379
Internal vs. external dimensions, 350–356
primary feelings and, 352–353
reframing process and, 355–356
responsibility analysis and, 350–352
spheres of control and, 353–355
See also Positive vs. negative dimensions
Interpersonal indicators, 336–338
Interpersonal processes, 455–457
building relationships, 456
ensuring acceptance, 455–456
establishing interaction, 457
Inter-rater reliability, 124
Interruption
of automatic responses, 236
of problem patterns, 316
See also Behavior interruption strategies
Interventions
art-based, 376

community-based, 463–465
modeling, 300–301
problem-solving, 303–307
role-playing, 301
skill development, 308–309
support-focused, 447–466
symbolic expressive, 375–377
Interviewing families, 93–106
exercise on, 103–106
follow-up to, 102–103
posing questions, 97–102
setting up questions, 96–97
targeting questions, 94–96
Intimacy
autonomy and, 31
observing patterns of, 107–108
Intrusiveness, 149
Investments
family, 109
hidden, 335
Invisible cultures, 81–83
Invitation modes, 209–210
Irrefutable positions, 249

**J**
Judgment sensitivity, 421

**K**
Kinship supports, 383
Knowledge
incorporation of new, 289–290
integrating data with, 178
Known groups validity, 125

**L**
Laddering, 347–348
Leader role, 453
Learned helplessness, 420
Learning-based outcomes, 44
Legends, family, 109
Legislation, violence-related, 83–84
Lesbian or gay families, 81–83
Level of fit, 420–423
Lewin, Kurt, 266
Limitable outcomes, 31–32, 40, 58, 71
Limits, categories of, 42
Lineal questions, 98
Linking process, 96
Locus of control, 282
Logical consequences, 47
Logical outcomes, 288

Loose boundaries, 23
Lost child role, 406
Loveable outcomes, 31–33, 39–40, 71
Loyalties, family, 147

**M**
Malefic attributions, 166
Manipulative situations, 384–385
Marketable skills, 395–396
Mascot role, 405
Meaning
attributing, 176–179, 367–368
generalizing, 177–178
reframing, 284–285
self-generating, 367–368
systems of, 22
Media involvement, 441
Mediation support, 64, 422
Mentally ill/disabled parents, 403–404
Metaphors, 370–373
client-generated, 370–371
concrete, 372–373
family, 123
therapist-constructed, 371–372
Minimizing discussion, 217
Minor validations, 157
Miracle questions, 279–280
Modeling interventions, 300–301
Modulating affect, 96, 280–282
restraining change for, 281
shaggy dog strategy for, 281–282
Monetary outcomes, 318
Monitoring progress, 195
Monopolizing conversations, 114
Mood regulation, 39
Morale, 22
Motivation, 261–263
disentangling array of, 351
feelings related to, 262, 270–272
tuning-in process and, 261–262
Multiagency work, 415–446
autonomy issues and, 420, 423
case advocacy and, 434–438
class advocacy and, 438–445
collaborative support and, 423–434

Multiagency work *(continued)*
exercises related to, 432–433, 437–438, 443–445
family stresses due to, 416–419
formal services and, 419–423
level of fit and, 420–423
system messages/approaches in, 418
theories related to, 415–416
*See also* Service providers
Multiple perspectives, 218–221
Multiproblem or high-risk families
adaptive challenges and, 397–409
case advocacy for, 434–438
class advocacy for, 438–445
collaborative support for, 423–434
community-based work for, 462–465
exercises on working with, 407–409, 432–434
formal support services for, 419–423
group programs for, 411–412, 450–459
in-home support for, 411, 412, 459–462
multiagency work and, 415–446
resource challenges and, 395–397
support-focused intervention and, 447–466
systemic stresses on, 416–419
theories related to, 393–394
treatment approaches for, 409–413
Multisystemic treatment, 411, 412–413
Mystery themes, 329

**N**
Narrative organization, 176–177
Narrow mandates, 420
Natural consequences, 47
Needs
expressed, 158
shared, 249
Negative energy, 241–246
Negative interpretations, 356
*See also* Positive vs. negative dimensions

Negative reinforcement, 47–48
Negotiation
external relationships and, 384–385
sibling relationships and, 33
Neighborhood, 140
Neutralization strategies
for divisive issues, 217–218
for negative energy, 241–246
Noble positions, 249
Nonverbal indicators, 338–339
Normalization, 456
Normative behavior, 27, 100, 101, 147, 454
Normative questions, 99–100, 101
Normed test, 125
Nurturing functions, 33, 58–62, 71
assessment of, 152–158, 188–189
caregiving acts, 59, 60–61
cultural influences on, 77–79
ineffective parenting and, 402
mental illness/disability and, 404
parental support, 59
physical contact, 59–60
substance abuse and, 404
verbalizations, 59, 61–62

**O**
Objectification, 167
Objectives, 194–195
Observational perspective questions, 100
Observing family processes, 93, 106–121
actions/interactions, 112–118
affective expression, 111–112
belief and value systems, 108–110
communications, 115–116
control mechanisms, 114–115
difference management, 117–118
exercise on, 118–121
intimacy and sharing, 107–108
support functions, 116–117
task accomplishment, 113–114

tension management, 110–111
Obsessive thinking, 165
Omnipotence, 166–167
Ontic relationship changes, 19
Opening statement, 216–217
Operant conditioning, 317
Optimal direction, 8
Option evaluations, 307–308
Ordeal strategies, 319–320
Organizing information, 176–177
Outcomes
contingency contracts and, 318
evaluation of, 306–307, 429
inscription strategies and, 44
loveable and limitable, 31–33, 39–40, 71
parenting functions and, 32–33, 41
reflecting logical, 288
Overcompensation, 148
Overcontrol, 166
Overgeneralizing beliefs, 344
Overlapping themes, 223–226, 242

**P**
Pairing stimuli, 320
Paradoxes, 260
Paranoid thinking, 165
Paraprofessionals, 464
Parental functions, 37–68
access, 62–65, 71, 79–81
cultural influences on, 71–83
discipline, 42–51, 71, 73–74
exercise on evaluating, 65–67
guidance, 51–58, 71, 74–77
ineffective parenting and, 402–403
mental illness/disability and, 403–404
nurturing, 58–62, 71, 77–79
outcomes and, 39–40, 41
substance abuse and, 404–405
theories related to, 37–38
Parental functions framework, 130, 147–159
access function assessment, 155–158
discipline function assessment, 147–149
guidance function assessment, 150–152

nurturing function
assessment, 152–155
Parental substance abuse,
404–407
Parental subsystem, 31–33
Parent-child engagement, 156
Partial responses, 420
Past adaptation, 335
Pattern interruption strategies,
316
Peer supports, 383, 464
Permeability of boundaries, 23
Personal knowledge, 107
Personification, 283–284
Perspective taking
focusing and, 237
guidance function and,
51–53
interactive positioning
and, 291
multiple perspectives and,
218–221
nonblaming perspectives
and, 239
overlapping themes and,
223–226
questions related to, 101
validation and, 238–239
Physical closeness, 107
Physical contact, 59–60
Planning
group programs and, 450
problem solving and, 306,
429
support programs and, 465
Playfulness, 110, 154, 155
Play therapy, 376–377
Polarized positions, 221
Polarized thinking, 165
Political processes, 178
Politicians, 442
Posing questions, 97–102
Positional power, 28
Positioning, 259–294
alliance skills and, 270–272
communicating visions in,
272–273
exercises on, 263–265,
268–270, 285–287,
291–292
explanation of, 260
force field analysis and,
266–268
homeostasis and, 261
interactive, 274, 287–292
juxtaposing visions in,
273–274

motivation and, 261–263,
270–272
punctuated, 274–287
skills required for, 270–274
strategies of, 274–292
visions of change and,
265–270, 272–274
Positive illumination, 241
Positive reinforcement, 45–47,
321
Positive vs. negative
dimensions, 356–360
discipline function and, 148
guidance function and, 151
nurturing function and, 154
positive reframing and,
356–357
solution focusing and,
357–358
strength coupling and,
359–360
strength finding and,
358–359
*See also* Internal vs. external
dimensions
Postponing discussion, 217
Postures, 107–108
Power
assertion strategies, 48–49
reframing sense of, 355–356
types of, 27–28
Powerlessness, 164
Power systems, 27–28
Praise-focused rewards, 46–47
Predetermined frameworks,
175, 177
Predictive validity, 125
Preliminary engagement,
205–232
building investment,
214–231
challenges of, 206–208
exercises on, 212–213,
221–223, 229–231
tentative engagement,
208–213
theories related to, 206, 207
Presentation rules, 110
Pressuring, 114, 208
Presupposition setup, 96
Primary feelings
change motivation and, 262
questions related to, 101
tuning in to, 352–353
Primary felt perspective,
219–220
Privilege hierarchies, 109

Proactive positioning, 150
Probing, 65
Problem definition, 249–250,
304, 428
Problem solving
exploring in families,
138–139, 141
guidance function and, 150
interventions based on,
303–307
managing differences in, 118
steps in process of, 54,
304–307, 427–429
tension management and,
53–55, 110
Process identification
questions, 99
Processing systems
challenging, 342–348,
360–362
direct change strategies and,
327–363
highlighting themes/patterns
in, 335–342
identifying themes/patterns
in, 329–334
observation of, 107, 330
punctuated positioning and,
280–285
response system framework
and, 35
shifting from action systems
to, 237–238
*See also* Action systems
Projective techniques, 93,
121–123
draw a family, 122
family dances, 123
family metaphors, 123
family sculpting, 122
Promotion skills, 40
Protection, 155
Provision patterns, 117
Provocation, 351
Proximity management, 16,
158
Psychoeducational groups, 308
Psychometric methods of
risk assessment,
161–162
Public health programs, 460
Punctuated positioning,
274–287
action system strategies,
275–280
processing system strategies,
280–285

Punishment
   patterns of, 109–110
   utility of, 147
Purpose, sense of, 223–231

**Q**

Questionnaires, 93, 123–126
   reliability of, 124
   types of, 125–126
   validity of, 124–125
Questions
   affect system, 101–102
   behavior system, 99–100
   belief system, 100–101
   exception-focused, 239
   family-based, 94
   interaction system, 98–99
   miracle, 279–280
   posing, 97–102
   scaling, 102, 277–278
   self-report, 237
   setting up, 96–97
   targeting, 94–96
   types of, 97–98

**R**

Rational focus, 436
Reactions
   automatic, 235–241, 244–246
   intensity of, 331
Reconstructing beliefs,
      343–344
Redirection, 237
Redundant processes, 420
Reentry rituals, 158
Referent power, 28
Referrals, 420
Reflecting skills, 340
Reflexive questions, 98
Reframing strategies, 284–285,
      355–356
   de-escalation process and,
      426–427
   externalization issues and,
      355–356
   positive vs. negative polarity
      and, 356–357
Reinforcement strategies,
      45–48
   control mechanisms and, 114
   negative reinforcement and,
      47–48
   operant conditioning and, 317
   positive reinforcement and,
      45–47, 321
   weight-shifting strategies as,
      317–321

Relational outcomes, 318
Relational power, 28
Relational thinking, 4–5
Relationships
   attraction formation in,
      10–13
   boundary formation in, 11,
      13–15
   building in groups, 456
   formalization of, 11, 15–17
   four-cell assessment of,
      145–146
   response system of, 35
Relative influence strategies,
      276–277
Reliability, 124, 161
Religion, 76–77
Reluctant members, 220–221
Repeated themes, 330–331
Replenishment systems, 16
Resources
   cultural systems and, 81
   external activation of,
      379–389
   family challenges and,
      395–397
   internal activation of, 366–379
   priority setting for, 16
   task accomplishment and, 113
Respect rules, 110
Response systems, 15, 16, 34–
      35, 36, 37, 95–96, 98, 107,
      150, 162, 207, 209, 224, 329
Responsibility
   analysis of, 347, 350–352
   attributions of, 108
   group agreements about, 453
   parental beliefs about, 147
   reframing in situations, 356
Restraining change, 281
Retaliation, 114
Reverse-scored items, 126
Rewards
   power based on, 28
   reinforcement and, 321
   types of, 46–47
Rights of others, 40
Rigid boundaries, 23
Risk assessment, 130, 159–171
   actuarial approaches to,
      160–161
   clinical approaches to,
      162–164
   dangerousness indicators in,
      166–168
   emergence of risk and,
      168–169

exercise on, 169–171
   high immediacy indicators
      in, 164–166
   psychometric methods of,
      161–162
Rituals, family, 16, 22–23, 108
Roadblocks, 421–422
Role-playing interventions, 301
   exercise on, 301–302
Roles
   beliefs about, 153
   development of social, 56–57
   expectations about, 150
   *See also* Family roles
Romantic relationships,
      145–146
Rounds, group, 457
Routine rituals, 23
Rubs, 143–144
Rules
   hierarchies of, 147
   highlighting, 335–336
   safety, 42, 110
   situational, 42
   *See also* Family rules

**S**

Safety, 250
Safety rules, 42, 110
Sanctioning
   cultural systems of, 74
   of relationship input, 17
Scaling questions, 102,
      277–278
Scapegoat role, 405
Scheduling strategies, 315
Sculpting, family, 122
Secondary emotions, 112, 262
Secondary felt perspectives,
      219, 220
Seeking-out behavior, 158
Self-concept, 39, 141
Self-control, 151
Self-empowerment, 436
Self-report questions, 237
Self-talk, 346
Sense of purpose, 223–231
   exercise on building,
      229–231
   framing process and,
      226–229
   overlapping themes and,
      223–226
Service contracts, 195
Service providers
   autonomy issues and, 420,
      423

case advocacy and, 434–438
class advocacy and, 438–445
collaborative support and, 423–434
family stresses and, 416–419
formal supports and, 419–423
level of fit with, 420–423
messages and approaches of, 418
multiproblem families and, 416–419
referrals to, 420
*See also* Multiagency work; Support
Setting up questions, 96–97
Shaggy dog strategy, 281–282
Shame, 164, 421
Shared experiences, 227
Shared needs/desires, 249
Shared problem definition, 249–250
Shared values/beliefs, 16
Sharing
observing in families, 107
promoting in groups, 457
Shifting focus, 217, 237–238, 330, 426
Sibling subsystem, 33
Situational rewards, 46
Situational rules, 42
Skill development interventions, 308–309
Slogans, family, 109
Social appropriateness, 40
Social fit, 12
Social illumination, 50
Social institutions, 140
Socialization problems, 402
Social resources, 81
Social roles, 56–57, 79
Social support. See Support
Solicitation patterns, 117
Solutions
focusing on, 357–358
potential, 178–179, 305
Somatizing, 111
Spanking, 48
Special occasion rituals, 22
Spheres of control, 353–355, 429–431
Split half reliability, 124
Spousal relationship, 10
Spousal subsystem, 30–31
Stalking behavior, 167
Standardized questionnaires, 123–126

reliability of, 124
types of, 125–126
validity of, 124–125
Standardized services, 421
Standards, family, 109, 138, 140–141
Status quo motivations, 385
Stimuli, pairing, 320
Stories
collaborative, 373
family, 108–109, 374–375
thematic, 373–374
Storytelling techniques, 373–375
assigning storytelling homework, 375
developing thematic stories, 373–374
eliciting family stories, 374–375
Strategic discipline, 49
Strategic model of practice, 365
Strength coupling, 359–360
Strength finding, 358–359
Strength-focused framing, 422
Stress
access function and, 157
discipline function and, 148
financial resources and, 396
multiagency services and, 416–419
multiple stressors and, 407–409
Structured questionnaires. *See* Standardized questionnaires
Subgroups, 456
Substance use/abuse
parental functions and, 404–407
violent behavior and, 166, 406
Subsystems
boundaries of, 25–26
organizing data into, 176
parental, 31–33
sibling, 33
spousal, 30–31
Suggestions, embedded, 290
Summary setup, 97
Supervising support partners, 465
Support
active, 63
advocacy, 64
assessment of, 155

collaborative, 423–434
cultural systems of, 80
empowerment-enhancing, 63
engaging systems of, 382–384
formal systems of, 419–423
functional changes in, 19
matrix of, 383–384
mediation, 64
mental health and, 449
multiproblem families and, 397, 416–419
observing functions of, 116–117
parental nurturing and, 59
seeking in families for, 139
sources of, 383
spousal, 30
types of, 382
*See also* Service providers
Support-focused intervention, 447–466
community-based work and, 462–465
group work and, 450–459
in-home work and, 459–462
principles for, 448–450
theories related to, 447–448
Symbolic expression, 112, 375–377
Systemic family stressors, 416–419
Systemic theories, 20–34
boundary management in, 23–26
energy processes in, 21–23
exercise on identifying, 33–34
family interaction patterns in, 29–30
intermember exchanges/control in, 26–28
overview of critical concepts in, 21
subsystem functions in, 30–34

**T**

Tabling forward, 236
Targeting questions, 94–96
Tasks
accomplishing, 113–114
assigning, 309–310
developmental, 8–9
Teaching, 151
Telephone invitation, 210
Tension management, 16, 22
differences and, 53–54

Tension management *(continued)*
  interactive engagement
    and, 236
  observation of, 110–111
Tentative engagement,
    208–213
  exercise on, 212–213
  facilitating interest, 210–211
  invitation mode, 209–210
  tuning-in phase, 208–209
Test-retest reliability, 124
Tests
  reliability of, 124
  types of, 125–126
  validity of, 124–125
Themes
  attributing meaning to,
    176–179
  identification of, 174–176,
    242, 329–334
  overlapping, 223–226, 242
  repeated, 330–331
Theoretical domains, 177
Theories, 3–4, 6–7
  developmental, 7–20
  exercise on identifying,
    33–34
  integrating data with, 178
  practice frameworks and,
    34–35
  systemic, 20–34
Therapist-constructed
    metaphors, 371–372
Thinking
  access function and, 156
  discipline function and, 147
  engagement concerns and,
    214
  guidance function and, 150
  linking body sensations and,
    346
  nurturing function and,
    152–153
  potential roadblocks based
    on, 421
  response system framework
    and, 35
  risk assessment and, 165,
    166–167, 168, 169
  shifting focus to, 238
Third-party invitation, 210
Threats, 166, 168
Time-out strategies, 313–314
Token economies, 46
Token rewards, 46
Touch, 155

Training support partners, 465
Transitional tracking, 103
Treatment approaches
  group treatment, 411–412
  in-home support, 411, 412
  multiproblem families and,
    409–413
  multisystemic treatment,
    411, 412–413
  traditional, 409–411
Treatment goals, 192–200
  contracted elements and, 195
  establishing objectives for,
    194–195
  exercise on setting, 199–200
  formulating statements for,
    193–194
  sample contract for, 196–199
Triadic questions, 97–98
Triangulation, 29–30, 43–44,
    148–149
Tuning-in process
  motivation and, 261–262
  parental functions and, 153
  role-playing and, 301
  tentative engagement and,
    208–209

**U**
Uncertainty, managing, 39
Undermining
  discipline, 149
  input, 16–17
Unique outcomes, 275–276
Updating, 65

**V**
Validation
  continuation of, 241–242
  experience/perspective,
    238–239, 426
Validation setup, 97
Validity, 124–125, 161
Values
  cultural, 76–77
  family-influenced, 22
  observation of, 108–110
  outcomes based on, 44, 318
  rigidity of, 156
  shared, 16
  *See also* Beliefs
Verbalizations, 59, 61–62
Verbal shaping rewards, 47
Violence
  cultural issues and, 83–84
  curbing in children, 40

family/domestic, 83–84, 162,
    163, 398–401
  ignore and explode cycles of,
    110–111
  intergenerational, 398
  legislation related to, 83–84
  past patterns of, 167
  public use of, 167
  risk assessment of, 162, 163,
    164–169
  substance abuse and, 166,
    406
Visceral reactions, 175
Visions of change, 265–270
  balanced view of, 266–268
  communicating about,
    272–273
  exercise on using, 285–287
  identification of, 265–266
  juxtaposing, 273–274
  motivating feelings and,
    270–272
  uncovering alternative,
    278–280
Visualization strategies, 368–369
Volunteers, 464
Vulnerability tolerance, 153–154

**W**
Weapons use, 167
Weight-shifting strategies,
    317–324
  behavioral contracting,
    320–321
  contingency contracting,
    317–319
  establishing ordeals, 319–320
  exercise on using, 321–324
  pairing stimuli, 320
  reinforcing behavior, 321
White, Michael, 278, 282
Win-lose framing, 421
Win-win situations, 227
Withdrawal strategies
  control mechanisms and, 115
  withdrawal of love, 44–45
Withholding input, 16
Women, battered, 400–401
Working through others,
    379–389
*Working with Families: An
    Integrative Model by Level of
    Need* (Kilpatrick &
    Holland), 394, 416, 448
Written invitations, 210
Written stories, 374